Music in American Life

Books in the series:

Only a Miner: Studies in Recorded Coal-Mining Songs
ARCHIE GREEN

Great Day Coming: Folk Music and the American Left
R. SERGE DENISOFF

John Philip Sousa: A Descriptive Catalog of His Works
PAUL E. BIERLEY

The Hell-Bound Train: A Cowboy Songbook
GLENN OHRLIN

*Oh, Didn't He Ramble: The Life Story of Lee Collins as
Told to Mary Collins*
FRANK J. GILLIS AND JOHN W. MINER, EDITORS

American Labor Songs of the Nineteenth Century
PHILIP S. FONER

Stars of Country Music: Uncle Dave Macon to Johnny Rodriguez
BILL C. MALONE AND JUDITH MC CULLOH, EDITORS

*Git Along, Little Dogies: Songs and Songmakers of the
American West*
JOHN I. WHITE

A Texas-Mexican Cancionero: *Folksongs of the Lower Border*
AMÉRICO PAREDES

San Antonio Rose: The Life and Music of Bob Wills
CHARLES R. TOWNSEND

Early Downhome Blues: A Musical and Cultural Analysis
JEFF TODD TITON

*An Ives Celebration: Papers and Panels of the
Charles Ives Centennial Festival-Conference*
H. WILEY HITCHCOCK AND VIVIAN PERLIS

Sinful Tunes and Spirituals: Black Folk Music to the Civil War
DENA J. EPSTEIN

Sinful Tunes and Spirituals

I told them everything was sinful which was not done
with a single eye to God's glory.

George Whitefield's *Journal*, December 6, 1739

SINFUL TUNES AND SPIRITUALS

Black Folk Music to the Civil War

DENA J. EPSTEIN

UNIVERSITY OF ILLINOIS PRESS

Urbana Chicago London

Publication of this work was supported in part by
a grant from the Andrew W. Mellon Foundation.

© 1977 by the Board of Trustees of the University of Illinois
Manufactured in the United States of America

Library of Congress Cataloging in Publication Data

Epstein, Dena J
    Sinful tunes and spirituals.

    (Music in American life)
    Bibliography: p.
    Includes index.
    1. Afro-American music—History and criticism.
2. Spirituals (Songs)—History and criticism.
I. Title.
ML3556.E8   784.7′56′009   77–6315
ISBN 0-252-00520-1

To the
BLACK AND UNKNOWN BARDS . . .
SLAVE SINGERS, GONE, FORGOT, UNFAMED.
    —James Weldon Johnson

. . . .

Contents

· ·

Illustrations

Musical Examples

Preface

For generations black folk music has had enormous popular appeal in the United States and around the world. Understandably it has inspired many writers to expound its meaning, significance, and aesthetics. Tracing its history, however, has been more difficult because of a lack of historical evidence. This lack puzzled me, since there was a historical record of slavery which should throw light on the development of the music that originated therein. As far as I could learn, no systematic search of this material for its musical content had ever been made. It would not be an easy task, for such a search would involve the examination of a heterogeneous literature made up of slave narratives, travel accounts, memoirs, letters, novels, church histories, and polemics on slavery, but no other approach seemed likely to provide the source material so badly needed. About 1953 I decided to make the attempt, limiting the search to the period which seemed most in need of documentation: the earliest era that ended in 1867 with the appearance of the first published collection, *Slave Songs of the United States*. After 1872 the tours of the Fisk Jubilee Singers provided more accessible accounts.

I was not an ethnomusicologist; my knowledge of African musics was limited, and I had no way of knowing what could be found. But the application of library techniques to a search of this kind seemed well worth trying. Without more evidence, no real progress could be made in tracing the development of this music or in resolving the controversies about it. Gathering primary source material and making it available seemed to be a worthwhile objective in itself. The interpretation of whatever material might be uncovered was a matter for the future.

If I had any illusions that the search would be a short one, they were discarded very early, as I discovered that many of the books had neither indices nor tables of contents. The only way to learn if they contained any information was to scan them page by page. All too often that scanning would reveal not one word about music, for there was no way of predicting which sources were likely to be fruitful. A great many reminiscences by white Southerners never mentioned the blacks among whom they spent their lives—but there was always the hope that exceptional diarists would turn up, as indeed they did. As time passed, a few generalizations became possible. Planters as a group seemed preoccupied with politics and crops, having little curiosity about the lives of their slaves; however, southern ladies were more interested in their surroundings and the events of their daily lives, which might include slave customs and amusements. Works concerned with slave religion, recreation, or morale might mention music. Descriptions of Christmas or harvest festivities, the high points of the slave year, frequently involved music and sometimes dancing. If the writer was an apologist for slavery, it was necessary to corroborate his facts and disregard his interpretation of them. The writings of abolitionists, on the other hand, however sincere their concern for the welfare of the slaves, usually reflected little direct experience with plantation slavery or its music. One of my initial hunches, that touring actors or musicians would be discerning reporters of slave music, proved almost completely wrong. Very few of them so much as mentioned the subject.

There were long, tedious stretches of fruitless examination, periods of discouragement when I was almost ready to concede that the historic record really did not exist—but then, when I least expected it, a significant document would be uncovered. There was Solomon Northup's description of his life as a slave fiddler, with the transcription of a fiddle tune on the last page of his narrative, *Twelve Years a Slave*. There was a detailed account of a corn husking accompanied by corn songs in George Tucker's novel, *The Valley of Shenandoah*, and notated words and music of two slave songs in an autobiographical novel, James Hungerford's *The Old Plantation and What I Gathered There in an Autumn Month*. There was the report of a case filed in the Chancery Court of Louisville, Kentucky, in 1844, involving three professional slave musicians who took their instruments, music, and clothing and escaped on a steamboat to Cincinnati, included in Helen Catterall's *Judicial Cases Concerning American Slavery and the Negro.* Their owner sued the proprietor of the steamboat for damages—and lost. Most of the documents specified the time and place of the events described, indispensable information for tracing the music's development. Many earlier discussions have been seriously flawed by the assumption that conditions existing just before the Civil War could be extended backward in time. Slavery was not a static institution; it experienced historic change, as did the music that developed out of it.

Under conditions of slavery, the social structure of the southern states tightly circumscribed the life of plantation slaves, severely restricting their contacts with the outside world. This virtually closed society was shattered by the Civil War, which brought the slaves into contact with circumstances and people previously unknown. An incidental by-product of this social revolution was the emergence into public knowledge of the music of the slaves, particularly the body of songs that came to be known as Negro spirituals.

Among the multitude of wartime reports of the freedmen and their ways, the most revealing centered on the circumstances and people associated with the historic first published collection, *Slave Songs of the United States* (1867). Since the reports from the antebellum period seemed sufficient to establish the uninterrupted tradition of Afro-American music from its African beginnings, its existence after 1860 could hardly be in question. The genesis of the first collection, however, had never been investigated, although its editors had been severely criticized. It seemed worthwhile to illuminate the circumstances surrounding this seminal volume, the areas where most of the songs were collected and the people most directly involved.

The senior editor, William Francis Allen, had been an eminent historian, but his musical background was not known. His manuscript diary covering the Civil War years had been in the Library of the State Historical Society of Wisconsin for almost fifty years, but no one had ever examined it for its musical content. Charles Pickard Ware's letters were found conveniently published in a volume called *Letters from Port Royal Written at the Time of the Civil War* (1906), hidden behind the disguise of his initials. These were supplemented by family papers and reminiscences made available by his granddaughter, Caroline Farrar Ware. The third editor, Lucy McKim

Garrison, proved to be the most elusive, although she was related to a number of eminent men. Eventually I was directed to Miss Eleanor Garrison of Santa Barbara, California, who had a remarkable collection of family papers, now in the Smith College Library —a veritable treasure-trove of American cultural history.

By 1962 I had accumulated enough material to provide a survey of source material. "Slave Music in the United States before 1860" was published in two parts in Music Library Association *Notes* for 1963. A sketch entitled "Lucy McKim Garrison, American Musician" appeared in the same year in the *Bulletin of the New York Public Library*. Some of these published findings were expected: descriptions of dances, worksongs, instruments, and spirituals. More surprising was the evidence of a much greater prevalence of secular music than had previously been reported. Deeply disappointing was the almost total lack of any documentation for the colonial period when the Africans were newly arrived in the New World, or any indication of the process by which the music was acculturated.

The search continued with renewed emphasis on records from 1619 to 1800, but the results from a much more intensive examination were still meager: a few pious objections to slave dancing, some vague references to their singing, advertisements for runaways who played the fiddle, and the reports of a very few clergymen who made efforts to convert blacks. This lack of information was discouraging, but even more troubling was my inability to explain it. Not until I realized the slow growth rate of the black population did I understand why the blacks made little impact on travelers and other witnesses.

So matters stood in 1969 when I read Orlando Patterson's *The Sociology of Slavery*, a description of slave life in Jamaica, which suggested a possible new direction for the search. Patterson cited numerous contemporary descriptions of African music and dancing in Jamaica; there, as in other West Indian islands, the black population increased at a much faster rate than on the mainland. Were West Indian accounts relevant for the United States? In the seventeenth and eighteenth centuries they certainly were, for both France and Britain considered all their colonies in the New World as part of the same colonial structure. The colonies shared a common relationship with the mother country, close commercial ties, and a constant interchange of population, both black and white. Contemporary descriptions of these colonies intermixed them, making little distinction between the islands and the mainland. After the American Revolution their paths separated, but earlier they had much in common. In the hope of compensating for the deficiency in mainland colonial records, a search was made in the literature of the French and British West Indies for contemporary descriptions of African dancing, instruments, and music, with results that far exceeded my highest hopes. Best of all, these reports were quite consistent with the fragmentary accounts from the mainland. For the first time it was possible to demonstrate from contemporary documents the introduction of African music in the New World, its survival for generations in some areas, and its transformation into something different—Afro-American or Creole music.

This book includes a substantial mass of historical evidence, much of it previously unknown to musicologists and historians of black culture, presenting a picture of the development of black folk music in the United States. Since some of the documents illuminate several different aspects of the music which are discussed in widely separated parts of the text, they may be cited more than once. Extra evidence which substantiates points presented in the text can be found in the "Additional Sources" at the ends of most chapters. They are indicated in the text by (AS 1), (AS 2), etc.

The book does not pretend to be complete, for no one person could possibly examine every potential source of information, especially after the surge of interest in black studies greatly increased the volume of new publications and reprints. Certain types of material were excluded, such as newspapers and manuscripts, not because they held no promise, but because time and strength had their limits. No attempt was made to correlate the written material with field recordings or oral history interviews. The Slave Narrative Collection gathered by the Federal Writers' Project in the 1930's was published too late for a careful examination, but it undoubtedly includes much valuable material. These and other documents yet to be examined may throw further illumination on aspects of the subject that remain unclear.

A NOTE ON ILLUSTRATIONS

The illustrations were selected as historic documents, using the same criteria as the quotations included in the text. Thus a contemporary drawing of black dancers and instruments made in Virginia in 1853 was preferred to a more polished painting by a better-known artist, "The Bones Player," by William Sidney Mount (1856), which had less significance as historical evidence. Similarly, numerous genre paintings of black fiddlers, banjo players, and dancers from the mid-nineteenth century, such as Christian

Mayr's "Kitchen Ball at White Sulphur Springs" (1838, in the North Carolina Museum of Art, Raleigh), were passed over despite their authentic charm because the activities they illustrated had been documented at an earlier date. Artists' imaginative conceptions of what could have existed earlier have been excluded, such as E. W. Kemble's pictures of Congo Square in New Orleans that illustrated George Cable's *Century Magazine* articles of 1886.

In addition to pictures, music has been reproduced to permit the examination of primary documents that are now extremely scarce. However, a plan to include a number of pieces of sheet music that may have been black folk music was abandoned for two reasons. First, many of them are already available in modern editions, such as the Brown University Library's *Series of Old American Songs* (Providence, 1936) and Hans Nathan's *Dan Emmett and the Rise of Early Negro Minstrelsy* (Norman: University of Oklahoma Press, 1962), which includes "The Bee-Gum" (Baltimore: G. Willig, Jr., 1833). Second, these versions put into conventional standard notation by unknown arrangers could not be identified as folk music with any certainty. The whole question of the relationship of black folk music to Negro minstrelsy is a knotty one, still to be disentangled. For those who wish to pursue this matter futher, two songs in the Driscoll Collection at the Newberry Library in Chicago may be of interest: "Aunt Milly. A Popular Virginia Melody," arr. W. E. Liddle (Boston: H. Prentiss, c 1844) and "Come Back, Steben, A Negro Cavatina, as sung by a Kentuckian" (Philadelphia: Lee & Walker, c 1848).

ACKNOWLEDGMENTS

My debt to my fellow librarians who patiently answered my letters and questions cannot be overestimated. At the outset my local public library in Linden, New Jersey, provided general literature and invaluable inter-library loan service. I spent long days in the New York Public Library, especially in the divisions for American History, Genealogy, Rare Books, Manuscripts, and the Schomberg Collection of Negro History. Later I consulted the collections at the Library of Congress, Cornell University, the American Antiquarian Society, Widener Library at Harvard, Smith College, the Free Library of Philadelphia, the Pennsylvania Historical Society, the Newberry Library, and the University of Chicago. Libraries consulted by correspondence included the Massachusetts Historical Society, the University of the West Indies, the Caroliniana Library of the University of South Carolina, the Southern

Historical Collection at the University of North Carolina, the Germantown, Pennsylvania, Historical Society, and many others. Invaluable manuscripts were located among the McKim Papers at the New York Public Library and at Cornell; the Garrison Family Papers at Smith College and Houghton Library, Harvard University; Library of the State Historical Society of Wisconsin, the Library of Congress, Rutgers University, and the Pierpont Morgan Library, who generously granted permission to quote from these materials. To all of them, my most grateful thanks.

Many individuals graciously responded to a stranger's letters asking for information about long-ago people and events. From the Garrison family, I am deeply grateful to the late Mrs. Hendon Chubb (formerly Mrs. Philip McKim Garrison), Miss Eleanor Garrison, and Lloyd K. Garrison, among others. Caroline Farrar Ware shared her knowledge and her family papers with me. A number of historians were generous with suggestions and advice, notably Willie Lee Rose, John Anthony Scott, Sidney Kaplan, Joseph Logsdon, John Blassingame, and Winthrop D. Jordan. Special thanks are due Eva Maddox, who typed the entire manuscript. The supportive interest and encouragement of my family never faltered through the years. To my husband, Morton, and my children, William and Suzanne, I owe more than I can say.

Successive chairmen of the Department of Music at the University of Chicago encouraged and sponsored my work: Leonard B. Meyer, Howard Mayer Brown, and Robert L. Marshall, as did John Hope Franklin, chairman of the Department of History, and Hans Lenneberg, Music Librarian. Without their support the project could not have been completed. Other colleagues and friends who encouraged me were William Lichtenwanger, Frank C. Campbell, H. Wiley Hitchcock, Donald W. Krummel, the late Sidney Kramer, Miriam Studley, and Edward Reilly, of Colonial Williamsburg.

Above all, I am grateful to the American Council of Learned Socieites, the Illinois Arts Council, an agency of the state, and the National Endowment for the Humanities for their generous support which made completion of this study possible. The conclusions, findings, etc., do not necessarily represent their views.

—D. J. E.

Sinful Tunes and Spirituals

. . . .

....

Prologue: The African Heritage and the Middle Passage

The beginnings of African dancing and music are lost in the mists of antiquity; statues and pictures bear witness that they were known to the Greeks and the Romans.[1] During the fourteenth century a sophisticated and learned Arab historian, Ibn Khaldun, wrote of the Africans: "They are found eager to dance whenever they hear a melody."[2] In the next century, when the Portuguese under Prince Henry the Navigator began the European exploration of Africa, reports of African singing were included in their chronicles. The official account of the landing in Portugal of a group of captured Africans from about 1445 described their singing sympathetically:

> But what heart could be so hard as not to be pierced with piteous feeling to see that company? For some kept their heads low and their faces bathed in tears, looking one upon another ... others made their lamentations in the manner of a dirge, after the custom of their country. And though we could not understand the words of their language, the sound of it right well accorded with the measure of their sadness.[3]

1. Snowden, *Blacks in Antiquity*, pp. 106, 165, 190–91. Full citations for all footnote items are given in the bibliography.

2. Ibn Khaldùn, *Introduction to History*, p. 63.

3. Zurara, *Discovery and Conquest of Guinea*, I, 81. Sir Arthur Helps gave a slightly different translation in his *Spanish Conquest in America*, I, 38: "... others made their lamentations in songs, according to the customs of their country, which, although we could not understand their language, we saw corresponded well to the height of their sorrow."

These reports were mere fragments, demonstrating little but the existence of the music and its great emotional appeal at a time when European knowledge of Africa in general was hardly more than an amalgam of legend with a few facts drawn from ancient authorities and the accounts of early travelers.[4] By the beginning of the seventeenth century, however, when the first blacks arrived in the colony of Virginia, commercial relations between England and Africa were becoming increasingly profitable, and interest in Africa was widespread. An employee of the Company of Adventurers of London trading to Guinea and Benin, Richard Jobson, published a lively description of his travels, including descriptions of the music and instruments he observed.

> There is, without doubt, no people on the earth more naturally affected to the sound of musicke then these people . . . they use singing of Songs unto their musicke, the ground and effect whereof is the rehearsall of the auncient stocke of the King . . . and recounting over all the worthy and famous acts by him . . . singing likewise *extempore* upon any occasion is offered. . . . They have little varietie of instruments, that which is most common in use, is made of a great gourd, and a necke thereunto fastned, resembling, in some sort, our Bandora; but they have no manner of fret, and the strings they are either such as the place yeeldes, or their invention can attaine to make, being very unapt to yeeld a sweete and musicall sound, notwithstanding with pinnes they winde and bring to agree in tunable notes, having not above sixe strings upon their greatest instrument: In consortship with this they have many times another who playes upon a little drumme which he holds under his left arme, and with a crooked sticke in his right hand, and his naked fingers on the left he strikes the drumme. . . . [5]

Jobson's description of "their most principall instrument, which is called Ballards" will be deferred until the balafo is discussed. He continued with details about dancing and the treatment of "professional" musicians, to whom he applied the term "Juddy," apparently a variant of "griot." His description included many of the elements used by later writers to characterize African music: long narrative histories, extemporaneous singing, and various instruments, among them a gourd with a neck and up to six strings, and drums.

Descriptions of African music until fairly recently—the end of the

4. A convenient summary of English knowledge of Africa at the time of the settlement of North America is Eldred D. Jones, *Elizabethan Image of Africa*.

5. Jobson, *Golden Trade*, pp. 105–8. The pertinent section has been included in Eileen Southern's *Readings in Black American Music*, pp. [1]–3. For additional contemporary descriptions of African music and dancing, see Thompson, *African Art*, pp. 30–41.

nineteenth century—tended to regard it as one music with specific characteristics, instead of many musics, some of them still imperfectly known. For our purposes, however, contemporary descriptions are meaningful despite their lack of precision, for they document the existence of the music and provide a frame of reference for the descriptions of that music in the New World.

Many Portuguese and Spanish descriptions of music in Africa and of African music in the New World were written before 1800,[6] but this account will be confined to the reports of the French and the English, who had direct impact on the area which was to become the United States. In 1721 an Englishman, John Atkins, arrived in Sierra Leone; later he wrote:

> *Dancing* is the Diversion of their Evenings: Men and Women make a Ring in an open part of the Town, and one at a time shews his Skill in antick Motions and Gesticulations, yet with a great deal of Agility, the Company making the Musick by clapping their hands together during the time, helped by the louder noise of two or three Drums made of a hollowed piece of Tree, and covered with Kid-Skin. Sometimes they are all round in a Circle laughing, and with uncouth Notes, blame or praise somebody in the Company.[7]

This improvised "blame or praise" was to be transported to the Americas, becoming a standard feature of festive singing on holidays and of all kinds of worksongs from corn songs in Kentucky to calypso songs in Trinidad. In 1749 a Frenchman, Michel Adanson, was attended by "guiriots . . . the name the negroes give to musicians and drummers of this country,"[8] an early report of a term that is still in use.

Other English reporters included Nicholas Owen, a slave dealer in Africa from 1746 to 1757, who wrote in his journal that the blacks played an instrument called "bangelo" and drums,[9] and Anna Maria Falconbridge, who wrote from Granville Town, Sierra Leone, on June 8, 1791, of an instrument "resembling our guitar, the country name of which is bangeon."[10] Whether Owen's "bangelo" was related to Mrs. Falconbridge's "bangeon," and either or both to the banjo, is still conjectural.

Another observer of African music and instruments was a physi-

6. See Stevenson, "Afro-American Musical Legacy."

7. Atkins, *Voyage*, p. 53.

8. Adanson, "Voyage," p. 612. A fascinating discussion of *griots*, the professional musicians of twentieth-century Senegal, appears in Paul Oliver's *Savannah Syncopators*.

9. Owen, *Journal*, p. 52.

10. Anna Maria Falconbridge, *Narrative*, p. 80.

cian, Thomas Winterbottom, who was in Sierra Leone from July, 1792, until April, 1796. His perceptive comments are too long to be quoted in full:

> Music . . . is seldom listened to alone, but is generally used as an accompaniment to the dance. Drums are their most common instruments, and are of various kinds; some of these are six feet in length, and are composed of the trunk of a large tree hollowed, and covered at both ends with a sheep or goat's skin. . . . Another kind of drum, called eekilling, consists of the trunk of a tree hollowed out, but having both ends closed with wood, and in the side a longitudinal slit, upon which they beat alternately with two sticks. . . . They have also a smaller kind of drum, about two feet long, hollow at both ends, and covered with skins, but contracted in the middle like an hour glass. This is carried under the left arm, when walking, and is beaten upon with a stick. . . . Upon the Gold Coast they make a kind of drum by covering a large calabash with a skin; this is hung round the neck, and beat upon with the flat hand. When rowing in canoes also, they generally sing during the whole time, and one of the passengers accompanies the song with a small drum. One of the rowers sings a couplet, somewhat in a recitative voice, which is closed by a chorus in which they all join. When there are several rowers the couplet is repeated by a second person, and concluded by a general chorus. The subject of the song is either a description of some love intrigue, the praise of some woman celebrated for her beauty, &c. or it is of a satirical cast. . . . They are commonly impromptu, seldom the result of much study, and frequently describe the passengers in a strain either of praise or of the most pointed ridicule.[11] Besides the above, they have the banja or merrywang, as it is called in the West Indies, and the Dundo. . . . Besides the tabor or tamborine, which Europeans have borrowed from the Africans, they have also taken from them another instrument, frequently used in the British army, called a triangle, which is a piece of iron of that form beat upon by a rod of the same metal, and used with the drum. These sounds . . . [are accompanied] by . . . shouting and clapping of hands. . . . [12]

In contrast to Winterbottom's wealth of detail was a brief statement in the autobiography of an African who had lived in England for many years:

> We are almost a nation of dancers, musicians, and poets. Thus every great event, such as a triumphant return from battle, or other cause of public rejoicing is celebrated in public dances which are accompanied with songs and music suited to the occasion. . . . We have many musical instruments, particularly drums of different kinds, a piece of music which resembles a guitar, and another much like a stickado.[13]

11. This description of boat songs is strikingly similar to descriptions of the boat songs on the tidal rivers in the vicinity of Charleston, S.C., throughout the nineteenth century.

12. Winterbottom, *Native Africans*, I, 111–14. Biographical information from the new introduction by John D. Hargreaves and E. Maurice Backett, I, v, xiii.

13. Equiano, *Life*, I, 8.

It is hard to estimate the impact of these accounts on the public in Europe or in mainland North America. During the eighteenth and nineteenth centuries racist polemics proclaimed the total lack of culture in Africa, but travelers continued to publish factual accounts of what they had seen. For example, an 1834 account was written by a man who "resided and travelled in nearly all the colonies and settlements which he professes to describe," basing his opinions on "personal observation."

> The amusements which the negroes most esteem next to conversation, are music and dancing. . . . Their musical instruments are drums, flutes, and horns, and a kind of rude guitar. They have also professional and itinerant musicians called Guiriots. These people hire themselves by the day or month to any one that is disposed to entertain them, and their business is to accompany him wherever he goes, and to sing his praises and proclaim his virtues (as impartially as European tombstones do those of the dead) to the bystanders.[14]

These accounts, only a few of the many that exist, should be sufficient to demonstrate the continuous existence of native African musics, recognized by contemporary European travelers as displaying distinctive qualities. As the nineteenth century progressed, European literature on Africa increased in volume, and more information became available. With the onset of modern anthropology and ethnomusicology, serious study of these musics began.

For many years the proponents of African influences in American music based their theories on the supposition that the transported slaves remembered the music they had known in Africa and constructed instruments modeled on those they recalled. It was generally accepted that they could not have brought any physical objects with them. A typical statement accompanied a recording of Afro-American music: "The drums were brought to this country by Africans more in their minds and in their creative skills than in any physical sense, because . . . it was impossible for them to bring anything but themselves." [15] While the Africans undoubtedly did make in their new "home" some instruments which they had known in Africa, it is possible to document another means of accounting for African instruments in the New World: the prevailing practice for more than 150 years—from 1693 to 1860—of encouraging the captives to dance aboard slave ships as a means of preserving their health. The mortality rate in the slave trade was staggering, and it behooved even the most brutal slaving captain to take some measures to ensure the profitable arrival of his cargo. Dancing served

14. Howison, *European Colonies*, I, 94.
15 James, brochure notes for *Afro-American Music*, p. 1.

the twofold purpose of providing physical exercise in a limited space and of combatting the widespread danger of depression, a recognized forerunner of suicide or revolt.

Accounts of dancing on Spanish or Portuguese slaving voyages may yet be found, for those nations were active in the trade prior to other countries. The earliest report found so far, however, dates from the 1693 voyage of the ship *Hannibal* of London. The commander, Thomas Phillips, wrote: "We often at sea in the evening would let the slaves come up into the sun to air themselves, and make them jump and dance for an hour or two to our bagpipes, harp, and fiddle, by which exercise to preserve them in health." [16] Captain Phillips described the use of instruments which probably belonged to the crew, providing for the blacks a mid-Atlantic exposure to Western instruments.

The first general encyclopedia to be published, Chambers's (1728), confirmed the general acceptance of this practice: "Negro's: a Kind of Slaves which make a considerable Article in the modern Commerce. . . . As soon as the Ship has its Complement [of slaves], it immediately makes off; the poor Wretches, while yet in sight of their Country, fall into Sickness, and die. . . . The only sure means to preserve 'em, is to have some Musical Instrument play to 'em, be it ever so mean." [17] Chambers's distinguished successor, Diderot's *Encyclopédie*, virtually repeated this helpful information, adding that any instrument would do, even a vielle or a musette.[18]

Dancing and singing figured in the examination of witnesses on the African slave trade before a select committee of the House of Commons in 1791. James Towne, carpenter of His Majesty's Ship *Syren*, who had been on the coast of Africa in 1760/61, 1767, and 1768, testified:

> They [the slaves] were kept in irons, and in the afternoon, after being fed, the boatswain and the mate . . . make them dance; and if they do not, they had each of them a cat to flog them, and make them do it which I have seen exercised repeatedly. . . .
>
> Have you ever heard the Slaves singing, and have you been acquainted with the subject of their song? I have. I never found it any thing joyous, but lamentations. What I did not understand I made it my business to learn what the subject was [He had earlier testified: "I knew their language nearly as well as English." (p. 21)] and from their information it was complaints for having been taken away from their friends and relations.

16. Thomas Phillips, "Voyage Made in the *Hannibal*," from Churchill, *Collection of Voyages and Travels* (1732), reprinted in Donnan, ed., *Documents*, I, 392.
17. Chambers, *Cyclopaedia*, II, 623.
18. *Encyclopédie*, XI, 80, "Negres."

Ecroyde Claxton, surgeon, who had been in Africa in 1788, gave similar testimony about dancing, whereupon he was asked: "Did the Slaves on board your vessel ever amuse themselves by singing?" He replied:

> I believe they very seldom amuse themselves by it—they were ordered to sing by the captain, but they were songs of sad lamentations. The words of the songs used by them were, Madda! Madda! Yiera! Bemini! Madda! Aufera! that is to say, they were all sick, and by and by they should be no more; they also sung songs expressive of their fears of being beat, of their want of victuals, particularly the want of their native food, and of their never returning to their own country—I could mention their own words.[19] (AS 1)

Alexander Falconbridge, a surgeon who shipped on four voyages to Africa for slaves from 1780 or 1781 to 1787,[20] published his own account in addition to testifying before the select committee:

> Exercise being deemed necessary for the preservation of their health, they [slaves on board ship] are sometimes obliged to dance, when the weather will permit their coming on deck. If they go about it reluctantly, or do not move with agility, they are flogged; a person standing by them all the time with a cat-o'-nine-tails in his hand for that purpose. Their musick, upon these occasions, consists of a drum, sometimes with only one head; and when that is worn out, they do not scruple to make use of the bottom of one of the tubs [in which their food is served]. . . . The poor wretches are frequently compelled to sing also; but when they do so, their songs are generally, as may naturally be expected, melancholy lamentations of their exile from their native country.[21]

The practice of dancing the slaves was not confined to British slave ships; the Dutch and French did it, too. (The practices of the Spanish and Portuguese are not considered here.) The private slave trade carried on by the Dutch between 1734 and 1802 was well documented by the records of the Middelburgsche Commercie Compagnie, a Zeeland-based slaving firm. The "instructions of the directors . . . to their captains were very explicit about hygienic procedures. . . . Right before the end of the journey the slaves were stimulated to dance and sing in order to lower the tensions. No wonder only a few slave mutinies on M.C.C. slavers are recorded."[22] The Dutch West India Company issued similar instructions, requiring compulsory physical exercise at regular intervals, with wooden drums carried aboard to assist in keeping the slaves in

19. Great Britain, Parliament, House of Commons, *Minutes of the Evidence . . . Respecting the African Slave Trade*, XXXIV, 14, 20, 22, 34, 36.
20. *Ibid.*, p. 214.
21. Alexander Falconbridge, *Account*, p. 23.
22. Emmer, "Dutch Slave Trade," pp. 742–43.

"buoyant spirits" and to deemphasize the nature of their bondage.[23] (AS 2)

A few more contemporary descriptions may remove any remaining doubt that the practice was indeed common. Sir William Young wrote from St. Vincent's on December 7, 1791:

> Three Guinea ships being in the harbour, full of slaves from Africa, I testified a wish to visit the ships previous to the sale. . . . I was disgusted with a general jumping or dancing of the negroes on the deck, which some, and perhaps many of them, did voluntarily, but some under force or control; for I saw a sailor, more than once, catch those rudely by the arm who had ceased dancing, and by gesture menace them to repeat their motion, to clap their hands and shout their song of Yah! Yah! which I understood to mean "Friends." . . . I insisted on the dance being stopped. . . .[24]

In February, 1796, George Pinckard wrote from Carlisle Bay, Jamaica:

> A slave-ship, belonging to North America, and bound to Savanna in Georgia, had arrived from the coast of Guinea . . . and was lying very near to us, with a cargo of negroes on board. . . . [We] took off a boat . . . and went to visit the Guineaman. . . . In the daytime they were not allowed to remain in the place where they had slept, but were kept mostly upon the open deck, where they were made to exercise, and encouraged, by the music of their beloved banjar, to dancing and cheerfulness.
>
> We saw them dance, and heard them sing. In dancing they scarcely moved their feet, but threw about their arms, and twisted and writhed their bodies. . . . Their song was a wild yell, devoid of all softness and harmony, and loudly chanted in harsh monotony.[25]

Sir William and George Pinckard merely visited slave ships, but John Riland, to his horror, was ordered to travel on one. After studying at Christ Church, Oxford, he received "my father's edict . . . [with] the appalling information, that I must sail first in a slave-ship from Liverpool to the windward coast of Africa; and thence, with a living cargo, to Port Royal" in Jamaica. When they sailed on May 6, 1801, the cargo consisted of 170 males and 70 females. On May 24:

> The captain again wanted the slaves to dance; but they did not seem disposed to comply with his wish. He began to dance himself, by way of setting them an example; but they shewed no inclination to follow it, till the *cat* was called for. Then, indeed, they began to sing and skip about. A few, however, were content to have the *cat* smartly applied across their

23. Goslinga, *Dutch in the Caribbean*, p. 38.
24. Young, "Tour," in Edwards, *History*, III, 268.
25. Pinckard, *Notes*, I, 97–103.

shoulders several times, before they would so much belie their feelings as to make merry, when their heart was sad. . . .

Sometimes a drum was carried on the main-deck, to the music of which the men sung and danced. Being fixed to one spot, by means of the chain . . . their dancing consisted only of beating the deck violently with the foot which was at liberty. The women were not in irons. . . . They were frequently ordered to dance and sing; . . . though it was a difficult matter at times to prevail on them to engage in it. . . . [The captain] was at great pains . . . to induce them to take exercise; which they did, often with much reluctance. . . . An air of dejection appeared in the faces of most of them. . . . They were very averse to any kind of exercise; and, when they danced, their whole aim seemed to be to make noise enough to please the captain; . . . The songs which accompanied their dancing consisted only of one stanza, constantly repeated and loudly vociferated; . . . Some of the women used to sing very sweetly, and in a plaintive tone, when left to themselves. The subject of their songs I could not learn. . . . [26]

By the time of John Riland's voyage, the practice of "dancing the slaves" on shipboard was so widely known that it became one of the clichés of didactic literature. "The Sorrows of Yamba," a poem, was included in a collection of sermons, tracts, and dialogues "recommended to all masters and mistresses to be used in their families." It described life in Africa and the horrors of the slave ship as a prelude to the supreme indignity:

> At the savage Captain's beck
>   Now like brutes they make us prance;
> Smack the cat about the deck,
>   And in scorn they bid us dance.[27]

A strange verse to find among sermons dealing with the duty of obeying one's master! Its sympathy with the slave indicates that it might have been written during the second half of the eighteenth century, probably in England, when the Enlightenment was in full sway, and the stereotype of the brutish, happy slave had not yet been standardized.

The end of the legal slave traffic in 1808 had little impact on the well-established practice of encouraging the slaves to dance on shipboard to preserve their health. Captain Canot, the prototype of slaving captains, wrote in his journal on March 15, 1827: "During afternoons of serene weather, men, women, girls and boys are allowed to unite in African melodies, which they always enhance by an extemporaneous *tom-tom* on the bottom of a tub or tin kettle."[28] On the eve of the Civil War, a slave ship, the bark *Wildfire*, was

26. Riland, *Memoirs*, pp. 46–60.
27. "Sorrows of Yamba," in Meade, ed., *Sermons*, p. 184.
28. Canot, *Captain Canot*, pp. 99–104.

Upon one of their Feſtivals when a great many of the Negro Muſicians were gathered together, I deſired Mr. *Baptiſte*, the beſt Muſician there to take the Words they ſung and ſet them to Muſick, which follows.

You muſt clap Hands when the Baſe is plaid, and cry, *Alla, Alla.*

African music in Jamaica. Source: Sir Hans Sloane, *A Voyage to the Islands of Madera, Barbados, Nieves, S. Christopher and Jamaica, with the Natural History of the . . . Last of These Islands. . . .* London: Printed by B. M. for the Author, 1707. I, l–li. Courtesy of the Newberry Library.

Koromanti.

Meri Bonbo

mich langa meri wa langa.

taken in tow by an American ship in sight of Cuba and brought to Key West, Florida, on May 20, 1860. On board were 510 native Africans from the River Congo. *Harper's Weekly* deplored the poor physical condition of many of the "passengers," but added comments that would have been equally appropriate a century and a half earlier: "The well ones . . . were ready at any moment to join in a song or dance. . . . Their singing was monotonous. The words we did not understand."[29] The incongruity of African singing and dancing during the horrors of a slave voyage made it unbelievable to abolitionists, but it was true nonetheless, a link with the past that was gone among the brutalities of the awful present. Even the slave trade had to make some compromises to keep its cargo alive long enough to reach the market.

The instruments which accompanied this dancing could have been almost anything from Captain Phillips's bagpipe, harp, and fiddle of 1693 to the bottom of a tub in which their food was served, but contemporary observers reported that African instruments were also used, being collected and brought on board for this specific purpose. Present evidence is insufficient to indicate how widespread this practice was, but it seems beyond doubt that slave captains for purely pragmatic reasons were unwitting agents in transmitting African instruments to the New World. George Pinckard wrote from Carlisle Bay, Jamaica, in February, 1796, of the dancing of the slaves to "the music of their beloved banjar" an instrument of demonstrable African origin.[30] Still more convincing was the statement made by Bryan Edwards, a resident of the West Indies for over thirty years, in describing the Middle Passage: "In the intervals between their meals, they [the slaves] are encouraged to divert themselves with music and dancing; for which purpose such rude and uncouth instruments as are used in Africa, are collected before their departure. . . ."[31]

Memories of that dreadful voyage, enlivened occasionally by intervals of familiar singing and dancing, were handed down from father to son, emerging in the reminiscences of former slaves. Uncle Ephraim, the grandson of a native of the Ivory Coast, retold the story of his grandfather's voyage to Virginia, a dreary, stormy crossing with much illness. Finally the winds calmed down, and the slaves were allowed to come up on deck: "Keeps dozen or so chain togedd'ah. Feed 'em good, an' dey sits on de deck watchin' de sun go

29. "Africans of the Slave Bark, 'Wildfire,' " p. 344.
30. Pinckard, *Notes*, I, 103.
31. Edwards, *History*, II, 116.

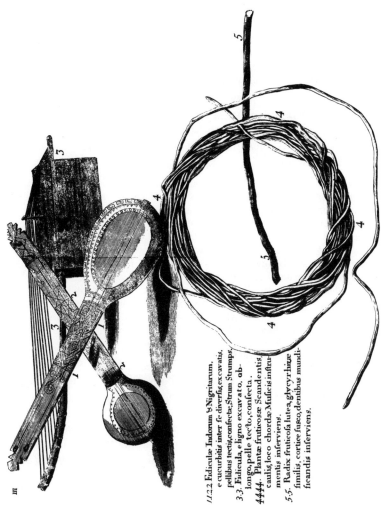

III

1122. Fidiculæ Indorum & Nigritarum,
e cucurbitis inter se diversis, excavatis,
pellibus tectis, confectæ, Strum Strumps.

3.3. Fidicula, e ligno excavato, ob-
longo, pelle tecto, confecta.

4444. Plantæ fruticosæ Scandentis,
caulis, loco chordæ Musicis instru-
mentis inserviens.

5.5. Radix fruticosa lutea, glycyrhizæ
similis, cortice fusco, dentibus mundi-
ficandis inserviens.

African instruments in Jamaica. Source: Sloane, *Voyage*, I, plate 3. Courtesy of the Newberry Library.

down an' de moon come up. Den dey sings. One sings, an' de res' hum, lak. What dey sing? Nobody don' know. It's not ou'ah words. Dey sing language what dey learn in Africa when dey was free!"[32]

Once the slaves debarked in the New World, music, dance, and instruments would provide vivid means of recalling their lost homeland. These remnants of their culture were early recognized by planters as potent means of acclimating them, so (initially, at least) their arts were encouraged. And when slaves were transported by water between the West Indies and the North American mainland, music and dancing were again permitted, if not encouraged. A glimpse of this activity was provided by a German naturalist, Johann David Schoepf, who sailed from St. Augustine, Florida, to Providence in the Bahamas on March 29, 1784. After describing in great detail the tropical fauna he saw, Schoepf wrote about the slaves on board who were being sent to market in the Bahamas:

> Another sort of amusement was furnished us by several among the negroes on board, native Africans. One of them would often be entertaining his comrades with the music and songs of their country. The instrument which he used . . . he called *Gambee*: a notched bar of wood, one end of which he placed against his breast. In his right hand he held a small stick of wood, split lengthwise into several clappers . . . in his left hand also a small thin wooden stick, unsplit. Beating and rubbing both of these, vigorously and in time, over the notches of the first stick, he produced a hollow rattling noise, accompanied by a song in the Guinea tongue. . . . The Guinea negroes are extremely fond of this rude, barbaric music, and sing or hear their folk-songs never without the greatest excitement; and they are at such times capable of any enterprise. Hence in Jamaica, and elsewhere, where there are many Guinea slaves, this sort of music and song is forbidden. . . . [33]

The music which arrived in the New World with the African slaves survived with them the trauma of exile, forced labor, and alienation. Wherever the Africans were taken, the music went with them, merging to a degree with the white man's culture, but never losing its distinctive qualities. How it was modified by its new surroundings and how it modified the music of the whites is a fascinating aspect of music in the Americas.

32. Orland Kay Armstrong, *Old Massa's People*, p. 52.
33. Schoepf, *Travels*, II, 260–61.

ADDITIONAL SOURCES

AS1. The abstract of this evidence was published separately, including a section on "Method of . . . exercising the Negroes. . . . After meals they are made to jump in their irons. This is called dancing by the slave dealers. . . . The above account of . . . dancing,* and singing the slaves, is allowed by all the evidences as far as they spake to the same points. . . ." * "The necessity of exercise for health, is the reason given for compelling the slaves to dance. . . ." *Abstract of the Evidence*, pp. 44–46. See also [Clarkson,] *Substance of the Evidence*, pp. 18, 32, 36, 45, 53, 65, 76, 135. The index entry "Slaves compelled to dance" is followed by the references 14, 20, 32, 35, 44, 53, 134, and 135.

AS2. For comparable practices among the French, see Garneray, *Voyages—Souvenirs de ma Vie Maritime* (1851), quoted in Mousnier, *Journal de la Traité des Noirs*, pp. 202–3; and Robin, *Voyages*, III, 167–70. See also *Description d'un Navire Négrier* (1789), pp. 9–10, quoted in Vaissière, *Saint-Domingue*, p. 161. A description of the practice without specifying the nationality of the slavers appears in Frossard, *Cause des Ésclaves Nègres*, I, 264, 275–76.

PART ONE

Development of Black Folk Music to 1800

1

. . . .

Early Reports of African Music in
British and French America

A chronic difficulty in discussing African music in the New World
has involved documenting its earliest period. Descriptions of music
in Africa and aboard slave ships prove that the music existed and
that it came to the New World with the slaves, but they fail to
answer other questions—how long it persisted in its new
environment, and how it was transformed into something now
called Afro-American. Authentic answers to these questions are not
at all easy to find, for the published literature on the thirteen
colonies says very little about the black population and still less
about its music. Seemingly Ralph Ellison's Invisible Man was already invisible.

If the search for contemporary descriptions of black music is
confined to mainland North America, an anomalous situation is
revealed: the blacks arrived in the colonies in 1619, but almost
nothing about their music has been found before the end of the
seventeenth century, when they were already playing the fiddle.
Very fragmentary accounts of music and dancing have been found
from the mainland during the seventeenth century—not enough, by
themselves, to present a convincing case that African music and
dancing continued among the Africans after their arrival in the
thirteen colonies. This lack of contemporary description becomes
comprehensible when one realizes that the black population of the

mainland colonies grew very slowly throughout the seventeenth century, and that it was widely dispersed among a much larger white population. Consider this description of the growth of the black population of Virginia: "In 1624, there were only 22 Negroes in Virginia. . . . In 1640, they had not increased to more than 150. Nine years later, when Virginia was inhabited by 15,000 whites, there were still only 300 Negroes. . . . In 1715 the population of all the [mainland] colonies with the exception of South Carolina was overwhelmingly composed of a white yeomanry, ex-indentured servants and wage earners."[1] Ulrich Bonnell Phillips had written in 1918: "For two generations [after their arrival in North America] the Negroes were few, they were employed alongside the white servants, and in many cases were members of their masters' households. They had by far the best opportunity which any of their race had been given in America to learn the white men's ways. . . ."[2] Conversely, they would have had difficulty preserving their own culture.

But there were other colonies in the West Indies that shared with the mainland a common relationship to the mother country. "The colonists in the two areas were the same sorts of people, and the same kinds of men provided the planning and financing. In fact, entrepreneurs in England frequently had simultaneous interests in Virginia, Bermuda, and the West Indies."[3] Moreover the two areas shared close commercial ties and a constant interchange of populations, both black and white. In the seventeenth and eighteenth centuries both Britain and France regarded all their colonies in the New World as part of the same colonial structure, regardless of where they were located. Barbados and South Carolina, the French Antilles and Louisiana were closer in their interests, their plantation systems, and their exchanges of population than, say, Massachusetts and South Carolina. While in Virginia the Negroes were few, in the islands they were a large majority. Considering these factors, it seems reasonable to look to contemporary accounts of the West Indies for illumination on aspects of black life on the mainland that were ignored in local sources. Happily, accounts of the West Indies yield rich descriptions of African dancing, instruments, and

1. Marvin Harris, "Origin of Descent Rule," in *Slavery in the New World*, ed. Foner and Genovese, pp. 51–52. South Carolina, settled in 1670, was the only mainland colony where there was a black majority. Being settled so late in the seventeenth century, however, it did not materially alter the statement as to conditions before 1700. Cf. Wood, *Black Majority*.

2. Ulrich Bonnell Phillips, *American Negro Slavery*, p. 75.

3. Pomfret and Shumway, *Founding the American Colonies*, p. 304.

music, far beyond expectation. For example, a description of all the British colonies in the New World written by a single author merely mentioned "Negro servants" in Virginia, but in discussing Barbados the writer dwelt on the blacks in considerable detail, particularly their religion, instruments, and music, commenting that "Negro servants [in Virginia] . . . are but a few, in comparison to the Sugar-Plantations."[4] In 1708, when this report appeared, there were so few blacks in Virginia that they did not dominate the landscape or the culture, whereas in the sugar islands they were all pervasive.

England and France in the seventeenth century were far more interested in the West Indies than in North America, for the most elementary financial reason: enormous fortunes were to be made from sugar.[5] Contrast the slow growth of Virginia, described earlier, with Oldmixon's account of Barbados: "The Character of this Island was such, as drew over Multitudes to see and inhabit it; insomuch that twenty Years after the first Settlement was made there [ca. 1625], the Militia of the Country were more in Number than that of *Virginia* is now [1708], tho the Place is not a fiftieth Part so big."[6]

The cultural heritage brought from Africa, common to the slaves both on the mainland and in the islands, met with less overt opposition in the islands and so was able to maintain itself freely and for a longer time.[7] The conditions in the islands which were conducive to the preservation of African cultural patterns included absentee landowning, with an accompanying lack of interest in the leisure activities of the slaves; frequent influxes of new arrivals from Africa; and a very high proportion of blacks to whites, ranging from 5:1 to as high as 25:1.[8] The blacks on the mainland, relatively fewer in number and dispersed among a much larger white population, did not all come directly from Africa; slaves already "seasoned" in the West Indies were considered more desirable, since they could al-

4. Oldmixon, *British Empire in America*, I, 113, 118, 122–24; II, 289.

5. ". . . it is to be observ'd, that of all the Colonies which these three European Nations [the English, the French, and the Dutch] have planted in America, those . . . in the *Caribby-Islands* are of greatest account, and . . . the most advantageous upon the score of Trade." [Rochefort,] *History*, p. 158.

6. Oldmixon, *British Empire in America*, I, 113.

7. Dunn, *Sugar and Slaves*, pp. 250ff. "The West Indian slave, barred from the essentials of European civility, was free to retain as much as he wished of his West African cultural heritage. Here he differed from the Negro in Virginia or New England, who was not only uprooted from his familiar tropical environment but thrown into close association with white people and their European ways. It is not surprising, therefore, that blacks in the sugar islands preserved more of their native culture than blacks in North America."

8. Eric Williams, *From Columbus to Castro*, pp. 104–7.

ready understand some English or French and had become accustomed to plantation labor.

However, the descriptions of African music from the islands were quite consistent with the more fragmentary accounts surviving from the mainland, as will be demonstrated in the pages to come. They present a picture of the persistence and development of this music in the colonies of the New World: Barbados, Jamaica, Antigua, Virginia, and South Carolina—all British—and Martinique, Saint-Domingue (Haiti), Guadeloupe, and Louisiana—all French. (The colonies of other countries are not considered, since they had less impact on what was to become the United States.) Whether the colonies were British or French, on the mainland or in the islands, the culture of the slaves was initially African and, as seen through the eyes of European observers, seemingly homogeneous. In an attempt to demonstrate this, contemporary accounts from different geographic areas will be presented in roughly chronological order, with interruptions in that order to permit the development of specific topics. Since African music persisted much longer in some areas than in others, a strictly chronological organization cannot be maintained.

First come the very earliest reports from both French and British colonies. The dance called *la calinda* and its associated instrument, the *banza*, once introduced, will be followed throughout their history to show the persistence of a dance and an instrument, both African in origin. There follows a discussion of other African dances, drums and other African instruments (notably the balafo, an African xylophone), the legal restrictions on their use, funeral practices, and African festivals in the northern colonies on the mainland (such as Pinkster), concluding with worksongs and other kinds of singing.

The chronology begins about 1640. Charles I was struggling to stay on the throne of England and Louis XIV was yet uncrowned when Jean-Baptiste Du Tertre, a young Dominican monk, was sent as a missionary to France's new overseas possessions in the West Indies. His descriptions of what he saw there over a period of six years formed part of one of the first detailed histories of the Antilles by a Frenchman. Although the cultivation of sugar was just beginning and the importation of Africans was not yet the flood it was to become, Du Tertre devoted a chapter of his four-volume work to "Des Recreations des Négres."

He described the gatherings of Negroes on Sundays and festivals to dance in the styles of their native countries, singing their own songs (which he found "tres-desagreable"). The accompaniment was provided by a drum made from the trunk of a hollowed tree, with the skin of a "loup marin" stretched over the opening. One of the Negroes held this instrument between his legs and played upon it with his fingers "comme sur un tambour de basque"; after he played a phrase ("couplet"), the dancers sang a refrain, alternating throughout. Another instrument was made from a calabash filled with little stones, which Du Tertre thought was played very skillfully and found more agreeable. The exertions of the dancers astonished the good father, who marveled at how little fatigue the Negroes seemed to feel after spending a whole afternoon in this manner. Indeed, he reported that the dancing sometimes continued throughout the night, the slaves not separating from each other until it was time to begin work.

While the men and women were dancing "de toute leur force," the children formed a separate group of dancers, imitating the postures of their fathers and mothers and mimicking their gestures; they continued dancing and singing until they fell asleep.[9]

Du Tertre described events which he witnessed before 1656, when he left the Antilles for the last time, including a complex of cultural elements which now would be regarded as characteristically African: drums made from hollowed tree trunks covered with skin and held between the drummer's legs, the alternation between a solo performer and a chorus, and dancing which continued for an extended period. The calabashes filled with stones could have derived either from Africa or from the Caribs.[10]

The next reporter, Richard Ligon, left England on June 16, 1647, "bound for the Indies in hopes to mend his fortunes . . . [which had suffered in the Civil War in England. He] was already a man of more than 50 years . . . a shrewd, very accurate observer of the West Indian scene."[11] Since he claimed to know well the instrumentalists at Black Friars, it has been speculated that he may have been a professional musician, a supposition reinforced by the discovery that he was the executor named in the will of John Coprario (or Cooper), Master of Music for King Charles I.[12] His account, dated "Upper Bench Prison, July 12th, 1653," where he was imprisoned for debt, is worth quoting at length:

> The Negres . . . are fetch'd from severall parts of *Africa*, who speake severall languages, and by that means, one of them understands not

9. Du Tertre, *Histoire Générale des Antilles*, II, 526–27.
10. Lillian Moore, "Moreau de Saint-Méry and Danse," pp. 231–59.
11. Goveia, *Historiography*, pp. 26–27.
12. Field, "Musical Observations from Barbados," p. 565.

another. . . . We had an excellent Negre in the Plantation, whose name was *Macow*, and was our Chiefe Musitian; a very valiant man, and was keeper of our Plantine-groave. . . .

On Sunday they rest, and have the whole day at their pleasure. . . . In the afternoon on Sundayes, they have their musicke, which is of kettle-drums, and those of severall sises; upon the smallest the best musician playes, and the others come in as Chorasses: the drum all men know, has but one tone; and therefore varietie of tunes have little to doe in this musicke; and yet so strangely they varie their time, as 'tis a pleasure to the most curious eares, and it was to me one of the strangest noyses that ever I heard made of one tone; and if they had the varietie of tune, which gives the greater scope in musicke, as they have of time, they would do wonders in that Art. . . .

I found *Macow* very apt for it himselfe, and one day comming into the house (which none of the *Negroes* use to doe, unlesse an Officer, as he was,) he found me playing on a Theorbo, and sinking to it which he hearkened very attentively to; and when I had done took the Theorbo in his hand, and strooke one string, stopping it by degrees upon every fret, and finding the notes to varie, till it came to the body of the instrument; and that the neerer the body of the instrument he stopt, the smaller or higher the sound was, which he found was by the shortening of the string, considered with himselfe, how he might make some triall of this experiment upon such an instrument as he could come by; having no hope ever to have any instrument of this kind to practise on. In a day or two after, walking in the Plantine grove . . . I found this *Negro* . . . sitting on the ground, and before him a piece of large timber, upon which he had laid crosse, six Billets, and having a handsaw and a hatchet by him, would cut the billets by little and little, till he had brought them to the tunes, he would fit them to; for the shorter they were, the higher the Notes which he tryed by knocking upon the ends of them with a sticke, which he had in his hand. When I found him at it, I took the stick out of his hand, and tried the sound, finding the six billets to have six distinct notes, one above another, which put me in a wonder, how he of himselfe, should without teaching doe so much.[13] I then shewed him the difference between flats and sharpes, which he presently apprehended, as between *Fa*, and *Mi*: and he would have cut two more billets to those notes, but I had then no time to see it done, and so left him to his own enquiries. I say this much to let you see that some of these people are capable of learning Arts.

On Sundaies in the afternoon, their Musick plaies, and to dancing they go, the men by themselves, and the women by themselves, no mixt dancing. . . . their hands having more of motion than their feet, & their heads more than their hands. They may dance a whole day, and neer heat themselves; yet, now and then, one of the activest amongst them

13. "Richard Ligon had marveled at a balafo made by Macow and thought that the clever slave had invented it there in Barbados, whereas it was an instrument that had a history in Africa."—Bridenbaugh, *No Peace Beyond the Line*, p. 235. Whether the tuning that Ligon observed was traditional or whether Macow was adapting his instrument to the tuning he had learned from Ligon's theorbo must be left to others to determine.

will leap bolt upright, and fall in his place again, but without cutting a capre. When they have danc'd an hour or two, the men fall to wrastle, (the Musick playing all the while) . . . the women leave of their dancing, and come to be spectatours of the sport.

When any of them die, they dig a grave, and at evening they bury him, clapping and wringing their hands, and making a dolefull sound with their voyces. . . . For their Singing, I cannot much commend that, having heard so good in *Europe*; but for their voices, I have heard many of them very loud and sweet.

Ligon commented on the musical interests of the whites with much less enthusiasm:

And though I found at *Barbados* some, who had musicall mindes; yet, I found others, whose souls were so fixt upon, and so riveted to the earth and the profits that arise out of it, as their souls were lifted no higher; and those men think, and have been heard to say, that three whip-Sawes, going all at once in a Frame or Pit, is the best and sweetest musick that can enter their ears; and to hear a Cow of their own low, or an Assinigo bray, no sound can please them better. But these men souls were never lifted up so high, as to hear the musick of the Sphears, nor to be judges of that Science, as 'tis practised here on earth. . . .[14] (AS 1)

If more settlers in the colonies had been as sensitive and as articulate as Ligon, the extant record of the music of the Africans would have been far richer. However, pioneer conditions such as existed everywhere in the Western hemisphere at this time were not conducive to sensitive appreciation of the arts. Most of the settlers were fully occupied with the business of their daily activities, and the written records they left behind commonly say nothing about the music of the blacks, even though it may have been a constant accompaniment to their leisure hours.

The first official attempt to suppress African dancing and instruments was reported by Adrien Dessalles, who had access to the Archives Coloniales. There he found that the Conseil Souverain de Martinique issued an ordinance on May 4, 1654, prohibiting "danses et assemblées de nègres." This sweeping prohibition, so contrary to the natural inclinations of the black population, apparently proved impossible to enforce. On August 16, 1678, a planter named Greny was charged by the lieutenant of the island with having permitted a large gathering of Negroes at the wedding of one of his slaves; the "kalenda" had lasted from morning to night. One Lieutenant Nicolas Regnandin, who had been sent to disperse the crowd, was

14. Ligon, *True & Exact History*, pp. 46–49, 50, 52, 107. Ligon's descriptions of Sunday festivities and funerals were repeated virtually word for word in Samuel Clarke's *True and Faithful Account*, p. 69.

insulted and obliged to mount his horse in a hurry, somehow having antagonized the slaves. The Conseil then restated its prohibition, this time specifying "kalendas" by name. Dessalles inserted his own explanation of the term, here roughly translated: the *kalenda* was a gathering of Negroes where they danced in their own style to the sound of a drum and an instrument they called *banza*. The drum was often a cask or barrel, sometimes the first piece of wood they could find; it is a dance most lascivious and tiring.[15] These incidents, explained Dessalles, led to the inclusion of Article 16 in the Code Noir of 1685; the article forbade the gatherings of slaves, by day or night, on the property of their masters or elsewhere.[16] Further statements of the prohibition which mentioned the dance by name ("un Calenda" or "Kalenda") were issued on August 5, 1758,[17] and on May 23, 1772.[18]

Before following the career of the *banza* and *la calinda*, which continued throughout the eighteenth century and well into the nineteenth, the remaining reports from the seventeenth century should be considered. One published in 1680 was written by the Reverend Morgan Godwyn, who went to Virginia in 1665, becoming the minister of Marston parish in York County. After a short stay he returned to England, horrified by the abject state of the Negroes and Indians. His book was a plea that they be instructed and baptized, but incidentally he revealed that the Africans on the mainland performed African dances just as they did in the islands.

> Nothing is more barbarous, and contrary to Christianity, than their . . . *Idolatrous Dances*, and *Revels*; in which they usually spend the *Sunday*. . . .
> And here, that I may not be thought too rashly to impute Idolatry to their *Dances*, my conjecture is raised upon this ground . . . for that they use their Dances as a *means to procure Rain*: Some of them having been known to beg this Liberty upon the Week Days, in order thereunto. . . . [19]

A dialogue between a slave and his master published in 1684 testified that the dances of the slaves were already diverting the planters, in a tradition that led to the minstrel theatre.

> MASTER. Come hither, *Sambo* . . . make us *some Sport*, let us see one of your *Dances*, such as are used in your own Country, with all your odd Postures and Tricks for Diversion; I have heard you are the best at it of all my People.

15. Dessalles, *Histoire Générale des Antilles*, III, 296–97.
16. Moreau de Saint-Méry, *Loix et Constitutions*, I, 417.
17. *Ibid.*, IV, 234.
18. *Ibid.*, V, 384.
19. Godwyn, *Negro's & Indians Advocate*, p. 33.

SLAVE. *Boon Master*! If you will have me Dance upon mine Head, or Caper on the top of the House, I must do it, though I break my Neck; for you are become Lord both of my *Feet*, and every part of me. . . .

The slave begs to be excused because he is weary, admitting that on Sundays "amongst our selves, [we] endeavor to *forget* our Slavery, and skip about, as if our Heels were *our own*, so long sometimes, till our Limbs are almost as weary with that, as with working; But that is not my present case. . . ."[20] The language was not African, but the dancing certainly was.

In 1687 Richard Blome described the dancing on Barbados in much the same terms that Richard Ligon had used thirty years earlier:

> Every *Sunday* (which is the only day of Rest, and should be set apart for the Service of God) they employ either in . . . making Ropes . . . or else spend the Day in Recreation, as Dancing or Wrestling . . . in their Dancing they use Antick Actions, their hands having more of motion than their feet, and their head than either; nor do the men and women dance together, but apart; the Musick to which they dance being a sort of Kettle-Drums, one bigger than another, which makes a strange and various noise, but whether harmonious I leave to the Judgement of the Reader.[21]

Dancing in Jamaica was very similar. Sir Hans Sloane, who accompanied the Duke of Albemarle to that island as his physician in September, 1687, wrote after his return to England in 1689:

> The Negroes . . . will at nights, or on Feast days Dance and Sing; . . . They have several sorts of Instruments in imitation of Lutes, made of small Gourds fitted with Necks, strung with Horse hairs, or the peeled stalks of climbing Plants or Withs. These Instruments are sometimes made of hollow'd Timber covered with Parchment or other Skin wetted, having a Bow for its Neck, the Strings ty'd longer or shorter, as they would alter their Sounds. . . . They have likewise in their Dances Rattles ty'd to their Legs and Wrists, and in their Hands, with which they make a noise, keeping time with one who makes a sound answering it on the mouth of an empty Gourd or Jar with his Hand. Their Dances consist in great activity and strength of Body, and keeping time, if it can be. They very often tie Cows Tails to their Rumps, and add such other odd things to their Bodies in several places, as gives them a very extraordinary appearance. . . . They formerly on their Festivals were allowed the use of Trumpets after their Fashion, and Drums made of a piece of a hollow Tree, covered on one end with any green Skin, and stretched with

20. [Tryon,] "Discourse in Way of Dialogue," in his *Friendly Advice*, pp. 146–48.

21. [Blome,] *Present State of His Majesties Isles*, pp. 39–40. Blome's intermixing of mainland and island colonies in his title demonstrates seventeenth-century attitudes toward the colonies. The same passage appeared also in [Crouch,] *English Empire in America*, pp. 176–77.

Thouls or Pins. But making use of these in their Wars at home in Africa, it was thought too much inciting them to Rebellion, and so they were prohibited by the Customs of the Island.[22]

So before 1700 the British as well as the French issued prohibitions, not of the dancing itself, but of drums, trumpets, and other loud instruments.

La Calinda AND THE Banza

Dessalles reported the earliest reference found (1654) to a dance and an associated instrument that were to have a long and distinguished career in Creole culture: la calenda (or calinda) and the banza. From Jamaica Sir Hans Sloane described an instrument he called the "strum-strum," which seems to have been closely related to the banza, judging from its picture. He also described dancing, but gave it no distinctive name. La calenda was more fully described by another French monk, Jean Baptiste Labat, who went to Martinique as a missionary in 1694. His description may be found conveniently translated into English by Reginald Nettel in his "Historical Introduction to 'La Calinda.' "[23] Since Nettel's point of departure was Delius's version of la calinda in his opera Koanga, he omitted Labat's description of the instruments: two drums made from two tree trunks of unequal length, each with an open end and one covered with skinlike parchment. The larger, called "le grand tambour," was three or four feet long and fifteen or sixteen inches in diameter. The smaller, called the "baboula," was about the same length, but eight or nine inches in diameter. The drummers held them between their legs and played them with the four fingers of both hands. The larger provided the basic beat, while the smaller was played as fast as possible.

He also described other instruments. Some of the slaves had already learned to play the violin well, and they had a kind of guitar, made from half a calabash covered with a piece of skin and with a long neck. Four strings were raised on a bridge above the skin. This instrument was played by plucking and striking the strings. Labat gave it no name, but other accounts called it banza.

Labat suggested that the African dances, which he regarded as "dèshonnêtes," "indecentes," "lascives," "cette danse infame," could be replaced by teaching the slaves the minuet or the courante, which would satisfy their love of dancing in an innocent way. But he

22. Sloane, Voyage, I, xlviii–xlix, lii.

23. Nettel, " 'La Calinda,' " pp. 59–62. "Calinda" and "Bamboula" are both listed as "African Words" in Read, Louisiana-French, pp. 118, 120.

concluded ruefully that, in spite of all he could do, they were still dancing the *calenda*: the old, the young, and even the children. It seemed as if they had danced it in the wombs of their mothers.[24]

Labat described the French islands, and John Oldmixon the British, but the African dancing and instruments were common to them both. Oldmixon described the changes which had taken place in Barbados since Richard Ligon's time, slightly more than a half-century earlier:

> Sundays are the only Days of Pleasure to the Negroes . . . the Generality of them dance, or wrestle all Day, the Men and Women together. In Mr. *Ligon's* time, the Men danc'd by themselves, and the Women by themselves, but 'tis not so in ours. They have two Musical Instruments, like Kettle-Drums, for each Company of Dancers, with which they make a very barbarous Melody. They have other Musical Instruments, as a *Bangil*, not much unlike our Lute in any thing, but the Musick; the *Rookaw*, which is two Sticks jagg'd; and a *Jinkgoving*, which is a way of clapping their Hands on the Mouth of two Jars. These are all play'd together, and accompany'd with Voices, in a most terribly harmonious manner.[25]

The *bangil* to the English was the *banza* to the French.

Thirty years later the dancing and instruments remained about the same.

> On *Sundays* . . . towards the Evening . . . some hundreds of them [the slaves] will meet together, according to the Customs of their own Country (many of which they retain) with Strum-Strums and Calibashes, which they beat and make a horrid Noise with (tho' some of the *Creol* Negroes are esteem'd for keeping just Time, and playing very well on the Violin). . . .[26]

Substantially the same details as Labat had described in 1698 were given in Diderot's *Encyclopédie* under the headings "Calinda" (II, 474 [1758]), "Negres" (XI, 2nd ed., 66 [1768]), and "Tamboula" (XV, 874 [1765]), the last written by le Romain, identified in the preliminary discourse as chief engineer on the island of Grenada. Le Romain added that the "tamboula," a type of large drum, was always accompanied by one or two kinds of guitars with four strings which were called "banzas."[27] While the volumes of the *Encyclopédie* were appearing in France, Thomas Jefferys reported

24. Labat, *Nouveau Voyage*, IV, 152–60.
25. Oldmixon, *British Empire in America*, I, 123–24.
26. *Importance of Jamaica*, p. 19.
27. *Encyclopédie.* "Le Romain (first name and dates unknown) Mentioned at the end of the Preliminary Discourse as . . . the chief engineer of the West Indian island of Grenada. Very little is known of him." *Encyclopedia Selections: Diderot, D'Alembert and a Society of Men of Letters*, trans. Hoyt [and] Cassirer, p. 396.

an English approximation of "la calinda," "the *Calendoe*, a sport brought from the coast of *Guinea*, and attended with gestures which are not entirely consistent with modesty, whence it is forbidden by the public laws of the islands."[28] This term apparently did not achieve any currency, for it has not been found in any other source. English-speaking authors, when they discussed African dancing in the West Indies, usually used no specific names for the dances. For example, a poem dated "Basseterre [St. Kitts], Jan., 1763" mentioned the instrument by name, but not the dance.

> On festal days; or when their work is done;
> Permit thy slaves to lead the choral dance,
> To the wild banshaw's* melancholy sound.
> Responsive to the sound, head, feet, and frame
> Move awkwardly harmonious; hand in hand
> Now lock'd, the gay troop circularly wheels,
> And frisks and capers with intemperate joy,
> While those distinguish'd for their heels and air,
> Bound in the centre.... [29]

The poet's explanatory footnote read: "*Banshaw*. This is a sort of rude guitar, invented by the Negroes. It produces a wild pleasing melancholy sound."

Reginald Nettel's "Historical Introduction to 'La Calinda' " also included a translation of Moreau de Saint-Méry's description of the dance in his *Déscription . . . de la Partie Française de l'Isle Saint-Domingue . . .* ,[30] concerning events almost a hundred years later than those described by Père Labat. Yet they are remarkably consistent; the descriptions of the instruments are virtually identical. Moreau de Saint-Méry was as convinced of the African origins of the dance and music as Labat had been.

Between these two accounts the dance had been observed on the mainland in Louisiana. Le Page du Pratz, who had firsthand experience as a planter in that colony in 1758, wrote: "Nothing is more to be dreaded than to see the Negroes assemble together on Sundays, since, under pretence of Calinda, or the dance, they sometimes get together to the number of three or four hundred, and make a kind of Sabbath, which it is always prudent to avoid; for it is in those tumultuous meetings that they . . . plot their rebellions."[31]

28. Jefferys, *French Dominions*, II, 192. "Thomas Jefferys . . . became geographer to the Prince of Wales in 1746 and in 1760 to the king. He was the leading British chart and mapmaker of his day. . . ." Cumming, *British Maps of Colonial America*, p. 45. See also Goveia, *Historiography*, p. 74.

29. Grainger, *The Sugar-Cane; A Poem*. In Alexander Chalmers, *Works of the English Poets*, XIV, 12, lines 582–90 of book 4 of the poem.

30. Moreau de Saint-Méry, *Déscription*, I, 44.

31. Le Page du Pratz, *History of Louisiana*, pp. 380, 384, 387.

La calinda in one of its forms or something very similar to it survived in New Orleans into the nineteenth century, according to Hélène Allain's *Souvenirs d'Amérique et de France, Par une Créole.* She justified a long quotation (pp. [132]–70) from Moreau de Saint-Méry's book on Haiti on the grounds that the descriptions, including *la calinda*, fitted her recollections of New Orleans. Her account leaves something to be desired, since she reported what she had heard, not what she herself saw:

> I myself have heard a great deal in New Orleans of Negro dances. . . . At the time that we lived on the corner of Rue du Quartier and Rue Conde [1836–55] . . . the Negroes danced again [?] at Place Congo. It was a holiday for them every Sunday evening, and whites and blacks, slaves and masters, pressed themselves against the heavy gate that separated the dancers from the crowd. I never saw them myself, nor knew anyone who had seen them, but I believe . . . that these dances were identical with those one reads about in the description [i.e., Moreau de Saint-Méry]. Our Louisiana Negroes yield nothing to the Negroes of the older colonies: dances, songs, proverbs—they have inherited all.[32]

The vagueness of Allain's account was typical of most of the evidence about African dancing in New Orleans after 1835, but her claim that the culture of the Louisiana Negroes had much in common with that of the Negroes of the French West Indies will be supported by many other contemporary witnesses in the pages that follow.

The precise nature of *la calinda* and its choreographic history are still to be determined,[33] but the instrument most closely associated with it, the *banza* or banjo, seems to have been the most widely reported and longest lived of all the African instruments in the New World. A tabular summary of its literature appears in an appendix, and the more interesting and significant contemporary descriptions now follow in chronological order. They will disprove the legends that have grown up about the banjo—that it originated in the United States, that it was invented by minstrels in New York, and that it was totally unknown to the slaves. But only the folk banjo will be considered; the commercial banjo has another story.

Earlier accounts have described the *banza* and the *strum-strum*. Oldmixon's description of the *bangil* published in 1708 in an account of Barbados was repeated by Charles Leslie in 1740, without ac-

32. [Allain,] *Souvenirs d'Amérique*, pp. 171–73, my rough translation. Errors in the translation of this passage in Epstein, "African Music in British and French America." p. 73, were kindly noted by Henry A. Kmen in a letter to the author dated Feb. 19, 1974. They have been corrected here.

33. Other descriptions of la calinda appear in Lillian Moore, "Moreau de Saint-Méry and Danse," and Peytraud, *L'Esclavage*, pp. 232–35. Descriptions of African dancing in nineteenth-century New Orleans will be given in ch. 7.

knowledgment and now attributed to Jamaica.[34] (Apparently the instruments were as common in 1740 as they had been in 1708.) By 1754 the "banjer" was given as a means of identifying a runaway slave.[35] *Merry-wang* was the term used by Edward Long in 1774 for a "rustic guitar of four strings . . . made with a calibash . . . [with] a dried bladder, or skin . . . spread across the largest section; and . . . a handle . . . [ornamented] with a sort of rude carved work, and ribbands"[36]—this description from Jamaica. Nicholas Creswell saw the same kind of instrument in Maryland in 1774 and called it a banjo.[37]

The Reverend Jonathan Boucher, a Loyalist refugee from the American Revolution, devoted his later years to philology, beginning a supplement to Dr. Johnson's dictionary which he did not live to complete. Since "banjo" was near the beginning of the alphabet, this confirmed Tory's recollections of it were preserved:

> *Bandore, n.* A musical instrument . . . in use, chiefly, if not entirely, among people of the lower classes. . . . I well remember, that in Virginia and Maryland the favourite and almost only instrument in use among the slaves there was a *bandore*; or, as they pronounced the word, *banjer*. Its body was a large hollow gourd, with a long handle attached to it, strung with catgut, and played on with the fingers. . . . My memory supplies me with a couplet of one of their songs, which are generally of the improvisatori kind; nor did I use to think the poetry much beneath the music:
>
> Negro Sambo play fine *banjer*,
> Make his fingers go like handsaw.[38] (AS 2)

In 1755 a *Virginia Gazette* advertisement for a runaway slave specified "plays exceedingly well on the Banger, and generally carries one with him."[39] When Thomas Jefferson wrote his *Notes on the State of Virginia* in 1781, he included his only comment on the music of the blacks, mentioning in a footnote: "The instrument proper to them is the Banjar, which they brought hither from Africa, and which is the original of the guitar, its chords being precisely the four lower chords of the guitar."[40] In March, 1784, Johann David Schoepf saw this same instrument aboard a ship carrying slaves to market in Providence in the Bahamas:

34. [Leslie,] *New History of Jamaica*, p. 310.
35. Advertisement in *Maryland Gazette*, July 25, 1754, cited in "Eighteenth Century Slaves," p. 210.
36. [Edward Long,] *History of Jamaica*, II, 423.
37. Creswell, *Journal*, p. 19, entry for May 29, 1774, Nanjemoy, Md.
38. Boucher, *Glossary*, p. BAN.
39. *Virginia Gazette*, Feb. 18, 1775, p. [3], col. 2; see also *ibid.*, Jan. 8, 1780, p. [2], col. 3.
40. Jefferson, *Notes on the State of Virginia*, p. 257.

Banjo-like instrument painted by Samuel Jennings (active in Philadelphia 1787–ca. 1792). Detail from *Liberty Displaying the Arts and Sciences* (1792). Courtesy of the Library Company of Philadelphia.

Another musical instrument of the true negro is the *Banjah*. Over a hollow calabash (*Cucurb lagenaria L.*) is stretched a sheepskin, the instrument lengthened with a neck, strung with 4 strings, and made accordant. It gives out a rude sound; usually there is some one besides to give an accompaniment with the drum, or an iron pan, or empty cask, whatever may be at hand. In America and on the islands they make use of this instrument greatly for the dance. Their melodies are almost always the same, with little variation. The dancers, the musicians, and often even the spectators, sing alternately.[41]

In Antigua the same name was used for the same instrument:

Negroes are very fond of the discordant notes of the banjar . . . somewhat similar to the guittar, the bottom, or under part, is formed of one half of a large calabash, to which is prefixed a wooden neck, and it is strung with cat-gut and wire. This instrument is the invention of, and was brought here by the African negroes, who are most expert in the performances thereon, which are principally their own country tunes, indeed I do not remember ever to have heard any thing like European numbers from its touch. [It is played with] The toombah . . . similar to the tabor, and has gingles of tin or shells; to this music (if it deserves the name) I have seen a hundred or more dancing at a time. . . . [42]

Other reporters who took it for granted that the instrument was of African origin included Bryan Edwards[43] and Thomas Fairfax.[44] Illustrations show the common features that persisted over a century and more: Sloane included an engraving of a "strum-strum" in his *Voyage* of 1707, and the anonymous watercolor *The Old Plantation*, from around 1800, included a similar instrument. As the term "banjo" became standardized in English-speaking areas, *banza* continued to be used by the French. A vitriolic attack on the slaves of the French colonies published in 1810 included their method of making *banzas* as an example of their barbarism:

As to guitars, which the Negroes call *banza*, see what they consist of: they cut lengthwise through the middle of a calabash. . . . This fruit is sometimes eight inches and more in diameter. They stretch upon it the skin of a goat which they adjust around the edges with little nails; they make two holes in this surface; then a piece of lath or flat wood makes the handle of the guitar; they then stretch three cords of *pitre* (a kind of hemp taken from the *agave* plant, vulgarly called *pitre*), and the instrument is finished. They play on this instrument tunes composed of

41. Schoepf, *Travels in the Confederation*, II, 261–62.
42. Luffman, *Brief Account of . . . Antigua*, pp. 135–36. Letter XXX, dated "St. John's, Antigua, March 14, 1788."
43. Edwards, *History*, II, 84. Edwards's description of the *banja* was quoted by Thomas Winterbottom to describe an African instrument. See prologue.
44. Fairfax, *Journey from Virginia to Salem*, p. 2.

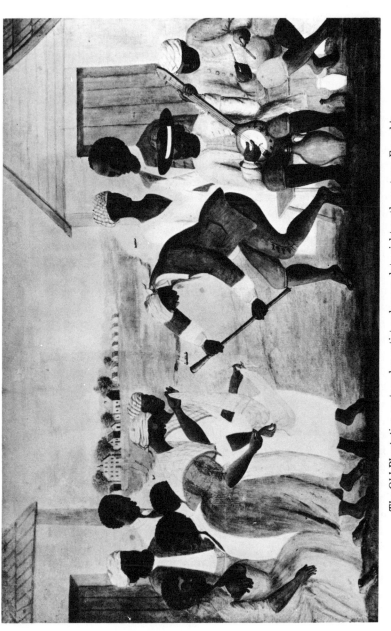

The Old Plantation, watercolor, artist unknown, late eighteenth century. Found in Columbia, S.C. African instruments, postures, possibly sacred dance; European dress. Reproduced by permission of the Abby Aldrich Rockefeller Folk Art Collection, Colonial Williamsburg.

three or four notes, which they repeat endlessly; this is what Bishop
Grégoire calls sentimental and melancholy music; and which we call the
the music of savages.[45]

After 1810 the banjo continued to be mentioned frequently, but in
an offhand manner, as if it were too well known to require detailed
descriptions.[46] The documents already cited should be sufficient to
demonstrate that the banjo was derived from Africa; that those in
the best position to know, including Thomas Jefferson, believed it
was an African instrument; and that it had a continuous existence
in the West Indies and on the North American mainland from the
late seventeenth century until well after the advent of the minstrel
theatre. The folk banjo has maintained itself in the folk tradition
down to this day, fretless banjos being sometimes preferred to their
commercial counterparts by rural performers in Virginia and the
Carolinas.[47]

OTHER AFRICAN DANCING[48]

African music has always been intimately associated with dance,
and frequently descriptions of dancing are the only evidence that
music was also present. This was especially true in the New World,
where the dancing led to a (frequently unfavorable) reaction while
the music was ignored. For example, Dr. Francis Le Jau, an
Anglican missionary in South Carolina, deplored the persistence of
Sunday dances in the first decade of the eighteenth century. What
had been essential to the slaves in the West Indies had not disappeared completely on the mainland, despite the many forces, both
sacred and secular, opposed to it. Le Jau wrote from Goose Creek on
October 20, 1709: "I[t] has been Customary among them [our
Slaves] to have their ffeasts, dances, and merry Meetings upon the
Lord's day, that practice is pretty well over in this Parish, but not
absolutely: I tell them that present themselves to be admitted to
Baptism, they must promise they'l spend no more the Lord's day in
idleness, and if they do I'l cut them off from the Communion." On
June 13, 1710, he again wrote to the secretary of the Society for the
Propagation of the Gospel in Foreign Parts (S.P.G.): "The Lord's
day is no more profaned by their dancings at least about me." And
again on August 30, 1712: "I hope the Dancings upon Sundays are

45. [Tussac,] *Cri des Colons*, p. 292. My rough translation.
46. For a fuller discussion of the history of the banjo, see Epstein, "Folk Banjo."
47. J. Roderick Moore, "Folk Crafts," pp. 22–29. See also Glassie, *Pattern in Material Folk Culture*, p. 24.
48. For a general discussion, see Emery, *Black Dance*. See also Moore, "Moreau de Saint-Méry and Danse."

quite over in this Neighborhood."[49] It seems to have been an uphill struggle.

In 1712 the Reverend John Sharpe wrote from New York that indifference to converting the slaves was so great that Christian slaves "are buried in the Common by those of their country and complexion without the office; on the contrary the Heathenish rites are performed at the grave by their countrymen."[50]

An anonymous "Inhabitant of His Majesty's Leeward Carribee-Islands" wrote to the Bishop of London on November 29, 1729, about a problem common to all the colonies: the conversion of the slaves to Christianity. "The Field-Slaves . . . on Sundays . . . whatever Orders may be made against it (at least in the *Leeward-Islands*) divert themselves with Singing, Playing, and Dancing after their several Country Modes. . . ."[51]

The Reverend George Whitefield wrote on January 23, 1739/40, "To the Inhabitants of Maryland, Virginia, North and South-Carolina, Concerning Their Negroes": "I have great reason to believe that most of you, on Purpose, keep your Negroes ignorant of Christianity; or otherwise, why are they permitted thro' your Provinces, openly to prophane the Lord's Day, by their Dancing, Piping and such like?"[52]

These fragmentary accounts from the early eighteenth century tell little more than that Africans danced in a manner that was considered heathenish in South Carolina, New York, the Leeward Islands, Maryland, Virginia, and North Carolina. It is significant that dancing was that widespread, although the reports give no idea of the degree of acculturation the dances may have shown. However, the official account of the 1739 Stono insurrection in South Carolina reported dancing, singing, and beating drums, which, under the circumstances, must have been African.

> On the 9th day of September last being Sunday which is the day the Planters allow them to work for themselves, Some Angola Negroes assembled, to the number of Twenty; at a place called Stonehow. . . . Several Negroes joyned them, they calling out Liberty, marched on with Colours displayed, and two Drums beating, pursuing all the white people they met with, and killing Man Woman and Child. . . . They increased every minute by new Negroes coming to them, so that they were above Sixty, some say a hundred, on which they halted in a field, and set to dancing, Singing and beating Drums, to draw more Negroes to them,

49. Le Jau, *Carolina Chronicle*, pp. 61, 77, 120–21.
50. Sharpe, "Proposals," p. 341.
51. *Letter to . . . the Lord Bishop of London*, pp. 12, 90–94.
52. Whitefield, *Three Letters*, Letter III, p. 14.

thinking they were now victorious over the whole Province, having marched ten miles & burnt all before them without opposition. . . . [53]

A tantalizing hint of African religious music came from the records of the Superior Council of Louisiana, September 9, 1743, in the case of the slave Jeannot. A mutilated document told of a mutiny against Jeannot's master and a threat to set fire to his cabin. "A service was sung in negro style and language two months before the day of his disappearance, wherefore he prays that Jeannot be arrested and imprisoned to be interrogated. . . . "[54] The official record breaks off there, with no further details about the service and no clue as to Jeannot's fate.

While reports from mainland North America usually were silent about the degree of acculturation shown in the dancing of the Africans, in Jamaica the culture was unmistakeably African. Edward Long, son of English landed gentry, "played a Cremona violin,"[55] and presumably knew as much about European music as other gentlemen amateurs. When he described the music and dancing of the slaves in his *History of Jamaica* of 1774, he knew he was dealing with non-European music:

> Their tunes for dancing are usually brisk, and have an agreeable compound of the *vivace* and *larghetto*, gay and grave, pursued alternately. They seem also well-adapted to keep their dancers in just time and regular movements. The female dancer is all languishing, and easy in her motions; the man, all action, fire and gesture; . . . In her paces she exhibits a wonderful address, particularly in the motion of her hips, and steady position of the upper part of her person; the execution of this wriggle, keeping exact time with the music, is esteemed among them a particular excellence; and on this account they begin to practise it so early in life, that few are without it in their ordinary walking. As the dance proceeds, the musician introduces now and then a pause or rest, or dwells on two or three *pianissimo* notes; then strikes out again on a sudden into a more spirited air. . . . [56]

In Virginia sometime before the Revolution African instruments were still in use, Negro dances being accompanied by a "banjor (a large hollow instrument with three strings), and a qua-qua (somewhat resembling a drum)."[57] With such instruments it seems reasonable to suppose that African dances such as were pictured in the anonymous watercolor *The Old Plantation*[58] would have been

53. Genl. Oglethorpe to the Accotant, Mr. Harman Verelst, Oct. 9, 1739, in Candler, comp., *Colonial Records*, XXII, pt. 2, p. 235.
54. "Records of the Superior Council of Louisiana," p. 145.
55. Howard, ed., *Records and Letters of . . . the Longs*, I, 123.
56. [Edward Long,] *History of Jamaica*, II, 242.
57. Smyth, *Tour*, I, 46.
58. Little, *Rockefeller Folk Art Collection*, p. 132.

performed. Very little is known of the evolution of new dance steps, possibly to the music of traditional African instruments—music which could well have been changing at the same time. Perhaps sources still to be investigated will throw light on these developments.

While the Revolution was in progress in 1779, Alexander Hewatt wrote of the Negroes of South Carolina:

> The negroes of that country, a few only excepted, are to this day as great strangers to Christianity, and as much under the influence of Pagan darkness, idolatry and superstition, as they were at their first arrival from Africa. . . . Sundays and holidays are indeed allowed the negroes in Carolina. . . . Holidays there are days of idleness, riot, wantonness and excess; in which the slaves assemble together in alarming crowds, for the purposes of dancing, feasting and merriment.[59]

Hewatt appeared to be objecting to the dancing as a desecration of the Sabbath, as the Reverend Francis Le Jau had done seventy years earlier; but whereas the dancing in 1708 almost certainly had been African, its character in 1779 cannot be stated with confidence. The fact that the slaves were still pagans is suggestive but not conclusive—conversion to Christianity would not have been a necessary precondition for learning European dances. But nothing in Hewatt's account would rule out African dancing to African instruments which were reported in South Carolina as late as 1805. The slave population of all the mainland colonies at the time of the Revolution was a heterogeneous mixture of new arrivals from Africa, thoroughly acculturated slaves, the children of parents who had been born on the mainland, and every possible intermediate gradation. Variations in the degree of acculturation would have been the norm, not the exception.

African singing was heard in South Carolina about 1782 by General William Moulton, who stopped at his own plantation on his way to Charleston to be present at its evacuation by the British:

> On my entering the place, as soon as the negroes discovered that I was of the party, there was immediately a general alarm and an outcry through the plantation that, "Massa was come! Massa was come!" . . . I stood in the piazza to receive them. They gazed at me with astonishment . . . and every now and then some one or other would come out with a "Ky!" and the old Africans joined in a war-song in their own language of "Welcome the war home."[60]

By 1788 the Negro dances, particularly those after work in the evening, gave rise to a controversy among the whites which persisted

59. [Hewatt,] *Rise and Progress*, II, 100, 103.
60. Society for the Preservation of Spirituals, *Carolina Low-Country*, p. 94.

as long as slavery itself. The apparent contradiction between the miseries of slavery and such vigorous dancing and singing created great problems in the thinking of Europeans and their American descendants. Rationalist opponents of slavery theorized from their studies that dancing and singing could not exist in slavery, that the claim of their existence was just another proslavery canard; the defenders of slavery would point to the dancing and singing as proof that slavery was really not so bad after all. Franklin's friend, Dr. Benjamin Rush, argued: "We are told by their masters, they are the happiest people in the world, because they are 'merry,'" whereas "The singing and dancing to which the negroes in the West-Indies are so much addicted, are the effects of mirth, and not of happiness. . . . Instead of considering the songs and dances . . . as marks of their happiness, I have long considered them as physical symptoms of *Melancholy Madness*, and therefore as certain proofs of their misery."[61] (AS 3) A similar argument was put forth by Thomas Clarkson in his prize-winning *Essay on the Slavery and Commerce of the Human Species.* According to Clarkson, Negro dances in the West Indies "are so far from proceeding from any uncommon degree of happiness . . . that they proceed rather from an *uncommon depression of spirits*, which makes them even sacrifice their rest for the sake of experiencing *for a moment*, a more joyful oblivion of their cares." Gilbert Francklyn asked (not unreasonably) how walking several miles to and from a dance after work could demonstrate "the insupportable fatigue they underwent the day before."[62] That the dancing and singing could be interpreted to demonstrate qualities of the blacks other than simple happiness was only rarely suggested.

An account from Jamaica published in 1790 gave an eyewitness report, without trying to theorize about it:

> Notwithstanding all their hardships, they are fond of plays and merriment; and if not prevented by whites, according to a law of the island, they will meet on Saturday-nights, hundreds of them in gangs, and dance and sing till morning; nay, sometimes they continue their balls without intermission till Monday-morning; I have often gone, out of curiosity, to such meetings, and was highly diverted; . . .[63] (AS 4)

61. Rush, "Diseases Peculiar to Negroes," p. 82.
62. Francklyn, *Answer,* pp. 205–6. Letter VIII, dated Nov. 30, 1788. Clarkson's essay was published anonymously as *An Essay on the Slavery and Commerce of the Human Species, Particularly the African, Translated from a Latin Dissertation, which was Honoured with the First Prize in the University of Cambridge, for the Year 1785, with Additions.*
63. Moreton, *Manners and Customs,* pp. 155–56.

Long after acculturated dancing was common on the eastern seaboard of the mainland, African-style dancing was reported by a traveler from the shores of the Washita [Ouachita] River in Louisiana. One dance followed the capture of a wildcat sometime before 1833:

> When all was ready for the dance, one of them [the Negroes] tuned a large guitar, made from a calabash strung with cat-gut, and began to strum as on a Moorish mandolin. Another Negro overturned a brass pot normally used for milking, and struck on it a long drumroll that lost itself in the woods. Soon at a signal from the guitar player, the dance began: before long there was rapid stamping, the dancers striking their thighs and their hands in time, pirouetting by themselves, or stopping suddenly in a posture of surprise and pleasure; by and by a general circle was formed. . . .
> "Now dance the dance of the Congos!" demanded their leader. . . . Three old Negroes tuned their *banjas*, and three others began to beat the rhythm. . . . [64]

Such African dancing in the backwoods would be repressed by the growing settlement of the area. When Fredrika Bremer visited New Orleans in 1851, she was disappointed to see no dancing. "I have heard much said about the happiness of the negroes in America, of their songs and dances, and I wish, therefore, for once to see . . . their festivals. In South Carolina and Georgia the preachers have done away with dancing and the singing of songs. In Louisiana there is no preaching to the slaves; perhaps they may there sing and dance." But once arrived there, she could only complain that "I have now traveled in search of these negro festivities from one end of the slave states to the other, without having been lucky enough to meet with, to see, nay, nor even to hear of one such occasion. I believe, nevertheless, that they do occur here and there on the plantations."[65] Later, in Cuba, she had her wish, and the dancing was comparable to that described in other parts of the New World:

> The spectators stood in a ring around the dancers, one or two couples accompanying the dance with singing, which consisted of the lively but monotonous repetitions of a few words which were given out by one person in the circle, who seemed a sort of *improvisatore*, and who had been chosen as leader of the song. Each time that a fresh couple entered the dance, they were greeted by shrill cries, and the words and tune of the song were changed. . . .

She wrote again on April 23, 1851:

64. Pavie, *Souvenirs Atlantiques*, II, 319–20. My rough translation.
65. Bremer, *Homes of the New World*, Letter XXIX, Cincinnati, Dec. 16 [1850], II, 116–17; Letter XXXI, New Orleans, Jan. 20 [1851], II, 249.

The dance was altogether similar in character to the dances which I have already described. The negroes stood in a ring and sang, monotonously and inharmoniously, but with measured cadence, the words and the tune which a young negro gave out. In the centre of the ring two or three dancing couples flourished about, leaping and grimacing, the men with much animation . . . the dance was one continuous, monotonous improvisation. A number of little children joined in the ring. . . .[66]

The detail of children joining in the ring, first described by Du Tertre before 1656, "imitating the postures of their fathers and mothers and mimicking their gestures," tells much of how this style of dancing was transmitted from one generation to another.

The recollections of former slaves frequently refer to dancing, but only rarely do they specify the kind of dancing. Robert Anderson, who was born in Green County, Kentucky, on March 1, 1843, recalled an occasion when the master's family had gone to Louisville and the overseer permitted the slaves to invite their friends from neighboring plantations for a big dance. "We had a regular jubilee which lasted the greater part of the night. We danced the dances like the white folks danced them, and then danced our own kind of dances."[67] The precise nature of these dances must be conjectured; Lynne Emery in *Black Dance* offers a number of possibilities, ranging from African survivals like the buzzard lope through jigs, ring dances, and cake walks to reels and quadrilles. The music which accompanied it must have been as varied in style and degree of acculturation as the dance itself.

66. *Ibid.*, Letter XXXIV, Ariadne Inhegno, Mar. 7 [1851], II, 325–28, 379–83; Letter XXXVI, San Antonio de los Bagnos, May 3 [1851], II, 410–11.
67. Anderson, *From Slavery to Affluence*, pp. 32–33.

ADDITIONAL SOURCES

AS1. A year after Ligon's book was published, a rival to Du Tertre's book appeared, Charles de Rochefort's *Histoire Naturelle et Morale des Antilles de l'Amerique . . . Avec un Vocabulaire Caraïbe* (Rotterdam, 1658). Although it was quite inferior to Du Tertre's history (Goveia, *Historiography*, pp. 23–26), it achieved something Du Tertre did not—an English translation, which appeared in 1666. Although Rochefort was more interested in the Caribs than in the Africans, he too commented on the blacks and their recreations:

> They are great Lovers of Musick, and much pleas'd with such Instruments as make a certain delightful noise, and a kind of harmony, which they accompany with their voices. . . . In the Island of S. *Christophers* . . . they met on Sundays and Holidays after Divine Service . . . [spending] the remainder of that day, and the night following, in dancing and pleasant discourses . . . it was commonly observ'd,

that after they had so diverted themselves, they went through their work with greater courage and chearfulness . . . and did all things better than if they had rested all night long in their huts. (Rochefort, *History*, p. 202.)

AS2. The glossary proper was preceded by some general remarks: "There is, properly, no dialect in America. There are, however, both on the continent and in the islands, some singularities of speech. . . . A List of some of the most remarkable and common, collected during my residence in Virginia and Maryland nearly thirty years ago, is here set down . . . [including] a *Bandore* (pronounced *Banjor*; a rude musical instrument, made of the shell of a large gourd, or pumpion, and strung somewhat in the manner of a violin; it is much used by Negroes . . ." (p. xlix).

Boucher recalled scenes he witnessed before the Revolution, as did other writers. John Ferdinand Dalziel Smyth remembered the "banjor (a large hollow instrument with three strings)," and John Davis, a "banger." Cf. Smyth, *Tour*, I, 46 (reprinted as "Manner of Living of the Different Ranks of Inhabitants of Virginia," *American Museum* 1 [Mar., 1787]: 247), and Davis, *Travels*, pp. 378–79.

David Dalby, reader in West African languages at the School of Oriental and African Studies at the University of London, regards banjo as the result of a convergence with *bandore* of the Kimbundu *mbanza*, "stringed musical instrument (whence also black Jamaican English *banja* and Brazilian Portuguese *banza*). " He does not mention the French usage. See "The African Element in American English," in Kochman, ed., *Rappin' and Stylin' Out*, p. 177.

AS3. Dr. Rush also wrote in a pamphlet exchange with Richard Nisbet: "The Amusements, Songs &c. of the Negroes, are urged as signs of their Happiness, or Contentment in Slavery. . . . Although some of their Songs, like those of *civilized* Nations, are Obscene and Warlike, yet I have been informed that many of them, as well as their Tunes, are of a most plaintive Nature, and very expressive of their Misery." [Rush,] *Vindication of the Address*, p. 30. Nisbet's pamphlet, also published anonymously, *Slavery Not Forbidden by Scripture*, was issued in Philadelphia in the same year.

AS4. Moreton continued:

When dancing, they form themselves into a circular position, adjoining some of their huts, and continue all in motion, singing so loud, that of a calm night they may be heard at about two miles distance—thus:

Hipsaw! my deaa! you no do like a-me!
You no jig like a-me! you no twist like a-me!
Hipsaw! my deaa! you no shake like a-me!
You no wind like a-me! Go, yondaa! . . .

It is very amazing to think with what agility they twist and move their joints: —I sometimes imagined they were on springs or hinges, from the hips downwards; whoever is most active and expert at wriggling, is reputed the best dancer.

For a discussion of the word "hipsaw" on the mainland as well as in the islands, see Cassidy, " 'Hipsaw' and 'John Canoe'," pp. [45]–46.

This twisting, shaking, and jigging which the early missionaries found so lascivious is not unknown today. The late Marshall Stearns described it as "pelvic movement," an essential feature of African dancing: Stearns, *Jazz Dance*.

A circle dance similar to that described by Moreton was reported by Moreau de Saint-Méry from Saint-Domingue as a *Calenda* (*Description*, I, 45) while Albert, Baron von Sack saw its counterpart in Paramaribo, Surinam, in 1806.

On the first of January the free negroes, by permission of the government, meet in a large place near the citadel, and have a dance; their dances vary according to the different negro tribes, though all consist principally in the muscular movement of their heads, and arms, turning of their bodies, accompanied by very quick steps, keeping time very exactly to the music. . . .

After discussing the instruments, he continued:

The most curious thing is, that the musicians are as much in motion as the dancers, and all mark the time most expressively with their feet, accompanied with the motion of the whole body, so that those who perform the music may complain the next day of being as much fatigued as the dancers themselves; besides, those negroes who cannot get partners, will dance round a tree, or even to their own shadows . . . A lady lately arrived in the colony, came for a moment to see this negro dance; but she was obliged to quit it, as she declared that her eyes were so affected by the rapidity of the motions . . . that her head became dizzy, and she was afraid if she staid but a short time longer, that she should faint away.

Letter dated: Paramaribo, January 1st, 1806, in Sack, *Narrative*, p. 62.

2

More Black Instruments
and Early White Reaction

DRUMS AND OTHER AFRICAN INSTRUMENTS

In the earliest reports of Africans in the New World, drums were
the most important instruments. Du Tertre (1656), Ligon (1653),
Blome (1687), and Sloane (1689) all mentioned drums in association
with other African instruments. Nor were the drums all alike. Some
were made from trunks of hollowed trees with skins stretched across
the opening (Du Tertre, Labat, and Sloane); others were kettle-
drums "of severall sizes" (Ligon and Blome). Despite the legal restrictions on their use, African drums persisted in the islands and,
despite all the statements to the contrary, on the mainland as well,
although hemmed in by many more restrictions. References to
African drums in mainland North America were uncommon, but
they did occur, accompanying the same sorts of activities that were
described in accounts from the West Indies. For example, the judicial records of Somerset County, Maryland, 1707-11, included a
complaint that slaves were "Drunke on the Lords Day beating their
Negro drums by which they call considerable Number of Negroes
together in some Certaine places."[1]

The official report of the Stono revolt of 1739, already discussed in
connection with dancing, also mentioned drumming which was sure-

1. Somerset County Judicials, 1707-11, quoted in Menard, "Maryland Slave
Population," p. 37.

African drum from eighteenth-century Virginia; exhibit 1368 of the Sloane bequest of 1753. Now in the British Museum. Reproduced through the courtesy of the Trustees of the British Museum.

ly African in nature. But perhaps the most convincing evidence that African drums persisted on the mainland is the existence of a drum itself. This drum has survived, not in the United States, but in England, where it became part of the private museum collection belonging to Sir Hans Sloane, the same man who had African music notated in Jamaica before 1689. Although his manuscript catalog of the collection has survived, it yields no information as to when the objects became part of the collection. The earliest verifiable acquisition date is 1753, when the British nation purchased the large and varied collections belonging to Sir Hans; these collections formed the nucleus for the British Museum. Among the objects from America was item 1368, "An Indian drum made of a hollowed tree carv'd the top being brac'd with peggs and thongs with the bottom hollow from Virginia." So ran the manuscript catalog entry, corrected by a modern curator: "Although described as Indian, this drum was more probably made by Negroes and may even have been brought from Africa. The drum is typical of the Ashanti of Ghana."[2] Similar drums are also found among the Africans in Guyana, where they are called "apinti," a derivation of the Ashanti "mpinti."[3] Accounting for such widespread distribution on grounds other than African origin seems impossible. Descriptions from the second half of the eighteenth century and later demonstrate the persistence of these drums despite all the restrictions placed upon them. (AS 1)

Other African instruments also crossed the Atlantic. Some are described by William Beckford, who lived in Jamaica for thirteen years before departing in 1777:

> Their musical instruments, if such they may be called, consist of a bonjour . . . a kind of Spanish guitar; a cotter, upon which they beat with sticks; a gomba, which they strike with their hands; a drum; a box filled with pebbles, which they shake with their wrists; and . . . the jaw-bone of an animal from which is produced a harsh and disagreeable sound: and it may easily be imagined, when these all together join in chorus, and are accompanied by a number of voices, what kind of music must . . . fill the ear.

He singled out for special mention

> the Caramantee-flutes . . . made from the porous branches of the trumpet-tree . . . about a yard in length, and of nearly the thickness of the upper part of a bassoon: they have generally three holes at the bottom; are held, in point of direction, like the hautboy; and while the right hand

2. Braunholtz, *Sloane and Ethnography*, p. 35; pl. 17. See also Bushnell, "Sloane Collection," pp. 676–77; and Bastide, *African Civilization*, p. 12. I am indebted for the Bushnell citation to Dr. Klaus Wachsmann.
3. Hurault, *Africains de Guyane*, pl. 40, 42, 47; p. 219.

stops the holes, in the left is shaken, by one of the party, a hollow ball that is filled with pebbles. . . . I have frequently heard these flutes played in parts; and I think the sounds they produce are the most affecting, as they are the most melancholy, that I ever remember to have heard. The high notes are uncommonly wild, but yet are sweet; and the lower tones are deep, majestic, and impressive.

The bender is an instrument upon which the Whydaw negroes, I believe, in particular, excel. It is made of a bent stick, the ends of which are restrained in this direction by a slip of dried grass; the upper part of which is gently compressed between the lips, and to which the breath gives a soft and pleasing vibration; and the other end is graduated by a slender stick that beats upon the nerve, if I may so express it, and confines the natural acuteness of the sound, and thus produces a trembling, a querulous and a delightful harmony.

Later he remedied an omission in his description of the bender: "a slender stick which the player . . . presses to the string a little below his mouth, to graduate the vibration." The "bender" as Beckford described it apparently was a form of musical bow, an instrument common in Africa.

Beckford had a better appreciation of the value of these instruments than most of his contemporaries, for he considered them worthy of the attention of Dr. Burney:

In the elegant and learned work which Doctor Burney has composed and published upon the History of Music, it would, I conceive, have been a matter of pleasure and curiosity, if the description of these different instruments had found a place; and if he had signified his ideas how, and upon what a scale of composition, they might, with advantage and effect, have been employed: a description that would have even given variety to a work which already voluminously new, and that has scarcely room for fresh attractions![4]

Beckford, like Ligon before him, provided a refreshing exception to the rule of indifference or contempt which most Europeans of his time displayed toward the culture of the Africans.

Moreton, by contrast, was patronizing, unwilling to concede that African instruments were anything but "imitations" of European instruments: "Their music is composed of any thing that makes a tinkling sound; a hollow cane, or bamboo, with holes in it, in imitation of a fife; an herring-barrel, or tub, with sheep-skins substituted for the heads, in imitation of a drum, called a gumbay. . . ."[5] (AS 2) The German naturalist Johann David Schoepf was matter-of-fact,

4. Beckford, *Descriptive Account,* II, 387; I, 217–18, 216; II, 387; I, 220. Burney's *History* was published 1782–89.
5. Moreton, *Manners and Customs,* p. 155.

describing musical instruments with the same precision and de-
tachment with which he noted the tropical flora and fauna, each
with its correct Latin name.

In 1797 Moreau de Saint-Méry described very much the same
combination of instruments that Labat had described almost a
hundred years before: various sizes of drums made from hollow
trees, calabashes filled with seeds, and the *banza*.[6] By 1800 African
drums had become part of the local color in the West Indies, called
upon by writers of fiction to provide authentic backgrounds for their
stories. In a volume described as "among the most authentic stories
of West-Indian life" was a tale about a beautiful heroine who had
been imprisoned by her wicked father in a remote plantation in the
northern mountains of Jamaica during an uprising of Maroons. The
one-dimensional heroine seemed to come to life as she described

> noises which, I was informed, are the signals used by the Maroons and
> runaway negroes to collect their numbers or hold their councils. Some-
> times it was a few dull notes struck in a particular manner on their
> gombay or drum, answered by the same number of strokes from another
> quarter. At another time, it was the sullen sound of a great shell; which
> is, they say, used every where by the savages as a war signal; and this was
> answered by hollow human voices from different parts. . . . I hear again
> the gombah in the woods. . . . The conchs and gomgoms of the Maroons
> suddenly broke the silence of the night. . . .[7]

Lady Maria Nugent, wife of the governor of Jamaica, heard
"bonjoes, drums, and tomtoms" during the Christmas celebration
in 1804; earlier, when visiting a settlement of Maroons (descendants
of escaped slaves who lived in independent communities), she had
heard "all sorts of rude instruments. . . . The Coromantee flute is a
long black reed, has a plaintive and melancholy sound, and is played
with the nose."[8]

Baron von Sack, in describing the New Year's festivities of 1806 in
Paramaribo, Surinam, saw these instruments:

> The musical instruments are chiefly pieces of hollow trees, the up-
> per part covered with leather like a drum, and are beaten with sticks; but
> these instruments are in different forms to vary the sound; the negro
> females who are not engaged in dancing, have strings with sounding nut
> shells, which they clap to with their hands, and sing a chorus to it; the
> most curious thing is, that the musicians are as much in motion as the

6. Moreau de Saint-Méry, *Déscription*, I, 44.

7. Charlotte Turner Smith, *Letters*, II, 93–94, 101, 139.

8. Nugent, *Journal*, pp. 219, 75. The editor added in a footnote: "No other visitor
to the Maroons seems to have mentioned a nose flute, nor have I traced any mention
of one in the Gold Coast area."

dancers . . . so that those who perform the music may complain the next day of being as much fatigued as the dancers themselves. . . . [9]

The African instruments which were seen throughout the West Indies from the seventeenth century to the nineteenth were thus equally at home on the mainland of South America, in an area that remains a center of New World African culture to this day.

The prohibition of drums, ignored to a great extent on the islands and in South America, was more strictly enforced on the North American mainland, but one should not conclude that even there the edicts were completely effective. Drums continued to be played, some secretly, some in the open. A description of a Sunday morning in New Orleans dated May 1, 1808, told of "twenty different dancing groups of the wretched Africans. . . . They have their own national music, consisting for the most part of a long kind of narrow drum of various sizes, from two to eight feet in length, three or four of which make a band."[10] In 1811 an uprising took place in St. John the Baptiste, about fifty miles above New Orleans, with an army of insurgents consisting of "nearly 500 men and women . . . divided into companies commanded by officers. Their objective was the sack of New Orleans. They were goaded to a frenzy by the beating of drums and iron kettles, accompanied by the barbarous shrill notes of reed quills."[11]

As the nineteenth century advanced, Africans in the West Indies continued to prefer their native music to the more "civilized" European music and instruments. When Matthew Lewis gave a holiday to his Negroes in Cornwall, Jamaica, in 1816, he saw no European instruments at all. "The music consisted of nothing but Gambys (Eboe drums), Shaky-shekies, and Kitty-katties; the latter is nothing but any flat piece of board beat upon with two sticks, and the former is a bladder with a parcel of pebbles in it. But the principal part of the music to which they dance is vocal. . . ."[12] The following year a Methodist missionary, Mr. Gilgrass, described Sundays in Jamaica: "Those that neither work, nor go to market, will sleep, smoak segars, and dance to a tomtom. . . ."[13] Isaac Holmes, who visited Louisiana in 1821, saw very similar dancing to drums:

> In Louisiana, and the state of Mississippi, the slaves have Sunday for a day of recreation, and upon many plantations they dance for several

9. Albert, Baron von Sack, *Narrative*, p. 62.
10. Schultz, *Travels*, p. 197.
11. Fossier, *New Orleans*, pp. 368–69.
12. Lewis, *Journal*, pp. 73, 81. Entry for Jan. 6, 1816.
13. Richard Watson, *Defence*, p. 60.

hours during the afternoon of this day. The general movement is in what they call the Congo dance; but their music often consists of nothing more than an excavated piece of wood, at one end of which is a piece of parchment, which covers the hollow part on which they beat; this, and the singing . . . of those who are dancing, and of those who surround the dancers . . . constitute the whole of their harmony.[14]

While only very few reports of African-style drums have been found from the mainland after 1821, in the islands they continued to be extremely popular. The celebration which followed the completion of the year's sugar-making in Jamaica was called "crop over." This description was published in 1828:

> Immediately . . . the negroes assembled in and around the boiling house, dancing and roaring for joy, to the sound of the gumba. . . . This favourite instrument of music, the gumba, consists of a square box, with a piece of sheep's skin on each end, and though only beat with a single stick, and incapable of marking any tune, yet the negroes seemed delighted with it, and danced in the true African fashions . . . at the same time, singing as loud as their lungs would permit. . . .

At Christmas, "field negroes from the country flocked into the town . . . severally accompanied with their favourite gumba and a fife. Though the sound of the gumba is any thing but pleasant, the principal actors drew numbers of spectators around it."[15]

Descriptions of African drumming and instruments continued to be common in reports from the West Indies,[16] but the already quoted account of a dance along the Washita [Ouachita] River in Louisiana was unusual on the mainland for its almost purely African flavor.[17] Yet African drumming must have continued surreptitiously in the United States, since interviews collected by the Federal Writers' Project in the 1930's describe it vividly. Wash Wilson, who was born a slave in Louisiana near the Ouachita Road, was interviewed when he was ninety-four years old. He and his family had been brought to Texas before the Civil War, which broke out when he was about eighteen. He described corn shuckings in Louisiana that included instruments which were lineal descendants of those reported in the seventeenth century:

> Dere wasn't no music instruments. Us take pieces of sheep's rib or cow's jaw or a piece iron, with a old kettle, or a hollow gourd and some horse-hairs to make de drum. Sometimes dey'd get a piece of tree trunk and

14. Holmes, *Account*, p. 332. Other accounts from New Orleans will appear in ch. 7.
15. *Marly; or, A Planter's Life in Jamaica*, pp. 46, 293.
16. Cf. Alexander, *Transatlantic Sketches*, p. 112; Rolph, *Brief Account*, p. 21; Willis, *Health Trip*, p. 410; Day, *Five Years' Residence*, I, 47.
17. Pavie, *Souvenirs Atlantiques*, II, 319–20.

hollow it out and stretch a goat's or sheep's skin over it for de drum. Dey'd be one to four foot high and a foot up to six foot 'cross. In gen'ral two niggers play with de fingers or sticks on dis drum. Never seed so many in Texas, but dey made some. Dey'd take de buffalo horn and scrape it out to make de flute. Dat sho' be heard a long ways off. Then dey'd take a mule's jaw-bone, and rattle de stick 'cross its teeth. Dey'd take a barrel, and stretch a ox's hide 'cross one end and a man sat 'stride de barrel, and beat on dat hide with he hands and he feet and iffen he get to feelin' de music in his bones, he'd beat on dat barrel with his head. 'Nother man beat on wooden sides with sticks.[18]

Another unit of the Writers' Program in Savannah, Georgia, collected evidences of African survivals among the coastal Negroes; this important collection of interviews has been insufficiently appreciated by students of black studies. Among reports of African songs, dances, and folk customs are descriptions of drum-making: "In Brownville we found a man who knew how to make the old time drum. He made one for us out of a hollow log, across the end of which he tightly stretched a goat skin. He fastened the skin to the log by means of a number of wooden pegs. Unlike modern drums, this one was taller than it was wide, measuring about eighteen inches in length and ten inches in diameter." The drum-maker, James Collier, a middle-aged, well-educated Negro, said he had made a number of drums in this primitive manner.[19] The technique for making African drums which was displayed in coastal Georgia in the 1930's had survived undocumented for many generations, offering convincing evidence of a continuing tradition that existed underground, apparently unknown to the local whites.

Other African instruments were also reported in the United States: the musical bow, the quills or panpipes, and the balafo, a xylophone. The musical bow is frequently described in books on African instruments, but so far only one contemporary report of it has been found in the United States—from Granada, Mississippi in February, 1858:

> Paul [a slave] was a good dancer and singer, and could play upon various musical instruments. The most curious of these was one which he called a "song-bow," a simple contrivance, consisting of a string stretched tight from one end to the other of a long, flexible, narrow board or bow, and which the performer breathed upon in such a way as

18. Federal Writers' Project, *Slave Narratives*, XVI: Texas, pt. 4.
19. Writers' Program, Georgia, *Drums and Shadows*, p. 62. Another informant, F. J. Jackson, gave instructions for drum-making: "Yuh cut duh lawg an tak a deah hide an stretch obuh duh hole. Den yuh cut a hoop ban dat could lock roun du lawg. Den yuh cut strips uh deah hide and make bans tuh hole duh head cuvvah tight." —p. 101. References to drums recur throughout the entire volume.

to cause a musical vibration, while at the same time he sang. The song and accompaniment were strangely blended, and the effect was not unpleasant.[20]

The quills, or panpipes, apparently had wide currency. Bill Home of Fort Worth, Texas, who was born on June 17, 1850, near Shreveport, Louisiana, told how the quills were made in his youth: "We plays de quill, made from willow stalk when de sap am up. You takes de stick, and pounds de bark loose and slips it off, den split de wood in one end and down one side, puts holes in de bark, and put it back on de stick. De quill plays like de flute."[21] Panpipes of course were not confined to Africa, but they were widely played there, and their use in the above-mentioned slave insurrection of 1811 seems more likely to have derived from Africa than from Europe or ancient Greece.

THE BALAFO

Most of these African instruments were relatively portable and simple to make, so their transportation to or reconstruction in the New World is not too surprising. More astonishing is the discovery that the balafo, an African xylophone, (AS 3) had wide currency in the New World.

European travelers in Africa found the balafo an interesting subject for the delectation of their readers. Richard Jobson wrote of his trip in 1621:

> I would acquaint you of their most principall instrument, which is called Ballards made to stand a foot above the ground, hollow under, and hath uppon the top some seventeene woodden keyes standing like the Organ, upon which hee that playes sitting upon the ground, just against the middle of the instrument, strikes with a sticke in either hand, about a foote long, at the end whereof is made fast a round ball, covered with some soft stuffe, to avoyd the clattering noyse the bare stickes would make: . . . the sound that proceeds from this instrument is worth the observing, for we can heare it a good English mile, the making of this instrument being one of the most ingenious things amongst them: for to every one of these keyes there belongs a small Iron the bignese of a quill, and is a foote long, the breadth of the Instrument, upon which hangs two gourdes under the hollow, like bottles, who receives the sound, and returnes it again with that extraordinary loudnesse. . . .[22]

20. Venable, "Down South Before the War," p. 498.
21. Yetman, *"Peculiar Institution,"* p. 170. William Harden, born on Nov. 11, 1844, in Savannah, heard "Mary Had a Little Lamb" for the first time "when a negro boy on my uncle's plantation in Bryan County played it on a rudely constructed set of 'Pipes of Pan.'" Harden, *Recollections,* p. 48. And Joel Chandler Harris, creator of Uncle Remus, never heard a plantation Negro play a banjo, but "I have heard them make sweet music with . . . Pan pipes . . ." Joel Chandler Harris, "Plantation Music," p. 505.
22. Jobson, *Golden Trade,* pp. 106–7.

Balafo in West Africa, sketched by William Smith, surveyor for the Royal Africa
Company, 1726. Frontispiece in his *New Voyage to Guinea*. London: J. Nourse,

Other descriptions of the balafo in Africa have been found, perhaps the most notable being that of William Smith (1726), who not only described it, but had an engraving made.[23]

The earliest known account of the balafo in the New World was Richard Ligon's above-quoted tale of a Negro making a musical instrument which Ligon thought the man had invented, but which was clearly a balafo.[24] The appearance of this instrument in Barbados seems surprising, perhaps because of our ignorance of the richness of slave musical life; but that it should also appear in eighteenth-century Virginia must alter our conceptions of the acculturated life which mainland slaves were supposed to have led. An indentured servant and schoolmaster, John Harrower, wrote in his journal on March 25, 1775:

> At noon went to Newpost to see Mr. Martin Heely Schoolmaster for Mr. [Alexander] Spotswood's Children, and after Dinner I spent the afternoon with him in conversation & hearing him play the Fiddle. He also made a Niger come & play on an Instrument call'd a Barrafou. The body of it is an oblong box with the mouth up & stands on four sticks put in bottom, & cross the [top?] is laid 11 lose sticks upon [which?] he beats.[25]

The term "barrafou" cannot have been so uncommon that the ordinary newspaper reader in Virginia was unfamiliar with its meaning, for the *Virginia Gazette* for March 22, 1776, used the expression in showing its contempt for Lord Dunmore's invitation to the slaves to desert their masters and come aboard his ships anchored in the York River:

> We hear that lord Dunmore's *Royal Regiment of Black Fusileers* is already recruited, with runaway and stolen negroes, to the formidable number of 80 effective men, who, after doing the drudgery of the day (such as acting as scullions, etc. on board the fleet) are ordered upon deck to perform the military exercise; and, to comply with their *native* warlike genius, instead of the drowsy drum and fife, will be gratified with the use of the sprightly and enlivening *barrafoo*. . . .[26]

Christmas, 1791, was celebrated on the island of St. Vincent by a ball; the opening dance was a minuet, accompanied by "two excellent fiddles . . . and [a] tamborine," with eighteen couples taking part. Then

23. William Smith, *New Voyage to Guinea*, p. 21 and frontispiece. See also Merolla, *Voyage to Congo*, in Pinkerton, ed., *Interesting Voyages and Travels*, XVI, 245.

24. Ligon, *True & Exact History*, pp. 48–49.

25. Harrower, *Journal*, p. 89. I am indebted to Edward M. Riley for calling my attention to this journal.

26. Purdie's Williamsburg *Virginia Gazette*, Mar. 22, 1776, quoted in Jordan, *White Over Black*, p. 303.

a new party of musicians are arrived with an African Balafo, an instrument composed of pieces of hard wood of different diameters, laid in a row over a sort of box; they beat on one or the other so as to strike out a musical tune. They played two or three African tunes; and about a dozen girls, hearing it sound, came from the huts to the great court [where the dance was held], and began a most curious and lascivious dance, with much grace and action. . . .[27]

What a contrast in cultures!

The balafo was seen in Surinam in 1806 by Baron von Sack, who wrote of the bush Negroes: "Among their instruments, which consist mostly in different sorts of drums, there was one in particular which I had not seen before: it was made of different sounding woods cut into several sticks of various sizes, and laid upon two pieces of wood: this instrument is played with two little sticks. . . ."[28] As late as 1823 the word "balafou" was still known well enough in Jamaica to have meaning for the general reader, who would understand a passing reference: "The Africans struck up a song of welcome, accompanying it with the tones of the balafou."[29] Further research may add to our knowledge of the career of this African instrument in the New World.

LEGAL RESTRICTIONS ON INSTRUMENTS

Almost as soon as the Africans arrived in the New World, their white masters began to worry about their dancing and instruments. The action of the Conseil Souverain de Martinique of May 4, 1654, prohibiting "danses et assemblées de nègres" has already been discussed. Charles de Rochefort attributed this prohibition not to the noise or the conspiracies that might be hatched, but to the poultry and fruit that disappeared during these gatherings. So, despite the fact that "it was commonly observ'd, that after they had so diverted themselves, they went through their work with greater courage and chearfulness, without expressing any weariness, and did all things better than if they had rested all night long in their huts . . . the *French* General thought fit to forbid these nocturnal assemblies. . . ."[30] The English reacted in the same fashion. When Sir Hans Sloane was in Jamaica in the late 1680's, he made this observation: "They formerly on their Festivals were allowd the use of Trumpets after their Fashion, and Drums. . . . But making use of these in their Wars at home in Africa, it was thought too much inciting them to Rebel-

27. Young, "Tour," in Edwards, *History*, III, 276.
28. Albert, Baron von Sack, *Narrative*, pp. 82–83.
29. *Koromantyn Slaves; or, West Indian Sketches* (London: Hatchard and Son, 1823), p. 85, cited in Cassidy and Le Page, *Dictionary of Jamaican English*, p. 21.
30. [Rochefort,] *History*, p. 202.

lion, and so they were prohibited by the Customs of the Island."[31] By 1699 the laws of Barbados included the following provision: "Whatsoever Master, &c. shall suffer his Negro or Slave at any time to beat Drums, blow Horns, or use any other loud instruments, or shall not cause his *Negro-Houses* once a Week to be search'd, and if any such things be there found, to be burnt . . . he shall forfeit 40 s. Sterling."[32] The St. Kitts slave acts of 1711 and 1722 prohibited the slaves from "holding dangerous assemblies or from communicating at a distance by beating drums or blowing horns,"[33] while the 1717 slave act of Jamaica "forbade the gathering of slaves by the beating of drums and blowing of horns, although they could meet together for 'any innocent amusement.' "[34]

The mainland colonies were also concerned about the gathering of crowds of slaves, and Maryland took action as early as 1695. "Of the provisions of the act of 1695, to restrain the frequent assemblages of negroes, we know nothing; but the law soon expired. In 1723 the Assembly considered the evils resulting from the large meetings of negroes on 'Sabbath and other Holy-days,' and enacted that the courts should begin at once . . . to suppress tumultuous meetings of slaves."[35] South Carolina took similar action, ordering the constables of Charlestown to search the streets on Sundays and holidays to disperse crowds of Negroes, and even authorizing them "to enter into any house. . . to search for such slaves."[36] In other words, all gatherings of slaves, indoors or out, were suspect. But, after the Stono insurrection, the colony of South Carolina passed the more stringent Slave Act of 1740; it incorporated many of the provisions of earlier slave acts from the West Indies, most notably the banning of "wooden swords, and other mischievous and dangerous weapons, or using or keeping of drums, horns, or other loud instruments, which may call together, or give sign or notice to one another of their wicked designs or purposes."[37] Classing drums, horns, and other loud instruments with dangerous weapons indicated the fears

31. Sloane, *Voyage*, I, lii.
32. In *Abridgement of the Laws*, p. 239.
33. C.O. 240/2, St. Kitts Acts, no. 2 of 1711, clause XIV; no. 52 of 1722, clause XIV, cited in Goveia, *Slave Society*, p. 156.
34. "An Act for the more effectual punishing of Crimes committed by Slaves," 4 Geo I, c. 4 (1717), pp. 113–16, cited in Gipson, *British Isles and American Colonies*, p. 199.
35. Brackett, *Negro in Maryland*, p. 100.
36. South Carolina, Laws, Statutes, etc., *Statutes at Large*, VII (1840): 354, "An Act for the Better Ordering and Governing of Negroes and Slaves . . . ratified . . . the seventh day of June . . . 1712."
37. *Ibid.*, p. 410. These laws continued in force through the antebellum period.

and suspicions that became associated with African music and dancing. (AS 4)

Fear and suspicion were not the only factors involved, however; the relative sizes of the black and white populations were also a factor. The West Indian slave masters were not noted for their bravery, but they became convinced of the wisdom of permitting their slaves to dance and drum under normal conditions. The mainland colonies, with the exception of Louisiana, found it possible strictly to enforce the regulations, judging from the relative absence of drums and drumming in accounts from the mainland. (The utilization of slaves as drummers in the militia, an acculturated kind of drumming, is not relevant here, but will be discussed later.)

As the eighteenth century progressed, additional laws were designed to enforce control of the slave population, to prevent them from gathering in crowds, and to discourage them from dancing (presumably African dances) and drumming. In 1794 the General Assembly of North Carolina passed an act forbidding slave owners to permit slaves or free Negroes to gather "for the purpose of drinking and dancing,"[38] while slaves in St. John's Parish, Louisiana, were prohibited in 1849 "from beating the drum or dancing after sundown."[39] Dancing in 1849 was less likely to have been purely African.

Irrational though it may have been, the fear of drumming as a signal of insurrection persisted up to the outbreak of the Civil War. During the 1860 Democratic convention in Charleston, the New York delegation sent its band to serenade some visiting dignitaries at ten o'clock one evening. "It was stopped in the midst of its performance, and forbidden to use its drums. . . . The chief of police, in full uniform, appeared on the scene . . . politely explained the rule, and the reason of it, saying, 'Play any music you like, if you can dispense with your drums. Their sound at this hour would arouse the whole city.' "[40] The New York bandsmen were governed by a ruling devised almost two hundred years earlier for the control of African slaves newly arrived in the West Indies.

38. Brewer, "Legislation Designed to Control Slavery," p. 160.
39. St. John's Parish, Minutes of the Police Jury, Aug. 13, 1849, MS, cited in Moody, *Slavery on Louisiana Sugar Plantations*, p. 89.
40. Mason, "Visit to South Carolina," p. 244.

ADDITIONAL SOURCES

AS1. Edward Long wrote (*History of Jamaica*, II, 423-24):

> The *goombah* ... is a hollow block of wood, covered with sheep-skin stripped of its hair. The musician holds a little stick, of about six inches in length, sharpened at one end like the blade of a knife, in each hand. With one hand he rakes it over a notched piece of wood, fixed across the instrument, the whole length, and crosses with the other alternately, using both with a brisk motion; whilst a second performer beats with all his might on the sheep-skin, or tabor.

From Antigua John Luffman wrote on March 14, 1788 (*Brief Account of Antigua*, p. 136):

> The toombah is similar to the tabor, and has gingles of tin or shells; to this music ... I have seen a hundred or more dancing at a time, their gestures are extravagant, but not more so than the principal dancers at your Opera-house, and, I believe, were some of their steps and motions introduced into the public amusements at home, by French or Italian dancers, they would be well received ... their agility and surprising command of their limbs, is astonishing. ...

Peter Marsden was also impressed by the dancing, but less by the instruments (*Account*, p. 34): "They used formerly to have no other instrument than a bow with two or three wires, which they struck with a stick, making a noise strangely dissonant and uncouth." A coffee plantation on Saint-Domingue also saw dancing to drumming. The author displayed his attitude toward the slaves in his casual statement,

> I shall ... treat this interesting subject [i.e., Negroes and cattle] as I would have done in 1788. ... On Saturday or Sunday evening, the negroes are allowed to dance upon the platforms [used for drying coffee] ... till nine o'clock. ... [on] New Year's Day. ... The morning just begins to dawn, when a hurricane of drums, of discordant shouts, and African songs, awake the master from his slumbers. ... [The slaves] go to dress themselves in their best cloaths; they return and begin to dance ... the ball breaks up to give time for breakfast. ... The dance is resumed with redoubled alacrity. ... [In the evening] the dance rages more and more lively and swift. Every nerve is in motion, every exertion raised to the utmost. All ... keep pace with the drums, now beating with ten-fold quickness. ...

Laborie, *Coffee Planter*, pp. 157, 178, 181–83.

AS2. Other descriptions of African instruments in the West Indies included those of Bryan Edwards, who listed, in addition to "the Banja or Merriwang,"

> the *Dundo*, and the *Goombay*; all of African origin. The first is an imperfect kind of violincello; except that it is played on by the fingers like the guitar; producing a dismal monotony of four notes. The Dundo is precisely a tabor; and the Goombay is a rustic drum; being formed of the trunk of a hollow tree, one end of which is covered with a sheep's skin. From such instruments nothing like a regular tune can be expected, nor is it attempted.

See his *History*, II, 84.

The instruments of Barbados were described by George Pinckard (*Notes*, p. 127) in 1796:

> The instrumental parts of the band consist of a species of drum, a kind of rattle, and the ever-delighting banjar. The first is a long hollow piece of wood, with a dried sheep-skin tied over the end; the second is a calabash containing a number of small stones, fixed to a short stick which serves as the handle; and the third is a coarse and rough kind of guitar. While one negro strikes the banjar, another

shakes the rattle with great force of arm; a third sitting across the body of the drum, as it lies lengthwise upon the ground, beats and kicks the sheep-skin at the end, in violent exertion with his hands and heels; and a fourth sitting upon the ground at the other end, behind the man upon the drum, beats upon the wooden sides of it with two sticks. Together with these noisy sounds, numbers of the party of both sexes bawl forth their dear delighting song with all possible force of lungs; from the *tout ensemble* of the scene, a spectator would require only a slight aid from fancy to transport him to the savage wilds of Africa. On great occasions the band is increased by an additional number of drums, rattles, and voices.

AS3. Marcuse, *Musical Instruments*, p. 32. Her reference to Laborde is to his *Essai*, I, 217–18. The *Encyclopédie* included "Balafo" as a term defined in its *Supplément* of 1776, "a kind of instrument of the Negroes, that very much resembles our 'claque-bois,' with this difference, that beneath the keys they suspend some calabashes which augment the sound . . . Another name for *balafo* is *ballard*" (I, 759; my translation).

AS4. Further provisions forbidding "slaves to assemble together, and beat their military drums, or blow their horns or shells" were enacted in Jamaica as XIX, XX, and XXI of the New Consolidated Acts passed December 6, 1788. (Jamaica, Laws, Statutes, etc., *New Act of Assembly*, p. 7.) On March 2, 1792, a Consolidated Slave Act was again passed, with the same provision, and again on December 22, 1826. See Edwards, *History*, II, 167; and Jamaica, Laws, Statutes, etc., *Consolidated Slave Law*, pp. 19–20.

Elsa Goveia summarized the West Indian police regulations, saying slaves

> were forbidden to beat drums and blow horns, since these were means of communication which might be used to help runaways. All such activities were dangerous, too, as a means of concerting uprisings—another reason for the existence of these laws. Not all of them were enforced at all times with equal rigor. Slave dances, feasts, and drumming were often allowed. . . . The laws remained in force, however, and they were used when necessary to prevent or to control emergencies."

See her "West Indian Slave Laws," pp. 120–21. For further developments in South Carolina, see Henry, *Police Control*, p. 150. The Georgia law, probably also deriving from the aftermath of the Stono rebellion, was similar:

> And as it is absolutely necessary to the safety of this province, that all due care be taken to restrain the wandering and meeting of negroes, and other slaves, at all times, and more especially on Saturday nights, Sundays, and other holydays, and their using and carrying mischievous and dangerous weapons, or using and keeping *drums, horns, or other loud instruments*, which may call together or give sign or notice to one another of their wicked designs or intentions; . . . and whatsoever master or owner or overseer shall permit or suffer his or their slave or slaves at any time hereafter to *beat drums, blow horns, or other loud instruments* . . . shall forfeit thirty shillings sterling for every such offense. . . .

Georgia, Laws, Statutes, etc., *Codification*, p. 813. Codes for other states were not examined.

3

The Role of Music
in Daily Life

After recounting the singing and dancing which took place on holidays and at harvest celebrations, European reporters of African customs in the New World occasionally described the funerals, which seemed wholly heathenish by their own standards. Instead of the sad decorum of an English or French interment, the Africans sang and danced. Some Europeans took the trouble to inquire as to whether these customs had been brought from Africa, and what they meant to Africans. Many more, however, regarded this behavior as just one more example of the barbarism and lack of decent sensibility of "benighted" and "uncivilized" people. Later the abolitionists interpreted these customs as evidence of the joy with which the slaves greeted the end of suffering and servitude for one of their number. It was widely explained that the Africans believed they would return to Africa after death.

Obviously, the complex beliefs and customs surrounding death and burial involve much more than music. But music was and is an integral part of such ceremonies, and so contemporary descriptions of slave funerals can be appropriately cited as part of their music. Richard Ligon was one of the earliest observers, writing at a time when no common means of communication had yet been developed. He wrote: "The Negres . . . are fetch'd from severall parts of *Africa*, who speake severall languages, and by that means, one of them understands not another.... When any of them die, they dig a grave, and at evening they bury him, clapping and wringing their hands, and making a dolefull sound with their voyces."[1] There is no way of knowing if Ligon's description of the music as "dolefull" was a reflection of his own reaction, or if indeed these early ceremonies reflected greater sadness than those described by others. The next reporter, writing from New York in 1712, did not concern himself with the emotions of the slaves; the Reverend John Sharpe stated baldly that Christian slaves did not receive what he regarded as decent burial: "They are buried in the Common by those of their country and complexion without the office, on the contrary the Heathenish rites are performed at the grave by their countrymen...."[2]

In 1740 Charles Leslie displayed little sympathy or understanding when describing Jamaican funerals:

> the Customs they use at their Burials. . . . When one is carried to his Grave, he is attended with a vast Multitude, who . . . sing all the way. . . . When they come to the Grave . . . the Negroes sacrifice a Hog . . . all the while they are covering it [the body] with Earth, the Attendants scream out in a terrible manner, which is not the Effect of Grief, but of Joy; they beat on their wooden Drums, and the Women with their Rattles make a hideous Noise. . . .[3] (AS 1)

From Bridge Town, Barbados, Nicholas Creswell observed on September 16, 1774: "These poor beings [slaves] . . . have a hell on earth. It appears that they are sensible of this, if one may judge from their behavior at their funerals. Instead of weeping and wailing, they dance and sing and appear to be the happiest mortals on earth."[4]

Despite the higher proportion of whites on the mainland, conditions (at least in some areas) during the eighteenth century were not very different. Janet Schaw wrote from Point Pleasant, North Carolina, in 1775: "The Negroes assembled to perform their part of the funeral rites [for their mistress] which they did by running, jumping, crying and various exercises. . . ."[5] Her animus toward the blacks, clearly evident in other portions of her journal, colored her choice of words. She was hardly a sympathetic observer. In 1793 Bryan Edwards was more perceptive, writing: "Their funeral songs

---

1. Ligon, *True & Exact History*, pp. 46, 50, and repeated in Clarke, *True and Faithful Account*, p. 69.
2. Sharpe, "Proposals," p. 355.
3. [Leslie,] *New History of Jamaica*, pp. 308–9.
4. Creswell, *Journal*, p. 40.
5. [Schaw,] *Journal*, p. 171.

too are all of the heroic or martial cast; affording some colour to the prevalent notion that the Negroes consider death not only as a welcome and happy release from the calamities of their condition, but also as a passport to the place of their nativity. . . ."[6]

George Pinckard described a Negro funeral in Barbados in 1796:

> Grief and lamentations were not among them: nor was even the semblance thereof assumed. No solemn dirge was heard; no deep-sounding bell was tolled: no fearful silence held. It seemed a period of mirth and joy! Instead of weeping and bewailing, the attendants jumped and sported, as they passed along, and talked and laughed, with each other, in high festivity. The procession was closed by five robust Negro fishermen, who came behind playing antic gambols, and dancing all the way to the grave. . . . The body was committed to the grave . . . without either prayer or ceremony; and the coffin, directly, covered with earth. . . . During this process an old Negro woman chanted an African air, the multitude joining in chorus. It was not in the strain of a solemn requiem, but was loud and lively. . . .[7]

Another description from Jamaica in 1809 included many details that seemed distinctly African, concluding with an account of the festivities after the interment. This bears comparison with the use of marching bands at funerals in New Orleans toward the end of the nineteenth century:

> At their funerals they use various ceremonies: among which is the practice of pouring libations, and sacrificing a fowl on the grave of the deceased; a tribute of respect. . . . During the whole of this ceremony many fantastic motions and wild gesticulations are practised, accompanied with a suitable beat of their drums, and other rude instruments while a melancholy dirge is sung by a female, the chorus of which is performed by the whole of the other females with admirable precision, and full-toned, and not unmelodious voices. . . .
>
> When the deceased its interred, the plaintive notes of sympathy and regret are no longer heard; the drums resound with a livelier beat, the song grows animated and cheerful; dancing and apparent merriment commences, and the remainder of the night is spent in feasting. . . .[8]
> (AS 2)

Reports from the mainland, while milder in their Africanisms, were nevertheless sometimes distinctly non-European. For example, a letter from Virginia in 1816, long after the separation of the United States from the British colonial structure, has more in common with the reports from the West Indies than with the funeral customs of the Virginia whites: "When a slave dies, the master gives

6. Edwards, *History*, II, 85.
7. Pinckard, *Notes*, pp. 130–32.
8. [Stewart,] *Account of Jamaica*, p. 179.

the rest a day, of their own choosing, to celebrate the funeral. This, perhaps a month after the corpse is interred, is a jovial day with them; they sing and dance and drink the dead to his new home, which some believe to be in old Guinea."[9] Yet Virginia was one of the oldest mainland colonies, long removed from a frontier condition. The African survivals that persisted in the West Indies were less prominent in mainland North America, but they did not disappear completely. Nineteenth-century reports of African customs will be presented later, but it is pertinent to mention here that the tenacity of African funeral customs, long after they were officially "stamped out," was demonstrated in the field reports which the Georgia Writers' Program collected in the 1930's. Focusing on customs and beliefs of "African origin," the Program reported on the use of drums in funeral ceremonies: "The mourners beat the drum while on the way to the cemetery; after arriving they marched around the grave in a ring and beat the drum and shouted. . . ."[10] The persistence of such customs in the face of hostile authority (in the forms of churches and local government) has yet to be fully explored. All too often the few whites who observed these ceremonies misunderstood their cultural and religious significance, considering them as either amusing or sacrilegious.

PINKSTER AND OTHER AFRICAN CELEBRATIONS IN THE NORTH

As the complaint from the Reverend John Sharpe made clear, the slaves in the northern colonies also continued their own African celebrations in a somewhat attenuated fashion; their festivities resembled in many details the dancing and singing which was such a prominent part of West Indian life. Although no contemporary descriptions of Pinkster celebrations have yet been found, there is no reason to question the authenticity of traditions of a distinctive black holiday, which was widely reported in secondary sources. Dictionaries of American English are in agreement that the word "pinkster" or "pinxter" is related to the Dutch name for Whitsuntide or Pentecost—*Pfingsten* in German—and that the word came to America with the early Dutch settlers.[11] Initially the term had no specific connotations relating to the blacks; it was a holiday for the Dutch. As in the English tradition of Boxing Day, the servants were given the days immediately following the holiday for their own

9. [Knight,] *Letters*, p. 77.
10. Writers' Program, Georgia, *Drums and Shadows*, p. 62. See also pp. 67, 71, 106–7, 125, 127, 130, 140–41, 143, 155, 180, 184.
11. Craigie and Hulbert, *Dictionary of American English*, III, 1747; Mathews, *Dictionary of Americanisms*, II, 1249.

celebration, and that day (or days) came to be known as Pinkster. The earliest cited reference to the word dates from William Dunlap's diary for 1797, where he appears to be referring to a general holiday rather than one specifically for blacks: "The settlements along the river are dutch, it is the holiday they call pinkster & every public house is crowded with merry makers."[12]

The lack of contemporary references to a phenomenon that must have been widely known has been explained by the editors of *American Notes & Queries*: "Precise and systematic references to its early history are noticeably absent, for social historians, two centuries ago, were highly arbitrary in their choice of material, and if they saw fit to skip over the commonplace things, they did so."[13] The celebration seems to have originated about or before 1750, according to this article, although there must have been smaller, less organized festivities out of which such a general holiday grew. The earliest description of a specifically black holiday is given in a novel, *Satanstoe*, by James Fenimore Cooper. The book was originally published in 1845 but purported to describe events of 1757, including a Pinkster celebration just outside the city of New York:

> Nine tenths of the blacks of the city, and of the whole country within thirty or forty miles, indeed, were collected in thousands in those fields, beating banjos, singing African songs. . . . The features that distinguish a Pinkster frolic from the usual scenes at fairs . . . however, were of African origin. It is true, there are not now, nor were there then, many blacks among us of African birth; but the traditions and usages of their original country were so far preserved as to produce a marked difference between this festival, and one of European origin. Among other things, some were making music, by beating on skins drawn over the ends of hollow logs, while others were dancing to it. . . . This, in particular, was said to be a usage of their African progenitors.[14]

A typical secondary account appeared in the *Bi-Centennial History of Albany* (1886):

> Mr. Williams says "Pinkster Day" was in Africa a religious day, partly pagan and partly Christian, like our Christmas day. Many of the old colored people, then [1815?] in Albany, were born in Africa, and would dance their wild dances and sing in their native language.
>
> "Pinkster" festivities took place usually in May, and lasted an entire week. It began the Monday following Whit-Sunday . . . and was the Carnival of the African race. . . . The main and leading spirit was "Charley of the Pinkster Hill," who was brought from Angola, in the Guinea Gulf, in his infant days. . . .

12. Cited in Mathews, *Dictionary of Americanisms*.
13. "Sassafras and Swinglingtow," p. 35.
14. James Fenimore Cooper, *Satanstoe*, pp. 66–67.

The dancing music was peculiar. The main instrument was a sort of "kettle-drum," a wooden article called an eel-pot, with a sheep-skin drawn tightly over one end. Astride this sat Jackey Quackenboss, beating lustily with his hands, and repeating the ever-wild, though euphonic cry of "Hi-a-bomba, bomba, bomba," in full harmony with the trumming sounds of his eel-pot.[15]

An account such as this must have been based on interviews or on manuscript accounts derived from oral tradition, if not from firsthand witnesses. Research in colonial archives and manuscript records is badly needed to satisfactorily document this rich cultural tradition.

WORKSONGS AND OTHER KINDS OF AFRICAN SINGING

There has been less controversy about the African origins of Afro-American worksongs than about the roots of spirituals or jazz, even though most of the songs were collected in the twentieth century in what D. K. Wilgus has characterized as "a period of decay."[16] In the absence of contemporary documents, the willingness of scholars to accept their African provenance while denying that of other types of Afro-American music seems at first puzzling. But explanations do present themselves. The scholars who were concerned with the white "forerunners" of spirituals or with the origins of jazz viewed worksongs as outside their area of interest and perhaps as irrelevant. No one arguing in favor of white origins for Afro-American music has extended his argument to worksongs. Newman Ivey White, in discussing "the very earliest" of Negro secular songs, speculated: "They were probably too simple and incoherent to be thought worthy of notice by any white person who encountered them"[17]—a theory that is supported by the many published opinions on the monotony of slave singing, since worksongs tend to sound monotonous to anyone not engaged in the task at hand. There was probably an element of intellectual snobbery involved, too, with some condescension toward rough workmen who were not expected to produce songs likely to interest educated people.

When worksongs began to attract students of folk music, these collectors and scholars took it for granted that the songs represented the continuation of a tradition that originated in Africa, however

15. Howell, *Bi-centennial History of Albany*, p. 725. For similar accounts, see Caulkins, *History of Norwich*, p. 330; Weise, *History of Troy*, pp. 63–64; Mary Gay Humphreys, *Catherine Schuyler*, p. 39; Olson, "Social Aspects," pp. 66–77. Even John Fanning Watson's *Annals of Philadelphia* included only a secondary account.
16. Wilgus, *Anglo-American Folksong Scholarship*, p. 320.
17. White, *American Negro Folk-Songs*, p. 148.

much it had been acculturated. The need for documentary proof never occurred to them. However, even on the basis of the documents now available, their instincts appear to have been correct. It is still not possible to document a specific worksong's origin in Africa and its persistence in the New World, although documentation of that sort may turn up some day. But it is possible to present contemporary reports of worksongs in Africa and the same types of songs in the New World, songs which have never been attributed to any other influence than the African. When more reports have been collected, it may be possible to trace the acculturation of worksongs.

Accounts of travelers in Africa usually stressed the music which accompanied ceremonies and dancing—the music which would have been performed in their presence and which would have made the greatest impression. Rarely do they mention the singing which regulated work in the fields or in boats, but no one should interpret their reports as evidence that worksongs did not exist. A Philadelphia surgeon who took part in a slaving voyage to Africa in 1749–51 wrote in his diary on July 11, 1750: "Early this morning the King of the Fantees . . . sent his Canoe wth. 12 negroes for me . . . [and] from the Ship to the Shore I was attended with the Singing of them."[18] A responsible scholar of the history of the blacks in colonial South Carolina postulated a direct connection between such boat songs and those that were sung in South Carolina.

> Slender boats . . . were the central means of transportation in South Carolina for two generations while roads and bridges were still too poor and infrequent for easy land travel. They were hollowed from a single cypress log by Negroes or Indians, who were then employed . . . to pole, row, or paddle them through the labyrinth of lowland waterways. . . . As the traditional historian of the crown colony [Edward McCrady] explained . . . "there was a naval officer too, to each planter's household, and he was called the patroon—a name no doubt brought from the West Indies. The patroon had charge of the boats. . . . He, too, trained the boat hands to the oar and taught them the plaintive, humorous, happy catches which they sang as they bent to the stroke." The earliest rowing songs were probably African remnants recalled by the patroon. . . .[19]

A fascinating speculation which cannot at present be supported by documentation is that the slaves who successfully grew rice in coastal South Carolina had learned their techniques in Africa.

> In summer, when Carolina blacks moved through the rice fields in a row, hoeing in unison to work songs, the pattern of cultivation was not one imposed by European owners but rather one retained from West African

18. Wax, "Philadelphia Surgeon," p. 478.
19. Wood, *Black Majority*, pp. 124, 202. McCrady's study was *The History of South Carolina Under the Royal Government, 1719–1776* (New York, 1899), p. 516.

forebears. . . . There was a strikingly close resemblance between the traditional West African means of pounding rice and the process used by slaves in South Carolina. . . . Even the songs used by the slaves who threshed and pounded the rice may have retained African elements.[20]

No details of the singing of worksongs have yet been found from colonial South Carolina, but they were reported in the West Indies:

> The Negroes, when at work in howing [sugar] Canes, or digging round Holes to plant them in, (perhaps forty Persons in a row) sing very merrily, *i.e.* two or three Men with large Voices, and a sort of Base Tone, sing three or four short lines, and then all the rest join at once, in a sort of Chorus, which I have often heard, and seemed to be, *La, Alla, La, La,* well enough, and indeed harmoniously turned.[21]

Descriptions of songs regulating field work recur, but with less frequency than descriptions of boat songs, perhaps because the Europeans who provide these records saw less of the fieldhands or paid less attention to them. Jean Baptiste Thibault de Chanvalon, who went to Martinique in 1751, reported that there was no work without singing, which had the advantage of forcing the lazy ones to keep up with the others.[22] Le Page du Pratz, who planted in Louisiana in 1758, wrote: "When I surprised them singing at their work . . . I said to them chearfully, Courage, my boys, I love to see you merry at your work; but do not sing so loud, that you may not fatigue yourselves."[23] Peter Marsden wrote from Jamaica in 1788: "All the time the negroes are busy with the crop, they make so much noise in singing that they may be heard a great way off."[24] Two reports appeared in 1790, those of Moreton and Beckford:

> When working, though at the hardest labour, they [the slaves] are commonly singing; and though their songs have neither rhime nor measure, yet many are witty and pathetic. I have often laughed heartily, and have been as often struck with deep melancholy at their songs.[25]

> When the mill is at work at night [grinding sugar], there is something affecting in the songs of the women who feed it; and it appears somewhat singular, that all their tunes . . . are of a plaintive cast. Sometimes

20. Wood, *Black Majority*, pp. 61–62. Compare this with a letter written from St. Helena Island, Apr. 12, 1862, a very early wartime reaction of a Northerner to the Sea Islands: "Sixty-eight hands are . . . planting sweet potatos, swinging their hoes in unison, timed by a jolly song, words undistinguishable."—signed E.P. [Edward S. Philbrick or Edward Pierce?], "Extracts from Letters of Teachers and Superintendents, 2d series," Educational Commission for Freedmen, *1st Annual Report*, p. 31.

21. William Smith, *Natural History of Nevis*, pp. 230–31, Letter IX.

22. [Chanvalon,] *Voyage*, p. 67.

23. Le Page du Pratz, *History of Louisiana*, p. 384.

24. [Marsden,] *Account*, p. 36.

25. Moreton, *Manners and Customs*, p. 152. The account concludes with the words of a song inspired by "the Overseer's barbarity to them."

you may hear one soft, complaining voice; and now a second and a third chime in; and presently . . . a full chorus is heard to swell upon the ear, and then to die away again to the first original tone. [Apparently this was a song not to regulate the rate of work, but to pass the time.]

The style of singing among the negroes is uniform; and this is confined to women; for the men very seldom, excepting upon extraordinary occasions, are ever heard to join in chorus. [This observation is not corroborated elsewhere.] One person begins first, and continues to sing alone; but at particular periods the others join: there is not, indeed, much variety in their songs; but their intonation is not less perfect than their time.[26]

Berquin-Duvallon, who visited Louisiana in 1802, complained that the Negroes there did not seem as happy as those in Saint-Domingue, as shown by the songs they sang at their work.[27] Other reporters were less critical. Clement Caines wrote of the workers on his own Leeward Islands estate (1804): "The slaves then work in a long string, and follow each other in regular order. Some one takes the lead and breaks out with a song, to which there is always a chorus. In this they all join, and the union of such a number of voices, produces a very animated and pleasing effect." His description of the subjects of their songs—improvised comments on his treatment of them—while following an African tradition, must have been sung in a language he understood, and so illustrate the beginnings of acculturation.[28] In 1817, a traveler in Santo Domingo described "several negroes, singing songs of Congo [as they] were pounding the root of the manioc."[29] As late as 1842 Victor Schoelcher, the French abolitionist and biographer of Händel, wrote of worksongs as "une importation africaine," describing how each "atelier" had its "chanteur ou chanterelle" who, by setting the rhythm of the work, lessened fatigue and encouraged comrades to respond with a refrain.[30]

So much for field songs. The boat songs which were an early part of the South Carolina scene remained a feature of life in the Sea Islands until after the Civil War. Only reports from before 1800 which may have described African music will be considered here. An account of Edisto Island, South Carolina, near Charleston, was published in 1809; it described the slaves as they had been forty years earlier: "In their voyages to the city they were wont to beguile the time and toil of rowing with songs and extravagant

26. Beckford, *Descriptive Account*, II, 120–21.
27. Berquin-Duvallon, *Vue de la Colonie Espagnole*, p. 274.
28. Caines, *History*, I, 110–11.
29. Montule, *Voyage*, p. 25, Letter VI, dated "Santo Domingo, the 26th February, 1817."
30. Schoelcher, *Des Colonies Françaises*, p. 23.

vociferations. . . ."[31] In 1777 Elkanah Watson was sent from Providence, Rhode Island, to South Carolina on a business mission. He crossed Winyaw Bay in a ferry "manned by four jolly . . . negroes . . . a distance of four miles. . . . The poor fellows amused us, the whole way, by singing their plaintive African songs, in cadence with the oars."[32] Other accounts of later boat songs in a continuing tradition will be described subsequently.

In addition to the accounts of field songs and boat songs, there were a few general comments on African singing and songs. Thomas Clarkson wrote in 1785: "Their abilities in musick are such, as to have been generally noticed. . . . They have . . . tunes of their own composition. Some of these have been imported among us; are now in use; and are admired for their sprightliness and ease, though the ungenerous and prejudiced importer has concealed their original."[33] If only Clarkson had specified the songs he had in mind!

Ten years later, slaves in Louisiana were heard "singing Jacobin songs which threatened the lives of the officials of the province. In one of the more popular songs, the slaves sang of the time when they would become republicans and freedmen, promised to guillotine the 'swine governor' and hang the treasurer and auditor."[34] Nothing can now be said as to the degree of acculturation displayed by the music of these songs, but certainly the guillotine sounds like French influence. A false alarm of a slave uprising was described by Charles Janson between 1793 and 1806. He was staying with a friend in Madison Court-House, Virginia, when they were "greatly alarmed by an uncouth singing of the Negroes, apparently about a mile distant. We listened attentively, and fancied the noise grew nearer." They armed themselves, "apprehending an attack, and conceiving that it was the negro-war song." When they reached the local tavern, they found a card game in progress, and "upon our mentioning the cause of our alarm, they burst into a laugh, informing us that it was only a harvest-home of the negroes."[35] To Janson's ears the music sounded menacing, but to the natives it was clearly a familiar if not welcome sound that frightened them not at all.

An account of African singing in North Carolina about 1800 was given by the pioneer historian John Spencer Bassett, who was told of the incident by

31. "Appendix No. 1. A Statistical Account of Edisto Island," Ramsay, *History of South-Carolina*, p. 545.
32. Elkanah Watson, *Men and Times of the Revolution*, p. 52. I am indebted to Miss Miriam Studley, formerly of the Newark Public Library, for this citation.
33. [Clarkson,] *Essay*, p. 170.
34. Cabildo Books, "Minutes for May 2, 1795," cited in McConnell, *Negro Troops*, pp. 26–27.
35. Janson, *Stranger in America*, p. 406.

an intelligent gentleman, who was a large planter in the eastern part of the State. . . . This incident was related to my informant by the gentleman who was overseer on this plantation when the incident occurred. . . . About the beginning of this century when the large Collins plantation on Lake Phelps, Washington County, was being cleared a number of negroes just from Africa were put on the work. . . . They were kept at night in cabins on the shore of the lake. At night they would begin to sing their native songs, and in a short while would become so wrought up that, utterly oblivious to the danger involved, they would grasp their bundles of personal effects, swing them on their shoulders, and setting their faces towards Africa, would march down into the water singing as they marched till recalled to their senses only by the drowning of some of the party. The owners lost a number of them in this way, and finally had to stop the evening singing.[36]

African singing could be prohibited by the owners, but they had no way of enforcing the prohibition at times and in places unknown to them, where the singing continued surreptitiously. On the islands, the owners tolerated whatever the Africans wanted to sing.

It is well known that the Negroes will make a song out of any thing. On one occasion, I listened to a party of old women, boys and girls, singing the following in our kitchen:
O massa! O massa! one Monday morning they lay me down,
And give me thirty-nine on my bare rump. O massa! O massa![37]

The words were English, but the call-and-response form, the improvisatory character of the words, and the relation of the song to the lives of the singers were African.

A few writers attempted to characterize African singing in general. Lacking specialized knowledge of the differences between various African musics, their conclusions were hardly reliable, yet they identified some of the distinguishing elements that modern ethnomusicologists have recognized. Chanvallon remarked on the Africans' ability to prolong or shorten the words to fit the music, and on their extended repetition of the same music either for dancing or to regulate work. Three or four words were repeated alternately by the soloist and the chorus; five or six measures of melody might be the extent of a song. Curiously, he made no comment on the rhythm; perhaps his eighteenth-century ears could not comprehend the complexities of what they heard? Finally he divided the songs into two groups: tender and warlike.[38]

Edward Long, who "played a Cremona violin," was able to appreciate some of the qualities of this exotic music:

36. Bassett, *Slavery in the State of North Carolina*, pp. 92–93.
37. Thomas Cooper, *Facts Illustrative . . . Negro Slaves in Jamaica*, p. 18n.
38. [Chanvallon,] *Voyage*, p. 67.

They have good ears for music; and their songs, as they call them, are generally *impromptu*, without the least particle of poetry, or poetic images, of which they seem to have no idea. The tunes consist of a *solo* part, which we may style the recitative, the key of which is frequently varied; and this is accompanied with a full or general chorus. Some of them are not deficient in melody; although the tone of voice is, for the most part, rather flat and melancholy. Instead of choosing panegyric for their subject-matter, they generally prefer one of derision, and not unfrequently at the expence of the overseer, if he happens to be near, and listening; this only serves to add a poignancy to their satire, and heightens the fun. In the crop season, the mill-feeders entertain themselves very often with these *jeux d'esprit* in the night-time; and this merriment helps to keep them awake.[39] (AS3) [In the sugar-grinding season, the boiling kettles were kept going twenty-four hours a day.]

A Swiss traveler, Girod-Chantrans, visited Saint-Domingue in 1782, commenting that he preferred the music of the native Africans, especially from the Congo, to that of the Creoles. He particularly admired the precision of movement, the execution and harmony when several of them sang together, the ornaments (*les murmures variés*), the long, sustained tones, and the dialogue between the soloist and the chorus. Compared with these, he found the songs of the Creoles uninteresting.[40] His taste was far more eclectic than that of most Europeans of the time, and the norm of European taste was imposed upon the Africans who sought to rise in the social scale. Despite their overwhelming preponderance in the population of the West Indies, the Africans were faced with the necessity for some kind of accommodation with the white masters. Just as the need for communication weakened the position of African languages, so in music and dancing European elements crept in, little by little. Except in isolated communities of runaway slaves, the process of acculturation was unavoidable. However, the evidence makes it abundantly clear that African music and dancing not only were transported to the New World but also persisted there for generations. Even after they were acculturated, recognizable elements continued to persist in public, and it seems unquestionable that many more survived surreptitiously. The written record may be only the tip of the iceberg.

39. [Edward Long,] *History of Jamaica*, II, 423.
40. [Girod-Chantrans,] *Voyage*, pp. 192–93. 14th letter from Saint-Domingue, 1782. My translation. A German translation appeared in 1786: *Reisen eines Schweizers in verschiedene Kolonien von Amerika während dem letztern Krieg* (Leipzig: A. F. Höhme, 1786), pp. 145–46.

ADDITIONAL SOURCES

AS1. A less localized description of a Negro funeral in the West Indies was published in verse in 1767 by John Singleton as book 3 of his *General Description* (pp. 115–18):

> But see what strange procession hither winds . . .
> Like gentle waves hundreds of sable heads
> Float onwards . . .
> Behold the white-rob'd train in form advance
> To yonder new-made grave. Six ugly hags . . .
> In wild contorsive postures lead the van;
> High o'er their palsied heads, rattling, they wave
> Their noisy instruments; whilst to the sound
> In dance progressive their shrunk shanks keep time.
> With more composure the succeeding ranks,
> Chanting their fun'ral song in chorus full,
> Precede the mournful bier. . . .

After the interment,

> . . . the mourners form a spacious ring,
> When sudden clangours, blended with shrill notes,
> Pour'd forth from many a piercing pipe . . .
> Thus do these sooty children of the sun . . . perform
> Their fun'ral obsequies, and joyous chaunt,
> In concert full, the requiem of the dead;
> Wheeling in many a mazy round, they fill
> The jocund dance, and take a last farewell
> Of their departed friend, without a tear.

William Beckford disapproved of the slave funeral customs current in Jamaica, not only on religious principles, but also on the grounds of health and morality: "It is notorious that more slaves are ruined in principle and health, at those dances which are allowed at the burials of their dead, than by any other intercourse or occupation whatever" (*Remarks Upon the Situation of Negroes*, p. 82). In the same year Gilbert Francklyn agreed "that their funerals are attended with music and dancing" (*Answer*, p. 213), and Peter Marsden commented, "After the interment of a corpse, they always dance and sing dolefully; but there is no knowing what they say on these occasions" (*Account*, p. 34). See also Moreton, *Manners and Customs*, p. 156.

AS2. A later account of an African funeral in Jamaica was written by Michael Scott, who was there between 1806 and 1810 and again from about 1818 until 1822. *Tom Cringle's Log*, in which the account appeared, was originally published in 1833. The persistence of African cultural patterns until well into the nineteenth century is striking.

> [In Kingston, Jamaica] a negro funeral came past, preceded by a squad of . . . black vagabonds, singing and playing on gumbies, or African drums, made out of pieces of hollow trees, about six feet long, with skins braced over them, each carried by one man, while another beats it with his open hands.

Later, a description of a wake in the Negro houses:

> No white person ever broke in on these orgies . . . the negroes are very averse to their doing so . . . a loud drumming which, as I came nearer, every now and then sunk into a low murmuring roll, when a strong bass voice would burst forth into a wild recitative; to which succeeded a loud piercing chorus of female voices, during which the drums were beaten with great vehemence; this was succeeded by

another solo, and so on. . . . Before the door a circle was formed by about twenty women . . . sitting on the floor, and swaying their bodies to and fro, while they sung in chorus the wild dirge already mentioned, the words of which I could not make out; in the centre of the circle sat four men playing on the *gumbies*, or the long drum formerly described, while a fifth stood behind them, with a conch-shell, which he kept sounding at intervals.

[Scott,] *Tom Cringle's Log*, pp. 131, 145–47. This account was fictitious, although it was based on firsthand experience. The words of the song were included.

AS3. Bryan Edwards echoed the ideas that Long had published twenty-three years earlier; whether consciously, who can say?

Their songs are commonly *impromptu*, and there are among them individuals who resemble the *improvisatore*, or extempore bards, of Italy; but I cannot say much for their poetry. Their tunes in general are characteristic of their national manners; those of the Ebos being soft and languishing; of the Koromantyns heroic and martial. At the same time, there is observable, in most of them, a predominant melancholy, which, to a man of feeling, is sometimes very affecting.

At their merry meetings, and midnight festivals, they are not without ballads of another kind, adapted to such occasions; and here they give full scope to a talent for ridicule and derision, which is exercised not only against each other, but also, not unfrequently, at the expence of their owner or employer; but most part of their songs at these places are fraught with obscene ribaldry, and accompanied with dances in the highest degree licentious and wanton.

History, II, 85. Yet Edwards disagreed with the prevailing opinion that Africans were especially talented in music. "In vocal harmony they display neither variety nor compass," and so on and on (II, 84).

4

....

The Acculturation of African
Music in the New World

African culture in its native surroundings may have reflected some
influence from Europe or Asia,[1] but when the African was seized and
put aboard a slave ship, the exposure to European influences became inevitable. When he landed in the New World, communication in language became the most urgent problem for master and
slave, but it was only one acculturative problem among many. The
culture of the Africans had been violently disrupted; even in areas
where they greatly outnumbered the whites, their lives could never
be the same. The rate of acculturation varied greatly from colony to
colony, determined largely by the ratio between black and white
populations. Where the blacks were in the majority, they were able
to retain more of their native culture. Richard S. Dunn neatly
summed up the situation:

> The West Indian slave, barred from the essentials of European civili-
> ty, was free to retain as much as he wished of his West African cultural
> heritage. Here he differed from the Negro in Virginia or New England,
> who was not only uprooted from his familiar tropical environment but
> thrown into close association with white people and their European
> ways. It is not surprising, therefore, that blacks in the sugar islands
> preserved more of their native culture than blacks in North America.
> The West Indian slaves learned enough broken English to communicate

1. For a study of one aspect of this subject, see A. M. Jones, *Africa and Indonesia*.

with their overlords, but they were always bilingual and retained their tribal dialects. The large number of West African languages prevented easy communication among the slaves, so they evolved a common creole patois, compounded of English and African elements, which was unintelligible to their masters.[2]

Although music will be singled out for detailed discussion here, it was always a part of a complex of cultural elements, constantly undergoing modification. To follow the course of its acculturation, it will be necessary to rely largely on West Indian accounts, because reports from the mainland are at best fragmentary, and indeed have not been found at all for many areas. The known reports indicate that the pattern on the mainland was similar to that in the islands. Although the two areas displayed basic differences, the seventeenth- and eighteenth-century similarities are more significant for our purposes. The discussion of acculturation will begin with the African's introduction to his new environment, followed by the acculturation of African music in the New World as a whole; developments in New Orleans, an atypical city for the mainland; and (in the following chapter) conversion to Christianity.

THE ARRIVAL OF AFRICANS AND THEIR MUSIC

Africans were widely dispersed among a much larger population of whites in all the mainland colonies except South Carolina. They usually were separated from shipmates, their sole tie with home, almost as soon as they landed in a strange and hostile land; frequently they arrived at the place of their bondage alone or in small groups. To communicate with those around them, they had to learn a new language as soon as possible. Their adjustment to the new surroundings was considered an individual problem, of very little concern to the man who had bought them. Attempts to reconstruct the adjustment problems of newly arrived slaves in North America are now being made from advertisements for runaway slaves and similar sources.[3]

In the West Indies, however, slaves arrived in groups. Planters found it advantageous to introduce them to their new environment by a series of techniques which (they hoped) would permit a transition without serious illness or death. These techniques apparently were evolved over a period of time. Du Tertre did not consider the

2. Dunn, *Sugar and Slaves*, p. 250.
3. The problem of cultural change among Africans in the colonial era received perceptive attention from Gerald W. Mullin in his *Flight and Rebellion,* and "Rethinking American Negro Slavery."

problem at all, merely contrasting the dancing and singing of the Africans with the sadness of the captive Israelites in Babylon.[4] Richard Ligon did not discuss what means, if any, were taken to help them adapt. In the early years of settlement the planters may have been fully occupied with their own adjustment and struggle to survive. At any rate, the earliest known mention of a considered policy on acclimating the slaves dates from 1786, although the practices described probably had evolved earlier. Gordon Turnbull, an apologist for slavery, described the "Guinea negroe's arrival in one of the islands": "It is not uncommon for these newly arrived guests to mingle in the dance, or to join in the song, with their country people." When the new Negroes were brought "home to the plantation," they were allowed to recover (if possible) from the rigors of the voyage in a slaver, and to discover fellow countrymen among their new associates. "In the evenings they sing and dance, after the manner of their own nation, together with the old negroes who happen to be from the same country, one or two of whom are commonly instrumental performers, in these very noisy, but very joyous assemblies."[5] Turnbull's purpose in writing was to vindicate the planters "from the charge of inhumanity," but his account can be corroborated, and there seems no reason to doubt that the planters encouraged African singing and dancing as a means of raising the spirits of the new arrivals.[6]

In Louisiana the same pattern evolved. "Negroes bought from the importers and carried home by the purchasers are ordinarily treated differently from the old ones. They are only gradually accustomed to work. They are made to bathe often, to take walks . . . and especially to dance; they are distributed in small numbers among old slaves in order to dispose them better to acquire their habits."[7] The author explained that these attentions were ordinarily due to self-interest, rather than to sentiments of humanity.

The ties formed between shipmates or natives from the same country were noticed and used by the slaveowners for their own advantage. Newly purchased Negroes were assigned to "one, two or

4. Du Tertre, *Histoire Générale des Antilles*, II, 526.

5. [Gordon Turnbull,] *Apology*, pp. 21–25.

6. An account from 1797 says of the newly arrived slaves: "Having reached the abodes of their several owners, they are soothed by meeting with their countrymen; and some of the old negroes are instructed to cheer and console them, by talking to them in their own language, and representing that, by good conduct, they may ensure good treatment . . ."–Pinckard, *Notes*, II, 457.

7. Robin, *Voyages*, III, 166–70. Translation by Ulrich Bonnell Phillips in *A Documentary History of American Industrial Society*, ed. Commons, Phillips et al., II, 31,

three strangers . . . of their own colour [who] will lead from forty to fifty newly purchased from one end of the Island to the other; they will dance and sing throughout the journey. . . ."[8]

Of all the aspects of African music in the New World, the most difficult to document has been its acculturation—that is, its transition from being purely or almost purely African to a form recognizable as something different: Afro-American, Jamaican, Creole, or whatever term was devised for this new and hybrid music. The process began immediately on board the slave ships, with exposure to the European instruments that happened to be aboard. The dancing on board (sometimes little more than jumping up and down on the same spot) could not have remained unaffected by its surroundings, but no reports of conscious efforts to influence it have been found. As early as 1694 Père Labat had suggested replacing African dances with the minuet or courante, but he admitted that his attempts were unsuccessful. Even at this early date he wrote that some of the slaves played the violin well and earned extra money by playing at get-togethers (*assemblées*), presumably of the whites.[9] The Africans had taken up European instruments successfully.

In Virginia as well, slaves were valued for their fiddling prowess by the 1690's. A case in the records of Accomac County tells of a slave fiddling for a dance at the home of the Reverend Thomas Teakle in his absence. The dance started on a Saturday night and continued until nearly eleven o'clock on the following morning. When Mr. Teakle returned home and learned of the desecration of his house by a dance while church services were in progress, he commenced legal proceedings against his daughter's friends, thereby providing documentation of an event[10] which otherwise would have gone unrecorded, as no doubt many similar events did. As the eighteenth century progressed, increasing numbers of slaves in the islands and on the mainland learned to play Western instruments and to dance European dances, not necessarily as a substitute for their native recreations, but as a supplement to them. The descriptions of African and European musics and dancing existing side by side demonstrate the process by which acculturation proceeded.

A report from Guadeloupe, based on documents in the Archives Nationales, made a distinction between the dances of the town and

---

8. Beckford, *Remarks upon the Situation of Negroes*, p. 10.

9. Labat, *Nouveau Voyage*, IV, 158–59.

10. Accomac County Records, v. 1690–97, pp. 161ff., quoted in Bruce, *Social Life of Virginia*, pp. 181–84. See also Wise, *Ye Kingdome of Accawmacke*, pp. 322–24.

those of the countryside. In the early days, African dances occurred everywhere, but after 1750 they were restricted to the countryside and the "new" Negroes fresh from Africa, while the Creole Negroes in the towns adopted French dances.[11] A certain English soldier was stationed in Guadeloupe until June, 1763, when the Glorious Peace of Paris restored that island to the French. He wrote in his journal:

> Some of the Mulattoes can play indifferently well on the violin; they have likewise a kind of tabor, it hath but one head, and all round the hoop are fixed small pieces of tin; the manner of playing is to hold the instrument with one hand, and beat on the parchment head with the fingers of the other, according to the tune of the violin; others are singing to the tune; and some beat on the boards at the side of the hut in which the ball is kept, and others will clap their hands, all which instrumental and vocal music together makes a most hideous concert. Their chief dances are minuets and jigs, and some of the Creole slaves will dance a minuet tolerably well, after the French mode. . . . The women will dance down two or three men in a jig. . . .[12]

This account is difficult to interpret, with its description of Negroes dancing "minuets" to a combination of African and European instruments, followed by minuets "afrer the French mode." The use of "jig" is also ambiguous, for both African and European dances were called jigs in the eighteenth century (of which more will be said later on).

Later the soldier described a slave wedding where the guests, after dancing with the bride, put money "into the violin," which was given to the bride when the wedding was over. (This seems to imply a banjo-like instrument.) He continued:

> But these weddings, as well as balls, are only kept up by the Creole slaves; the raw negroes, have not wherewith to do so, but assemble in another part of the plantation, and divert themselves after their own country manner. Their chief instrument of music is a small cask, on one end is fastened a sheep or goat skin, with the hair off, and the musician sits across like Bacchus, beating on the head with his hands; all the assembly gather around him, and sing to the tune which he beats, which indeed is all at random, and the instrumental and vocal musick make a most terrible discord. . . .[13]

What is significant here is not whether the African music was discordant, but that Creole slaves were celebrating a wedding in one part of the plantation while the "raw" Negroes gathered elsewhere to "divert themselves after their own country manner." This jux-

11. Satineau, *Histoire de la Guadeloupe*, pp. 275–76.
12. *Soldier's Journal*, pp. 106–7.
13. *Ibid.*, p. 109.

taposition of African and European instruments, music, and dancing was reported from all the islands, both French and English, until well into the nineteenth century, and more rarely from the mainland.

Diderot's *Encyclopédie*, in the article "*Amérique*—Negres, considérée comme esclaves dans les colonies de l'Amérique," reported that the Negroes loved dancing passionately; those of each country gathered to dance in the style of their nation, but the dance that the Creoles liked the best and which was most popular among "les Nations naturalisées" was *la calenda*, which was considered important enough to have an entry of its own under "C."[14] It seems fair to assume that this article had reference to French possessions, probably in the islands and Louisiana. Accounts from other sections of the mainland were usually less explicit. Hennig Cohen, who has made a careful study of the *South Carolina Gazette* from 1732 to 1775,[15] reported that it contained

> a wealth of information on the sports and pastimes of the pleasure-loving population. . . . Little information, however, is to be found in the *Gazette* or other colonial newspapers regarding exclusively Negro diversions. This is not surprising for such entertainments were usually of so mild a nature that they held no interest for the newspaper reader or they were illegal and hence a closely guarded secret. Few references to any kind of clandestine social gatherings of Negro slaves before the Revolutionary war have been noted.

Cohen, however, did find one such description in an essay signed "Stranger" in the *Gazette* for September 17, 1772:

> The *Stranger* had once an opportunity of seeing a Country Dance, Rout, or Cabal of *Negroes*, within 5 miles distance of this town [Charleston], on a Saturday night. . . . It consisted of about 60 people . . . provided with Music, Cards, Dice, &c. The entertainment was opened, by the men copying (or *taking off*) the manners of their masters, and the women those of their mistresses, and relating some highly curious anecdotes, to the inexpressible diversion of that company. They then *danced*. . . . The *Stranger* is informed, that such assemblies *have been* very common, and that the company has sometimes amounted to 200 persons, even within one mile's distance of this place. . . .[16]

Although this is the only known description from the colonial period, it implies that gatherings of between sixty and two hundred Negroes for dancing of some unspecified character, and other diversions, were common within a mile of Charleston. The account of

14. *Encyclopédie*, XI, 66.
15. Cohen, *South-Carolina Gazette*.
16. Cohen, "Negro 'Folk Game,' " pp. 183–84.

"take offs" of masters and mistresses sounds very like the African tradition of derisive singing and mimicking. It seems likely that the dancing at such a clandestine gathering would have been quite different from the impromptu dancing that Philip Fithian found in his schoolroom on January 30, 1774, when he dispersed a group of Negroes and two of the Carter boys.[17] Yet each kind of dancing exemplified a stage of acculturation; if we knew more details, the process by which it progressed would become clearer.

A vivid account of a Jamaican Christmas celebration with African and European dancing was published in 1788:

> At Christmas the slaves are allowed three days holiday. . . . The . . . negroes and mulattoes pay a visit to the white people . . . one of them attends with a fiddle, and the men dress in the English mode, with cocked hats, cloth coats, Holland shirts, and pumps. They dance minuets with the mulattoe and other brown women, imitating the motion and steps of the English, but with a degree of affectation. . . . But their own way of dancing is droll indeed; they put themselves into strange postures, and shake their hips and great breasts to such a degree, that it is impossible to refrain from laughing, though they go through the whole performance with profound gravity, their feet beating time remarkably quick; two of them generally dance together, and sometimes do not move six inches from the same place.[18]

Another account of Negro dances was from 1790: "Their music is composed of any thing that makes a tinkling sound; a hollow cane, or bamboo, with holes in it, in imitation of a fife; an herring-barrel, or tub, with sheep-skins substituted for the heads, in imitation of a drum, called a gumbay; but sometimes more 'grandy balls,' as they are called, are honoured with a tabret and violin. . . ."[19]

One of the most remarkable descriptions of the visible acculturative process was Sir William Young's journal entry describing the Christmas festivities on St. Vincent in 1791:

> In the evening I opened the ball in the great court, with a minuet with black Phillis . . . our music consisted of two excellent fiddles . . . and . . . tamborin . . . there stood up about eighteen couple. . . . This moment a new party of musicians are arrived with an African *Balafo*, an instrument composed of pieces of hard wood of different diameters, laid on a row over a sort of box; they beat on one or the other so as to strike out a good musical tune. They played two or three African tunes; and about a dozen girls, hearing their sound, came from the huts to the great court, and began a curious and most lascivious dance, with much grace as well as action; of the last, plenty in truth.[20]

17. Fithian, *Journal & Letters*, entry for Jan. 30, 1774, pp. 61–62.
18. [Peter Marsden,] *Account*, pp. 33–34.
19. Moreton, *Manners and Customs*, p. 155.
20. Young, "Tour," in Edwards, *History*, III, 276.

On the mainland the proselytizing efforts of the Great Awakening and the evangelical revivals of the late eighteenth century were to some extent substituting religious exercises for dancing; however, New Orleans remained unaffected by such developments. "A gentleman of accurate observation, a passenger in a New Orleans boat" described what he saw on Sundays in 1799:

> Sunday, Feb. 24 . . . we saw vast numbers of negro slaves, men, women, and children, assembled together on the levee, druming, fifing, and dancing, in large rings.
> Sunday, March 3 . . . we found upwards of one hundred negroes of both sexes assembled on the levee, fiddling, dancing and singing.[21]

The juxtaposition of African and European dances and instruments side by side was frequently described in the islands, but only two examples of it have been found on the mainland. The first was a Christmas celebration similar to many described in the West Indies. It was observed in Georgetown District, South Carolina, in 1805 by young John Pierpont, newly arrived from Litchfield, Connecticut, to take up his duties as tutor at Colonel William Allston's Monjetta Plantation. Here again the evangelical revival had not yet made its influence felt.

> Decr 25th. Throwought the state of South Carolina, Christmas is a holiday, together with 2 of the succeeding days . . . for the Negroes.
> . . . On my first waking, the sound of serenading violins & drums saluted my ears, and for some time continued. . . . During almost the whole of the second and 3d afternoons, the portico was crowded with these [?] dancers . . . fiddlers & drumming. . . . Some of them who were native Africans did not join the dance with the others, but, by themselves gave us a specimen of the sports & amusement with which the benighted & uncivilized children of nature divert themselves. . . . Clapping their hands was their music and distorting their frames into the most unnatural figures and emiting the most hideous noises in their dancing. . . .[22]

The other account was from New Orleans, where on March 3, 1808, the Negroes danced a *bamboula* as part of the Mardi Gras celebration. Or rather, there were two groups, side by side, one dancing a *bamboula*, and the other a contre-danse.[23]

This overt competition between the two cultures did not long continue in most parts of the mainland; only in Place Congo in New

---

21. "Voyage from Pittsburgh to New Orleans," in Cuming, *Sketches*, pp. 333, 336.
22. John Pierpont, *Journal*, pp. 10–13, MS, Pierpont Morgan Library, New York. Quoted with permission of the Pierpont Morgan Library. Pierpont was J. P. Morgan's grandfather. See also Ravitz, "Pierpont and Slave's Christmas," pp. 383–86.
23. Laussat, *Mémoire*, p. 395.

Orleans was the African tradition able to continue in the open. But in the islands the competition went on. A Jamaican account published in 1809 discussed the music traditionally performed at funerals, "a suitable beat of their drums, and other rude instruments while a melancholy dirge is sung by a female, the chorus of which is performed by the whole of the other females with admirable precision and full-toned and not unmelodious voices." The report then makes evident that the slaves were quite familiar with European music but preferred their own. "This species of barbarous music is indeed more enchanting to their ears than all the most exquisite notes of a Purcell or a Pleyel; and however delighted they might appear to be with the finest melody of our bands, let them but hear at a distance the uncouth sounds of their own native instruments, and they would instantly fly from the one to enjoy the other."[24]

Another work by the same author published in 1823 described the progress of acculturation:

> Their music is very rude; it consists of the *goombay* or drum, several rattles, and the voices of the female slaves, which, by the bye, is the best part of the music. . . . The drums of the Africans vary in shape, size, &c. according to the different countries, as does also their vocal music. In a few years it is probable that the rude music here described will be altogether exploded among the creole negroes, who shew a decided preference for European music. Its instruments, its tunes, its dances, are now pretty generally adopted by the young creoles. . . . A sort of subscription balls are set on foot, and parties of both sexes assemble and dance country dances to the music of a violin, tambarine, &c. But this improvement of taste is in a great measure confined to those who are, or have been, domestics about the houses of the whites, and have in consequence imbibed a fondness for their amusements, and some skill in the performance. . . .[25]

In 1823, Christmas at Jamaica's Orange Grove plantation began with a fiddler, but in the evening

> they again assembled on the lawn before the house with their gombays, bonjaws, and an ebo drum. . . . Some of the women carried small calabashes with pebbles in them, stuck on short sticks, which they rattled in time to the songs. . . . They divided themselves into parties to dance, some before the gombays, in a ring. . . . Others performed . . . before the ebo drummer. . . . On all these occasions of festivity the mulattos kept aloof . . . and some of the pious . . . also objected to participate in the heathen practices of their ancestors. . . . I was a little quizzed for remarking that the planters would be called to account by

24. [Stewart,] *Account of Jamaica*, p. 178.
25. Stewart, *Past and Present State*, p. 272.

the reformers in England for letting the negroes dance on Christmas-day. . . . Mr. Graham told me there would be a rebellion in the island if any attempt was made to curtail the enjoyments of the blacks, even on religious principles.[26]

By 1825 reporters were beginning to refer to African music in the past tense: "When a negro wishes to give a dance . . . those of the old school preferring the goombay and African dances, and those of the new, fiddles, reels, &c. . . . The various African amusements, in which the negroes formerly took so much delight, are not now kept up with spirit, and Joncanoe himself is getting out of fashion."[27] In 1828 African music was considered extinct:

> About twenty years ago, it was common on occasions of this kind [the celebrations of the end of the cane-cutting] to see the different African tribes each a distinct party, singing and dancing to the *gumbay*, after the rude manners of their native Africa; but this custom is now extinct. The fiddle is now the leading instrument with them, as with the white people, whom they imitate; they dance Scotch reels, and some of the better sort (who have been house servants) country-dances. . . . [There follows a discussion of the influence of the missionaries on Christmas dances.] The young people, however still indulge in some amusements on this occasion. . . . They have always with them . . . a fiddle, a drum, and a tambourine, frequently boys playing fifes. . . .[28]

Frederic Bayley corroborated this statement by Barclay as

> natural, interesting, and true; and though I believe it is more particularly relative to Jamaica, it will also apply to nearly all the other islands. . . . For instance, I believe in one or two of the Leeward Islands it is more usual for the august assembly of sable revellers to carry on their gaieties on the green lawn before the dwelling of the proprietor, than to take possession of one of the rooms in the house. The music also is sometimes of wonderful variety. An empty barrel . . . with a large piece of parchment over the top, a kettledrum, a tambourine, a pipe, a *gumbay* or *bonja*, with sundry other instruments, and these aided by the vocal efforts of men and women, boys and girls . . .

Bayley did not consider the music barbarous or call it mere noise, unlike many of his contemporaries. "I must now, however, charge the slaves with a crime of which . . . they are seldom guilty, namely that of producing inharmonious and nonaccordant sounds; on the contrary, they have, generally a good ear for music, they sing or whistle with wonderful correctness any tune they may have heard, they dance in excellent time, and are altogether very intelligent

26. Cynric R. Williams, *Tour*, pp. 23–29.
27. De la Beche, *Notes*, pp. 40–42. ". . . observed . . . during my residence there from the 20th of December, 1823, to the 28th of December, 1824."—p. 3.
28. Barclay, *Practical View*, pp. 10–11.

persons in any thing connected with music."[29] It is curious that Bayley should endorse Barclay's report as "true," including as it does the statement that African dancing was extinct, and follow it with his own report of just such dancing in the Leeward Islands. It must be concluded that African dancing in the West Indies persisted long after country dances became popular, and that the repeated reports of its death were probably exaggerated. Acculturation proceeded at an erratic pace, the attractions of African rhythm overcoming both religious and cultural objections to the outlandish and old-fashioned behavior patterns. ("Outlandish" is here used in its colonial sense of originating in Africa.)

A report of both musics being performed simultaneously was published in 1831, but the date of the occasion was unclear. (The author arrived in Jamaica in 1814 and implied that he was describing events during his year's seasoning at Industry coffee plantation, but the book's title was *Jamaica in 1831*.) During the Christmas holidays the Negroes took over the manager's house for their celebration, a traditional dropping of the customary separation of the races: "The Mongolas, the Mandingos, the Ebos, the Congoes, &c., &c., formed into exclusive groups, and each strove to be loudest in the music and songs . . . peculiar to their country. . . . These African groups took up the sides and corners of the hall, whilst the Creoles occupied the centre and piazzas . . . the Creoles danced to fife and drum. . . ."[30] In New Orleans in 1831 the same dancing in groups was taking place.

> Every Sunday the negroes of the city and of the surroundings meet in a place called *The Camp*. It is a huge green field on the bank of a lake about three leagues from New Orleans. It takes only a few minutes to get there by a railroad. . . . At The Camp . . . negroes . . . are gathered in a large number of distinct groups; each has its own flag floating atop a very tall mast, used as a rallying point for the group . . . [for the] dance. . . . They make their music by beating and rolling their sticks on their drums. . . .[31]

A holiday celebration on the Meerzorg sugar plantation on the coast of British Guiana presented another instance of African and acculturated slaves performing their own musics, side by side: "Two or three musicians . . . with fiddle, tambourine and drum, strike up some lively jigs, at the same time thumping the floor vigorously with their heels. . . . Outside the house, in the moonlight, a musician seated himself with his drum on the grass, and commenced

29. Bayley, *Four Years' Residence*, p. 437.
30. Kelly, *Jamaica in 1831*, pp. 20–21.
31. Joyaux, ed., "Forest's Voyage," p. 468.

singing an African air, when a circle of men and women, linked hand in hand, danced round him with rattling seeds on their legs and joined in the chorus."[32]

The same complex was reported from Jamaica in the same year: "Sunday dances in Kingstown are not now common, but in the country they frequently occur. . . . The native African[s] . . . dance their own African dances to the drum, while the creole negroes consider the fiddle genteeler, though of an evening among themselves they will sing, dance, and beat the drum, yet they would not produce this instrument at a grand party. Fiddles and tambourines, with triangles, are essential there."[33]

New Year's celebrations on the island of St. Thomas shared many of these characteristics.

> It is the custom here, especially among the coloured persons, to celebrate the old year's night with music, dancing, singing, and in short, making a great noise. . . . Some of them . . . put up a tent of cocoanut leaves, and dance there during the night. Many of them again dance in their own rooms, which are certainly very small, and are so full that the dancers have scarcely room to move. The dances of the negroes are of one sort: turning and moving about—they have no regular dances. Their principal instrument is called the Gombee. This is a small barrel, the bottom of which being taken out, a goat skin is drawn over the rim. They must have one on purpose continually knocking on this Gombee, which sounds very hard and makes a great deal of noise. But this music and sort of dancing is more a custom amongst the lower class of negroes and slaves, for amongst the well-educated persons they have learnt dancing, have very good music, and often give balls like the white inhabitants.[34]

As the nineteenth century progressed, reporters of the West Indian scene expressed their bias against African culture with increasing sharpness, growing ever more certain that any assumption of European behavior patterns was a positive improvement, and that all aspects of African life were crude, mean, and uncivilized. Yet these prejudiced writers could convey much valuable information, filtered through their narrow ethnocentric opinions. For example, an account published in 1843 described African dances, singing, and instruments that were recognizably similar to those reported during the seventeenth century by Du Tertre and Labat, using the word "contortions" to characterize the dancing, but then giving an objective description of the steps.

> Their nightly dances or plays, which were frequent and general, were of a character the most licentious. They were usually accompanied by a band of the most rude and monotonous music, composed of instruments

32. Alexander, *Transatlantic Sketches*, pp. 60–61.
33. Carmichael, *Domestic Manners*, I, 292.
34. Nissen, *Reminiscences*, p. 165.

of African manufacture. The assemblage on such occasions consisted of
both sexes, who ranged themselves in a circle round a male and female
dancer, and performed to the music of their drums.

The songs were sung by the other females of the party; one alternately
singing, while her companions repeated in chorus; the singers and
dancers observing the exactest precision as to time and measure. On
some occasions the dance consisted of stamping the feet, accompanied by
various contortions of the body . . . on others, the head of each dancer
was erect, or occasionally inclined forward; the hands nearly united in
front; the elbows fixed, pointing from the sides; and the lower extremities being held firm, the whole person moved without raising the feet
from the ground. Making the head and limbs fixed points, they writhed
and turned the body upon its own axis, slowly advancing towards each
other, or retreating to the outer part of the circumference. . . . On public
holidays, particularly those of Christmas . . . each of the African tribes
upon the different estates formed itself into a distinct party. . . . They
paraded or gambolled in their respective neighborhoods, dancing to the
rude music. . . .

In the towns, such processions were preceded by a tall athletic
man . . . John Connu. . . . Several companions were associated with
him as musicians, beating banjas and tomtoms, blowing cow-horns,
shaking a hard round black seed, called Indian shot, in a calabash,
and scraping the bones of animals together. . . .[35]

This quotation is illuminating for the detailed description of African
dance steps written at a time when they were supposed to have been
completely superseded by European dances, except in the most
remote country regions.

These recognizably African dances and music persisted in the
West Indies long after they had been either superseded or suppressed in the United States. Similar dancing and music continued
in Cuba, where they were witnessed in 1851 and then compared to
music of blacks in the Charleston vicinity by an admittedly conventional witness, Fredrika Bremer. She wrote from Charleston on May
1, 1851:

Since I have seen in Cuba the negroes in their savage, original state—
seen their dances, heard their songs, and am able to compare them with
what they are at the best in the United States, there remains no longer a
doubt in my mind as to the beneficial influence of Anglo-American
culture on the negro. . . . The sour crab is not more unlike our noble,
bright, Astrachan apple, than is the song of the wild African to the song
of the Christian negro in the United States, whether it be hymns that he
sings or gay negro [minstrel] songs that he has himself composed. . . .
There is a vast, vast difference between the screeching improvisation of
the negroes in Cuba, and the inspired and inspiring preaching of the
Savior . . . which I have heard extemporized in South Carolina, Georgia,
Maryland, and Louisiana. And low and sensual is that lawless life, and

35. Phillippo, *Jamaica*, pp. 241–43.

intoxication of the senses in those wild negro-dances, and those noisy festivities to the beat of the drum, compared with that life, and that spiritual intoxication in song and prayer, and religious joy, which is seen and heard at the religious festivals of the negro people here.[36]

Yet African music and dancing were apparently not all bad. Bremer's ambivalence toward them was made evident in a curious paragraph which followed by a few pages the diatribe just quoted. She described an idyllic vision of young white women teaching black children the songs and dances "as they are practiced in their native land; those songs, for instance, with the chorus, which seems to be the heart of all songs among the natives of Africa. . . ."[37] Why couldn't the children learn the songs from their mothers and fathers, as they had done since blacks arrived in the New World? Bremer probably envisioned the young white women carefully screening out those words and gestures that offended white evangelical mores. But what is significant is that even such a conventional person recognized something worth preserving in the songs and dances of "their native land"—a glimmer of cosmopolitan tolerance amid her self-assured conviction that her taste and ideas were unassailable.

ACCULTURATION IN NEW ORLEANS

In many ways New Orleans was atypical of mainland cities. It had never belonged to the English and, until after the Louisiana Purchase in 1803, it had been ruled by either the Spanish or the French. Culturally and economically it seemed closer to the Caribbean territories of France or Spain than to the mainland colonies or the United States, and its absorption after the Purchase was a gradual process. Throughout the eighteenth century and the first quarter of the nineteenth, in Louisiana and the sugar islands there were many similarities in the conditions of slaves' lives. The toleration of Sunday dances until well into the nineteenth century was symptomatic of a laissez faire attitude toward black recreational activities which was more typical of French Catholicism than of the English evangelical sects.

Louisiana was settled after 1700, later than most of the English seaboard colonies or the French Caribbean island colonies. Many techniques of plantation management that had been developed on the islands were transported to Louisiana; the process was intensified around 1800 by the flood of refugees from Saint-Domingue

36. Bremer, *Homes of the New World*, II, 442–44.
37. *Ibid.*, p. 450.

after the slave uprising there. These factors may help to explain the persistence of Sunday dancing in Place Congo in New Orleans almost one hundred years after the practice had ended in South Carolina and Virginia, as well as the African dancing which continued in Louisiana well into the nineteenth century.

An excellent start toward documenting the development of black folk music in Louisiana has been made by Henry Kmen.[38] His examination of local newspapers and archival documents has surpassed any comparable study in exhuming contemporary local records. The discussion here will attempt to relate his findings and other local documents to the reports of foreign travelers, and to comparable material from the French West Indies, in order to demonstrate the interrelationships between the two geographic areas.

The French sociologist Roger Bastide has studied African influences throughout the Americas, finding much stronger influences in Central America and the Caribbean than in the United States. But he does distinguish two main centers within the continental United States: the Sea Islands–coastal region of Virginia, and the area centered around New Orleans. He finds a double-level culture in Louisiana, "Dahomean in religion (*Vaudou* cult) and Bantu as regards its folklore (the *calenda* dance)."[39] We have already seen that the method of "seasoning" the newly arrived Africans in Louisiana was very similar to that practiced in the West Indies, that dancing in large rings was observed on the levee in New Orleans in 1799, and that bamboulas and contre-danses were danced side by side in 1808. A more detailed history of black folk music in New Orleans and Louisiana to 1819 will now be presented.

The earliest reports from Louisiana said almost nothing about the blacks. Sister Marie Madeleine Hachard de Saint Stanislas, writing in 1727, complained of the manners of the residents, but she did not so much as mention the slaves.[40] Jean Bochart, Chevalier de Champigny, in 1744 wrote only that "our Negroes were procured from the Islands, or from *Guinea*"[41]—an indication that trading relations with the islands were commonplace. Le Page du Pratz

38. Kmen, *Music in New Orleans*, and his "Roots of Jazz."
39. Bastide, *African Civilizations*, pp. 11–12. Bastide theorizes that the Gullah Islands and Virginia seem "to have been occupied by a cultural group which originated in the former Gold Coast, now Ghana. The types of drum found in Virginia during the mid-eighteenth century (and now on display in the British Museum), together with the practice of naming children after their birthday, both provide clear cultural links with the Fanti-Ashanti civilisation."
40. Hachard, *Relation*, letter from New Orleans dated Oct. 27, 1727.
41. [Champigny,] *Present State*, p. 26.

described his planting experiences in Louisiana in 1758, including passing references to "Calinda, or the dance" and worksongs; he was almost the only eighteenth-century Frenchman in Louisiana to provide even these meagre details.[42]

While Louisiana was governed by the Spanish, the tradition of Sunday dances for the slaves was codified into law. In 1792 Baron de Carondelet, the Spanish governor, proclaimed that Sundays were reserved for the slaves' recreation; in 1795 another ordinance restricted amusements to Sunday, with planters being forbidden to permit "strange negroes to visit their plantations after dark. . . ."[43] An English visitor, Francis Baily, arrived in New Orleans on June 6, 1797, and was struck by the manner of observing the Sabbath in a Roman Catholic country.

> Scarcely had the priest pronounced his benediction, ere the violin or the fife struck up at the door, and the lower classes of people indulged themselves in all the gaiety and mirth of juvenile diversions. Singing, dancing, and all kinds of sports were seen in every street. . . . The lower sort of people . . . look forward with the highest pleasure for Sunday— particularly amongst the negroes, who in *this* country are suffered to refrain from work on that day. Here, arrayed in their best apparel . . . they would meet together on the green, and spend the day in mirth and festivity. . . .[44]

There is no reason to believe that the festivities did not include singing and dancing, just because Baily did not specify them. Many other observers did—for example, the anonymous visitor of 1799, already quoted, saw "vast numbers of negro slaves . . . druming, fifing, and dancing, in large rings."

By 1802 Negro fiddlers were already a feature of the public balls that made the "Carnaval" a gala season.[45] The non-observance of the Sabbath also impressed John F. Watson, who arrived in New Orleans on May 26, 1804. He saw the same kind of dancing on the levee that had been reported in 1799:

> Sabbaths are not observed—all stores are open in the forenoon, and at night there are balls and sometimes plays, &c. . . .
> I often see negroes put up for sale, and I see vessels loaded with them for sale also. In the latter they are made to dance and seem lively and healthy to enhance their value. They assemble in great masses on the

42. Le Page du Pratz, *History of Louisiana*, p. 387.
43. Cf. Martin, *History of Louisiana*, II, 112; Stoddard, *Sketches*, p. 335. Kmen, *Music in New Orleans*, p. 226, states: "As early as 1786 the law forbade slaves to dance in the public squares on Sundays and holy days until the close of evening service." This law could not have been strictly enforced.
44. Baily, *Journal*, p. 314.
45. [Berquin-Duvallon,] *Travels*, p. 27.

levee on Sundays, and make themselves glad with song, dance and merriment.[46]

After the Louisiana Purchase, new "Ordinances of Police" refined and extended the previous legal restrictions on such matters as slave funerals, dancing, and singing in the streets:

Art. 9.—As to the custom observed by several Africans and people of colour of assembling during the night, on occasion of the death of some of their acquaintance, those meetings shall be tolerated only when confined to the relations of the deceased, and when everything is conducted at them with decency. But if the tranquility of the neighborhood be disturbed with cries, singing or dancing, &c. on such occasions, the Commissary of Police and the patrols, are required to take up all persons found at such meetings after the hour of retreat. . . .

Art. 10.—It shall not be lawful for any slaves in town and suburbs to meet together for the purpose of dancing and amusing themselves, (except on Sundays, at such places only as may be therefore appointed by the Mayor, and no where else), under the penalty of ten lashes against every slave delinquent.[47]

Another ordinance governing slaves "employed as hirelings by the day" forbade them "to quarrel among themselves . . . to shout or sing a loud obscene song, or, in short, to do any thing . . . that may disturb public tranquility. . . ."[48]

Reports of the manner of observing the Sabbath continued to be a stock feature of travelers' accounts of New Orleans. The traditions of a Roman Catholic country, combined with the amusements of the slaves, seemed to have a never-ending fascination for those who were accustomed to the sober and sedate English or New England Sabbath. On May 1, 1808, Christian Schultz, Jun., told what he had seen while strolling "in the rear" of New Orleans on Sunday afternoon:

Twenty different dancing groups of the wretched Africans, collected together to perform their *worship* after the manner of their country. They have their own national music, consisting for the most part of a long kind of narrow drum of various sizes, from two to eight feet in length, three or four of which makes a band. The principal dancers or leaders are dressed in a variety of wild and savage fashions, always ornamented with a number of tails of the smaller wild beasts. . . . These amusements continue until sunset, when one or two of the city patrole show themselves with their cutlasses, and the crowds immediately disperse.[49]

46. John Fanning Watson, "Notitia," p. 232.
47. New Orleans, Ordinances, etc., *Police Code*, pp. 48–50. Approved Mar. 14, 1808.
48. *Ibid.*, p. 254.
49. Schultz, *Travels*, II, 197.

The precise locale of the dancing Schultz saw has not been determined. It is not known when the mayor decided on what became known as "Congo Square" as the approved location for these festivities. The reports that mentioned the levee obviously antedated that decision, and a number of later reports were vague about the location.

Another form of acculturation was recorded in 1811: the first appearance in print in North America of the Creole French patois known as gombo. Gombo was to be much used as local color in nineteenth-century accounts of Louisiana by George Cable and others, but it was also spoken throughout the French Caribbean and must have developed much earlier, perhaps in the seventeenth century. Its linguistic history has unfortunately not been much studied—a serious deficiency, since it is surely a prime example of acculturation in the French colonies. How little is known about it is illustrated by the significance attached to its appearance in a pamphlet printed in Philadelphia in 1811, forty-eight years before its first printing in Louisiana.[50] This pamphlet, *Idylles et Chansons, ou Essais de Poésie Créole, par un Habitant d'Hayti*, included versions of two songs, "Lizette to quité la plaine" and "Pauvre piti Mamselle Zizi," that were very popular in both Louisiana and the French West Indies. Their appearance in 1811 seems less impressive, however, when it is known that Jean Jacques Rousseau used "Lizette to quité la plaine" about 1740 to demonstrate a system of musical notation which he had invented.[51] Nothing is known about how he learned the song, but he was aware of its derivation, calling it "Chanson Negre." The one stanza of text given in the facsimile of his manuscript, while closer to classical French, was substantially the same as that given in the 1811 version, where it was called "Chanson Creole" and included five stanzas of eight lines each. The first quatrain of stanza 3 is notable for the words "Bamboula" and "Calinda":

> Dipi mo pêrdi Lizette,
> Mo pa batte Bamboula,
> Bouche a moi tourné muette,
> Mo pa dansé Calinda.[52]

The enormous time lag between Rousseau's use of the song and its printed appearance in America illustrates the difficulties inherent in

50. Tinker, "Gombo," pp. 51–53.
51. "Example of Jean-Jacques Rousseau's system of musical notation," reproduced in De Beer, *Rousseau*, p. 22.
52. Tinker, "Gombo," p. 71.

attempting to document aspects of folk culture. Songs such as these may well have been sung at Place Congo on Sunday afternoons, gradually replacing the African songs that began the cultural cycle.

New ordinances relating to the slaves were approved by the mayor in October, 1817. They substantially re-enacted those of 1808:

> Art. 6. The assemblies of slaves for the purposes of dancing or other merriment, shall take place only on Sundays, and solely in such open or public places as shall be appointed by the mayor; and no such assembly shall continue later than sunset. . . .
>
> Art. 9. If any slave shall be guilty of whooping or hallooing any where in the city and suburbs, or of making any clamorous noise, or of singing aloud any indecent song, he or she shall receive for each . . . such offence . . . 20 lashes. . . .[53]

J. G. Flügel, a German traveler, wrote from New Orleans on February 16, 1817: "Towards evening I went with Pierre to see the negroes dance. Their dances are certainly curious, particularly to a European. I shall give a more detailed account of them sometime in the future." On April 11 he wrote again: "Gildemeister of Bremen . . . told me that three of the negroes in the group closest to us were formerly kings or chiefs in Congo. I perceive in them a more genteel address. They are richly ornamented and dance extremely well."[54]

Another traveler, Johann Buechler from St. Gall, Switzerland, arrived in New Orleans on May 15, 1817, remaining until June 13. His colorful account of the Sunday dancing of the Negroes added many details:

> Now I want to tell my readers a little about the comical shows the Negroes present behind the city each Sunday if the weather is good at 4 o'clock in the evening at large open places at various different locations, where they have a good time and anyone can look on without being hindered. The males clothe themselves in oriental and Indian dress, with a Turkish turban of various colors, red, blue, yellow, green and brown, with a sash of the same sort around the body to cover themselves; except for that they go naked. The women clothe themselves, each according to her means, in the newest fashions in silk, gauze, muslin, percale dresses. . . . They dance in the most wonderful way, form a circle and make on all sides the most wonderful bending gestures with their bodies and knees . . . this routine . . . lasts from 4 to 6:30, for their own amusement.

The author apparently used the terms "oriental and Indian" to describe any mode of dress that was not European. There must have

53. Fearon, *Sketches of America*, pp. 276–78. An identical text appeared in Yates, *Colonial Slavery*, pp. 16–17. The official text has not been seen.

54. [Flügel,] "Pages from a Journal," pp. 427, 432. The detailed account has not been located.

been considerable variation in dress, the men being more exotic, the women more fashionable.

Later, from Cuba, the author compared that island's dancing with what he had seen in New Orleans: "Every Sunday they [the slaves] have free time after supper to dance, just as they did in New Orleans, but here [in the countryside] without clothing, and the same familiar comical music.... In the city of Havannah they do the same, but inside a garden and dressed, at least those one can see."[55] Buechler specifically stated that the dancing took place "at various different locations," while Latrobe, writing a year later, implied that it was restricted to one place, perhaps what became known as Place Congo.

Another traveler who arrived in mid-June, 1818, was shocked by the dissipation in New Orleans: "Here ... the Sabbath is devoted to recreation. On this day the negroes assemble, and amuse themselves and spectators by dancing."[56] Nor was this kind of amusement confined to New Orleans. In that year in St. Louis

> the colored people, both free and bond ... all alike were without religious instruction. The Sabbath to them was a relief from toil. There was an open space of a square or more, between Main and Second streets. ... Here the negroes were accustomed to assemble in the pleasant afternoons of the Sabbath, dance, drink, and fight, quite to the annoyance of all seriously disposed persons. On the 11th of April, 1818 ... the late William Clark, Governor of the Territory ... alluding to the scenes of dancing, riot, drunkenness, and fighting on the Sabbath ... stated that the preceding summer, he had to call out a military company three times to suppress riots amongst this class.[57]

St. Louis had been settled by the French, but it adopted American ways more quickly than New Orleans.

In 1819 a letter from New Orleans reported that "on sabbath evening the African slaves meet on the green, by the swamp, and rock the city with their Congo dances."[58] "The green" quite likely was Place Congo, now called Beauregard Square. The longest and most detailed account found, however, was from the diary of Benjamin Latrobe, the architect and engineer who had supervised the rebuilding of the Capitol after the war of 1812. In the entry dated

55. [Buechler,] *Land- und Seereisen*, pp. 129–30, 160–61 (translation by Dena and William Epstein). Another German traveler, J. Valentin Hecke, was inspired to poetry by the New Orleans Sabbath, with its fiddles, drums, and dancing in rings. Cf. his *Reise durch die Vereinigten Staaten*, II, 155.
56. Evans, *Pedestrian Tour*, in Thwaites, *Early Western Travels*, VIII, 336.
57. Peck, *Forty Years of Pioneer Life*, p. 90. Section dated Feb. 28, 1856.
58. [Knight,] *Letters*, p. 127.

"Feb'y 21st, 1819," he discussed the "Mode of keeping Sunday in New Orleans and reasonings thereon."

A bill was moved, I think, in the last session of the Legislature to put down the practice of dancing & shop keeping prevailing here on Sunday. . . . My accidentally stumbling upon the assembly of Negroes which I am told every Sunday afternoon meets on the Common in the rear of the city. . . . Approaching the common I heard a most extraordinary noise, which I supposed to proceed from some horse mill, the horses trampling on a wooden floor. I found, however, on emerging from the houses onto the Common, that it proceeded from a crowd of 5 or 600 persons assembled in an open space or public square. I . . . crowded near enough to see the performance. All those who were engaged in the business seemed to be *blacks*. I did not observe a dozen yellow faces. They were formed into circular groupse in the midst of four of which, which I examined (but there were more of them), was a ring, the largest not 10 feet in diameter. In the first were two women dancing. They held each a coarse handkerchief extended by the corners in their hands, & *set* to each other in a miserably dull & slow figure, hardly moving their feet or bodies. The music consisted of two drums and a stringed instrument. An old man sat astride of a cylindrical drum about a foot in diameter, & beat it with incredible quickness with the edge of his hand & fingers. The other drum was an open staved thing held between the knees & beaten in the same manner. They made an incredible noise. The most curious instrument, however, was a stringed instrument which no doubt was imported from Africa. On the top of the finger board was the rude figure of a man in a sitting posture, & two pegs behind him to which the strings were fastened. The body was a calabash. It was played upon by a very little old man, apparently 80 or 90 years old.

The women squalled out a burthen to the playing at intervals, consisting of two notes, as the negroes, working in our cities, respond to the song of their leader. [i.e., call-and-response] Most of the circles contained the same sort of dancers. One was larger, in which a ring of a dozen women walked, by way of dancing, round the music in the center. But the instruments were of a different construction. One, which from the color of the wood seemed new, consisted of a block cut into something of the form of a cricket bat with a long & deep mortice down the center. This thing made a considerable noise, being beaten lustily on the side by a short stick. In the same orchestra was a square drum, looking like a stool, which made an abominably loud noise; also a calabash with a round hole in it, the hole studded with brass nails, which was beaten by a woman with two short sticks.

A man sung an uncouth song to the dancing which I suppose was in some African language, for it was not French, & the women screamed a detestable burthen on one single note. The allowed amusements of Sunday have, it seems, perpetuated here those of Africa among its inhabitants. I have never seen anything more brutally savage, and at the same time dull & stupid, than this whole exhibition. Continuing my walk about a mile along the canal, & returning after Sunset near the

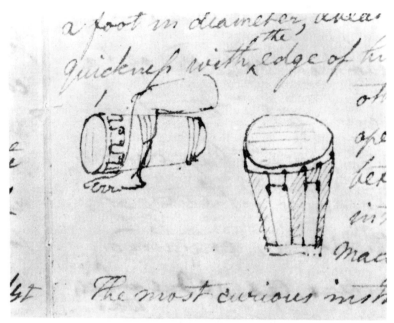

Sketches of African drum, in manuscript journal of Benjamin Henry Latrobe. Entry for Feb'y 21st, 1819, from New Orleans, describing "the assembly of Negroes . . . every Sunday . . . on the Common." Reproduced by permission of the Papers of Benjamin Henry Latrobe, Maryland Historical Society.

same spot, the noise was still heard. There was not the least disorder among the crowd, nor do I learn on enquiry, that these weekly meetings of the negroes have ever produced any mischief.[59]

Latrobe accompanied his diary entry with sketches, among the very few contemporary drawings of African instruments that have survived from the mainland. His description agreed in many particulars with similar accounts from the West Indies—the dancing, the kinds of instruments, the call-and-response singing.

The records of acculturation in New Orleans extended well into the nineteenth century, with African instruments and dancing being performed in public long after they were suppressed in other regions. Latrobe's account, while the highlight of the historical record, was succeeded by other reports that described less graphically the continuation of the same activities he had seen. In order to avoid chronological confusion, the balance of this discussion will be deferred.

59. Latrobe, *Impressions*, pp. 49–51.

Description and sketches of African instruments, from Latrobe journal, Feb. 21, 1819.

5

Conversion to Christianity

One can hardly overstate the importance of conversion to Christianity in the acculturation of blacks in the New World. It was an essential precondition for the emergence of the Negro spiritual, a body of song that occupied a central position in nineteenth-century black American folk music. African religious beliefs and musical practices undoubtedly continued to make their contribution, combined and intermixed with Christian doctrine to form a distinctive and universally appealing body of song.

The earliest reports of Africans in the New World describe them as pagans and show little attempt to understand their religion. Differences in culture and language created a chasm between blacks and whites; for the planters, a laissez faire policy was easiest to implement. In the English colonies Sunday dances were initially permitted after church services—but that practice may have originated to prevent interruption of the services, rather than from any thought of encouraging the Africans to attend church themselves. Ligon and his contemporaries apparently felt no concern for the souls of the slaves. It was left to clergymen to raise the question of converting the Africans to Christianity, and they found it a difficult and thankless task for many years. The saintly pious slave personified by Uncle Tom did not evolve until the second quarter of the nineteenth century.

Morgan Godwyn among the English and Du Tertre and Labat among the French exhorted the colonists to provide for the salvation of their bondsmen, but with very limited success. Language difficulties were a major obstacle; the slaves' preference for their own gods was another. For many years after the Africans had learned some English or French (in the West Indies, at least) they had little cause to value Christianity, and their masters took no interest in their religious welfare. Moreover, since admission into the Anglican church required an understanding and acceptance of its basic tenets, knowledge of both the English language and the catechism was a precondition. The Catholic church did not require as much preparation for admission, and its ceremonies offered more possibilities for the blending of religious practices. However, in both French and English colonies the replacement of African religious patterns by Christian practices progressed very slowly.

In mainland North America during the seventeenth century, individual Africans were probably converted to Christianity by the families with whom they lived. Such individual conversions were a normal expression of traditional Christian practice, rather than part of an organized missionary or evangelical movement—a natural consequence of living in family units. Morgan Godwyn's plea of 1680 for the instruction and conversion of the Negroes and Indians was not implemented in the southern colonies until after the beginning of the eighteenth century.

The first organized attempt to convert the Africans to Christianity in the mainland colonies was the incidental result of an attempt to strengthen the Anglican church. In 1701 the Church of England set up the Society for the Propagation of the Gospel in Foreign Parts (S.P.G.), a central body to provide missionaries for the colonies in the New World. These missionaries were primarily concerned with ministering to the emigrant members of the Church of England, but from the outset they assumed the obligation of teaching the blacks as well, insofar as circumstances made that possible.

The first missionary to the Province of Carolina, the Reverend Samuel Thomas, was appointed by the S.P.G. on July 3, 1702. He wrote in his first letter from Carolina, "I have here a multitude of ignorant persons to instruct . . . and many Negroes, Indians to begin withall." He requested Bibles and Books of Common Prayer "to give to the poor Negroes," reporting later, "By my encouragement about 20 Negroes have learned to read, and I am acquainting them as I have opportunity with the Principles of the Christian Religion."[1] He

1. Samuel Thomas, "Letters," pp. 225, 280.

drafted a document for the S.P.G. to justify his efforts; in it he
described conditions at the beginning of the eighteenth century:

> There are in the Province of South Carolina somewhat more than one
> thousand slaves, eight hundred of which can speak English tollerably
> well, and are capable of Christian Instruction, many of 'em are desirous
> of Christian knowledge, great numbers of these can come to the places of
> our Publick Worship. . . . It is indeed much to be lamented that the
> generality of our Planters are no great friends to the design of giving their
> slaves Christian instructions. . . .[2]

Thomas's successor, Dr. Francis Le Jau, was the man who recorded the existence of Sunday dances by the slaves in his letters to
the secretary of the S.P.G.[3] His report of the slaves' eagerness to be
instructed was corroborated by the Reverend E. Taylor of St. Andrew's, South Carolina, who wrote to the secretary in 1713: "The
desire of the slaves for instruction was so general that but for the
opposition of the owners there seems no reason why the whole of
them should not have been brought to Christ."[4] A survey of religious
conditions among the Negroes in the mainland colonies was taken in
1724, when the representative of the Bishop of London included this
question among the queries sent to the clergy: "Are there any
Infidels, bond or free, within your Parish; and what means are used
for their conversion?" Some of the answers from Virginia provide
glimpses of conditions in one of the oldest mainland colonies.

> Our Negroe Slaves imported daily, are altogether ignorant of God and
> Religion, and in truth have so little Docility in them that they scarce
> ever become capable of Instruction; but . . . I have examined and im-
> proved Several Negroes, Natives of Virginia. . . . [from James City Parish]
> I have several times exhorted their Masters to send such of them as
> could speak English to Church to be catechised but they would not.
> Some masters instruct their Slaves at home . . . but not many such.
> [Bristol Parish] The Negroes . . . cannot . . . be said to be of any Religion
> for as there is no law of the Colony obliging their Masters or Owners to
> instruct them in the principles of Christianity . . . the poor creatures
> generally live and die without it. [Wilmington Parish] A great many
> Black bond men and women infidels that understand not our Lan-
> guage nor me their's. [Christ Church Parish][5]

These typical comments demonstrated not only the indifference of
the planters, but also a total lack of interest and understanding

2. "Documents Concerning . . . Thomas," pp. 39–47.
3. Cf. ch. 2.
4. Society for the Propagation of the Gospel in Foreign Parts, *Classified Digest*,
p. 16.
5. Perry, ed., *Historical Collections*, I, 265, 267, 278, 283. See also Jernegan,
"Slavery and Conversion."

toward the culture and beliefs of the Africans. Eighteenth-century clergymen could not be expected to show tolerance toward non-Christian religious beliefs. To them, paganism was an undifferentiated mass of ignorance, not another form of religion. But these men were the most likely source of sympathy and help available to the Africans in the New World, and their values were adopted by many slaves as the best avenue to accommodation.

In his study "Slavery and Conversion in the Colonies," Marcus Jernegan came to the conclusion that "the number of slaves who were even nominal Christians bore a very small proportion to the total number.... It is evident that the comparatively few clergymen and missionaries who took an interest in the conversion of slaves, could make little impression on the whole slave population," simply because of the distances between plantations and the other duties of their office.[6] David Humphreys wrote in 1730 that the S.P.G. felt responsible for converting the Negroes and had instructed, baptized, and admitted to Communion "some hundreds ... But alas! what is the instruction of a few hundreds, in several years, with respect to the many thousands uninstructed, unconverted, living, dying, utter Pagans.... The greatest obstruction is, the masters themselves do not consider enough, the obligation which lies upon them, to have their slaves instructed. Some have been so weak as to argue, the Negroes had no souls; others, that they grew worse by being taught, and made Christians."[7] George Whitefield, the Methodist evangelist, cited the persistence of Sunday dances in 1739 as evidence that the masters were deliberately refusing to have their slaves instructed: "I have great reason to believe, that most of you, on Purpose, keep your Negroes ignorant of Christianity."[8]

This indifference to the conversion of the slaves continued into the mid-eighteenth century. Peter Kalm, a Swedish traveler, wrote on December 6, 1748: "The masters of these Negroes in most of the *English* colonies take little care of their spiritual welfare, and let them live on in their pagan darkness. There are even some, who would be very ill pleased at, and would by all means hinder their Negroes from being instructed in the doctrines of Christianity...."[9] Thus, although there were undoubtedly individual conversions before 1750, it seems unlikely that any widespread entry of Negro slaves into the Church took place. This would of course have made

6. Jernegan, "Slavery and Conversion," p. 525.
7. David Humphreys, *Historical Account*, pp. 90–91.
8. Whitefield, *Three Letters*, Letter III, p. 15.
9. Kalm, *Travels*, pp. 201–2.

even more unlikely the beginnings of any Christian Afro-American religious folksong.

With the Great Awakening the dissenting sects outside the Anglican church (Presbyterians, Baptists, and Methodists) began to extend their influence in the South. Evangelical clergymen like Samuel Davies, a Presbyterian of Hanover, Virginia, became active in converting the Negroes. *"Ethiopia has also stretched forth her Hands unto God.* There is a great number of Negroes in these parts; and sometimes I see a 100 & more among my Hearers. I have baptized about 40 Adults of them within these three years. . . ."[10] "The Books I principally want for them [the Negroes] are, *Watts's Psalms and Hymns,* and *Bibles.* . . . I cannot but observe, that the *Negroes,* above all the Human Species that I ever knew, have an Ear for Musick, and a kind of extatic Delight in *Psalmody*; and there are no books they learn so soon, or take so much Pleasure in. . . ."[11]

When the books were sent, Davies acknowledged them, saying, "The books were all *very acceptable*; but none more so than the *Psalms* and Hymns, which enabled them to gratify their peculiar taste for *Psalmody.* Sundry of them have lodged all night in my kitchen; and, sometimes, when I have awakened about two or three a-clock in the morning, a torrent of sacred harmony poured into my chamber. . . . In this seraphic exercise, some of them spend almost the whole night."[12] In a letter to "J. F." dated August 26, 1758, Davies described the results of his instruction: "I can hardly express the pleasure it affords me to turn to that part of the gallery where they [the Negroes] sit, and see so many of them with their Psalm or Hymn Books, assisting their fellows, who are beginners, to find the place; and then all breaking out in a torrent of sacred harmony, enough to bear away the whole congregation to heaven."[13]

Davies's experience was paralleled by that of another letter-writer, "the Rev. Mr. Hutson at *South Carolina,*" to the same Mr. J. F. on July 11, 1758: "I must confess that the vital part of Religion among us at this time, seems to be chiefly among them [the Negroes]. . . . I understand that several of them meet once a week and spend some time in singing, praying, and reading the Bible. . . ."[14] The Reverend Mr. Todd, also of Hanover, told of his success on November 18: "The sacred hours of the Sabbath, that used to be spent in frolicking, dancing, and other profane courses, are now em-

10. Davies, *State of Religion,* p. 23.
11. Davies' letter of June 28, 1751, to "Mr. Bellamy of Bethlem in New-England" in Fawcett, *Compassionate Address,* appendix, p. 37.
12. Davies to J. F., Mar. 2, 1756, quoted in Pilcher, *Davies,* p. 112.
13. Davies, *Letters,* p. 14.
14. *Ibid.,* p. 15.

ployed in attending upon public ordinances, in learning to read at home, or in praying together, and singing the praises of God and the Lamb."[15] Again and again, praying and singing psalms were described as the supplanters of Sunday dances which, in the eighteenth century, may very well have been African in character.

A Reverend Mr. Wright of Cumberland County, Virginia, described similar experiences in January, 1761: "My Landlord tells me ... they heard the *Slaves* at worship in their lodge, singing Psalms and Hymns in the evening, and again in the morning, long before break of day. They are excellent singers, and long to get some of Dr. *Watts's Psalms* and *Hymns.* . . ."[16] Although the attempts at conversion were not yet general, they had increasing impact—a fact reflected obliquely in an advertisement for a runaway slave published in 1767: "Hannah, about 35 years of age. . . . She pretends much to the religion the Negroes of late have practised. . . ."[17] Yet Davies himself admitted that he and his colleagues did not reach all the slaves: "The Negroes in Virginia who have embraced the Gospel, or who are under any promising impressions, are generally in the bounds of our congregations. In other parts of *Virginia* where there are no Dissenters, there are indeed many thousands of Negroes who are neglected or instructed just according to the character of the established Clergy in their several parishes."[18]

The activities of the Presbyterians, led by Davies, inspired the Anglican clergy to increase their activity among the Negroes. William Knox wrote two tracts entitled "Of the Negroe Slaves in the Colonies," complaining that "the owners of slaves will not suffer them to assemble together in large bodies, nor to have much intercourse with one another; indeed few owners of Negroes will suffer them to go to the catechist at all, because his house being a sort of general rendezvous for them. . . . the planters in the country would never consent to let their several gangs meet together." He added: "The Negroes in general have an ear for musick, and might without much trouble be taught to sing hymns, which would be the pleasantest way of instructing them, and bringing them speedily to offer praise to God."[19] Thus a common practice of nineteenth-century camp-meeting evangelists and plantation missionaries was anticipated in 1768.

The Methodists also were active among the slaves, especially

15. *Ibid.*, p. 17.
16. *Ibid.*, p. 29.
17. Advertisement signed Stephen Dence, *Virginia Gazette*, Mar. 26, 1767, p. [3], col. 1.
18. Davies, *Letters*, p. 9.
19. Knox, *Three Tracts*, pp. 36, 39. A new edition was issued in 1789.

Bishop Francis Asbury, whose *Journal* frequently mentioned the Negroes who attended his services and Harry Hosier, his black assistant exhorter. In New York on November 17, 1771, Asbury wrote, "To see the poor Negroes so affected is pleasing, to see their sable countenances in our solemn assemblies, and to hear them sing with cheerful melody their dear Redeemer's praise, affected me much. . . ."[20] Other entries tell of religious excitement presaging the frenzied emotion of the camp meeting:

> The house was greatly crowded, and four or five hundred stood at the doors and windows, and listened with unabated attention. . . . I was obliged to stop again and again, and beg of the people to compose themselves. But they could not; some on their knees, and some on their faces, were crying mightily to God all the time I was preaching. Hundreds of Negroes were among them, with the tears streaming down their faces.[21]

In South Carolina on February 8, 1793, "Our congregation consists of five hundred souls and upwards; three hundred being black."[22]

Asbury was not unique. Freeborn Garrettson, another Methodist itinerant, reported thus: "I preached to about five hundred whites, and almost as many blacks who stood without; . . . tears trickled down the faces of many, both white and black. . . ."[23]

The second half of the eighteenth century saw the continued authority of the established church, as well as the growing influence of the dissenting sects. While emotional religious meetings were taking place, other groups continued their accustomed practices, including dances and other amusements on Sunday. The evangelists of the eighteenth century apparently did not object to secular music and dancing, as long as they did not interfere with the proper observance of the Sabbath; however, there was wide disagreement as to what a proper observance required.

---

20. Asbury, *Journals and Letters*, I, 9–10. See also I, 56–57, 89, 403.

21. *Ibid.*, I, 222, from White's chapel [Virginia?].

22. *Ibid.*, p. 747. See also:

Maryland . . . *Monday* [Dec.] 7 [1772] . . . We lodged at Robert Thompson's, when I spoke closely to the poor Negroes, who took some notice of what was said.

Tuesday, [Dec.] 8. . . . In the evening the Negroes were collected, and I spoke to them in exhortation (I, 56–57).

Virginia . . . *Monday* [May] 21 [1781] . . . Harry Hosier spoke to the Negroes, some of whom came a great distance to hear him. . . (I, 403).

23. Garrettson, *Experience and Travels*, entry from Roanoak [*sic*], N.C., May 20, 1777. "In September I went to North-Carolina, to travel Roan-oak circuit . . . I would often set apart times to preach to the blacks, and adapt my discourse to them alone . . ."–p. 76. See also [Jarratt,] *Brief Narrative*, pp. 30–34.

Philip Fithian, who left his studies for the Presbyterian ministry to tutor the children of Robert Carter of Nomini Hall, Westmoreland County, Virginia, was struck by the differences in Sunday observance between New Jersey and Virginia. His journal entry for July 10, 1774, compared them: "A Sunday in Virginia dont seem to wear the same Dress as our Sundays to the Northward—Generally here by five o-Clock on Saturday every Face (especially the Negroes) looks festive & cheerful—All the lower class of People, & the Servants, & the Slaves, consider it as a Day of Pleasure & amusement & spend it in such Diversions as they severally choose. . . ."[24] If Fithian had been indignant instead of tolerant, he might have described in detail the diversions chosen by the slaves, and our slender stock of information would have been enriched.

But despite the labors of Samuel Davies and Francis Asbury, many slaves were still unaffected by any missionary effort. In 1774 Elhanan Winchester wrote of his experiences: "I was minister for several years upon the river PeeDee, in South Carolina. Till I came thither no attempts had been made in that settlement to convert the slaves, as I could ever learn . . . for not one had ever been baptized there in the memory of man. . . ."[25] Alexander Hewatt described conditions in South Carolina and Georgia five years later:

[The Negroe slaves] are . . . kept in heathen ignorance and darkness, destitute of the means of instruction, and excluded in a manner from the pale of the Christian church. . . . Masters of slaves under the French and Spanish jurisdictions, are obliged by law to allow them time for instruction, and to bring them up in the knowledge and practice of the Catholic religion. Is it not a reproach to the subjects of Britain, who profess to be the freest and most civilized people upon earth, that no provision is made for this purpose, and that they suffer so many thousands of these creatures, residing in the British dominions, to live and die the slaves of ignorance and superstition? [He mentioned the efforts of the Society for the Propagation of the Gospel in Foreign Parts.] But it is well known, that the fruit of their labours has been very small and inconsiderable. . . . the negroes of that country, a few only excepted, are to this day as great strangers to Christianity, and as much under the influence of Pagan darkness, idolatry and superstition, as they were at their first arrival from Africa.[26]

Impediments to missionary activity continued to exist: the distances separating plantations from each other, language problems among the new arrivals, and the limited number of clergymen to serve the whites, let alone the Negroes. But the rising tide of evan-

24. Fithian, *Journal & Letters*, p. 137.
25. Winchester, *Reigning Abominations*, p. 25n.
26. [Hewatt,] *Rise and Progress*, II, 98–100.

gelism had increasing impact on the established church during the closing years of the eighteenth century, and concern for salvation grew steadily more general. Attention to the slaves' souls would carry with it a conscious or unconscious determination to curtail their native amusements, especially on Sundays. Conversion to Christianity would bring with it a greatly expanded acculturation involving language, dress, style of singing and disapproval of so-called heathen practices.

A number of publications exhorted the Anglican clergy in America to intensify their efforts to convert the slaves, attempting to answer the objections which had been offered ever since the Bishop of London's queries of 1724. Sixty years later the incumbent Bishop complained about the failure of efforts to convert the slaves in Barbados, even those on the trust estate belonging to the Society for the Propagation of the Gospel in Foreign Parts. He attributed the failure partly to

> the accession of fresh slaves . . . either hired from other estates, or imported from Africa. These are so many constant temptations in their way to revert to their former heathenish principles and savage manners, to which they have always a strong propensity; and when this propensity is continually inflamed by the solicitations of their unconverted brethren, or the arrival of new companions from the coast of Guinea, it frequently becomes very difficult to be resisted, and counteracts, in a great degree, all the influence and exhortations of their religious teachers.

After contrasting "the almost unrestrained licentiousness of their manners" and the "dissoluteness in which they are permitted to live" with the "pure and undefiled religion" of Christianity, Bishop Porteus offered from London some helpful suggestions to his brethren in the field, suggestions that with respect to music virtually outlined the syncretic process of acculturation:

> Many of the Negroes have a natural turn for music, and are frequently heard to sing in their rude and artless way at their work. This propensity might be improved to the purposes of devotion . . . by composing short hymns . . . set to plain, easy, solemn psalm tunes, as nearly resembling their own simple melody as possible. . . . These might be used not only in church, but when their task was finished in the field, and on other joyous occasions. This would make them see Christianity in a much more pleasing light than they generally do . . . and would be found probably a much more effectual way of fixing their attention . . . than any other that can be devised.

He also recommended that the catechist could increase his effectiveness by mingling even in their entertainments, their festivities, and amusements, and turning every little incident into an instrument of moral and religious improvement. This kind of familiar and friendly intercourse with their slaves, the French planters in general, but especially their ecclesiastics, cultivate in a much higher degree than the English, and the advantages . . . are exceedingly important.

He urged that time be allowed for recreation and argued against any ban on it, returning to his previous interesting suggestion:

Even instruction itself may in *some* degree be made an amusement by the means suggested above; that is by the help of a little sacred melody adapted to the peculiar taste and turn of the Africans; than which nothing would be more likely to secure their attendance at church, and to draw them off from their heathenish Sunday recreations abroad, by providing them with others full as agreeable to them, and much more harmless, at home.[27]

Less elaborate arguments were also advanced for the conversion of the slaves: "The First, and principal Difficulty, which you alledged against attempting to instruct Adult *Negroes* imported was their strong Attachment to the idolatrous Rites and Practices of their own Country." The answer to this objection was invariably: persevere.

But perhaps you will say, "the *Negroes* are utter Strangers to our Language, and we to theirs." But

Do not many of the Negroes, who are grown Persons when imported, even of themselves attain so much of our Language, as to enable them to understand, and be understood in Things which concern the ordinary Business of Life?[28]

These arguments demonstrate the existence at the time of the American Revolution of a diverse slave population; some could not speak English, and some were attached to the "idolatrous Rites and Practices of their own Country." Too many discussions of slavery and slave religion have focused exclusively on the period immediately before the Civil War, postulating a homogeneous slave population which may have existed more in fancy than in fact.

Toward the end of the eighteenth century the increased and sustained efforts of the clergy of all churches to convert the slave population resulted in a gradual increase in the number of black church members. In 1782 a Richmond newspaper published an advertisement for two slaves who had run away on May 1, 1781, "when the British troops were there"; the slaves were characterized

27. Porteus, "Essay," pp. 174–75, 182–87.

28. *Letter to an American Planter*, pp. 5–7. See also "Bishop of London's Letter," in Humphreys, *Historical Account*, pp. 21–31.

as "much given to singing hymns."[29] Sunday observance gradually became much stricter. The casual attitude toward Sundays observed by Philip Fithian in 1774 grew into the more rigid observance found by Johann David Schoepf in Charleston ten years later: "The feast of the Sunday is strictly observed at Charleston. No shop may keep open; no sort of game or music is permitted, and during the church service watchmen go about who lay hold upon any one idling in the streets, (any not on urgent business or visiting the sick), and compel him to turn aside into some church or pay 2 shillings 4 pence; no slave may be required to work on this day."[30]

The consequences of this swelling evangelical effort were described by a Methodist preacher on Grensville Circuit in Virginia. His journal contains repeated mentions of black religious singing.

> Tuesday [July] 23 [1789] . . . evening the dear black bretheren began to sing as they ware in their cottage. I went to join them, we went to prayer. . . .
> Saturday [August] 15 . . . Some time in the Night—I judge near the Middle watch—I awaked in raptures of Heaven by the sweet Echo of Singing in the Kitchen among the dear Black people (who my Soul loves.) I scarcely ever heard anything to equal it upon earth. I rose up and strove to join them—ah—I felt the miserably weight of oppression intolerable upon my heart—while the proud whites can live in luxury . . . the African upholds him by his Swet and labour . . .—and if they serve the Lord God it must be in the dead of night. . . .
> Friday [August] 21 . . . the Evening several blacks came to meet me, as they cannot come to preaching in the day they came out many of a night.
> Sunday [August] 30 . . . the dear black people was filled with the power & spirit of God and began with a great Shout to give Glory to God—this vexed the Devil. He entered into the cruel whitemen with violence (who) eagerly ran into the Church with sticks clubs and caines—abeating and abusing the poor Slaves the outcast of Men for praising of God—O America how she groans under the burden of Slavery. . . .[31]

(Few ministers in the South were so outspoken in their condemnation of slavery, even in their diaries. The Methodists opposed slavery initially, but their opposition did not long continue, and by 1830 southern public opinion had so solidified on the subject that opposition, even by the clergy, was all but impossible.[32])

As the eighteenth century drew to a close, resistance to converting the slaves was disappearing, although organized missionary ac-

29. *Virginia Gazette, or, American Advertiser*, June 22, 1782, quoted in Stoutamire, *Music of the Old South*, p. 44.
30. Schoepf, *Travels*, II, 222.
31. Meacham, "Journal, Pt.1," pp. 79, 88, 90, 94.
32. See Eaton, *Freedom of Thought*.

tivity did not begin until somewhat later. Reports of Christian slaves became more frequent, along with comments on their love of music and on the feasibility of teaching them to sing hymns. What had been confined to a few Presbyterian ministers in 1750 was now quite general. John Leland wrote in his *Virginia Chronicle* of 1790:

> The poor slaves, under all their hardships, discover as great inclination for religion as the free-born do, when they engage in the service of God, they spare no pains. It is nothing strange for them to walk 20 miles on Sunday morning to meeting, and back again at night. They are remarkable for learning a tune soon, and have very melodious voices. . . . they're remarkably fond of meeting together, to sing pray and exhort and sometimes preach, and seem to be unwearied in the procession. . . .[33]

The acceptance by some blacks of the conventional evangelical attitude toward dancing and other amusements was demonstrated in a speech delivered by a black man, Abraham Johnstone, before he was hanged for his crimes in 1797. It could have been (and perhaps was) written by a white missionary: "Above all my dear friends avoid frolicking, and all amusements that lead to expense and idleness. . . ."[34] Dancing, whether African or European, was lumped together with idleness, extravagance, and sin—all deplored by the truly religious.

The conversion to Christianity, an essential prerequisite for the development of the Afro-American spiritual, was not completed by 1800. After the turn of the century some indifference and outright opposition to religious instruction for the slaves continued, but it was a declining position. The majority of southern whites were themselves to be converted in the evangelical revival that began with the century, and they were soon convinced that religion for the slaves was not only morally correct, but financially profitable as well.

33. Leland, *Virginia Chronicle*, p. 11.
34. Johnstone, *Address*, p. 28.

6

. . . .

Acculturated Black Musicians
in the Thirteen Colonies

Before the end of the seventeenth century, Africans in the New World were playing European instruments well and performing for the dancing of whites. Nothing has been found to indicate that Africans played European instruments in Africa, although it was not impossible for them to have done so. It seems more likely, however, that they acquired that skill in America, as those Africans who went to Europe learned it there.[1] Du Tertre did not mention blacks playing the violin, but by 1694 Labat thought some of them could play well, and in Virginia at about the same time a slave belonging to Captain Richard Bailey was in demand as a fiddler throughout the neighborhood. This slave, whose name was not recorded, became the center of an already mentioned legal controversy when he played for a dance at the home of the Reverend Thomas Teakle in his absence. No one knows how many other slave fiddlers were playing in the colonies at this time, but by the mid-eighteenth century they were a normal feature of the social scene.

During the eighteenth century, neither gentleman amateurs nor professional musicians played for dancing or other casual entertainments. That job belonged to servants, and many white indentured servants and black slaves could play quite well.[2] Advertisements for runaways often specified, among other means

1. Walvin, *Black and White*, pp. 70–71.
2. Cripe, *Jefferson and Music*, p. 7.

of identification, the ability to play well on certain instruments, particularly the fiddle.[3] The earliest such advertisement found so far dated from 1734 and indicated a degree of acculturation which was thought worthy of notice: "Runaway the 26th of June, last, from Samuel Leonard of Perth Amboy, in New Jersey . . . Wan [Juan?] He is half Indian and half negro; He had on when he went away a blue coat. He plays the fiddle, and speaks good English and his country Indian."[4] Advertisements which included fiddle-playing as a recognizable characteristic appeared regularly in the *Virginia Gazette* from the 1730's on. One slave named Will, a "Carpenter, Sawyer, Shoemaker, and Cooper," carried with him "a lopping Ax, and a Fiddle."[5] Tom, who was "country-born," i.e., born in Virginia, "plays very well on the Violin."[6] David Gratenread, who "plays the fiddle extremely well," owned his own instrument, for "I believe he carried his fiddle with him,"[7] whereas Billie "can play on the violin, which he carried away with him,"[8] the ownership not being stated. A Virginia-born Negro was described thus in 1768: "He makes fiddles, and can play upon the fiddle, and work at the carpenters trade."[9] Playing the fiddle provided ready employment for a slave making his way to freedom; an advertisement published almost a year after Samuel Berry ran away said petulantly: "It is needless to mention his cloathing, as he has been out so long, and as he plays the fiddle, he has many opportunities of changing his dress."[10] Many masters considered fiddling good for the morale of the slaves and encouraged it. Jack, a shoemaker, "is fond of the violin, and has taken with him a new one, which his master lately gave him."[11] Those who ran away surely did not fit the stereotype of the happy-go-lucky contented

3. "Eighteenth Century Slaves," pp. 176, 181, 206. See also Stoutamire, *Music of the Old South*, pp. 27, 32.

4. *American Weekly Mercury*, Oct. 24, 1734, quoted in Johnston, *Race Relations*, p. 276n.

5. *Virginia Gazette*, May 5, 1738, p. [4], col. 1.

6. *Ibid.*, Dec. 5, 1745, p. [4], col. 1.

7. *Ibid.*, May 7, 1767, p. [3], col. 3. He ran away again in 1774; *ibid.*, Feb. 17, 1774, p. [3], col. 2.

8. *Ibid.*, Aug. 4, 1768, p. [3], col. 2.

9. *Ibid.*, Aug. 18, 1768, p. [3], col. 2.

10. *Ibid.* (Rinn), July 18, 1771, p. [4], col. 1.

11. *Ibid.*, May 20, 1773, p. [2], col. 2. Other advertisements mentioning fiddles appeared on Mar. 27 and Apr. 24, 1746; May 4, 1769; May 14, 1772; Jan. 28, 1775; etc. For numerous references to slaves as musicians, see Cappon and Duff, *Virginia Gazette Index*, II, 1079. This index, however, does *not* include a reference to the "two African-originated musicians, flutists, from the household of Baron Botetourt, the late governor general of Virginia, and their African-style concerts," which was attributed to the *Virginia Gazette* of 1753 in John Rublowsky's *Music in America* and cited in John Lovell's *Black Song*, p. 67. No evidence has been found that the story appeared in the *Virginia Gazette* or that such concerts took place.

slave, yet they frequently played the fiddle. We must presume the existence of numerous other slave fiddlers whose presence was never recorded in an advertisement.

Although some masters encouraged fiddling and dancing as wholesome recreation, the stricter evangelical sects were already denouncing dancing as sinful, and the fiddle was acquiring a degraded reputation. There is no way of knowing, of course, to what degree black fiddlers played African music or added an African coloration to European tunes. That Negro jigs entered the repertory of white fiddlers and fifers is demonstrated in a number of tutors and collections of pieces.[12] (More will be said about this black-to-white influence later.) But black fiddlers in the North were regarded as marginal vagabonds outside the bounds of respectable society. In the New York "slave conspiracy" of 1741, much of the testimony about the alleged plot dealt with Negroes dancing, fiddling, and drumming, as if that in itself were evidence of dissolute habits that could lead to serious crimes. The evidence against one of the accused, Cuffee, was that a witness had seen "when the flames of the house blazed up very high, he huzza'd, danced, whistled and sung. . . ." Jamaica, another accused man, was usually described as "fiddling" or "with his fiddle." In his summation, the attorney general commented, "This horrid scene of iniquity has been chiefly contrived and promoted at meetings of negroes in great numbers on Sundays"[13]—meetings similar to those which were blamed for similar results in Jamaica and other West Indian islands. No satisfactory description of the Sunday meetings of slaves in the North has been found, and there is no basis for evaluating the degrees of acculturation displayed. That they may have resembled the Pinkster celebrations seems possible, but until more information is uncovered, little more than speculation is possible.

Not all fiddlers were men. Clarinda, in later life "a pious coloured woman of South Carolina," was born in 1730. She was brought up "in a state of ignorance unworthy of a Christian country," as evidenced by the fact that "she learned to play on the violin, and, usually, on the first day of the week, sallied forth with her instrument, in order to draw persons of both sexes together, who, not having the fear of God before their eyes, delighted like herself, in sinful and pernicious amusement. . . ." Once while dancing she

12. See, for example, "Pompey ran away. Negroe Jig" in *Selection of . . . Airs*, I, 57; "Negro Dance" in Riley, *Flute Melodies*, I, 31; "Congo—A Jig" in Darling, arr., *Little Keyboard Book*, p. 11. Arranged from a manuscript book, probably for fiddle, see p. v.
13. Horsmanden, *New-York Conspiracy*, pp. 76, 86, 98, 93. See also pp. 148–49, 192, 213, 238, 255.

"was seized with fits, and convulsively fell to the ground. From that moment, she lost her love of dancing, and no more engaged in this vain amusement." She became a preacher, the leader of a flock, and led a blameless life until she died at the age of 102.[14] This story of a reformed fiddler is remarkable chiefly because it concerns a woman. Such tales of conversion are a standard feature of religious literature in nineteenth-century America.

In the eighteenth century, slave fiddlers played for the dancing and amusement of both whites and blacks—usually not at the same time, of course, Impromptu dances were only rarely described, but there can be no doubt that they did occur. Nicholas Creswell, on his way to Barbados aboard the schooner *John* in 1774, was invited to a barbecue by a pilot boat which came alongside. He went with the captain and had a fine time: "These Barbecues are Hogs, roasted whole. This was under a large Tree. A great number of young people met together with a Fiddle and Banjo played by two Negroes, with Plenty of Toddy. . . . I believe they have danced and drunk till there are few sober people amongst them."[15] Another Englishman, Robert Hunter, writing from Baltimore in 1785, told just how casual such affairs could be. "We sent for a violin in the evening and had a most agreeable dance. . . . After the poor Negro's fingers were tired of fiddling, I took the violin and played them the 'Pleasures of Youth' and the 'Savage Dance.' " A month later at a wedding in Blandfield, Virginia, he danced "cotillions, minuets, Virginia and Scotch reels, country dances, jigs, etc., till ten o'clock,"[16] without mentioning the race of the musicians.

A legendary figure among eighteenth-century slave fiddlers was Sy (or Simeon) Gilliat, reputed to have been the fiddler at the Governor's Palace in Williamsburg during Baron Botetourt's regime. Gilliat was unquestionably the most popular society fiddler in Richmond for two generations, but no confirmation of his association with the Governor's Palace has yet been found by the staff of Colonial Williamsburg;[17] the sole authority that he was "court fiddler" were his own statements, made many years later in Richmond. Gilliat's career was described by Samuel Mordecai in his *Richmond in By-Gone Days*, written many years after Gilliat's death, but contemporary obituaries testify to his great popularity.

14. A[bigail] Mott, comp., *Biographical Sketches*, pp. 74–81.
15. Creswell, *Journal*, p. 30. The schooner was anchored in the St. Mary's River, the boundary between Georgia and Florida. Journal entry dated July 26, 1774.
16. Hunter, *Quebec to Carolina*, pp. 179–81, 206–7.
17. Letter to the author from Edward M. Riley, Director of Research, Colonial Williamsburg, Inc.

The death notice in the Richmond *Patriot* for October 16, 1820, lamented the passing of Simeon Gilliat, "a man of color, very celebrated as a Fiddler, and much caressed by polished society who will long deplore the loss."[18]

Most slave fiddlers played by ear, but some of them had lessons, more or less formal, arranged by themselves or (like the instruments) provided by their masters. The only known description of the way in which slave fiddlers learned to play came from Saint-Domingue (Haiti), but it could apply equally well to any mainland colony.

> The good ears of the Negroes give them the first qualification of a musician . . . many are good violinists. That is the instrument they prefer. Many certainly play it only by rote, that is, they learn by themselves, imitating the sounds of a tune, or they are taught by another Negro, who explains only the position of the strings and the fingers, with no thought of notes. They learn very quickly, for example, that *Si* is on the third string where the first finger is used, and in hearing a melody, remember what they have learned. This method is used by country fiddlers, and those of France cannot outdo them for volume of sound, capacity for drinking, or the ability to sleep without interrupting their playing.[19]

A unique document describes, in his own words, the training of a black musician of the eighteenth century. John Marrant was born in New York on June 15, 1755, and at the age of five was taken by his mother to St. Augustine, where he learned to read and spell. After some time spent in Georgia, he went to Charles Town to learn a trade. Such mobility indicates that he must have been free.

> In Charles-Town, as I was walking one day, I passed a school, and heard music and dancing, which took my fancy very much, and I felt a strong inclination to learn the music. I went home, and informed my sister, that I had rather learn to play upon music than go to a trade. . . . She persuaded me much against it, but her persuasions were fruitless. . . . Finding I was set upon it, and resolved to learn nothing else, she agreed to it, and went with me to speak to the man, and to settle upon the best terms with him she could. He insisted upon twenty pounds down, which was paid, and I was engaged to stay with him eighteen months. . . . The first day I went to him he put the violin into my hand, which pleased me very much, and, applying close, I learned very fast, not only to play, but to dance also; so that in six months I was able to play for the whole school. In the evenings . . . I used to resort to the bottom of our garden, where it was customary for some musicians to assemble to blow the

18. Clipping in the files of the Valentine Museum, Richmond; also in the file is a manuscript poem, beginning "Ye sons of mirth, attend his bier. Sy's fiddle ye no more will hear. . . ." Cf. Mordecai, *Richmond*, pp. 251–52, 352–54.

19. Moreau de Saint-Méry, *Déscription*, I, 51. My rough translation.

French horn. Here my improvement was so rapid, that in a twelve-month's time I became master of both the violin and of the French horn, and was much respected by the Gentlemen and Ladies whose children attended the school, as also by my master. This opened to me a large door of vanity and vice, for I was invited to all the balls and assemblies that were held in the town, and met with the general applause of the inhabitants. . . . I was now in my thirteenth year. . . .

Marrant tried to change his ways by learning a trade, but "every evening I was sent for to play on music." On one such occasion, he passed a meeting where George Whitefield was preaching. His friends persuaded him to "Blow the French horn among them," but just as Marrant was lifting his horn to his shoulder, Whitefield announced his text, looking directly at him: "Prepare to meet they God, O Israel." Like Clarinda before him, and many sinful fiddlers to come after, Marrant was struck to the ground both speechless and senseless, thus ending his musical career.[20] His conversion adheres to the traditional pattern for such a religious experience, but the description of his musical apprenticeship has no counterpart among black autobiographies of his time.

Marrant's choice of the French horn may seem surprising to twentieth-century readers, but that instrument was not unknown to slave musicians. An advertisement for a slave to be sold testified: "plays extremely well on the *French* horn."[21] Another was even more informative: "To be sold, A valuable young handsome Negro fellow, about 18 or 20 years of age, has every qualification of a genteel and sensible servant, and has been in many different parts of the world. He shaves, dresses hair, and plays on the *French* horn. He lately came from *London*, and has with him two suits of new clothes, and his *French* horn, which the purchaser may have with him."[22] Hardly the traditional picture of a slave. Another advertisement, this time for a runaway, said in part: "He is a Native of *Africa*, speaks *English* tolerably . . . and plays on the *French* Horn."[23] Another European instrument that figured in advertisements for runaway slaves was the flute. One slave in Boston could "play on the flute . . . and speaks good English,"[24] while another "plays well upon a *flute*, and not so well on a violin. This is to desire

20. Marrant, *Narrative*, pp. [7]–11. See also Porter, ed., *Early Negro Writing*, p. 402; and Kaplan, *Black Presence*, pp. 95–99. This otherwise superb volume does not mention black musicians.

21. *Virginia Gazette*, Mar. 28, 1766, p. [4], col. 1.

22. *Ibid.*, July 23, 1767, p. [3], col. 1.

23. *Ibid.*, Apr. 1, 1773, p. [3], col. 3.

24. Boston *Evening Post*, Oct. 3, 1748, quoted in "Eighteenth Century Slaves," p. 165.

Detail showing instruments, from an engraving of a painting of Negroes dancing in the Island of Dominica, by Agostino Brunyas (or Augustin Brunias, or Abraham Brunias), published in 1779. Brunyas returned from the Lesser Antilles in 1778. Source: Bryan Edwards, *The History, Civil and Commercial, of the British Colonies in the West Indies. . . .* London: Printed for J. Stockdale, 1794. Courtesy of the Rare Book Room, University of Illinois Library at Urbana-Champaign.

all Masters and Heads of Families not to suffer said Negro to come into their Houses to teach their Prentices or Servants to play. . . ."[25]

The violin, French horn, and flute were used largely for dancing, although perhaps the horn was used in hunting as well. But blacks also learned to play military instruments—trumpet, fife, and drum —and in the eighteenth century they were welcomed into the militia as essential musicians. The Assembly of the colony of Virginia provided for the militia in an act of 1723, including as Article IV: "Such free Negroes, Mulattos or Indians, as are capable, may be listed and emploied as Drummers or Trumpeters. . . ."[26] Slaves were not eligible, as might be expected, but the use of free blacks in such a capacity seems to indicate the shortage of able-bodied men in the colony, the lack of capable musicians, and the effect of the long tradition of black military musicians in England.[27]

In South Carolina, where frontier conditions still prevailed, one slave auctioned in 1740 was versatile enough to be "a good Groom, waiting Man, Cook, Drummer, Coachman, and hacks Deer Skins very well."[28] Virginia slaves, though ineligible for the militia, apparently found some legal opportunities to drum. The *Virginia Gazette* in 1766 carried an advertisement for a Negro named Damon, who "speaks good *English*, was born in the *West Indies*, beats the drum tolerably well, which he is very fond of, and loves liquor. . . ."[29]

In the northern colonies the enlistment in the militia of Negroes, both slave and free, as trumpeters or drummers was also common. In Framingham, Massachusetts, Nero Benson, a slave, served as trumpeter in Captain Isaac Clark's troop in 1725.[30] Barzillai Lew of Chelmsford, Massachusetts, served as a musician in both the French and Indian War and in the Continental Army, 22nd Regiment, under Captain Ford.[31] The colonies, both North and South, enlisted Negroes as drummers during the Revolution;[32] on May 6, 1777, the

25. *Ibid.*, Oct. 24, 1743, quoted in "Eighteenth Century Slaves," p. 206.

26. Virginia (Colony) Laws, Statutes, etc., *Exact Abridgment*, "Ann. 1723, cap. 2, p. 334," p. 189.

27. Cf. Walvin, *Black and White*, pp. 70–71.

28. *South Carolina Gazette*, Apr. 11, 1740, quoted in Wood, *Black Majority*, p. 104.

29. *Virginia Gazette*, Apr. 4, 1766, p. [4], col. 1.

30. Barry, *History of Framingham*, pp. 63n., 181. A portrait of "Negro [*sic*] Benson, trumpeter to the King's Militia at Framingham, Mass., in 1725" was exhibited by the Negro History Associates in "An Introduction to the Negro in American History: An Exhibition," Sept. 9–Oct. 19, 1969, at the New York Cultural Center.

31. Wilkes, *Missing Pages*, reprinted in *Negro Soldier*, p. 27. See also pp. 31, 47.

32. See Quarles, *Negro in American Revolution*, p. 77: "A typical assignment of Negro soldiers was that of drummer. In Captain Rufus Lincoln's company of the Seventh Massachusetts Regiment the drummer was Jabez Jolly of Barnstable, who,

Virginia Assembly passed another act providing for the enlistment of free Negroes as drummers or fifers.[33]

Isaac, one of Thomas Jefferson's slaves at Monticello, described an interracial fife-and-drum team that played at the Governor's Palace in Richmond during Jefferson's term as governor of Virginia.

> Bob Anderson a white man was a blacksmith. Mat Anderson was a black man and worked with Bob. Bob was a fifer; Mat was a drummer. . . . The soldiers at Richmond . . . would come every two or three days to salute the Governor at the Palace, marching about there drumming & fifing. . . . Mat went into the kitchen to see Mary Hemings. He would take his drum with him into the kitchen & set it down there. Isaac [then six years old] would beat on it & Mat larnt him how to beat. . . . He was then big enough to beat the drum, but couldn't raise it off the ground; would hold it tilted over to one side and beat on it that way.[34]

THE AFRICAN JIG, A BLACK-TO-WHITE EXCHANGE

Up to this point, we have been concerned with the presence of African music and dancing in the New World and the impact of European culture upon them. The impact of African culture upon European music and dancing in the colonial period has been even more difficult to document, although American culture today is a living demonstration of that influence. In an era when many people were preoccupied with preserving elements of their European heritage in an alien, not to say hostile, environment, it is hardly surprising that they recorded very little of an influence which they could not publicly acknowledge. To an eighteenth-century gentleman or lady, "going native" would have been as uncongenial as it was to a British civil servant in India a century later.

Yet evidence has been found to indicate that these ladies and gentlemen did indeed dance Negro dances, not just occasionally but with some regularity—"usual" was the term found in contemporary accounts. Not enough is known about the dance to draw any conclusions about it; at this stage the documents must be allowed to speak for themselves. The kind of interracial gathering in which

---

young as were drummers generally, was either eighteen or nineteen when he enlisted on December 9, 1779. William Nickens, who came from a Northern Neck, Virginia family . . . served as drummer for 'three or four years.' In South Carolina a payroll of Captain Samuel Wise's First Company of Rangers for the month of September 1775 lists 'Negro Bob (drummer).' "

33. Hening, ed., *Statutes of Virginia*, IX, 280, quoted in Quarles, *Negro in American Revolution*, p. 58.

34. "Memoirs of a Monticello Slave," in Bear, ed., *Jefferson at Monticello*, pp. 7, 10.

such dances might have been learned was described by Philip Fithian in his journal entry for Sunday, January 30, 1774:

> This Evening the Negroes collected themselves into the School-Room [a detached outbuilding], & began to play the *Fiddle*, & dance. . . . I went among them, *Ben* [Benjamin Carter, the eldest son, a quiet, studious boy of eighteen] & *Harry* [the Councillor's nephew, Harry Willis] were of the company—Harry was dancing with his Coat off—I dispersed them however immediately.[35]

This group of Negroes, with two young sons of the household, were probably not dancing the minuet or even country dances. It is far more likely that the boys were learning to dance what became known as "Negro jigs."

About a year later Nicholas Creswell attended a ball in Alexandria, Virginia, where he saw "about 37 ladies dressed and powdered to the life. . . . Betwixt the Country dances they have what I call everlasting jigs. A couple gets up and begins to dance a jig (to some Negro tune) others comes and cuts them out, and these dances always last as long as the Fiddler can play. This is sociable, but I think it looks more like a Bacchanalian dance than one in a polite assembly."[36] Creswell's description included elements usually ascribed to African dancing: couples succeeding each other in demonstrating their ability, with the dance lasting as long as the energy of the participants.

Another description was published in Dublin in 1776. In discussing the women of Virginia, the anonymous author wrote:

> They are immoderately fond of dancing. Towards the close of an evening, when the company are pretty well tired with country-dances, it is usual to dance jigs; a practice originally borrowed, I am informed, from the Negroes.*
> *These dances are without any method or regularity; a gentleman and lady stand up, and dance about the room, one of them retiring, the other pursuing, then perhaps meeting, in an irregular fantastical manner. After some time, another lady gets up, and then the first lady must sit down, she being, as the term is, cut out; the second lady acts the same part which the first did, till somebody cuts her out. The gentlemen perform in the same manner.[37]

It seems unlikely that this dance could have been the popular English dance of the sixteenth century, "introduced in America,

35. Fithian, *Journal & Letters*, pp. 61–62.
36. Creswell, *Journal*, pp. 52–53.
37. *Concise Historical Account*, p. 213. The passage also appears in Franklin, *Philosophical and Political History*, p. 91.

Music of a Negro jig danced by whites. Source: *A Selection of Scotch, English, Irish and Foreign Airs, Adapted for the Fife, Violin or German Flute....* Glasgow: J. Aird, 1782. I, 57. Courtesy of Forbes Library, Northampton, Mass.

where they were imitated by Negroes and gradually transformed into the grotesque dances of the minstrel shows."[38] The writers of the above reports were either English or Irish men who presumably could recognize English or Irish jigs when they saw them. Not one contemporary witness has associated the Negro jig with jigs known in the British Isles, although they used the same word for both, leading to unfortunate ambiguity.

A tantalizing cameo of the African strain in colonial culture is provided by the contrast between Thomas Jefferson and his brother, Randolph.[39] Thomas Jefferson, who regarded European music as "a delightful recreation for the hours of respite from the cares of the day,"[40] who played the violin and stressed music in the education of his daughters and his granddaughters, "seemed not the least bit curious about or interested in" the music of the black people by whom he was surrounded throughout his life.[41] In his voluminous correspondence and other writings, he mentioned the music of the blacks only once, in his *Notes on the State of Virginia*. On the other hand, his brother Randolph, about whom we know almost nothing, was described by the former Monticello slave, Isaac, as "a mighty simple man: used to come out among black people, play the fiddle and dance half the night."[42] Randolph, with no pretensions to be anything but a country gentleman, was able to relax and enjoy the company of black people, while his brother Thomas, with greater intellectual pretensions and more refined tastes, never recognized the distinctive qualities of the black music all around him.

38. "Jig," *Harvard Dictionary of Music*, p. 448. No distinction between various kinds of jigs was made in the *Oxford English Dictionary*, nor do those dictionaries of the dance that were consulted mention an African dance by this name. It appears that the term was peculiar to the American colonies and has not survived in recognized dance terminology.

39. *Thomas Jefferson and His Unknown Brother Randolph.*

40. Thomas Jefferson to Nathaniel Burwell, Mar. 14, 1818, quoted in Cripe, *Jefferson and Music*, p. 2.

41. *Ibid.*, p. 92.

42. "Memoirs of a Monticello Slave," in Bear, ed., *Jefferson at Monticello*, p. 22.

Reports of the African jig were not restricted to the eighteenth century, although some of them are too vague to be more than suggestive. For example, Whitman Mead attended a dance in Tarborough, North Carolina, in February, 1817. People there danced "North Carolina camper downs, or what would be more descriptive, scamper dances. . . . It would require a much more intimate acquaintance with them than I ever expect to possess, to describe them properly. The best account I can give of them is, scamper, scamper, scamper."[43] Not a very satisfactory description.

The South Carolina poet William J. Grayson included a description of a jig at Christmastime in his defense of slavery in heroic couplets, "The Hireling and the Slave":

> . . . Then clear the barn, the ample area fill,
> In the gay jig display their vigorous skill;
> No dainty steps, no mincing measures here—
> But hearts of joy and nerves of living steel,
> On floors that spring beneath the bounding reel;
> Proud on his chair, with magisterial glance
> And stamping foot, the fiddler rules the dance;
> Draws, if he nods, the still unwearied bow,
> And gives a joy no bearded bards bestow. . . .[44]

It is not clear whether Grayson's use of the word "reel" has any significance other than poetic; his description could have been of any square dance on the frontier, but he was describing life in the Sea Islands and coastal South Carolina, where the gentry did not dance in the barn.

The best description of this dance was written in 1876 by Henry W. Ravenel of South Carolina, in a description of his childhood and youth in which he tried to recapture a portion of the old life that was gone. He had been born in 1814 and lived on the ancestral Ravenel plantation in a house built in 1716. Pooshee, the plantation, was in St. John's Berkeley, about forty miles from Charleston.

> The jig was an African dance and a famous one in old times, before more refined notions began to prevail. However it was always called for by some of the older ones who had learned its steps, and never failed to raise shouts of laughter, with applause of the performers. For the jig the music would be changed. The fiddle would assume a low monotonous tone, the whole tune running on three or four notes only (when it could be heard,) the stick-knocker changed his time, and beat a softer and slower measure. Indeed only a few could give the "knock" for proper effect.

43. Mead, *Travels*, p. 67.
44. Grayson, *Hireling and Slave*, p. 52.

It was strictly a dance for two, one man and one woman on the floor at a time. It was opened by a gentleman leading out the lady of his choice and presenting her to the musicians. She always carried a handkerchief held at arm's length over her head, which was waved in a graceful motion to and fro as she moved. The step, if it may be so called, was simply a slow shuffling gait in front of the fiddler, edging along by some unseen exertion of the feet, from one side to the other—sometimes courtesying down and remaining in that posture while the edging motion from one side to the other continued.

Whilst this was going on, the man danced behind her, shuffling his arms and legs in artistic style, and his whole soul and body thrown into the dance. The feet moved about in the most grotesque manner stamping, slamming, and banging the floor, not unlike the pattering of hail on the housetop. The conflict between brogan and the sanded floor was terrific. It was hard work, and at intervals of five or ten minutes, he was relieved by another jumping into the ring with a shout, and shuffling him out. . . . When there was a relay of fiddlers the dancing would be kept up night and day with intermissions for meals and rest.

This was rather the Christmas of thirty or forty years ago [1836 or 1846] than of later days. There was dancing and merrymaking up to the time of emancipation, but it was in a more subdued form, and under the protest from some of the elders.[45]

The "shuffling, edging along by some unseen exertion of the feet, from one side to the other" sounds remarkably like the descriptions of "shouts," religious dances from the same general area, as described during and immediately after the Civil War. The possibility that the African jig was the secular equivalent of the sacred dance, the "shout," deserves consideration and investigation.

Three examples of Negro jigs reduced to musical notation have been found: "Pompey Ran Away," "Negro Dance," and "Congo—A Jig."[46] All lack any distinctive African flavor, sounding much like other non-African dances. Presumably much was lost in the transcription, as the tunes were filtered through the ears and musical sensibilities of a musician bred in the European tradition. Perhaps only the dance steps retained African elements, but it is at least possible that African aspects of the tunes may still be identified.

45. Ravenel, "Recollections," pp. 768–69.
46. See note 12, above.

PART TWO

Secular and Sacred Black Folk Music, 1800–1867

7

··

African Survivals

The year 1801 was more than a convenient chronological dividing line between two centuries; it also differentiated between the old and the new in several areas that dramatically affected the music of the blacks. The West Indies were now politically separate from the United States, and the close interrelations that had existed between them disintegrated as they went their separate ways. The invention of the cotton gin in 1793 and its rapid spread throughout the South changed a declining economy into a booming Cotton Kingdom based on chattel slavery. And the end of the legal slave trade in 1808 drastically reduced the influx of new slaves entering the country from Africa or the West Indies. No one knows how many slaves were smuggled in after the end of the legal trade, but undoubtedly the number was substantially lower than the legal trade had been.

Ties with Africa persisted in the memories of slaves who had been born there, and the memories they handed down to their children. However, the Europeanization of the mainland slaves was irreversible, not only because whites outnumbered blacks in most states, but also because the black population was increasingly composed of people born in the United States. A black population of 4,441,830 reported in the census of 1860 had developed from a total of 399,000 slaves imported into British North America.[1] The nineteenth-cen-

1. Curtin, *Atlantic Slave Trade*, p. 75.

tury U.S. plantation system was characterized, therefore, by a booming cotton economy dependent entirely on slave labor, a labor supply restricted largely to natural increase, and an internal slave trade which replaced the foreign. All these factors had heavy implications for the acculturative process and the development of black culture, of which black music was a prominent component.

PERSISTING MUSICAL AND CULTURAL PATTERNS

Despite the declining number of fresh arrivals from Africa or the West Indies and the growing proportion of the blacks who had been born in the United States, African cultural patterns persisted, largely unseen by whites. During the 1930's the Georgia Writers' Program collected much evidence of African survivals among the coastal Negroes[2]—survivals which must have persisted throughout the preceding period, although little documentation has been found. The reasons why so few documents have been found can be conjectured. Literate nineteenth-century blacks tended to focus their writings on matters that would contribute to the progress of their race (the horrors of slavery and the readiness of slaves for freedom), while folklore and anthropology were the hobbies of amateurs, rather than academic disciplines. Rare was the observer who recorded evidence of African musical instruments or culture before 1860 (AS 1). On a walking "ramble" to New Orleans in 1858, one W. H. Venable saw an instrument in Granada, Mississippi, which aroused his curiosity:

> Paul [a slave] was a good dancer and singer, and could play upon various musical instruments. The most curious of these was one which he called a "songbow," a simple contrivance, consisting of a string stretched tight from one end to the other of a long, flexible, narrow board or bow, and which the performer breathed upon in such a way as to cause a musical vibration, while at the same time he sang. The song and accompaniment were strangely blended and the effect was not unpleasant.[3]

This seems unquestionably to be related to the African musical bow.

Another contemporary reporter was the pioneer sociologist Daniel Robinson Hundley, who published his *Social Relations in Our Southern States* in 1860. Having grown up on a plantation in northern Alabama, Hundley was educated at Bacon College in Kentucky, the University of Virginia, and Harvard College.[4] He had this to say about African survivals in slave music: "The religious

2. Writers' Program, Georgia, *Drums and Shadows.*
3. Venable, "Down South," p. 498.
4. Eaton, *Waning of Old South*, p. 4.

and love-songs of the negroes are not so peculiar and striking as those wild choruses and lullaloos, which their fathers must have brought with them from Africa, but the words and meaning of which are no longer remembered."[5] Ironically, in the childhood memories of aristocratic southern whites we find descriptions of events that usually must have been kept secret from white adults. They represent the tips of the cultural iceberg; we can only guess what was beneath the surface of plantation life.

The recollections of the childhood of Henry William Ravenel, planter, botanist, and writer of South Carolina (1814–87), described the life at Pooshee, with a community of about two hundred slaves:

> There was a never-failing fund of interest in the old Negroes' stories, which they were very fond of telling. Some (the native Africans) told of the "old country," which they could remember . . . the story of their capture and march to the coast—of the "middle passage" . . . many of them would show the "tattoo" marks of royalty seared upon the faces and bodies. . . . Crazy Will and Old Surry were two crazy native Africans. . . . One of his [Will's] pastimes was a peculiar dance. As he proceeded, it seemed to absorb him with a frenzy of excitement. He used two light rods in his hands, and with these he would make passes at some imaginary person, all the while looking steadily at the sun. It was probably the lingering shadow of some war dance he had seen or known in his native land. . . . We called it the "javelin dance."[6]

The daughter of a rice planter of Broughton Island, Macintosh County, near Darien, Georgia, wrote:

> One of our friends owned a real African princess. She must have been over a hundred when I knew her. . . . We dearly loved her songs, which were African ones, thrown into rough English by herself. One was about two birds, one having challenged the other to remain on a rock in the river, whilst the challenger stayed in a tree where it could get worms from the trunk. The idea was that the one who held out longest without leaving its position would be the victor. Of course the bird in the tree won, the poor bird on the rock collapsing from hunger.[7] (AS 2)

Jacob Stroyer was born a slave on a plantation twenty-eight miles southeast of Columbia, South Carolina, in 1849. He described Christmas celebrations where "some who were born in Africa, would sing some of their songs, or tell stories of the customs in Africa."[8] (AS 3)

Letitia Burwell, the daughter of a Virginia planter, wrote about a mulatto cook, "Aunt Fanny," a pillar of the church who dumb-

5. Hundley, *Social Relations*, p. 348.
6. Ravenel, "Recollections," pp. 750, 774–75.
7. Conrad, "Reminiscences," p. 168.
8. Stroyer, *My Life*, p. 47.

founded her master's family by abandoning her "civilized" habits when death approached.

> Several days before her death. . . . Her room was crowded with Negroes who had come to perform their religious rites around the death bed. Joining hands they performed a savage dance, shouting wildly around her bed. This was horrible to hear and see, especially as in this family every effort had been made to instruct their negro dependants in the truths of religion. . . . But although [Aunt Fanny was] an intelligent woman, she seemed to cling to the superstitions of her race.
> After the savage dance and rites were over . . . I went, and said to her: . . . "we are afraid the noise and dancing have made you worse."
> Speaking feebly, she replied: "Honey, that kind of religion suits us black folks better than your kind. What suits Mars Charles' mind, don't suit mine."[9] (AS 4)

In South Carolina, as a Union victory approached during the last year of the war, "a brooding, smouldering feeling of apprehension and suppressed excitement" was conveyed to the whites by the singing of the slaves.

> We young people had always been fond of occasionally going to the negro prayer meetings, but I remember a slight thrill of alarm one night that winter when D. and I heard very wild singing at their church . . . and looking in saw a scene of barbaric frenzy that I have since thought the howling Dervishes reminded me of. The men sat around clapping and singing deep monotonous notes, but the women were shuffling and leaping in a circle, clapping their hands high in the air, their heads thrown back so that some of their turbans had fallen off, and singing in high, shrill tones, strange spiritual songs such as, "I'll pick up my work and I'll lay um down, no man can hender me." [Song 14 in *Slave Songs of the United States*?] They really looked wrought up to frenzy; the sweat pouring down their faces and eyes glittering.[10]

Since Elizabeth Coxe had lived all her life among these Africans, she must have felt some change in their behavior that caused her apprehension, even though they were singing a "spiritual song" in a church she had visited many times.

Even in a dialect narrative written to amuse white readers—hardly a reliable source for authentic folk tradition—there are references to dances that seem to have been derived from African animal dances: "dogshort, pulled-de-root, beat de mule," culminating in a "snake dance." It was "a queer kin' er dance . . . a turrible dance . . . hist my skirt on up de right, en crossed my feets."

---

9. [Burwell,] *Plantation Reminiscences*, p. 57.

10. Coxe, *Memories*, pp. 54–55. The plantation was Belvidere, belonging to Charles Sinkler, Mrs. Coxe's father. She was apparently a sister of Anne Sinkler Fishburne, quoted in AS 2.

Crossing the feet was what distinguished secular dancing from the "shout," but it had powerful attractions. "Fo' I knowed it de las' one er dem gals wuz histin' dey skirts, en crossin' dey feets, en tryin' dey bes' to git de steps. . . ." "Miss Mouse," the narrator, was transmitting traditional African dance steps to the whole crowd, with the result that the preacher and the elders of the church brought charges against her of "dancin' . . . singin' reel chunes . . . dance de dogshort, en pull-de-root, en cut de pigeon wing . . . *hist her skirt en CROSS her feets.*"[11]

An exotic custom apparently brought from Jamaica (where it still continues), or perhaps from Africa, was the John Canoe festival, part of the Christmas celebration in sections of North Carolina before the Civil War. The festival required its own distinctive combination of instruments:

> Every child rises early on Christmas morning to see the Johnkannaus. Without them, Christmas would be shorn of its greatest attraction . . . companies of slaves [gather] from the plantations. . . . Two athletic men, in calico wrappers, have a net thrown over them. . . . Cows' tails are fastened to their backs, and their heads are decorated with horns. A box, covered with sheepskin, is called the gumbo box. A dozen beat on this, while others strike triangles and jawbones, to which bands of dancers keep time. For a month previous they are composing songs, which are sung on this occasion. These companies, of a hundred each, turn out early in the morning, and are allowed to go round till twelve o'clock, begging for contributions. . . . It is seldom a white man or child refuses to give them a trifle. If he does, they regale his ears with the following song:—
>
> > "Poor massa, so dey say;
> > Down in de heel, so dey say;
> > Got no money, so dey say;
> > Not one shillin', so dey say;
> > God A'mighty, bress you, so dey say."[12]

The parallel with African songs of derision is evident. (AS 5)

An incident that demonstrated the disintegration of the customary dominance of the European master over the African servant was reported shortly after Emancipation by Elizabeth Allston of South Carolina. She and her mother visited her brother's plantation after they had heard reports that the blacks there had become "turbulent and excited." After being refused entrance to the house, Mrs. Allston asked for the keys and was refused again.

11. Hobson, *In Old Alabama*, pp. 111–12, 119, 126. This questionable source can be corroborated in other, more authentic documents.

12. Jacobs, *Incidents*, pp. 179–80. For a fuller discussion of the tradition, see Ira De A. Reid, "John Canoe Festival," and Cassidy, " 'Hip-saw' and 'John Canoe.' "

Mamma and I walked slowly down the avenue to the public road, with a yelling mob of men, women, and children around us. They sang sometimes in unison, sometimes in parts, strange words which we did not understand, followed by a much-repeated chorus:

> "I free, I free!
> I free as a frog!
> I free till I fool!
> Glory Alleluia!"

They revolved around us, holding out their skirts and dancing—now with slow, swinging movement, now with rapid jig-motions, but always with weird chant and wild gestures.[13]

The strange words which she did not understand, and some which she misunderstood, may have been in some African language. Elizabeth Allston had studied piano and singing in Charleston before the war and gave music lessons after it, but her ignorance of or indifference to the survivals of African culture among which she lived characterized her stratum of society. She expressed no curiosity about that culture, and her reaction when she could not avoid noticing its existence was a compound of uncomprehending fear, hostility, and defensiveness.

BLACK MUSIC IN NEW ORLEANS, 1820–67

The earlier discussion of the acculturation of African music in New Orleans extended to Latrobe's description of 1819, which reflected the persistence of African music and dancing there long after it had been suppressed or acculturated in other parts of the country. Although French Catholic influence was losing its primacy as Louisiana became steadily more Americanized, nevertheless tolerance toward Sunday dancing continued there, in striking contrast to the eastern states. Another 1819 report was far less informative than Latrobe's, illustrating the indifference of the usual traveler toward the dancing of the blacks.[14] In 1821 Isaac Holmes described Sunday dances on the plantations; his details were few, but enough to indicate that African influences were still dominant:

> In Louisiana, and the state of Mississippi, the slaves have Sunday for a day of recreation, and upon many plantations they dance for several hours during the afternoon. . . . The general movement is in what they call the Congo dance; but their music often consists of nothing more than an excavated piece of wood, at one end of which is a piece of parchment which covers the hollow part on which they beat; and the

13. Pringle, *Chronicles of Chicora Wood*, pp. 269–73. For her musical training, see pp. 179–80; for her teaching, p. 310.
14. [Knight,] *Letters*, p. 127. Letter dated New Orleans, 1819.

singing or vociferation of those who are dancing, and of those who surround the dancers, constitute the whole of their harmony.[15]

Another report came from Timothy Flint, a Harvard-trained missionary who visited New Orleans in 1823:

> Every year the Negroes have two or three holidays, which in New Orleans and the vicinity, are like the "Saturnalia" of the slaves in ancient Rome. The great Congo-dance is performed. Every thing is license and revelry. Some hundreds of Negroes, male and female, follow the king of the wake, who is conspicuous for his youth, size, the whiteness of his eyes, and the blackness of his visage. For a crown he has a series of oblong, gilt-paper boxes on his head, tapering upwards, like a pyramid. From the ends of these boxes, hang two huge tassels.... All the characters that follow him ... have their own peculiar dress, and their own contortions. They dance, and their streamers fly, and the bells that they have hung about them tinkle....[16]

"Congo dances" in "a back square" were mentioned in 1823, and again in 1835, when Joseph Ingraham learned from a passer-by that the "treeless green" he saw was called "Congo Square." "Here ... the coloured 'ladies and gentlemen' are accustomed to assemble on gala and saints' days, and to the time of outlandish music, dance"— but he was too early to see for himself.[17] Henry Kmen believes the dancing was discontinued shortly after 1835, presenting substantial evidence for his conclusions,[18] but no contemporary statement of the action has yet been found, and some of the evidence is at least ambiguous. Hélène d'Aquin Allain, who lived in New Orleans between 1836 and 1855, wrote in her anonymous memoirs:

> At the time when we lived at the corner of Rue du Quartier and Rue Conde ... one spoke always ... [of] the Negroes dancing again at Place Congo! It was a holiday for them, every Sunday evening, and whites and blacks, slaves and masters, pressed against the heavy gate that separated the dancers from the crowd. I myself never saw them, nor did I know anyone who had, but I believe ... that these dances were identical with those one reads about in the description [Moreau de Saint-Méry's book on Haiti].... Our Louisiana Negroes yield nothing to the Negroes of the older colonies; dances, songs, proverbs—they have inherited all.[19]

Colonel James Creecy first came to New Orleans in October, 1834. His description of Congo Square remained unpublished until after his death in 1860 with no indication of when it was written, so it is less than ideal as evidence of chronology:

15. Holmes, *Account*, p. 332.
16. Flint, *Recollections*, p. 140.
17. Greene, *Journals*, p. 123; [Ingraham,] *South-West*, I, 162.
18. Kmen, "Roots of Jazz," pp. 11ff.
19. [Allain,] *Souvenirs d'Amérique*, pp. [171]–73, my rough translation.

North of Rampart street . . . is the celebrated Congo Square, well enclosed, containing five or six or perhaps more acres, well shaded, with graveled walks and beautiful grass plats, devoted on Sunday afternoons to negro dances and amusement. . . . The lower order of colored people and negroes, bond and free, assemble in great numbers in Congo Square, on every Sunday afternoon in good weather, to enjoy themselves in their own peculiar manner. Groups of fifties and hundreds may be seen in different sections of the square, with banjos, tom-toms, violins, jaw-bones, triangles, and various other instruments from which harsh or dulcet sounds may be extracted; and a variety, indeed, of queer, gro-tesque, fantastic, strange, and merry dancers are to be seen . . . most fancifully dressed, with fringes, ribbons, little bells, and shells and balls, jingling and flirting about the performers legs and arms, who sing a second or counter to the music most sweetly; for all Africans have melody in their souls; and in all their movements . . . the most perfect time is kept, making the beats with the feet, heads, or hands, or all, as correctly as a well-regulated metronome! Young and old join in the sport and dances. One will continue the rapid *jig* till nature is exhausted; then a fresh disciple leaps before him or her and "cuts out" the fatigued one. . . .[20] Hundreds of nurses, with children of all ages, attend, and many fathers and mothers. . . . Every stranger should visit Congo Square . . . once at least, and, my word for it, no one will ever regret or forget it. . . . The gaieties continue till sunset; and at the "gun-fire" the whole crowd disperse. . . .[21]

Un Voyage à la Nouvelle-Orléans, probably published during the 1840's, mentions cannon fire in "la place Congo" as a curfew for the Negroes, but does not mention dancing.[22] By 1845 the square was called "Circus Place . . . once known as *Congo Park* . . . where the negroes, in olden times, were accustomed to meet . . . the unsophis-ticated break-down, and double-shuffle of these primitive days have ceased. . . ."[23] In 1855 an article in *De Bow's Review* recalled the dancing without giving it a date: "We who have heard the *tom-tom* beat, and witnessed the mystic dance of thousands of native Africans and their lineal descendants in Congo-Square, New Or-leans. . . ."[24]

While Kmen's assertion that African dancing in Place Congo was discontinued sometime before the Civil War is undoubtedly correct, his evidence for "shortly after 1835"[25] is less than convincing. We

20. This description has many similarities with those of the "African jig" in ch. 6.
21. Creecy, *Scenes in South*, pp. 19–23. For the date of his arrival in New Orleans, see p. 9. In discussing the Mardi Gras celebration, he wrote: "This carnival . . . has been more than once forbidden, as well as the Congo Square dances . . ."—p. 45. The description of Congo Square was quoted by Mrs. Mary Schoolcraft in her novel, *Black Gauntlet*, pp. 31–33.
22. Berjot, *Voyage*, p. 16. Date supplied by the Library of Congress.
23. Norman, *New Orleans and Environs*, p. 182.
24. "African Slave Trade," p. 20.
25. Kmen, "Roots of Jazz," p. 11.

can hope that additional documents will yet be found to resolve a number of clouded points: the date when dancing was first banned in Place Congo, the date when it was resumed, and the date of its final, permanent discontinuance. But even if the dancing did cease shortly after 1835, that date cannot be regarded as the terminal date for African music and dancing in New Orlenas; private surreptitious African dancing would not have been affected by the ban on public dancing in Congo Square. Reports of such dancing are extremely rare, but that indicates nothing about its frequency. Those reports that have been found are commonly associated with voodoo rites, ceremonies that were frowned on by the authorities and ostracized by polite society. Their very nature made it prudent for participants to keep them secret. One account published in 1875 described a rite of fifty years earlier in terms strikingly similar to comparable reports from Haiti:

> An old Negro . . . astride on a cylinder made of thin cypress-staves hooped with brass and headed by a sheepskin. With two sticks he droned away on a monotonous ra-ta-ta, ra-ra-ta-ta, while on his left sat a Negro on a low stool, who with two sheep-shank bones, and a Negress with the leg-bones of a buzzard or turkey, beat an accompaniment on the sides of the cylinder. Some two feet from these arch-musicians squatted a young Negro vigorously twirling a long calabash . . . filled with pebbles. [After the ceremony] . . . back to his tam-tam, his accompaniers right and left, and the gourd-musician with his rattle. A banjo-player too. . . .[26]

Charles Dudley Warner, the American editor, visited New Orleans for the first time in March, 1885. He witnessed "the barbaric rites of Voudooism" at noon in "a small frame house . . . just beyond Congo Square, an incantation rather than a dance. . . ."

> A colored woman at the side of the altar began a chant in a low, melodious voice. It was the weird and strange "Danse Calinda." . . . The chant grew, the single line was enunciated in stronger pulsations, and other voices joined in the wild refrain. . . . The singing became wilder and more impassioned, a strange minor strain, full of savage pathos and longing . . . the chant had been changed for the wild *canga*, more rapid in movement than the *chanson africaine*. . . .[27]

Outside New Orleans, African influences continued in what had been French territory. A descendant of a Creole family recalled plantation New Year's celebrations which resembled comparable occasions in eighteenth-century Saint-Domingue:

> Their musical instruments were, first, a barrel with one end covered with an ox-hide,—this was the drum; then two sticks and the jawbone of

26. Marie B. Williams, "Night with Voudous," p. 404. The author, aged fifteen, accompanied a servant from the West Indies to the rites.

27. Warner, *Studies*, pp. [75]–82.

a mule, with the teeth still on it,—this was the violin. The principal musician bestrode the barrel and began to beat on the hide, singing as loud as he could. He beat with his hands, with his feet, and sometimes, when quite carried away by his enthusiasm, with his head also. The second musician took the sticks and beat on the wood of the barrel, while the third made a dreadful music by rattling the teeth of the jawbone with a stick. Five or six men stood around the musicians and sang without stopping. . . . These dancing-songs generally consisted of one phrase, repeated for hours on the same air.[28]

Fortier gave no date for such a performance, and other contemporary descriptions of plantation dances, though rather vague, imply possibly a higher degree of European influence. Salomon de Rothschild merely commented that Mr. McCall, the owner of Evan Hall, provided a wagon to take his Negroes "to a nearby town where they can dance" on Sundays. William Howard Russell, the correspondent for the London *Times*, visited a Mr. Roman in Natchez, Mississippi, on June 14, 1861.

As we passed the house . . . slaves [were] going off to a dance at the sugarhouse . . . the scraping of fiddles was audible. It was Sunday, and Mr. Roman informed me that he gave his negroes leave to have a dance on that day. The planters who are not Catholics rarely give any such indulgence to their slaves . . . four couples were dancing a kind of Irish jig to the music of the negro musicians—a double shuffle and a thumping ecstasy. . . .[29]

Russell probably used the term "Irish jig" to describe the general character of the dancing, rather than to identify a specific set of steps.

28. Fortier, "Customs and Superstitions," pp. 136–37. Virtually the same passage appeared in his *Louisiana Studies*, pp. 126–27.
29. Rothschild, *Casual View*, p. 112; Russell, *Pictures of Southern Life*, pp. 93–96.

ADDITIONAL SOURCES

AS1.

So far as we can now tell . . . abolitionists had little appreciation for what a later age would call "black culture." They did not find anything precious or vital or especially worth cherishing in the black man's peculiar way of life—if indeed they thought it at all peculiar. They took for granted that blacks would share the common American culture. Their observation led them to believe that blacks held similar expectations. They expected them to be sober and thrifty, to work hard, to be law-abiding, to educate their children, to attend church faithfully.

Dillon, *Abolitionists*, p. 73.

Some references to African survivals have been found. In a letter from Virginia dated 1816, one man wrote about the slaves:

[They have] their poison-doctors, and their conjurors. Some become wizards, by chewing live coals, first gathering the saliva. . . . When a slave dies, the master gives the rest a day, of their own choosing, to celebrate the funeral. This, perhaps a month after the corpse in interred, is a jovial day with them; they sing and dance and drink the dead to his new home, which some believe to be in old Guinea.

[Knight,] *Letters*, pp. 75, 77. His is very similar to descriptions of funerals in Jamaica.

AS2. A similar reminiscence came from Charles Seton Henry Hardee, who was born on August 9, 1830, and moved to Savannah in 1835. One of the servants who came with his family to Savannah was named Jinny:

She was no longer young, and we called her "Mom Jinny." She was a native African, and claimed to be the daughter of an African prince. When she was ten or twelve years old, she said she was captured by a strolling band of slave-hunters, while she was in the woods near her home gathering sticks to make a fire to cook with. . . . She used to tell many amusing stories and sing many funny songs about animals, birds and insects. There was one that had a dozen or more verses, each ending with a chorus. I remember only two verses of this song. One of them ran thus:

> "Dare's a ting dey call him de 'Gater.'
> He lib on the lan' as well as de water.
> · He go chingering, chingering, chingering,
> Charigo, chingering, chingering chaw."

And the other:

> "Dare's a little ting dey call 'im de chigger,
> He lib on the lan' and he bitee po' nigger.
> He go chingering, chingering, chingering,
> Charigo, chingering, chingering chaw."

"Reminiscences," pp. 159, 165–66.

Another account from South Carolina was similar:

Often we children would draw up on three-legged stools and listen with rapt absorption to Maum Hetty's tales of the Guinea Negroes of whom her father was one before he was brought as a slave to Carolina. Sometimes she taught us scraps of native African songs, and when we were able to count to ten in African we concluded that our education was complete indeed.

Fishburne, *Belvidere*, p. 25.

AS3. A New York *Times* report of the commencement exercises at Hampton Institute in 1875 told of a speech made by Joseph Towe, "a full-blooded negro from North Carolina," on "Old Time Music of the Negroes":

He stated that the beautiful melodies [spirituals?] which so much delighted every lover of music when sung by the negroes were derived from native African airs, and that an old negro still lived in North Carolina who spoke the African languages, and knew more of these melodies than any other negro in the South. . . . The student stated, what no doubt is true, that as the negroes are emancipated and become educated, they are dropping this old music which belongs to the days of slavery, and that, unless they are preserved in type, these sweet melodies are destined to entirely pass away.

New York *Times*, June 15, 1875, reprinted in Washington, *Papers*, II, 58–60.

AS4. Many southern whites were depressed by the rejection of white pastors by the blacks after Emancipation, one of them commenting on the situation of the Reverend Alexander Glennie, English rector of All Saints Parish in Waccamaw,

South Carolina: "Strange to say, after the Civil War, no negroes listened to his preaching, but would shout and sing after their own fashion, and surround themselves with their old African superstitions." (Alston, *Rice Planter and Sportsman*, p. 48.)

AS5. A description of John Canoe in Jamaica appears in Long's *History* (II, 424): "In the towns, during Christmas holidays, they have several tall robust fellows dressed up in grotesque habits, and a pair of ox-horns on their head, sprouting from the top of a horrid sort of vizor, or mask, which about the mouth is rendered very terrific with large boar-tusks.... He dances at every door, bellowing out John Connu! with great vehemence...." Another is in *Marly* (pp. 293–94).

Roger Abrahams sees evidence of the St. George Mummer's Play or the Christmas Bull, European peasant traditions, being superimposed on the African traditions. See his "Shaping of Folklore Traditions," pp. 461–62.

8

. . . .

Acculturated Dancing
and Associated Instruments

Despite the persistence of African dancing, European dances and instruments were known to blacks before 1700. By the beginning of the nineteenth century, black dancing accompanied by fiddle, banjo, and other instruments was a common sight in the slave states. The dancing probably combined both African and European elements, while those instruments that derived from Europe were very likely played in increasingly acculturated styles.

John Bernard, an English actor, toured the United States a number of times. Around 1800 he left Virginia for Charleston, noticing en route the passion of the slaves for dancing:

> The negroes have . . . been . . . known to walk five or six miles after a hard day's work to enjoy the pleasures of flinging about their hands, heads, and legs to the music of a banjo, in a manner that threatened each limb with dislocation. [He observed a dance at which the Negroes] laughed, jumped, danced, and sang all their favorite ditties—"The Praise of Bumbo," "Virginny Nigger Berry Good," "I Lost My Shoe in an Old Canoe," etc., etc.[1]

(None of these songs has been traced.)

Evidence to prove that slaves danced may seem wholly unnecessary, but responsible witnesses seriously maintained that slaves did *not* dance, but only sang hymns. This contradiction grew in part

1. John Bernard, *Retrospections*, pp. 207, 214.

from religious opposition to dancing (to be discussed later) and from the antislavery axiom that slaves were unhappy, from which it was believed to follow that they did not dance. Proslavery advocates, on the other hand, cited the dancing of the slaves as proof that they were the happiest people on earth. Neither position was wholly wrong: slaves were unhappy, but they danced just the same—to forget their misery, to derive fresh strength in order to survive, and to obtain release from the frustrations and tensions of their daily existence. Dancing before 1800 was documented in preceding chapters; later accounts reported dancing in Raleigh, North Carolina, in 1815; in Red Church, Louisiana, in June, 1822; and in many other parts of the South until the outbreak of the Civil War.[2] (AS 1) Proslavery novels regularly featured slave dancing, but their credibility as evidence is questionable. While it seems likely that the stricter evangelical sects' prohibition of secular dancing may have led to the development of the "shout," and that secular dancing became less pervasive as the antebellum period drew to a close, it never stopped completely.

Even in the Sea Islands, where numerous witnesses agreed that by 1862 secular music had virtually disappeared, a report of a dance has been found. The manuscript, a handwritten newspaper compiled for the author's family at home in the North, was impressively entitled "The Port Royal Gazette." Its "editor," Isaac W. Brinckerhoff, a lay missionary, went south with the first group of "occupation" teachers and superintendents, leaving New York on March 5, 1862. On March 15 he wrote from Beaufort, South Carolina:

> One means of amusement to which the Negroes, the irreligious portion of them, are addicted, is that of the dance. . . . A party of us strolled out by early moonlight to find the dance. We found it in one of the Negro huts—a room ten feet by twelve. The congregation consisted of about twenty-five blacks. One was fiddling, another was making time upon the floor with two sticks, & two were dancing. The ease with which the dancers handled their heels, so to speak, was astonishing. . . . From appearances one would judge that these poor blacks knew no other joy. O that the light of civilization & Christianity may soon enter their darkened minds.[3]

In 1862 slave dancing was observed in Chatham County, North Carolina, in the camp of the First South Carolina Volunteers near

2. *Raleigh Register*, Feb. 10, 1815, quoted in Guion Griffis Johnson, *Ante-bellum North Carolina*, p. 701; Teas, "Trading Trip," p. 391.

3. Isaac W. Brinckerhoff, "The Port Royal Gazette," I, no. 4 (MS, Rutgers University Library), pp. [2–3].

Beaufort, and in Augusta, Georgia. In this last instance a slave's irrepressible desire to jig betrayed him to the authorities, who commandeered him to work on Confederate fortifications.[4] Finally a Yankee officer recruiting for black regiments wrote in his diary on May 22, 1864: "We have found that Sunday is the best time to recruit as the darkeys have places where they all come together to have a dance or 'shindig,' as it is called and . . . gather from the distance of five or six miles."[5] So, despite the unquestionable influence of the evangelical sects, dancing continued throughout the antebellum period and during the war itself.

PATTING JUBA

Handclapping to mark rhythm was a staple element in African music, reported by European travelers with convincing frequency. In 1621 Richard Jobson wrote of the circle surrounding the dancers, "the standers by seeme to grace the dancer, by clapping their hands together after the manner of keeping time. . . ."[6] The practice known as "patting juba" was an extension and elaboration of simple handclapping, raising it to the level of a self-contained accompaniment for dancing. It seems quite likely that the prohibition of drums in the colonies contributed to the development of this less threatening rhythmic device. Its existence in Africa or in the West Indies has not been investigated, but the absence of any reference to it in Frederic Cassidy's comprehensive *Dictionary of Jamaican English*, either under "juba" or "patting," certainly implies that the practice was unknown by that name in that island. Although patting has been described throughout the southern United States, it was not associated with the minstrel threatre. No one appears to have claimed that juba was really an archaic English practice.

From its name and its limited resources—"striking the hands on the knees, then striking the hands together, then striking the right shoulder with one hand, the left with the other—all the while keeping time with the feet, and singing"[7]—patting might be assumed to be very old. No eighteenth-century descriptions of it have been found, however; the earliest known reference to the practice dates from the 1820's. Henry Bibb, who was born in May, 1815, to a slave mother in Shelby County, Kentucky, deplored the encouragement

4. Tyson, *Institution of Slavery*, pp. 12–13; Higginson, *Army Life*, pp. 23–24; Morgan, *How It Was*, p. 120.
5. Henry Whitney, 2d Lieut., 45th U.S. Colored Troops, Diary (MS, Rutgers University Library), pp. 61–62.
6. Jobson, *Golden Trade*, p. 107.
7. Northup, *Twelve Years a Slave*, p. 219.

On the other hand, every one who has noticed a Southern negro's "patting" will have been apt to hear an
effect of the same nature as in Haydn's movement,
produced by omitting the stroke, of foot or of hand,
which the hearer expects to fall on the accented note at
the first of the bar, thus :

Patting Juba, as notated by Sidney Lanier in *The Science of English Verse.* New
York: C. Scribner's Sons, 1880, p. 189. Courtesy of the Joseph Regenstein Library,
University of Chicago.

by the slaveholders of secular amusements, such as dancing, patting
"juber," singing, and playing the banjo.[8]

By the 1830's serious attention was being paid to its rhythmic
patterns, not by musicians, but by poets who were fascinated by its
metrical complexities. On December 5, 1835, Beverly Tucker wrote
to Edgar Allan Poe:

> I do not know to what to liken those occasional departures from regular
> metre which are so fascinating. They are more to my ear like that
> marvellous performance—"clapping Juba," than anything else. The beat
> is capriciously irregular; there is no attempt to keep time to *all* the
> notes, but then it comes so pat & so distinct that the cadence is never
> lost. . . . Such irregularities are like rests and grace notes. They must be
> so managed as neither to hasten or retard the beat. The time of the bar
> must be the same, no matter how many notes are in it.[9]

Another of Poe's friends, Thomas Holly Chivers, was also taken
with "a Jig which must be accompanied by a measured clapping of
the thighs and alternately on each other. . . . There is no such
rhythm as this in the Greek Poetry—nor, in fact, in any other Nation
under the sun. There is no dance in the world like that of Juba—the
name of that [illegible] provoking jig . . . the very climax of
jocularity. . . ."[10] And Sidney Lanier, in discussing the function of
pauses in poetry, found "Juba" a potent example:

> I have heard a Southern plantation "hand," in "patting Juba" for a
> comrade to dance by, venture upon quite complex successions of
> rhythm, not hesitating to syncopate, to change the rhythmic accent for
> a moment, or to indulge in other highly-specialized variations of the

8. Bibb, *Narrative*, p. 23.
9. Poe, *Complete Works*, XVII, 22.
10. Woodberry, ed., "Poe-Chivers Papers," p. 555.

current rhythmus. Here music . . . is in its rudest form, consisting of rhythm alone; for the patting is done with hands and feet, and of course no change of pitch or of tone-color is possible.[11]

One William B. Smith reported a persimmon beer dance from Prince Edward County, Virginia, some years before 1838. At that event were "two athletic blacks . . . clapping *Juber* to the notes of the banjor. . . . I have never seen Juber clapped to the banjor before. . . . The clappers rested the right foot on the heel, and its clap on the floor was in perfect unison with the notes of the banjor, and palms of the hands on the corresponding extremities. . . ." The account included the words of a song, beginning "Juber up and Juber down, Juber all around de town."[12]

A graphic description of "patting juba" from 1851 was written by Lewis Paine, who was born in Smithfield, Rhode Island, in 1819 and went to work in Upson County, Georgia, in the summer of 1841:

> Some one calls for a fiddle—but if one is not to be found, some one "pats juber." This is done by placing one foot a little in advance of the other, raising the ball of the foot from the ground, and striking it in regular time, while, in connection, the hands are struck slightly together, and then upon the thighs. In this way they make the most curious noise, yet in such perfect order, it furnishes music to dance by. . . . It is really astonishing to witness the rapidity of their motions, their accurate time, and the precision of their music and dance. I have never seen it equaled in my life.[13]

"Patting" was reported in Mississippi in 1851; in Louisiana in the 1850's by Solomon Northup; near Granada, Mississippi, in 1858; in Newbern, North Carolina, in 1862; and on Craney Island, Virginia, near Norfolk, in 1863.[14] Other reports, not restricted to any particular locale, have also been found. For example: "The plantation slaves . . . Generally . . . have no instruments, but dance to the tunes and words of a leader, keeping time by striking their hands against the thighs, and patting the right foot. . . ."[15] A description in a novel conformed to the details found in firsthand reports:

> Now the dancing began in good earnest. . . . As they were disappointed about the violin they had expected, one of the negroes stood . . . to "*pat*

11. Lanier, *Science of English Verse*, pp. 186–87, 247.

12. William B. Smith, "Persimmon Tree and Beer Dance," pp. 59–60. See also an extended description of a Juber dance in an autobiographical novel, Hungerford, *Old Plantation*, pp. 196–99.

13. Paine, *Six Years*, pp. 179–80.

14. "A Mississippi Planter," "Management of Negroes," p. 625; Venable, "Down South," p. 497; "Extracts from a letter written by a Private"; Swint, ed., *Dear Ones*, pp. 89–90, letter dated Sept. 30, 1863.

15. John Dixon Long, *Pictures of Slavery*, p. 18.

juber." This is much the same thing we have seen among the negroes of Nubia and the Upper Nile. One foot, resting on the heel, is brought a little in advance of the other, and the ball is made to strike, or pat in regular time; while, as an accompaniment, the hands are struck smartly together, and then upon the thighs. In all the sounds, and the motions that respond to them, there is such perfect time, as only the negro could preserve, with these simple means.[16]

An intermediate stage between "patting" and the use of instruments, not on a cultural scale but as a matter of expediency, has already been mentioned in connection with dancing—"making time upon the floor with two sticks." William Cullen Bryant saw a dance in Barnwell District, South Carolina, on March 29, 1843, where one of the Negroes provided music for the others by "whistling, and beating time with two sticks upon the floor."[17] Such sticks were used not only when no instruments were available, but also to supplement instruments. Thus at Eutaw plantation in South Carolina during the Civil War "Every day of Christmas week, in the afternoon, the negroes danced in the broad piazza until late at night, the orchestra consisting of two fiddlers, one man with bones, and another had sticks with which he kept time on the floor, and sometimes singing."[18] Dancing, acculturated to an unknown degree, continued through the Civil War, with or without instrumental accompaniment. The types of instruments used will now be considered.

DRUMS, QUILLS, BANJO, BONES, TRIANGLE, TAMBOURINE

In the discussion of African survivals, the persistence of drums was described. During the antebellum period drums were rarely mentioned in connection with acculturated music, except in a negative sense. For example, the Georgia legal code of 1845 reiterated the ban on "drums, horns, or other loud instruments, which may call together or give sign or notice to one another of their wicked designs and intentions";[19] this passage dates back to the South Carolina Slave Act of 1740, and to still earlier Codes Noir in the West Indies. As already mentioned, drums after dark signaled slave insurrection in South Carolina as late as 1860. The omnipresent drums of the West Indies were not heard on the mainland—not even at slave dances, where other percussive devices (sticks, bones, tambourines, and clapping) had to take their place.

16. [McDougall,] *Shahmah*, pp. 276–77.
17. Bryant, *Letters*, pp. 86–87.
18. Coxe, *Memories*, p. 89.
19. Georgia, Laws, Statutes, etc., *Codification*, p. 813. Statutes for other states were not examined.

Panpipes, or quills, as they were called by the Negroes, are widely found in Negro Africa,[20] and Harold Courlander included them among the instruments discussed in his *Negro Folk Music, U.S.A.*, where he complained about their lack of documentation. Some contemporary descriptions for what Courlander described as "elementary panpipes, usually made of reeds,"[21] exist in the Slave Narrative Collection. A former slave who was born near Shreveport in 1850 told how to make one: "We plays de quill, made from willow stalk when de sap am up. You takes de stick, and pounds de bark loose and slips it off, den split de wood in one end and down one side, puts holes in de bark, and put it back on de stick. De quill plays like de flute."[22] There must have been several varieties of panpipes, of which this was only one. Courlander described another: "Three or four reeds were used, with the player hooting an occasional tone beyond their range." "The various reeds are not joined, but are held together in the hand in playing position." That kind of quill was reported by James Bolton of Oglethorpe County, Georgia:

> After supper we used to gather around and knock tin buckets and pans. We beat them like drums. Some used their fingers, and some used sticks for to make the drum sounds and most always somebody blowed on quills. Quills was a row of whistles made out of reeds or sometimes they made them out of bark. Every whistle in the row was a diffunt tone, and you could play any kind of tune you wants if you had a good row of quills they sure did sound sweet.[23] (AS 2)

The early history of the banjo has been presented, a table of sources in chronological order is given in an appendix, and a more detailed account is given elsewhere.[24] After 1810 the banjo continued to be mentioned frequently, but descriptions of it were only occasional, as if it were too well known to require detailed reports. An 1832 novel of plantation life, *Swallow Barn*, featured a slave "banjoe" player who could both improvise and sing requested songs, performing for the dancing of his fellow slaves and serenading the young ladies of the household.[25] Elements that contributed to the minstrel theatre were clearly foreshadowed here. Dancing to the music of the banjo was a commonplace in antebellum fiction, travel accounts, and genre paintings, both before and after the minstrels

20. Nettl, *Folk and Traditional Music*, p. 140.
21. Courlander, *Negro Folk Music*, p. 217.
22. Yetman, "*Peculiar Institution*," p. 170, interview with Bill Homer.
23. Courlander, *Negro Folk Music*; interview with James Bolton by Sarah Hall at Athens, Ga., in 1937, in Killion and Waller, eds., *Slavery Time*, pp. 24–25.
24. Epstein, "Folk Banjo."
25. Kennedy, *Swallow Barn*, I, 110–13.

appeared on the American scene; but reports of how a banjo was made using a gourd or, more rarely, wood, were less frequent. A former slave who reached Canada in 1855 wrote of life in King George County, Virginia, before he escaped in the summer of 1854: "We generally made our own banjos and fiddles. . . . When we made a banjo we would first of all catch what we called a ground hog, known in the north as a woodchuck. After tanning his hide, it would be stretched over a piece of timber fashioned like a cheese box. . . ."[26]

Henri Herz, the pianist who toured the United States from 1845 to 1851, was much impressed with the banjo—"the favorite instrument of the blacks in the United States, just as the marimba is of the blacks in Brazil."[27] Descriptions of the method for making a banjo appeared in a novel set on a plantation between New Orleans and Baton Rouge in May, 1851 [28] (where the *banza* was not unlike that described by Labat in 1698), and in the autobiography of John Allen Wyeth, who was taught how to make a banjo at the age of eleven in 1856:

> The banjo was the real musical instrument of the Southern negroes, not the fancy silver and nickel rimmed article with frets seen now on the minstrel stage or in the shops, but a very crude device, which I believe to be of native origin. . . . [It] was made from a large gourd with a long straight neck. . . . The bowl of the gourd was cut away on a plane level with the surface of the neck, the seed and contents removed, and over this, like a drumhead, a freshly tanned coon-skin was stretched, fastened, and allowed to dry. The five strings of home-made materials passing from the apron behind over a small bridge near the middle of the drumhead were attached to the keys in proper position on the neck.[29]

Fretless banjos are still made by rural musicians in Virginia and the Carolinas.[30]

The word "banjo" was also applied to an instrumental ensemble by a British traveler, Robert Playfair, who wrote from "Virginia Springs" on Sunday, July 30, 1848:

> Sometimes a little quadrille was made up from the juniors of the party, when three negro musicians were sent for to play the banjo, as it is called, which consisted of three instruments, a violin, a tambourine, I think, and the third the skull of an ass, played upon by a collar-bone of the same animal, sounding not unlike the Spanish castanets.

26. [Goldie,] *Sunshine and Shadow*, p. 62.
27. Herz, *Travels*, p. 75.
28. Mercier, *L'Habitation*, p. 52.
29. Wyeth, *With Sabre and Scalpel*, pp. 61–62.
30. Cf. J. Roderick Moore, "Folk Crafts," pp. 22–29; and Glassie, *Pattern in Material Folk Culture*, p. 24.

> Those men were probably slaves . . . they seemed clever, good-humoured, and contented.[31]

It is curious that this instrumental combination did not include a banjo.

The development of the commercial banjo during the nineteenth century and its popularization by the minstrel theatre are related to black folk music, but are not integral parts of it.[32]

The banjo became associated exclusively with the minstrel theatre in the popular mind, and its African origins were forgotten; likewise the bones, triangle, and tambourine were part of the caricature of blacks that white men created to entertain other white men. The supposition that the early minstrel theatre was modeled on improvised slave entertainments is credible but not yet proven. In any case, the minstrel theatre is outside the scope of black folk music, however closely it may have been related. The claim that Negroes never played bones, triangle, or tambourine is relevant and can be disproved. Earlier, in a discussion of the John Canoe festival in North Carolina, the instruments that were described included "triangles and jawbones," while recollections of slave dances in Louisiana also included jawbones played along with violins and other instruments. Bernhard Karl, Duke of Saxe-Weimar-Eisenach, attended a ball on a plantation near Columbia, South Carolina, in December, 1825, surely well before the advent of the minstrel theatre. "I found there a numerous and splendid society. But the music was of a singular kind; for the blacks, who two days ago played very well at the governor's, were now drunk, and could not make their appearance. This was the reason that the whole music consisted of two violins and a tamborine. . . ."[33] A Northerner's letter from Savannah, Georgia, dated March 28, 1853, commented on the Negroes: "Two accomplishments they all have—whistling and playing on the bones—both of which are going on under my window at this moment, as they always do."[34]

FIDDLERS

Black slaves' talent and skill on European instruments, particularly the fiddle, were demonstrated before 1700, and black fiddlers be-

31. Playfair, *Recollections*, p. 174. No other use of "banjo" in this way has been found; and it is possible that Playfair misunderstood his informants.
32. Arthur Woodward, "Joel Sweeney," pp. [7]-[11]. Cf. Toll, *Blacking Up*, p. 44.
33. Bernhard Karl, *Travels*, I, 212.
34. [Pyle?,] "Letters," pp. 125–26. Reprinted in Schwaab, ed., *Travels*, II, 528.

came as pervasive a part of the plantation legend as black banjo players. But there was more depth to the careers of black performers than the minstrel troupes would lead one to suspect, or than the plantation myth would allow. These obscure musicians at times achieved what would have been a professional status if their earnings had remained in their own hands. Many of them earned a reputation for excellence that extended for miles around. Some had homemade fiddles, and others, store-bought ones, but most were encouraged by their masters to play for the dancing of their fellow slaves, as well as for white visitors or dancing parties. In the rural South the slave fiddler seems to have been a necessary support to dancing and other recreations—despite the adamant disapproval of the evangelical sects who equated the Devil with fiddling, and who predicted eternal damnation for the fiddler.

An upstate New York master made a contract with his slave in the early part of the nineteenth century. The document specified, among other things, that the slave was to leave his fiddle with his master and not go fiddling except on holidays or with his master's permission.[35] In his case, his other work came first. An English traveler on his way from Augusta, Georgia, to Charleston, South Carolina, in February, 1817, stopped for the night at the only house where lodgings could be obtained for many miles. The gentleman of the house being away, his wife and three children did the honors. "In the evening a black fiddler amused us for awhile, and I danced four reels in company with the girls and their brother. The country people of Georgia and Carolina are alike fond of the violin and the dance."[36]

On occasion violins were used by slave traders. In 1822 James H. Dickey, hearing music, discovered a slave convoy marching to the sound of two violins played by the first couple.[37] His report of this incident was frequently reprinted, nowhere more effectively than in Amos Dresser's *Narrative*, where a picture of the coffle accompanied his account of his imprisonment in Sumner County, Tennessee. A local resident, rummaging through a box which he had left in a carriage,

35. Van Epps, "Slavery in Glenville, N.Y.," *Sixth Report of the Town Historian* (Glenville, N.Y., 1932), pp. 7–8, cited in Zilversmit, *First Emancipation*, p. 31.

36. Mead, *Travels*, p. 29.

37. Rankin, *Letters*, p. 46. Letter dated Sept. 30, 1824. This incident was also cited by Lydia Maria Child in her *Appeal*, p. 33. An Englishman, George William Featherstonhaugh, saw a coffle of slaves traveling toward the Mississippi River in 1834, led by slave fiddlers who played lively tunes to lift the morale of the group. See his *Excursion*, I, 46.

Chained slaves led by two fiddlers. Source: *The Anti-Slavery Record*, February, 1835, p. [13]. Courtesy of the Joseph Regenstein Library, University of Chicago.

found, among the other pamphlets, a February number of the Anti-Slavery Record, with a cut representing a drove of slaves chained, the two foremost having violins, on which they were playing—the American flag waving in the centre, whilst the slave-driver, with his whip, was urging on the rear.... In a short time it was noised about that I had been "circulating incendiary periodicals among the free colored people, and trying to excite the slaves to insurrection."... Mr. S. [the local carriage repair-man], on this occasion, told me that the scene represented in the cut was one of by no means unfrequent occurrence—that it was accurate in all its parts, and that he had witnessed it again and again. Mr. S. is himself a slaveholder, though as he says, opposed to slavery in principle . . . and one of the committee of vigilance which afterwards sat in judgment upon me.[38]

Most fiddlers, however, played for dancing. In 1833 an Englishman wrote that "every negro is a musician from his birth. A black boy will make an excellent fiddle out of a gourd and some string. . . . The supreme ambition of every negro is to procure a real violin. . . . An instrument of music seems necessary to their existence."[39] (AS 3) A similar opinion came from one Ebenezer Baldwin: "In music, it is believed that Africans have exhibited more decided marks of general or national taste than exists among the

38. Dresser, *Narrative*, pp. 6–7.
39. John Finch, *Travels*, pp. 237–38.

whites ... they have almost individually a correct ear.... The rudest of them, without teaching, whistle, and sing, and play on the jews-harp and banjo, and with a little practice master that difficult instrument, the violin...."[40] Caroline Howard Gilman was the wife of the Unitarian minister of Charleston, South Carolina; though Massachusetts bred, she adapted herself to the mores around her. Although her descriptions of blacks were more detailed than those of other antebellum Southern writers, she was still patronizing in her attitude, as shown in her account of a slave fiddler:

> We possessed the usual plantation luxury of a fiddler. I do not feel bound to say how many tunes Diggory played, nor how well a few visits to town had initiated his quick eye and ear into the tunes and figures of some newly-introduced cotillons. . . . Diggory, alas! in his musical science and dancing oratory was but a specimen of our city ball-room performers. Unacquainted with the science of music, though gifted with decided musical powers, they play antics with the "high heaven of sound," while sawing violins. . . . The South is certainly far, far behind the civilized world in music of this character, and there seems little hope of a remedy.[41] (AS 4)

What Diggory's life must have been like was told by another slave fiddler, Solomon Northup. A free Negro of New York, Northup was kidnapped in 1841 and sold into slavery which lasted until 1853, when his Northern friends were finally able to rescue him from a cotton plantation in Louisiana. Fortunately, Northup was a good fiddler.

> My master often received letters, sometimes from a distance of ten miles, requesting him to send me to play at a ball or festival of the whites. He received his compensation, and usually I also returned with many picayunes jingling in my pockets. . . .
> Alas! had it not been for my beloved violin, I scarcely can conceive how I could have endured the long years of bondage. It introduced me to great houses—relieved me of many days' labor in the field—supplied me with conveniences for my cabin—with pipes and tobacco, and extra pairs of shoes. . . . It heralded my name round the country—made me friends, who, otherwise would not have noticed me—gave me an honored seat at the yearly feasts, and secured the loudest and heartiest welcome of them all at the Christmas dance.[42]

40. Baldwin, *Observations*, p. 19.
41. Caroline Howard Gilman, *Recollections*, pp. 76–77.
42. Northup, *Twelve Years a Slave*, pp. 216–17. Northup was not unique; Gus Smith, who was born in 1845 near Jefferson City, Mo., told a Federal Writers' Project interviewer when he was 92: "In times of holidays, we always had our own musicians. Sometimes we sent ten or twelve miles for a fiddler. He'd stay a week or so in one place and den he would go on to de next farm, maybe four or five miles away, and dey had a good time for a week."—Yetman, *"Peculiar Institution,"* p. 282.

ROARING RIVER.

A REFRAIN OF THE RED RIVER PLANTATION.

"Harper's creek and roarin' ribber,
  Thar, my dear, we'll live forebber;
Den we'll go to de Ingin nation,
All I want in dis creation,
  Is pretty little wife and big plantation.

CHORUS.

Up dat oak and down dat ribber,
Two overseers and one little nigger."

Fiddle tune (?) described as being sung accompanied by patting. Source: Solomon Northup, *Twelve Years a Slave.* Auburn, N.Y.: Derby and Miller, 1853, p. [337]. Courtesy of the New York Public Library, Astor, Lenox and Tilden Foundations.

More sophisticated, better trained musicians were the cause of a legal action filed in October, 1844, in the Chancery Court of Louisville, attaching the steamboat *Pike* "to recover damages for the unauthorized transportation of . . . three slaves, Reuben, Henry and George, on board said steamboat from Louisville to Cincinnati, whence they escaped to Canada." The slaves were described as

> between nineteen and twenty-three years of age, well trained as dining room servants and scientific musicians, in which capacity they had been in the habit, for some years, of playing together on various instruments, at balls and parties . . . each of them was worth $1500. . . . They were taken on board the *Pike*, at Louisville, about the last of January, 1841, when they had with them, besides their clothes, musical instruments and books of the value of about $250; that from Cincinnati . . . they escaped to Canada, and . . . the complainant had expended from $700 to $1000 in fruitless efforts to recover them.

The defendant charged that the complainant had allowed the slaves to go to Louisville to live with one Williams, a free Negro, in order to learn music, and that afterwards he gave them written permission to accompany him to any part of the South, "even so far as New Orleans." "It appears that . . . Henry and Reuben . . . were with him once in Cincinnati, Ohio, once and perhaps twice in Madison, Indiana, and two or three times in New Albany, Indiana [i.e., in free states], playing as musicians, at balls and other entertainments." For about two years before their escape, none of them had been under the care of Williams, but "were stationed at Lexington as their headquarters, with liberty to go to the neighboring towns to play as musicians, and to give their master what they made beyond their expenses. . . ." The complainant, Mr. Graham, stated that it would cost $500 to supply their services as musicians for a single season at his hotel at Harrodsburg Springs. The judge ruled that the jury had a right in assessing damages "to take into consideration their qualities as musicians . . . their acquirements in literature as well as in music, their habits of . . . independence, the liberties which had been allowed them, and the effect of all these circumstances not only upon the value of their services, but also in generating a restlessness under restraint, and a desire of freedom. . . ."[43]

These three slaves were obviously highly skilled men, moving about and hiring their own time in a most atypical way. We know too little about slave musicians to be dogmatic, but these arrangements can hardly have been customary. In the larger towns it was not uncommon to find an advertisement like the following:

43. Catterall, *Judicial Cases*, I, 365–68.

FOR HIRE, either for the remainder of the year, or by the month, week, or job, the celebrated musician and fiddler, GEORGE WALKER. All persons desiring the services of George, are notified that they must contract for them with us, and in no case pay to him or any other person, the amount of his hire, without a written order from us.—George Walker is admitted, by common consent, to be the best leader of a band in all eastern and middle Virginia.[44]

The relation of professional musicians, who were also slaves, to black folk music in the United States is a matter which has hardly been mentioned. However, Reuben, Henry, and George of the 1844 Louisville case and George Walker were not unique. An unpublished document describes the musical education of another slave, Robin, who was the "property" of John Laurence Manning, governor of South Carolina from 1852 to 1854. Governor Manning described the training of Robin in a letter dated November 17, 1856, in response to a request for information about his musicians, who must have achieved some local reputation. The letter told of the recognition of Robin's talent while he was still a child. "Upon a shingle strung, with the hairs of the horse and with a bow made from a twig and horse hairs, Robin first gave evidence of his musical capacity; and I determined at once to cultivate whatever talent . . . he might possess." Robin was trained by two teachers, Mr. Hedwig and Mr. Traul, possibly German emigrés, about whom no information could be found.

> Under their tuitions his progress was such as to cause me great gratification. At home—without a teacher, & without any knowledge of music on my part his progress astonished myself & those of my friends who watched his improvement. I then determined to give him still further advantages, and . . . I procured the services of Mr. Dauer who for two successive summers superintended the musical education of Robin and taught beside his brothers Henry, Sanders and Edward. The three latter were taught chiefly by Robin without assistance from a superior teacher until Mr. Dauer took charge of them under whose care they have arrived at the excellence which they now exhibit. . . . A large portion of the elementary instruction of the others has been due to him [Robin], subject to the supervision of Mr. Dauer. . . .[45]

Governor Manning's letter gave no clues to the type of music played by Robin and his brothers, and there is no reason to believe that

44. Adv. of Toler & Cook, General Agents, in the *Richmond Daily Enquirer*, June 27, 1853, quoted in Bancroft, *Slave-Trading*, p. 155.
45. John Laurence Manning, letter dated "Clarendon, 17th Nov 1856," MS, South Caroliniana Library, University of South Carolina. MS, apparently a draft, with many corrections and cancellations. None of the teachers mentioned could be identified in standard music reference books.

their sphere of activities extended beyond the local neighborhood. But at least one slave became a national celebrity—Thomas Greene Bethune, popularly known as Blind Tom. While his concert career as a pianist and his published compositions place him outside the scope of a study of folk music, it may be noted that a serious study of his career is still to be written.[46]

These professional or quasi-professional musicians were able to emerge from the anonymity of slavery through a complex of circumstances that are still little understood. Between them and their fellow slaves was every possible gradation of musical experience, just as the instruments they played ranged from nothing but their bare hands and their bodies (patting juba) to combinations of instruments not usually associated with the status of slaves. For example, two Englishwomen reported from Montgomery, Alabama, in December, 1853, "about sixty negroes, all dancing . . . to the music of two violins and a banjo . . . a negro was standing on a chair, calling out what figures were to be performed in the Virginia Reel. . . ."[47]

The mass of fieldhands probably rarely heard musicians like these, who usually played for the entertainment of whites or city blacks. A fieldhand might have considered himself fortunate had he worked for the planter who contributed his views on management to De Bow's Review: "I must not omit to mention that I have a good fiddler, and keep him well supplied with cat-gut, and I make it his duty to play for the Negroes every Saturday night until 12 o'clock. . . . Charley's fiddle is always accompanied with Ihurod on the triangle and Sam to 'pat.' "[48] "A Small Farmer" contributed the third article to this series, saying in part: "I have a fiddle in my quarters, and though some of my good old brethren in the church would think hard of me, yet I allow dancing; ay, I buy the fiddle and encourage it. . . . I know the rebuke in store about dancing, but I cannot help it. I believe Negroes will be better disposed this way than any other."[49]

A former slave from Clarksdale, Mississippi, reported that "De same old fiddler played for us dat played for de white folks."[50] Another ex-slave, this time from Georgia, recalled that "music was furnished by slaves who were able to play the banjo or the fiddle," commenting also that the slaves "usually bought these instruments

46. Cf. The Nation 1 (Aug. 10, 1865): 162; and (Oct. 19, 1865): 508. Geneva Southall has announced that she is writing just such a study. See her "Blind Tom," p. [141].
47. Jane M. and Marion Turnbull, American Photographs, II, [60]–72.
48. "A Mississippi Planter," "Management of Negroes," p. 625.
49. "A Small Farmer," "Art. III—Management of Negroes," pp. 371–72.
50. Yetman, "Peculiar Institution," p. 190.

themselves and in some cases the master bought them," but he had made his own.[51]

The accounts cited are all more or less authentic, in contrast to the numerous novels, written as replies to *Uncle Tom's Cabin*, that hoped to demonstrate the great happiness of the slaves by picturing them dancing and singing. A good example of this type of effusion was Martha Haines Butt's *Antifanaticism: A Tale of the South* (Philadelphia: Lippincott, Grambo, 1853).

In addition to the instruments that were widely associated with the Negroes, slaves were sometimes described as playing unusual instruments, such as bagpipes. The highlight of the wedding of Caroline Wylly to James Hamilton Couper in December, 1827, was reputed to have been the playing of Johnny, "Mr. Couper's Negro choral man—'a marvel, a wonder' who played the bagpipes."[52]

In moments of stress, the sound of a cavalry trumpet could be mistaken for that made by "those long tubes used by boatmen." During the intense excitement around the so-called Denmark Vesey insurrection, a communication appeared in the Charleston *Courier* for June 21, 1822, telling the story of a slave named Billy; he had been unjustly accused of blowing his boatman's horn to arouse the troops, who took the sound for the signal of an uprising. In reality the trumpet blast came from a drunken trumpeter who wished to see what effect a blast of his horn might have. Although Billy was found asleep, and "no evidence was given whatever as to a motive for sounding the horn, and the horn was actually found covered and even filled with cobwebs," he was condemned to death and hung.[53]

INSTRUMENTAL COMBINATIONS

Plantation instrumental combinations varied according to the material at hand. In 1806 Thomas Ashe visited a ball in Wheeling, where music was provided by "two bangies, played by negroes . . . and a lute . . . [played by] a Chickasaw."[54] A fictional account of a "barbacue," published in 1824, specified music for dancing played by "two fiddlers and one fifer, all black."[55]

The militia fifers and drummers of the eighteenth century led to

---

51. Federal Writers' Project, *Slave Narratives*, "Georgia Narratives," IV, pt. 4, p. 194.
52. Fancher, *Lost Legacy*, pp. 152–53.
53. Lofton, *Insurrection*, pp. 162–65. See also Wade, "Vesey Plot," in Hoover, ed., *Understanding Negro History*, p. 80.
54. Ashe, *Travels*, p. 100.
55. [Tucker,] *Valley of Shenandoah*, II, 121.

all-black bands early in the nineteenth century. The professional bands of the northern cities, such as Frank Johnson's (AS 5), were clearly not composed of folk musicians, but even in the South such bands were not unknown. In Shreveport an exception was made to the rigorous regulations governing the night-time meetings of slaves in order to permit evening practice of the Shreveport Ethiopian Band, and in Montgomery a Negro band was trained by a musician hired by four white citizens.[56] (AS 6)

It is not now known how many of these regularly organized black bands existed during the nineteenth century, but impromptu instrumental groups must have been even more common. "Two negroes playing on violins, and a third upon a bass" played for dancing in Lebanon Springs [New York or Massachusetts?] in July, 1832.[57] Caroline Howard Gilman, the Charleston novelist who was quoted on slave fiddlers, also described a party where the music was provided by "violins, harsh clarinets, jingling tambarines, crashing triangles, with the occasional climax of a *base* drum."[58] A more primitive, more African combination was observed in middle Florida in 1837–38: "The orchestra is provided with a sort of mandolin made of a gourd, and a horse's jaw bone, the teeth of which are scraped with a hollow stick."[59]

In 1843 Henry Benjamin Whipple, future Bishop of Minnesota, visited St. Marys, Georgia, while on a trip for his health. In his journal he recorded a lively description of the Christmas festivities on the plantation of General Clinch. Tambourine and fiddle provided music for a dance, and on the twenty-seventh the Negroes had a parade, with a band composed of "3 fiddles, 1 tenor & 1 bass drum, 2 triangles & 2 tamborines."[60] In a rose-colored view of slavery, the author described a group led by a fiddler which also included a banjo, "hollow sticks, like castanets, but five times as large, hollow, and more musical; and . . . a base on . . . [a] hollow drum."[61] This purported to describe scenes in Tennessee; contemporary reminiscences of Orange County, North Carolina, recalled an open air dance for whites, with a black band composed of two fiddles, flute, banjo, triangle, and castanets.[62] A fictional account of a black

56. Wood, ed., *Charter . . . and Laws of . . . Shreveport*, p. 54, quoted in Taylor, *Negro Slavery*, pp. 228–29; Sellers, *Slavery in Alabama*, p. 121.
57. Coke, *Subaltern's Furlough*, I, 204.
58. Caroline Howard Gilman, *Recollections*, p. 76.
59. Castelnau, "Essay on Middle Florida," p. 243.
60. Whipple, *Southern Diary*, pp. 50–51.
61. Ingraham, *Sunny South*, p. 106.
62. Avirett, *Old Plantation*, p. 99.

Negro dance sketched by Lewis Miller of York, Pa., while on a trip to Virginia in 1853. Instruments both European (fiddle) and African (banjo and bones); posture and dance steps, more Europeanized than in the eighteenth-century watercolor of *The Old Plantation*; dress, European. Courtesy of the Virginia State Library.

Christmas celebration in Louisiana in 1861 called for fiddle, two banjos, tambourine, tin pan, and "*kettle*-drum."[63]

Southern whites' reminiscences of antebellum days sometimes refer to the instruments played by slaves:

> My grandfather, Alfred Hatch . . . [lived at] His Arcola plantation, of three thousand acres . . . on the Warrior River, six miles above Demopolis [Alabama?]. . . . At night Jim Pritchett with his fiddle, Mingo with his triangle, and Mose with his banjo, came up from the quarters, and made music for the happy belles and beaux. They danced cotillions and the Lancers, winding up with the Virginia Reel. . . . Jim was a noted mimic, as well as a fiddler, and usually wound up with an improvisation of his own, which he called "The Dying Coon," in which his voice added to the witchery of his bow the shouts of the hunters, the baying of the dogs and the snarls and dying wail of the fighting [rac]coon.[64]

Another reminiscence told of slave dances in South Carolina with an "orchestra consisting of two fiddlers, one man with bones and another had sticks with which he kept time on the floor."[65] A long tribute to slave musicians appeared in the Richmond *Times-Dispatch* in 1921, recalling such groups as fiddle, banjo, and tambourine ("A trio of this kind . . . furnished all the music required at the average dancing parties"), or "a string band of four violins, one fiddle (or bass, I suppose they called it), two banjos, two tambourines and mandolin." However, most of the dances were "one-fiddle" affairs. The author commented that, while most of these musicians played by ear, some "were taught . . . to play by note and do sight reading well enough to pick up a new piece of music and play it at once."[66] The former slaves also recalled with affection the music that brightened what leisure time they had: "Slaves usually amused themselves by . . . playing music on tin cans, Jew's harps, or any kind of instrument which they could get that would produce sound . . . a banjo . . . an accordion . . . fiddles, fifes and sometimes a drum. This same music was often carried to the home of the master when company came."[67]

63. Victor, *Maum Guinea*, p. 37.
64. Benners, *Slavery and Its Results*, pp. 22, 25–26.
65. Coxe, *Memories*, p. 89.
66. Bryce, "Dusky 'Fiddlers.' "
67. Cade, "Out of the Mouths of Ex-Slaves," pp. 333–34. Similar reports recur in the slave narratives collected by the Federal Writers' Project.

ADDITIONAL SOURCES

AS1. Other slave dances were reported near Richmond, Virginia, at Christmas, 1832 (Henry, "Yankee Schoolmistress," p. 129); on St. Simon's Island, Georgia, in 1838–39 (Kemble, *Journal*, pp. 96–97); near Natchez in 1849 ([Robinson,] "Negro Slavery," p. 382); in Kentucky in 1850 (Drake, *Letters*, pp. 16–17); and in Mobile in 1851 (*Mobile Daily Advertiser*, Nov. 14, 1851, quoted in Wade, *Slavery in Cities*, pp. 90, 104).

The case of the *State of North Carolina* v. *Boyce* in December, 1849, illustrated a clash between overzealous patrollers and a more tolerant planter over dancing. A witness, one Roberts, stated that on Christmas night, 1846,

> he and other patrollers went to the defendant's plantation between 8 and 9 o'clock . . . [in] the house in which Boyce lived, [they] found therein twelve or fifteen negroes of whom one was fiddling, and the others dancing . . . that Boyce was in the house . . . and several children of the defendant . . . were enjoying themselves in the dance with the negroes. . . .

Despite the presence of Boyce and his children, the patrol felt justified in whipping the Negroes—an opinion not shared by the judge, who stated: "It would really be a source of regret, if contrary to common custom it were to be denied to slaves, in the intervals between their toils, to indulge in mirthful pastimes . . . children of the family might, in Christmas times, without the least impropriety, countenance the festivities of the old servants of the family by witnessing, and even mingling in them." Quoted in Catterall, *Judicial Cases*, II, 139–41.

AS2. Bolton continued: "Saturday night we played and danced, sometimes in the cabins and sometimes in the yards. . . . We danced the 'Turkey Trot' and 'Buzzard Lope,' and how we did love to dance the 'Mary Jane.' We would get in a ring and when the music started we would begin working our foots while we sang, 'You steal my true love, an' I steal your'en' " (*ibid.*, p. 25).

Another former slave, Georgia Baker, born in Taliaferro County, Georgia, recalled Saturday nights "when slaves got together and danced. George blowed the quills, and he sure could blow grand dance music on them" (*ibid.*, p. 11).

AS3. The Slave Narrative Collection includes the reminiscences of Henry Wright, ninety-nine years old, who described making a fiddle: "I made a fiddle out of a large sized gourd—a long wooden handle was used as a neck, and the hair from a horse's tail was used for the bow. The strings were made of cat-gut." (Georgia Narratives, IV, pt. 4, p. 200).

AS4. Diggory was also described in Mrs. Gilman's magazine for children, *The Southern Rose*, for January 9, 1836, where he was accompanied by "a tall, stout, fellow beating a triangle, and another drumming with two long sticks on a piece of wood." The description of the dancing includes many African elements. See Saint-Amand, *Balcony in Charleston*, p. 57. The tradition of slave fiddlers continued into the Civil War; witness the report of an Englishman from "Conwayboro', Norry Co., N. E. South Carolina. . . . Here the coachman, 'Prince,' is a capital fiddler; his favourite tunes are 'Dixie Land' and country dances" (Malet, *Errand to the South*, p. 49). Free Negroes traditionally had also been fiddlers, according to Bassett, *Slavery in North Carolina*, p. 359.

AS5. William J. Brown, born in Providence, Rhode Island, in 1814, tried to organize a band among his friends during his teens, modelling his plans on the "colored band, led by Henry [Frank?] Johnson," visiting Providence from Philadelphia (*Life*, pp. 54–81). A writer in 1834 commented, "They have formed many superior bands, and are much patronized for their skill in our larger cities" (Baldwin, *Observations*, p. 19). And a music journal reminisced in 1883, "Forty years ago nearly every regimental band in New York was composed of black musicians" (*American Art Journal* 39 [May 19, 1883]: 80).

AS6. During the Civil War, good bands were considered all but essential to the black regiments:

> An old officer of the *Regular* army told me yesterday that with a good band of music he could lead the 1st South Carolina Regiment up to and over any breastworks in the land which was within the range of possibility to carry. If we are to have a large army of negroes—and I have not the least doubt we are—it will be wise to furnish every regiment with a good band. Brass instruments would be better, but if they cannot be had, let a full drum corps be provided . . . the sanitary condition of the troops who are accustomed every day or two to listen to good music, is much better than those who hear nothing but the discordant strains of cracked drums and split fifes. It was poor economy to take from the army the good bands most of the regiments brought with them. . . . If music is a necessity to the white soldier, much more so will it prove to the negro. On long marches and fatiguing campaigns it will prove meat and drink . . . [N.Y.] Tribune.

Reprinted in *National Anti-Slavery Standard* 23 (Mar. 21, 1863), p. [3], col. 3–4.

9

. . . .

Worksongs

FIELD WORK AND DOMESTIC CHORES

After 1800, descriptions of worksongs became more numerous, associated with a variety of different occupations ranging from field labor through domestic chores such as flailing rice, grinding hominy, spinning, and making baskets, to more industrial employments such as loading cargo, processing hemp or tobacco, and firing engines. Most common among contemporary reports were boat songs to regulate rowing, and corn or other harvest songs. Some of these songs provided rhythmic regulation of the rate of labor; others passed the time and relieved boredom, but all of them provided fuel for the perennial argument about whether the slaves were happy. Apologists for the "peculiar institution" seemed compelled to convince the world that the slaves were not only well fed and healthy, but the happiest people in the world. An early response to this defense of slavery presented a position that would recur in abolitionist literature:

> But we are further told that slaves show by their actions that they are happy. They sing, laugh, dance and make merry. He is a shallow smatterer in human nature, who does not understand this, that mirth is often rather the effort of the mind to throw off trouble than the evidence of happiness. It shows the man wishes to be happy, and is trying for it, and is oftener the means of use to get it than the proof that it exists. . . . In illustration of this fact we insert a fact from Dr. Channing of Boston.

"I once passed a colored woman at work on a plantation, who was singing apparently with *animation*, and whose general manners would have led me to set her down as the happiest of the gang. I said to her, your work seems pleasant to you. She replied, no, massa. Supposing that she referred to something particularly disagreeable in her immediate occupation, I said to her, tell me then, what part of your work is not pleasant She answered with emphasis—'No part pleasant. We forced to do it.' "[1] (AS 1)

There is evidence that slave masters regarded the singing of their slaves as an inducement to greater exertion. In an essay entitled "Management of Negroes" and signed Agricola, the author wrote: "When at work I have no objection to their whistling or singing some lively tune, but no *drawling* tunes are allowed in the field, for their motions are almost certain to keep time with the music."[2] This would seem to confirm Fanny Kemble's statement, although she was anathema to slaveholders:

> I have heard that many of the masters and overseers on these plantations prohibit melancholy tunes or words, and encourage nothing but cheerful music and senseless words, deprecating the effect of sadder strains upon the slaves, whose peculiar musical sensibility might be expected to make them especially excitable by any songs of a plaintive character, and having any reference to their particular hardships. If it is true, I think it a judicious precaution enough. . . .[3]

Frederick Douglass summed up his view of the matter:

> Slaves are generally expected to sing as well as to work. A silent slave is not liked by masters or overseers. *"Make a noise,"* *"make a noise,"* and *"bear a hand,"* are the words usually addressed to the slaves when there is silence amongst them. This may account for the almost constant singing heard in the southern states. There was, generally, more or less singing among the teamsters, as it was one means of letting the overseer know where they were, and that they were moving on with the work.[4]

A former slave recalled that not all the songs were nonsensical. "Boss like for de slaves to sing while workin'. We had a jackleg slave preacher who's hist de tunes. Some was spirituals."[5]

Not many descriptions of field hands singing at work have been found, possibly because the travelers who wrote so many of the accounts rarely saw them at work. But a description written by a planter in the Leeward Islands would have been equally appropriate

1. Aaron, a Slave, *Light a Truth of Slavery*, pp. 17–18.
2. Agricola, "Management of Negroes," p. 361.
3. Kemble, *Journal*, p. 129.
4. Douglass, *My Bondage*, p. 97.
5. Yetman, *"Peculiar Institution,"* pp. 221–22, narrative of Andy Marion of South Carolina, born in 1844.

for the mainland: "The slaves then work in a long string, and follow each other in regular order. Some one takes the lead and breaks out with a song, to which there is always a chorus. In this they all join, and the union of such a number of voices, produces a very animated and pleasing effect."[6] Only one description has been found of slaves singing in the cotton fields, although no movie of plantation life would have been considered complete without such music:

> From Branchville we took the direct route to Charleston by way of the South Carolina Railroad. . . . We saw cotton fields stretching away on either side as we passed . . . The negroes were at work in the fields, picking cotton and stowing it in long baskets. [Most accounts mentioned long bags tied to the pickers' waists.] They worked in gangs, or companies. . . . While at work in the cotton fields, the slaves often sing some wild, simple melody, by way of mutual cheer, which usually ends in a chorus, in which all join with a right hearty good will, in a key so loud as to be heard from one plantation to another, and the welkin is made to ring for miles with musical echoes. . . . I could not comprehend the words of the songs or choruses. . . .[7]

Another description of fieldhands singing was from a letter written in St. Helena Island, off the South Carolina coast, in 1862: "Sixty-eight hands in the potato field planting sweet potatoes, swinging their hoes in unison, timed by a jolly song, words undistinguishable. They work with a good will, and plant about thirteen acres during the day."[8]

Grinding grain, spinning and weaving, basket-making, and nursing children all were accompanied with songs. A northern teacher, stationed at Beaufort, South Carolina, during the war, described the process of grinding hominy:

> This hominy was ground between two flat stones, one of which was stationary and the other was moved by hand by means of an upright stick inserted in a groove in the stone. It was a slow and tedious process, but always enlivened by the songs and jokes of the colored people, when grinding. Two or three always came together, as one could not move the stone alone. . . . There were people grinding corn . . . every hour, day and night. Boys and girls would come in procession with their "fanners" filled with corn perched on the top of their heads. Singing and laughing and joking they would wait for hours for a turn to grind. . . . At night the older people came. . . . All night long I could hear the whizzing of the wheel and the shouts of the people. . . . All kept time by clapping their hands and stamping their feet. . . .[9]

6. Caines, *History*, I, 110–11.
7. "Life and Travel in the Southern States," in Schwaab, ed., *Travels*, II, 491.
8. "Extracts from Letters of Teachers and Superintendents," p. 31. Letter dated Coffin's Point, St. Helena Island, Apr. 12, 1862, signed E. P.
9. Botume, *First Days*, pp. 135–36.

Lucy McKim's historic letter of November 1, 1862, also mentioned grinding hominy: "As the same songs are sung at every sort of work, of course the *tempo* is not always alike. On the water, the oars dip 'Poor Rosy' to an even andante; a stout boy and girl at the hominy-mill will make the same 'Poor Rosy' fly, to keep up with the whirling stone; . . ."[10] Flailing rice was another activity done rhythmically to music, as were spinning and weaving.[11] A child braiding a straw basket sang as he worked, and a nurse dressing a stubborn child distracted it by singing.[12]

INDUSTRIAL AND STEAMBOAT WORKERS

The South was primarily an agricultural region, but some industries closely allied to staple crops flourished. As early as 1830 hemp factories were thriving in Lexington, Kentucky:

> At one of the principal bagging and balerope establishments, there are employed from 60 to 100 negroes, of all ages . . . some of whom contrive to . . . drown the noise of the machinery by their own melody. . . . The leader would commence singing in a low tone—"Ho! Ho! Ho! Master's gone away." To which the rest replied with rapidity, "Ho! Ho!—chicken-pie for supper, Ho! Ho!—Ho! Ho!" . . . When they get tired of this, anyone who had a little fancy—and precious little would answer the purpose, would start something equally as sentimental; to which the rest again responded, at the same time walking backward and forward about their spinning, with great regularity, and in some measure keeping time with their steps. . . .[13]

The hemp spinners did not attract as much attention from tourists as did the tobacco workers in Richmond. William Cullen Bryant saw them in 1843 and quoted his guide on the repertory: "Their taste is exclusively for sacred music; they will sing nothing else."[14] Fredrika Bremer, who was in Richmond in June, 1851, became ecstatic: "I heard the slaves, about a hundred in number, singing at their work in large rooms; they sung quartettes, choruses, and anthems, and that so purely, and in such perfect harmony, and with such exquisite feeling, that it was difficult to believe them self-taught. . . . The slaves were all Baptists, and sung only hymns."[15]

10. Lucy McKim [Garrison], "Songs of the Port Royal 'Contrabands,' " p. 255. This communication is sometimes referred to as "A letter on Negro singing."

11. Cate, *Early Days*, p. 117; Yetman, "*Peculiar Institution*," p. 163, narrative of Tempie Herndon, aged 103, from Chatham County, N.C.

12. "Planter's Son," p. 18; Bodichon, *American Diary*, pp. 120–21.

13. [A New England Traveller,] "Original Correspondence," Lexington, Ky., Oct. 16 [1830], reprinted in Louisville *Journal*, Nov. 29, 1830, typescript, misc. papers H (Filson) quoted in Starobin, *Industrial Slavery*, p. 18.

14. Bryant, "Tour," in his *Prose Writings*, II, 25–26.

15. Bremer, *Homes of the New World*, II, 509–10. Other reports confirming the exclusively sacred repertory were: Jane M. and Marion Turnbull, *American Photographs*, II, 214–17; [Hopley,] *Life in the South*, I, 152.

Although Bryant had been told, "They must sing wholly of their own accord; it is of no use to bid them do it," a slave who had worked there himself described an overseer as "altogether a very good man; was very fond of sacred music, and used to ask me and some of the other slaves, who were working in the same room, to sing for him . . . which we were generally as well pleased to do, as he was to ask us. . . ."[16]

Before the days of steamboats, stevedores loaded sailing vessels. An Englishman saw them working in Savannah in 1817: "Along the wharves they [slaves] are to be seen transporting the cargoes of ships to and from the warehouses. They accompany all their labour with a kind of monotonous song, at times breaking out into a yell, and then sinking into the same nasal drawl."[17] A different kind of labor was witnessed in the harbor of Mobile forty years later:

> I have been amused by observing the crew stowing the cargo. . . . When the stowed bales [of cotton] in the hold are in contact with the upper deck, another layer has to be forced in. This is effected, bale by bale, by powerful jack-screws, worked by four men. . . . The men keep the most perfect time by means of their songs. These ditties, nearly meaningless, have much music in them, and as all join in the perpetually recurring chorus, a rough harmony is produced, by no means unpleasing. I think the leader improvises the words . . . he singing one line alone, and the whole then giving the chorus, which is repeated without change at every line, till the general chorus concludes the stanza. . . .[18]

Sailors and dockworkers were frequently a cosmopolitan group who exchanged songs as they worked together: Englishmen, Irishmen, West Indian blacks, and mainland slaves.[19] The origin of some of their songs cannot be established with confidence.

Steamboats on inland rivers normally included a good many blacks among their crews. The most picturesque were the firemen, who worked in a veritable inferno below decks. Fredrika Bremer was taken to see them on the Mississippi River in 1850, after being asked if she would like to "hear the negroes of the ship sing." She was led to the lowest deck,

> where I beheld a strange scene. The immense engine-fires are all on this deck, eight or nine apertures all in a row; they are like yawning fiery throats, and beside each throat stood a negro naked to his middle, who flung in fire-wood. Pieces of wood were passed onward to these feeders by other negroes, who stood up aloft on a large open place between them and a negro, who, standing on a lofty stack of firewood, threw down with

16. Bryant, "Tour"; Henry Box Brown, *Narrative*, pp. 17-21.
17. Mead, *Travels*, pp. 13-14.
18. Gosse, *Letters*, p. 306.
19. Hugill, *Shanties*, pp. 7-17. For the West Indian tradition, see Abrahams, *Deep the Water*.

vigorous arms food for the monsters on deck. Lerner H.[arrison] encouraged the negroes to sing; and the negro up aloft on the pile of fire-wood began immediately an improvised song in stanzas, and at the close of each, the negroes down below joined in vigorous chorus. It was a fantastic and grand sight to see these energetic black athletes lit up by the wildly flashing flames from the fiery throats, while they, amid their equally fantastic song, keeping time most exquisitely, hurled one piece of fire-wood after another into the yawning fiery gulf.[20] (AS 2)

Other reports describe boat-hands standing on the freight and singing. Frederick Law Olmsted saw them aboard the St. Charles leaving New Orleans in 1853,[21] and Daniel Hundley, while on board an Alabama River steamboat going from Mobile to Montgomery, heard "the wildest and most striking negro song . . . we ever listened to. . . . As we began to near the wharf, the negro boatmen collected in a squad on the bow of the boat, and one dusky fellow, twirling his wool hat above his head, took the lead in singing, improvising as he sang, all except the chorus, in which the whole crew joined with enthusiasm."[22]

BOAT SONGS

Boat songs were used to regulate rowing or poling boats in coastal and inland waters, as distinguished from sailing vessels and steamboats. This practice had been reported before 1800, and such reports continued throughout the antebellum period. They were distributed from Maryland to Florida along the eastern seaboard, particularly between the coastal islands and the mainland, and on inland rivers; the greatest concentration of reports came from Charleston and its environs, including the Sea Island region.

William J. Grayson, author of *The Hireling and the Slave*, which summed up the proslavery argument in heroic couplets, was born in Beaufort, South Carolina, in 1788. As an old man, he recalled from his boyhood

the canoes of six, eight, ten or twelve oars, in which planters were accustomed to visit the city [Charleston]. . . . Nor was the accompaniment of music wanting. . . . The singers were the negro oarsmen. One served as chief performer, the rest as chorus. The songs were partly traditionary, partly improvised. They were simple . . . consisting of one line only and the chorus. The singer worked into his rude strain any incident that came in his way relating to the place of destination, the passengers on board, the wife or sweetheart at home, his work or

20. Bremer, *Homes of the New World*, II, 174.
21. Olmsted, *Cotton Kingdom*, pp. 270–71. Originally published as *A Journey in the Seaboard Slave States* (1856).
22. Hundley, *Social Relations*, p. 345.

amusement. . . . The voices were generally good, the tunes pleasing and various, sometimes gay, sometimes plaintive. They were sung *con amore*. . . .[23]

A secondary account from 1930 added details that cannot be confirmed by contemporary sources:

These boats were rowed by slaves, who seemed to feel that the reputation of their masters depended on their skill in rowing and singing, for they invariably sang as they rowed. . . . There was . . . a desire on the part of the slaves to sing the best songs. The oarsmen of one plantation would never sing the songs belonging to another plantation, but would try to compose a song that would be finer than that sung by the neighboring oarsmen. So well did these songs become known on the plantations, that, when a boat had passed in the night, one would know the plantation to which it belonged by the songs that were being sung.[24]

In 1808 John Lambert traveled from Purrysburgh, the stage coach terminus, to Savannah, a distance of twenty-five miles by water.

We . . . were rowed by four negroes, for canoes are not paddled here as in Canada. They seemed to be jolly fellows, and rowed lustily to a boat-song of their own composing. The words were given out by one of them, and the rest joined chorus at the end of every line. It began in the following manner:

	Chorus:
"We are going down to Georgia, boys,	Aye, Aye.
To see the pretty girls, boys;	Yoe, Yoe.
We'll give 'em a pint of brandy, boys,	Aye, Aye.
And a hearty kiss, besides, boys.	Yoe, Yoe.
&c. &c. &c."	

The tune of this ditty was rather monotonous, but had a pleasing effect, as they kept time with it at every stroke of their oars. The words were mere nonsense; anything, in fact, which came into their heads.[25]

William Faux wrote from Charleston on June 7, 1819: "I noticed to-day the galley-slaves all singing in chorus, regulated by the motion of their oars; the music was barbarously harmonious. Some were plaintive love-songs. The verse was their own, and abounding either in praise or satire, intended for kind or unkind masters."[26] And Basil Hall was rowed down the Altamaha River from Darien, Georgia, in March, 1828, by five Negroes "in a canoe some thirty feet long, hollowed out of a cypress tree. . . . They accompanied their

23. Grayson, "Autobiography," pp. 24–25.
24. Cate, *Our Todays and Yesterdays*, pp. 157–58. "The Negroes improvised as they sang, . . . never singing the songs of another plantation."—Lovell, *Golden Isles*, p. 230.
25. Lambert, *Travels*, II, 253–54.
26. Faux, *Memorable Days*, pp. 77–78.

labor by a wild sort of song, not very unlike that of the Canadian voyageurs, but still more nearly resembling that of the well-known Bunder-boatmen at Bombay."[27]

An autobiographical novel recalled boat songs in southern Maryland in 1832, reproducing both words and music. When a passenger requested "Round' de Corn, Sally," she was told, "Dat's a corn song; un we'll hab ter sing it slow ter row to." Sing it they did, improvising words to fit the members of the party, as well as the mournful "Sold off to Georgy." The episode again illustrated the flexibility of slave music; just as "Poor Rosy, Poor Gal" could be sung fast to grind hominy and slow to row by, a corn song could also be adapted for rowing. Hymns were to be modified for the same purpose where conversion made secular songs unacceptable.[28]

Caroline Howard Gilman described a similar scene in one of the first magazines for children, *The Rose Bud, or Youth's Gazette*, in a ballad entitled "The Plantation":

> ... Yon skiff is darting from the cover;
> And list the negro's song,
> The theme, his owner and his boat,
> While glide the crew along.
>
> And when the leading voice is lost,
> Receding from the shore,
> His brother boatmen swell the strain,
> In chorus with the oar....[29]

One more description of a boat song will be quoted. This one occurred on a trip up the St. John's River in Florida; the boat carried a load of muskets for the settlers who were endangered by the advancing Seminole Indians, circumstances which place the incident about 1835:

> As we shot ahead, over the lake-like expanse of the noble river, the [dozen stout rowers] negroes struck up a song to which they kept time with their oars; and our speed increased as they went on, and become warmed with their singing. The words were rude enough, the music better, and both were well-adapted to the scene. A line was sung by a leader, then all joined in a short chorus; then came another solo line, and another short chorus, followed by a longer chorus, during the singing of which the boat foamed through the water with redoubled velocity. There seemed to be a certain number of lines ready-manufactured, but after this stock was exhausted, lines relating to surrounding objects were extemporized. Some of these were full of rude wit, and a lucky hit

27. Hall, *Travels*, II, 228.
28. Hungerford, *Old Plantation*, pp. 183–92.
29. C. G. [Caroline Howard Gilman?], "A Ballad," pp. [149]–51.

ROUN' DE CORN, SALLY.

1. Hooray, hooray, ho! Roun' de corn, Sally! Hooray for all de lub-ly la-dies!

Roun' de corn, Sal-ly! Hooray, hoo-ray, ho! Roun' de corn, Sal-ly!

Hoo-ray for all de lub-ly la-dies! Roun' de corn, Sal-ly!

Dis lub's er thing dat's sure to hab you, Roun' de corn, Sal-ly!

He hole you tight, when once he grab you, Roun' de corn, Sal-ly!

Un ole un ug-ly, young un prit-ty, Roun' de corn, Sal-ly!

You need-en try when once he git you, Roun' de corn, Sal-ly!

2. Dere's Mr. Travers lub Miss Jinny;
   He thinks she is us good us any.
   He comes from church wid her er Sunday,
   Un don't go back ter town till Monday.
       Hooray, hooray, ho! etc.

3. Dere's Mr. Lucas lub Miss T'reser,
   Un ebery thing he does ter please her;

Corn song, included in James Hungerford, *The Old Plantation, and What I Gathered There in an Autumn Month*. New York: Harper, 1859, p. 191. This autobiographical novel was set in 1832. Courtesy of the New York Public Library, Astor, Lenox and Tilden Foundations.

SOLD OFF TO GEORGY.

1. Farewell, fel-low-sarvants! O - ho! O - ho! I'm gwine way to leabe you; O -
ho! O - ho! I'm gwine to leabe de ole coun -ty; O -
ho! O - ho! I'm sold off to Geor- gy! O - ho! O - ho!

2. Farewell, ole plantation, (Oho! Oho!)
Farewell, de ole quarter, (Oho! Oho!)
Un daddy, un mammy, (Oho! Oho!)
Un marster, un missus! (Oho! Oho!)

3. My dear wife un one chile, (Oho! Oho!)
My poor heart is breaking; (Oho! Oho!)
No more shall I see you, (Oho! Oho!)
Oh! no more foreber! (Oho! Oho!)

Another song from Hungerford's *Old Plantation*.

always drew a thundering chorus from the rowers, and an encouraging
laugh from the occupants of the stern-seats. Sometimes several minutes
elapsed in silence; then one of the negroes burst out with a line or two
which he had been excogitating. Little regard was paid to rhyme, and
hardly any to the number of syllables in a line; they condensed four or
five into one foot, or stretched out one to occupy the space that should
have been filled with four or five; yet they never spoiled the tune. This
elasticity of form is peculiar to the negro song.[30]

Most of these descriptions, ranging up to 1853 in date, deal with
secular songs, usually improvised; however, a few mention that
hymns were sometimes used for this purpose. Caroline Howard
Gilman described a boat song improvised about the boat being
rowed and, later in her novel (1838), described blacks singing a hymn
on a flatboat.[31] Fanny Kemble described a number of secular boat

30. [Kinnard,] "Who Are Our National Poets?" p. 338. Other descriptions of boat
songs are in Caroline Howard Gilman, *Recollections*, pp. 69–70, 106–7; Kemble,
Journal, pp. 106–7, 127–29, 159, 218–19; Lyell, *Second Visit*, I, 244–45; Bremer,
America of the Fifties, p. 150; [Schoolcraft,] *Letters*, p. 13; Torian, ed., "Ante-Bellum
and War Memories," p. 351; and [David Brown,] *Planter*, pp. 85–87.
31. Caroline Howard Gilman, *Recollections*, pp. 69–70, 106–7.

songs, some of them nonsensical, as well as one "they call Caesar's song . . . an extremely spirited war-song, beginning 'The trumpets blow, the bugles sound—Oh, stand your ground!' It has puzzled me not a little to determine in my own mind whether this title of Caesar's song has any reference to the great Julius, and, if so, what may be the Negro notion of him, and whence and how derived."[32] At least as likely is the possibility that Caesar was a black, named in the classical tradition as so many were, and that the song may have had religious connotations. Consider the version of "Michael Row the Boat Ashore" from Hilton Head:

> Michael haul the boat ashore
> Then you'll hear the horn they blow.
> Then you'll hear the trumpet sound.
> Trumpet sound the world around. (and so on)[33]

Fredrika Bremer wrote from Charleston on June 10, 1850, of "the hymns composed by the negroes themselves, such as they sing in their canoes."[34] From all of this it seems reasonable to conclude that sacred texts gradually replaced secular texts in boat songs as the century progressed. By the time Northerners arrived in the Sea Islands in 1862, most of the songs were sacred. Many of the Northerners were unaware of a tradition of secular music among the blacks and sincerely believed that they sang only hymns, relegating all frivolous and worldly music to the minstrel theatre.

But the songs were used in the same way. The first group of teachers and superintendents arrived in Beaufort, South Carolina, on March 9, 1862; the first description of a boat song by a member of the group was dated March 18, telling of a trip to Port Royal Island: "Our rowers sing as they row, their own songs—some impromptu and all religious—about the Saviour and the kingdom. Their oars dip in the sparkling water, keeping time to the song."[35] The boat songs were a staple part of the letters and diaries of these Northerners, for whom they provided a never-ending source of pleasure and comment. James Miller McKim wrote to his wife about them on June 9, 1862; Charlotte Forten wrote of them repeatedly in 1862 and 1863.[36] Harriet Ware observed in a letter dated January 1, 1863, "The

32. Kemble, *Journal*, pp. 218–19.
33. [Allen, Ware, and Garrison,] *Slave Songs*, p. 24.
34. Bremer, *America of the Fifties*, p. 150.
35. Walker, "Journal," p. 19.
36. James Miller McKim, letter to his wife headed "Pope's Plantation, St. Helena's Island, June 9, 1862," MS, New York Public Library; Forten, *Journal*, pp. 126–28, 157, 161, 169, 170, 173. See also her letter dated Nov. 20, 1862, in *The Liberator* 32 (Dec. 12, 1862): 199.

singing while they row always sounds differently from [that] at any other time to me, though they always sing the same, religious songs."[37] And one James P. Blake wrote from Hilton Head, South Carolina, on December 19, 1864:

> Coming over from St. Helena yesterday, in a row-boat with about twenty of them [freedmen], they were singing all the way strange responsive chants or melodies, of which the women would sing the burden, and the stout oarsmen every once in a while burst out with the refrain, "An I heard from Heaben to-day." These songs, much to my surprise, were all cheerful in their tendency, and all in the major key. I had read much of the plaintive airs of the slaves; but have not heard one since I came among them. . . .[38]

The preface to *Slave Songs of the United States* discussed boat songs in some detail, listing the tunes most commonly used for rowing (of which only "Michael Row the Boat Ashore" referred specifically to boats) and describing rather precisely the speed of the rowing.[39] The practice did not die out with the end of slavery. In 1874, to cite only one reference, teachers at Hampton Institute in Virginia wrote of the "slow dip of oars and the weird, rich singing of the negro boatmen. . . ."[40]

CORN, CANE, AND OTHER HARVEST SONGS

Boat songs were described as call-and-response improvisations, and corn songs shared this general pattern. The *Dictionary of American English* defined corn song as "almost always a song with a chorus . . . kept up continuously during the entire time the work is going on. . . ."[41] Corn was one of the staples from Virginia to Texas; even the most intensively cultivated cotton or sugar plantation set aside some land for growing this indispensable grain, and the songs that made the shucking pass more quickly were widely and fondly remembered.

The earliest known mention of corn songs appeared in one of the first novels of plantation life, George Tucker's *The Valley of Shenandoah* (1824). In this story, set in Virginia in 1796, a planter explained to a visitor:

> The corn songs of these humble creatures would please you . . . for some of them have a small smack of poetry, and are natural at expressions of kind and amiable feelings—such as, praise of their master, gratitude for

37. Pearson, ed., *Letters from Port Royal*, p. 134.
38. *Freedmen's Record* 1 (Feb., 1865): 28.
39. [Allen, Ware, and Garrison,] *Slave Songs*, pp. xvi–xvii.
40. Armstrong and Ludlow, *Hampton and Its Students*, p. 11.
41. Craigie and Hulbert, eds., *Dictionary of American English*, II, 630.

his kindness, thanks for his goodness, praise of one another, and, now and then, a little humorous satire. The air of these songs has not much variety or melody, and requires not more flexibility of voice than they all possess, as they all join in the chorus. Some one . . . strikes up, and singly gives a few rude stanzas, sometimes in rhyme, and sometimes in short expressive sentences, while the rest unite in chorus, and this he continues, until some other improvisatore relieves him. One of the favourite occasions, on which their talent for music and poetry is thus exercised, is when they are 'shocking' out the Indian corn—at which time, all the negroes of the plantation, and sometimes many from the neighborhood, are assembled, and sit up nearly the whole night. This is a practice prevailing more or less throughout this state [Virginia], and, I believe, the other slave states; but it prevails most in the lower country, where the negroes are in the greatest numbers, and the plantations the largest; and yet, there are thousands among us, who never attended a corn-shocking, or even heard a corn song—so entirely separated are the two classes of black and white, and so little curiosity does that excite, which is, and always has been, near us. . . . No wonder, then, the rude ditties of our hewers of wood and drawers of water, should not provoke curiosity, or interest humanity.[42]

A vivid description from 1841 quoted the songs at length:

The negroes at the corn huskings or picking matches, when they are singing one of their wild songs, often made as they go along. The leader sings his part, and all hands join in the chorus, so that they can sometimes of a calm day or evening, be heard at least three miles. . . . We give the reader a part of one of their wild songs. . . .

"Leader.—I loves old Virginny.   Chorus.—So ho! boys! so ho!
L. I love to shuck corn.   C. So ho, &c.
L. Now's picking cotton time.   C. So ho, &c.
L. We'll make the money, boys.   C. So ho, &c.
L. My master is a gentleman.   C. So ho, &c.
L. He came from the Old Dominion.   C. So ho, &c.
L. And mistress is a lady.   C. So ho, &c.
L. Right from the land of Washington.   C. So ho, &c.
L. We all live in Mississippi.   C. So ho, &c.
L. The land for making cotton.   C. So ho, &c.
L. They used to tell of cotton seed.   C. So ho, &c.
L. As dinner for the negro man.   C. So ho, &c.
L. But boys and gals it's all a lie.   C. So ho, &c.
L. We live in a fat land.   C. So ho, &c.
L. Hog meat and hominy.   C. So ho, &c.
L. Good bread and Indian dumplins.   C. So ho, &c.
L. Music roots* and rich molasses.   C. So ho, &c. *Sweet potatoes.
L. The negro up to picking cotton.   C. So ho, &c.
L. An old ox broke his neck.   C. So ho, &c.
L. He belong to old Joe R----.   C. So ho, &c.
L. He cut him up for negro meat.   C. So ho, &c.

42. [Tucker,] *Valley of Shenandoah*, II, 116–18.

L. My master say he be a rascal.	C. So ho, &c.
L. His negroes shall not shuck his corn.	C. So ho, &c.
L. No negro will pick his cotton.	C. So ho, &c.
L. Old Joe hire Indian.	C. So ho, &c.
L. I gwine home to Africa.	C. So ho, &c.
L. My overseer says so.	C. So ho, &c.
L. He scold only bad negroes.	C. So ho, &c.
L. Here goes the corn boys.	C. So ho, &c."

The first leader having sung out his song, all at once a second leader will break out with his, and begins unceremoniously, perhaps with—

"General Washington was a gentleman.	C. Here goes the corn.
L. I don't love the pedlars.	C. Here goes the corn.
L. They cheat me in my rabbit skins.	C. Here goes &c.
L. When I bought their tin ware.	C. Here goes &c."

The author then tells of a minister who made his slaves work on Sunday.

The negroes put him into their corn songs; and, said this excellent gentleman, "Sir, I assure you it is now twenty-five years since that happened, and they are not yet done singing their song about the old parson." Let us then also give the reader a part of it.

"L. The parson say his prayers in church.	C. It rain, boys, it rain.
L. Then deliver a fine sermon.	C. It rain, boys, &c.
L. He cut the matter short my friends.	C. It rain, boys, &c.
L. He say the blessed Lord send it.	C. It rain, boys, &c.
L. Now's the time for planting bacco.	C. It rain, boys, &c.
L. Come, my negroes, get you home.	C. It rain, boys, &c.
L. Jim, Jack, and Joe and Tom	C. It rain, boys, &c.
L. Go draw your plants and set them out.	C. It rain, boys, &c.
L. Don't you stop a moment, boys.	C. It rain, boys, &c.
L. 'Twas on a blessed Sabbath day.	C. It rain, boys, &c.
L. Here's a pretty preacher for you.	C. It rain, boys, &c."

Poor fellow; *we are told* that he was actually sung out of the neighborhood.[43]

The derision and flattery in these songs seems to be related to similar qualities in the calypso songs of Trinidad, and improvised songs throughout the West Indies, South America, and in Africa itself. This aspect will be pursued later in a discussion of satire in the songs.

Many other descriptions of corn shuckings have been found, dis-

43. Thornton, *Inquiry*, pp. 120–22. This same incident and a variant of the song with some identical lines was cited by Anna Hoppe in 1935 in her reminiscences. She did not give any date for the incident, but said merely that her father had been a clergyman in the slaveholding states from 1855 on. If Thornton was correct in dating the incident twenty-five years before he wrote, (i.e., 1816), the longevity of the song was quite remarkable for an improvised corn song. Anna Hoppe's account is given in the section on satire in the next chapter.

tributed from Virginia and South Carolina to Missouri and Texas (AS 3); novels replying to *Uncle Tom's Cabin* commonly described them (with varying degrees of authenticity) as proof of the happiness of the slaves. A particularly synthetic and unconvincing picture, with song lyrics to match, appeared in Robert Criswell's *Uncle Tom's Cabin Contrasted with Buckingham Hall*.[44]

The son of a "very substantial Eastern Shore (Maryland) family" returned to his native Talbot County during the Civil War, aware that life would never be the same again. He wrote in his diary on November 3, 1863, upon hearing the Negroes sing at a corn husking on a neighboring farm:

> Their songs at a distance in the clear frosty air of the fall, at night have a sad but pleasing effect. . . . I felt that probably for the last time I had heard the songs of the negroes at one of their only convivial gatherings, songs and sounds which I have been familiar with from my infancy. Old things are passing away. What characterized our society here, the presence of slavery, is being rapidly removed.[45]

Few corn songs were notated in the nineteenth century to preserve their music for posterity. "Round' de Corn, Sally" was notated by James Hungerford of Maryland in his novel, *The Old Plantation, and What I Gathered There in an Autumn Month*; a version from Virginia was collected by William Francis Allen and included in *Slave Songs of the United States*, along with another corn song, "Shock Along, John," from Maryland.[46] Allen commented on the lack of secular songs among the Port Royal freedmen, adding, "In other parts of the South, 'fiddle-sings,' 'devil-songs,' 'corn-songs,' 'jig-tunes,' and what not, are common. . . . We have succeeded in obtaining only a very few songs of this character."[47] It appears that no one tried to collect them in those areas where they were widely sung. When the teachers from Hampton Institute made the attempt in 1874, they were unsuccessful. They walked to the isolated cabin of a man named Harry Jarvis and asked him to sing

> "Some plantation songs of a different kind from the spirituals; some of those you used to sing at your work, you know; at corn-huskings or on the water. . . . Can you sing us some?"
>
> "Not o' dem corn-shuckin' songs, madam. Neber sung none o' dem sence I 'sperienced religion. Dem's wicked songs."

44. Criswell, *Uncle Tom's Cabin Contrasted*, pp. 65–67, including texts of two songs, "Sing Darkeys, Sing" and "Shucking ob de Corn."
45. Samuel Alexander Harrison, "Journal," p. 136.
46. p. 191; pp. 67–68; songs 87, 86.
47. *Ibid.*, p. x. Barrow, "Georgia Corn-Shucking," pp. 873–78, included five song texts with the music of two.

"I have heard some of your people say something of that sort, but I didn't suppose they could *all* be wicked songs. Are there no good ones?"

"Nuffin's good dat ain't religious, madam. Nobody sings dem corn-shuckin' songs arter dey's done got religion."[48]

Boat songs with religious texts have been reported; hymns were sung in tobacco factories and to grind corn by; but of all the accounts of corn huskings found so far, only Booker T. Washington has reported corn songs with sacred texts. The whole atmosphere must have been too secular, too closely associated with the good food and drink and a dance to come.

Other crops gave rise to somewhat similar harvest celebrations. In Louisiana, as in the West Indies, sugar plantations celebrated the close of the grinding season with a holiday featuring the "cane-song—which is improvised by one of the gang, the rest all joining in a prolonged and unintelligible chorus . . . 'most musical, most melancholy.' "[49] The cane song apparently did not accompany work, but was recreational, as was the persimmon beer dance.[50] The tradition of secular worksongs, inhibited by the disapproval of secular music on the part of the stricter evangelical sects, reasserted itself after the turn of the twentieth century, when secular songs began to seem less sinful. The songs recorded in prison work-camps of the southern states were lineal descendants of the nineteenth-century worksongs, but, since genteel nineteenth-century collectors did not frequent prisons, we may never know what was sung there before the new breed of collectors led by John Lomax appeared.

SINGING ON THE MARCH

The occasions on which slaves could have been said to march were carefully regulated by the authorities, for nothing was more feared than large groups of slaves moving about on their own. Movements within the plantation included the "marching" of labor gangs out to the fields, or up to the "big house" to receive weekly allotments of rations. Under the conditions of slavery, there were very few group expeditions into the world outside the plantation, and those few were usually unpleasant. With the end of the overseas slave traffic in 1808, the domestic slave trade took on new importance, as slaves from the overpopulated states like Virginia were moved to the fresh cotton territories in Alabama, Louisiana, Mississippi, Arkansas, and

48. Armstrong and Ludlow, *Hampton and Its Students*, p. 113.
49. [Ingraham,] *South-West*, I, 241.
50. William B. Smith, "Persimmon Tree and Beer Dance," pp. 58–61.

Texas. Some migrations were organized by planters moving their entire households and working forces, but other coffles were led by slave traders transporting groups of slaves to better markets. The means of travel could be by water, by wagon, or later by railroad, but the cheapest was on foot. The earliest description of such a slave coffle, singing as it walked, came from Portsmouth, Virginia. As George Tucker stood on the courthouse steps, he saw "a group of about thirty Negroes, of different ages and sizes, following a rough looking white man. . . . They came along singing a little wild hymn of sweet and mournful melody. . . . 'It's nothing at all but a parcel of Negroes, sold to Carolina, and that man is their driver, who has bought them.' "[51] One Thomas Shillitoe wrote of an incident he observed near Mount Vernon, Kentucky, in 1829: "This morning we were met by a company of slaves, some of them heavily loaded with irons, singing as they passed along; this, we were informed, was an effort to drown the suffering of mind they were brought into, by leaving behind them wives, children, or other near connexions and never likely to meet them again in this world."[52] The coffle gang was a sight that even proslavery Southerners found distressing and unpleasant, while abolitionists featured it as a standard item in their propaganda. The "Song of the Coffle Gang" appeared in several antislavery songsters with "Words by the Slaves":

> This song is said to be sung by Slaves, as they are chained in gangs when parted from friends for the far South—children taken from parents, husbands from wives, and brothers from sisters:
>
> > See these poor souls from Africa
> > Transported to America:
> > We are stolen, and sold to Georgia, will you go along with me?
> > We are stolen and sold to Georgia, go sound the jubilee. . . .[53]

Peter Bruner, who was born a slave in Winchester, Clark County, Kentucky, in 1845, described slave coffles traveling by riverboat:

> The slave traders would buy the slaves at market and take them down the river on a boat. Then he would tell them to start up a song, and then I would hear them begin to sing:
>
> > "O Come and let us go where pleasure never dies,
> > Jesus my all to Heaven is gone,
> > He who I fix my hopes upon.

51. [Tucker,] *Letters*, pp. 29–34.
52. Shillitoe, "Journal," p. 461.
53. Clark, *Liberty Minstrel*, pp. 22–23. An identical text appeared also in *Anti-Slavery Songs*, p. 37; and in William Wells Brown, comp., *Anti-Slavery Harp*, p. 29.

> His track I see and I'll pursue
> The narrow road till him I view
> O come and let us go,
> O come and let us go where pleasure never dies."

... Those that refused to sing they would throw that big whip in among them and make them sing.[54]

This text, derived from an English hymn attributed to John Cennick (1718–55), with interpolations, was possibly atypical of songs sung under these conditions. Since Bruner's account is undated, all that can be fixed about it is that he was describing events late in the antebellum period. Besides singing, slave traders also used fiddles to raise the spirits of their coffles, a practice discussed in an earlier chapter.

Nehemiah Caulkins described singing under more pleasant conditions in southeastern North Carolina sometime before 1839:

> When the slaves get a permit to leave the plantation, they sometimes make all ring again by singing the following significant ditty, which shows that after all there is a flow of spirits . . . [that] enables them to forget their wretchedness.
>
> > Hurra, for good ole Massa,
> > He giv me de pass to go to de city
> > Hurra, for good ole Missis,
> > She bile de pot, and giv me de licker.
> > Hurra, I'm goin to de city.[55]

Frederick Douglass described similar singing in eastern Maryland before 1845, when he escaped:

> Slaves are generally expected to sing as well as to work. A silent slave is not liked by masters or overseers. . . . This may account for the almost constant singing heard in the southern states. . . . On allowance day, those who visited the great house farm were peculiarly excited and noisy. While on their way, they would make the dense old woods, for miles around, reverberate with their wild notes. . . . In all the songs of the slaves, there was ever some expression of praise of the great house farm; something which would flatter the pride of the owner, and, possibly, draw a favorable glance from him.
>
> > "I am going away to the great house farm,
> > O yea! O yea! O yea!
> > My old master is a good old master,
> > O yea! O yea! O yea!"

54. Bruner, *Slave's Adventures*, p. [11].
55. Nehemiah Caulkins, "Personal Narratives," in Weld, *American Slavery As It Is*, p. 13. This song text was also reported from St. Louis County, Mo., Jan. 1, 1834, in William Wells Brown, *My Southern Home*, p. 96.

This they would sing, with other words of their own improvising—jargon to others, but full of meaning to themselves.[56]

Douglass's impassioned interpretation of the meaning of these songs to the men who sang them far exceeds in eloquence and sensitivity any other comparable statement in the literature.

I did not, when a slave, understand the deep meaning of those rude and apparently incoherent songs. I was myself within the circle; so that I neither saw nor heard as those without might see and hear. They told a tale of woe which was then altogether beyond my feeble comprehension; they were tones loud, long and deep; they breathed the prayer and complaint of souls boiling over with the bitterest anguish. . . .

I have often been utterly astonished, since I came to the north, to find persons who could speak of the singing, among slaves, as evidence of their contentment and happiness. It is impossible to conceive of a greater mistake. Slaves sing most when they are most unhappy. The songs of the slave represent the sorrows of his heart; and he is relieved by them, only as an aching heart is relieved by its tears. At least, such is my experience.[57]

John Dixon Long, a Philadelphia clergyman, was less personally involved in these songs, but his interpretation complements Douglass's.

Listen to his songs while seated on his ox-cart hauling wood, or splitting rails. . . . his holiday songs and his self-made hymns. His songs do not always indicate a happy state of mind. He resorts to them in order to divert his thoughts from dwelling on his condition. . . . The songs of a slave are word-pictures of every thing he sees, or hears, or feels. The tunes once fixed in his memory, words descriptive of any and every thing are applied to them, as occasion requires. . . . Imagine a colored man seated on the front part of an ox-cart, in an old field, unobserved by any white man, and in a clear loud voice, ringing out these words . . .

> "William Rino sold Henry Silvers;
>   Hilo! Hilo!
> Sold him to de Georgy trader;
>   Hilo! Hilo!
> His wife she cried, and children bawled,
>   Hilo! Hilo!
> Sold him to de Georgy trader;
>   Hilo! Hilo!"

Here is a specimen in the religious vein.

> "Working all day,
> And part of the night,

56. Douglass, *My Bondage*, pp. 97–98. Other editions of Douglass's autobiography have slightly different versions of this passage. Cf. his *Narrative*, pp. 36–38, and *Life and Times*, pp. 62–63.

57. Douglass, *Narrative*, pp. 37–38.

> And up before the morning light.
> Chorus.—When will Jehovah hear our cry,
>   And free the sons of Africa?"[58]

A year after Long's book was published, W. H. Venable, on his "ramble" to New Orleans, recorded from Kentucky one of the most vivid descriptions of singing on the march:

> On Christmas Eve, a gang of colored hands from the 'Iron works,' came in joyfull procession to Mount Sterling. Their captain headed the line, improvising and singing in a loud voice, such couplets as:
>
>> "Oh Lord have mercy on my soul,
>> De hens and chickens I has stole."
>
> At the close of each line the whole squad would join in a jubilant chorus, animating to hear. . . . [They] were coming home to spend the holidays. . . . After the week . . . the reluctant company returned, in slow procession, and again they sang, but now in mournful strain. The leader, improvising his solo as before, changed its tenor to suit his mood:
>
>> "Fare ye well, ye white folks all!"
>
> The wild, sad chorus came swelling from the marching column, as from some melodious instrument:
>
>> Chorus.—"Wo - o - o - o - o - o!"
>> Solo.—"And fare ye well, ye niggers too!"
>> Chorus.—"Wo - o - o - o - o - o!"
>> Solo.—"I holler dis time, I holler no mo!"
>> Chorus.—"Wo - o - o - o - o - o!"
>
> Thus went on the strange song and chorus, as the slaves filed back to their labor, tramp, tramp, tramp; and the tones grew fainter in the distance, till at last the dying "Wo - o - o - o - o - o!" was lost in the silence of the winter night.[59]

The near relation of such songs to those used in boating, loading cargo, or other kinds of group work is unmistakable. When blacks entered the army, the same kind of song was put to military service.

Thomas Wentworth Higginson, who wrote *Army Life in a Black Regiment*, also wrote an article entitled "Drummer Boys in a Black Regiment" for *The Youth's Companion* in 1888. In the course of it he described his regiment's march to the ferry that took it to picket duty.

> Very often the drummer boys would sing a song, and each of the ten companies that followed would be singing a different one, so that if I reined up my horse to watch them pass, each song would take the place

58. John Dixon Long, *Pictures of Slavery*, pp. 197–98. These song texts have not been found elsewhere.
59. Venable, "Down South," p. 490.

of another in my ear, like the music of successive military bands in a long procession. . . .

Sometimes the drummer boys would make up songs as they went along, mixing lines of their own hymns with descriptions of what they were actually doing, and all shouting out the chorus very loud:

> "O! we're gwine to de Ferry,
>   De bell done ringing;
> Gwine to de landing,
>   De bell done ringing;
> Trust, believer,
>   De bell done ringing;
> Satan's behind me,
>   De bell done ringing;
> 'Tis a misty morning,
>   De bell done ringing;
> O! de road am sandy,
>   De bell done ringing!"[60]

This mixture of sacred and secular themes and images, also used in boat songs, developed in the Sea Island region, where secular music was supposed to have been eliminated.

STREET CRIES AND FIELD HOLLERS

An urban form of improvised song was the street cry, usually sung to call attention to goods or services for sale. Few contemporary descriptions of them have been found in the literature, although it seems reasonable to assume that they were common in all sizable towns. In his autobiography William Wells Brown, the first black novelist, described the street cries of Norfolk, Virginia:

[In] the market . . . the costermongers, or street-vendors, are the men of music, "Here's yer nice vegables—green corn, butter beans, taters, Irish taters, new jess bin digged; come an' get 'em while dey is fresh. Now's yer time; squash, Calafony quash, bess in de worl'; come an' git 'em now' it'll be Sunday termorrer, an' I'll be gone to church. Big fat Mexican peas, marrer fat squash, Protestant squash, good Catholic vegables of all kinds."

"A woman with some really fine strawberries" combined a religious refrain with an improvised "sales-pitch":

> "I live fore miles out of town,
>   I am gwine to glory.
> My strawberries are sweet an' soun',
>   I am gwine to glory.
> I fotch 'em fore miles on my head,

60. Higginson, "Drummer Boys," p. 465.

> I am gwine to glory.
> My chile is sick, an' husban' dead,
>   I am gwine to glory.
> Now's de time to get 'em cheap,
>   I am gwine to glory.
> Eat 'em wid yer bread an' meat,
>   I am gwine to glory.
> Come sinner get down on your knees,
>   I am gwine to glory.
> Eat dees strawberries when you please,
>   I am gwine to glory."[61]

Long after the Civil War ended slavery, street cries remained an attractive feature of the markets in such centers as Charleston and New Orleans, judging from accounts of the cities written after 1900, such as Harriette Leiding's *Street Cries of an Old Southern City*, i.e., Charleston.[62]

Field hollers have been collected and recorded in recent years,[63] but few known descriptions of them antedate the Civil War. Perhaps the people who heard them then did not know how to describe them, or possibly they did not consider them worth mentioning. Frederick Law Olmsted was impressed by what he heard in January, 1853, somewhere in South Carolina between Wilmington, North Carolina, and Charleston. Asleep in a passenger car on the railroad, he was awakened by loud laughter at about midnight; looking out, he saw that the loading gang of Negroes had made a fire:

> Suddenly one raised such a sound as I never heard before: a long, loud, musical shout, rising and falling and breaking into falsetto, his voice ringing through the woods in the clear, frosty night air, like a bugle-call. As he finished, the melody was caught up by another, and then, another, and then, by several in chorus. . . . After a few minutes I could hear one urging the rest to come to work again, and soon he stepped towards the cotton bales, saying, "Come, brederen come; let's go at it; come now, eoho! roll away! eeoho-eeoho-eeoho-weeioho-i!"—and the rest taking it up as before, in a few moments they all had their shoulders to a bale of cotton, and were rolling it up the embankment.[64]

It is difficult to decide whether field hollers were what Daniel Hundley had in mind when he wrote of the "wild choruses and lullaloos" of the Negroes which were more "peculiar and striking" than their religious and love songs, and which "their fathers must have brought with them from Africa, but the words and meaning of which are no longer remembered."[65]

61. William Wells Brown, *My Southern Home*, pp. 209–11.
62. Leiding, *Street Cries*.
63. Courlander, *Negro Folk Music*, pp. [80]–88.
64. Olmsted, *Journey*, II, 19–20.
65. Hundley, *Social Relations*, p. 348.

ADDITIONAL SOURCES

AS1. See also Weld, *American Slavery As It Is*, p. 13n: "Slaves sometimes sing, and so do convicts in jails under sentence, and both for the same reason. Their singing proves that they *want* to be happy, not that they *are* so. It is the *means* that they use to make themselves happy, not the evidence that they are so already. Sometimes, doubtless, the excitement of song whelms their misery in momentary oblivion. He who argues from this that they have no conscious misery to forget, knows as little of human nature as of slavery."

AS2. The refrain "of the firemen" was reported in 1851 as

almost invariably sung by negroes when they have anything to do with or about a fire, whether it be while working at a New Orleans fire engine or crowding wood into the furnaces of a steamboat . . .
>   Fire on the quarter-deck,
>   Fire on the bow.
>   Fire on the gun-deck,
>   Fire down below.

The last line is given by all hands with great voice and volume, and as for the chorus itself, you will never meet or pass a boat, you will never behold the departure or arrival of one, and you will never witness a New Orleans fire, without hearing it.

"Every-Day Commerce," in Schwaab, ed., *Travels*, II, 398. See also Lanman, *Adventures*, II, 150.

AS3. Thomas Holley Chivers wrote to Edgar Allan Poe on March 12, 1853, of a corn song he wrote for his father's slaves before 1828 (quoted in Hubbell, *South*, p. 555). Other descriptions, some with snatches of song texts, are found in: Bryant, *Letters*, pp. 84–87, from Barnwell District, South Carolina; Hensel, *Christiana Riot*, p. 22, describing events in Baltimore County, Maryland, in 1849; Lanman, *Haw-Ho-Noo*, pp. 142–43; Avirett, *Old Plantation*, pp. 144–45, from tidewater North Carolina; "The Old Plantation: A Poem," p. [65], on Putnam County, Georgia; Fedric, *Slave Life*, pp. 47–51. An extended description from the diary of Judge Cabell Chenault is quoted in Coleman, *Slavery Times*, pp. 70–77; William Wells Brown, *My Southern Home*, pp. 91–95, from Missouri; "Narrative of Wash Wilson," in Federal Writers' Project, *Slave Narratives*, Texas, XVI, 195; Yetman, *"Peculiar Institution,"* p. 259, North Carolina; p. 267, Georgia; pp. 124–25, Alabama; Wyeth, *With Sabre and Scalpel*, p. 58, from Alabama. In Booker T. Washington's reminiscences of his childhood, just before the Civil War, he mentioned corn-shuckings as one of the year's festivities:

When all were assembled . . . some one individual, who had already gained a reputation as a leader in singing, would climb on top of the mound and begin at once, in clear, loud tones, a solo—a song of the corn-shucking season—a kind of singing which I am sorry to say has very largely passed from memory and practice. After leading off in this way, in clear, distinct tones, the chorus at the base of the mound would join in, some hundred voices strong. The words, which were largely improvised, were very simple and suited to the occasion, and more often than not they had the flavor of the camp-meeting rather than any more secular proceeding. Such singing I have never heard on any other occasion. There was something wild and weird about that music, such as will never again be heard in America.

Washington, "Christmas Days," p. 395.

10

. . . .

Distinctive Characteristics of
Secular Black Folk Music

WHISTLING

Another kind of music used to pass the time was whistling. Sidney Lanier notated the music of whistling in his guidebook to Florida,[1] and a graphic description of the whistling of Negroes in Lynchburg, Virginia, appeared in the *New York Mercury* in 1859:

> Of course, there is a very large negro population in Lynchburg . . . when not asleep [in the evening they] keep up a continual whistling. All along the streets, come the note of this boy-beloved music. . . . The Lynchburg blacks . . . whistle in a manner well calculated to "soothe the savage breast." It is the tunes of the plantations where they were born, and hope to die; of the factories, where the song lightens their labor; and each is given with an accuracy, and even sweetness, which the instrument cannot always achieve. The negroes stand with their backs to the palings and walls, their hands in their pockets, and . . . whistle away the evening hours. Other gangs pass, whistling their loudest and best, which incites the first to displays of their fullest capacity; and thus the concert goes on. At an early hour, however, the whistling is hushed. . . .[2]

IMPROVISATION

The improvisatory character of slave singing, both sacred and secular, at work and at play, has been fully documented. The

1. Lanier, *Florida*, pp. 30–31.
2. Patten, "Scenes in Old Dominion," p. 8, reprinted in Schwaab, ed., *Travels*, II, 541.

You should hear him! With the great aperture of his mouth, and the rounding vibratory-surfaces of his thick lips, he gets out a mellow breadth of tone that almost entitles him to rank as an orchestral instrument. Here is his tune:

It is a genuine plagal cadence. Observe the syncopations marked in this air: they are characteristic of negro music. I have heard negroes change a well-known melody by adroitly syncopating it in this way, so as to give it a *bizarre* effect scarcely imaginable; and nothing illustrates the negro's natural gifts in the way of keeping a difficult *tempo* more clearly than his perfect execution of airs thus transformed from simple to complex accentuations.

Dick has changed his tune: *allegro!*

Da capo, of course, and *da capo* indefinitely; for it ends on the dominant. The dominant is a chord of progress: no such thing as stopping. It is like dividing ten by nine, and carrying out the decimal remainders: there is always one over.

Thus the negro shows that he does not like the ordinary accentuations nor the ordinary cadences of tunes: his ear is primitive. If you will follow the course of Dick's musical reverie—which he now thinks is solely a matter betwixt himself and the night, as he sits back yonder in the stern alone—presently you will hear him sing a whole

Negro whistling notated by Sidney Lanier in his *Florida . . . a Complete Hand-book and Guide.* Philadelphia: J. B. Lippincott, 1876. Courtesy of the Joseph Regenstein Library, University of Chicago.

chapter dealing with worksongs especially gives many examples, which need not be repeated. Here follow only a few characteristic descriptions, chosen to show the continuity of this tradition and its flexibility in almost any situation. Books on African music usually comment on the tradition of improvisation in many cultures, while contemporary accounts of Africa demonstrate its longevity. In 1621 Richard Jobson commented that "singing . . . *extempore* upon any occasion is offered, whereby the principall may be pleased; wherein diverse times they will not forget in our presence to sing in the praise of us white men."[3] In the 1790's Thomas Winterbottom also noted this tradition: "Among the Foolas there is a set of people called singing men, who, like the ancient bards, travel about the country singing the praises of those who chuse to purchase renown, or venting their sarcasms upon such as have offended them."[4]

The practice of improvisation in the New World was not reported in connection with African music and dancing, probably because the European auditors did not understand either the words or the musical practice. But descriptions of night-long dances, beginning with the earliest accounts of African music in the New World, surely allow for variation in the music which went unnoticed by the reporter. The earliest known mention of the technique of improvising in mainland North America (if we accept the date set for the fiction) was in one of the first novels of plantation life, set ostensibly in 1796. Corn songs were described as "natural at expressions of kind and amiable feelings—such as, praise of their master, gratitude for his kindness, thanks for his goodness, praise of one another, and now and then, a little humorous satire."[5] This idyllic account did not concern itself with the inner feelings of the slaves, but, as far as it went, undoubtedly implied the existence of a practice of improvisation. More revealing of the relation between master and slave and the license allowed in song was an 1804 account from the Leeward Islands, which described field work:

> The slaves then work in a long string, and follow each other in regular order. Some one takes the lead and breaks out with a song, to which there is always a chorus. In this they all join. . . . These songs are not without their jibes; sometimes too levelled at the master, and then they are sung with peculiar vivacity, when the negroes come under his window or near his house. They remind him of promised and ungiven holidays, additional allowance or change in the kind of their food, when long sameness has rendered variety desirable.*

3. Jobson, *Golden Trade*, pp. 105–8.
4. Winterbottom, *Native Africans*, I, 108.
5. [Tucker,] *Valley of Shenandoah*, II, 116–17.

> The facility with which the negroes dress every occurrence in rhime, and give it a metre, rude indeed, but well adapted to the purpose of raillery or sarcasm, is no slight proof of genius perhaps; as well as of vivacity.

The footnote is perhaps the most significant detail, since the actions of a child very likely represent a deeply ingrained tradition:

> *The Author was sung all over his estate by a little slave, not six years old, and she told her mistress, that she had been singing her master; because he did not give her a black dog (the smallest description of coin in the West Indies) which he had promised her.[6]

"Singing the master," apparently regarded by this author as self-explanatory, has not been mentioned in any other source found so far.

Many of the accounts of worksongs already quoted contained elements of improvisation. In the chapters on sacred music the same techniques will be observed, having been readily adapted to singing sacred texts when the demands of evangelical religion made secular songs taboo. A perceptive observer commented:

> The blacks themselves leave out old stanzas, and introduce new ones at pleasure. Travelling through the South, you may, in passing from Virginia to Louisiana, hear the same tune a hundred times, but seldom the same words accompanying it. This necessarily results from the fact that the songs are unwritten, and also from the habit of extemporizing, in which the performers indulge on festive occasions.[7]

W. H. Venable, who was quoted in connection with marching, was equally revealing on improvisation.

SATIRE

Many descriptions of improvisatory singing comment on the satiric license taken by the singers, who felt free to express in song sentiments that could never be spoken. Alan Merriam has described a number of incidents of this kind in various parts of Africa;[8] calypso songs from the West Indies are noted for this kind of social commentary, and such songs were (and still are) also recorded in the United States. Boat songs, corn songs, and other kinds of repetitive songs designed to lighten labor or pass the time were ideally suited for the insertion of satiric or derisive lines. Rather than repeat passages already quoted, I shall quote from the reminiscences of a

---

6. Caines, *History*, I, 110–11.
7. [Kinnard,] "Who Are Our National Poets?" p. 336.
8. Alan P. Merriam, "African Music," in Bascom and Herskovitz, eds., *Continuity and Change*, pp. 51, 55.

woman whose father served as a clergyman in the slaveholding states beginning in 1855:

> The slaves on the plantations usually expressed approval or disapproval of the master's conduct in their wild songs, sometimes ringing out his praises, and at other times in the spirit of revenge, when they felt abused. . . . At the corn huskings and picking matches these songs were often made as they went along. . . .
>
> No master had a right to make his slave work on Sunday, except in the ordinary household offices. However, we know of a minister, who also planted tobacco. It had not rained until late in the year, and the tobacco plants could not be set out. During the service on Sunday there came a fine rain. After the service was over, having thanked God for his blessing, the minister called on his Negroes to be off home and go to planting at once. This the Negroes considered such a flagrant violation of morality and such a bad example, that they put him into their corn songs. We were told, that he was actually sung out of the neighborhood:—

> *Leader:* "Twas on a blessed Sabbath day.
> *Chorus:* It rain, boys, it rain.
> *Leader:* The parson say his prayers in church. *Chorus.*
> *Leader:* He cut the matter short, my friends. *Chorus.*
> *Leader:* Now's the time for planting 'bacco. *Chorus.*
> *Leader:* Come my Negroes get you home. *Chorus.*
> *Leader:* Go draw your plants and set them out. *Chorus.*
> *Leader:* 'Twas on a blessed Sabbath Day. *Chorus.*
> *Leader:* Here's a pretty preacher for you, etc." *Chorus.*[9]

This text published in St. Louis in 1935 is closely related to the version in Chapter 9 that appeared in Washington in 1841. Many of the leader's lines and the choral refrain are identical.

STYLE OF SINGING

Available sources are most unsatisfactory regarding the style of singing or of instrumental music, probably because few of the observers were sensitive to details of musical performance. An unmusical traveler could mention a musical instrument in passing, and so record its existence without knowing or caring much about it. But when he tried to describe how it sounded or the singing that went with it, he was likely to say only, "I cannot give you the least idea of it."

William Beckford, who left Jamaica in 1777, did attempt to describe what he had heard: "The style of singing among the Negroes, is uniform. . . . One person begins first, and continues to sing alone; but at particular periods the others join; there is not, indeed, much

9. Hoppe, *Negro Slavery*, pp. 30–32. Cf. ch. 9, note 43.

variety in their songs; but their intonation is not less perfect than their time."[10] Beckford was almost the only reporter who consciously tried to describe the style of singing. Many reports give only a glimpse, or portray an isolated aspect of the performance. A Russian diplomat visited a Negro Methodist church in Philadelphia sometime between 1811 and 1813, reporting that "every psalm the entire congregation, men and women alike, sang verses in a loud, shrill monotone. This lasted about half an hour. . . . Afterwards . . . all rose and began chanting psalms in chorus, the men and women alternating, a procedure which lasted some twenty minutes."[11] Another fragmentary account described the singing of stevedores on the wharves of Savannah, Georgia, in 1817: "They accompany all their labour with a kind of monotonous song, at times breaking out into a yell, and then sinking into the same nasal drawl."[12]

In describing boat songs Fanny Kemble wrote: "They all sing in unison, having never, it appears, attempted or heard any thing like part-singing. Their voices seem oftener tenor than any other quality, and the tune and time they keep, something quite wonderful; such truth of intonation and accent would make almost any music agreeable. . . ."[13]

These reports all seem to describe monophonic singing, yet some reporters insisted they sang in parts. More on this will be found in the reports written during the Civil War, when the singing of the slaves attracted more attention from Northerners in the South for the first time. Further discussion of musical style will be deferred until a later chapter.

OTHER SECULAR MUSIC

Our knowledge of antebellum black secular music is still sadly defective. Little is known about the music of the urban centers of the North; very little secular music was notated anywhere until after the Civil War. Scraps of song texts were included in travel accounts and similar narratives, including fiction, but, since the focus of this work is on music, no attempt was made to collate or study them.[14] One tantalizing question that needs more attention concerns the use of songs as signals, both in connection with the

10. Beckford, *Descriptive Account*, II, 121.
11. Svi'nin, *Picturesque United States*, p. 20.
12. Mead, *Travels*, pp. 13–14.
13. Kemble, *Journal*, p. 127.
14. See, e.g., Davis, *Kennedy*, pp. 20–21, "Quashee's Seditious Ode." Several interesting texts are also given in Victor's *Maum Guinea*, pp. 76–77, 108–9, et passim.

Underground Railroad[15] and in other affairs kept secret from whites.

Many sources remain to be explored, particularly newspapers, magazines, and manuscripts. *De Bow's Review* in 1855 reported:

> Negro melodies. There have appeared at sundry times in sundry journals of the south papers upon this subject, with most copious illustrations selected from the cabins of the cane and cotton-fields and from the canoes and flat-boats of the creeks and bayous of the south. We should be very glad if our subscribers would furnish us with any specimens that are well authenticated, whether in print or in manuscript. Many gems in their way could be picked up without an effort....[16]

None of these "sundry papers" has been discovered by modern scholars, nor is it known if *De Bow's* readers responded to this invitation.

Manuscript sources, of which the Slave Narrative Collection assembled by the Federal Writers' Project in the 1930's is a prime example, also remain virtually untapped.

15. See, e.g., H. B. Parks, "Follow the Drinking Gourd," in Dobie, *Follow de Drinkin' Gou'd*, pp. [81]–84; and Bradford, *Harriet*, pp. 27–28, 51–52, passim.
16. "Negro Melodies," pp. 335–36.

11

The Religious Background of
Sacred Black Folk Music, 1801–67

A heated, confused, and prejudice-ridden controversy over the origins of the Negro spiritual has been carried on for years by professors of English literature, musicologists, and theologians, none with adequate backgrounds in American history or African music and culture. In the absence of reliable evidence, much of the literature they produced was speculative, sincere, and no doubt well meaning, but lacking a firm basis in established fact. A good summary of the situation before the surge of interest in black studies was written by D. K. Wilgus in 1959:

> There is no trustworthy evidence before the Civil War. There are few examples of American Negro tradition that we can accept as pure. Too little is known of African song, and analyzable elements seem to prove little. Critics of Negro song have not been competent in all the required fields and have usually based their arguments on only a part of the evidence. Even all the evidence is not enough, for there are elements in the songs to which we are not able to apply objective analysis.[1]

Moreover, many writers seemed to assume that slavery and Christianity were much the same in 1860 as they had been earlier—that conditions at the outbreak of the Civil War could be extended back in time to the beginning of the century, and perhaps even further.

1. Wilgus, *Anglo-American Folksong Scholarship*, "Appendix One: Negro-White Spiritual," pp. 345–64.

But slavery, like the church, was a historically evolving system rather than a static, changeless institution, and the conditions that existed in 1860 were not those of sixty or a hundred years earlier.

To understand the genesis of the Negro spiritual, it is necessary to consider the religious forces that helped to shape it. The eighteenth-century efforts at converting the blacks to Christianity, already described, were followed after 1800 by an increasingly successful evangelical movement that advocated religious instruction for the slaves under white supervision and control. The independent black churches that had begun during the eighteenth century were largely circumscribed in the South, although they continued to grow in the North. Even such useful adjuncts as black class leaders within white congregations were viewed with suspicion by southern whites. Their effectiveness and convenience were outweighed by the dreadful possibility that they might think and act for themselves, instead of limiting their teachings to approved texts that explained God's will in terms of serving master well on earth and reaping a reward in heaven. The characteristic indifference or hostility of slaveowners toward religious instruction for their slaves was superseded by a period of ambivalence prior to the socially approved position of the mid-nineteenth century: full, enthusiastic support for missions to the slaves. This chapter will consider the impact of evangelical religion on the slave population through all these stages in turn, beginning with the vestiges of opposition to religious instruction after 1800, continuing with black participation in the camp-meeting movement, missions to the slaves, the survival of independent black religious groups in the South, and, finally, the opposition to secular music and dancing. The next chapter contains material more directly related to the music: the emergence of distinctive black religious music of two specific types, the spiritual and the shout; attempts to suppress black religious singing; and, finally, black funeral customs.

OPPOSITION TO RELIGIOUS INSTRUCTION OF SLAVES

With the growing influence of the evangelical sects after 1800, opposition to religious instruction of the slaves diminished but failed to disappear completely. Some vestiges of eighteenth-century enlightenment still continued to exist, together with a casual indifference to the behavior of the slaves outside of working hours. In 1837 Charles Ball, a former slave, described conditions he had experienced at the beginning of the century:

There has always been a strong repugnance amongst the planters, against their slaves becoming members of any religious society.... They fear the slaves, by attending meetings, and listening to the preachers may imbibe the morality they teach, the notions of equality and liberty, contained in the gospel....

At the time I first went to Carolina, there were a great many African slaves in the country, and they continued to come in for several years afterward [i.e., until 1808].... Many of them believed there were several gods; some of whom were good, and others evil.... I knew several who must have been, from what I have since learned, Mohamedans.... There was one man on this plantation, who prayed five times every day, always turning his face to the east....

There is, in general, very little sense of religious obligation, or duty, amongst the slaves on the cotton plantations; and Christianity cannot be, with propriety, called the religion of these people.

[On Saturday night] Our quarter knew but little quiet . . . singing, playing on the banjoe, and dancing, occupied nearly the whole community, until the break of day. Those who were too old to take any part in our active pleasures, beat time with their hands, or recited stories of former times . . . in Africa....

On Sunday afternoon we had a meeting . . . sang and prayed; but a great many of the people went . . . in search of fruits. . . .[2]

Many of the elements in this description can be corroborated by other accounts. As late as 1810 Daniel Coker, minister of the African Methodist Episcopal Church in Baltimore, wrote that some masters were still refusing to permit religious instruction to their slaves. "Some, I said, for thank God, all masters are not so abominably wicked; for, I remember hearing dear old Bishop Asbury the last time he preached in the African church in . . . Baltimore, say, that in some parts of the southern states, there are some owners of slaves who take pleasure in seeing their servants get religion."[3]

Others continued to be indifferent. Basil Hall visited a rice plantation near the Combahee River in South Carolina in March, 1828. He was told by the owner,

"We don't care what they do when their tasks are over—we lose sight of them till next day. Their morals and manners are in their own keeping. The men may have, for instance, as many wives as they please, so long as they do not quarrel about such matters."

I asked if they had any religion?

"I know little about that," he said; "there may perhaps be one or two methodists in a hundred. Preachers are never prevented, by me at least, from coming amongst the negroes, upon a distinct and express

2. Ball, *Slavery*, pp. 164–65, 201–3.
3. Coker, *Dialogue*, pp. 33–34.

stipulation, however, that they do not interfere with the duties of the slaves. . . ."[4]

Besides opposition or indifference to converting the slaves, a still rarer attitude was tolerance of African mores and customs. Zephaniah Kinglsey, a slave dealer resident in Florida, recommended respect for the privacy of slaves:

> About twenty-five years ago [1804?], I settled a plantation on St. Johns river, in Florida, with about fifty new African negroes, many of whom I brought from the coast [of Africa] myself. . . . I never interfered with their connubial concerns, and domestic affairs, but let them regulate these after their own manner. . . . I encouraged as much as possible dancing, merriment and dress, for which Saturday afternoon and night, and Sunday morning were dedicated. . . . A man, calling himself a minister, got among them. It was now sinful to dance, work their corn or catch fish, on a Sunday . . . all pastime or pleasure in this iniquitous world was sinful. . . . I cannot help regretting that honest well meaning men, with so much ability to do good . . . should so misapply their, talents as to subvert all natural and rational happiness, and endeavor to render our species miserable.[5]

A South Carolina planter who shared Kingsley's opinion that religion was harmful for Negroes broke up their religious meetings and

> induced them to occasional meetings for the purposes of merriment. He had fiddles and drums for their use, [and] promoted dancing. . . . Innocent amusement, when under proper regulations . . . conduce to morality and virtue. . . . If those who used to follow the abominable slave trade, found it to their advantage . . . to produce gaiety in their miserable captives, by causing them to listen to and dance at the sound of some instrument, there must be some virtue in the practice; or else, in their cupidity, they never would have thought of this.[6]

This belief that religion was harmful while secular music and dancing were morally beneficial was most uncharacteristic of South Carolina in 1836; equally unusual at that time was the acknowledgement that music and dancing had played a role in the slave trade.

Those slaveholders, however, who now approved the evangelization of their slaves were almost unanimous in opposing black preachers on both religious and political grounds. Bishop Asbury had encouraged his black assistant, Harry Hosier, to exhort before both black and mixed congregations; after 1800, however, black

4. Hall, *Travels*, II, 216.
5. [Kingsley,] *Treatise*, pp. 14–15.
6. Herbemont, "On Moral Discipline," pp. 71–74.

class leaders were regarded with great suspicion as potential leaders of insurrection. In 1822, in the wake of the abortive Denmark Vesey conspiracy in Charleston, a local resident denounced all missionaries, white as well as black:

> We are exposed to still greater perils, by the swarms of Missionaries, white and *black*, that are perpetually visiting us, who, with the Sacred Volume of God in one hand ... scatter ... with the other, the fire-brands of discord and destruction, and *secretly* disperse among our Negro Population, the seeds of discontent and sedition. It is an acknowledged fact, that some of these religious itinerants ... have, by means of *Tracts* and other modes of instruction, all professedly *religious* in their character, excited among our Negroes such a spirit of dissatisfaction and revolt.... Those who are intimately acquainted with the efficient causes of the late intended Insurrection in Charleston ... know ... what a powerful agency was put into operation by the dispersion among our Negroes, of *religious magazines, news paper paragraphs* and *insulated* [isolated?] *texts of scripture....*[7]

The author did approve, however, of slaves attending regular services at Presbyterian or Episcopal churches where special segregated sections were provided for them. Zephaniah Kingsley dared to put into words the dread that his Charleston colleague only implied. "All the late insurrections of slaves are to be traced to influential preachers of the gospel, (as, for instance at Barbados and Demarara,) to white preachers, (missionaries) from England. Vesey, who instigated the Charleston plot, was an exhorting brother. Gualla [i.e., Gullah] Jack or Jack the Conjurer was a priest in his own country...."[8]

At a later date, in the atmosphere generated by camp meetings and the rapid growth of evangelical sects, opposition to organized religion and missionary work was not a socially acceptable position; few indeed were the men courageous enough to maintain it. White Southerners had to reconcile the conscientious duty of providing the consolations of religion for their slaves with as much assurance as possible that religious instruction would not go too far. The wide opposition to "noisy enthusiastic" meetings of blacks was based not only on a desire for stricter theological interpretations, but also on a concern about what the black preachers might be saying. Another South Carolinian attributed the Vesey conspiracy directly to Negro preachers:

> *None of the Negroes belonging to the Protestant Episcopal Church were concerned in the late conspiracy.* To what cause is this to be attributed?

7. [Holland,] *Refutation*, pp. 11–12.
8. [Kingsley,] *Treatise*, p. 13.

... Is it because the coloured leaders in that Church were not permitted to expound the Scriptures, or to exhort, in words of their own; to use extemporary prayer, and to utter at such times, whatever nonsense and profanity might happen to come into their minds? ...

When the coloured class-leaders in the Protestant Episcopal Church were allowed to meet for religious exercises,* they were accustomed to use *no other worship* than the regular course prescribed in the Book of Common Prayer, for the day. Hymns, or Psalms out of the same book were sung, and a printed sermon read. ... No extemporary address, exhortation, or prayer, was permitted, or used. ...

The event which gave rise to these "considerations," had its origin and seat, chiefly in the *African Church*. . . .[9]

*These meetings have been discontinued since the event alluded to.

The strict control over the service exercised by the Episcopal Church would have prevented (or at least kept to a minimum) any blending of African religious practice with the formal order of worship, or any expression of ethnic cultural preferences except in ways too subtle to be detected. The development of any distinctive black religious song would thus have been tightly circumscribed.

Even among the less formal Baptists and Methodists, there was widespread opposition to permitting blacks to worship as they chose. The more genteel objected to practices that were traditional at camp meetings, claiming that noisy, enthusiastic meetings were not a proper expression of religious feeling and disturbed the peace. Thomas H. Jones, a slave for forty-three years, described an attempt to suppress a religious meeting near Wilmington, Delaware, in 1824:

> [After a Sunday "class" meeting] A good many of us went . . . to a brother's cabin, where we began to express our joy in happy songs. The palace of General Dudley was only a little way off, and he soon sent over a slave with orders to stop our noise, or he would send the patrollers upon us. We then stopped our singing, and spent the remainder of the night in talking, rejoicing and praying. . . . I was then nearly eighteen years old.[10]

James W. C. Pennington, who received a D.D. degree from the University of Heidelberg while he was still a fugitive slave, described the conditions he had known before he escaped from slavery in Maryland in 1827:

> Neither my master or any other master within my acquaintance made any provision for the religious instruction of his slaves. They were not worked on the Sabbath. . . . [but] I never knew him to say a word to one of us about going to church . . . or a future state. But there were a

9. *Practical Considerations*, pp. 33–36.
10. Thomas H. Jones, *Experience*, pp. 26–27.

number of pious slaves . . . and several of these my master owned; one
. . . was an exhorter. . . . He could not read . . . but he knew a number
of "spiritual songs by heart," of these he would give two lines at a time
very exact, set and lead the tune himself. . . .

The Methodists at one time attempted to evangelize the slaves in our
neighborhood, but the effort was sternly resisted by the masters. They
held a camp meeting. . . . But one of their preachers . . . was arrested and
tried for his life . . . [he was] acquitted. . . .[11]

The 1845 Georgia statutes provided "Negroes not to assemble
under pretence of divine worship" and "persons of color not allowed
to preach without written license," stipulating that "no person of
color, whether free or slave, shall be allowed to preach, to exhort, or
join in any religious exercise with any persons of color, either free or
slave, there being more than seven persons of color present. . . ."[12]
Even in laissez faire New Orleans the police arrested a dozen blacks
in a makeshift church, charging that they "have been in the habit of
repairing to this place for the purpose of joining in singing hymns
and cantiques which was followed by sermons, the subject of which
was of the most inflammatory character."[13] The black churches
that were able to persist in the face of this opposition will be
described later.

CAMP MEETINGS

Bishop Asbury's protracted meetings continued from the eighteenth century into the era of the camp meeting proper. Before the
colossal Cane Ridge Kentucky camp meeting of August, 1801, he
wrote in his journal on February 25: "Our tabernacle is crowded
again: the minds of the people are strangely changed; and the
indignation excited against us is overpast: the people see and confess
that the slaves are made better by religion; and wonder to hear the
poor Africans pray and exhort."[14] From the first camp meeting,
contemporary accounts reported the presence of black worshippers.
An "extract of a letter from a gentleman to his sister in Philadelphia, dated Lexington, Kentucky, August 10, 1801," described the
historic Cane Ridge meeting: "I hasten to give you an account of the
revival of religion . . . the meeting . . . took place at Kainridge, in
Bourbon county. . . . [there were two preaching stands for whites]
and about 150 yards in a south course from the [meeting] house

11. Pennington, *Fugitive Blacksmith*, pp. 66–68.
12. Georgia, Laws, Statutes, etc., *Codification*, pp. 814, 840.
13. *New Orleans Daily Delta*, June 12, 1846, as cited in Wade, *Slavery in Cities*, pp.
83–84.
14. Asbury, *Journal*, III, 11.

was an assembly of black people, hearing the exhortations of the blacks."[15] The pattern set at Cane Ridge continued in the many camp meetings that followed. The Reverend Samuel M'Corkle described a meeting at Randolph, Rowan County, North Carolina, in January, 1802:

> A speaker [rose] to give a short parting exhortation: and wonderful to tell, as if by an electric shock, a large number in every direction, men, women and children, white and black, fell and cried for mercy ... a poor black man with his hands raised over the heads of the crowd, and shouting, "Glory, glory to God on high" ... another black man prostrate on the ground, and his aged mother on her knees at his feet ... a black woman, grasping her mistress' hand and crying ... [at another meeting at Jersey, North Carolina, June 4–8, 1802] near three thousand people attended. ... Nothing very unusual ... appeared, until Sunday evening, when a stout Negro-woman, who had been all day mocking the mourners, fell ... in a state of horror and despair. ... In this state, she continued with intervals, for three hours. ... She often roared out, "O hell! hell! hell! Thy pangs have seized me! O torment! torment! ..." She said she saw hell-flames below, herself hung over by a thread, and a sharp, bright sword drawn to cut it through. ... Such an exercise I never beheld, and I have seen not less than a thousand. ... at last she shouted, "Glory, glory.". ...[16]

Other descriptions of camp meetings included Negro participants as a matter of course. Lucius Bellinger, an itinerant Methodist preacher, recalled a quarterly meeting at Pine Grove, South Carolina, about 1830: "Old Pine Grove had never seen such a turn out for many years. ... The people ... came in crowds. ... singing as the old-time Methodists used to sing. ... The negroes are out in great crowds, and sing with voices that make the woods ring."[17]

Twenty years later, on May 7, 1850, Fredrika Bremer was greatly impressed with the contributions of the blacks to a camp meeting held in a wood eighteen miles from Charleston:

> In the middle of a thick wood ... not a house to be seen. ... It swarms with people, in particular with blacks ... an open space, in the centre of which rises a great long roof, supported by pillars, and under which stand benches in rows, affording sufficient accommodation for four or five thousand people. ...
>
> By degrees the people begin to assemble ... the white people on one side, the black on the other; the black being considerably more numerous than the white. ... [There were] certainly from three to four thousand persons. They sang hymns—a magnificent choir! Most likely the sound proceeded from the black portion of the assembly, as their

15. Sweet, *Religion*, pp. 610–11.
16. "Letters by the Rev. Samuel M'Corkle, North Carolina," written in Jan. and June, 1802, in Foote, *Sketches*, pp. 391–92, 402–4.
17. Bellinger, *Stray-Leaves*, p. 17.

number was three times that of the white, and their voices are naturally beautiful and pure.... Past midnight ... we went the round of the camp, especially on the black side. And here all the tents were still full of religious exaltation, each separate tent presenting some new phasis. We saw in one a zealous convert, male or female, as it might be, who with violent gesticulations gave vent to his or her newly-awakened feelings, surrounded by devout auditors; in another we saw a whole crowd of black people on their knees, all dressed in white, striking themselves on the breast, and crying out and talking with the greatest pathos; in a third women were dancing "the holy dance" for one of the newly-converted. ... In a fourth, a song of the spiritual Canaan was being sung excellently....

At sunrise ... an alarm ... gave the sign for the general rising. At half past five I was dressed and out. The hymns of the negroes, which had continued through the night, were still to be heard on all sides.

[Later] The hymns were ... fervent and beautiful on the side of the negroes' camp. ... Their musical talents are remarkable. Most of the blacks have beautiful, pure voices, and sing as easily as we whites talk. ... These religious camp-meetings ... are the saturnalia of the negro slaves....

At five in the afternoon we returned to Charleston by a train which conveyed certainly two thousand persons, two thirds of them blacks. They sang the whole way, and were in high spirits.[18] (AS 1)

There is no room for doubt that blacks and whites worshipped and sang together in an atmosphere highly charged with emotion at camp meetings during the first half of the nineteenth century. That the participants were mutually influenced seems inescapable. Songs, parts of songs, and ways of singing must have been exchanged, without the excited folk knowing or caring who started what. The assumption that the blacks learned all their songs from the whites has not been proved, nor has documentation been found to prove the opposite. What seems most likely is that many blacks found in the camp meeting not only their first extensive experience with Christianity, but also a religious atmosphere better suited to their needs than anything else available. The call-and-response style of singing so familiar to them was ideally suited to the participatory service of the camp meeting, where vast numbers of people required musical responses that they could learn on the spot. The blacks were there, and their contribution is still to be evaluated fully.

MISSIONS TO THE SLAVES

During the first two or three decades of the nineteenth century, camp meetings and the normal activities of organized congregations provided most of the religious experiences available to the slaves. In

18. Bremer, *Homes of the New World*, I, 306–17.

towns blacks were admitted to church services and were seated in segregated sections, often in a gallery. The service intended for the white congregation was heard by them as well, with only an occasional special service conducted for their benefit. In rural areas, where the majority of the slave population lived, plantations were frequently isolated from each other, and the planter decided what religious facilities were to be available on his place. They could vary from none at all to the provision of a special praise-house especially for the use of the slaves. Rural churches were frequently too small to accommodate large groups of slaves. As the century advanced, it became increasingly common for at least the house servants to take part in prayers with the master's family. In more pious families the ladies conducted Sunday schools for the slave children, reading the Bible and teaching the catechism; all the slaves were expected to worship with the family.

Sporadic attempts to set up missionary stations in plantation areas occurred before an organized movement materialized. An abortive attempt to evangelize the slaves had been made by the South Carolina Conference of the Methodist church in 1809, but regular missions were not begun until 1829.[19] An appraisal of the situation was made in 1834: "In the vast field extending . . . from the Atlantic to the Ohio, there are, to the best of our knowledge, not twelve men exclusively devoted to the religious instruction of the negroes! . . . The negroes have no regular and efficient Ministry; as a matter of course, *no Churches: neither is there sufficient room in white Churches for their accommodation.* We know of but five Churches in the slave-holding States, built expressly for their use."[20]

As late as August 15, 1832, a minister still wrote of Sabbath observance in terms of Sunday dances: "I have rarely, for several years, seen it made by them [the blacks] a day of amusement, as I am told it formerly was."[21] A drive to evangelize the slaves was underway that envisioned their conversion under complete white supervision and control. Opposition to independent black churches was shared by all the denominations in the South, in keeping with their endorsement of chattel slavery. Methods of converting large numbers of plantation slaves to the strictly enforced tenets of the Presbyterian and Methodist churches of the South became a topic of great pastoral interest.

19. William Pope Harrison, *Gospel Among Slaves*, pp. 137, 149.
20. "Report of the [Presbyterian] Synod," pp. 174–75.
21. Bailey, *Issue*, p. 13.

The Presbyterian Church, for example, sponsored a protracted meeting at Midway Church in Liberty County, Georgia, in November, 1844.

> Friday and Saturday were given to the Negroes for religious worship. . . . Planters who were and who were not members of the Church, united cordially in it. Services were held . . . twice a day for the negroes. . . . The house could not contain the people: more were *without* than *within*. On Sabbath, they attended from all parts of the County. The gallery of the white Church was filled, the colored Church was filled, and perhaps as many remained around the doors and windows of the Churches, as had been accommodated with seats within. Such a congregation of negroes had not been assembled in the county for many years. The greatest order and propriety of behaviour prevailed. . . . The moral effect upon the negroes has been of the most satisfactory kind. It has given them increased respect and attachment to their owners. . . . No attempt was made to play upon their feelings, or "to get up an excitement.". . .[22]

A leader in the missions movement in Liberty County, the Reverend Charles Colcock Jones, tried valiantly to discourage all spontaneity and emotional response on the part of the black congregations:

> The public worship of God should be conducted *with reverence and stillness on the part of the congregation*; nor should the minister— whatever may have been the previous habits and training of the people —encourage demonstrations of approbation or disapprobation, or exclamations, or responses, or noises, or outcries of any kind during the progress of divine worship; nor boisterous singing immediately at its close. These practices prevail over large portions of the southern country, and are not confined to one denomination, but appear to some extent in all. . . . I cannot think them beneficial.[23] (AS 2)

The Reverend Mr. Jones not only wished his black congregations to remain silent during the spoken parts of the service; he also wished them to sing only approved hymns:

> To give variety and interest to . . . the Sabbath school [for Negroes], it is proper to teach the scholars *hymns and psalms, and how to sing them.* They are extravagantly fond of music; and this taste may be turned to good account in their instruction. . . . One great advantage in teaching them good psalms and hymns is that they are thereby induced to lay aside the extravagant and nonsensical chants, and catches and hallelujah songs of their own composing; and when they sing, which is very often while about their business or of an evening in their houses, they will have something profitable to sing.[24]

22. Association for the Religious Instruction of the Negroes in Liberty County, Georgia, *Ninth Annual Report*, pp. 12–13.
23. Charles Colcock Jones, *Suggestions*, pp. 39–40.
24. Charles Colcock Jones, *Religious Instruction*, pp. 265–66.

"Lining out" was a device much used by the missionaries and black class leaders to teach the approved psalms and hymns to their black congregations. The practice had originated in English and colonial churches when books were scarce; each line was read or intoned by the minister or some other person before it was sung by the congregation. Although in nearly all white churches the practice died out in the mid-nineteenth century, in black congregations it continued and is still observed in some churches, particularly in rural areas. It was used in some camp meetings, and by 1818 a small Baptist church in Woodville, Mississippi, was being criticized by an emigrant from Massachusetts: "They sung in ancient style, lineing the Psalm . . . both white and black, frequently making discordant sounds, grating to an ear accustomed to correct music."[25]

As the missionary movement got under way, the plans included "lining out" as an approved educational device. "As they [the slaves] have no books, the hymns should be given out by one or two lines, that they may join in the exercises."[26] (AS 3) The intention of the evangelizing missionaries was to impart to the slaves that kind of religion most congenial to the plantation owners. Their efforts had an enormous impact on the slave population, but the movement did not succeed in stamping out all traces of African cultural patterns, or the desire for independent black religious groups.

BLACK RELIGIOUS GROUPS

Even on plantations regularly visited by white missionaries, black deacons or class leaders assisted by leading prayer meetings, catechizing, visiting the sick, and functioning in the absence of the ordained minister. Where the black exhorter and the people wished, some independence of worship could be maintained, whatever the church prescribed. A former slave described his activities as an exhorter in the vicinity of Heathsville, Virginia, before 1836:

> Soon after I was converted I commenced holding meetings among the people, and it was not long before my fame began to spread as an exhorter. I was very zealous, so much so that I used to hold meeting all night, especially if there were any concerned about their immortal soul. . . . The way in which we worshiped is almost indescribable. The singing was accompanied by a certain ecstasy of motion, clapping of hands, tossing of heads, which would continue without cessation about half an hour; one would lead off in a kind of recitative style, others joining in the chorus. . . . When Nat Turner's insurrection broke out, the colored people were forbidden to hold meetings among themselves. . . . Not-

25. Pearse, *Narrative*, p. 68. Pearse was born in Massachusetts in 1786 (p. 10).
26. Clay, *Detail*, p. 4.

withstanding our difficulties, we used to steal away to some of the quarters to have our meetings.[27]

In spite of these restrictions, some organized black congregations continued to exist. For example, the Sharp Street Methodist Church in Baltimore was visited on July 19, 1835, by a New Englander, Ethan Allen Andrews, who reported:

> The preacher, this morning, was an old colored man. . . . The responses . . . became, in some instances, so sudden and piercing, as to be even startling to one unaccustomed to such an accompaniment; but they plainly served to arouse the attention of the assembly in a remarkable degree. . . . The singing . . . was excellent. . . . There is, in some of the African voices, a wild and touching pathos, which art can never reach.[28]

A more detailed report of a Negro church service in Lexington, Virginia, was written by a member of a deputation from the Congregational Union of England and Wales:

> The building, called a church, is without the town, and placed in a hollow, so as to be out of sight. . . . It is a poor log-house, built by the hands of the negroes, and so placed as to show that they must worship by stealth. It is, perhaps, 20 by 25; with boarding and rails breast-high, run around three sides, so as to form galleries. To this is added a lean-to, to take the overplus. . . . The place was quite full, the women and men were arranged on opposite sides. . . .
>   By the law of the State, no coloured persons are permitted to assemble for worship, unless a white person be present and preside. . . . At this time, two whites and two blacks were in the pulpit. One of the blacks . . . gave out Dr. Watt's beautiful Psalm, "Show pity, Lord; oh Lord, forgive," &c. They all rose immediately. They have no books, for they could not read; but it was printed on their memory, and they sang it off with freedom and feeling. There is much melody in their voices; and when they enjoy a hymn, there is a raised expression of the face, and an undulating motion of the body, keeping time with the music, which is very touching. . . . This was the first time I had worshipped with an assembly of slaves; and I shall never forget it. . . .[29]

Another visitor from the British Isles wrote of the preference of the slaves for all-black churches:

> The reluctance of slaves to worship in the same congregation with their masters, is unfavorable to the interests of true piety. That there is such a reluctance, every one knows who has had much to do with . . . slavery. . . . The negro of our southern States prefers going to a church or meeting composed of people of his own colour, and where no whites appear. Slaves, also, sometimes prefer places of worship where greater latitude is

27. James L. Smith, *Autobiography*, pp. [162]–65.
28. Ethan Allen Andrews, *Slavery*, pp. 89–93.
29. Reed and Matheson, *Narrative*, I, 217–22.

allowed for noisy excitement . . . than would be tolerated in the religious assemblies of white people.[30]

Reports from plantation owners corroborated the existence of exclusively black meetings. R. F. W. Allston wrote from Georgetown District, South Carolina, in May, 1845: "By the rules of my plantation the Methodists and Baptists have prayer-meetings at given houses, each twice in the week, besides Sunday, when they meet, and pray, and sing together. These meetings are exclusively for the negroes on my own plantation. I have had this custom for 15 years, and it works well. . . ." From North Santee, James H. Ladson reported, "Persons of colour are not allowed to preach, although it is occasionally done amongst themselves. . . . Meetings for prayer and singing are frequent. . . ."[31]

These comments make it clear that the laws against religious meetings of blacks were not rigidly enforced. A specific statement to that effect, insofar as the state of South Carolina was concerned, was made in 1848: "The 2d section of the Act of 1800, which prohibited meetings for the religious or mental instruction of slaves, or free negroes, mulattoes, or mestizos, before the rising of the sun or after the going down of same . . . [are] now . . . dead letters. Religious meetings of negroes, with only one or more white persons, are permitted by night as well as day."[32] The requirement of a white's presence must have irritated some blacks, but this kind of accommodation was unavoidable in the antebellum South, unless the meetings were kept completely secret from the whites.

Fredrika Bremer observed the evening worship of the Negroes of Columbia, South Carolina, in May, 1850:

> One evening . . . I was present at the evening worship of the negroes, in a hall which that good, right-thinking minister had allowed them to use. . . . [It was not] until the singing of one of the hymns composed by the negroes themselves, such as they sing in their canoes . . . that the congregation became really alive. They sang so that it was a pleasure to hear, with all their souls and with all their bodies in unison; for their bodies wagged, their heads nodded, their feet stamped, their knees shook, their elbows and their hands beat time to the tune and the words which they sang with evident delight. One must see these people singing if one is rightly to understand their life.[33]

A visiting English clergyman, Russell Lant Carpenter, preached in Dr. Samuel Gilman's Charleston, South Carolina, church on Sun-

30. Baird, *Religion*, p. 77.
31. Charleston, Citizens, *Proceedings*, pp. 34–35, 51–55.
32. O'Neall, *Negro Law*, p. 24.
33. Bremer, *Homes of the New World*, I, 393–94.

day, April 7, 1851. (Gilman was the husband of Caroline Howard Gilman, whose writings have been cited frequently in these pages.) In the evening

> I attended a religious meeting of Negroes, in a large upper room adjoining Dr. Gilman's house, which lasts from seven to half-past nine o'clock. Mrs. G. makes a point of attending. . . . The service was conducted by two old black men. . . . A prayer-meeting for the women followed. . . . Hymns were sung, but with little credit to their musical powers. When they were told to sing "more spiritually" (spiritedly?), they gave us one or two characteristic songs: one was a sort of Easter recitative. The minister walked among them and gave out a line, such as—"I go before you to Galilee;" then the rest sung "Hallelujah!" with great zeal. The burden of another song was to this effect—"We shall have nothing at all to do but ring Jerusalem;" and they did "ring Jerusalem" with amazing animation, the old men gesticulating, and the others waving to and fro and singing with the greatest earnestness.[34]

Charles Colcock Jones's son-in-law, the Reverend Robert Mallard, wrote to his wife about a Negro service he witnessed in Chattanooga in 1859. His reactions were characteristic not only of a Presbyterian minister, but of white southern society generally.

> I was much interested, and yet at the same time shocked, by a spectacle which I witnessed two nights ago. Hearing singing in the neighborhood of the hotel, I went to the church from which it proceeded. It belongs to the white congregation of a Cumberland Presbyterian church. I stood at the door and looked in—and such confusion of sights and sounds! The Negroes were holding a revival meeting. Some were standing, others sitting, others moving from one seat to another, several exhorting along the aisles. The whole congregation kept up one loud monotonous strain, interrupted by various sounds: groans and screams and clapping of hands. One woman specially under the influence of the excitement went across the church in a quick succession of leaps: now down on her knees with a sharp crack that smote upon my ear the full length of the church, then up again; now with her arms about some brother or sister, and again tossing them wildly in the air and clapping her hands together and accompanying the whole by a series of short, sharp shrieks. I was astonished that such proceedings were countenanced in even a Cumberland church. . . . Considering the mere excitement manifested in these disorderly ways, I could but ask: What religion is there in this? . . . Some allowance, of course must be made for the *excitability* of the Negro temperament. What better, indeed, could we expect of those who only imitate (somewhat exaggerating it, of course) the conduct of some of their masters, who should know better?[35]

34. Carpenter, *Observations*, pp. 33–37, part of a letter addressed "To the editor of the *Christian Reformer*," dated "Neath, Aug. 23, 1851."
35. Letter from Rev. R. Q. Mallard to Mrs. Mary S. Mallard, Chattanooga, May 18, [1859], in Myers, ed., *Children of Pride*, pp. 482–83.

Mallard agreed with his father-in-law on how church services should be conducted. To them it was the height of impiety and desecration for members of the congregation to punctuate the remarks of the minister with individual or group responses. Many of the activities which horrified genteel Protestants in the United States were characteristic of African cultures—general participation in the singing (and dancing), wide dependence on short musical units and on antiphonal or responsorial techniques (call-and-response), improvisation, clapping, and bodily movement.[36]

A later description of a black church service written by a Union solider vividly pictured the participation of the congregation. This service took place in a white church in Tigerville, Louisiana, in 1863, in a church made available to the blacks by Union forces:

> The church is crowded; doors and casements choked with joyous black people . . . many . . . of them were once forbidden to meet for purposes of worship, lest . . . Insurrection might arise. . . . I cannot more than indicate the chorus attending every effective pause [in the exhortation]; a curious monotoned vocal symphony, which, like some long-drawn congregational "Amen!" responded in a sort of humming chant. The rhythmic melody of this low refrain of mingling voices cannot be realized without a hearing of it. It is not so much an audible syllablizing, as a suppressed hum, like inward singing.[37]

The congregation in Tigerville was more "civilized," more restrained, than the one in Chattanooga, but the basic desire for participation was the same.

On the periphery between folk and European-influenced, "scientific" music were the church choirs in major southern cities, notably the choir of the First African Baptist Church of Richmond. The white pastor, Robert Ryland, took great pride in the singing of this choir, realistically acknowledging that the choir, and not his preaching, attracted visitors to the church:

> The choir, consisting of about thirty, is seated in the front gallery. Just below the pulpit, you see a few intelligent strangers, white persons of the highest class. . . . These persons have come in to witness the novel scene, and to hear the singing of the choir and congregation. They expect nothing of special interest in the preaching . . . the singing is the great attraction. The whole assembly is united in an old fashioned, spiritual song, and the zeal, the harmony, the fervor, the number and volume of voices, all tend to excite feelings of devotion. The pastor now rises to give out a hymn. It is lead by the choir and joined by the whole multitude *standing.* . . . [After a prayer] is a hymn of their own selection, sung by the choir, all of whom are members of the church. They study and

36. Nettl, *Folk and Traditional Music*, "Music of Black Africa," pp. 128, 140ff.
37. Duganne, *Camps and Prisons*, pp. 80, 82.

O Lord, bless our Pastor, Stand by him and preserve him, &c.

Prayer chanted by a member of the First African Baptist Church, Richmond, notated by George F. Root in his "Congregational Singing among Negroes," *New-York Musical Review and Choral Advocate* 6 (March 29, 1855): 107. Courtesy of Music Division, New York Public Library.

practice music on scientific principles, have the best works on psalmody that the country affords, and take a generous pride in excelling in their noble art. . . . [After the benediction] the whole congregation resume the spiritual songs, which resemble the sound of many waters.[38]

But even here, the congregation enjoyed bodily movement and strong rhythm. About 1851 an Englishwoman visited the church, reporting:

> On the Sunday we went to the African Baptist church [in Richmond]. It is entirely supported and attended by coloured people, most of whom are free. Their minister, Mr. Rylands, is a white man. . . .
> After the departure of the minister, there was an amateur performance of singing and exhortation, in which a few old people got very much excited, swinging their bodies about, stamping their feet, and shaking hands frantically with everybody near them, myself amongst the rest.[39]

OPPOSITION TO SECULAR MUSIC AND DANCING

In the late 1840's travelers began to report that blacks sang only religious songs, implying that this was a distinctively black religious practice.[40] During and after the Civil War, when Northerners first heard and collected Negro spirituals, they frequently repeated this statement as characterizing their experiences. The early collectors worked in areas that had been strongly evangelized, and their experience seems to have been largely responsible for the widely expressed impression that the slaves had no secular music. Unquestionably they had great difficulty in gathering any secular songs. When Helen W. Ludlow of Hampton Institute attempted to persuade a former slave to sing corn songs for her, she was told,

---

38. [Ryland,] "Reminiscences," [289]–92. The composer, George F. Root, praised the singing of the congregation of this church for its general participation and its adherence to conventional norms in his "Congregational Singing Among Negroes," p. 107. See also "Congregational Singing in Richmond, Va.," p. 333.

39. Marianne Finch, *Englishwoman's Experience*, pp. 297–99.

40. For example, the claim that tobacco workers in Richmond sang only hymns. Cf. Bremer, *Homes of the New World*, I, 369, entry for May 25, 1850, and Bryant, "Tour," in his *Prose Writings*, II, 23–26, Mar. 2, 1843.

"Nuffin's good dat aint religious, madam. Nobody sings dem corn-shuckin' songs after dey's done got religion."[41] Not everyone associated this belief with the blacks; Sir Charles Lyell attributed the silencing of "twenty violins" to the Methodist missionaries,[42] but he was an exception.

The prejudice against secular music, and especially against dancing, has not been traced to Africa, where such distinctions between sacred and secular cannot be said to have existed. This is one case where the blacks appear to have been influenced by the whites, for a prejudice against dancing can be documented among white evangelicals from the early eighteenth century. In 1739 George Whitefield, the English evangelist, wrote in his journal his disapproval of dancing. On Christmas Day he wrote from Newborn [sic], North Carolina, "It grieves me to find that in every little town there is a settled dancing-master, but scarcely anywhere a settled minister . . . dreadful. . . ." On New Year's Day, 1740, he described his futile efforts to convince his hostess of the sinfulness of dancing:

> It being New Year's Day, several of the neighbors were met together to divert themselves by dancing country dances . . . a woman was dancing a jig. . . . I endeavored to shew the folly of such entertainments, and to convince her how well pleased the devil was at every step she took. For some time she endeavored to outbrave me; neither the fiddler nor she desisted; but at last she gave over, and the musician laid aside his instrument. . . . [A long controversy ensued, with Whitefield having the pleasure of the last word.] Notwithstanding all that had been said, after I had gone to bed, I heard their music and dancing. . . .[43]

The Great Awakening of the mid-eighteenth century was characterized by "a horror of dancing, fox-hunting, and card-playing" on the part of "many dissenting groups."[44] These attitudes were shared by Bishop William Meade of the Protestant Episcopal Church of the Diocese of Virginia, who wrote with indignation of an incident that occurred soon after he entered the ministry on February 24, 1811. He had been asked to officiate at a wedding, and later he was invited to stay for refreshments: "At a place where I expected, and had a right to expect, more respect, the fiddle and dances were introduced into the room where I was sitting, without any warning. . . . As soon as I could, I escaped, and ordering my horse . . . went several miles to a neighbor's house. My conduct was well under-

41. Armstrong and Ludlow, *Hampton and Its Students*, p. 113.
42. Lyell, *Second Visit*, I, 269–70, entry for Dec. 31, 1845.
43. Whitefield, *Journals*, pp. 378–82.
44. Middleton, "Colonial Virginia Parson," p. [425].

stood, as I wished it to be, and I have never since been thus treated."[45] (AS 4)

This condemnation of dancing was neither eccentric nor an isolated phenomenon, but widespread and quite general among both white and black converts to various evangelical sects. Devereux Jarratt, for example, was born in New Kent County, Virginia, near Richmond in 1732/3. After a youthful enjoyment of such diversions as cards, racing, and dancing, he repented and turned to religion. During a visit to his home,

> all the black people on the plantation, seemed overjoyed at my coming.
> . . . They knew I have been very fond at company . . . and wished to
> entertain me with frolic and dance. This proposal I rejected . . . they soon
> discovered . . . that my mind was turned to religion . . . they thought I
> carried matters quite too far. We all ought to be good, say they, but sure
> there can be no harm in *innocent mirth*, such as dancing, drinking, and
> making merry, &c.
>
>   . . . .
>
> When I say I have still a good ear for music, and relish for harmonious
> sounds, I need not tell you I mean vocal music and such only as is
> employed in the solemn worship of God.—In my younger days, it is true,
> I learned to play on the violin; yet, after I came to serious reflection, and
> saw the pernicious use, to which the music of that instrument was
> generally applied, I conscientiously laid it aside, and to this day, I shut
> my ears against it. I think I have not heard a tune on the violin, more
> than once, for near 30 years.[46]

In an address delivered at the African Masonic Hall, Boston, on February 27, 1833, Maria W. Stewart applied these same principles to the special circumstances of the blacks:

> I would implore our men, and especially our rising youth, to flee from
> the gambling board and the dance-hall; for we are poor, and have no
> money to throw away. I do not consider dancing as criminal in itself, but
> it is astonishing to me that our young men are so blind to their own
> interest and the future welfare of their children, as to spend their hard
> earnings for this frivolous amusement; for it has been carried on among
> us to such an unbecoming extent, that it has become absolutely disgusting. . . . These polite accomplishments will never enroll your names
> on the bright annals of fame. . . . Then, O ye sons of Africa, turn your
> mind from these perishable objects, and contend for the cause of God
> and the rights of man. . . . Let our money, instead of being thrown away
> as heretofore, be appropriated for schools and seminaries of learning for
> our children and youth. . . .[47]

45. Johns, *Memoir*, p. 85.
46. Jarratt, *Life*, pp. 42–43, 7–8.
47. Maria W. Stewart, "Address," in Porter, ed., *Early Negro Writing*, p. 132.

Even the aristocracy was not immune to this kind of social pressure. Mrs. Roger Pryor, wife of a Confederate brigadier-general, wrote of her childhood in Charlottesville, Virginia, in the 1840's. Not even the presence of the University of Virginia was insurance against this kind of provincialism.

> There was a crusade against all card-playing and dancing. The pendulum was swinging far back from an earlier time when . . . the dancing-master held long sessions, travelling from house to house. To have a regular dancing party with violins and cotillon, was like "driving a coach-and-six straight through the Ten Commandments!" My aunt, however, had the courage of her convictions, and allowed me small and early dances in our parlor, with only piano music. Old Jesse Scott lived at the foot of the hill—but to the length of introducing him and his violin we dared not go. As it was, after our first offence, a sermon was preached in the Presbyterian church against the vulgarity and sin of dancing.[48]

So generally accepted was this attitude that it appeared in many domestic novels as a normal component in the make-up of a good Christian. In one of the novels written as a reply to *Uncle Tom's Cabin*, disapproval of dancing was attributed to both the saintly black hero and an Episcopal minister. Uncle Robin told his master, "I doesn' go whar dar's dancin' an' fiddlin," referring to a dance for the blacks; the minister was asked "whether a little family dance, for the amusement of the young [white] people would be disagreeable to him. . . . [He replied] I have no consent to give or withhold . . . if the Major and Mrs. Scott are willing, and a dance is gotten up, I cannot consent to remain here and witness it, but will have my horse brought out, and go home." Much discussion ensued as to whether members of the church, black and white, should or could dance.[49]

The question of dancing was an emotionally charged one for all devout people, but especially for the whites who wished to make decisions for blacks. Articles on plantation management discussed the wisdom of permitting dancing, along with other matters of good discipline:

> I must not omit to mention that I have a good fiddler, and keep him well supplied with cat-gut, and I make it his duty to play for the negroes every Saturday night until 12 o'clock. They are exceedingly punctual in their attendance at the ball, while Charley's fiddle is always accompanied by Ihurod on the triangle and Sam to "pat."
>
> I also employ a good preacher, who regularly preaches to them on the Sabbath day, and it is made the duty of every one to come up clean and decent to the place of worship.[50]

48. Pryor, *My Day*, pp. 54–57.
49. Page, *Uncle Robin*, pp. 155, 159ff.
50. "A Mississippi Planter," "Management of Negroes," p. 625.

This statement inspired a reply from "A Small Farmer":

> I have a fiddle in my quarters, and though some of my good old brethren
> in the church would think hard of me, yet I allow dancing; ay, I buy the
> fiddle and encourage it, by giving the boys occasionally a big supper. . . .
> [If I had more money] I would build a house large enough, and use it for
> a dance-house for the young, and those who wished to dance, as well as
> for prayer-meetings, and for church on Sundays. . . . I know the rebuke in
> store about dancing, but I cannot help it. I believe negroes will be better
> disposed this way than any other. . . .[51]

The efforts made by the evangelical sects to discourage secular
music and dancing were widely reported. Sir Charles Lyell's account
has already been mentioned. Moncure Conway, born near Fal-
mouth, Virginia, recalled: "In all the twenty-three years of my life
in the land of Slavery [1832–54] I never saw a Negro-dance. . . . The
slaves of the Border States are almost invariably members of the
Baptist and Methodist societies, which are particularly rigid in
denying them such amusements. . . . I have rarely known their
enthusiasm enlisted in any thing except prayer-and-experience
meetings and funerals."[52] Fredrika Bremer visited the plantation of
Joel Poinsett near Charleston in April, 1850. Hoping to witness slave
dancing, of which she had heard much, she visited the slave quarters
on a Sunday evening, but all she heard was

> a sound as of prayer and zealous exhortation. . . . I have since heard that
> the Methodist missionaries, who are the most influential and effective
> teachers and preachers among the negroes, are very angry with them for
> their love of dancing and music, and declare them to be sinful. And
> whenever the negroes become Christian, they give up dancing, have
> preaching meetings instead, and employ their musical talents merely on
> psalms and hymns. This seems to me a very unwise proceeding on the
> part of the preachers. . . .[53] (AS 5)

A South Carolinian recalled the conversion of a fiddler from his
boyhood:

> Griffin was a fiddler whose reputation extended far beyond the boun-
> daries of his master's plantation. Not only did he furnish music for his
> own people at their annual "cake-walks," but he helped often to furnish
> music at the dances of the white race. That fact . . . made him an
> aristocrat. . . . When he left home . . . for the Smyrna camp meeting,
> Griffin was in a jolly, good humor. He called back to one of his fellows: "I
> don't mind camp meetin', ef dey des let me play my fiddle." In two hours
> Griffin was picked up at the foot of Crosby's Hill on Rocky River in an
> unconscious condition and minus one ear. Regaining consciousness, he

51. "A Small Farmer," "Art. III—Management of Negroes," pp. 371–72.
52. Conway, *Testimonies*, pp. 3–4.
53. Bremer, *Homes of the New World*, I, 285, 289–90.

declared: "Dis is de judgment ob de Lord; I'll nuver tech dat fiddle ag'in." And he didn't.[54]

A former slave, Willis Winn, born March 10, 1822, reported a similar conversion: "I was always wild and played for dances but . . . after I married I quieted down. When I joined the church, I burned my fiddle up."[55] (AS 6)

A few slaveowners disapproved of the extreme social pressure that prevented some slaves from dancing when they wished to. James H. Hammond, for instance, penciled in his plantation manual: "Church members are privileged to dance on all holyday occasions; and the class-leader or deacon who may report them shall be reprimanded or punished at the discretion of the master."[56] Christmas was celebrated near Danville, Virginia, in 1855 with a dance, despite the strong feeling against it. "The Judge, though a strict church member, would not forbid such as were so disposed, to have a dance . . . although the amusement was not approved of by many of the older persons, and the churches condemned, yet it began to be tolerated."[57] And a New England "school-marm" reported her conversation with a Negro minister in Gordonsville, Virginia, in March, 1870:

"Miss Chase, is there anyting in the Bible in favor of Dancing," he said to me one day. "There is nothing in the Bible against it," I said. "Doesn't it say, 'you must become a new creature and lay aside old things,' " he said. . . . [After much talking on both sides] Mr. Tibbs inquired, "Well, Miss Chase, do you suppose God dances?" I could not resist . . . saying, "Do you suppose he eats three meals a day?" I told Mr. T. . . . the legitimate objections to dancing, and made him acknowledge that raising the feet with a light, rapid motion, is in itself no more sinful than walking. "But, then, there's the fiddle, you know," he said. "But the fiddle is not wicked," I replied. "I think it is," he said.[58]

Despite the few tolerant thinkers, the more common attitude was expressed in the thirteenth annual report of the white Association for the Religious Instruction of the Negroes in Liberty County, Georgia, in 1848:

And *the amusements* of the negroes deserve notice. The chief amusement, and that to which they become passionately fond is *dancing*. No

---

54. Clinkscales, *On the Old Plantation*, pp. 8–12.
55. Yetman, "*Peculiar Institution*," pp. 330–33.
56. MS, Hammond Papers, Library of Congress, quoted in Ulrich Bonnell Phillips, *American Negro Slavery*, p. 315.
57. Farmer, *Virginia*, pp. 17, 29.
58. Swint, ed., *Dear Ones*, pp. 246–47.

one will deny that it is an amusement of the world, and not of the Church. Fiddlers and dancers are not sober and devout persons; neither are those, whatever be their professions, who encourage them. . . . With the negroes dancing is a dissipating, demoralizing amusement, and is so viewed by those who are the really serious, virtuous and pious among them. Their dances are not only protracted to unseasonable hours, but too frequently become the resort of the most dissolute and abandoned, and for the vilest purposes. I do not think religion or good morals can flourish on a plantation where this amusement is permitted, and Christian owners should be the last persons to give it countenance.[59]

While the pious opponents of secular music and dancing won a partial victory in the areas that were described by Northerners after the Civil War, for the South as a whole neither side ever won complete dominance, and the controversy never really ended. (AS 7)

59. Association for the Religious Instruction of the Negroes in Liberty County, Georgia, *13th Annual Report*, p. 22.

ADDITIONAL SOURCES

AS1. The scenes described by Miss Bremer were by no means exceptional, as two additional quotations demonstrate.

But by no class is a camp-meeting hailed with more unmixed delight than by the poor slaves. It comes at a season of the year when they most need rest. It gives them all the advantages of an ordinary holiday, without its accompaniments of drunkenness and profanity. Here they get to see their mothers, their brothers, and their sisters from neighboring plantations; here they can sing and jump to their hearts' content.

When properly conducted more can be said in favor of camp-meetings than against them. . . . Camp-fires blazing in every direction . . . the groans and sobs of penitent sinners; the shout and rapture of the new convert; the rejoicing of friends; the deep, melodious organ-like music welling from a thousand African throats. . . .

John Dixon Long, *Pictures of Slavery*, pp. 159–60.
Another reminiscence was written many years later:

When I was a boy, I attended a yearly camp meeting held by the Cumberland Presbyterian Church near my home. . . . At every service the negroes were present in large numbers in a special section reserved for them, and many of them made professions of religion. Their singing was inspiring and was encouraged and enjoyed by the white congregation, who would sometimes remain silent to listen.

McNeilly, *Religion and Slavery*, pp. 83–84.

AS2. This attempt to discourage all congregational participation in the service except for formal responsive readings and hymns was shared by northern missionaries, black ministers of the more conservative school, and even by Union army officers, who were put in charge of refugee camps. The Reverend David Todd wrote from Pine Bluff, Arkansas, on July 4, 1864, about Colonel John Eaton, an army chaplain named superintendent of freedmen by General Grant: "When Colonel Eaton was here, he spoke at one of the meetings of the colored people on the idea that noise was not religion. We have exhibitions of dynamics in some of the meetings of the colored people, that I think savor little of devotion or edification. Such exercises are valued by some of the colored people, while others can see a purer want in their souls" (*American Missionary* 8 [Sept., 1864]: 216).

AS3. In Charleston in 1851, "lining out" was used by the Episcopal rector when he conducted a service at a "negro church": "Charleston May [10th, 1851] . . . We all went to a negro church. . . . The congregation responded and sang the Te Deum with Mr. G[lennie]. Some had books & could read, but as all could not, he would read two lines of a hymn & then they would all sing them & so on!!" (Easterby, ed., "South Carolina," p. 131).

"Lining out" continued in black churches after the Civil War. Belle Kearney, who was born near Vernon, Mississippi, in 1863, wrote in her memoirs:

> Some brother . . . begins the service by "lining out" a hymn, his voice intoning and dimly suggesting the tune with which the congregation follows,—one of those wild, weird negro airs, half chant and dirge, so full of demi-semi-quavers that only the improvisator-soul can divine it, yet, so full of strange, sweet melody and pathos, rendered in their marvelously tuneful voices, it is no wonder a suppressed emotion begins to communicate itself through the audience.

Kearney, *Slaveholder's Daughter*, p. 57.

AS4. Another example of Bishop Meade's attitude toward dancing was his republication of an undated dialogue, perhaps from the eighteenth century, between two slaves, Sambo and Toney, who had come from Africa on the same ship, and were separated only after the death of their first master. The dialogue concerns Sambo's attempt to convert Toney, whom he has not seen for a long time—an artificial but possibly contemporary projection of what pious whites thought blacks should think.

> Toney—Why Sambo, do you want me for leave off dance, and sing and frolic? Hey, Sambo, I can't leave them off, I love them too much; besides, Sambo, I know nothing 'bout this gospel and praying and all these things. . . . I am no such bad man as you think . . . True I love dance and frolic;—sure, Sambo, it's no harm, for make merry now and then . . . Is no body good but them praying sort a people?
>   Sambo—No body who allow themselves in such things as you plead for, can be good . . .
>   Toney—I tell you, Sambo, I never steal from any body but master, and that no harm, if he no find it out; . . . as for frolic and dance I love them for true. . . . I don't love this praying and going to meeting. What have we black people for do with that? the minister he never say any thing to us. . . .
>   [Later on Toney continues]—wicked thoughts come in my mind, I say, I don't care, I will dance and sing. I will take pleasure, God Almighty no expect black man should be like white man;—besides, don't white men dance and sing; yes, and curse and swear too, and he no fear going to hell. I am no worse than other people. . . . in the night . . . When I been going up to the negro's houses, I hear the fiddle, they been dance in the driver's house. O brother, I cant tell you how I feel. Before when I hear fiddle, I feel good, now my heart turn against it. I say to myself, Ah poor people! you're dancing to hell: I go by fast as I could, when I come to uncle Davy's house, I think I hear him pray. O go softly and listen. . . .

Meade, *Sermons*, pp. 197-206. Another edition attributed the authorship to the Reverend [Edmund] Botsford, *Sambo and Toney, a Dialogue Between Two Africans in South Carolina* (Philadelphia: D. Hogan, 1816). This copy in the Library Company of Philadelphia is Item 1398 in the bibliography, *Afro-Americana, 1553-1906*.

AS5. A visitor to the South in the summer of 1855 reported to the Hartford *Republican*: "There has been a great revival on the plantation [Botten Garden], and all are very pious. They sing nothing but hymns" (Parsons, *Inside View*, pp. 276-77). And the Reverend Robert Mallard quoted a letter from a fellow minister who described the changes in recreation on his father's plantation: "Previously the plantation resounded with the . . . merry strain of the fiddle, the measured beat of the 'quaw sticks,' and the rhythmical shuffling and patting of the feet in the Ethiopian jig. Now, the fiddle and the quaw sticks were abandoned, and the light, carnal song gave way to psalms and hymns" (*Plantation Life*, pp. 162–63).

AS6. Daniel Hundley commented in 1860, "It is notable what a change for the better Christianity produces in even the most degraded of them [the slaves]. They readily give up their banjos, their fiddles, their double-shuffles, and breakdowns, and are eager to learn what is right and becoming" (*Social Relations*, p. 349). By 1892 this pervasive evangelical belief had dwindled into a "Negro superstition." The *Journal of American Folk-lore* (V, 329–30) published an item entitled "Negro Superstition Concerning the Violin":

> The "Boston Transcript," October, 1892, affirms that for many years, and even long before the war, playing the fiddle and the banjo had been dying out among the negroes, owing to a superstition that "de devil is a fiddler." . . . It is . . . thought unbecoming, at least, for a "chu'ch member" to play the violin, if not actually an audacious communication with Satan himself. But it involves neither deadly sin nor any spiritual risk whatever to play the accordeon or "lap organ," as they call it. . . .

AS7. The antagonism between secular music and dancing and evangelical religion was epitomized in a fictional description of a slave prison published in 1836. The hero, Archy Moore, was awaiting sale in the slave depot of Savage, Brothers & Co. in Washington, D.C.

> Day came—the prison-door was unlocked, and we were let out into the enclosure about it. . . . A tall young fellow . . . produced a three stringed fiddle, and after preluding for a few moments, struck up a lively tune. The sound of the music soon drew a large group about him, who provided themselves with partners and began a dance. As the fiddler warmed to his business, he played faster and faster, and the dancers, amidst laughs and shouts and boisterous merriment, did their best to keep up with the tune.
> It is thus that men . . . betake themselves to artificial excitements. Too often, we sing and dance, not because we are merry, but in the hope to be so; and merriment itself is seldomer the expression and the evidence of pleasure, than the disguise of weariness and pain. . . .
> But the entire company did not join the dancers. As it happened, it was Sunday, and a part of them seemed to entertain conscientious scruples about dancing on that, and for ought I know, upon any other day. The more sober part of the company gradually collected together in the opposite corner of the prison-yard; and a sedate young man . . . struck up a Methodist psalm. . . . He was soon joined by several others; and as the chorus swelled, the sound of the psalmody almost drowned the scraping of the fiddle and the laughter of the dancers. . . .

Hildreth, *The Slave*, pp. 135–37. This novel was widely assumed to be a real slave narrative, giving rise to considerable controversy, although the author never claimed that it was true.

Another treatment in fiction of the opposition to secular music and dance was written by a white woman, Harriet E. Prescott, and published in 1865 in a sketch called "Down the River" in the *Atlantic Monthly* (XVI, 469). The heroine was described as "of pure race . . . an indigenous outcrop of African soil . . . a dancer . . . tossing a tambourine, and singing wild, meaningless songs." (Because the author found the songs meaningless, apparently she assumed everyone did.)

> She used to whirl and spring on the grass-plot of an evening, the young masters and mistresses smiling and applauding from the verandah. . . .

It was not, however, an indiscriminate assemblage even there that encouraged her rude art.... The more decorous of the slaves gave small favor to the young posturer, although the patronage she received from the house enabled her to meet their disapprobation defiantly....

Prescott then compared the steps of sacred and secular dancing realistically, if one disregards her rhetoric:

It was not that the frowning ones did not go through many of the same motions themselves; but theirs were occasioned by the frenzy of religious excitement, where pious rapture and ecstasy were to be expressed by nothing but the bodily exertion of the Shout; the objectless dance of the dancer was a thing beyond their comprehension, dimly at first, and then positively, associated with sin.... For the religion of the Shout she had no absorbents whatever; she furtively watched it, and openly ridiculed it....

12

Distinctive Black Religious Music

SPIRITUALS

Many of the missionaries who wished to stamp out black secular
music and dancing hoped to substitute for them approved evangelical hymns, the appropriate music for the serious, pious congregations they envisaged. But, as everyone who has ever heard a spiritual or a gospel song knows, it didn't quite work out that way. The
fiddle may have been silenced and the dancers forbidden to cross
their legs, but the droning hymnody was transformed into something quite different. Whatever it may have been initially (and that
we may never know, for no missionary focused his attention on the
transformation of this music), by the time contemporary reporters
described it, black sacred music shared many points of stylistic
similarity with secular black music: rhythmic complexity, gapped
scales, overlapping of leader and chorus, bodily movement, extended repetition of short melodic phrases—all now recognized as
characteristics of African musics. These distinctive qualities presented insoluble problems to the early collectors of slave music, who
were able to do little more than notate the general outline of the
melody. Nineteenth-century transcriptions of the music display few
distinctive features that would differentiate it from white nineteenth-century music. Contemporary descriptions demonstrate,
however, that there were widely perceived differences, although
they could not be analyzed in those days before the invention of
recording.

As early as 1819 a severe critic of camp meeting "excesses," John F. Watson, attributed what he considered objectionable aspects of the music to the influence of the "illiterate *blacks*":

> We have too, a growing evil, in the practice of singing in our places of public and society worship, *merry* airs, adapted from old *songs*, to hymns . . . most frequently composed and first sung by the illiterate *blacks* of the society. . . . In the *blacks'* quarter [of a camp meeting], the colored people get together, and sing for hours together, short scraps of disjointed affirmations, pledges, or prayers, lengthened out with long repetition *choruses*. These are all sung in the merry chorus-manner of the southern harvest field, or husking-frolic method of the slave blacks; and also very like the Indian dances. With every word so sung, they have a sinking of one or other leg of the body alternately, producing an audible sound of the feet at every step, and as manifest as the steps of actual negro dancing in Virginia, &c. If some in the mean time sit, they strike the sounds alternately on each thigh.[1]

What had been seen at camp meetings in 1819 continued to be widely observed throughout the South. When Darwin's friend, Sir Charles Lyell, visited Hopeton plantation near Darien, Georgia, in 1845, he commented, "At the Methodist prayer-meetings, they are permitted to move round rapidly in a ring . . . presenting first the right hand and then the left, in which manoeuvre, I am told, they sometimes contrive to take enough exercise to serve as a substitute for the dance. . . ."[2] The leaping and jumping of the early camp meetings seem to have been gradually subdued into possibly less obtrusive movements during the service, with a "holy dance" or "shout" permitted afterwards. The documentation of this development is still to be found, but other white reporters of black religious practices, though unquestionably biased, recorded impressions of the similarities between the sacred and secular music of the blacks. One report, although published in 1894, could have been equally appropriate for the antebellum period:

> The negro race seems to be the most religious of any in the world, and he falls into the exercises of singing and praying, &c., throwing himself into it with all the enthusiasm that he did in the old time corn songs and the dance. A prominent Methodist D. D., who traveled in the South on a tour of observation, turning his attention particularly to the colored race, after much observation said, "It seems to me that the negro has taken to religion as a matter of amusement, in place of his former employment of banjo playing, singing and dancing."[3]

1. [John Fanning Watson,] *Methodist Error*, pp. 15–16.
2. Lyell, *Second Visit*, I, 270.
3. Michaux, *Sketches*, pp. 23–24.

This Methodist minister must have found it inconceivable that there could be any question as to what was fitting and proper behavior during a church service, but the distinctions between sacred and secular that were so clear to him were not part of African tradition. Practices that seemed irreligious to whites were perfectly proper to devout and conventional blacks.

Another manifestation of the lack of distinction between sacred and secular was the incorporation of "secular" text in what were basically religious songs. For example, a version of "Swing Low, Sweet Chariot," published in 1903, included this third stanza:

> Banjos pickin', jewsharps zoonin',
> All de hebbenly ban' a-chunin',
> Swing low, sweet charriyut.
> Sing en shout bofe night en day,
> Stop jus long ernuff to pray,
> Swing low, sweet charriyut.[4]

Banjos and Jew's harps were as secular in their associations as the fiddle, but in this song they play for the "hebbenly ban'," a mingling of images wholly foreign to nineteenth-century Protestant hymnody. (It is possible that this stanza was constructed by the white author as a humorous example of ignorance. Certainly no banjos or fiddles were found in *Slave Songs of the United States*.)

John Watson's complaint about the songs "frequently composed and first sung by the illiterate *blacks*" is the earliest known mention of distinctive black religious music. His description ("short scraps of disjointed affirmations . . . with long repetition *choruses*") could have referred to what came to be known as Negro spirituals, although he did not use the term. Indeed, that term, as distinct from "spiritual song," has not been found before the Civil War, but its absence should not be interpreted as proof that the songs did not exist. Reports of black religious singing before the Civil War often do not distinguish between songs from denominational hymnals and those that were original. (AS 1) When references to distinctive black religious songs began to appear, they were casual and offhand, implying that the songs were too well known to require detailed description. In view of the controversy that has grown up about the spirituals, it seems worthwhile to quote available descriptions of

4. Hobson, *In Old Alabama*, pp. 159–60. This book was an "Uncle Remus" type of reporting black folklore, condescending in tone, but nevertheless reporting dance steps, song texts (other than this), and folk traditions that can be corroborated in other, more dispassionate sources. This particular text has not been found elsewhere.

distinctive black religious song, however vague, since they represent the gleaning of a most extended search in contemporary sources.

In the summer of 1821 Levi and Vestal Coffin, cousins, organized a Sunday school for slaves at New Garden, North Carolina. As Levi recalled many years later, "One of Thomas Caldwell's slaves, called Uncle Frank . . . made a long and fervent prayer. . . . Then the negroes broke out with one of their plantation songs, or hymns, led by Uncle Frank; a sort of prayer in rhyme, in which the same words occurred again and again."[5] Since Coffin moved to Indiana in 1822, the events could not have occurred much later, although his recollection may not have been completely reliable after the lapse of fifty-five years.

In 1830 a description of the black population of Charleston, South Carolina, was published by a Scottish trader, born and educated in Glasgow, who lived in the United States from 1822 until 1828. He spent considerable time in Charleston and, in a patronizing manner, summarized his impressions of the black population:

> The coloured people chiefly attend the Methodist and Baptist meetings. . . . The sermons occasionally, but the prayers always, are intermingled with the yelling and hooting of the Negroes . . . [who] make use of a thousand . . . gestures, quite indecorous in a place of worship. . . . Upon the evening of a Sunday, the song of praise may frequently be heard to issue from the hovel of the Negro, whilst all is quiet in the mansions of the wealthy. . . . The religious fervor of the Negroes does not always break forth in strains the most reverential or refined. The downfall of the archfiend forms the principal topic of their anthems. A few lines recollected at random may serve as an example, as—

> > "Sturdy sinners, come along,
> > "Hip and thigh, we'll pull him down.
> > "Let us pull old Satan down,
> > "We shall get a heavenly crown," &c., &c.

> Or,

> > "Old Satan, come before my face
> > "To pull my kingdom down.
> > "Jesus come before my face
> > "To put my kingdom up.
> > > "Well done, tankee, Massa Jesus.
> > > Halleluja," &c.[6]

Another account, this time from a slave narrative, told the "true" story of the youth of Dinah on a plantation about two miles from Petersburg, Virginia, around 1830. "Now and then she went with other slaves to hear a service (of what sort I cannot gather from her

---

5. Coffin, *Reminiscences*, pp. 69–71.
6. Neilson, *Recollections*, pp. 258–59.

description) in a room near the court-house. . . . Young and artless slaves were encouraged to sing whatever hymns or songs they knew . . . as those generally expressed their own genuine feelings on the ills of slavery."[7] (So scanty are the records that even one as unsatisfactory as this is worth recording.) An account from 1834, while not attributing the authorship of the songs to the blacks, refers to "native harmony" as if it were something distinctive: "To hear at night . . . the songs of Zion, at a distance, caroled in tones of sweetest melody by many co-mingled voices, when native harmony outvies instructed skill . . . such is the melody with which night after night the Negroes charm the ear. . . ."[8]

Another account from 1834 appeared in one of the earliest magazines for children, *The Southern Rose Bud*, written by the northern-born Charleston author Caroline Howard Gilman. The description of slave children singing hymns came from a serial story intended "For My Youngest Readers." Called "The Country Visit," the story told of an outing on a nearby plantation, where three Charleston children saw everyday sights such as cotton picking. The tenth chapter was entitled "Singing Hymns," with the footnote: "It may add to the interest of these little sketches to know that the writer has witnessed the scenes she describes."

> George and James and Clara loved to hear the young negroes sing the hymns taught them by the old ones. The place the little choir chose for their singing seat was beneath a circle of cedar trees; they selected it themselves. . . . George . . . counted sixteen children. . . .
>
> There was a whispering among the young blacks for a few moments, and then they began with a shout, clear and ringing—

> "Master Jesus is my Captain,
> "He is my all in all,
> "He give me grace to conquer,
> "And take me home to rest.

> "I'm walking on to Jesus,
> Hallelujah!
> "I'm walking on to Jesus,
> Hallelujah!"

> The boys and Clara grew sleepy, but negroes will sit up all night singing if permitted, and Clara's papa had to tell them to go to bed. The infants were asleep in the larger children's arms. They parted off, each to their house, and as they went they sang,

> "Don't you hear the Gospel trumpet
> Sound Jubilee?"[9]

7. Simpson, *Horrors*, pp. 28–29.
8. Sims, *View of Slavery*, pp. 25–26.
9. *Southern Rose Bud* 2 (Aug. 9, 1834): 199.

In 1842 Charles Colcock Jones, a leader in missions to the slaves, advocated displacing the slaves' own religious songs with approved hymns by such writers as Isaac Watts: "One great advantage in teaching them good psalms and hymns is that they are thereby induced to lay aside the extravagant and nonsensical chants, and catches and hallelujah songs of their own composing; and when they sing, which is very often while about their business or of an evening in their houses, they will have something profitable to sing."[10] "Their own composing" leaves no room for doubt that Jones attributed these songs to the slaves themselves.

One Ella Storrs Christian wrote in her diary: "When Baptist Negroes attended the church of their masters, or when their mistress sang with them, they used hymn books, but in their own meetings they often made up their own words and tunes. They said their songs had 'more religion than those in the books.' "[11]

The first notice of these songs found in a musical journal leaves much to be desired in specific detail, but again is unambiguous as to the originality of the songs:

> Many of the slave melodies are well known at the north, but not much is said about their sacred music. Many of them sing all common psalm tunes with accuracy, and in addition there are verses evidently original. When you hear them you are half inclined to laugh at their queerness, and yet cannot but be affected at the sincerity and thrilling tones of the singer. Here is a specimen:
>
> > "Oh, Satan he came by my heart,
> > Throw brickbats in de door,
> > But *Master Jesus* come wid brush,
> > Make cleaner dan before."
> > *Another*, (spoken) "My soul leap, and my soul dance."
> > (sung) "My soul leap, and my soul dance."[12]

A clergyman, the Reverend James Waddell Alexander, D.D., was born in 1804 in Louisa County, Virginia, and wrote of slave singing in 1847:

> The fondness of the black race for music is proverbial. It is rare to meet with a negro who does not sing. . . . We have listened to a great variety of sacred music . . . but if we were summoned to declare which of all seemed most like the praise of God, we should reply, the united voices of a thousand slaves. . . . As the Southern servants can seldom read, and, therefore, have no use of hymn-books, the memory must be the sole depository of their sacred song. It is known that they largely fre-

10. Charles Colcock Jones, *Religious Instruction*, pp. 265–66.
11. Christian, *Diary* (MS), p. 59, quoted (without date) in Sellers, *Slavery in Alabama*, p. 300. The manuscript diary has not been located.
12. *Musical Gazette* (Boston) 1 (July 6, 1846): 91.

quent the assemblies of illiterate and enthusiastic persons, and catch up snatches of hymns, which are full of error, if not of absurd irreverence...[13]

The Reverend Mr. Alexander, despite his superior attitude toward the songs of the blacks, acknowledged that blacks had their own songs, transmitted by oral tradition.

A British Methodist, James Dixon, sailed from Liverpool for the United States on April 8, 1848. He subsequently described the music at a service he conducted in a black Pittsburgh church. "After the sermon the people sang some of their own peculiarly soft and melancholy airs. This excited them; and we had a remarkable scene. They leaped, I know not how high, and in a manner one would have thought impossible. But, more than this, they danced to their own melody, and in perfect time. . . . This looked strange to us sober people. . . ."[14]

During the 1850's descriptions of the distinctive religious songs of the blacks became more common. Fredrika Bremer visited two black churches in Cincinnati on November 27, 1850. In the morning she attended "a negro Baptist Church belonging to the Episcopal creed" where the "negro aristocracy of the city" conducted a service that was "quiet, very proper and a little tedious. The hymns were beautifully and exquisitely sung." But in the afternoon the service at the African Methodist Church in a black neighborhood was quite different:

I found in the African Church African ardor and African life. The church was full to overflowing, and the congregation sang their own hymns. The singing ascended and poured forth like a melodious torrent, and the heads, feet and elbows of the congregation moved all in unison with it, amid evident enchantment and delight in the singing. . . .

The hymns and psalms which the negroes have themselves composed have a peculiar *naive* character, childlike, full of imagery and life. Here is a specimen of one of their popular church hymns:

> "What ship is this that's landed at the shore!
>   Oh, glory halleluiah!
> It's the old ship of Zion, halleluiah,
> It's the old ship of Zion, halleluiah,
> Is the mast all sure, and the timber all sound?
>   Oh, glory halleluiah!
> She's built of gospel timber, halleluiah,
> She's built, &c.

13. Alexander, "Thoughts on Family Worship," in Charles Colcock Jones, *Suggestions*, p. 56. Alexander's forenames and facts of birth are given in *Suppressed Tract!* p. 70.

14. Dixon, *Personal Narrative*, p. 94.

"What kind of men does she have on board?
    Oh, glory halleluiah!
They're all true-hearted soldiers, halleluiah,
They're all, &c.

"What kind of Captain does she have on board?
    Oh, glory halleluiah!
King Jesus is the Captain, halleluiah,
King Jesus, &c.

"Do you think she will be able to land us on the shore?
    Oh, glory halleluiah!
I think she will be able, halleluiah,
I think, &c.

"She has landed over thousands, and can land as many more,
    Oh, glory halleluiah!" &c., &c.

After the singing of the hymn, which was not led by any organ or musical instruments whatever, but which arose like burning melodious sighs from the breasts of the congregation, the preacher mounted the pulpit.[15]

In the same year, 1851, a Reverend C. F. Sturgis, of Greensboro', Alabama, described black religious singing, presumably in the Deep South:

The negro is a great singer, and he sings religious songs in preference to any other; indeed, unless now and then a comic song, often, as I suspect, falsely attributed to them, they sing but few others. They sing at their work, at their homes, on the highway, and in the streets; and, in the large majority of cases, their songs have a decidedly religious character. How common to see an old woman at her work, "*lining out*" a hymn to herself, and then singing it in a spirit of rapt abstraction from earth and all earthly things.[16]

John D. Long, a Methodist minister in Maryland, published this description in 1857: "The prayer-meetings of the more degraded class of slaves are conducted after the following manner: The colored exhorter or leader calls on two or three in succession to pray, filling up the intervals with singing tunes and words composed by themselves."[17]

Another description dated "Macon, Georgia, 1858" gave more details:

15. Bremer, *Homes of the New World*, II, 157–60. The text quoted is similar to no. 125 in *Slave Songs* while related white versions were given by George Pullen Jackson in *Spiritual Folk Songs*, nos. 191, 210. Miss Bremer's account continued with a detailed description of the sermon and the congregation's interjections during it.
16. Sturgis, "Melville Letters," in *Duties of Masters to Servants*, p. 100.
17. John Dixon Long, *Pictures of Slavery*, p. 383.

Their [the Negroes'] hymns, or religious chants, might furnish a curious book. The words are generally very few, and repeated over and over again; and the lines, though very unequal, are sung with a natural cadence that impresses the ear quite agreeably. Most of them relate to the moment of death, and in some of them are simple and poetic images which are often touching. The following occur to me without any pains at selection:

> "Oh, carry me away, carry me away, my Lord!
> Carry me to the berryin' [burying?] ground,
> *The green trees a-bowing.* Sinner, fare you well!
> I thank the Lord I want to go.
> To leave them all behind. [repeat 1st 2 lines][18]

Native southern whites wrote little in the antebellum period about the sacred music of the blacks. Literally hundreds of letters and reminiscences were examined, page by page, with a most disappointing yield of meaningful information. One explanation was offered by George Tucker of Virginia in 1824: "There are thousands among us who never . . . even heard a corn song—so entirely separated are the two classes of black and white, and so little curiosity does that excite, which is, and always has been, near us. . . . No wonder, then, the rude ditties of our hewers of wood and drawers of water, should not provoke curiosity or interest humanity."[19] For the natives the songs lacked the novelty and exoticism that attracted the travelers, and familiarity deadened appreciation. Besides the ethnocentrism so characteristic of most nineteenth-century whites, these Southerners had the problem of preserving their European culture under difficult conditions—a problem exacerbated for many of them by their aristocratic pretensions. In their writings one finds two apparently contradictory views of this music: close at hand it was often dismissed as mere noise or uncivilized barbarism, but at a distance it became beautiful, melancholy, and nostalgic. The comments of Mary Boykin Chesnut, while more perceptive than most, are typical of this attitude. Her diary entry for October 13, 1861, described a service she attended with her husband's family at a Negro church on their plantation, Mulberry, near Camden, South Carolina:

> [There was] a very large black congregation. . . . Jim Nelson, the driver . . . a full-blooded African, was asked to lead in prayer. He became wildly excited, on his knees, facing us with his eyes shut. He clapped his hands at the end of every sentence, and his voice rose to the pitch of a shrill

18. Edward Alfred Pollard, *Black Diamonds*, pp. 28, 35–36.
19. [Tucker,] *Valley of Shenandoah*, II, 118.

shriek, yet was strangely clear and musical, occasionally in a plaintive minor key that went to your heart. Sometimes it rang out like a trumpet. I wept bitterly. It was all sound, however, and emotional pathos.... The words had no meaning at all. It was the devotional passion of voice and manner which was so magnetic. The Negroes sobbed and shouted and swayed backward and forward, some with aprons to their eyes, most of them clapping their hands and responding in shrill tones: "Yes, God!" "Jesus!" "Savior!" "Bless de Lord, amen," etc. It was a little too exciting for me. I would very much have liked to shout, too. Jim Nelson when he rose from his knees trembled and shook as one in a palsy, and from his eyes you could see the ecstasy had not left him yet. He could not stand at all, and sank back on his bench.....

Suddenly, as I sat wondering what next, they broke out into one of those soul-stirring Negro camp-meeting hymns. To me this is the saddest of all earthly music, weird and depressing beyond my powers to describe.

Yet on March 13 of the following year she wrote: "The best way to take Negroes to your heart is to get as far away from them as possible."[20]

A remarkably graphic description of slave music in 1856 was printed in Edinburgh in 1860. The author, Laurence Oliphant, had toured the southern United States in company with the editor of the London *Times*, John Thadeus Delane, summarizing his impressions of "the negro in the Southern States of America" with more detail than almost any other account of the antebellum period. For this reason, and because of the scarcity of the original, it seems appropriate to quote him at some length:

At the period of my visit, in consequence of a series of revivals, the result of perpetual camp-meetings, the negroes had assumed a certain air of solemn gravity and sobriety, a good deal at variance with the natural vivacity of their dispositions—a characteristic, however, which they never manage effectually to smother.

On some plantations in South Carolina they had given up dancing, held constant prayer-meetings, and never sang anything but their own sacred compositions. These chants break with their pleasant melody the calm stillness of evening, as we glide down the broad bosom of the Wacamaw, and our crew with measured stroke keep time to the music of their own choruses. The words, however, are more original than the music. Here are specimens taken down as they were sung:—

> "Oh, I takes my text in Matthew,
> And some in Revelation;
> Oh, I know you by your garment—
> There's a meeting here tonight,"

This is the entire effusion, and is constantly repeated, the last line being the chorus; some, however, are more elaborate:—

20. Chesnut, *Diary*, pp. 148–49, 199.

"In that morning, true believers,
                    In that morning,
We will sit aside of Jesus
                    In that morning,
If you should go fore I go,
                    In that morning,
You will sit aside of Jesus
                    In that morning,
True believers, where your tickets
                    In that morning,
Master Jesus got your tickets
                    In that morning."

And so on, with a number of variations, often extempore, but with the same refrain ever recurring, and joined in by all. Sometimes the metre is less regular, as—

"I want to sing as the angels sing,
                    Daniel;
I want to pray as the angels pray,
                    Daniel;
I want to shout as the angels shout,
                    Daniel.
O Lord, give me the eagle's wing.
What time of the day,   Daniel?
In the lion's den,   Daniel?
I want to pray,   Daniel.
O Lord, give me the eagle's wing."

The sense of the above is more difficult than usual to discover, and affords some notion of the superficial character of their knowledge of Scripture. Here is one, however, where a definite idea is intended to be conveyed. It is supposed to be sung by a believer on his deathbed, and the air is singularly touching:

"Master Jesus send for me—
                    Lord, I must go;
Dem archangels send for me—
                    Lord, I must go.
Fare de well, my broders—
                    Lord, I must go;
General Jesus send for me—
                    Lord, I must go.
Fare de well, my sisters—
                    Lord, I must go.
Weeping Mary send for me—
                    Lord, I must go;
Sister Martha send for me—
                    Lord, I must go."

Generally, indeed, the airs were appropriate to the spirit of the composition; some of them were sung with great vehemence and unction, and

from the excitement of tone and manner, the susceptibility of the Negro
to appeals of this nature to his devotional instincts was evident. The
sacred names were generally screamed rather than sung, with an almost
ecstatic fervour. The two following were clearly great favourites:

> "The heavenly bell is ringing loud,
> I wish it was ringing for me;
> Broders walking to New Jerusalem,
> Sisters walking to New Jerusalem,
> Doubters walking to New Jerusalem.
> Oh, the heavenly bell is ringing loud,
> I wish it was ringing for me;
> Sarah's walking to New Jerusalem,
> Elias' walking to New Jerusalem,
> Heroes walking to New Jerusalem.
> Oh, the heavenly bell," &c. &c.

And—

> "Broders, don't you hear the horn?
> Yes, Lord, I hear the horn;
> The horn sounds in jubilee.
> Sisters, don't you hear the horn?
> Yes, Lord, I hear the horn;
> The horn sounds from the door.
> Mourners, don't you hear the horn?
> Yes, Lord, I hear the horn;
> The horn sounds like broder Tony's horn."

It does not require the last line of the latter composition to prove its
originality; indeed, all of them differ very much from the Nigger
Melodies, popularly so called [i.e., minstrel songs], both in the character
of the music and words. Nor does any attempt at rhyme enter into their
construction.[21]

By 1856, the year of Oliphant's visit, the form of the spiritual as
we know it was fully developed. The first specimen he quoted,
beginning "Oh, I takes my text in Matthew," was included in *Slave
Songs of the United States* as number 11 with the title "There's a
Meeting Here To-night." The two following texts are obviously
intended to be sung in call-and-response style, even the layout of the
lines implying an overlap of the solo and the chorus. The final two
texts seem to require a response as well, a response which may have
been elided in the transcription. Oliphant, like many other com-
mentators, complained that the texts were hard to understand,
overlooking the improvisatory nature of the singing and the primary
importance of the rhythm, with a double-level meaning that eluded

21. Oliphant, *Patriots and Filibusters*, pp. 140–43. A substantial biographical
sketch of Oliphant, describing the circumstances of his travel in the United States, is
given in the *Dictionary of National Biography*.

him. His comments about the sacred names being screamed rather than sung implied the rough, strained vocal quality characteristic of African singing, rather than European. When his report was published in 1860, it summarized what was known of distinctive black religious music before the Civil War.

ATTEMPTS TO SUPPRESS BLACK RELIGIOUS SINGING

In the minds of many southern whites, black preachers and distinctive black religious singing were a potential cover for insurrectionary activities. The hysteria against black preachers after the Denmark Vesey conspiracy was described in an earlier chapter; even more overwhelming was the reaction to the Nat Turner conspiracy of 1831. This latter event led to the passage in many southern states of laws which forbade blacks to preach, to assemble for religious purposes unless whites were present, or even for others to teach blacks to read and write. In his first message to the Virginia Legislature after the insurrection Governor Floyd asserted:

> The most active incendiaries among us . . . have been the negro preachers. . . . Those preachers . . . have been the channels through which the inflammatory pamphlets and papers brought . . . from other states, have been circulated among the slaves. . . . Through the indulgency of the Magistracy and the laws, large collections of slaves have been permitted to take place, at any time through the week, for the ostensible purpose of religious worship, but in many instances, the real purpose, with the preachers, was of a different character; . . . The public interest requires that the negro preachers be silenced. . . .[22]

The controls which silenced their preachers would also be used to prevent many blacks from singing as they wished to. Thomas H. Jones's experience in 1824 has already been cited. The aftermath of the Nat Turner insurrection was described graphically by Charity Bowery, a former slave who was born at Pembroke, North Carolina, about 1774:

> The brightest and best men were killed in Nat's time. Such ones are always suspected. All the colored folks were afraid to pray in the time of old Prophet Nat. There was no law about it; but the whites reported it round among themselves that, if a note was heard, we should have some dreadful punishment; and after that, the low whites would fall upon any slaves they heard praying, or singing a hymn, and often killed them before their masters or mistresses could get to them.

> I asked Charity to give me a specimen of their hymns. In a voice cracked with age . . . she sang:

22. *Journal of the Senate of Virginia*, 1831, pp. 9–10, as quoted in Johnston, *Race Relations*, pp. 135–36.

> A few more beatings of the wind and rain,
> Ere the winter will be over—
>   Glory, Hallelujah!
> Some friends has gone before me,—
> I must try to go and meet them—
>   Glory, Hallelujah!
> A few more risings and settings of the sun,
> Ere the winter will be over—
>   Glory, Hallelujah!
> There's a better day a coming—
> There's a better day a coming—
>   Oh, Glory, Hallelujah!

With a very arch expression, she looked up, as she concluded, and said, "They wouldn't let us sing that. They wouldn't let us sing that. They thought we was going to *rise*, because we sung 'better days are coming.' "[23]

Another former slave, Charlotte Brooks, was brought from Virginia to Louisiana to be sold about 1855. Her reminiscences described the spirituals that had been sung in Virginia and the conditions that she found in Louisiana: "When I came to Louisiana I did not go to church any more. Every body was Catholic where I lived, and I had never seen that sort of religion that has people praying on beads. . . . I could never hear any of the old Virginia hymns sung here . . . I remember . . . a minister . . . in Virginia . . . used to sing, 'O where are the Hebrew children? Safe in the promised land.' . . ." After a time another slave from Virginia was bought by a neighbor and began to hold prayer meetings.

> "Would your marster allow you to hold prayer-meetings on his place?"
> "No, my child; if old marster heard us singing and praying he would come out and make us stop. . . . Marster used to say God was tired of us all hollering to him at night." . . . None of us listened to him about singing and praying. . . . Sometimes when we met . . . we would put a big wash-tub full of water in the middle of the floor to catch the sound of our voices when we sung. When we all sung we would march around and shake each other's hands, and we would sing easy and low, so marster could not hear us. . . . Aunt Jane used to sing, 'Jesus! the name that charms our fears.' . . . [and] 'Guide me, O thou great Jehovah.' . . . (AS 2)

The second was a standard hymn, not a spiritual, as may be the first; I have not been able to identify it in any hymnal. The reminiscences included the words of several spirituals, interspersed with other standard hymns:

23. Child, "Charity Bowery," pp. 42–43.

> 'In the valley, in the valley,
>   There's a mighty cry to
> Jesus in the valley;
>   So weary, so tired, I wish
> I was in heaven, hallelu.'

And

> 'On Jordan's stormy banks I stand, and cast a wistful eye.'
> ... We all used to sing a hymn like this:

> 'My God delivered Daniel, Daniel, Daniel;
> My God delivered Daniel,
>   And why not deliver me too?
> He delivered Daniel from the lion's den,
> Jonah from the belly of the whale,
> The three Hebrew children from the fiery furnace,
>   And why not deliver me too?'...

> 'O brother, where was you?
> O brother, where was you?
> O brother, where was you?
>   When the Lord come passing by?
> Jesus been here,
> O, he's been here,
> He's been here

> Soon in the morning;
> Jesus been here,
> And blest my soul and gone.'

> 'When my heart first believed,
> What a joy I received,
> What a heaven in Jesus's name!'[24]

None of these songs seems complete, but even from these fragments it is possible to conclude that Charlotte Brooks and her friends sang both standard and folk hymns. There is no indication that they made any distinction between the two.

Former slaves recalled the limitations placed on their singing. For example, Fanny White of Texas remembered that "on a Bowie County, Texas, farm, slaves were allowed to hold church services on Wednesday nights, Sunday and Sunday nights. They were not allowed to preach or sing loud for fear of disturbing their mistress."[25] Alice Sewell, who was born in Montgomery on November 13, 1851, recollected: "Dey didn't allow us to sing on our plantation, 'cause if we did we just sing ourselves happy and get to shouting and dat would settle de work." Lucretia Alexander, at the age of eighty-nine,

24. Albert, *House of Bondage*, pp. 2–6, 9–12, 26–33.
25. Cade, "Out of the Mouths of Ex-Slaves," p. 327.

said: "My father would have church in dwelling houses and they had to whisper. . . . They used to sing their songs in a whisper, and pray in a whisper." Eighty-seven-year-old Henry Cheatam of Clay County, Missouri, reported: "At nighttime us just went to our cabins and went to bed, 'cause we weren't allowed to do no singin'. Most of de singin' was done in de fields."[26] Similar recollections are scattered through the Slave Narrative Collection of the Federal Writers' Project. One other report from 1864 demonstrated that these conditions existed right through the Civil War. The narrative came from "a colored lady, now engaged in teaching one of the Freedmen's schools in Washington," but the area in which the incident took place was not identified.

> We were just in time for a great camp-meeting. All the people of the country were there, and many whites and blacks professed conversion. . . . For several nights after the meetings, the slaves had prayer-meetings in their houses, and sang and shouted greatly to the disturbance of the master. One evening the noise had been greater than ever, and, in the midst of it, the master sent for the leading black man. . . . "Dick," said the planter, "what is the meaning of this hideous noise? If you were whipped by devils, you could not make a more horrible howling. Now, Dick, I can bear a great deal, but more of this I cannot stand. Now I say, Dick, stop it. . . ." "Yes, massa; but the blessed gospel is from God, and if He command us to pray, and you command us not to pray, what shall we do, massa?"[27]

The conflict between what was regarded as acceptable behavior by the whites and the blacks was a potent force in shaping the style and content of black religious music. The progress of this conflict can only be dimly perceived as yet, and we must await the uncovering of further evidence to understand fully how it proceeded. What is clear is that African elements in religious singing were recognized and described as early as 1819, although they must have existed earlier, antedating by decades the first published reference to a "Negro spiritual."

THE SHOUT

The bodily movements that accompanied black religious music bothered most whites who observed them. Nineteenth-century congregations usually sat quietly in their pews during church services, preserving a strict decorum. (Quakers, of course, were even more restrained, permitting no music at all in their meetings.) But while many observers commented on the rhythmic movements

26. Yetman, "*Peculiar Institution*," pp. 261–62, 11–13, 55–56.
27. *National Anti-Slavery Standard* 25 (Oct. 15, 1864), p. [1], col. 5.

which punctuated black church services, only a few fragmentary
references have been found to the "shout," or sacred dance, before
the Civil War. The earliest known description dates from 1845 on
the Hopeton plantation of James Hamilton Couper in Georgia, not
far from St. Simon's Island, where Fanny Kemble stayed. On New
Year's Eve, Sir Charles Lyell wrote:

> Of dancing and music the Negroes are passionately fond. On the Hope-
> ton plantation above twenty violins have been silenced by the Metho-
> dist [Baptist?] missionaries. . . . At the Methodist prayer meetings, they
> are permitted to move round rapidly in a ring, in which manoeuvre, I
> am told, they sometimes contrive to take enough exercise to serve
> as a substitute for the dance, it being, in fact, a kind of spiritual *bou-
> langer*. . . .[28]

Sir Charles received the impression that there was a direct connection between the ban of secular dancing and the development of the
shout, as it came to be called. Other visitors were never told this, or
connected the shout with African ritual.

Among the fragmentary references to some kind of sacred dance,
not always identifiable as a shout, were "they danced to their own
melody, and in perfect time" (Pittsburgh, 1848); and "the holy
dance" (Macon, 1850).[29] An unidentified lady who spent the summer
of 1855 in the South wrote a letter which was published in the
Hartford *Republican*: "I have just been to visit a plantation, 'Bot-
ten Garden' . . . the slaves . . . took hold of hands, forming a circle,
and went round a tree, singing, 'I'm gwine away up yonder,' 'See
God, feedin on de lambs!' and 'When I get ober Jordan, I'll be a hero
den.' . . ."[30]

A Methodist minister in Maryland was thoroughly disapproving
in his description, but two details identify the true shout: it took
place after, not during, a church service, and it was a ring dance.
Following the close of the prayer-meeting, "At a given signal of the
leader, the men will take off their jackets, hang up their hats, and tie
up their heads with handkerchiefs; the women will tighten their
turbans, and the company will then form a circle around the singer,
and jump and bawl to their heart's content. . . ."[31] An unidentified
Englishman visited Beaufort, South Carolina, in 1860, although his
description was not published until 1863. He reported a discussion with a local Episcopal clergyman on the slaves' "religious con-
ventions":

28. Lyell, *Second Visit*, I, 269–70.
29. Dixon, *Personal Narrative*, p. 94; Bremer, *America of the Fifties*, p. 119.
30. Quoted in Parsons, *Inside View*, p. 276.
31. John Dixon Long, *Pictures of Slavery*, p. 383.

"Heathenish! quite heathenish! ... Did you ever see a *shout* ...?"
I responded in the negative, and inquired what it was.

"Oh, a dance of negro men and women to the accompaniment of their own voices. It's of no particular figure, and they sing to no particular tune, improvising both at pleasure, and keeping it up for an hour together. I'll defy you to look at it without thinking of Ashantee or Dahomey; it's so suggestive of aboriginal Africa."

I had an opportunity, subsequently, of witnessing the performance in question, and can indorse the lazy gentleman's assertion.[32]

This is the earliest known use of the term "shout."

FUNERALS

The music traditionally accompanying slave funerals elicited harsh criticism from most devout whites, who felt that the rhythm and what they regarded as cheerfulness were wholly inappropriate for times of mourning. Rare was the nineteenth-century person who made any attempt to grasp an alien attitude toward death. Much more understanding was Charles Leslie, who discussed the burial customs of the blacks in Jamaica in the early eighteenth century:

> They have no Idea of Heaven, further than the Pleasures of returning to their native Country, whither they believe every Negro goes after Death: This Thought is so agreeable, that it chears the poor Creatures. ... They look on Death as a Blessing: 'Tis indeed surprising to see ... some of them ... meet their Fate, and be merry in their last Moments; they are quite transported to think their Slavery is near an End, and that they shall revisit their happy native Shores, and see their old Friends and Acquaintances. ... When one is carried out to his Grave, he is attended with a vast Multitude. ... They sing all the way ... all the while they are covering it with Earth, the Attendants scream out in a terrible manner, which is not the Effect of Grief, but of Joy; they beat on their wooden Drums, and the Women with their Rattles make a hideous Noise ... they return to Town, or the Plantation, singing after their manner, and so the Ceremony ends.[33]

Leslie was describing customs completely untouched by Christianity, and although he used pejorative words like "terrible" and "hideous," his approach is one of curiosity rather than disapproval.

32. "Englishman in South Carolina," p. 114. A much later discussion which distinguished between various kinds of "shouts" can be found in Society for the Preservation of Spirituals, *Carolina Low-Country*, pp. 199–201.

33. [Leslie,] *New History*, pp. 307–10. The changes brought by time were discussed by R. R. Madden in 1835: "A negro burial used formerly to be as joyous a solemnity as an Irish wake. There was dancing, singing, drinking, feasting. ... But these happy times are gone: the negroes are no longer permitted to bury their dead by torchlight; to dance over their departed friends, and to frighten the isle from its propriety with barbarous music."—Madden, *Twelvemonth's Residence*, I, 371 [i.e., 137]. Twentieth-century continuations of these practices were described in Beckwith, *Black Roadways*, pp. [70]–87.

Certainly he displayed none of the horror or disgust that was the common reaction of nineteenth-century whites to music that had undergone far more acculturation.

In 1835 a "Taxable Citizen of Ward Four" wrote to the *Southern Patriot* of Charleston: "There are sometimes every evening in the week funerals of negroes accompanied by three or four hundred negroes and a tumultuous crowd of other slaves who disturb all the other inhabitants in the neighborhood of burying grounds. . . . It appears to be a jubilee for every slave in the city. . . . such is frequently the crowd and noise made by them that carriages cannot safely be driven that way."[34]

Another, less agitated, description appears in the diary of Caroline B. Poole, a native of Cambridge, Massachusetts, who taught school in Monroe, Ouachita County, Louisiana, for two years. The entry for March 16, 1837, read: "This eve'g a negro of Mr. H. Bry's died suddenly—about 9 ocl'k. . . . Heard a sound of distant music. It was a lament for the dead. . . . The negroes assemble & spend a great part of the night praying & singing."[35]

Fanny Kemble witnessed a slave funeral on St. Simon's Island off the coast of Georgia during the winter of 1838–39:

> Yesterday evening the burial of the poor man Shadrach took place. . . . The coffin was laid on trestles in front of the cooper's cottage, and a large assemblage of the people had gathered round, many of the men carrying pine-wood torches. . . . Presently the whole congregation uplifted their voices in a hymn, the first high wailing notes of which—sung all in unison, in the midst of these unwonted surroundings—sent a thrill through all my nerves. . . .[36]

Peter Randolph, an "emancipated slave," discussed the practice in Virginia about 1855: "Customs of the slaves, when one of their number dies. They go to the overseer, and obtain leave to sit up all night with their dead, and sing and pray. This is a very solemn season. First, one sings and another prays, and this they continue every night until the dead body is buried."[37] Frederick Law Olmsted witnessed a Negro funeral in the vicinity of Washington, D.C., in 1853:

> On a Sunday afternoon I met a negro funeral procession, and followed after it to the place of burial. . . . The hearse halted at a desolate place, where a dozen colored people were already engaged heaping the earth over the grave of a child, and singing a wild kind of chant. [After a

34. *Southern Patriot* (Charleston) for Sept. 19, 1835, as quoted in Howell Meadows Henry, *Police Control*, p. 144.
35. Padgett, "Yankee School Teacher," p. 677.
36. Kemble, *Journal*, pp. 112–13.
37. Randolph, *Sketches*, p. 49.

sermon] an old negro . . . raised a hymn, which soon became a confused chant—the leader singing a few words alone, and the company then either repeating them after him or make a response to them, in the manner of sailors heaving at the windlass. I could understand but very few of the words. The music was wild and barbarous, but not without a plaintive melody. A new leader took the place of the old man, when his breath gave out (he had sung very hard, with much bending of the body and gesticulation), and continued until the grave was filled, and a mound raised over it.[38]

Funeral practices continued to be about the same after 1860, according to reports by two white women, one a southern aristocrat and the other a New England schoolmarm. Mrs. Roger A. Pryor, wife of a Confederate officer, spent the month of July, 1861, at The Oaks, residence of Dr. Izard Bacon Rice. In Charlotte County, Virginia, the somewhat isolated plantation was seventy miles from Richmond and "miles away from the nearest railroad depot." She described the funeral of one of the old "servants":

> We had a long, warm walk behind hundreds of negroes, following the rude coffin in slave procession through the woods, singing antiphonally as they went one of those strange, weird hymns not to be caught by any Anglo-Saxon voice. . . . Words of immortal comfort to the great throng of negro mourners who caught it up, line after line, on an air of their own, full of tears and tenderness,—a strange, weird tune no white person's voice could ever follow [even though she described lining out the hymns herself].[39]

Elizabeth Hyde Botume, who taught school in the Sea Islands, reported the funeral of a Negro soldier:

> A young colored sergeant just returned from the army died, and was buried at midnight. He . . . died a little after dark. His friends immediately assembled and held a watch-meeting, which they call "a setting-up." All night long we could hear their solemn chanting and clapping of hands, as they beat the time. They had a praise-meeting before the house, as they believe the spirit remains with the body until daylight, when it takes leave and goes home to the heavenly Father as the morning stars go out.
>
> The comrades of the young sergeant wished to bury him with military honors, so they waited until the next night at midnight. They had a long procession, with torches and a muffled drum. Then all the women and children straggled along, singing their spirituals. It was a sombre sight. . . .[40]

38. Olmsted, *Journey*, I, 26–29. A description of "the night funeral of a slave" without any distinctive musical detail appeared in *De Bow's Review* 20 (Feb., 1856): 218–21.

39. Pryor, *My Day*, pp. 146, 157–58.

40. Botume, *First Days*, pp. 222–23.

AS1. Typical of the reports that did not attribute distinctive music to the black worshippers was William Faux's travel account of 1819. On Sunday, July 18, he visited a black Methodist congregation in Georgetown, South Carolina: "At half a mile distant, we could distinctly hear their devotional songs. We found a mighty assemblage of priests and priestesses, for all preached, prayed and sung together. The pious prayers, and sensible, cheerful singing of the poor negroes, (who are, however, apt to rise into wild enthusiasm), are very honourable to black capabilities. . . ." The implication of original songs "honourable to black capabilities" is strong. Later, on May 11, 1820, he visited a black church in Philadelphia [?], probably Richard Allen's Bethel A.M.E. Church:

> After sermon they began singing merrily, and continued, without stopping, one hour, till they became exhausted and breathless. "Oh! come to Zion, come!" "Hallelujah, &c." And then, "O won't you have my lovely bleeding *Jasus*," a thousand times repeated in full thundering chorus to the tune of "Fol de rol." While all the time they were clapping hands, shouting and jumping, and exclaiming, "Ah Lord! Good Lord! Give me *Jasus*! Amen." . . . At the close, one female said, striking the breasts of two male friends, "We had a happy time of it."

Faux, *Memorable Days*, pp. 109, 420.

AS2. The reference to a washtub to catch the sound of voices described a folk practice widespread throughout the slave states. Eighty-eight-year-old Fannie Moore of Moore, South Carolina, told how "de niggers slip off and pray and hold prayer-meetin' in de woods, den dey turn down a big wash pot and prop it up with a stick to drown out de sound of de singin'." Marriah Hines, 102, of Norfolk, Virginia, was more fortunate; she and others were allowed to have prayer meetings every Wednesday night at church. " 'Cause some of the masters didn't like the way we slaves carried on we would turn pots down and tubs to keep the sound from going out. Den we would have a good time, shouting, singing, and praying just like we pleased." Clara Young, 95, of Huntsville, Alabama, reported the same practice: "De meetin's last from early in de mornin' till late at night [on Sundays]. When dark come, de men folks would hang a wash pot, bottom upwards, in de little brush church house us had, so's it would catch de noise and de overseer wouldn't hear us singin' and shoutin'." See Yetman, *"Peculiar Institution,"* pp. 224–25, 166–67, 334–35.

This practice was also applied to the sound of dancing. "The old trick played on the master by turning a huge pot with its mouth upon the floor of the master's residence, in order to deaden the noise while the negroes danced, was considered a part of the slave's right" (Turner, "Slavery in Edgecombe County," p. 27). Dorothy Scarborough quoted Dr. Boyd, "head of the Baptist Publication Society for the colored people, Nashville, Tennessee," in 1925 on "a peculiar practice to prevent their singing from being heard at the big house. They would turn an iron washpot upside down on the dirt floor and put a stick under it . . . they thought the sound would be muffled under the pot" (Scarborough, *On the Trail*, p. 23). For additional discussion of the practice in slave narratives, see J. Ralph Jones, "Portraits," pp. 129, 270.

PART THREE

The Emergence of Black Folk Music during the Civil War

13

. . . .

Early Wartime Reports and the First
Publication of a Spiritual with Its Music

The descriptions of black folk music written before the Civil War
were scattered and intermittent, without continuity or general impact. Many of the reports quoted in earlier chapters were not published until long after the war, so their contents were unknown to
contemporaries. The "black" music known to the public at large was
the music of the "Negro minstrels," which was accepted as the authentic music of the plantation slaves. The country as a whole was
still hardly aware that any body of black religious music existed.
Many travelers from abroad expected to find the slaves singing
songs like "Old Black Joe," which they assumed the slaves themselves had written. Typical of this naïveté was Fredrika Bremer's
letter from Columbia, South Carolina, of May 25, 1850:

> Another young negro . . . sang with his banjo several of the negro songs
> universally known and sung in the South by the negro people, whose
> product they are, and in the Northern States by persons of all classes,
> because they are extremely popular. . . . Many of the songs remind me of
> Haydn's and Mozart's simple, artless melodies; for example, "Rosa
> Lee," "Oh, Susannah," "Dearest May," "Carry Me Back to Old Vir-
> ginny," "Uncle Ned," and "Mary Blane." . . . [Needless to say, these are
> all minstrel songs, two of them by Stephen Foster.] These songs have
> been made on the road; during the journeyings of the slaves; upon the
> rivers, as they paddled their canoes along or steered the raft down the

stream; and, in particular, at the corn-huskings. . . . Yes, all these songs are peculiarly improvisations, which have taken root in the mind of the people. . . .[1]

The general confusion of minstrel songs with authentic folk music was understandable, since the slaves quickly took up such songs and sang what they learned was expected of them. As no one knows how much of the early minstrel music did derive from folk music, and many minstrel songs later entered the folk repertory and were transmitted orally,[2] disentangling one from the other is a herculean task. The German traveler Moritz Busch, who has been credited with publishing one of the first groups of Negro song texts in German translation, gathered what appear to be principally minstrel songs (they cannot all be identified) and rendered them freely, transforming "The Yellow Rose of Texas" into "Gelbe Röslein von Indiana."[3] Few contemporary accounts by Southerners distinguished between authentic slave music and the products of the minstrels, while few people outside the South during the antebellum period knew enough about slave music to make such a distinction. In short, public knowledge of black folk music before the Civil War was largely confined to minstrel music which was attributed to the slaves. (AS 1)

With the outbreak of the war, forces were set in motion that would inevitably bring large numbers of Northerners into direct contact with plantation slaves. The occasional comment of the antebellum period was superseded by a stream of reports of Negro singing as newspaper reporters found it to be colorful copy, and soldiers began writing letters home. As the war progressed, educated, sympathetic teachers and superintendents were sent into areas from which the native whites had fled, permitting the Negroes to dominate the landscape as they had in Barbados in the seventeenth century. Circumstances located the most notable educational experiment of the Civil War on isolated islands behind the Confederate lines where there was little of interest; this situation helped to

1. Bremer, *America of the Fifties*, pp. 141–42.
2. White, *American Negro Folk-Songs*.
3. Busch, *Wanderungen*, I, [250]–80. The song texts translated into German include "O Sussianna," "Onkel Ned," "Feuer brunten! Ho!," "Schlimme Zeit in Alt-Virginien," "Dort im alten Carolina," and others less recognizable. This chapter was omitted from the English translation; the summary of the omitted chapters says incorrectly that it includes "translations into German of thirteen Negro spirituals."—*Travels*, p. xviii. Busch's collection begins with a text he claimed derived from Africa, "Horch, was blasen die Frumfrums so?" with the chorus, "Und all' ihr Weiber jauchzt Lu-lu!/Lustig Leben in Timbuktu' " (pp. 258–59).

focus the attention of Northerners on the freedmen and their strange songs.

In an attempt to recapture the impact made by the wartime reports of slave music, this chapter will present only the earliest published reports of contact between plantation slaves and people from the North—soldiers, newspaper reporters, missionaries, and teachers.

Open hostilities began with the surrender of Fort Sumter to the Confederate forces on April 14, 1861. In May the first refugee slaves entered the Union lines at Fortress Monroe, a Virginia fort commanding the entrance to Chesapeake Bay. When General Benjamin Butler, in command of the fort, was asked to return the slaves to their masters, he refused, claiming them as "contraband of war"—a phrase which delighted the North and became a new synonym for slave. News of his decision spread by "grapevine telegraph," bringing large numbers of slaves into Fortress Monroe and Hampton, the neighboring town. They were given rations and put to work on fortifications, but they were still in great need of clothing, shelter, and every imaginable kind of social service.

On August 3, 1861, the first systematic attempt to provide help was initiated by the American Missionary Association; its treasurer, Lewis Tappan, wrote to General Butler "making inquiries and suggestions as to the means of relief." Butler replied on August 10, welcoming any efforts the Association might make.[4] On August 21 the chaplain of the First Regiment of New York State Volunteers, P. Franklin Jones, wrote to the Young Men's Christian Association of New York, describing the "destitute and desolate" conditions of the contrabands around Fortress Monroe and suggesting the need for a "good and faithful missionary." An employee of the YMCA, the Reverend Lewis C. Lockwood, brought the letter to the American Missionary Association and was himself sent to investigate the situation. Since he was being sent to a theatre of war, he first had to be approved by the Assistant Secretary of War in Washington. That accomplished, he went on to Fortress Monroe, arriving on September 3, 1861.[5] On that day he heard the music of the blacks for the

---

4. American Missionary Association, *History*, pp. 11–12. The same facts in somewhat greater detail appear in "The American Missionary Association among the Freedmen," p. 18.

5. *American Missionary* 5 (Oct., 1861): 241. Special supplement, quoted in Richard Bryant Drake, "American Missionary Association," p. 9. Lockwood's date of commission was Sept. 1, 1861. See American Missionary Association, *16th Annual Report*, p. 32.

first time. The strong impression it made on him was an integral part of his first report on his mission:

> Last evening . . . on the piazza of the hotel, I overheard music, and directed my footsteps thither, and in a long building, just outside the entrance of the Fortress, I found a number of colored people assembled for a prayer-meeting. The brother who led in the concluding prayer had a sing-song manner, but his sentiments and expressions were very scriptural and impressive. He prayed that He who brought Israel out of Egypt, Jonah out of the mouth of the whale, and Daniel out of the den of lions, might bring them out into full deliverance, spiritually and temporally.
>
> I told my mission in few words, and the message was received with deep, half-uttered expressions of gladness and gratitude. They assured me that this was what they had been praying for; and now that "the good Lord" had answered their prayers, they felt assured that some great thing was in store for them and their people. There are some peculiarities in their prayer-meetings. Their responses are not boisterous; but in the gentle, chanted style. . . . The themes are generally devotional; but they have a prime deliverance melody, that runs in this style:

> > "Go down to Egypt—Tell Pharoah
> > Thus saith my servant, Moses—
> > Let my people go."

> Accent on the last syllable, with repetition of the chorus, that seems every hour to ring like a warning note in the ear of despotism.[6]

This was the first published report of what we know as "Go Down, Moses."

Lockwood's letter was dated September 4. An even earlier report to the New York *Commercial Advertiser* was reprinted in *Dwight's Journal of Music* for September 7:

> Contraband Singing.—It is one of the most striking incidents of this war to listen to the singing of the groups of colored people in Fortress Monroe, who gather at their resorts after nightfall. . . . I passed around by the Fortress chapel and adjacent yard, where most of the "contraband" tents are spread. There were hundreds of men of all ages scattered around. In one tent they were singing in order, one man leading, as extemporaneous chorister, while some ten or twelve others joined in the chorus. The hymn was long and plaintive, as usual, and the air was one of the sweetest minors I ever listened to. . . . One verse ran thus:

> > "Shout along, children! Shout along, children! Hear the dying Lamb.
> > Oh! take your nets and follow me For I died for you upon the tree!
> > Shout along, children! Shout along, children!
> > Hear the dying Lamb!"

> There was no confusion, no uproar, no discord—all was as tender and

6. *National Anti-Slavery Standard* 22 (Oct. 12, 1861), p. [3], col. 2.

harmonious as the symphony of an organ. . . . [signed] C. W. D.–N.Y. Com. Ad.[7]

This kind of newspaper dispatch was to become a common feature of the reports from the theatre of war, sometimes inserted within a description of military action or camp life. For example, a dispatch attributed to the correspondent of the New York *Times* headed "More about the Contrabands/Beaufort and Vicinity/From *The Tribune*" said in part: "There was a jubilee last night in the negro quarters at Seabrook, dancing and singing around fires that they build, and inside of captured Fort Walker a religious meeting was held and thanks offered to God for their deliverance. . . ."[8]

The social forces unleashed by the war led directly to the emergence of the Negro spiritual, as agents of the national government on wartime duty reported the deep impressions made upon them by the songs they heard. The Reverend Lewis Lockwood had heard "Go Down, Moses" at Fortress Monroe on September 3, 1861. By December 2 he had sent an extended text of the song to the secretary of the YMCA in New York, who in turn sent it to the New York *Tribune* with a letter describing its circumstances. We cannot know how much the text was edited in transit, but this version appears to have been the first publication of the complete text of a Negro spiritual. This historic document was republished in the *National Anti-Slavery Standard* under the heading: THE CONTRABANDS' FREEDOM HYMN:

> The following curious hymn comes to us from the Secretary of the Young Men's Christian Association, who received it from the Missionary among the contrabands at Fortress Monroe. It will be seen that there is evidence in this hymn that the slaves in a considerable part of Virginia, at least, have had a superstitious faith in being freed some time in the future. The air to which the hymn is sung is in the minor key, and very plaintive:
>
> *To the Editor of the N.Y. Tribune:*
>
> SIR: I this evening received the accompanying song from the Rev. L. C. Lockwood, recently employed by the New York Men's Christian Association in its army work, and at present laboring under the auspices of the American Missionary Association, among the slaves at Fortress Monroe.
>
> Mr. Lockwood publicly referred to this song during his late visit to this city, and upon his return to the Fortress took it down *verbatim* from the dictation of Carl Hollosay, and other contrabands.
>
> It is said to have been sung for at least fifteen or twenty years in

---

7. *Dwight's Journal of Music* 19 (Sept. 7, 1861): 182. This text does not appear to have been included in *Slave Songs*, nor has C. W. D. been identified.

8. *National Anti-Slavery Standard* 22 (Nov. 30, 1861), p. [1], col. 3.

Virginia and Maryland, and perhaps in all the slave States, though stealthily, for fear of the lash; and is now sung openly by the fugitives who are living under the protection of our government and in the enjoyment of Mr. Lockwood's ministry.

The verses surely were not born from a love of bondage, and show that in a portion, if not in all the South, the slaves are familiar with the history of the past, and are looking hopefully toward the future.

Yours respectfully,

New York, Dec. 2, 1861.   Harwood Vernon.

_____

LET MY PEOPLE GO.
A SONG OF THE "CONTRABANDS."
When Israel was in Egypt's land,
    O let my people go!
Oppressed so hard they could not stand,
    O let my people go!

CHORUS—O go down, Moses,
    Away down to Egypt's land,
And tell King Pharaoh
To let my people go!

Thus saith the Lord bold Moses said
    O let my people go!
If not I'll smite your first born dead
    O let my people go!

No more shall they in bondage toil,
    O let my people go!
Let them come out with Egypt's spoil,
    O let my people go! . . .[9]

These are only three of the twenty stanzas accompanying Harwood Vernon's letter, all of them in standard grammatical English. Lockwood made no attempt to preserve the dialect, nor did he have a modern editor's respect for the integrity of the text, for he supplied a substantially different version for the sheet music edition. (Both versions are given in an appendix.)

Even before the sheet music edition appeared, however, other published dispatches from the theatre of war included reports of Negro songs, frequently cast in some kind of dialect. In the same issue of the *National Anti-Slavery Standard* that printed the first text of "Go Down, Moses" there also appeared a dispatch from the correspondent of the New York *Tribune* dated December 4 from Port Royal, South Carolina:

> The negro relish for all sorts of fun, their keen appreciation of the ludicrous side of every incident, and their love for music, and rude natural talent for it, are all more or less familiar. Their genius in

9. *Ibid.* (Dec. 21, 1861), p. [4], col. 5.

improvisation was comically illustrated in the case of Capt. Cuthbert, a rebel officer, who came over in a boat, last week, with a number of his slaves, from St. Helena Island, and was taken on St. Phillips by a party of the 79th New York Highlanders, who are encamped at Bay Point. The delight of the negroes at their unexpected liberation was only equalled by their sense of the misfortune which had overtaken the captain, and finally found expression in the following lyrical refrain.

> "De Northmen dey's got massa now,
> De Northmen dey's got massa now,
> De Northmen dey's got massa now,
> Glory Hallelujah!"

The next column on the same page had a dispatch from the correspondent of the *Times*, describing the same incident. After a more detailed account of the capture of Captain Cuthbert, the account went on:

While he was rowed off a prisoner in his own boat, and by his own slaves, these burst out into singing, to the tune of one of their rude hymns, making the versicles as they went along:

> "O Massa a rebel, we row him to prison.
> > Hallelujah.
> Massa no whip us any more,
> > Hallelujah.
> We have no massa now; we free.
> > Hallelujah.
> We have the Yankees, who no run away.
> > Hallelujah.
> O! all our old massas run away.
> > Hallelujah.
> O! massa going to prison now.
> > Hallelujah.

Cuthbert, who had come to the island for the sake of preventing the escape of his slaves ... had ... scrupulously maintained that the negroes loved their masters, and wanted no freedom; but when these exulting chants were sung in his hearing, he acknowledged that so long as the Union forces remained the South Carolinians were in danger from their slaves. He has been sent North, a prisoner.[10]

The publication of a sheet music edition of "Go Down, Moses" was announced on December 14, less than two weeks after the letter transmitting the text to the New York *Tribune*. It was the first true Negro spiritual to be published with its music. The notice read:

The Song of the Contrabands.—"O let my People go"—words and music obtained through the Rev. L. C. Lockwood, Chaplain of the Contrabands at Fortress Monroe, arranged by Thomas Baker. Pub-

10. *Ibid.*, p. [1], col. 5–6.

lished by Horace Waters, 481 Broadway. This song, Mr. Lockwood says, has been sung for about nine years by the slaves of Virginia. He has done well to send it North, where it cannot fail to awake fresh sympathy for the bondman.[11]

The publication notice in *The American Missionary* added: "It would be worth hearing if sung by a hundred or two. . . . It is a sweet melody. Price 25 cents, with harp and piano accompaniment."[12] Possibly the accompaniment could be played on the harp, but the copies I have seen do not mention that instrument, and piano seems more likely.

On the reverse of the title page is a caption title above the music, reading:

THE SONG OF THE CONTRABANDS.
"O LET MY PEOPLE GO."

This Song, originated among the Contrabands, and was first heard sung by them on their arrival at Fortress Monroe; and was introduced here by their Chaplain: Rev. L. C. Lockwood.
Arranged by Thomas Baker.

At the bottom of page 5 appears: "N.B. This Song has been sung for about nine years by the slaves of Virginia. L. C. L." The text differs radically from the version reported to the New York *Tribune*, although both versions were attributed to the same source. (They are reproduced in an appendix.) At least one later edition was issued, including a parody, "The Lord Doth Now to this Nation Speak," written by "Moses," not otherwise identified. This edition was advertised as "just published" on January 11, 1862.[13] The parody was a topical political argument in favor of emancipation. Whoever he may have been, "Moses" was clearly not a "contraband" himself.

At first the song seemed to be having some impact on the public. Lockwood reported to the American Missionary Association that it "has been sung at the Sabbath-school celebration in Rev. Henry Ward Beecher's Church, and in other places."[14] In March the sheet music was offered for sale at the Anti-Slavery Office in Phila-

11. *Ibid.*, (Dec. 14, 1861), p. [3], col. 5.
12. *American Missionary* 6 (Jan., 1862): 12.
13. *National Anti-Slavery Standard* 22 (Jan. 11, 1862), p. [3], col. 6, adv. The title page differed from the earlier edition by having the following phrase inserted after Thomas Baker's name: "Also have Published/The Lord Doth Now, to This Nation Speak,/A Parody on the "SONG OF THE CONTRABANDS." In this edition, pp. 6–7 contain the added version "Words by Moses, Music Arr'd by T. Baker." Stanzas 1–2 are accompanied by a melodic line, the chorus by a two-part chorus, on p. 6; stanzas 3–12 are on p. 7.
14. *American Missionary* 6 (Feb., 1862): [30].

delphia,[15] and by April 5 both the original song and its parody were available in a collection of anti-slavery songs published by Horace Waters, *The Harp of Freedom*.[16] (AS 2) In spite of these early signs of growing public acceptance, the song seems to have made little impression outside antislavery circles. Although it has inspired people throughout the world by its stirring music and its enspiriting words, it held no appeal when it first appeared in print. For this a good deal of the blame must fall upon the arrangement made by Thomas Baker. Apparently an Englishman, Baker must have been a capable violinist, for he was the leader of the band of virtuosi that Louis Jullien brought from England to America in August, 1853. The series of concerts they gave created a sensation, and some members of the orchestra settled in the United States, making notable contributions to the rise of instrumental music in this country.[17] Baker's name is not to be found in any musical reference book, nor is it known whether he settled in the United States. Nothing has been found about him after 1862.

It seems more than likely that Baker knew nothing about the original song. Since we know nothing of Lockwood's musical attainments, we can only surmise what sort of version he supplied to Baker. It must have been feeble indeed for Baker to have devised his arrangement in 6/8 time, with a weak accent on the first syllable of "Pharaoh," and generally making a wishy-washy ballad of what was in most other versions a truly splendid song. "Go Down, Moses" was not included in *Slave Songs of the United States*; it had to wait until *Jubilee Songs* of 1872 for a satisfactory version.[18] (AS 3)

Lewis Lockwood, the man responsible for the publication of "Go Down, Moses," seems to have been quite unaware of the historic significance of that action. He remained an obscure missionary, laboring in the state of Delaware in September, 1863 and 1864.[19] A

15. *National Anti-Slavery Standard* 22 (Mar. 1, 1862), p. [3], col. 6, adv.

16. *Ibid.*, (Apr. 5, 1862), p. [3], col. 6, adv.

17. Carse, *Life of Jullien*, pp. 76–78. Among the emigrant musicians who had impact on the development of music in the United States were Edward and Friedrich Mollenhauer; musicians resident in America who were added to the nucleus Jullien brought with him included G. F. Bristow, U. C. Hill, and Theodore Thomas. Baker was associated with Horace Waters as early as 1853 with the publication of "The Dying Words of Little Katy"; or, "Will He Come? . . . Written by Solon Robinson . . . Music by Horace Waters . . . Arranged for the Piano Forte, by Thomas Baker, Leader of Jullien's Band" (New York: H. Waters, 1853).

18. [Seward, comp.,] *Jubilee Songs*, pp. 22–23. The text is identical with that first published in December, 1861, with the addition of four stanzas that are not related to the flight from Egypt.

19. *National Anti-Slavery Standard* 24 (Sept. 12, 1863), p. [3], col. 5; *American Missionary* 8 (May, 1864): 120.

friend of his, Arthur Buckminster Fuller, told of attending contraband religious meetings at Fortress Monroe with him, commenting:
"They are a little more demonstrative than I am accustomed to or
suits my taste. . . . [He was chaplain of the 16th Massachusetts
Regiment.] The other day I attended a funeral of one of their
number. . . . They chanted many of their plantation religious songs.
O, they were so mournful, so despairing (who wonders at that?) in
their view of this life; but they changed to wild paeans when they
spoke of an immortal state."[20] No further information about Lockwood has been found.

Since "Go Down, Moses" was not included in *Slave Songs of the
United States*, nor did any of the Northerners who collected slave
songs in the Sea Island area report hearing it, it may not have been
sung there. But it was heard at places other than Fortress Monroe
during the war. A dispatch from Philadelphia dated May 26, 1862,
signed M. [James Miller McKim?] told of a visit to the "contraband" school near the Capitol in Washington. After an evening
session in which the teacher drilled the class from a wall chart,
getting collective answers, the class was asked what they would like
to sing during a recess. The choice was "Go Down, Moses."

> Someone began, in a low tone. One by one the others joined, and soon
> the whole school swelled the chorus of
>
> > "O go down Moses
> >   Away down to Egypt's land,
> > And tell King Pharaoh,
> >   To let my People go.
> >
> > "Thus saith the Lord, bold Moses said,
> >   O let my people go;
> > If not, I'll smite your first-born dead,
> >   O let my people go.
> >
> > "No more shall they in bondage toil,
> >   O let my people go;
> > Let them come out with Egypt's spoil,
> >   O let my people go," etc., etc.[21]

The folk version sung by the contrabands themselves was more
direct and moving than either of the published versions filtered
through the hands of white "improvers."

20. Fuller, *Chaplain Fuller*, pp. 199–200.
21. *National Anti-Slavery Standard* 23 (May 31, 1862), p. [2], col. 6–p. [3], col. 1–2.

ADDITIONAL SOURCES

AS1. The review of *Slave Songs of the United States* in *The Nation* commented on the lack of knowledge of the true music of the slaves:

If intercourse between the two sections [of the United States] had been unrestricted . . . we should have had something besides the gospel of Christy. But the whites who attended the negro camp-meetings were present from other motives than a love of harmony; the planter's guest was naturally content to hear from a distance and to cherish as simply a pleasant recollection the airs that floated up to the house from the "nigger" quarter; and as for the wanderer who would have stopped to listen and note down, the suspicion of tampering with happy but credulous laborers was not to be incurred with impunity. Moreover, most men are curious, many and many again have a fondness for music, but those who are musically educated are seldom to be met with.

"Slave Songs of the United States" [unsigned review], *The Nation* 5 (Nov. 21, 1867): 411.

AS2. Because of its rarity, it may be worthwhile to describe *The Harp of Freedom* in more detail, utilizing a photographic reproduction of the copy in the Moorland-Spingarn Research Center, Howard University. A booklet of thirty-two pages, selling for five cents, "50 cents per doz., $3 per 100," it must have been intended for a mass market. The title page read: "Harp of Freedom: (Part I,) a New and Superior Collection of Anti-Slavery, Patriotic and 'Contraband' Songs, Solos, Duets and Choruses. Most of the words and music were written expressly for this work, to correspond with the times; and should be sung by the million, in order to awaken a deep interest in behalf of the 'contrabands' whom God, in his providence, has cast upon the Free North, to clothe and educate. New York: Published by Horace Waters, no. 481 Broadway, c1862." None of the other songs were attributed to the contrabands, and most of them appear to be old tunes with new topical texts, set to feeble arrangements. It is easy to understand why this songster failed to kindle the enthusiasm that greeted *The Battle Cry of Freedom*, published a few months later.

AS3. Before the Jubilee Singers existed, a version of "Go Down, Moses" reached Geneva, Switzerland, in French translation. It formed the basis of a discussion of the moral and intellectual qualities of the Negroes as conducted at a meeting on March 29, 1866, of the Comité Genevois en Faveur des Esclaves Affranchis. How the song's text reached Geneva is not yet known.

O Moïse, descends! descends au loin dans la terre d'Égypte, et dis au roi Pharaon: Laise aller mon peuple!—Et toi! recule, recule et laisse aller mon peuple.

Pharaon se met en travers de la route . . . Laisse aller mon peuple!—Pharaon et ses armées s'engloutissent. Laisse aller mon peuple!—Tu peux me retenir ici; mais là-haut, tu ne peux rien sur moi. Laisse aller mon peuple!

O Moïse, étends ta main sur les eaux!—Laisse aller mon peuple. Et ne va pas te perdre dans le désert.—Laisse aller mon peuple! Ill en est Un qui siége en haut dans les cieux et qui répond a mes prières.—Laisse aller mon peuple!

Serment, *Question des Nègres*, pp. 44–45.

14

· ·

The Port Royal Experiment

HISTORICAL BACKGROUND

The earliest wartime reports of "contraband" singing from Fortress Monroe and other places, while friendly and sometimes sympathetic, were the results of rather superficial contacts. Newspaper reporters did not tarry in one place, and while Lockwood's mission at Fortress Monroe was planned along broad lines, he went on to other duties after little more than a year.[1] The American Missionary Association's activities continued, culminating in the founding of Hampton Institute, but Lockwood was not part of them. He had no further role in the history of black folk music.

In contrast, the Northerners who went to the Sea Islands off the coast of South Carolina remained in that isolated area for months and, in some cases, years. Their imaginations were captured by the conviction that they were part of a historic experiment of far-reaching consequences. Charles Ware, who went to Port Royal early in July, 1862, was still there in January, 1865; Laura Towne, who arrived in April, 1862, stayed until her death in 1901.[2] She was

1. He served as "an agent in Pennsylvania and New Jersey," before moving on to Delaware in 1863–64.—Cf. American Missionary Association, *17th Annual Report, . . .* Oct. 21st and 22nd, 1863 (New York, 1863), p. 37; *National Anti-Slavery Standard* 24 (Sept. 12, 1863), p. [3], col. 5, and *American Missionary* 8 (May, 1864): 120.
2. Pearson, ed., *Letters from Port Royal*, pp. 70, 120; Towne, *Letters and Diary*.

exceptional, of course, in her life-long commitment to the freedmen, but the Port Royal experiment attracted a notable group of intelligent, enthusiastic people, many of whom participated in the collection of the first published volume of slave music, *Slave Songs of the United States*. An understanding of how that volume came into being must consider the people and circumstances that made it possible.

The Sea Islands to which they came stretched along the coast of South Carolina and Georgia, separated from the mainland by salt creeks and marshes, level sandy land ideally suited to the growing of rice and long staple cotton of the highest quality. The islands had been popular among wealthy whites of the vicinity as summer residences when the ocean breezes made them more pleasant than Charleston and inland areas. (In the 1970's they are an even more popular winter resort.) Because the islands were separated from the mainland by water, the slaves there tended to live in isolation and to retain a higher proportion of Africanisms in their speech and culture than mainland slaves.[3] At the outbreak of the Civil War, the concentration of slaves on the Sea Islands was far above the ratio of whites to blacks for the South as a whole. The state census of South Carolina for 1860 listed for Beaufort District 939 property owners and 33,339 Negroes, including a few free men.[4]

Conditions at the beginning of the nineteenth century can be glimpsed in a description of the slaves on one of the Sea Islands, Edisto. Published in 1809, the profile was written by the Reverend Donald M'Leod, the incumbent of the local Presbyterian church. He estimated there were then 2,609 slaves on the island.

> Their vacant hours they are at liberty to spend as their discretion or caprice may dictate.... The island negroes appear to be more intelligent and speak better than their brethren of the main. [In 1860 and after, the opposite was generally reported.] Their frequent [social] intercourse with the city and the easier access they have to the white population may have created this difference. [This apparently puzzling remark may be explained by the fact that travel by water was so much easier in 1809 than travel by land; therefore island slaves serving as oarsmen could more easily reach Charleston than could slaves on an inland plantation. I have, however, no explanation as to why they had easier access to whites.] They are very susceptible of religious impressions, and repair to the churches in their best attire, and conduct themselves in a grave and orderly manner. [M'Leod apparently only observed their behavior in the white churches. What went on in the privacy of their own cabins or

3. There is an extensive literature on the culture of the Sea Island blacks, of which only two examples can be cited here: Guion Griffis Johnson, *Social History of Sea Islands*, and Guy Benton Johnson, *Folk Culture on St. Helena Island*.

4. Rose, *Rehearsal for Reconstruction*, pp. 115–16.

praise meetings he may not have known.] The more aged inhabitants observe that although they are treated with more lenity and indulgence [relative terms, to be sure], and in every respect fare better than they did 40 years ago; yet they do not appear to be happier in proportion. If dancing, frolic and dissipation be a sure indication of happiness, the observation is well founded. At the period alluded to [ca. 1769] in their voyages to the city they were wont to beguile the time and toil of rowing with songs and extravagant vociferations, and were accustomed to devote their holidays to dancing, dissipation and irregularities. . . . These practices they have in a great measure abandoned. . . . from an impression they have acquired that they are incompatible with a religious frame of mind.

What is significant here is that even as sedate an observer as M'Leod knew that the slaves had danced in the mid-eighteenth century, so that dancing must have been generally allowed and done in public. How much was African and how much European-influenced, we still do not know. His comments on the lenient treatment the slaves received were not borne out by other witnesses.

Laura Towne's impressions of Sea Island slavery, based on her observations from 1862 on, were summed up in the introduction to her *Letters and Diary*:

> Whatever the condition of the negroes elsewhere, it had been hard in reality in the Sea Islands. The cotton there was an imperious crop, requiring a full year's labor to prepare for market. The drivers were required to be severe. The slaves had been allowed no holidays except Christmas and Sundays, no rest but a few hours at night, and that shortened on Saturdays by the need of grinding at the hand-mill the weekly ration of one peck of corn, turn and turn about, until daylight. The older ones were dulled with incessant labor, the younger had had no chance to learn anything. . . . They could count no farther than ten, and that they did in this fashion, "one, two, five, eight, ten." . . . The houses were of rough boards, with small windows without glass. The floors were of sand and lime. At one side was an open hearth. In spite of doors and shutters large cracks let in the bitter winter cold. The older people slept in bunks, the younger on the floor. The cooking-utensils usually consisted of a single pot; the food was hominy or peas and salt pork. Long oyster shells were used for spoons, and when the family had scraped the hominy from the pot, the dogs were allowed to clean it for the next meal. Such conditions were little short of those in a savage settlement on the Congo.[6]

In this setting and among these people, more slave songs, both words and music, were collected during the war than in any other area. It may seem strange that collecting was concentrated in such

5. Ramsay, *History of South-Carolina*, II, [539], 543–45. Rev. M'Leod had been ordained in 1794–cf. II, 559.

6. Towne, *Letters and Diary*, p. xiii.

an atypical, geographically restricted region as the Sea Islands, but explanations do present themselves. Although the Islands were behind the Confederate lines, life there was able to continue more normally than in most areas of fighting. Confederate raids were an omnipresent danger, but they occurred only occasionally, and actual fighting took place elsewhere. All contact with the North or the mainland was by water, usually by steamer to New York. A select group of well-educated, politically aware young Northerners were assigned to duty here where almost nothing of interest was to be seen, save the beauties of nature and the freedmen themselves. Interest in the freedmen was intense; when the day's work was over, the freedmen conducted "praise" meetings, and the Northerners wrote down the songs.

The Sea Islands came under Union occupation very early in the war. A week after the bombardment of Fort Sumter, President Lincoln proclaimed a blockade of the Confederate coast from Virginia to Texas. To make such an extensive blockade effective in the absence of an enormous navy, it was necessary for the North to capture harbors along the Southern coast, and Port Royal harbor, a fine natural port commanding the entrances to Charleston and Savannah, was a logical first choice. On November 7, 1861, the Union fleet under Commodore Dupont captured two earth forts; those whites who had not already left then fled to the mainland, leaving behind thousands of slaves and the largest cotton crop in years. The Union forces found themselves responsible for those thousands still on the plantations where they had toiled as slaves. The cotton crop also demanded attention, at a time when cotton was being withheld from the market as a war measure. The administration in Washington now had two more problems among the many demanding solution.[7]

Since the plantations, cotton, and slaves could all be considered abandoned property, responsibility fell to Secretary of the Treasury Salmon P. Chase to do something. He dispatched a young Boston attorney named Edward Pierce on a preliminary tour of investigation. Pierce had been at Fortress Monroe and had published a widely read report on the activities there.[8] His ability, antislavery convictions, and friendship with such figures as Senator Charles Sumner and Secretary Chase made him a logical choice for such a mission.[9]

7. Pearson, *Letters from Port Royal*, pp. [v]–vi; Rose, *Rehearsal for Reconstruction*, pp. 3–21.
8. [Pierce,] "Contrabands," pp. 626–40.
9. Rose, *Rehearsal for Reconstruction*, pp. 21–22.

On his return, volunteer groups were organized in the North to recruit teachers, missionaries, and superintendents for the abandoned plantations, and to raise money for their salaries and needed supplies of food, clothing, equipment, and seed. Antislavery people throughout the North quickly realized that the Sea Islands could provide a laboratory for a grand experiment to demonstrate that slaves could work and learn as free men. The first formal committee was the Educational Commission for Freedmen, organized in Boston on February 7, 1862;[10] it was followed on February 22 by a New York group called grandly the New York National Freedmen's Relief Association. These two organizations soon agreed to work jointly, and when the Port Royal Relief Committee was organized in Philadelphia on March 20, it worked harmoniously with both.[11]

These relief organizations played a vital role in bringing the future editors and contributors to *Slave Songs of the United States* into contact with the former slaves who provided the songs. Of the 114 teachers and superintendents sent South by the Educational Commission during its first year of operation, 97 went to Port Royal, including Charles P. Ware of Milton, Massachusetts, the contributor of the largest single collection of songs.[12] His sister Harriet had preceded him, and they were to meet Lucy McKim in the islands when she accompanied her father there on a tour of inspection for the Port Royal Relief Committee in June, 1862.[13] Ware's cousin, William Francis Allen, joined them as a teacher in November, 1863.[14]

EARLIEST PUBLISHED REPORTS

Port Royal received a good deal of attention in the press. The former slaves there were newsworthy, for they appeared more primitive and colorful than their mainland counterparts. Reporters found them good copy, and abolitionists sensed the propaganda value of reports about them and their ways. Soon the newspapers, periodicals, and publications of the relief societies all featured long

10. *Ibid.* Educational Commission for Freedmen, *First Annual Report*, p. [15].

11. All these developments are set in perspective in Rose, *Rehearsal for Reconstruction*, pp. 18ff. For the Port Royal Relief Committee, see McKim, *Freedmen*, p. 4.

12. "The largest and most accurate single collection in existence is probably that made by Mr. Charles P. Ware, chiefly at Coffin's Point, St. Helena Island."—[Allen, Ware, and Garrison,] *Slave Songs*, [Introduction,] p. iii.

13. Pearson, *Letters from Port Royal*, pp. vii, 16, 70; Epstein, "Garrison," 537–38, 543–44.

14. William Francis Allen, *Diary*, MS, State Historical Society of Wisconsin, entries for Nov., 1863.

discussions of the character and behavior of the Sea Island Negroes. Inevitably their songs and holy dances attracted much comment.

The earliest dispatches from Port Royal, printed in November and December, 1861, have already been given. But anecdotes about the "contrabands" of Port Royal were in circulation even earlier than that. On September 10, almost two months before the capture of the harbor, John Greenleaf Whittier wrote to Lydia Maria Child thanking her for some of these anecdotes, adding, "If I can do anything in prose or verse to aid the cause, I shall be glad. I wish somebody would write a song worthy of the people and the cause; I am not able to do it."[15] Despite his misgivings, Whittier made the attempt. The *Atlantic Monthly* for February, 1862, contained his poem, "At Port Royal. 1861," including the "Song of the Negro Boatmen"—his conception of what the boatmen *ought* to sing, not a re-creation of a genuine folksong. (AS 1) After a four-line stanza describing the scene, the poet focused on the singing boatmen:

> At last our grating keels outslide,
>   Our good boats forward swing;
> And while we ride the land-locked tide,
>   Our negroes row and sing.
>
> For dear the bondman holds his gifts
>   Of music and of song;
> The gold that kindly Nature sifts
>   Among his sands of wrong; . . .
>
> With oar-strokes timing to their song,
>   They weave in simple lays
> The pathos of remembered wrong,
>   The hope of better days,—
>
> The triumph-note that Miriam sung,
>   The joy of uncaged birds:
> Softening with Afric's mellow tongue
>   Their broken Saxon words.

The "Song of the Negro Boatmen" followed, written in dialect contrasting with the standard English which preceded it:

> Oh, praise an' tanks! De Lord he come
>   To set de people free;
> An' massa tink it day ob doom,
>   An' we ob jubilee.
> De Lord dat heap de Red Sea waves
>   He jus' as 'trong as den;

15. Underwood, *Whittier*, p. 235.

> He say de word: we las' night slaves;
> To-day, de Lord's freemen.
> De yam will grow, de cotton blow,
> We'll hab de rice an' corn:
> Oh, nebber you fear, if nebber you hear
> De driver blow his horn! . . .[16]

"At Port Royal," described as a "weak imitation of negro folk-song,"[17] is not considered one of Whittier's best poems, but his contemporaries were delighted with it. Lydia Maria Child's enthusiastic comments betrayed the conventional limitations of her judgments: "It is a complete embodiment of African humor, and expressed as they would express it, if they were learned in the mysteries of rhyme and rhythm."[18] (Presumably she meant conventional, regular rhythm.) Neither she nor Whittier visited Port Royal, and their conceptions of Africans must have been secondhand or based on contacts made in the North. His ideas of folksong seemed realistic to those of his contemporaries who heard the real thing, for Lucy McKim remarked in her letter to *Dwight's Journal of Music*: "Whittier 'builded better than he knew' when he wrote his 'Song of the Negro Boatmen.' It seemed wonderfully applicable as we were being rowed across Hilton Head Harbor among United States gunboats . . . I thought the crew *must* strike up 'And massa tink it day ob doom/And we ob jubilee.' "[19] It would be interesting to learn the sources of Whittier's ideas of Negro folksong, for the "Song of the Negro Boatmen" became one the most frequently reprinted poems inspired by the Civil War, set to music by a number of composers. (AS 2) This literary imitation of folk poetry prepared the public mind for the authentic songs themselves, which were still largely unknown; Whittier's poem reached far more people than Thomas Baker's deplorable arrangement of "Go Down, Moses."

After the publication of "At Port Royal. 1861," reports began to appear from teachers and superintendents at work among the freedmen; these included some comments on the music and singing of the blacks. Among the first was a letter dated March 26, printed in the *Liberator* for May 2, 1862.

The Liberated Slaves at Beaufort./Letter from one of the Teachers/ . . . Last Sunday we went to the Church on St. Helena Island; we had a school before church, at which nearly a hundred negroes, of all ages were

16. Whittier, "At Port Royal," pp. 244–45.
17. Mordell, *Quaker Militant*, p. 212.
18. John Albert Pollard, *Whittier*, p. 236.
19. Lucy McKim [Garrison], "Songs of the Port Royal 'Contrabands,' " pp. 254–55.

present. There being no one to preach, I was asked to say something; so I began the service by reading a hymn, two lines at a time, while a colored brother led the singing. By this time, there were three or four hundred negroes in the church . . . another hymn was doled out, two lines at a time. . . .

> [signed] E. [?] W. H.[20]

In the May 31, 1862, issue of the *National Anti-Slavery Standard* were two reports, the first probably written by Laura Towne:

> St. Helena Island, May, 1862
> . . . The martial spirit is spreading among the boys. I saw those belonging to this place having a rude kind of a drill the other day, and marching to *hymn* tunes. The air of "John Brown's Body" is one of the most popular and best known among the people here, but they sing other words to it.[21]

The other story was reprinted from *The Independent,* quoting correspondent Elias Smith:

> I witnessed . . . at Hatteras . . . a party of forty-two men, women and children arrived from South Creek on Pamlico river. After finding themselves really among friends, they joined in singing some of their simple chants and hymns; and when the party were being transferred to the shore, one of the women, with an infant at her breast, broke forth in exclamations of praise and thanksgiving to God, which in its simple pathos reminded me of the song of Miriam celebrating the deliverance of the children of Israel on the banks of the Red Sea. They walked in slow and solemn procession to Fort Clark, chanting as they went:
>
> > "Oh! ain't I glad to get out de wilderness."[22]

The element of biblical prophecy became a standard feature in discussions of Negro spirituals from this time on. But the firsthand observers also detected secular—and exotic—components. A correspondent of *The Tribune* was quoted: "Hilton Head, S.C., Headquarters of the 1st Regiment South Carolina Volunteers [a black regiment], July 7, 1862. . . . They sang several hymns. I thought I detected a spice of the native African in their rendering of the

20. *Liberator* 32 (May 2, 1862), p. 72, col. 5–6. The writer may have been Edward W. Hooper, of Boston, a Harvard graduate recruited by Edward Pierce. He did not contribute to *Slave Songs,* and may not have been musical. Certainly this letter displays no interest in music. After the close of the war he became treasurer of Harvard College. See Rose, *Rehearsal for Reconstruction,* pp. 50–51.

21. *National Anti-Slavery Standard* 22 (May 31, 1862), p. [2], col. 2. Could the "other words" have been "Say, Brothers, Will You Meet Us?" The letter was prefaced with an endorsement: "the writer [of the following letter], an accomplished Philadelphia lady, is a tried and true Abolitionist of the radical class, that she is now laboring among the freed blacks in South Carolina, wholly at her own charges; and that this letter, being addressed to the gentleman who acts as our Philadelphia Correspondent [James Miller McKim], may be relied upon. . . ."

22. *Ibid.,* p. [4], col. 4.

rhythm and choruses, and am certain of it with respect to the dances I witnessed at a later period in the evening."[23]

WARTIME PUBLICATION OF SONG TEXTS AND MUSIC

Newspaper reports, magazine articles, and letters from teachers sometimes included parts of song texts, along with comments on the music, the performance, or the meaning of the texts. Very few of these reporters from the theatres of war were trained musicians, but even more significant was their attitude toward the songs they were transmitting. No concept of the integrity of the text had yet evolved, and no one was likely to have any compunction about editing texts to prove a point or to make an impression. Friends of the freedmen viewed the songs less as folk culture than as evidence of the capacity of the ex-slaves for the higher things of life. In the 1860's most educated people considered folk poetry and music as a primitive stage in the development of literature and "scientific" music, meriting only their amused indulgence.

In refreshing contrast to this all-but-universal reaction was the sympathetic appreciation of a nineteen-year-old girl from Philadelphia. She made the next attempt to publish slave songs with their music, the first after the "Song of the 'Contrabands.' "

On November 1, 1862, Lucy McKim wrote her historic letter to John S. Dwight. He published it in his *Journal of Music* under the heading "Songs of the Port Royal 'Contrabands,' " often described as the first description of Negro spirituals to appear in print. First it was not, but in perception and sensitivity it was far in advance of anything that had preceded it. While her biography will appear later, it should be noted here that Lucy McKim was the only professional musician among the people known to have collected slave songs in this area during the Civil War. Although she was in the Sea Island area for only about three weeks, she was a well-trained musician by the standards of her day,[24] greatly impressed by what was to her an exotic but deeply moving music. Her abolitionist background made her receptive; her musical training prepared her for a respectful appreciation of a style she could not emulate. Her letter was the first to describe this music in terms of its style and technique, rather than focusing on religious or political aspects of slavery while regarding the music as indescribable. Unpretentious though it was, her letter recognized the historic importance of what she had heard, and did its best to describe the music itself:

23. *Ibid.*, 23 (July 26, 1862), p. [1], col. 3–4.
24. Epstein, "Garrison," pp. 532–36.

It is difficult to express the entire character of these negro ballads by mere musical notes and signs. The odd turns made in the throat; and the curious rhythmic effect produced by single voices chiming in at different irregular intervals, seem almost as impossible to place on score, as the singing of birds, or the tones of an AEolian Harp. The airs, however, can be reached. . . . Their striking originality would catch the ear of any musician.

. . . It is true there is a great deal of repetition of the music, but that is to accommodate the *leader*, who, if he be a good one, is always an improvisator. For instance, on one occasion, the name of each of our party who was present, was dexterously introduced.

She concluded by saying that the music could speak for itself "better than any one for it."[25]

She had accompanied her father, James Miller McKim, on his tour of inspection to the Sea Islands, leaving New York on June 2, 1862, and returning on the 28th.[26] In a letter of June 12 she wrote: "I have copied a number of the wild, sad songs of the Negroes—tunes & words both. . . ."[27] By "copied" it appears she meant reduced to musical notation. After her return to Philadelphia she asked the friends she had made in Port Royal to send her more songs, for Laura Towne wrote to Miller McKim on August 2 that she would be happy to collect songs for Lucy, but that she was no musician and could take down only the words. On September 24 Laura Towne wrote again, hoping the songs had been satisfactory, and offering to send more. "If the six she has undertaken are successful, in these hard times, she will surely want more by & by."[28] Lucy had decided to publish the songs in arrangements for voice and piano, but only two titles are known to have appeared. The first, "Poor Rosy, Poor Gal," was sent to Dwight with the letter of November 1, so it must have been engraved by then, although it was not announced in the *National Anti-Slavery Standard* until November 22. It was registered for copyright by her in the District Court in Philadelphia on December 27, along with the second song in the series, "Roll, Jordan, Roll." The deposit copies cannot be found in the Library of Congress, but copies of both were found in the Garrison house in West Orange, New Jersey, and other copies are known to exist elsewhere.

25. Lucy McKim [Garrison], "Songs of the Port Royal 'Contrabands,'" pp. 254–55.

26. McKim, *Freedmen of South Carolina*, p. 4.

27. MS excerpts from a letter written by Lucy McKim dated "St Helena's Island, June 12th [1862]," copied by Ellen Wright for William Beverly Chase, Garrison Family Papers, Sophia Smith Collection, Smith College Library. Original not found.

28. Letters, Laura Matilda Towne to James Miller McKim, Aug. 2 and Sept. 24, 1862, MSS, McKim Papers, Cornell University Library.

The common cover of both songs reads: "Songs of the Freedmen of Port Royal. Collected and Arranged by Miss Lucy McKim. 1. Poor Rosy, Poor Gal. 2. Roll, Jordan, Roll," with blank numbers 3–8 for additional titles. Both pieces have a Philadelphia imprint, with a blank space above the copyright claim, and the name "Geo. Swain," a Philadelphia music engraver, on the left side slightly above the level of Philadelphia. (AS 3)

Lucy McKim's versions of both words and music display substantial advance over the "Song of the 'Contrabands'" produced by Lewis Lockwood and Thomas Baker. Lockwood's version of the text had been edited with a heavy hand to make it acceptable to a genteel audience, while Lucy transcribed the words as she heard them, trying to capture the rhythm and sense of the text with some attempt at reproducing the dialect, but without a trace of pedantry. Where the "Song of the 'Contrabands'" was the product of a European professional musician who was unfamiliar with the style and understood it not at all, "Poor Rosy, Poor Gal" was arranged by a gifted amateur who had heard the song in its natural surroundings and tried to reproduce it with fidelity and sympathy. Her arrangements were for solo voice with unpretentious piano accompaniments: in "Poor Rosy" a banjo-like strumming, and in "Roll, Jordan, Roll" block chords with rolling octaves in the bass. The arranger's inexperience in proofreading is evident in the consistently misplaced sharps on page 4 of "Poor Rosy," but the arrangement is much truer to a folk original than a more elaborate version would have been. The refrain follows a short piano introduction, with the verse assigned alternately to "solo" and "chorus," although one voice could have sung the whole arrangement. (The melody was to be included in *Slave Songs of the United States* as a variant of another version collected by Charles P. Ware [p. 7].)

In contrast to Baker's conventional setting of "Go Down, Moses" for solo voice and four-part chorus, Lucy McKim provided performance directions that have a ring of authenticity for "Roll, Jordan, Roll." After a brief piano introduction, the refrain began with the direction "Chorus unison." The verse began with "Chorus of women," followed two lines later with "Chorus of men and women." The transition from C major to C minor is also highly unconventional for its time, the flatted third having a peculiarly exotic flavor. Then, strangely enough, just one measure later, the arrangement ends on a major chord. Is it possible the inexperienced arranger forgot to write the flat?

Songs of the FREEDMEN of Port Royal.

Collected and Arranged by

MISS LUCY Mc. KIM.

x

x

<table>
<tr><td>1 POOR ROSY, POOR GAL.</td><td>2</td></tr>
<tr><td>3</td><td>4</td></tr>
<tr><td>5</td><td>6</td></tr>
<tr><td>7</td><td>8</td></tr>
</table>

Lee Snow

Philadelphia.

"Poor Rosy, Poor Gal." Made available by the late Mrs. Hendon Chubb, West Orange, N.J.

POOR ROSY, POOR GAL.

N.º 4.   Arranged by Miss LUCY McKIM.

Poor   Rosy, poor gal!   Poor   Rosy, poor gal!   Poor   Rosy, poor gal!

Entered according to act of Congress A.D.1862 by L.M.ºKim in the Clerk's office of the District Court of the Eastern Dist: Court of Pa.

Heab'n shall a be my home.   Poor Rosy, poor gal!   Poor Rosy, poor gal!

Poor   Rosy, poor   gal!   Heab'n shall a be my home.   Be _ fore I spend one day in hell.

Solo.

Chorus.   Solo.   Chorus.

(Heab'n shall a be my home.)   I   sing and pray my soul away.   (Heab'n shall a be my home.)

Poor Rosy. 3.

Poor Rosy, poor gal! Poor Rosy, poor gal! Poor Rosy, poor gal! Heab'n shall a be my home.

2.

Got hard trial in my way!
Hard trial in my way,
Hard trial in my way,
    Heab'n shall a be my home
O! when I talk I talk wid God.
    Heab'n shall a be my home
O! when I talk I talk wid God.
    Heab'n shall a be my home
Poor Rosy, poor gal!
Poor Rosy, poor gal!
Poor Rosy, poor gal!
Heab'n shall a be my home.

3.

I dunno what de people want o' me,
Dunno what de people want o' me,
Dunno what de people want o' me,
    Heab'n shall a be my home.
O! dis day no holiday,
    Heab'n shall a be my home.
O! dis day no holiday,
    Heab'n shall a be my home.
Poor Rosy, poor gal!
Poor Rosy, poor gal!
Poor Rosy, poor gal!
Heab'n shall a be my home.

4.

A singin' an' emb'acin, talkin' too,
Singin' an' emb'acin talkin, too,
Singin' an' emb'acin talkin too,
    Heab'n shall a be my home.
O! when I walk, I walk wid God!
    Heab'n shall a be my home.
O! when I sleep, I sleep in God!
    Heab'n shall a be my home.
Poor Rosy, poor gal!
Poor Rosy, poor gal!
Poor Rosy, poor gal!
Heab'n shall a be my home.

Poor Rosy, 3.

Songs of the FREEDMEN of Port Royal.

Collected and Arranged by MISS LUCY McKIM.

Philadelphia.

"Roll, Jordan, Roll." Made available by the late Mrs. Hendon Chubb, West Orange, N.J.

ROLL, JORDAN ROLL.

Nº 2.

Tempo di marcia.

PIANO.

Chorus unison.

March, angels, march! March, angels, march! My soul am rise to heav'n Lord, where de heav'n Jording roll.

March, angels, march! March, angels, march! My soul am rise to heav'n Lord, where de heav'n Jording roll.

Chorus of women.

Little chilen sit_tin' on de Tree ob Life, Where de heav'n 'e Jor _ ding roll,___ Oh!

and women.

Roll, Jording, roll, Jording. Roll, Jording, roll! Little chilen sit_tin de Tree ob Life, Where de

heav'n e Jor_ding roll. Oh! Roll, Jording, roll, Jording. Roll, Jording, roll!

2.

March, angels, march!
March, angels, march!
My soul am rise to heaven, Lord,
   Where de heav'n e Jording roll.
Parson Fuller settin' on de Tree ob Life
   Where de heav'n 'e Jording roll.
Oh! roll, Jording, roll, Jording, roll, Jording, roll!

3.

March, angels, march!
March, angels, march!
My soul am rise to heaven, Lord,
   For to hear de Jording roll.
Little chil'en learn to fear de Lord,
   An' let yore day be long.
Oh! roll Jording, roll Jording, roll Jording, roll!

4.

March, angels march!
March, angels march!
My soul am rise to heaven, Lord,
   Where de heav'n 'e Jording roll.
Let no false or spiteful word
   Be found upon yore tongue.
Oh! roll, Jording, roll, Jording, roll Jording, roll.

   Roll, Jording roll!
   Roll, Jording roll!
Oh! Lord, I wish I been dar,
   To hear de Jording roll!

In *Slave Songs of the United States,* "Roll, Jordan, Roll" appeared as the first song, characterized as "one of the best known and noblest of the songs." As with "Poor Rosy," the version included was that collected by Charles Ware, with Lucy McKim's version given as a variant. They differ in several respects. The sheet music edition is in 4/4 time and the key of C major, while Ware's version is in 2/4 time and entirely in D major, without the flatted third, or the syncopation in the penultimate measure of the chorus. Both versions were collected in the Sea Islands, and there is no way of telling if the differences reflect to some extent the musical abilities of the collectors. Neither version, however, has the tune now usually associated with "Roll, Jordan, Roll," based on the ascending tones of the major triad. That tune appears in *Slave Songs* as number 15, "Lord, Remember Me" (p. 23).

These songs constitute a pioneer attempt to notate black folksongs and make them known to the public at large. Lucy McKim appreciated their immediate popular appeal despite their strangeness and the difficulties in transcribing them in conventional musical notation, commenting in her letter to Dwight, "They are too decided not to be easily understood. . . ." Yet little attention seems to have been paid to them aside from the notices in *Dwight's Journal of Music* and the *National Anti-Slavery Standard.* Her name was not known to the musical public, and in 1862 the songs may have seemed too strange and perhaps too controversial. Notices have not been found outside the abolitionist press, while the lack of advertisements probably reflected her lack of funds. That only two of a planned series of eight were published implied poor sales, for certainly her enthusiasm did not falter. It must be assumed that her effort succeeded in reaching very few people. A century was to pass before her historic role was recognized.

Far more influential in bringing to public notice the songs of the freedmen was an article published in the *Continental Monthly* in August, 1863. "Under the Palmetto" was written by Henry George Spaulding, a Unitarian minister who had visited Port Royal early in 1863. Spaulding described the war's impact on conditions in the Sea Islands under headings like "On the Plantations," "Home Life of the Freedmen," "Free Labor," "Religion of the Freedmen," "Schools and Education among the Freedmen," and "In Camp," with only four pages devoted to "Negro 'Shouts' and Shout Songs," including the melodies and partial texts of five songs: "O Lord, Remember Me," "Hold Your Light," "Dar's a Meetin' Here To-night," "Done wid Driber's Dribin'," and "O Brudder William, You Want to Get

Religion."[29] The impact of these songs may be estimated from a remark made in one of William Allen's letters to his family. On December 20, 1863, Allen described an evening service that had been held in his schoolroom: "After the services were over the people sang some of their peculiar hymns—'The Lonesome Valley' which I used to sing from the Continental last summer."[30]

Nothing is known of Spaulding's musical background, but apparently he was capable of notating the melodies himself, for he was also responsible for another publication, the next attempt to reproduce the music of a slave song. In April, 1866, Oliver Ditson & Co. of Boston published his "Times Hab Badly Change' Old Massa Now; Song of the Freedmen." Above the first line of music appeared an explanation: "The leading melody of this song was heard by the writer in Florida. It was sung by a negro, but the words could not be recognized. In the words here given the writer has attempted to express what seems to him to have been the general feeling of the freedmen since the close of the war."[31] The words, then, were not traditional and have no significance for the study of folksong. Unfortunately, the melody seems to have little more significance, for it cannot be associated with any recognized folk tune, nor does it have any of the characteristics of a black tune: syncopation, call-and-response form, strong rhythm, or repeated short melodic phrases. It sounds much like other sentimental ballads of its day—an opinion shared by an anonymous reviewer for *The Nation*, possibly Lucy McKim Garrison, who considered it "a latter-day composition, a song of the new regime, and an imitation of the popular 'negro melody' of white origin. It contains no traces of the peculiarly wild and melancholy character of the old-time plantation songs."[32] No other version of this song has been found.

Ditson's experience with Lucy McKim's and Spaulding's sheet music editions of slave songs may have conditioned the firm against further ventures of this type. At any rate, no other sheet music

29. [Spaulding,] "Under the Palmetto," pp. 188–203. Of the songs given by Spaulding, only "Done wid Driber's Dribin'" was not included in *Slave Songs*, although Spaulding was not listed as a contributor. His descriptions of singing and shouting were quite consistent with those of William Allen and Lucy McKim. Spaulding was educated at Phillips Academy, Andover, and Harvard, Class of 1860. During the Civil War he was a member of the U.S. Sanitary Commission. Cf. *National Cyclopaedia of American Biography*, XVIII, 28.

30. William Francis Allen, *Diary*, MS, State Historical Society of Wisconsin, entry for Dec. 20, [1863].

31. Spaulding, *Times Hab Badly Change' Old Massa Now*, p. 3. Registered for copyright by the publisher on Apr. 27, 1866. Copy in Library of Congress.

32. [Review of the above,] *The Nation* 2 (Mar. 29, 1866): 408.

editions of slave songs were attempted in the postwar period, and, as will be recounted later, Ditson refused to buy *Slave Songs of the United States*. The only other substantial publication to appear before *Slave Songs* was Thomas Wentworth Higginson's "Negro Spirituals," in the *Atlantic Monthly* for June, 1867,[33] five months before *Slave Songs* was published. Higginson gave texts without any music, generously making his collection available for the larger volume. A comparison of the two shows "field-collected variants of at least twenty of his thirty-seven songs," for which the music was supplied from other sources.[34] Higginson could not write music as far as we know, and his manuscript diary, unlike William Allen's, does not include any musical transcriptions.[35]

In addition to these published song texts, many fragments of descriptions of the music and sacred dancing of the freedmen of Port Royal were written in the letters of teachers, superintendents of plantations, and other visitors to the Islands. In the interests of a clearer picture of how Northerners responded to this music, these accounts will be combined with reports from other areas and arranged by the topics in the next chapter.

33. Higginson, "Negro Spirituals," pp. 685–94.
34. Bruce Jackson, ed., *Negro and His Folklore*, p. 82.
35. In the Houghton Library, Harvard University.

ADDITIONAL SOURCES

AS1. Whittier's biographer, Francis Underwood, epitomized a common nineteenth-century attitude toward folk poetry:

[The Negro oarsman] habitually sung, keeping time with the strokes. But though there might be occasional gleams of humor in their rude verses, an actual copy in print of what they sung would be insipid and tedious. . . . Whittier has filled the lines with good sense and point . . . while in fact the mental horizon hangs low over these black anachronisms, and very few of them could be made to understand the song, to say nothing of composing or singing it. . . . A song in imitation of the boatmen's solos, with their monotonous refrains, would be vapid. This is what the boatmen should have sung, if they had possessed the intelligence.

Whittier, pp. 235–36. What can one say of such smug superiority!

AS2. " 'Song of the Negro Boatmen' (from 'At Port Royal') appeared quite as often as Lowell's 'The Present Crisis' " (Pollard, *Whittier*, p. 256). It was set to music by a number of composers in 1862, such as Robbins Battell, J. W. Dadman [Dadmun?], L. O. Emerson, Ferdinand Mayer, H. T. Merrill, S. K. Whiting, and Edward Wiebé. See Currier, *Bibliography of Whittier*, pp. 582–83. Of these settings, three were still in print in 1870—those by Battell, Dadmun, and Merrill. See Board of Music Trade, *Complete Catalogue, 1870*, p. 121.

AS3. The bibliographic history of "Poor Rosy, Poor Gal" is more complicated than would be expected for an unsuccessful song published by an amateur without the backing of an established publisher. The edition published in Philadelphia without the name of a publisher has been found in two states. The first lists only "Poor Rosy," while the second lists also "2 Roll Jordan Roll." (This copy was made available by the late Mrs. Hendon Chubb from the Garrison house in West Orange, New Jersey.) A second edition, in the Harris Collection of American Poetry and Plays at Brown University in Providence, Rhode Island, has the totally unexpected imprint: Boston: Published by Oliver Ditson & Co., 277 Washington St., with secondary imprints: N. York, Firth Pond & Co.; Cin. J. Church Jr.; Boston, J. C. Haynes & Co.; Philada., J. E. Gould. Nothing has been found to indicate when Ditson took over the plates for the songs. With copies exceedingly scarce, no commercial edition had been anticipated. Even more surprising, in view of Ditson's refusal to buy *Slave Songs of the United States* in December, 1869 (see Wendell Garrison's letter to his brother William, Dec. 2, 1869, Garrison Family Papers, Smith College Library), both songs were still available with Ditson imprints in 1870, for they were listed as Ditson publications in the Board of Music Trade's *Complete Catalogue, 1870.*

Two copies of "Roll, Jordan, Roll" have been found after years of searching, both with identical imprints: Philadelphia: c 1862. One was made available by Mrs. Chubb, the other by James Fuld from an original in the possession of Thornton Hagert, Arlington, Virginia. Presumably copies were issued with a Ditson imprint, but none has yet been located.

15

....

Reports of Black Folk Music, 1863–67

The descriptions of black music by the two McKims, Spaulding, and Higginson have become fairly well known, cited in bibliographies and frequently reprinted, but other accounts in letters, newspaper reports, and memoirs are all but unknown. Those early accounts given in the preceding chapter were followed by many more, reflecting the varied temperaments and capabilities of the soldiers, teachers, missionaries, and others brought into contact with the freedmen by the fortunes of war. It was quite natural, however unfortunate, that many Northerners in the South concentrated on their daily duties, ignoring the music that at times surrounded them. Some who mentioned it could not understand it and disliked it; others listened with curiosity and pleasure but only a very few had sufficient musical training to write down an approximation of what they heard. Considering that these accounts were written in the midst of a war, it is impressive when we realize how many people found time to describe the music they heard and to try to reduce it to musical notation.

CRITICISM OF "THIS BARBARIC MUSIC"

Some Northerners' comments have a family resemblance to the uncomprehending early responses to jazz. A southern-born white clergyman living in Worcester, Massachusetts, expressed his disapproval of the blacks' "native songs" in 1863, equating them with the ignorance of slavery:

> We have heard these long enough, and we hope the good taste of the refined young ladies at Port Royal will substitute others more sensible and elevated in language. Northern people love to hear these songs as specimens of negro ignorance. Let us now endeavor to teach them something better. Here is a specimen which should not be tolerated in these schools:—
>
> "In de mornin' when I rise,
> Tell my Jesus, Huddy oh? . . ."
>
> We hope the day may soon come when all such illiterate, we will not say senseless songs will be discouraged by all who wish and are laboring for the true enlightenment of the African race.[1]

A visitor to the Sea Island schools in 1866, identified only as M. R. S., wrote of "these little barbarians . . . circling round in this fetish dance [a shout]," concluding, "These people are receiving an education through their songs which is incalculable. Our teachers discourage the use of their old barbaric chants, and besides our beautiful, patriotic and religious hymns teach the virtues of industry, truth, honesty and purity in rhyme and measure. . . ."[2]

One teacher in the Sea Islands, James P. Blake of New Haven, Connecticut, was equally convinced of the good being done in discouraging the singing of the people's own songs: "I have seen them [the children], when requested to sing some of their grotesque hymns, which were great favorites in slave-times, hide their heads while singing, and seem heartily ashamed of them."[3]

RECOGNITION OF A DISTINCTIVE FOLK MUSIC

However, the more perceptive teachers and other northern workers in the South instinctively recognized something of musical value in these songs, even though they could not fully understand them. Lucy McKim's letter to Dwight spoke for them.[4]

Among the perceptive newspaper correspondents was Charles Nordhoff of the New York *Evening Post*, who described the schools of Port Royal in his dispatch of March 25, 1863:

> The children in the schools. . . take great delight in singing, which is very properly a part of the daily routine. They have fine voices and an excellent ear for time; and some of the larger boys roar a deep bass. Besides the songs which have been introduced by the teachers, they

1. Hawkins, *Lunsford Lane*, p. 294.
2. M. R. S., "Visitor's Account," pp. 5–7.
3. Blake, Letter to "Miss Stevenson," p. 28.
4. Lucy McKim [Garrison], "Songs of the Port Royal 'Contrabands,' " pp. 254–55.

have their own, of which the melodies are always quaint, and often full
of music. "Roll, Jordan, Roll" has a glorious swing. The words mostly
tell of death, and the happier life beyond; and in fact all the songs I
heard, even among the boatmen and other grown people, related to
Scripture stories and religious sentiment.

One song, sung with peculiar force and unction, had for refrain an
aspiration for liberty which not even the masters, probably, ventured to
check. I remember but two lines:

> "I'll follow Jesus's ways, *No man can hinder me!*
> I'll do what Jesus says, *No man can hinder me!*"

The first stanza of another clings to me, as curious a bit of folk-song as
I ever met:

"Old massa Death He's a very little man,
He goes from door to door; He kills some souls,
And he woundeth some, Good Lord, remember me;
  Good Lord, remember me;
Remember me as the years roll round, Good Lord, remember me."[5]

Different ears heard different qualities. James P. Blake was surprised to hear cheerful songs. "These songs, much to my surprise,
were all cheerful in their tendency, and all in the major key. I had
read much of the plaintive airs of the slaves; but have not heard one
since I came among them."[6] The Freedmen's Inquiry Commission,
on the other hand, reported to the Secretary of War: "The negro
songs of South Carolina are, with scarcely an exception, plaintive,
despondent, and religious. When there mingles a tone of mournful
exultation, it has reference to the future glories of Zion, not worldly
hopes."[7]

William P. Stanton, a teacher at Gallatin, Tennessee, wrote of his
school:

Each days exercises are commenced by reading a chapter in the Bible,
and usually singing a hymn. Almost every colored person can sing, and
some of them have remarkably fine voices.... They have many hymns of
their own; some of which seem to be a sort of miscellaneous patchwork,
made up from the most striking parts of popular Methodist hymns;
others seem to be entirely original.... In addition to their hymns they
delight in singing patriotic Union songs, which they do with great spirit

5. *National Anti-Slavery Standard* 23 (May 2, 1863), p. [4], col. 1–3. This dispatch,
signed C. N., was later reissued as no. 1 of the series, "Papers of the day, collected and
arranged by Frank Moore": Nordhoff, *Freedmen of South Carolina,* pp. 9–10.

6. Blake, Letter to "Miss Stevenson," p. 28.

7. American Freedmen's Inquiry Commission, *Preliminary Report,* p. 10. The
Commission was composed of Robert Dale Owen, James McKaye, and Samuel
Gridley Howe.

and energy. By far the most popular piece with them is the "John Brown" song. . . .

An account published in 1870 was written by one Elizabeth Kilham; she had been a teacher in an unidentified part of the South just after the close of the war. Despite her irresistible urge to patronize the freedmen and make fun of them, her series of four articles, "Sketches in Color," had an immediacy and liveliness that convey much of the sound and emotion of the scenes she witnessed. She described a service in a Negro church addressed by General Oliver Otis Howard, head of the Freedmen's Bureau. After he left the church, the service continued in a scene of wild emotion, to her great disapproval:

> With the first note of the hymn, began a tapping of feet by the whole congregation, gradually increasing to a stamp as the exercises proceeded, until the noise was deafening; and as the excitement increased, one and another would spring from their seats, and jump up and down, uttering shriek after shriek; while from all parts of the house came cries of "Hallelujah;" "Glory to God;" "Jes' now Lord, come jes' now;" "Amen;" and occasionally a prolonged, shrill whoop. . . . Then in strange contrast to this, came . . . a chant, carried by full deep bass voices; the liquid soprano of the melody wandering through and above it. . . .

She described in great detail the rising excitement which repelled and frightened her, concluding:

> The distinctive features of negro hymnology, are gradually disappearing, and with another generation will probably be obliterated entirely. The cause for this, lies in the education of the younger people. . . . Already they have learned to ridicule the extravagant preaching, the meaningless hymns, and the noisy singing of their elders. Not perhaps as yet, to any great extent in the country; changes come always more slowly there, but in the cities, the young people have, in many cases, taken the matter into their own hands, formed choirs, adopted the hymns and tunes in use in the white churches. . . .
> A collection of negro hymns, will, a few years hence, be one of the "Curiosities of Literature." A fruitful question for the antiquarian will be, where and how did they originate? Were they composed as a whole, with deliberate arrangement and definite meaning, or are they fragments, caught here and there, and pieced into mosaic, hap-hazard as they come? . . . Watts and Newton would never recognize their productions through the transformation they have undergone at the hands of their colored admirers.

8. Western Freedmen's Aid Commission, *Second Annual Report*, p. 33. Mr. Stanton seems to have been unaware that the tune of the "John Brown Song" may have been known to the freedmen before it acquired that set of words.

... The colored people scarcely ever sing a hymn without a chorus, their favorite being, "Shall we know each other there?" This they sing with almost everything; ...[9]

As a reporter, Elizabeth Kilham was limited by her conventional reactions and fears, but she was far superior to the majority of Northerners who went South during the Civil War. Their letters and diaries frequently make no mention at all of the music that was to be heard around them, while those who did mention it usually confined themselves to brief statements, like Henry Villard, who visited the Sea Islands as a young war correspondent. He wrote in his memoirs, "A noteworthy characteristic was their proneness to express their moods of joy and sorrow in original songs, which indicated the natural musical gift of the race."[10] Fortunately the collectors of slave songs in the Sea Islands overcame whatever feelings of discomfort they may have felt with this music and the emotional religion that accompanied it, and learned to accept and value it.

THE SHOUT

Descriptions of the shout written before the Civil War were perfunctory and vague, making little attempt to explain how the practice began. A few more perceptive observers likened it to "Ashantee or Dahomey," but most cultured whites ridiculed the dance or described it as savage and uncivilized. The Northerners who participated in the Port Royal experiment were fascinated by what was to them the most exotic practice of the freedmen for which they were unable to get any clear explanation. The more conventional found the practice shocking, sacrilegious, and perhaps a bit frightening, and they hoped it would disappear in the light of true religion. But many were curious and admiring, rather than disapproving.

As early as the first annual report of the Educational Commission for Freedmen, the shout was described in a letter from a teacher:

Coffin Point Plantation, St. Helena [S.C.], March 17th, 1862. ... Three evenings a week and thrice on the Sabbath they [the freedmen] meet for prayer and praise. ... The younger usually wish to end the worship with a "shout"—a kind of slow, religious trot, accompanied by loud singing of a few lines or words repeated over and over again. The conclusion of the stanza or sentence is marked by a peculiar jerk of the body.[11]

9. [Kilham,] "Sketches in Color," pp. 304–9.
10. Villard, *Memoirs*, II, 24.
11. Letter signed W. C. G. [William Channing Gannett] in Educational Commission for Freedmen, *1st Annual Report*, pp. 25–26.

Other brief descriptions of the shout appeared throughout the war, varying in the degree of sympathy and understanding. Charles Nordhoff's account was one of the very few that equated it with camp meeting "exercises."

> They [the freedmen of South Carolina] all like to sing, are fond of devotional meetings, and have much of that curious excitability which is often developed in Western and Southern camp-meetings. What is called a "shout" is one way in which this excitement manifests itself; and this seems to be an effect of the same nature as what was called "the jerks" in the West and Southwest. . . .
> This excitability appears to many observers peculiar to the negroes; but I think the people here show it perhaps more readily than any whites I have seen; but any one who has been accustomed to camp-meeting scenes in Indiana or Ohio a dozen or twenty years ago, will find here, on occasion of a "shout," I am sure, something he is quite familiar with.[12]

Nordhoff's conclusion that the shout was very similar to the "jerks" seems to be a most superficial reaction. Both were unrestrained and emotional, especially in comparison with sedate nineteenth-century Protestant church services. However, the jerks were individual responses to intense religious excitement, while a shout was a ritualized group activity, with separate roles assigned to singers and dancers who performed music and steps that had become traditional for such occasions. The more detailed descriptions that follow will demonstrate that the shout was far from formless noise and random movement.

Charlotte Forten, the sensitive granddaughter of James Forten, a prominent black sailmaker of Philadelphia, arrived in the Sea Islands on October 28, 1862, to teach the freedmen. She described her experiences in an article, "Life on the Sea Islands," that was published in the *Atlantic Monthly* in 1864, including an account of a shout:

> On this, as on several other large plantations, there is a "Praise-House," which is the special property of the people. Even in the old days of Slavery, they were allowed to hold meetings here; and they still keep up the custom. They assemble on several nights of the week, and on Sunday afternoons. First, they hold what is called the "Praise-Meeting," which consists of singing, praying, and preaching. . . . At the close of the Praise-Meeting they all shake hands with each other in the most solemn manner. Afterward, as a kind of appendix, they have a grand "shout," during which they sing their own hymns. . . . [13]

Her description of a shout here was very vague, but she gave details elsewhere:

12. C. N., "The Freedmen of South Carolina," *National Anti-Slavery Standard* 24 (May 23, 1863), p. [4], col. 4.
13. Forten, "Life on the Sea Islands," p. 672.

In the evening, the children frequently came in to sing and shout for us. These "shouts" are very strange,—in truth, almost indescribable. It is necessary to hear and see in order to have any clear idea of them. The children form a ring, and move around in a kind of shuffling dance, singing all the time. Four or five stand apart, and sing very energetically, clapping their hands, stamping their feet, and rocking their bodies to and fro. These are the musicians, to whose performance the shouters keep perfect time. The grown people on this plantation did not shout, but they do on some of the other plantations. It is very comical to see little children, not more than three or four years old, entering into the performance with all their might. But the shouting of the grown people is rather solemn and impressive than otherwise. We cannot determine whether it has a religious character or not. Some of the people tell us that it has, others that it has not. But as the shouts of the grown people are always in connection with their religious meetings, it is probable that they are the barbarous expression of religion, handed down to them from their African ancestors, and destined to pass away under the influence of Christian teachings.[14]

Thomas Wentworth Higginson, the Unitarian clergyman from Worcester, Massachusetts, was colonel of the 1st Regiment, South Carolina Volunteers, the first black regiment to be mustered into service in the Civil War. He arrived in the Sea Islands on November 24, 1862. Under the stimulation of the novel surroundings and experiences and the historic events in which he played a part, the line-a-day diary which he had been keeping for years was expanded into a fuller record. On December 3 he wrote in his diary a description of a shout. This account provided the basis for a widely read article in the *Atlantic Monthly*, which in turn was included in his book-length account of his experiences, *Army Life in a Black Regiment*.[15] The published versions are more polished and have been reprinted frequently, but they lack the immediacy of the original diary entry, which has not been published until now:

> Dec. 3, 1862. . . . from a neighboring campfire comes one of those strange concerts half powwow, half prayer meeting, of which Eliza Dodge's "negro spirituals" & Olmsted's descriptions give each but a part.[16] These fires are often enclosed in a sort of little booth made neatly of palm leaves covered in at top, a native African hut in short; this at such times

14. *Ibid.*, p. 594.
15. Higginson, "Leaves," p. 527. Reprinted in his *Army Life*, pp. 17–18.
16. This, the earliest reference to "Negro spirituals" that has been found, set off a wide-ranging search for the mysterious "Eliza Dodge" and her association with them. No approach was fruitful, either in Worcester, Mass., or anywhere else. I was forced to consider the possibility that she might be fictitious, until I happened to notice in a genealogy of Caroline Howard Gilman's family that her third daughter was "Eliza Webb, b. Feb. 14, 1825; m. (1st) Pickering Dodge, of Salem, Mass. . . ."—Pierce, *Lillie Family*, p. 114. So Higginson's Eliza Dodge was Caroline Howard Gilman's daughter and Annie Bowen's sister, born in Charleston but with warm family ties in New England.

[dusk] is crammed with men singing at the top of their voices—often the John Brown song was sung, but oftener these incomprehensible negro methodist, meaningless, monotonous, endless chants, with obscure syllables recurring constantly & slight variations interwoven, all accompanied with a regular drumming of the feet & clapping of the hands, like castenets; then the excitement spreads, outside the enclosure men begin to quiver & dance, others join, a circle forms, winding monotonously round some one in the centre. Some heel & toe tumultuously, others merely tremble & stagger on, others stoop & rise, others whirl, others caper sidewise all keep steadily circling like dervishes, outsiders applaud especial strokes of skill, my approach only enlivens the scene, the circle enlarges, louder grows the singing about Jesus & Heaven, & the ceaseless drumming & clapping go steadily on. At last seems to come a snap and the spell breaks amid general sighs & laughter. And this not rarely & occasionally but night after night.[17]

Higginson did not say whether a traditional "praise" service had preceded this shout, but his description differs in many respects from the other contemporary descriptions, notably in the enumeration of the different kinds of steps performed. Most other descriptions refer only to a kind of shuffle, beginning slowly and very gradually quickening, in which the feet never cross.

That shocked visitor, M. R. S., saw a shout in a school held in an old cotton gin house in Beaufort on May 15, 1866:

After school the teachers gave their children permission to have a "shout."

This is a favorite religious exercise of these people, old and young. In the infant schoolroom, the benches were first put aside, and the children ranged along the wall. Then began a wild droning chant in a minor key, marked with clapping of hands and stamping of feet. A dozen or twenty rose, formed a ring in the centre of the room, and began an odd shuffling dance. Keeping time to this weird chant they circled round, one following the other, changing their step to quicker and wilder motion, with louder clappings of the hands as the fervor of the singers reached a climax. The words of their hymns are simple and touching. The verses consist of two lines, the first being repeated twice. Take for example:

> Nobody knows de trubble I sees,
> Nobody knows de trubble I sees,
> Nobody knows de trubble I sees,
>   Nobody knows but Jesus.

And again:

> We a huntin fo' a city to stay awhile,
> We a huntin fo' a city to stay awhile,
> We a huntin fo' a city to stay awhile,
>   O! Lord, de Believer got a home at last.

17. Higginson, *Diary*, MS, Houghton Library, Harvard University, entry for Dec. 3, 1862.

This clear and objective account was followed by an outburst of the discomfort and fear this strange sight inspired:

> As I looked upon the faces of these little barbarians and watched them circling round in this fetish dance, doubtless the relic of some African rite, I felt discouraged, thinking how much we had to do to bring them up to the level of our educated classes of the colored people in the free states. However, the recollection of the mental arithmetic seemed a more cheerful view of the matter. Thank God, that under these embruted faces there lies the unextinguished soul![18]

Excepting the entry from Higginson's diary, all these accounts were published before the appearance of *Slave Songs of the United States*, contributing to the public awareness of a distinctive black religious folk music. Other accounts written during the same years remained unpublished, some, like Higginson's diary, until now. Just as Higginson described a shout within days after his arrival in the Sea Islands, many of the teachers were equally struck by it. In April, 1862, Laura Towne wrote to her family:

> To-night I have been to a "shout," which seems to me certainly the remains of some old idol worship. The negroes sing a kind of chorus,—three standing apart to lead and clap,—and then all the others go shuffling round in a circle following one another with not much regularity, turning round occasionally and bending the knees, and stamping so that the whole floor swings. I never saw anything so savage. They call it a religious ceremony, but it seems more like a regular frolic to me, and instead of attending the shout, the better persons go to the "Praise House." This is always the cabin of the oldest person in the little village of negro houses, and they meet there to read and pray.... [19]

Her diary entry for the next day described the same scene:

> Last night ... we went to the "shout," a savage, heathenish dance out in Rina's house. Three men stood and sang, clapping and gesticulating. The others shuffled along on their heels, following one another in a circle and occasionally bending the knees in a kind of curtsey. They began slowly, a few going around and more gradually joining in, the song getting faster and faster, till at last only the most marked part of the refrain is sung and the shuffling, stamping, and clapping get furious. The floor shook so that it seemed dangerous. It swayed regularly to the time of the song. As they danced they, of course, got out of breath, and the singing was kept up principally by the three apart, but it was astonishing how long they continued and how soon after a rest they were ready to begin again.[20]

18. M. R. S., "Visitor's Account," p. 6.
19. Towne, *Letters and Diary*, p. 20. Letter dated "St. Helena's, Sunday, April 27, 1862."
20. *Ibid.*, p. 23.

Harriet Ware witnessed a shout at about the same time but on a different plantation, Pine Grove. She described on April 29 what she saw after a regular evening prayer service.

> They then shook hands all round, when one of the young girls struck up one of their wild songs, and we waited listening ... for twenty minutes more. It was not a regular "shout," but some of them clapped their hands, and they stamped in time. It was very difficult to understand the words, though there was so much repetition that I generally managed to make out a good deal, but could not remember it much, still less the music, which is indescribable, and no one person could imitate it at all. As we walked home we asked Cuffy if they considered the "shout" as part of their religious worship; he said yes, that "it exercise the frame." Mr. [William] G[annett] told him that some of the old people had told him they did not like the shouts, or think them religious, but he said old Binah did not object to them in the praise-house, but she did not like the shout "out in de world," *i.e.*, before they joined the Church. ... [21]

On May 4 she wrote:

> They had a "shout," which I had heard distinctly at three o'clock in the morning when I happened to wake up. They come from all the plantations about, when these meetings take place for the examination of new members. ... They do not begin till about ten o'clock Saturday night, when the examinations commence, and the other services, after which they keep up the shout till near daylight, when they can see to go home.[22]

Christmas, 1862, she reported, the men in Colonel Higginson's regiment had no taps, and shouted all night.[23]

When Lucy McKim and her father visited the Sea Islands in June, 1862, Laura Towne took them to see a shout, "which Mr. McKim was inclined to think was a remnant of African worship."[24]

Reuben Tomlinson, a scrupulously honest and capable abolitionist from Pennsylvania,[25] took a hard-headed, strictly business attitude toward the shout and other religious practices of the Negro which he deplored as taking too much of their time and energy. In a letter to James Miller McKim he wrote:

> Walker Plantation, Port Royal, S.C., Sunday Evng., Oct 5/62 ... I asked them [the children] to sing some of their own [songs] & at it they went. Soon they got from singing into shouting & dancing (which is part of their religious exercises) Some of the boys took their stand [?] against

21. Pearson, ed., *Letters from Port Royal*, pp. 22–28.
22. *Ibid.*, p. 34.
23. *Ibid.*, p. 124.
24. Towne, *Letters and Diary*, p. 67.
25. Cf. *Pennsylvania Freedmen's Bulletin* 1 (Feb., 1865): 13, and Williamson, *After Slavery*, p. 361.

the wall, & sung & beat time with their hands & feet, while the rest marched around, in a sort of double shuffle moving gradually faster & faster; until at last each joint in their bodies seemed to have strange collective [word illegible]. It was the most ludicrous & at the same time the most pitiful sight I ever witnessed. Little children that can scarcely stand alone will go around in this way by the hour. I soon stopped it; not because I thought there was any harm in it, in itself, but it seemed so entirely the result of their ignorance & servitude, it was painful to me. I strongly desire that some regulation may be adopted here with reference to the . . . Church organizations of these people, the limits within which they should enjoy them, ought to be rigorously defined. . . . The consequence [of preparations for a baptism] is that last week my two places were nearly deserted for three days.[26]

William Francis Allen's diary included several graphic descriptions of shouts. The first told of the Christmas celebration at his school in 1863. After the distribution of presents and some singing:

. . . Billy [a freedman] came to Mary [Mrs. Allen] and asked if she wouldn't like to have a "shout" so forthwith the tree was shoved into a corner and the floor cleared. This "shout" is a peculiar custom of these people, and is well described in that article in the Continental "Under the Palmetto". Mr. Eustis told me to-day that so far as he knew (and he is a native of South Carolina) it is not only peculiar to these islands, but to some plantations.[27] Perhaps it is of African origin, with Christianity engrafted upon it just as it was upon the ancient Roman ritual. At any rate, it arises from that same strange connection between dancing and religious worship which was so frequent among the ancients, and which we find in the dervishes, shakers, etc. These people are very strict about dancing, but will keep up the shout all night. It has a religious significance, and apparently a very sincere one, but it is evidently their recreation—just as prayer meetings are the only recreation of some people in the North. They do not have shouts very often, and were very glad to the excuse to have one in a large open room. We went to see their regular Christmas shout in Peg's house last night. They had a praise meeting first . . . At last they cleared the room and began, and a strange sight it was. The room is no more than ten feet square, with a fire burning on the hearth. . . . On one side of the room is a table, and in front of it stood young Paris (Simmons), Billy and Henry, who served as *band*. Billy sang or rather chanted, and the others "based" him as they say, while . . . [six dancers] moved round the room in a circle in a sort of shuffle. This is the

26. Reuben Tomlinson to James Miller McKim, Oct. 5, 1862, MS, Cornell University Library.

27. This supposition seems to have been incorrect. Although shouting was more common in the Sea Islands than elsewhere, something very similar was observed as far away as Texas. Sylvia King, a former slave 100 years old, reported from Fayette County, Texas: "De black folks gets off down in de bottom and shouts and sings and prays. Dey gets in de ring dance. It am just a kind of shuffle, den it get faster and faster and dey gets warmed up and moans and shouts and claps and dances. Some gets exhausted and drops out and de ring gets closer. Sometimes dey sings and shouts all night. . . ."—Yetman, "*Peculiar Institution*," pp. 198–201.

shout. Some moved the feet backward and forward alternately, but the best shouters—and Jimmy, I was told to-day, "is a great shouter," keep the feet on the floor and work themselves along over the floor by moving them right and left. It seemed tremendous work for them . . . and I saw that the most skillful ones moved very easily and quietly. The shouters seldom sing or make any noise except with their feet, but work their bodies more or less; while the singers clap their hands and stamp the right foot in time. . . . [Three others] sat or stood about and joined in the "base." When they had shouted in this way for several minutes, they stopped and walked slowly round while Billy sang a sort of recitative interlude; then, when he began a new tune, they started off again. And their shouting varied a little according to the tune. In some they kept along with scarcely any change, and in others they would half stop, with a jerk at every change in the tune, and shift the foot in advance from right to left or left to right. Presently Billy joined the shouters, and Henry led the singing. . . .—Today I was very glad to see the shouting again, to understand it a little better and catch the words. First there was a circle of the young people . . . Church members are sometimes unwilling to shout with outsiders. . . . I caught some of the words, which are evidently original.

"Jesus call and I must go—I cannot stay behin' my Lord," while the base sang "I must go." Another was "Pray a little longer, Jericho do worry me," while the base was "O Lord, yes my Lord." In singing this Billy sang very fast "Jericho, Jericho, Jericho, etc." while the shouting was very rapid and excited. Another "Bell do ring,—want to go to meeting; bell do ring, wan' to go to shoutin' ",—base "bell do ring" and here he sang in the same way "heaven bell" so fast that it sounded like "humbell—a—humbell—a—etc." These two were very fascinating. Another was mournful—"Jesus died—died on the cross," while the base was minor, "Jesus died", and the singer repeated "died, died, died, etc." as he did "Jericho", only slowly and mournfully. Altogether it was one of the strangest and most interesting things I ever saw.[28]

On March 30, 1864, Allen reported another shout, where they shouted to seven tunes: "Heaven bell, Archangel open de door, I can't stay behin' my Lord, Jesus die, Sinner turn, My body rack wid fever, and Jordan, roll.[29] The Heaven bell is a pretty good type of these tunes. The introduction is sung, and shouters standing still or clapping their hands. Then begins the second part, the regular shout."[30]

Many teachers described the enthusiasm with which children shouted, deploring what appears to have been a joyous continuation of their own culture. Allen's description is among the best, factual in

28. Allen, *Diary*, MS, State Historical Society of Wisconsin, entry for Dec. 25, [1863].

29. These are all in *Slave Songs*, although sometimes the titles are different: 27, Heaven bell a-ring; 44, Archangel, open the door; 8, I can't stay behind; 52, Shall I die?; 48, Turn sinner, turn O; 45, My body rock 'long fever; and 1, Roll, Jordan, roll.

30. Allen, *Diary*, Mar. 20, 1864.

its detail without any moralizing overtones: "[Gibb] and Abraham got up a 'shout,' which was as good as a play—Gibb leaning against a post singing, stamping and clapping his hands with all his might, while Abraham kicked up the dust—they 'shouted' together, back to back and round each other, ending in tumbling in a heap on the ground. As big-headed Edward . . . came up,—'Edward come base we,' cried Gibb in the midst of his delirium."[31]

Harriet Ware permitted her pupils to have a shout during a Christmas celebration in 1865, although she disapproved of the custom:

> I let the children sing some of their own songs in a genuine, shouting style, a sight too funny in the little things, but sad and disagreeable to me in the grown people, who make it a religious act. It is impossible to describe it—the children move round in a circle, backwards, or sideways, with their feet and arms keeping energetic time, and their whole bodies undergoing most extraordinary contortions, while they sing at the top of their voices the refrain to some song sung by an outsider. We laughed till we almost cried over the little bits of ones, but when the grown people wanted to "shout," I would not let them. . . .[32]

The true "ring shout" consisted of movement in a circle with the feet never crossed and usually not lifted from the ground, accompanied by a vocal "band" composed of lead singer and "basers" who sang only religious texts; it flourished in the Sea Islands and the adjoining coastal region, the area of the distinctive Gullah dialect.[33] Other kinds of "sacred dancing" reported from other areas were less developed in form, often little more than a bodily response to religious ecstasy. This less formal "sacred dance" was described by a former teacher who had taught in Alabama and Mississippi after the Civil War. A chapter of her reminiscences was entitled "The Heavenly Dance":

> It usually began when the preaching was nearly done. Aunt Chloe, or Dinah, would get blest, and seemed to be unable to contain the blessing, and would spring to her feet, and begin shaking hands with the nearest one to her, and in a moment the example would be contagious, and two-thirds of the congregation would rise to their feet, each shaking

31. *Ibid.*, Mar. 29, [1864].
32. Pearson, *Letters from Port Royal*, pp. 292–93.
33. This form of ring shout is well described in Courlander, *Negro Folk Music*, pp. 194–200. A possibly related "shouting style," in which the singers midway in a song "break into a wild combination of complex foot-stomping and hand-clapping rhythms," can be heard in Folkways record FS 3842, *Been in the Storm so Long*, recorded by Guy Carawan on Johns Island, S.C. This may be what George Gershwin observed on Folly Island in 1934. Cf. Ewen, *Gershwin*, p. 224.

hands with some other, the men on one side of the church, women on the other; and soon all would swing into the center of the church, in front of the pulpit, and shouts of some would rend the air, while those who could sing would sing as though their life depended on their making a noise, all the time swaying their bodies up and down and circling among each other, shaking hands, and moving feet as if keeping time to the music. The preachers would come down out of the pulpit, and stand ready for the hand shaking. All would seem either solemn, or joyous, and perhaps after twenty minutes of such exercise, the pastor would lift his hand, when instantly the noise would cease, while he pronounced the benediction, and the worshippers would pass out of the church.

When the teachers first saw it, they were dumb with amazement. One of the larger scholars, who had participated in the dance, passed near them, and said, "That's what is called the Heavenly dance." The songs usual on the occasion were

"I wonder Lord will I ever get to heaven
To walk them golden streets."

or

"I'm just at the fountain, Lord,
That never runs dry."[34]

The ring shout continued to be part of Sea Island life long after the close of the Civil War. Lydia Parrish found it there when she first visited the Islands in 1912; her encouragement helped the tradition to survive, although its form may have changed with the years.[35]

WORKSONGS

Although the most frequently reported worksongs in the antebellum period had been boat songs, and postwar reports demonstrated that the practice continued throughout the war, very few wartime descriptions of boat songs have been found. Whittier's synthetic but popular "Song of the Negro Boatmen" was the first to appear after the outbreak of the war. The next published reports were written by the McKims, who visited Port Royal between June 2 and 28, 1862.[36] James Miller McKim, a widely respected abolitionist from Philadelphia, was sent by the Port Royal Relief Committee to determine what supplies and services were needed. He was accompanied by his nineteen-year-old daughter, Lucy, who acted as

34. Waterbury, *Seven Years*, pp. 195-96.
35. Parrish, *Slave Songs of the Georgia Sea Islands*, pp. 54-[92]. Cf. also Cate, *Early Days*, and Society for the Preservation of Spirituals, *Carolina Low-Country*, pp. 198-201.
36. McKim, *Freedmen of South Carolina*, p. 4.

his secretary. In the public report he made on his return, McKim described the freedmen's songs. His remarks were reprinted in *Dwight's Journal of Music*:

> They [the freedmen] are a musical people. When they work in concert, as in rowing or grinding at the mill, their hands keep time to music. Their boat songs are the ones most frequently heard. The islands are made and permeated by rivers and creeks, and the boat furnishes the most common mode of locomotion.
>
> When the negroes begin to row, they at the same time begin to sing. All their songs are in the minor key. If one chances to begin on the major, it quickly saddens and passes into the minor. Their songs are all religious, barcaroles and all. . . .
>
> I said these songs were all in the minor key. This was a mistake. They have one that has a cheerful . . . ring. It is a new one, made, as they said, "since secesh times." It runs thus:
>
> No more driver call for me, . . .
>
> I first heard this song . . . going up from Hilton Head to Beaufort in a boat rowed by a half dozen men detailed from the first regiment of South Carolina volunteers. They were in fine voice and spirits, and the echoes came back from the inlets of Ladies' and St. Helena with fine effect.[37]

That McKim's daughter Lucy had accompanied her father to Port Royal was one of the most fortunate circumstances that could be imagined for American folk music, for her perceptive enthusiasm for the music she heard on this trip had far-reaching consequences. In a letter to editor Dwight, dated November 1, 1862, she added some comments of her own:

> having accompanied my father on his tour to Port Royal, and being much struck with the songs of its people. I reduced a number of them to paper. . . .[38]

Strangely enough, only one other report of worksongs published during the war has been found. It describes workers in the fields singing at their work: "Coffin's Point, St. Helena Island, . . . 1862. . . . April 3d.—Sixty-eight hands are in the potato field planting sweet potatos, swinging their hoes in unison, timed by a jolly song, words undistinguishable. They work with a good will, and plant about thirteen acres during the day."[39] The letters and diaries of the Northerners who were stationed in the Sea Islands included many descriptions of boat songs which continued to be sung as long as

---

37. *Ibid.*, pp. 11–13, reprinted as McKim, "Negro Songs," pp. 148–49.
38. Lucy McKim [Garrison], "Songs of the Port Royal 'Contrabands,' " pp. 254–55.
39. Letter signed E. P., "Extracts from Letters," in Educational Commission for Freedmen, *1st Annual Report*, p. 31.

they were needed to time the strokes of the oars. Early in her stay Harriet Ware wrote: "The negroes sang to us in their wild way as they rowed us across—I cannot give you the least idea of it."[40] At about the same time Laura Towne wrote in her diary: "Boats frequently pass by, the negro rowers singing their refrains. . . . Every now and then they shout and change the monotony by several very quick notes, or three or four long-drawn-out ones. One man sings a few words and the chorus breaks in, sometimes with a shout or interjectional note."[41]

New Year's Day, 1863, was made memorable by the promulgation of the Emancipation Proclamation, and a solemn and joyous celebration was held for all the inhabitants of the islands under federal rule. On the way to the festivities, Harriet Ware observed the four oarsmen who provided her transportation: "The men sang and we sang, as we wound our way through the marshbound creek. . . . They grew very much excited as they rowed and sung, shouting with all their might, and singing song after song the whole way home. The singing while they row always sounds differently from [that] at any other time to me, though they always sing the same, religious songs."[42] Dr. Seth Rogers, the surgeon of Colonel Higginson's regiment, described the singing of black men in uniform as they rowed:

> This morning, the adjutant and I, with eight oarsmen, went down to Hilton Head in our surf boat. . . . Our black soldiers sang as they rowed—not the songs of common sailors—but the hymns of praise mingled with those pathetic longings for a better world, so constant with these people. There are times when I could quite enjoy more earthly songs for them, even a touch of the wicked, but this generation must live and die in sadness.[43]

William Allen also heard boat songs, and added information that other people missed. Paris, one of the rowers, told him "the boatsongs were sometimes the same as the shouting songs, and sometimes only used for rowing." Allen added: "I haven't heard a single piece of music here that was not religious. . . . Phoebe divides all their music into 'sperituals' and 'running sperituals,' that is, shouting tunes."[44] Earlier Allen had been rowed across Station Creek: "The men sang most of the way as they rowed. It was curious to see how their rowing flagged—for they were quite tired—the moment the

40. Letter dated "Pine Grove, St. Helena, April 21 [1862], in Pearson, ed., *Letters from Port Royal*, p. 19.
41. Towne, *Letters and Diary*, diary entry: "Beaufort, S.C., April 17, 1862," p. 4.
42. Pearson, ed., *Letters from Port Royal*, pp. [128], 134, letter dated Jan. 1, 1863.
43. Rogers, "Letters," pp. 341–42.
44. Allen, *Diary*, entry for Saturday, Feb. 13 [1864].

singing stopped. It wasn't a very good set of singers, still I was very glad to hear them, for I have heard very little boat music. They sang 'Michael row', 'Hold your Light,' and several others, of which we were particularly struck by 'de Graveyard', 'Ober yonder' and 'I want to go home.' "[45]

In the fall of 1864, when Allen had left the Sea Islands and was on his way to Helena, Arkansas, he heard a different kind of boat song from hands on a Mississippi steamboat.

> They hauled off the planks, cast loose the hawser & slowly backed out, while the negro hands on the lower deck . . . began to sing—in the same mode as at Port Royal, the leader sitting on the bowsprit & whipping a figure of a buffalo which was before him, singing a line & the others taking it up after him. There was a wild, strange, irregular harmony about it,—less of a tune than [?] the songs at Port Royal.[46]

PERFORMANCE STYLE

From the contemporary reports that have been quoted, it is evident that very few observers before and during the Civil War were able to dissociate themselves from European norms of musical performance and to evaluate Afro-American music on its own terms. Most of these reporters were not particularly sensitive to details of musical style; even those who were professional musicians thought of music only in terms of European standards. The tense, strained vocal quality admired by Africans was described as shrieking, screaming, and mere noise. Sympathetic appreciation was quite exceptional; even comments on the manner in which the music was performed were rare. Before the publication of *Slave Songs of the United States*, only a few details were described in print. For example, Harriet Beecher Stowe described Sojourner Truth's conversion at a Methodist meeting in the North, where she sang the hymn "There Is a Holy City": "She sang with the strong barbaric accent of the native African,[47] and with those indescribable upward turns and those deep gutturals which give such a wild, peculiar power to the negro singing. . . ."[48]

A more meaningful account came from a New England minister, George H. Hepworth, who attended a church service in Carrollton, Louisiana, in February, 1863. A large number of refugee blacks,

45. *Ibid.*, entry for Sunday, Mar. 20, 1863.
46. *Ibid.*, entry headed: Cairo [Ill.], Sept. 22, Thursday [1864].
47. This would seem to be pure fantasy. Sojourner Truth was born in upstate New York. Her singing may have had strong African influences, but there is no evidence that Mrs. Stowe was qualified to recognize them.
48. Stowe, "Sojourner Truth," pp. 476–77.

not yet freedmen, had gathered there from "a radius of forty miles, and formed themselves into colonies with from one to five hundred in each; and were living on three-quarters Government rations, and working in every way in which they could." When he entered the rude church they had built, he found about a hundred blacks.

> For a few moments, perfect silence prevailed. . . . At length, however, a single voice, coming from a dark corner of the room, began a low, mournful chant, in which the whole assemblage joined by degrees. It was a strange song, with seemingly very little rhythm, and was what is termed in music a minor; it was not a psalm, nor a real song, as we understand these words; for there was nothing that approached the jubilant in it. It seemed more like a wail, a mournful, dirge-like expression of sorrow. At first, I was inclined to laugh, it was so far from what I had been accustomed to call music; then I felt uncomfortable, as though I could not endure it, and half rose to leave the room; and at last, as the weird chorus rose a little above, and then fell a little below, the key-note, I was overcome by the real sadness and depression of soul which it seemed to symbolize. . . . They sang for a full half-hour.—an old man knelt down to pray. His voice was at first low and indistinct. . . . He seemed to gain impulse as he went on, and pretty soon burst out with an "O good, dear Lord! we pray for de cullered people. Thou knows well 'nuff what we'se been through: do, do, oh! do, gib us free!" when the whole audience swayed back and forward in their seats, and uttered in perfect harmony a sound like that caused by prolonging the letter "m" with the lips closed. One or two began this wild, mournful chorus; and in an instant all joined in, and the sound swelled upwards and downwards like waves of the sea.[49]

A northern schoolteacher, Emily C. Blackman, wrote letters home describing her school on Dr. Tucker's plantation near Oka-lona, Mississippi. The letters were published in the *Independent Republican* of Montrose, Susquehanna County, Pennsylvania, and reprinted in the *Pennsylvania Freedmen's Bulletin*. The freedmen's Christmas celebration at the chapel on December 27, 1866, was almost entirely singing.

> Before separating we proposed to the blacks that they should let us hear some of their old tunes . . . and they proceeded to give them to us in their own inimitable style, swaying their bodies to and fro, and occasionally piercing the skies with their notes. For instance in the tune *Ortonville*, both men and women carried the soprano, and the need of variety of parts being felt, a few voices of the very highest register sang the whole tune an octave above the others. Fancy, if you can, the G, fourth line above the treble staff, sounded by the human voice![50]

49. Hepworth, *Whip, Hoe and Sword*, pp. 163–65.
50. *Pennsylvania Freedmen's Bulletin* (Apr., 1867): 12.

Here a traditional hymn tune, "Ortonville," by Thomas Hastings, was sung in a distinctive style.

Whitelaw Reid, a well-known journalist, made a tour of the South from May 1, 1865, to May 1, 1866, surveying conditions in the defeated Confederacy. In the course of his travels he observed the conditions and folkways of the blacks, coloring his comments with an unpleasant ethnocentricity, but with many accurate observations and details. In the church at St. Helena, South Carolina, where many of the slave songs had been gathered during the war, Reid heard an old man, leaning on his cane and swaying his body in time.

> He struck up, in a shrill, cracked voice, a curiously monotonous melody, in which, in a moment, the whole congregation were energetically joining.... The words were those of an old song, which our soldiers found them singing shortly after the fall of Bay Point [i.e., the capture of the Sea Islands in November, 1861]
>
>> "Ma-a-a-assa Fullah [Fuller], a sittin' on de tree ob life;
>> Ma-a-a-assa Fullah a sittin' on de tree ob life,
>>   Roll, Jordan, roll.
>> Ma-a-a-assa Fullah a sittin' on de tree ob life,
>>   Roll, Jordan, roll.
>> Ma-a-a-assa Fullah a sittin' on de tree ob life,
>>   Ro-o-oll, Jordan, roll,
>>   Ro-o-oll, Jordan, roll,
>>   Ro-o-oll, Jordan, roll." ...[51] (AS 1)

Reid also attended a service at a Negro church on a Louisiana cotton plantation in early April, 1866. After the sermon

> a young man, wearing the caped, light-blue army overcoat, rose and started a quaint chant. The congregation struck in and sung the line over. The young man chanted another line, and the congregation sang it after him; another was chanted, then sung; then another, and so on. It was exactly the old Scotch fashion of "lining out," except that instead of reading the line which the congregation was to sing, the leader delivered it in the oddest, most uncouth and sense-murdering chant ever conceived. Presently several of the older members joined the young man in the chant; then united with the chorus in thundering over the chanted line again.

The description continued with increasing disdain at the "hysteric excitement" and the "ludicrously perverted repetitions of the common forms of addressing the Deity." Finally the account concluded: "The rest joined in, in different keys, and the combination furnished a sort of chant, without one word in it, or one effort to

51. Whitelaw Reid, *After the War*, pp. 103–5.

articulate a word. . . . Singing and prayer alternated several times. The demeanor of all was earnest; and, so far as the emotions went, there could be no doubt of their sincerity."[52]

So much for the published reports. Those that remained unpublished are far more informative about how the music was performed. They will be given in roughly chronological order, beginning with one from Craney Island, Virginia, near Norfolk; it was written on September 30, 1863.

> Around one fire the boys had gathered to dance and make merry. The door of a fallen barrack was their spring-board, and upon it they performed their jigs and horn-pipes, keeping time to a variety of strange accompaniment the rapid and regular falling of the hands upon the knees, the beating of feet, or the pleasing accompaniment of a tenor and base voice singing alternate strains of music.[53]

This letter was written by Lucy or Sarah Chase of Worcester, Massachusetts, who wrote again from Norfolk on July 1, 1864: "It is very common for a large congregation to accompany the preacher, or prayer, by a wailing chant, swaying their bodies all the time, and often drowning the voice of the speaker. It is usually the women alone who are so unseemly."[54]

How a new song was created was described in a report from the camp of a black regiment near Petersburg, Virginia, just before the battle of the "Crater," July 30, 1864:

> Any striking event or piece of news . . . was followed by long silence. They sat about in groups, "studying," as they called it. . . . When the spirit moved, one of their singers would uplift a mighty voice, like a bard of old, in a wild sort of chant. If he did not strike a sympathetic chord in his hearers, if they did not find in his utterance the exponent of their idea, he would sing it again and again, altering sometimes the words or more often the music. If his changes met general acceptance, one voice after another would chime in; a rough harmony of three parts would add itself; other groups would join his, and the song became the song of the command.
>
> The night we learned that we were to lead the charge the news filled them too full for ordinary utterance. . . . They formed circles in their company streets and were sitting on the ground intently and solemnly "studying." At last a heavy voice began to sing, "We-e looks li-ike me-en a-a marchin' on, we looks li-ike men-er-war." Over and over again he sang it, making slight changes. The rest watched him intently; no sign of approval or disapproval escaped their lips, or appeared on their faces. All at once, when his refrain had struck the right response in their hearts, his group took it up, and shortly half a thousand voices were upraised. . . .

52. *Ibid.*, pp. 521–23.
53. Swint, ed., *Dear Ones*, pp. 88, 90.
54. *Ibid.*, pp. 117, 124.

SONG OF THE COLORED DIVISION BEFORE CHARGING INTO THE CRATER.

Source: Henry Goddard Thomas, Colonel, 2d Brigade, "The Colored Troops at Petersburg," *Century Magazine* 34, n.s. 12 (September, 1887): 778. Courtesy of the Joseph Regenstein Library, University of Chicago.

> The sound was ... weird ... when all the voices struck the low "E" (last note but one), held it, and then rose to "A" with a *portamento* as sonorous as it was clumsy. Until we fought the battle of the crater they sang this every night to the exclusion of all other songs. After that defeat they sang it no more.[55]

William Allen described the preaching of a noted black minister in Helena, Arkansas, with the congregational responses that accompanied him: "He very rarely passed out of the chanting tone— however fast he spoke, he still modulated his voice to the musical scale, & the women sitting around him, rocking & swaying & throwing up their arms, accompanied him with a murmuring croon, which swelled like an Eolian harp whenever he became excited, & was sometimes very sweet indeed."[56]

A perceptive girl on a plantation in southwest Georgia, between Albany and Thomasville, wrote in her journal on February 12, 1865:

> I went over to the quarter after dinner, to the "Praise House," to hear the negroes sing, but most of them had gone to walk on the river bank, so I did not get a full choir. At their "praise meetings" they go through with all sorts of motions in connection with their songs, but they won't give way to their wildest gesticulations or engage in their sacred dances before white people, for fear of being laughed at. They didn't get out of their seats while I was there, but whenever the "sperrit" of the song moved them very much, would pat their feet and flap their arms and go through with a number of motions. ... They call these native airs "little speritual songs," in contradistinction to the hymns the preachers read to them in church, out of a book, and seem to enjoy them a great deal more.[57]

Sidney Lanier was far more musical than most Southerners of his generation, and his comments on the music of the blacks were highly discerning and illuminating.

> Syncopations ... are characteristic of negro music. I have heard negroes change a well-known melody by adroitly syncopating it ... so as to give

55. Henry Goddard Thomas, "Colored Troops," pp. 777–78.
56. Allen, *Diary*, entry for Nov. 13 [1864].
57. Eliza Frances Andrews, *War-Time Journal*, pp. 89–90.

it a *bizarre* effect scarcely imaginable; and nothing illustrates the negro's natural gifts in the way of keeping a difficult *tempo* more clearly
than his perfect execution of airs thus transformed from simple to
complex accentuations.
   . . . Thus the negro shows that he does not like the ordinary accentuations nor the ordinary cadences of tunes . . . you will hear him sing a
whole minor tune without once using a semitone. . . . I have seen a whole
congregation of negroes at night, as they were worshiping in their church
with some wild song or other and swaying to and fro with the ecstasy
and glory of it, abandon as by one consent the semitone that *should*
come according to the civilized *modus*, and sing in its place a big lusty
whole tone that would shake any man's soul.[58]

Fanny Kemble's daughter, Frances Butler Leigh, had little of her
mother's sensitivity, musical susceptibility, or sympathy for the
Negroes. Frances Leigh's reminiscences[59] were full of hostility
toward the hands on the plantations she inherited from her father,
but her husband, an English clergyman, responded to the blacks
and their music with enthusiasm and understanding. James Wentworth Leigh wintered on St. Simons' and Butler Islands from 1873
to 1875,[60] before outside influences had had much effect. His descriptions of the music he heard were remarkable for the time in
which they were written.

It is the way they *sing* the words, and the natural seconds they take, and
the antiphonal mode they unconsciously adopt, also the remarkable
minors that many of their songs are sung in, which is almost impossible
to imitate. They have their boat songs, and their church songs, but
whatever they sing is of a religious character, and in both cases they
have a leader (in boating generally the stroke oar) who starts a line, the
rest answering antiphonally as a sort of chorus. They always keep
exquisite time and tune, and no words seem too hard for them to adapt
to their tunes, so that they can sing a long-metre hymn to a short-metre
tune without any difficulty. Their voices have a peculiar quality, and
their intonations and delicate variations cannot be reproduced on paper.
The leading singer starts the words of each verse or line, often improvising, and the others who base him, as it is called, strike in with a
refrain. The basers seem often to follow their own whims, beginning
when they please and leaving off when they please, striking an octave
above or below (in case they have pitched the tune too high or too low),
or hitting some other note that chords, so as to produce the effect of a
marvellous complication and variety, and yet with the most perfect time
and rarely with any discord.[61] . . . I once invited Arthur Sullivan to come

58. Lanier, *Florida*, pp. 30–31.
59. Frances Kemble Leigh, *Ten Years*, pp. 59, 254, 228–29.
60. Wright, *Kemble*, pp. 190–97. Cf. also Kemble, *Further Records*. Leigh is very
vague about dates.
61. This sentence is almost word for word a repetition of Allen's description from the
introduction to *Slave Songs*, p. v.

down and stay with us to hear their singing and to produce an oratorio to be called *The Queen of Sheba* or some such name, with these negro choruses introduced, but he was unable to find the time.

It is almost to be regretted that many of their old original tunes (which were, I suppose, of African origin) are rapidly being grafted on to the Modern Methodist melody. . . .[62]

Slave narratives and the memoirs of ex-slaves frequently refer to the music that helped the slaves to survive, but very few of those that have been examined give details of musical performance. One of the few that did was Robert Anderson's:

The colored people . . . have a peculiar music of their own, which is largely a process of rhythm, rather than the written music. Their music is largely, or was, of a minor strain, a sort of rhythmical chant. . . . While singing these songs, the singers and the entire congregation kept time to the music by the swaying of their bodies, or by the patting of the foot or hand. Practically all of their songs were accompanied by a motion of some kind.

The slaves knew nothing about music from the standpoint of a musician, but all of them could sing and keep time to music, improvise extra little parts to a melody already known, or make up melodies of their own. . . . Melodies . . . were improvised as a means of expressing their feelings.[63]

Accounts still to be uncovered may reveal more about the style of performance, while study of field recordings in relation to them will show those elements of style that have remained constant, as well as new elements that have entered the tradition.

INTRODUCTION OF "NEW" SONGS BY THE TEACHERS

As we have seen, not all teachers were impressed by the music of the freedmen. Some were narrow in their interests and conventional in their tastes, impressed with the correctness of their own ideas and their noble mission of bringing knowledge and culture to the benighted ex-slaves. Even those who were fascinated by the exotic music they heard were not averse to teaching their pupils new songs as part of a larger program of education. That they were diluting a folk tradition bothered them only occasionally. The letters describing teaching the children "new" songs displayed the whole range of attitudes toward the music, from full appreciation to aversion and distaste. The interaction between the teachers and pupils emerges from the letters written by the teachers.

62. James Wentworth Leigh, *Other Days*, pp. 155–57.
63. Anderson, *From Slavery to Affluence*, pp. 24–25.

Newbern, N.C., Dec. 22d, 1863 . . . I wish I could introduce you to this school as it appears in the morning, and let them sing to you one of their own native songs; afterwards one which they have just learned—"Rally round the Flag." They are delighted with our songs, and catch them readily.[64]

Beaufort, S.C., July 13, 1864 . . . We daily have new scholars. . . . Singing is taught, and as the colored people are naturally good timists, and have good voices, we enjoy the half-hour devoted to its practice. We mostly sing Sabbath-school songs from the *Golden Chain*; occasionally, when the singing drags, or they seem lifeless, I commence, "I can't stay behind my Lord," (one of their songs,) or "John Brown," [also one of "their" songs, although apparently she did not know it] which awakens all their enthusiasm, and they burst forth in their loudest, clearest and liveliest voices, making the old church ring with melody. When they come to the verse, "We'll hang Jeff Davis to a sour apple-tree," they quicken the time, and keep it so exact one can almost hear the march of the armies hastening to carry out the earnest resolve.[65]

It appears from this report that the teacher did not direct the singing; she merely started it, and the children took over.

A New Year's celebration was described in a letter from Newbern dated February 11, 1865:

They commenced by singing "Am I a soldier of the Cross," the chair "lining it off." . . . Just as the league was about ready to march out with their flags and banners, I set them [the children] to singing "Yes, we'll rally round the flag boys." The people below were unaccustomed to any singing, except their native hymns, and when my two hundred happy voices broke upon their ears, I think they wouldn't have looked more surprised or pleased if the roof had been lifted off, and they had seen and heard the heavenly choirs singing hallelujahs for their celebrations.[66]

The agent of the American Bible Society in Hampton, Virginia, the Reverend H. W. Gilbert, in his monthly report mentioned only the "new songs," ignoring the people's own songs. "Singing is taught in these schools by Rev. S. Tilden of Massachusetts; and I could not keep from weeping when I heard them sing so correctly the beautiful songs which they were taught. . . ."[67] A teacher wrote from Richmond on May 5, 1865, describing how her pupils had welcomed a troop of Union cavalry:

Sister and I were . . . just going into school . . . the children . . . were swarming the yard; when a body of cavalry appeared over the hill.

---

64. Letter signed S. M. Pearson, in New England Freedmen's Aid Society, *Extracts*, 4th ser., Jan., 1864, p. 11.

65. Letter signed Maria B. King, *American Missionary* 8 (Sept., 1864): 215.

66. Letter signed Anne C. G. Canedy, *Freedmen's Record* 1 (Mar., 1865): 39–40.

67. *American Missionary* 9 (May, 1865): 103.

"Yankee Doodle, children!" I cried; and immediately all the boys were whistling, and all the girls singing that as a welcome (clapping their hands in time) to the Yankees; who *were* "coming to town" and "a ridin' on their ponies." The tune never sounded so well to me before; their whistling is certainly very musical, and I wish you could have seen how pleased every soldier looked at this unexpected greeting. . . . But the neighbors, how they frowned upon the scene! 'Tis many a day since you had the privilege of hearing that good old tune, thought I; and but a few days ago, to hum it, would have led to the whipping-post.[68]

A visitor to Arlington, Virginia, reported on the school:

The *school* . . . was an object of interest to us. Everywhere the eyes of the children sparkled with the joy of being free; and this feeling seemed heightened here, by the peculiar character of the songs they sang. . . . One of them, called "Uncle Sam's School," was sung with a perfect gusto. . . . the schoolroom rang when happy voices swelled the chorus:—

"So come bring your books and slates,
    And don't be a fool;
For Uncle Sam is rich enough
    To send us all to school."[69]

Part of a donation from the Friends of the Poor, Leicester, Massachusetts, was spent on printing patriotic songs to be sung in the newly reopened schools of Charleston in 1865. The songs chosen were "America," "Rally round the Flag, Boys," and "The Star-Spangled Banner." "By this means the liberated slave children in this rebel city filled the school buildings with their music, and haunted the grass-grown streets with songs of loyalty."[70]

Emily C. Blackman wrote of teaching the children Sunday-school hymns: "I cannot tell you how heartily I rejoice in the ability to sing and play the melodion now as never before. The freedmen are perfectly charmed by the influence of music, and as I read aloud every verse before singing, and face them while playing . . . beautiful Sunday-school hymns and others of a kindred cast."[71] Similar songs were taught at Davis Bend, Mississippi, the former home of Jefferson Davis, president of the Confederacy: "[At] Sunday school . . . they have, or are beginning to have, the old Sunday school hymns sung, such as you sing in the Chicago schools, and it does my heart good to hear them. They are all very much taken with the new

68. Letter signed Sarah E. Chase, *Freedmen's Record* 1 (June, 1865): 99.
69. Unsigned report from Arlington, Va., *ibid.* (Oct., 1865): 161.
70. Letter dated Dec. 18, 1865, signed A. F. Pillsbury, *ibid.* 2 (Feb., 1866): 24–25.
71. Letter dated Feb. 16 [1867], signed Emily C. Blackman, *Pennsylvania Freedmen's Bulletin* (Mar., 1867): 9–10.

tunes. All this week I have heard the children humming and singing their songs. It is as if they were bubbling up all over the place."[72]

The accounts that remained unpublished during the war and the postwar period reflected much the same attitudes that characterized the published sources. A few responded to the slaves' music with sensitivity and perception, while many reporters failed to understand it and smugly regarded it as inferior to the "civilized" music of the whites. Charlotte Forten, a black teacher from Philadelphia, combined both these attitudes. While she was fascinated by the native music of the children she taught, she took pleasure in introducing them to "new" music, both as a teacher and as an abolitionist. In her diary she described teaching the new songs, and commissioning a new hymn for them. On November 10, 1862, she wrote, "We taught—or rather commenced teaching the children 'John Brown,' which they entered into eagerly. [Apparently she did not realize that the tune was probably already familiar to them.] I felt to the full the significance of that song being sung here in S.C. by little negro children, by those whom he—the glorious old man—died to save. Miss T[owne] told them about him."[73] On November 20 she wrote to John Greenleaf Whittier, asking him to write a Christmas hymn for the children to sing.[74] While she waited for the hymn to arrive, she helped Ellen Murray teach the children to sing "Sound the Loud Timbrel," which was chosen for sentimental reasons and presented some pedagogical problems. "Fear some of it is rather too difficult for them, but Miss M is determined they shall learn it, and I hope they will. It w'ld be so very appropriate."[75] On December 21 Whittier's hymn arrived, and she began teaching it to the children the next day. (The tune used was never specified.) "Commenced teaching the children Whittier's hymn. We told them who had written it; what a great friend he is to them, and that he had written it *expressly* for them. . . ."[76] By New Year's Day the children had learned both Whittier's hymn and "Sound the Loud Timbrel," singing them at the celebration which commemorated the Emancipation Proclamation.[77]

72. Letter dated May 22, 1867, signed C. P. Huntington, in American Missionary Association, *21st Annual Report*, pp. 58–59.

73. Forten, *Journal*, pp. 132–33.

74. *Ibid.*, p. 135.

75. *Ibid.*, p. 144. This hymn by Thomas Moore beginning "Sound the loud timbrel o'er Egypt's dark sea, Jehovah hath triumphed, His people are free" was very popular at Emancipation celebrations. It was set by a number of composers, and there is no way of knowing which setting was used in this instance.

76. *Ibid.*, pp. 149–50.

77. *Ibid.*, pp. 157–58.

In spite of her enthusiasm for teaching new songs, she had mixed feelings about their superseding the native songs of the people. At a Negro funeral on April 12, 1863, she commented: "We could see the crowd of people and hear them singing hymns;—not their own beautiful hymns, I am sorry to say. I do so fear these will be superseded by ours, which are poor in comparison, and which they do not sing well at all."[78] Charlotte Forten's ambivalence toward replacing the distinctive songs of the Sea Island freedmen characterized her anomalous position as one of the few black teachers to come from the North.

William Allen observed that the children in Helena, Arkansas, sang "precisely the same hymns as at Port Royal—I don't mean their own music, but the tunes taught them at school. They sang today 'In the Light' & 'Glory Be to God on High'—their two favorites on St. Helena."[79]

Sometime after Emancipation, the children in Buckeye School, Tennessee, were described by their teacher, Linda Slaughter:

> How I wish you could hear my children sing their strange, wild melodies, that bring back so vividly the old slave life with its toil and servile ignorance. Yet their old plantation songs are falling into disuse, and in their stead we hear chanted daily the hymns and psalms so familiar to Northern ears. Imagine if you can . . . voices of several hundred children . . . singing with wild energy and earnestness the teachers' improvised song, "We are free!"
>
> > Free! We are free! With a wild and joyous cry,
> > We children in our gladness are shouting far and nigh!
> > Free! We are free! Oh, let the tidings fly,
> > We are free to-day!
> >
> > Chorus—Glory, glory, Halleluiah, etc.
> > We are free to-day.[80]

This seems to have been sung to the tune of "John Brown's Body."

The teachers from the North considered the songs they taught as an integral part of the education they were bringing to the ignorant freedmen, much as the missionaries brought the Gospel to "darkest Africa." Their conscious sense of superiority seemed natural to educated men and women confronting illiterate, ragged, semicivilized (they thought) blacks in the 1860's, long before appreciation had developed for folk culture and folk art.

78. *Ibid.*, p. 183.
79. Allen, *Diary*, entry for Oct. 2, [1864].
80. Slaughter, *Freedmen*, p. 134.

ADDITIONAL SOURCES

AS1. After the body of the text was completed, this interesting report was found. It was written by a popular war correspondent, Charles Carleton Coffin, who had gone to Port Royal in March, 1863, in hopes of witnessing the recapture of Fort Sumter. One Sunday he attended a business meeting in the African Baptist Church,

> a plain wooden building . . . [with] two rows of benches . . . very much like the rude churches to be found in the thinly-settled prairies of Illinois. The congregation were singing when we entered,—
>
> > "Sweet fields beyond the swelling flood
> > Stand dressed in living green,
> > So to the Jews fair Canaan stood,
> > While Jordan rolled between."
>
> . . . It was the well-known tune "Jordan," sung by millions in times past and present. The women occupied one side of the house, the men sitting opposite. . . .
>
> On the following Sunday I was present at a service on Ladies' Island. . . . A hymn was lined off by Mr. Norton [the plantation superintendent, from Massachu-

ROLL JORDAN

Version of "Roll, Jordan, Roll" published in Charles Carleton Coffin, *Four Years of Fighting.* . . . Boston: Ticknor & Fields, 1866, p. 230. Courtesy of Joseph Regenstein Library, University of Chicago.

setts], after the fashion of our fathers. William, a stout, middle-aged man, struck into St. Martin's, and the congregation joined, not reading the music exactly as good old Tansur composed it, for there were crooks, turns, slurs, and appoggiaturas, not to be found in any printed copy. It was sung harshly, nasally, and dragged out in long, slow notes. . . .

After the exercises of the religious meeting were concluded, the chairs were set aside, and they began a "praise meeting," or singing meeting. Most of their music is plaintive. The piece frequently commences with a recitative by one voice, and at the end of the first line the chorus joins. The words are often improvised to suit the occasion.

A favorite song is "Roll, Jordan, roll," in which the progression of the melody is very descriptive of the rolling of waves upon the beach. There are many variations of the melody, but that here given is as I heard it sung by the negroes of Bythewood.

The verses vary only in recitation. If Mr. Jones is present, he will hear, "Mr. Jones is sitting on the tree of life." There is no pause, and before the last roll is ended the one giving the recitative places another personage on the tree, and thus Jordan rolls along.

As the song goes on the enthusiasm rises. They sing louder and stronger. The recitative is given with increased vigor, and the chorus swells with increasing volume. They beat time, at first, with their hands, then their feet. They rise from their seats. William begins to shuffle his feet. Anna, a short, thick-set woman . . . claps her hands, makes a short, quick jerk of her body, stamps her feet on the unaccented part of the measure, keeping exact syncopation. Catherine and Sancho catch the inspiration. They go round in a circle, shuffling, jerking, shouting louder and louder, while those outside of the circle respond with increasing vigor, all stamping, clapping their hands, and rolling out the chorus. William seems to be in a trance, his eyes are fixed, yet he goes on with a double-shuffle, till the perspiration stands in beads upon his face. Every joint seems hung on wires. Feet, legs, arms, head, body, and hands swing and jump like a child's dancing Dandy Jim. . . .

Thus it went on till nature was exhausted. When the meeting broke up, they all came round in procession, shaking hands with the superintendent and the strangers present, and singing a parting song,
"There's a meeting here to-night!"

The superintendent informed me that the children who attended school could not be coaxed to take part in those praise meetings. They had learned to sing Sunday-school songs, and evidently looked upon the plantation songs of their fathers and mothers as belonging to their bondage and not worthy to be sung now that they were free.

Coffin, *Four Years of Fighting*, pp. 224–31.

The music closely resembles the versions published by Lucy McKim and *Slave Songs of the United States*, while the details of performance corroborate descriptions written by William Francis Allen and Whitelaw Reid, among others.

16

···

Slave Songs of the United States:
Its Editors

As recently as 1959 a historian of folksong scholarship felt obliged to apologize for the editors of *Slave Songs of the United States*. "They were not folklorists, anthropologists, or musicologists. They knew little of the South, their acquaintance with the 'Western and Southern Camp-meetings' must have been superficial, and they knew nothing of folksongs among the white population." Yet, despite this "understandable ignorance,"[1] they produced a book of permanent historical value—a fact that seems to trouble academic folklorists. There is no reason why it should, for there was no academic discipline of folklore in the 1860's. In the United States there were no musicologists either, and what passed for anthropology at that time would not be accepted today. The systematic collection of European folk music had barely begun, while non-European musics were either ignored or misunderstood, being considered exotic manifestations of the primitive mind, barbaric and strange. The ethnocentricity of the nineteenth-century European tradition has been dissipated to a degree, but in the 1860's it was expressed politically in the "white man's burden," and religiously in the world mission movement. Musically, it led to the smug conviction that the only music worth hearing was its own.

1. Wilgus, *Anglo-American Folksong Scholarship*, p. 347.

Fortunately, there were exceptions to this norm. The editors of *Slave Songs of the United States* displayed concern for a music that they could not fully understand, but that they recognized as valuable, attractive, and eminently worth preserving from the hazards of time and historic change. Among the three of them were education, skills, and talents that made them as well qualified as any of their generation for the work they set out to do. The scholars who felt they must apologize for them knew virtually nothing about them, or they would have realized how unnecessary such apologies were.

WILLIAM FRANCIS ALLEN

William Francis Allen was born at Northborough, Massachusetts, on September 5, 1830, the son of the Reverend Joseph Allen, a Unitarian minister descended from five generations of farmers, and Lucy Clarke Ware, eldest daughter of Henry Ware, Hollis professor of divinity at Harvard.[2] The Ware family dominated the editing of *Slave Songs*, for Charles Pickard Ware, Allen's fellow editor, was his first cousin, the son of Henry Ware, Jr.[3] At an Atlantic Club dinner in 1859, the character of the Ware family was cited by Oliver Wendell Holmes as an example of his favorite theory of families: "Some families are constitutionally incapable of doing anything wrong; they try it as boys, but they relapse into virtue: as individuals, they attempt to do wrong, but the race is too strong for them and they end in pulpits. Look at the Wares, for instance; *I don't believe that the Wares fell in Adam*."[4] While the Allens were noted for cheerfulness, friendliness, and practicality, the Wares were intellectually vigorous, part of the colonial aristocracy of New England and one of its leading academic families. In his turn, William Allen was characterized by broad cultural interests, an inquiring mind, and deep human sympathies.

Despite a widespread impression that he was a musical illiterate, this was far from true. Allen grew up in a musical atmosphere, becoming a dedicated amateur. His sister Elizabeth recalled him as a boy of three, entertaining visitors by singing a very sentimental song; she also remembered that he wrote a political song for the Harrison campaign of 1840 when he was ten years old. His formal education included preparation at a home school in the Northbor-

2. Frankenburger, "Allen," in Allen, *Essays and Monographs*, pp. 3–4; *Dictionary of American Biography*, I, 211.

3. Emma Forbes Ware, *Genealogy*, p. 158.

4. Letter, Thomas Wentworth Higginson to his mother, July 10, 1859, in Higginson, *Letters and Journals*, p. 110.

William Francis Allen's manuscript version of "Nobody Knows the Trouble I See," Charleston, 1865. Original in State Historical Society of Wisconsin.

ough Parsonage, one year at Roxbury Latin School, and Harvard College, which he entered in 1847. During the summer of 1849, which he spent at home, he wrote to a classmate regarding the music he enjoyed when he was not working in the fields.

> We have got hold of some fine music of Mozart, Haydn, etc., and I enjoy a perfect elysium in raising my voice to unheard of pitch and sinking it beneath gloomy Acheron. I have been making violent efforts to play one of Beethoven's Waltzes on the piano, in which I succeed as well as might be expected. I pass pleasant minutes, too, in learning to play some of my mother's inexhaustible fund of Scotch tunes on the flute.[5]

There was no musical instruction at Harvard in his day, but before he graduated in 1851 he seems to have been proficient in sight-singing and in playing on the piano and flute. For three years after graduation he was a tutor for a wealthy family in New York, where he was able to hear many operas and concerts. Then, on September 7, 1854, he sailed for Europe, planning to stay two years or more, studying classical philology and history. He pursued his studies in Berlin, Göttingen, Rome, Naples, and Greece, hearing more operas and becoming friendly with Alexander Wheelock Thayer, the biographer of Beethoven. His Civil War letters reflected his familiarity with music and its notation, quite apart from the slave songs for which he inserted both words and music. For example, on March 25, 1864, he wrote from South Carolina: "In the woods I heard a bird with precisely the note of one in the Pastoral Symphony—'re-do, re-do, re-do.' " And on September 22, 1864, he graphically described all the various sounds he heard from a boat tied up at the pier at Cairo, Illinois, waiting to embark for Helena, Arkansas:

> Presently a *calliope* on the Jewess [another boat alongside] began to play "Rally round the flag," "Dixie," &c. & played very well too. Then a party of Germans on the Alton [still another boat] sang half a dozen of their part songs—so different from the scrambling, uproarious singing of Anglo-Saxons; & the fifer on the deck began to pipe up "Sweet Home" always sharping fa. . . . At last they sounded their whistle—not a single shriek like our eastern boats, but a ponderous & complicated thing, better called an ophicleide than a whistle; beginning with a hissing & rushing of steam, then groaning, screaming, wailing in all notes of the gamut, & ending at last in a combination of all—like a colossal boy endeavoring ineffectually to play on a gigantic harmonicon.[6]

His casual comment that the fifer always "sharped fa" indicated an excellent ear, a necessary prerequisite for the transcription of unfamiliar music.

5. Allen, *Essays and Monographs*, pp. 5–9.
6. Allen, *Diary*, MS, State Historical Society of Wisconsin.

William Francis Allen, 1830–89. Courtesy State Historical Society of Wisconsin.

In addition to his musical abilities, he brought to the Sea Islands the perspective of a trained historian who understood the changes going on around him, and the interest of a philologist for the strange Gullah dialect of the coastal Negroes. His later career as professor of history at the University of Wisconsin overshadowed his only excursion into folk music. Allen was the seminal influence in the education of Frederick Jackson Turner, who wrote of him: "I have never, in Johns Hopkins or elsewhere, seen his equal as a scholar." Allen regarded history

> as a search for the subsurface social and economic forces that shaped political behavior, a concept that was revolutionary in that day. . . . [His] research techniques were also progressive for his time. He preached the heretical doctrine that scholars should use every possible tool in their quest for the truth: to him the study of the past required a thorough knowledge of metaphysics, theology, military science, political economy and jurisprudence. . . . Societies, Allen taught, changed constantly, just as did the biological organisms then being popularized by Charles Darwin.[7]

A man of such broad interests, training, and understanding was surely as well qualified as anyone of his day to collect slave songs and to study their dialect.

Allen and his wife went south in November, 1863, to teach in the schools sponsored by the Educational Commission for Freedmen. In the Sea Islands he found his cousins, Harriet and Charles Ware, who had been there since April and July, 1862,[8] among other congenial antislavery workers who hoped to prove that the former slaves could work and learn as free men.[9]

His letters home formed a journal which was handed around a large circle of friends, relations, and church members, a fact that he recognized when he wrote from Memphis on September 26, 1864: "knowing that this journal will go to several towns." The letters were well written and full of interesting detail, well designed to hold the interest of a large, miscellaneous audience. At first he wrote general impressions of the people and the place, but on November 15, 1863, he wrote his first impressions of the music:

> Molly, Katy, Winsor and I went to the Praise House in the Quarters. . . . They were just beginning a hymn, which the preacher (a stranger), deaconed out, two lines at a time. The tune was evidently Old Hundred, which was maintained throughout by one voice or another, but cu-

7. Billington, *Turner*, pp. 31, 26.
8. Pearson, ed., *Letters from Port Royal*, pp. 16, 70.
9. Rose, *Rehearsal for Reconstruction*.

riously varied at every note, so as to form an intricate intertwining of harmonious sounds. It was something very different from anything I ever heard, and no description I have read conveys any notion of it. There were no *parts* properly speaking, only now and then a hint of a base or tenor, and the modulation seemed to be just the inspiration of the moment—no effort at regularity, only that one or two voices kept up the air—but their ears are so good, and the time is so perfectly kept (marked often by stamping and clapping the hands) that there was very seldom a discordant note. It might be compared to the notes of an organ or orchestra, where all harmony is poured out in accompaniment of the air; except that here there was no base.* Exhortation, prayer, another hymn, benediction, and then a "shouting song" I believe they call them, beginning "Good morning", at which all began to shake hands and move about the room in measure. The chorus was "Hallelujah," but the words were very hard to catch.

*Mary [his wife] says I draw it too strong. I tried to describe the *character* of the music and think I have—I haven't said that it was beautiful, and I must hear it again to form a fair judgment. She noticed more discord than I did.[10]

Allen had become interested in the music of the freedmen before he arrived in South Carolina, judging from the entries in his diary referring to H. G. Spaulding's article, "Under the Palmetto," which appeared the previous summer. Allen wrote on December 20, 1863: "After the services were over, the people sang some of their peculiar hymns—'The Lonesome Valley' which I used to sing from the *Continental* last summer." On March 14, 1864, he refreshed his recollection. "The *Continental* arrived the other day, and I was interested in looking at the music in 'Under the Palmetto.' I have heard all the pieces but one, and they are quite correct, except that he called them all 'shout tunes,' while only one of them is, and that he gives only in part, and that differently from what I have heard. It is as follows: ["Hold Your Light," words and music]."[11]

In July, 1864, Allen left the Sea Islands. In September he was sent to Helena, Arkansas, as an agent for the U.S. Sanitary Commission, the forerunner of the Red Cross, remaining there until February, 1865. In April he went to Charleston, South Carolina, as superintendent of schools.[12] After the war he taught at Antioch College, Yellow Springs, Ohio, during the academic year 1867-68.[13] In August, 1868, he joined the faculty of the University of Wisconsin, where he remained until his death in 1889. In a faculty of nine

10. Allen, *Diary*, MS, pp. 18–19.
11. *Ibid.*
12. *Freedmen's Record* 1 (July, 1865): 119.
13. *Dictionary of American Biography*, I, 211.

professors, he was expected to teach Greek, Latin, political economy, and history to a student body of 164, including 34 women.[14] The tablet in the First Unitarian Church of Madison is dedicated "In memory of William Francis Allen . . . A lover of flowers, poetry and music."[15]

CHARLES PICKARD WARE

Charles Ware, ten years younger than his cousin, William Allen, was born on June 11, 1840, the youngest child of Henry Ware, Jr., and his second wife, Mary Lovell Pickard.[16] The close ties between the Ware and Allen families had been demonstrated when Charles's older stepsister and brother were sent to live with the Allen family after the death of their mother in 1824, remaining until their father's remarriage in 1827.[17] Charles's sister Harriet, who also took part in the Port Royal experiment, was born in 1834. An interest in music seems to have run in the Ware family. Henry Ware, Jr., Charles's father, was a charter member of the Harvard Musical Association with John S. Dwight, and was elected its president in 1838 when the Association adopted a constitution. He continued as president until his death in 1843.[18] Another Henry Ware, a nephew, the son of John Ware, not only held a variety of offices during his membership from 1849 until his death in 1885, but also edited *Dwight's Journal of Music* during Dwight's year in Europe in 1860.[19] Charles's granddaughter, Caroline Farrar Ware, recalled that all the Ware children had piano lessons with Miss Emma Forbes, and described playing Schubert and Schumann piano duets with her grandfather as long as he lived.[20]

Charles Ware graduated from Harvard in 1862, and in July he joined his sister Harriet in the Sea Islands. Harriet's duties ranged from teaching school to distributing clothing, writing letters, and nursing the sick, but Charles at twenty-two was made superintendent of five plantations planted in corn and cotton.[21] As early as July 30 he mentioned collecting the songs of the freedmen, a

14. Margaret Loring Andrews Allen (Mrs. Wm. F. Allen), "The University of Wisconsin in the Days Soon after the Civil War," typescript, State Historical Society of Wisconsin.

15. Allen, *Essays and Monographs*, p. 13.

16. Emma Forbes Ware, *Genealogy*, pp. 157–58.

17. John Ware, *Memoir*, p. 156.

18. *Harvard Musical Association*, pp. [22]–23, [50]–56, 73.

19. Emma Forbes Ware, *Genealogy*, p. 234; *Harvard Musical Association*, passim; Cooke, *Dwight*, p. [168].

20. Conversation with Caroline Farrar Ware, Aug., 1961.

21. Pearson, ed., *Letters from Port Royal*, pp. 23–24ff., 71–73.

Charles Pickard Ware, at the age of 75 in 1915. Courtesy of Malcolm C. Ware, Brookline, Mass.

reference to a book he dreamed of writing: "I must also postpone to a future occasion my valuable analysis of the Negro character, with examples and illustrations, to be published on my return, to pass through eight editions . . . appended will appear 175 pages of Negro melodies, 'the only genuine and original,' already in process of selection, words and music complete."[22] It is not known whether he had already begun collecting songs or was merely joking. Whichever it may have been, in 1867 he was to contribute to *Slave Songs of the United States* what William Allen described as "the largest and most accurate single collection in existence. . . ."[23]

The musical equipment he brought to the task of collecting was indicated in a letter of September 9, 1862:

> I am going to try a little German and French, and some music. I have practised a little lately. I can soon learn to play glibly by ear; if I can learn to read rapidly enough to execute psalm tunes, I shall be satisfied. The piano is to be brought down into the sitting room; I should be perfectly satisfied, in a musical way, if I had some one to sing with. I do pine for musical food; even my own playing is as water to the thirsty land, or a sea breeze to the people of this region after a still morning with the mercury at 92°.[24]

He remained on St. Helena Island as a superintendent of plantations until April, 1865. His collection a reality, he wrote to his cousin, William Allen, in March, 1867:

> I have about 50 songs of St. Helena, words and music. . . . It has been suggested to me to publish these, and . . . I had decided to do so, & only put the matter off because I hoped to make a visit to St. Helena, where I might complete and correct my collection. Of course my collection is entirely at your service; I am very glad to have the editing performed by hands so much more competent to the work than mine. . . .

His unassuming attitude toward his work was probably justified. Allen, his senior by ten years, had completed his training in philology and history, and Wendell Garrison was an experienced editor. Ware's letter continued: "Let me know if I can assist you in any way;—perhaps I have more time than either you or Mr. Garrison. . . ." Allen and Garrison had apparently conceived the project of bringing into one general collection as many slave songs as possible, and Allen had approached Charles Ware for his collection. Ware's letter also contained a few details about his methods of transcribing

22. Letter, Charles Pickard Ware to his sister, Coffin Point, July 30, 1862, MS made available by Caroline Farrar Ware.

23. [Allen, Ware, and Garrison,] *Slave Songs*, p. iii.

24. Letter, Charles Pickard Ware to his sister, Sept. 9, 1862, MS made available by Caroline Farrar Ware.

Manuscript versions of songs omitted from *Slave Songs of the United States*, written by Charles Pickard Ware and mounted in his copy of *Slave Songs*. Made available by Caroline Farrar Ware.

the tunes. "I pitched the tunes so that none range higher than E, with one or two exceptions, in case of great compass in the tune, in favor of F. When I knew that the same tune was sung in two or three different ways—on different plantations,—I introduced these variations. Some of the tunes were somewhat difficult to write out, the musical accent & emphasis causing a little perplexity now & then."[25]

At twenty-six, Charles Ware merged his plan of publishing a collection of slave songs with the larger project proposed by Allen and Garrison, but his interest continued. In September he spent a Sunday afternoon helping Lucy Garrison read proof while she was visiting in Boston. Ellen Garrison, Lucy's sister-in-law, described him as "a fine young man who has spent three years among the Fr[eed]-men at the South, & is helping Lucy and others arrange the Slave Songs in a book."[26]

With the publication of *Slave Songs of the United States*, Charles Ware's public association with music ended, but his private interest in the music of the blacks continued. In the Houghton Library at Harvard, among the papers of Thomas Wentworth

25. Letter, Charles Pickard Ware to William Francis Allen, "Milton Hill, Mar. 21, 1867," MS, Cornell University Library.
26. Letter, Ellen Wright Garrison to Martha Coffin Wright, Sept. 17, 1867, MS, Garrison Family Papers, Sophia Smith Collection, Smith College Library.

Higginson, are a collection of Negro song texts, words only, in the handwriting of Charles Ware.[27] Nothing is known as to when they were written or how they came into the possession of Higginson. Eight of the twenty-six texts were included in *Slave Songs of the United States,* two in Higginson's article, "Negro Spirituals," in the *Atlantic Monthly* for June, 1867. Further, Ware annotated his own copy of *Slave Songs,* adding marginal comments and mounting in it manuscript versions of songs that were omitted as spurious.[28] As late as 1905 his interest in slave songs was still lively, as shown in a letter to him from William E. Barton, compiler of *Old Plantation Hymns* (1899): "I am very glad to hear from the man who did so good service in recording 'Slave Songs in America,' and I am glad to know that you cared for my article. . . ."[29]

Unlike William Allen's, his later career was not academic. After various attempts at law and teaching, including three years as an instructor of English at Harvard, he joined the American Bell Telephone Company in 1889 and remained in its employment until his retirement.[30] His Port Royal experiences remained fresh in his memory, and in 1911 he returned to South Carolina a collection of documents he had found in Coffin Point plantation in 1862. Since he was "unable to return them to their owners," he sent them to the South Carolina Historical Society.[31] He died in 1921, a year after his sister Harriet.[32]

LUCY McKIM GARRISON

In contrast to Allen, a trained historian and philologist, and Ware, a student fresh out of Harvard when he went to South Carolina, Lucy McKim Garrison was the only practicing musician among the Northerners who collected slave songs in the Sea Islands

27. Ms. fMS Am 1162.7, Higginson Papers, Houghton Library, Harvard University.
28. Made available through the generosity of Caroline Farrar Ware.
29. Letter, William E. Barton to Charles Pickard Ware, Aug. 2, 1905, MS made available by Caroline Farrar Ware.
30. Harvard University, *Historical Register,* p. 447; biography from the 50th anniversary report of the Harvard Class of 1862, provided by Stephen T. Riley, Massachusetts Historical Society, in 1958; letter to the author, Sept. 6, 1973, from Charles R. Morris, president, Milton Historical Society, Milton, Mass.
31. McCormack, "Provisional Guide," p. 54, Accession no. 452. One of the documents presented to the Society by Charles Ware was published as "Shipbuilding on St. Helena Island in 1816: A Diary of Ebenezer Coffin; contributed by J. H. Easterby," *South Carolina Historical and Genealogical Magazine* 47 (Apr., 1946): 117.
32. His death date was established by the Library of Congress; hers was provided by Charles R. Morris in his letter of Sept. 6, 1973.

during the Civil War.[33] She was born in Philadelphia on October 30, 1842, the first of two children of James Miller McKim, a well-known abolitionist, and Sarah Allibone Speakman, the daughter of Micajah Speakman, a substantial Quaker farmer of Chester County, Pennsylvania, whose home was a regular stop on the Underground Railroad. Growing up in the antislavery circle around Lucretia Mott, Lucy McKim was on the friendliest terms with the Mott grandchildren and with Ellen Wright, daughter of Martha Coffin Wright, Lucretia Mott's sister and co-inspirer of the first Woman's Rights meeting in 1848.

Nothing has been found about her early schooling and the beginning of her music lessons, but in April, 1857, she was attending Eagleswood School, conducted by the noted abolitionist Theodore Weld at Raritan Bay Union, a utopian colony near Perth Amboy, New Jersey. In the fall of 1857 fifteen-year-old Lucy began teaching piano at home, but later she returned to Eagleswood to study and teach, remaining there through 1860–61. At Eagleswood she studied violin with a fine emigré musician, Frederick Mollenhauer; her Philadelphia piano teachers were Benjamin Carr Cross, a prominent local pianist, and Carl Wolfsohn, widely respected as an interpreter of Beethoven sonatas and the works of Chopin, Schumann, and other European composers.[34] As a pianist and teacher, Lucy McKim had little importance, but she was well trained by the standards of her day, a sensitive musician who could appreciate the strange music that she was to hear in South Carolina.

Besides her musical training, she was memorable as an exemplar of a remarkable blend of cultural strains, characteristic of varied elements in American life. The educational theories of Bronson Alcott, the liberal Hicksite Quaker beliefs of Lucretia Mott, the practical antislavery convictions of her father and Theodore Weld —all these predisposed her to a deep sympathy for and a great interest in the newly freed ex-slaves in 1862. How much she knew of their music before she went South is not known. But she was aware

33. Much of the information on Lucy McKim Garrison is drawn from manuscript sources: her letters and those of her friends and family among the Garrison Family Papers, Sophia Smith Collection, Smith College Library; the McKim Papers in the Manuscript Divisions of the New York Public Library and Cornell University Library; and letters of various members of the Garrison family in the Houghton Library, Harvard University. For a fuller discussion of her life, with documentation, see Epstein, "Garrison," pp. 529–46.

34. Article on Carl Wolfsohn in F. O. Jones, ed., *Handbook of American Music and Musicians*, p. 177.

Lucy McKim Garrison, 1842–77. Courtesy Sophia Smith Collection, Smith College.

that it existed, for her father's brother, John McKim, who had lived in Georgetown, Delaware, since at least 1852, sent her a copy of a song "very much admired and sung by our colored people about here." Foreshadowing the difficulties of generations of folksong collectors, on August 4, 1860, the Reverend Mr. McKim wrote:

> As to the *Music*, I have done the best I could to reduce it to notes—but I fear I have not expressed the melody truly—. . . Perhaps by *fancying* the rich tones which a colored congregation can throw into their musical performances, and the various embellishments of *appogiaturas & after notes* they are so fond of—especially of making a decided *fall* on the last note of the air—Lucy can render the piece as we have it here—every day & all day long.[35]

More than likely she was also familiar with "Go Down, Moses," in the edition published by Lewis Lockwood, which was for sale at the Anti-Slavery Office in Philadelphia where Mr. McKim had his headquarters.[36]

In June, 1862, her father was sent to the Sea Islands to gather information for the Philadelphia Port Royal Relief Committee, and Lucy accompanied him as his secretary. Although she remained in this Union enclave for only three weeks, the impressions made on her by the songs of the freedmen were to have lasting effects on American music.

Her attempts to publish slave songs in sheet music editions and to make them known through her letter to *Dwight's Journal of Music* in 1862 have been discussed; these attempts met with little public acceptance. In *Slave Songs of the United States*, she is credited with only three variant versions of songs, "Roll, Jordan, Roll," "Poor Rosy," and "My Body Rock 'Long Fever" (No. 45), not as many as those contributed by the other two editors. Her contributions were of another kind.

After her return from South Carolina and her abortive attempt to make slave songs known to a wide public, she spent the remainder of the war years studying piano and giving lessons to pupils of her own. About July 1, 1864, she became engaged to the third son of William Lloyd Garrison, Wendell Phillips Garrison, who was born on June 4, 1840, and graduated from Harvard in 1861. After a

35. Letter, John McKim to James Miller McKim, Aug. 4, 1860, MS made available by the late Mrs. Hendon Chubb, West Orange, N.J. The song was not found with the letter, but it may have been "Wake Up, Jacob," contributed to *Slave Songs* by Miss Mary McKim, John McKim's daughter, from Delaware. John McKim was the "gentleman in Delaware" whose exceedingly interesting letter on slave singing was quoted on pp. vii–viii of the introduction to *Slave Songs*.

36. *National Anti-Slavery Standard* 22 (Mar. 1, 1862), p. [3], col. 6, adv.

succession of minor editorial and tutoring jobs, he was drafted on July 13, 1863; being a conscientious objector, he paid commutation money.[37] There is no record of their first meeting, but, since their fathers had collaborated since at least 1845, they may have known each other since childhood.[38] He wrote his brother William on July 2, 1864, when the engagement was official, that his mind had been made up since the winter of 1862–63. "My Pennsylvania trip last summer was a courtship which I had not courage to put into voice, and so proposed by letter on my return to Boston. [I was] Put off, but not rejected. . . ."[39]

Lucy described his visit in letters to Ellen Wright. Wendell made a good impression despite the hot weather by playing the "Raw Recruit" "madly on the piano" and by knowing "no end to Fr. & Ger. songs: voice tolerable,"[40] so he could not have been musically illiterate. Since he had yet to establish himself in a career, the marriage was deferred until he was assured of stable employment. That materialized when his future father-in-law helped in founding *The Nation* on July 6, 1865, with Edwin L. Godkin as editor and Wendell Garrison as literary editor.[41] They were married in Philadelphia on December 6, 1865, and in June, 1866, they formed a joint household with the senior McKims in Llewellyn Park, Orange, New Jersey.[42] Their proximity to the *Nation* office in New York City was essential to the gathering of *Slave Songs of the United States*.

In the early issues Lucy reviewed some books for *The Nation*, although her reviews were unsigned, like all of the magazine's contributions. A letter from Maria Mott Davis to James McKim in December, 1866, referred to "Lucy's notices of children's books in *The Nation*."[43] She probably also wrote two reviews that drew on

37. Harvard College, Class of 1861, *Fifth Report*, pp. 45–47. Garrison's own copy with ms. corrections and additions in his hand, now in Smith College Library.

38. Cf. Letter, William Lloyd Garrison to James Miller McKim, July 19, 1845, in Garrison, *Letters*, III, 307–8.

39. Letter, Wendell P. Garrison to William Lloyd Garrison II, July 2, 1864, MS, Garrison Family Papers, Smith College Library.

40. Letter, Lucy McKim to Ellen Wright, Aug. 31, 1863, MS, Garrison Family Papers, Smith College Library.

41. Frank Luther Mott, *American Magazines*, p. 333. See also Godkin, *Life and Letters*, II, 51–52.

42. *National Anti-Slavery Standard* 26 (Dec. 16, 1865), p. [3], col. 6; Charles Moore, *Life and Times*, p. 15, Appendix I. Chronology: entries for 1865–66.

43. Letter, Maria Mott Davis to James Miller McKim, Dec. 23, [1866?], MS, McKim Papers, Manuscript Division, New York Public Library. This letter may be referring to "Fiction for the Children," *The Nation* 3 (Dec. 13, 1866): 466–67, and "More Juvenile Fiction," *ibid.* (Dec. 20, 1866): 493. Still other reviews of children's books were recorded in payment vouchers and correspondence between Garrison and *Nation* contributors studied by William M. Armstrong, who established Lucy Gar-

her experiences in South Carolina, of *The Song-Book*, a collection of British and American songs, selected and arranged by John Hullah, and "Times Hab Badly Change' Old Massa Now, Song of the Freedmen," by H. G. Spaulding, which has been mentioned. The examples of American songs in *The Song-Book* did not meet the standard of the English selections, although "we have the amplest material and the broadest variety . . . [including] the beautiful and entirely unique negro melodies that are reaching us from every part of the South."[44] Spaulding's song was dismissed as "a latter-day composition . . . an imitation of the popular 'negro melody' of white origin. It contains no traces of the peculiarly wild and melancholy character of the old-time plantation song."[45]

About a year later Lucy and Wendell Garrison were both deeply involved in the culmination of her long enthusiasm, gathering the first comprehensive collection of slave songs to be published. Although the originator of the project cannot be identified with certainty, the available documents support a collaboration between the Garrisons and William Francis Allen, a frequent contributor to *The Nation*. *The Nation* office was used as a clearing-house, and Wendell Garrison did much of the corresponding with potential contributors, although his activity was never publicly acknowledged. He may have felt that he was merely acting as his wife's deputy during her pregnancy, for their first child, Lloyd McKim Garrison, was born while the book was in press.[46] Precisely what Lucy contributed beyond the variants of three songs was nowhere stated, but there can be little doubt that through her Wendell Garrison became interested in the songs and their publication. He had not visited the South and could not have heard the songs at first hand. Moreover, however fond of music he may have been, his musical experience was in no way comparable to hers. She apparently served as the intellectual catalyst who helped bring together a diverse group of collaborators. While William Allen wrote the preface and Charles Ware contributed the largest single collection, Lucy and Wendell Garrison corresponded far and wide with potential contributors, gathered the songs, and saw the work through the press. When Lucy

rison's connection with a three-part article, "Children's Books," issued as a supplement to *The Nation* 13 (Dec. 7, 1871): 388–90, 404–7. See New York Public Library *Bulletin* 73 (Apr., 1969): 268.

44. [Review of] "The Song-Book," *The Nation* 2 (Apr. 12, 1866): 471.

45. [Review of] Spaulding, "Times Hab Badly Change' Old Massa Now," *The Nation* 2 (Mar. 29, 1866): 408.

46. Letter, Wendell Phillips Garrison to William Lloyd Garrison II, May 4, 1867, MS, Houghton Library, Harvard University.

took the baby to Boston to visit his grandparents, she took the proofs along. Ellen Wright Garrison wrote her mother on September 17 that Charles Ware had Sunday dinner with them and "he & Lucy read proofs most of the afternoon."[47]

When the book was published, Lucy was twenty-five years old. Young Lloyd was followed by Philip McKim (September 28, 1869) and Katherine McKim (May 10, 1873).[48] Before the children were old enough to appreciate their mother's spirit and share her interests, her health gave way in a long illness. She died at thirty-four on May 11, 1877,[49] leaving behind three children, a pioneer work in American folk music, and an even greater promise unfulfilled.

47. Letter, Ellen Wright Garrison to Martha Coffin Wright, Sept. 17, 1867, MS, Garrison Family Papers, Smith College Library.
48. Harvard College, Class of 1861, *Fifth Report*, p. 46.
49. *Ibid.*; see also Wendell Phillips Garrison, *Garrison*, IV, 270.

17

Slave Songs of the United States:
Its Publication

THE CONTRIBUTORS

The identities of the contributors to *Slave Songs of the United States* can be determined in several ways. At the close of William Allen's introduction, on pp. xxxvii-xxxviii, the editors acknowledge the aid of a number of people, beginning with Colonel T. W. Higginson, who made available all the material he had published in the *Atlantic Monthly*, and continuing through many lesser names, some of whom it has not been possible to identify. In the table of contents, the title of each song is followed by the place where it was collected and the name of its collector.

Besides the book itself, information about its genesis can be found in the prospectus issued before publication and in a collection of letters sent to Cornell University in 1885 by Wendell Garrison as "part of the correspondence attending the publication of the 'Slave Songs of the United States,' in which my wife had a share." Garrison suggested they might "deserve a place in your freedmen's collection. Some of the writers are eminent. . . . But use your own discretion & consign them to the waste-basket if you judge best."[1] (AS 1) What

---

1. Letter, Wendell Phillips Garrison to Mr. Harris, Librarian of Cornell University, Oct. 29, 1885, MS, Cornell University Library. Garrison chose Cornell as the recipient of the McKim papers and this small group of manuscripts because it had accepted the Samuel May collection of antislavery material after it had been rejected by several major libraries. The May collection now constitutes one of its great treasures.

became of the rest of the correspondence and the original manuscripts contributed to the volume is not known. An extended search and correspondence has failed to uncover their whereabouts.

From these letters the process by which the volume was collected can be reconstructed. Once the idea of gathering the collection had been conceived, probably by William Allen and the Garrisons, they considered from whom songs could be obtained. Allen's first thought was of his cousin, Charles Ware; the earliest reference to the project found so far is the letter from Ware to Allen dated March 21, 1867, agreeing to make his collection available. Lucy wrote to her uncle, John McKim of Georgetown, Delaware, who had sent her a slave song in 1860; his reply of April 20, 1867, was quoted in the introduction to *Slave Songs*. Wendell Garrison wrote a series of letters to prospective contributors, of which we know only through the replies that have been preserved at Cornell. The earliest, dated April 24 [1867], was from Annie M. Bowen, wife of the Reverend Charles Bowen, a Unitarian clergyman of Tiverton, Rhode Island. Mrs. Bowen had been born in Charleston, South Carolina, the daughter of the Reverend Samuel Gilman, author of "Fair Harvard," and his wife, Caroline Howard Gilman, a leading Charleston writer who frequently described Negroes and their music.[2] Mrs. Bowen and her sister, Eliza Dodge, sang slave songs for their northern friends long before the Civil War, for Thomas Wentworth Higginson said that he had first heard a Negro spiritual from her lips "many years ago."[3] Higginson may have suggested her name to Garrison as a possible contributor.

Mrs. Bowen's letter to Wendell Garrison is important in the history of black folk music, since it is one of the few pieces of evidence linking *Slave Songs of the United States* to an antebellum knowledge of the songs and to an earlier collection which cannot now be located.

Mr. W. P. Garrison
Dear Sir,
   I received your letter with regard to the "Spirituals" and I shall be very happy to do any thing in my power towards furthering your project, but I am afraid, that if you have as many as 75 songs from my state, you must include the few that I know among them. I will send you a list of those that I know and you can compare them with what you have.
   I do not see how an Essay can be written, because I believe they have no history or a very short one. Some years ago, my mother, Mrs. Caroline Gilman, compiled some of them, and I believe wrote what she knew of

2. Pierce, *Lillie Family*, p. 114; McDowell, "Negro in Southern Novel," pp. 463–64.
3. *Freedmen's Record* 3 (Aug., 1867): [129]–30.

them, but I think the little arrangement was never published—I will write and ask her what her ideas were with regard to them, and if any one knows any thing about them she does, for she took an intense interest in the colored race from the time that she lived in Charleston at first [i.e., 1819] . . .

Annie M. Bowen

Roxbury, April 24th

The list of spirituals which followed included: "Lord Make Me More Patient," "Join Jerusalem Band," "See Brother Moses Yonder," "Sound the Trumpet Gabriel," "Paul & Silas Bound in Jail," "The Resurrection or Run, Mary, Run, Hallelujah," "Description of the Judgement Day," and "Good Bye My Sister, Good Bye, Hallelujah," all of which appear to have been included in *Slave Songs*. Mrs. Bowen then concluded, "It is possible that my mother may have heard some others in her sojourn in the Western part of So. Ca. during the War. I will enquire."[4]

No further reference to slave songs from western South Carolina has been found. The mention of Mrs. Gilman's manuscript collection of slave songs inspired a wide-ranging search for the manuscript, which could have been the earliest known collection. But no trace of it has been found, although many of Mrs. Gilman's papers are preserved in libraries ranging from the American Antiquarian Society to the South Carolina Historical Society. It is possible that she did make it available through her daughter, although her name is not acknowledged as a contributor. If she did, her collection could have been part of the manuscript of *Slave Songs of the United States*, which has not been found either. The presumption that Mrs. Gilman's collection was included in *Slave Songs* derived from two documents dating from August, 1867—the prospectus issued by the book's publisher, A. Simpson & Co., and an advance announcement appearing in *The American Freedman*. The prospectus, a four-page pamphlet including specimen pages, lists on page [4] the proposed contents of the book. Among the "spirituals" from the southeastern states is "Mrs. A. M. Bowen's Collection, (the earliest of all,)" while the same group is described in the advance announcement as "Mrs. Bowen's collection—about 6 (dating twenty years back)."[5] Mrs. Bowen could have described her own recol-

4. Letter, Annie M. Bowen to Wendell P. Garrison, Apr. 24, [1867,] MS, Cornell University Library.
5. Prospectus dated "Aug. 1st, 1867" from A. Simpson & Co., 60 Duane St., New York, made available by Caroline Farrar Ware; *American Freedman* [organ of the American Freedman's Union Commission] 2 (Aug., 1867): 262.

lected songs as "dating twenty years back" when she may have still been living in Charleston,[6] but it seems unlikely that she herself would have described it as "the earliest of all." Unless the phrase was added by the publisher as an aid to sales (which, of course, it could have been), its use seems to imply that Mrs. Gilman's collection was made available. That Mrs. Gilman was capable of writing songs in musical notation seems likely, for she wrote in an autobiographical sketch: "I taught myself the English guitar at the age of fifteen from hearing a schoolmate take lessons, and ambitiously made a tune. . . . By depriving myself of some luxuries, I purchased an instrument, over which my whole soul was poured in joy and sorrow for many years. . . ."[7]

Garrison could hardly have expected to uncover a collection like Mrs. Gilman's, gathered by a long-time resident of the Deep South many years before the outbreak of the War. What he probably expected and what he received were the combined gatherings of many Northerners who first experienced the music of the slaves during the War. Their backgrounds were as various as their wartime assignments, but they shared a strong interest in and curiosity about this music. Some of them, like Laura Towne, could collect only the words; others notated the music with greater or lesser success. We can only surmise how Garrison drew up the list of names to whom he wrote. Mrs. Bowen was probably suggested by Higginson; William Lee Apthorp, a "professor of music before the War," was suggested by John R. Dennett, who toured the South as a correspondent for *The Nation*. James Schouler wrote to Higginson in response to his article in the *Atlantic Monthly*, "Negro Spirituals." Many of the other contributors may have responded to a paragraph published in *The Nation* of May 30, 1867, requesting contributions:

> The proper folk-songs of this country should be sought, we suppose, among the aborigines, but the capacity of the Indian for music does not appear to be equal to his reputed capacity for eloquence. The negro possesses both these gifts in a high degree, and it is singular that no one up to this time has explored for preservation the wild, beautiful, and pathetic melodies of the Southern slaves. Their secular songs, or what purported to be such [i.e., minstrel songs], have in times past made their way into all mouths; but their "spirituals"—the genuine expression of their eminently religious nature—have only recently claimed attention.

6. Annie Margaret Gilman married the Reverend Charles Bowen in 1847, just twenty years before the publication of *Slave Songs*. See Arthur Gilman, *Family*, p. 114.

7. Caroline Howard Gilman, "Autobiography," in Hart, *Female Prose Writers*, p. 53.

We are able to announce a collection, based on the Port Royal hymnology, and including the songs of as many Southern states as are obtainable, which will be published either in the course of this year or at the beginning of the next. The words and (whenever possible) the music will be carefully reproduced, and it is the aim of the editors to make the volume complete in both respects. Any information relating to this subject will be very acceptable to them, and may be sent to Mr. W. P. Garrison, Box 6732, N. Y. Post-office.[8]

We do not know how many contributors responded to this notice. The letters at Cornell were all in response to personal communications, but they include only a small number of the names listed as contributors. Those people who have been identified were, with the exception of Mrs. Bowen, on duty in the South during and after the war in various capacities—as teachers, missionaries, army officers, or newspaper correspondents. Besides Higginson, two officers of his regiment, the 1st South Carolina Volunteers, contributed: Captain James S. Rogers and Lieutenant-Colonel Charles T. Trowbridge. Other army officers included Dr. William A. Hammond, Surgeon-General of the United States; the Reverend James K. Hosmer, who served as a private in the 52nd Massachusetts; and two major-generals, Truman Seymour and James H. Wilson. The Reverend Horace James was superintendent of Negro affairs in North Carolina; John Silsby, principal of colored schools in Selma, Alabama.[9] Many others were teachers in freedmen's schools: Charlotte L. Forten, Ellen Murray, James H. Palmer, T. Edwin Ruggles, Arthur Sumner, and Laura Towne. Kane O'Donnel was a newspaper correspondent, and the Reverend Frederick N. Knapp was on duty with the U.S. Sanitary Commission.

But even when a contributor's identity can be established, his musical competence remains an unknown quantity. He must have understood musical notation, for the music was included in all cases. No doubt there was considerable variation in the musical background of the contributors, but of those of which anything is known, a surprising number knew a good deal. The three editors were well qualified, as we have seen. James Schouler, who became a highly respected historian, described his life-long activity in music:

I showed early a fondness for music, and through life. . . . I would gather tunes and strains quickly by the ear. . . . My good parents, appreciating this love of music, allowed me . . . to attend for a term the best singing-school in the city [Lowell, Mass.]; and there I picked up some

8. "Notes. Literary," *The Nation* 4 (May 30, 1867): 428.
9. Horace James, *Annual Report*; entry in Amistad Research Center, *Author and Added Entry Catalog*.

excellent tunes adapted from such masters as Bellini, Weber, and De Beriot, which have stayed by me all my life. . . .

The anonymous editor of his essays continued the narrative:

He would improvise, would play on the piano whatever he heard elsewhere, catching a melody quickly and applying chords with an almost intuitive perception of thorough bass. [From piano lessons he progressed to studying the organ] . . . before he entered college he had written out with his own hand a choice collection of a hundred tunes, some of which were of his own arrangement. This manuscript book, still extant, he often used while conducting a choir. . . . [While an undergraduate at Harvard, 1855–59] The . . . rehearsals of the Handel and Haydn Society he enjoyed regularly . . . his thirst for good music was intense. . . . Most of his spare pocket-money in these college days . . . he would devote to classical works of music and standard authors. . . . Music . . . is an inseparable element of our author's nature. . . .[10]

It is evident that Americans of the Civil War generation were not all the musical illiterates they have been reputed to be, and the contributors to *Slave Songs of the United States* were as capable in their self-appointed task as any amateurs of their time in any country of the world.

PROBLEMS OF NOTATION

In these days of tape recorders, field recordings can capture a performance with all its peculiarities preserved for leisurely listening and study. Collecting folk music in the mid-nineteenth century was quite a different matter. No matter how enthusiastic a would-be collector might be, he was almost helpless unless he could reduce the sounds he heard to musical notation. True, Thomas Higginson made a great deal out of his collection of words without transcribing a note of music, treating the songs as poetry, and barely discussing the music or its performance.[11] But most collectors wished to transcribe the music which so impressed them—"copy" was a term frequently used—and those who were unable to do so were conscious of a serious deficiency. For example, Charlotte Forten, who was asked by Colonel Robert Gould Shaw for copies of some songs he had heard, did not complete the "copies" until after his regiment was

10. Schouler, *Historical Briefs*, pp. 170, 202–308. A publisher's note stated: "the Biography . . . is prepared from fresh and original materials supplied by the author himself."—p. 308.

11. Higginson, "Negro Spirituals," pp. 685–94; republished as ch. 9 of his *Army Life*. The prospectus of *Slave Songs* dated Aug. 1st, 1867, proposed a section III, "Words Without Music . . . most of the 'Spirituals' printed by Col. T. W. Higginson in the June *Atlantic*." This plan was abandoned in favor of including music for all the songs from the regiment, with the music supplied by other officers.

ordered away. After his death in the assault on Fort Wagner, she wrote to his mother: "I send them to you, thinking you might like to have them, as they were copied for him. I regret very much not being able to write the music, as the airs of many of them are very beautiful and touching."[12] Laura Towne was eager to send songs to Lucy McKim, but she was able to send only the words—"I am no musician unfortunately, & can give you no idea of the air."[13]

In that day the ability to write music was uncommon. Major-General Truman Seymour wrote to the Garrisons from Pensacola, Florida, in May, 1867:

> To find a person in this region who appreciated sufficiently such an object as yours, and was sufficiently cultivated in music to embody his wishes in a musical manner, would once have been as doubtful a task as the discovery of an Abolitionist—and is probably quite as doubtful now.
> If I can learn of any negro who is conversant with the distinctive melodies of his people, I may try to express them myself. But the duty of the hour, in "reconstructing" is itself absorbing.[14]

This difficulty was dwelt on by Wendell Garrison in his review of *Slave Songs* in *The Nation*: "Most men are curious, many and many again have a fondness for music, but those who are musically educated are seldom to be met with. To know two in one's circle of acquaintances (which may embrace several who can sing from notes at sight) is a rare thing."[15] Native southern whites suffered from the same disability. Eliza Frances Andrews wrote in her journal in February, 1865: "I mean to make a collection of these songs some day and keep them as a curiosity . . . the tunes are inspiring. They are mostly a sort of weird chant that makes me feel all out of myself when I hear it way in the night, too far off to catch the words. I wish I was musician enough to write down the melodies; they are worth preserving."[16]

But even transcribing the words was not simple. The Gullah dialect and the unconcern with syntax presented problems to the

---

12. Forten, *Journal*, p. 191; *Memorial, R[obert] G[ould] S[haw]*, p. 145. Letter to Mrs. Francis Shaw dated Philadelphia, Aug. 16, 1863. Copy in Rare Book Room, New York Public Library.

13. Letter, Laura Matilda Towne to James Miller McKim, Aug. 2, 1862, MS, McKim Papers, Cornell University Library.

14. Letter, Truman Seymour to Wendell P. Garrison (L. McK. G.), dated "Barrancas, Pensacola Harbor, Fla., May 13th, 1867," MS, Cornell University Library.

15. *The Nation* 5 (Nov. 21, 1867): 411. For the identity of the reviewer, see letter, Wendell Phillips Garrison to James Miller McKim, "Dear Father," dated Nov. 14, 1867, MS, McKim Papers, Cornell University Library.

16. Eliza Frances Andrews, *War-Time Journal*, entry for Feb. 12, Sunday [1865], p. 91.

collectors. Charlotte Forten wrote after a boat ride: "The boatmen sang several singular and beautiful hymns, which I have never heard before. Noted them down as well as I c'ld. C'ldn't understand the words very readily."[17] Undoubtedly others had the same problem.

Variant versions presented an intractable problem in a period when the concept of a "correct" version still was widespread. William Francis Allen described his growing awareness of this difficulty: "Songs often differ on different plantations, or are peculiar to them, and the 'Graveyard' they sang last night [on St. Helena] I hardly recognized, it was so different from the way our people sing it."[18]

But even if all these problems were solved—if the collector could write music, understand the words, and not be troubled with variant versions—the basic problem still remained: how to notate with conventional symbols a music that did not conform to conventional rules. Lucy McKim had expressed the dilemma in 1862.[19] Thomas Fenner echoed her sentiments in his preface to *Cabin and Plantation Songs, As Sung by the Hampton Students:*

> Tones are frequently employed [in the slave music of the South] which we have no musical characters to represent. Such, for example, is that which I have indicated as nearly as possible by the flat seventh, in *"Great Camp-meetin',"* *"Hard Trials,"* and others. These tones are variable in pitch, ranging through an entire interval on different occasions, according to the inspiration of the singer. They are rarely discordant, and often add a charm to the performance. It is of course impossible to explain them in words, and to those who wish to sing them, the best advice is . . . *go listen to a native.*[20]

A final problem was raised by Major-General James H. Wilson in a letter to Wendell Garrison: extensive editing of the songs in an effort to make them more acceptable to the reading public. This practice had a long tradition, going all the way back to Bishop Percy and his *Reliques of Ancient English Poetry.* Educated people were still likely to feel a compulsion to correct ungrammatical words, no matter how authentic, and editors often felt called upon to make their texts more "poetical" than they originally were. Wilson commented: "It seems to me that Mr. Higginson has 'finished' out a good many of these he has published in the Atlantic, with a good

17. Forten, *Journal,* entry for Saturday, Feb. 21 [1863], p. 169.
18. Allen, *Diary,* entry for May 3, 1864.
19. Lucy McKim [Garrison], "Songs of the Port Royal 'Contrabands,' " pp. 254–55.
20. Armstrong and Ludlow, *Hampton and Its Students.* Preface to the song section dated Hampton, Va., Jan. 1, 1874, p. [172].

deal more of elaboration than the negroes sang them—but . . . in
their general characteristics he has given them admirably. . . ."[21]
That Wilson was correct can be demonstrated by comparing the
published versions with those in Higginson's manuscript diary in the
Houghton Library at Harvard.

As Higginson made the texts more literary, so some collectors had
an irresistible urge to make the music more acceptable to conventional ears—an easier process than trying to record the music precisely as it was sung. William Lee Apthorp, who had been a "Prof. of
Music before the war," volunteered some advice to Wendell Garrison from his own experience:

> Perhaps I may be pardoned if I hint at a caution which I should not
> think it necessary to suggest, had I not seen the evil in several instances.
> It is this—the absolute correctness of the music as the freedmen sing it,
> and which must be preserved to give a correct and adequate idea of their
> songs is frequently marred, sometimes by faulty transcription by per-
> sons not sufficiently versed in the science of music, and sometimes by the
> tunes being taken down at second hand from the lips of others than the
> freedmen themselves, and sometimes again by attempts at modifying or
> correcting their natural and gracefully uncouth melodies . . . nearer
> conformity with the rules of musical composition. Any such attempts
> invariably destroy the peculiar individuality and nationality of the
> music.[22]

ASSEMBLING THE COLLECTION

The problems of reducing a single song to musical notation were
formidable enough, but still more difficult was the task of assembling a comprehensive collection of such songs from various local-
ities, collected by various hands. Those native Southerners who
came in contact with the slaves during the plantation era displayed
little interest in their folklore or their music; not until nostalgia
tinted their vision and made the past a golden era did they find
attractions there.[23] Caroline Howard Gilman was, of course, an
exception to this rule, with her collection of songs from about 1840.
In 1859 Edward A. Pollard, a journalist and outspoken secessionist,

21. Letter, Maj.-Gen. James Harrison Wilson to Wendell Phillips Garrison, Davenport, Iowa, June 11th, 1867, MS, Field-Garrison Autograph Collection, Library of
Congress. I am indebted to Prof. William H. Armstrong for calling my attention to
this letter.

22. For Apthorp's antebellum occupation, see letter, N. C. Dennett to Wendell P.
Garrison, Jacksonville, Fla., May 9, 1867, MS, Cornell University Library; letter,
William Lee Apthorp to Wendell P. Garrison, Jacksonville, Fla., May 24th, 1867, MS,
Cornell University Library.

23. Hubbell, *South*, pp. 686–87.

wrote of the slaves, "Their hymns, or religious chants, might furnish a curious book," in a volume which advocated the reopening of the slave trade![24]

Lucy McKim appears to have been the first person with both the necessary ability and the sustained enthusiasm to bring the project to fruition. Her initial project of publishing the songs in her own arrangements was not successful, but she tried other avenues as well. She wrote to *Dwight's Journal of Music* about them, and she sang them for friends at the home of Lucretia Mott.[25] It is probable that her interest infected her husband, for the first mention of the projected collection—Charles Ware's letter of March 21, 1867, to William Francis Allen—already implied an editorial collaboration between Allen and Wendell Garrison.[26] Lucy continued to play a seminal role, writing to her uncle John McKim and to Laura Towne. On April 13 Laura Towne wrote: "I had a letter from Lucy McKim Garrison the other day. She and others are going to get up a volume of Port Royal songs, and have sent to me for my collection. They are going to publish words and music together, perhaps with illustrations." And again on April 27: "Lucy McK. Garrison, who, with Charlie Ware and others, is going to publish words and music of all the freedmen's songs they can collect, and wants my collection to help out."[27] Though Laura Towne was no musician and could write only the words, her collection was requested nonetheless.

Other extant letters indicate that between March and June, 1867, Wendell Garrison was busy writing to every possible source of additional songs. John R. Dennett, a *Nation* contributor, wrote to Wager Swayne on behalf of the collection, and Thomas Wentworth Higginson not only made available the texts published in his *Atlantic* article, "Negro Spirituals," but also suggested Annie M. Bowen as a possible source of more songs. He alone of the people involved in making the collection seems to have known Mrs. Bowen before 1867. He had written in his *Atlantic* article, "I had for many years heard of this class of songs under the name of 'Negro Spirituals,' and had even heard some of them sung by friends from South Carolina." The identity of these friends may be inferred from the report of the Educational Commission's teacher's festival of July 11, 1867: "Col. T. W. Higginson took the chair. . . . [He] introduced to

24. Edward Albert Pollard, *Black Diamonds*, p. 35.
25. Letter, Martha Coffin Wright to "My dear Willy" [her son, William P. Wright], "Oaks, April 20th, 1863," MS, Garrison Family Papers, Smith College Library.
26. Letter, Charles Pickard Ware to William Francis Allen, "Milton Hill, Mar. 21, 1867," MS, Cornell University Library.
27. Towne, *Letters and Diary*, p. 181.

the audience Mrs. Charles Bowen, from whose lips, many years ago, he had first heard a 'negro spiritual.' With her husband and daughter she sang, very sweetly, an air and chorus."[28] Mrs. Bowen and her sister, Eliza Dodge, formed the link between the northern collectors of slave songs during the Civil War and the antebellum witnesses of the tradition represented by their mother, Caroline Howard Gilman.

While Garrison's correspondence was still in progress, on May 30, 1867, *The Nation* published the paragraph announcing the collection and inviting further contributions.

There was evidence that the collection was undertaken in the nick of time, as many observers prophesied. T. Edwin Ruggles, still in Port Royal, wrote thus on May 21, 1867, in response to a letter from Charles Ware: "I don't suppose we shall be able to make any new additions to your collection of negro songs. They sing but very little nowadays to what they used to. Do you remember those good old days when the Methodists used to sing up in that cottonhouse at Fuller's? Wasn't it good? They never sing any of them at the church, and very few in their praise-meeting."[29] If more correspondence from the contributors (and, best of all, the manuscripts contributed to *Slave Songs*) should be located, the methods of collecting and the nature of the music itself would become more clear to us.

PUBLICATION AND RECEPTION

As the gathering of the songs proceeded, editorial decisions were made and changed, and the search for a publisher began. Five days after Ruggles lamented the lack of singing in the Sea Islands, Wendell Garrison wrote to his mother of the progress being made: "I saw my friend Prof. Allen yesterday. Our collection of slave-songs is growing rapidly, and we shall produce, I think, a book of great value. Counting those with and those without accompanying music, I reckon that we shall have not fewer than 100 songs. Mr. Scribner, of New York, will probably be our publisher."[30] On June 26 he wrote to his brother Frank that Mr. Scribner was still undecided, and not until June 30 was there real progress to report:

> On Thursday Prof. Allen & I made our final call on Scribner to get a definitive answer in regard to our Slave Songs. Mr. S. lacked nothing in good will, but he said his regular business had assumed such proportions that he could not do justice to a side issue like ours—in which, besides he

28. Higginson, "Negro Spirituals," pp. [129]–30.
29. Pearson, ed., *Letters from Port Royal*, p. 328.
30. Letter, Wendell Phillips Garrison to "Dear Mother" [Helen Eliza (Benson) Garrison], "Anglelot, May 26, 1867," MS, Houghton Library, Harvard University.

did not see his way clear to a return for his outlay, tho' this alone wd. not have deterred him. I immediately laid the matter before the new firm of A. Simpson & Co. (formerly the Bradstreet Press), & there is a fair prospect of their taking hold of it. Bond (of the Co.) was a [Freedmen's?] Bureau agent at Norfolk, and they are publishers for Surgeon-Gen. Hammond, who is very friendly to me and to our enterprise, augurs well for it, recommends it, and has contributed about half-a-dozen mss. (he is a Marylander by birth.) Yesterday I recd. from the editor of the London Church Choirmaster a letter begging for a copy of the book when it should appear. He had seen my paragraph about it in the Nation, and wants to notice the book for his readers. We are sure of getting very conspicuous reviews in Eng. France & Germany.[31]

As the publication arrangements proceeded, still other letters arrived with suggestions and contributions, some from writers who had heard of the project only vaguely. Major-General James H. Wilson wrote Garrison on June 11, 1867: "I have seen it stated that you propose writing a volume on the subject of 'Negro Spirituals,' " giving general impressions of the singing he had heard in Port Royal during the war.[32] A Charleston resident, M.[?] W. Simmons, badly in need of money, offered to write "on the legendary tales and traditions of the Negroes," adding wistfully:

> I much regret not having preserved any of the *songs* of the negroes, which I used to hear in my you[th?]; my father having been a planter, & having passed my life among planters; and been one myself. They were often touching as they were simple & original. I only remember the following chorus of one of them. It used to sound very pathetic to my boyish ears
>
>> "How gloomy is the day!
>> No sadder sure can come—
>> Since Jenny's gone away
>> And Thomas left at home."
>
> It may not however be too late to recover & collect some of them; which if I were younger, I should set about doing; both to oblige you & to gratify my own desire to recall some of them.[33]

Poor Dr. Simmons wrote again and again, pleading for help to ease his poverty, and offering what he could in the way of helpful suggestions and saleable manuscripts:

31. Letter, Wendell Phillips Garrison to Francis Jackson Garrison, "Anglelot, June 26, 1867," MS; letter, Wendell P. Garrison to William Lloyd Garrison II, "Anglelot, Sunday, June 30/67," MS, both Houghton Library, Harvard University.

32. Letter, Maj.-Gen. James Harrison Wilson to Wendell Phillips Garrison, MS.

33. Letter, Dr. M. [?] W. Simmons to "Dear Sir" [Wendell Phillips Garrison?], "Charleston, June 22d./67," MS, laid in Wendell Garrison's copy of *Slave Songs*, made available through the generosity of Mrs. Hendon Chubb. Now in the Smith College Library.

You might increas your collection of songs, from the English Magazines & Reviews; but cannot now refer to the particular numbers or dates of the works containing them. The celebrated Georgiana—Duchess of Devonshire—published perhaps some thirty years ago—a version of an African song which at the time—attracted some attention . . . and was set to music, and sung in the fashionable circles of London.[34] A Lady Traveller, whose name I cannot recall also published about the same time, or not long after—a translation of a song, in praise of the exploits of "Damel"—the chief of a Tribe on the Coast. . . . The *name*, might be found in the *Indexes* of the Edinburgh, or Quarterly Reviews, one, or both of which, I think—contained the poem. I should have stated in my first communication—that I never met with any poems of this kind myself —among the negroes; or any *songs*, either of an *Exotic*, or heroic character. . . .

He then offered for publication a poem of his own, "stamped with an 'African originality,' & character—calculated to attract the attention of Psycologists and those who feel an interest in such manifestations of the imaginative & intellectual powers of the race. It contains some *introduced* ideas . . . but these are congruent, or in accordance with the general spirit of the piece."[35] Shades of Uncle Remus! There is no way of knowing how many similar letters were received but not preserved.

The first announcement found so far of the completed arrangements for publication appeared appropriately in *Dwight's Journal of Music*, the publisher of Lucy's letter about the songs of the contrabands in 1862. The paragraph, headed "The Songs of the Freedmen," a decent recognition of their changed status, appeared on July 20:

Our readers may remember that about five years ago we published a letter from Miss McKim, of Philadelphia, (now the wife of Mr. W. P. Garrison,) describing the songs which she had heard (and partly taken down) among the recently freed people of the Sea Islands. Much larger collections were afterwards made by Prof. Wm. F. Allen, of West Newton, and his cousin, Mr. Chas. P. Ware, of Milton. These three are now united, by common agreement, and have been very largely increased by accessions from all parts of the South. The basis still remains the "spirituals," such as were furnished the *Atlantic* by Mr. Higginson, who has kindly turned them over to the persons named above, that they may

34. This apparently refers to "Let us pity the poor white man," described in Mungo Park's *Travels in the Interior Districts of Africa . . . in the Years 1795, 1796, 1797*, paraphrased by Georgiana Cavendish, Duchess of Devonshire, and set to music by at least three composers. See Nathan, *Dan Emmett*, pp. 6-7. The settings ranged in date from 1798 to 1800.

35. Letter, M. [?] W. Simmons to "Dear Sir" [Wendell Phillips Garrison?], "Charleston, July 8th/67," MS, laid in Wendell Garrison's copy of *Slave Songs*. An intervening letter was dated July 7th/67.

publish them, words and music [Higginson of course had no music], in one volume. The collection will be edited by Prof. Allen, who has written a preface of some length to illustrate the songs. Messrs. A. Simpson & Co., of the Agathynian Press, 60 Duane street, New York, intend to give the work their imprint (a guaranty of the highest style of typography), provided they meet with sufficient encouragement. The cost per volume will probably not exceed $1.75, and will be much less to those taking several copies. Orders may be sent to the firm with the above address. No one will question the urgency of preserving these transient productions of a highly musical race, and they will commend themselves for actual enjoyment to all lovers of music, as well as to lovers of the curious.

There followed a reprinting of the paragraph from the May 30 issue of *The Nation*, inviting contributions to the collection.[36]

A. Simpson & Co. had legitimate concern about potential sales. Surely if such a well-established firm as Scribner's refused to take a chance, a much smaller firm had to be wary. One of the contributors, William Lee Apthorp, had written Garrison that he had thought of making a collection himself. Apthorp had written to Oliver Ditson about publishing it, "but he declined to undertake it," and Ditson was the largest music publisher in the country.[37] In an attempt to get advance orders, A. Simpson & Co. prepared a brochure of four pages, including a letter dated August 1, 1867, two specimen pages of words and music, and a proposed outline of the volume. The purpose of the brochure was explicitly stated: "The publishers, being desirous of ascertaining in advance how large an edition it will be necessary to print, take this mode of soliciting an order from you."[38]

The plan of the book as of August 1 differed in several points from the volume as it was finally published. "The collection will, probably, exceed one hundred in number, of which the music accompanies the words, besides some words without music, and some music without words." The book as finally published included 136 songs with both words and music, the words without music and music without words having been eliminated. An "Editors' Note" dated November, 1867, on pages 114–15 of *Slave Songs of the United States* explained the changes in part:

> The original arrangement of the foregoing collection has not been adhered to. Why the secular songs do not appear by themselves has been already explained. ["There are, however, so few of these that it has been decided to intersperse them with the spirituals under their respective States."–p. xx] That the division into parts is not strictly geographical

36. *Dwight's Journal of Music* 22 (July 20, 1867): 71–72.
37. Letter, William Lee Apthorp to Wendell P. Garrison, "Jacksonville, Fla., May 24th 1867," MS, Cornell University Library.
38. Prospectus made available through the generosity of Caroline Farrar Ware.

was caused by the tardy arrival of most of the songs contained in Part IV. Should a second edition ever be justified . . . these irregularities will be corrected.

It was proposed to print music without words, and words without music, each by themselves. But the first can hardly be said to have been obtained, unless "Shock along, John," No. 86, is an instance. The words without music which in one or two cases were kindly, and we fear laboriously, comm.inicated to us, presented no fresh or striking peculiarities, and we therefore decided against their admission.

[After a lengthy quotation from the letter from Gen. James H. Wilson, describing songs he had heard but could not record, the Note continued] These, certainly, are songs to be desired and regretted. . . . For fully a third of the songs recorded by Col. Higginson we have failed to obtain the music, and they may very well serve as a guide for future investigators.

An announcement of the forthcoming volume in the *American Freedman* for August, 1867, reflected the attitude toward the collection among abolitionist circles, who were rather ambivalent toward the music of slavery.

The announcement that there is soon to be published a large and tolerably complete collection of the Slave-songs of the South, will, we are sure, give pleasure to all whose good fortune it has been to hear these songs from the lips of the freedmen themselves, since the prison-house was opened by the strong arm of war. The basis of this new, and in all probability unique collection, is the united repertories of three persons, all qualified for the task, Prof. Wm. F. Allen, Mr. Chas. P. Ware, and Mrs. Lucy McKim Garrison, which have been greatly increased by contributions from all parts of the South. . . . The volume will have extraordinary claims on the public attention, and the service it performs for the freedmen, whose new duties and new aspirations compel them to put away the relics of an unhappy past, is such as will be appreciated most when the "spirit" has vanished from the Sea Islands, and the old barbarism been entirely replaced by the new civilization. Abroad we are certain that this collection will be eagerly welcomed, both by the friends of America and of the lovers of music, who will delight in the novelty and wild, sometimes melancholy, beauty of the Songs of slaves. Already, the bare announcement has developed an interest in England which we hope can be gratified in a very few months. . . .[39]

In September advertisements appeared in the *American Freedman* and in *The Nation*, the *Freedman* reproducing the specimen pages that had appeared in the brochure, and *The Nation* reproducing only one song, "Little Children, Then Won't You Be Glad?" with the welcome heading "In press."[40] Since Allen was teaching at

39. *American Freedman* [organ of the American Freedman's Union Commission] 2 (Aug., 1867): 262.
40. *Ibid.* (Sept., 1867): 287–88; *The Nation* 5 (Sept. 19, 1867): 241.

Antioch College in 1867–68, he probably was not available for chores of proofreading, but his co-editors each did their share. Not until November 8 could Wendell Garrison sigh with relief:

> To-day I have shaken off the last of our 136 Slave-songs. The printing of the book is to begin at once, and on the 15th we hope to be out. Our publishers are quite sanguine of a fine sale, & I hope they may not be disappointed. If they prosper to a 3d & 4th ed., we shall also. But the profits of the editors are divisible by 3.[41]

Six days later, however, he was still busy with last-minute details.

> Have done to-day the last proof-reading of our slave songs, which have been for some days passing through the press. The typography has been much hurried & disappoints me. Otherwise no fault can be found with the book. It ought to be bound by Monday.

He then discussed the arrangements that had been made for reviews—rather curious ones they seem today. "I am to review it for the *Nation*; Lucy for the *Independent*, Norton will do it for *N. A. Review*, & I hope Higginson for the *Atlantic*. Miss Forten for *Freedmen's Record*. Perhaps I can do something for the *Nat. Freeman's*. Now for large & rapid sales!"[42] Later he wrote, "The review of Slave Songs [in *The Nation*] was Lucy's & my patchwork. Lucy also reviewed the book for the *Independent*."[43] The practice of an author reviewing his own book was apparently regarded as perfectly normal.

But his expectations of favorable reviews and large sales were doomed to disappointment. As far as I have been able to determine, no review ever appeared in the *North American Review* or in the *Atlantic*. After Dwight's friendly paragraph about the book, it is surprising that no review appeared in *Dwight's Journal of Music* either. An advertisement in *The Nation* quoted reviews from the *Independent*, the *New York Citizen*, the *Brooklyn Standard*, the New York *Tribune*, the *World*, and *Le Messager Franco-Americain*.[44] Not all these publications have been available, and not all the reviews were located, but other reviews were found in *The Freedmen's Record*, the *National Anti-Slavery Standard*, *Lippincott's Magazine*, and one unidentified journal

41. Letter, Wendell Phillips Garrison to William Lloyd Garrison II, "Anglelot, Nov. 8, 1867," MS, Houghton Library, Harvard University.
42. Letter, Wendell Phillips Garrison to "Dear Father" [James Miller McKim], Nov. 14, 1867, MS, McKim Papers, Cornell University Library.
43. Letter, Wendell Phillips Garrison to "Dear Father" [James Miller McKim], Nov. 30, 1867, MS, McKim Papers, Cornell University Library.
44. *The Nation* 5 (Dec. 5, 1867): 462, adv.

found among Charles Ware's papers, now identified as the *Christian Examiner*. The evaluations of the volume ranged from enthusiastic praise to outright condemnation, with political and racial factors dominating the opinions.

The review in *The Nation*, the "patchwork" written by the two Garrisons, was outspoken in its abolitionist sympathies, but made some perceptive comments on the music and its background:

> This book . . . is a remarkable proof of the stringent separation of North and South, in consequence of slavery, before the war. Not a few of its songs, contributors testify, are at least a quarter of a century old, and the greater part . . . may easily be older. [Could these contributors have been Annie Bowen and John McKim?] A very small proportion belong to the Jim Crow category, the remainder being religious hymns or "spirituals." If intercourse between the two sections had been unrestricted . . . we should have had something besides the gospel of Christy. But the whites who attended the negro camp-meetings were present from other motives than a love of harmony; the planter's guest was naturally content to hear from a distance, and to cherish as simply a pleasant recollection, the airs that floated up to the house from the "nigger" quarter; and as for the wanderer who would have stopped to listen and note down, the suspicion of tampering with happy but credulous laborers was not to be incurred with impunity. Moreover, most men are curious, many and many again have a fondness for music, but those who are musically educated are seldom to be met with. . . .
>
> We utter no new truth when we affirm that whatever of nationality there is in the music of America she owes to her dusky children. Negro minstrelsy sprang from them, and from negro minstrelsy our truly national airs, of which "Yankee Doodle" and "The Star-Spangled Banner" are *not* specimens. The negroes in their turn imitate the whites, but they show their peculiar musical genius as much in their imitations as in their compositions. A "white tune," so to speak, adopted and sung by them —in their own way—becomes a different thing. The words may be simple mangled, but the music is changed under an inspiration; it becomes a vital force. Hence the difficulty of accrediting authorship; to say how much is pure African, how much Methodist or Baptist camp-meeting. Where did the camp-meeting songs come from? Why might they not as likely emanate from black as from white worshippers? . . .[45]

There are several remarkable statements in this review: that some of the songs "are at least a quarter of a century old, and the greater part . . . may easily be older"; that Negro minstrelsy was related to black folk music; and that black performances of "white tunes" were essentially changed. The final question about black and white influences in camp-meeting songs is as timely today as when it was written.

45. "Slave Songs of the United States," [unsigned review] *The Nation* 5 (Nov. 21, 1867): 411.

The review in *The Freedmen's Record* was also unsigned, but its nostalgic tone, recalling all the pleasant memories conjured up by the songs, points to Charlotte Forten as its author, as Wendell Garrison had predicted. Calling the collection "valuable and interesting," she commented: "We are very glad that these songs, which are too rapidly losing favor with the freedmen—are thus collected and preserved." Beyond such stock phrases as "wild, sad strains" and "their strange, barbaric dance" (the shout), she has little to say about the music. Only at the end does she offer new information: "The first edition is already very nearly, if not entirely, sold. The publishers are about to issue a second edition. . . ."[46]

Lucy Garrison's review in *The Independent*, again unsigned, described the spread of the music's reputation:

> Ever since the first occupation of a Southern port by our troops, the fame of the music of the negroes has been straggling slowly northward through all sorts of channels—through newspaper letters, magazine articles, through private description, and, occasionally, illustration. Specimens of the words of the songs have frequently been printed; specimens of the music, with three or four but illy-known exceptions, never till now. If only in the light of a curiosity, therefore, we welcome the volume before us—the first collection of negro songs, words and music, that has ever been attempted.[47]

Review after review stressed the *curious* aspect of the collection, as if even the most sympathetic critic could not quite conceive of these ungrammatical, strange songs as art worthy of appreciation on its own terms. That the grammatical structure might be somehow related to African norms never occurred to them, and only rarely did the concept of musical excellence outside the European tradition.

The *National Anti-Slavery Standard*'s review was more perceptive than might have been expected from a publication so partisan in purpose:

> Perhaps the most unique book of the season—certainly in its contents one of the most remarkable and valuable alike to observer and historical student. . . . These songs are . . . the wild, irregular, generally plaintive, though sometimes riant and rollicking "shouts" or "spirituals" from which the negro minstrelsy, so called, was conceived, and which all who have lived or travelled in the slave states have heard. The public have forgotten that many of the most beautiful airs that now exist among us were originally borrowed from the slaves. These plaintive strains seem

46. "Slave Songs of the United States," [unsigned review] *Freedmen's Record* (Dec. 1867): 185–86.

47. "The Hymnody of the Blacks," [unsigned review] *The Independent* 19 (Nov. 28, 1867), p. 2, col. 7–8.

to have been wrung from the negroes' life. Debarred from speech, the aspirations that the immortal soul—God's image in Ebony—was endowed with, found vent in music, grotesque often, strange always, but creative, original, striking, rich, pathetic and absorbing. . . .

The value of the collection can be readily seen when it is remembered that under the new regime, most of these "Shouts" or "speerchials" are dying out, passing away beneath the influence of education. Not that the love of music is passing from the negro's life, but when its next manifestation appears, it will be in a different, though perhaps not as original a form. . . . The editors have done their work conscientiously and well. Their collection will be of greater value hereafter, than even now.[48]

The review in the *New York Citizen* added little that was new, describing the words as "of the rudest and most primitive character" and the music as "very remarkable. Defying all the laws of musical composition . . . a wild, weird melody which is very fascinating. They bear no sort of resemblance to the so-called negro songs of the cork minstrels, and, as a rule, are much more attractive. The volume is well worth preservation, as it shows a phase of the slave-life of the South, which will soon entirely disappear."[49] But the review in *Lippincott's Magazine* was completely negative, beginning with a long discussion of the incapacity of the Negro for music! This unsigned review must be read to be believed. After the opening argument, the author considered the book itself:

> As regards the collection of tunes and words in the book under notice, we have played many of them on the piano [hardly an ideal method for evaluating a folksong], but have failed to discover melody in any of them, except where the *idea* of the tune was clearly traceable to some old hymn tune, to the composition of which no negro could lay claim. As to the words of the (so-called) hymns, they are generally so absurd and unmeaning, and often so absolutely profane (though, not so intended), that it would be well for the teachers in the schools and meeting-houses where they are sung to commence, as speedily as possible, the destruction of the entire lot, in the interest, temporal and spiritual, of the wards in their care. The simple hymns which are taught our children would be as readily learned by the colored people, and would, in time, convey some idea to their minds, which this collection cannot.
>
> It was hardly worth while to try to perpetuate this trash, vulgarity and profanity by putting it in print.[50]

Ethnocentricity could go no further.

48. "Notes from the Capitol—Personal and Literary," dated Washington, D.C., Dec. 11th, 1867, signed R. J. H. [Richard J. Hinton?], *National Anti-Slavery Standard* 28 (Dec. 21, 1867), p. 3, col. 1–2.

49. "Slave-Songs of the United States," [unsigned review] New York *Citizen* (Nov. 23, 1867), p. 3, col. 3–4.

50. "Literature of the Day: Slave Songs of the United States," [unsigned review] *Lippincott's Magazine* 1 (Mar., 1868): 341–43.

The review from the *Christian Examiner* found among Charles Ware's papers was signed H. G. S., probably Henry George Spaulding, the clergyman whose "Under the Palmetto" was one of the first attempts to record the words and music of the slave songs. This review is largely a discussion of slavery and its effects upon the former slaves, with not much comment on the songs themselves. Of the words, Spaulding was condescending—"we can hardly help laughing, in comparing the sublime opening of the twenty-third psalm, with the ridiculous translation in the 'Sperichils' of 'De Lord *is perwide*' . . . the Scriptural quotations and allusions make such ludicrous patchwork, as almost to destroy the real pathos of many of their peculiar versions and idioms." Only at the end does he discuss the music, and then to describe a rhythmic feature: "We were struck, when at Port Royal, with the peculiar mode of beating time in the 'shout', of which we find no mention in this work. Instead of clapping the hands in unison with the accented parts of the measure, the singers uniformly beat the time *in syncopation*; i.e. striking the hands together *immediately after* the accented notes were sung."[51]

The reviews, whether favorable or unfavorable, indicated a wider critical reception than had greeted Lucy McKim's two songs in 1862–63, but the response was far from overwhelming. Reviews did not appear in journals where they were expected; most music journals ignored the volume, as did the more popular magazines. Reviews in English, French, and German journals have not been located. Only publications especially interested in the freedmen were enthusiastic. The country did not seem to be ready for the music of the slaves, unrefined by genteel adaptors.

It is not known whether A. Simpson & Co. published the second edition which Charlotte Forten had predicted. Unfortunately, little is known about the firm, not even the length of time it was in business. Whatever the reason, Wendell Garrison wrote to his brother William on December 2, 1869, asking him to call on "John C. Haynes, at Ditson's, & ask him for me what decision he has come to in regard to purchasing Slave Songs."[52] Apparently Ditson's turned it down. An 1871 edition was issued by John Ross & Co., New York, possibly from the same plates and type as the Simpson edition. After that it sank into oblivion, all but forgotten, while the various volumes inspired by the Jubilee Singers became much more widely known. Not until 1929 was it reprinted, when Peter Smith began his

51. "Review of Current Literature. Miscellaneous," in unnamed periodical [*Christian Examiner* 84, n.s. 5 (Jan., 1868): 121–22], in Charles Pickard Ware Papers, made available through the generosity of Caroline Farrar Ware.

52. Letter, Wendell Phillips Garrison to William Lloyd Garrison II, Dec. 2, 1869, MS, Smith College Library.

career as a reprint publisher with *Slave Songs of the United States.* It has been in print ever since, finally recognized as the milestone in American folk music that it was.[53] The lukewarm response mixed with outright hostility that greeted its publication was followed by a long period of indifference. Ironically, the increased interest in folk music may have been partially responsible for this lack of appreciation. The published versions of 1867 were manifestly lacking in the rhapsodical qualities of field recordings; absent were the freedom and variety that could be captured in a recording. Many discussions of Negro folk music make no mention at all of the Allen collection, choosing not to evaluate the competence of the editors or the accuracy of the versions.

Only in recent years has the collection come to be fully appreciated. Rather than criticizing the editors for not following critical canons that did not exist in their lifetimes, critics now hail "the signal event" that the publication of *Slave Songs* was.

> This first collection of Negro folk songs was an exceptional achievement for the time. Plagued with the difficulties of notating folk music, the authors came to realize that they were dealing with a musical sensibility startlingly different from that encountered in Western music. But they were also aware of the existence of a different social reality underlying the songs, and their notes describe the relationship of leader to singing group, and even make a gesture at describing the social function of the music.[54]

Richard M. Dorson also expressed a very high opinion of their achievement:

> Though a pioneer volume, the *Slave Songs* set high standards. Unlike a good many later collections, it included musical scores with its one hundred and thirty-six texts. . . . the authors . . . discussed regional characteristics of Negro folk music throughout the Cotton Kingdom, a point virtually ignored by their successors. They described the unique "shout" of the Port Royal Islanders. . . . The collection established a canon for Negro spirituals of the Old South. . . .[55]

53. "OP Publishing," p. 37.
54. Whitten and Szwed, *Afro-American Anthropology*, p. 31.
55. Dorson, *American Folklore*, pp. 173–74.

ADDITIONAL SOURCES

AS1. The letters sent to Cornell by Wendell Garrison, and now bound in a copy of *Slave Songs*, were largely addressed to Garrison, including two from W[illiam] Lee Apthorp, Jacksonville and Tampa, Florida; and one each from Maria W. Benton, Selma, Alabama; Annie M. Bowen, Roxbury, Massachusetts; N. C. Dennett, "Cashier, Freedmen's Savings Bank," Jacksonville, Florida; Charlotte L. Forten, Boston; Kane O'Donnel, New York [?]; and T[ruman] Seymour, Maj.-Genl.,

U.S.A., Pensacola, Florida. Many of these were in response to a published notice asking for contributions to the projected collection.

In addition, there were several letters addressed to Lucy Garrison: one from her uncle, John McKim (the letter from "a gentleman in Delaware" quoted on pp. vii–viii of *Slave Songs*); and one from Laura Towne, St. Helena, South Carolina. There is also a letter from James Schouler to Thomas Wentworth Higginson, and one from Wager Swayne, Montgomery, Alabama, to John R. Dennett, New York. Concluding the group are two letters to William Francis Allen from Charles P. Ware. These letters reveal a good deal about the contributors and how the book was put together.

. . . .

Conclusion

It would be very satisfying to feel that the controversies and un-
certainties about black folk music have now been resolved, but
twenty years' research was not enough to find all the answers.
Documents have been found that establish certain facts beyond any
question. African musics were transplanted to the New World by
the second half of the seventeenth century. These musics maintained themselves and persisted, not unchanged, but still in recognizably distinctive forms, for over 150 years in the West Indies and
for a shorter time on the mainland. It should be remembered that
before the American Revolution all the British and French colonies
were part of the same colonial structure, sharing close relationships,
so it was reasonable to turn to West Indian accounts for information that could not be found in mainland reports. No attempt was
made, however, to develop an independent history of black music in
the West Indies or in Latin America. Contemporary documents
establish that African instruments were also transplanted, some as
remembered aspects of a lost life, and some as tangible objects
carried aboard slaving ships. Instruments common in Africa that
were seen and described in the United States and other parts of the
western hemisphere included drums of various kinds, rhythm sticks,
banjos, musical bows, quills or panpipes, and a form of xylophone
called the balafo.

Elements of musical performance and related cultural activities now recognized as distinctively African were widely observed throughout the West Indies and the mainland colonies before 1800: dance steps of many kinds, derisive or satiric singing, call-and-response form, bodily movement and hand-clapping to accentuate the rhythm of all kinds of music. Some of these elements were also known in Europe, but the comments of Europeans made clear that they regarded this music as exotic and unfamiliar. The banjo was considered an African instrument in the eighteenth century by many chroniclers, including Thomas Jefferson. It was reported in the West Indies as early as 1678 and continued to be widely distributed throughout the islands and on the mainland until long after the advent of the minstrel theatre. Enough documents are available to disprove conclusively some of the myths that have grown up about the banjo: that it originated in the minstrel theatre, that it was "invented" by white men in New York or Virginia, and that it was unknown to plantation slaves. These imaginative accounts of the banjo's history are enshrined in some of the most respectable reference books published only a few decades ago.

A theory preserved in many of those same reference books that was widely promulgated by prestigious scholars in the 1930's and 1940's can now be laid to rest: that the music of the blacks was wholly derived from European models. Conceived not only without knowledge of African musics, but unaware of a need for such knowledge, this theory was based largely on *published* music issued in an era when very little black folk music achieved publication. Not much black folk music was even reduced to musical notation, but the casual assumption that its influence was negligible is untenable. Contemporary reports leave no room for doubt that the music flourished and had great impact. Further evidence is needed to resolve questions of the *degree* of African influence in American music at different times and places, but the theory that European influences account for all the elements in Afro-American music has been refuted.

Sources now available also indicate the process by which the music of the Africans was acculturated into something different, a process that previously could be projected only theoretically. Numerous reports from the islands over a period of years describe Africans performing their native songs and dances to African instruments, while other nearby Africans were performing European dances to European instruments. On the mainland, where African instruments were more effectively suppressed, only two such reports have been found: a Christmas celebration in South Carolina in 1805, and Mardi Gras festivities in New Orleans in 1808. We still know very little about the playing of African instruments in private, although field recordings demonstrate that they are still being played. The banjo, of course, entered the mainstream of American culture so successfully that its African origins were forgotten, and it was claimed as a native American product.

Secular music flourished among the exiled Africans to a much greater degree than had been recognized. This included not only music for dancing, but also worksongs that accompanied rowing, corn husking, cotton picking, street vending, grinding, even spinning and weaving. In view of the omnipresence of secular music in the antebellum South, how is it possible to account for the widely stated belief that the slaves had no secular music and sang only hymns? Contemporary documents provide the background for this myth, explain how it came to be believed, and at the same time demonstrate that at no time was it really true. In the eighteenth century the growing evangelical sects increasingly attacked all secular music and dancing as "sinful." Their belief that church members should "put away the things of the world" and direct their thoughts to sacred matters expressed itself in bans on card-playing and fox-hunting as well as secular songs and dancing. These tenets were accepted by many whites and blacks, being a denominational, not a racial characteristic. Indeed, anthropologists maintain that there is little distinction between sacred and secular in African cultures, so it appears that this may be one concept that the blacks did acquire from the whites. As more and more blacks joined Christian churches, their worksongs were adapted to sacred texts, and the shout became a substitute for dancing. But "sinful" tunes never completely disappeared, despite the strenuous efforts to stamp them out.

Most antebellum Southerners expressed little interest in the black music heard around them, except to cite it as evidence of the happiness of the slaves. Abolitionists understandably did not believe that the slaves were happy; but they had difficulty in countering this argument, since they had little or no direct contact with plantation slaves. Adding to their dilemma was the emergence of the minstrel theatre, with its increasingly offensive portrayal of plantation slaves as mindless buffoons who spent their time singing and dancing on the old plantation. In the cultural climate of the mid-nineteenth century, with its serious religiosity, it seemed to them quite reasonable to believe that the slaves had no secular music or profane, frivolous pastimes.

Today we can understand that dancing and singing could coexist with forced labor and bitter suffering, providing the slaves with a psychological escape that helped them to survive. It no longer seems necessary to depict slavery as unrelieved misery in order to condemn it. What the singing and dancing represented to the slaves themselves is not fully understood, but there can be no doubt that secular music and dancing were widespread despite the religious opposition to them. Church members frequently refused to participate in them, but not all blacks were church members.

In view of the controversies over the origin of the Negro spiritual, it seemed desirable to document as fully as possible the earliest reports of blacks singing sacred songs and to attempt to distinguish between the songs they improvised themselves and those they learned from others. The documents that have been found do not resolve all the problems that have been raised, but they do illuminate some previously obscure areas and reduce the need for speculation. Very little can yet be documented about African religious practices in the United States and their syncretic merging with Christianity. Although black styles of singing probably had increasing influence, it does not seem likely that any large body of distinctive black *religious* song developed in the eighteenth century, since no sustained effort to convert the Africans was made. Individual blacks had been converted and admitted to Christian churches since the seventeenth century, a process that was accelerated in the mid-eighteenth century by a few nonconformist clergymen. Reports of psalm singing among blacks became more frequent, particularly in Virginia. As the century drew to a close, protracted meetings foreshadowed the camp meetings of the early nineteenth century, with blacks worshipping both with whites and by themselves, but the reports of what was sung are at best fragmentary.

The first known reports of distinctive black religious singing date from the early nineteenth century, somewhat earlier than the first organized program of missionary activities among plantation slaves. These reports are often very vague, sometimes little more than a quotation of the text. In general, however, the texts were not reprinted in this study; my primary objective was documenting the history of the music, and a voluminous literature on the texts is readily available.[1]

Much of the controversy about Negro spirituals has been based on the notated music published in the era before the introduction of

1. See Lehmann's *Negro Spirituals* and two excellent shorter articles, Levine's "Slave Songs and Slave Consciousness" and Stuckey's "Through the Prism of Folklore."

recorded sound. The earliest examples, the three pieces published by Sir Hans Sloane early in the eighteenth century and reproduced in this volume, display unmistakable African elements, in the opinion of Dr. Klaus Wachsmann. No such statement, however, can be made about later transcriptions. At a time when European folk music was not much studied, when anthropology was in its infancy and ethnomusicology had not even been conceived, there was little precedent for the transcribing of non-European music. Conventional musical notation was inadequate to capture the distinctive features of the music as it was performed, and the transcribers were struggling with a task wholly beyond their abilities. Whatever degree of acculturation may have existed, there were features in the music that could not be represented in standard notation. The more sensitive transcribers were quite aware that they were unable to capture all that they heard—notes outside the diatonic scale, what we now call "blue" notes, swoops, glissandos, and growls, and the overlapping of leader and chorus.

By no means were all the transcribers concerned with these unconventional sounds. Some were so confirmed in their adherence to European musical norms that they either did not hear the departures or did not feel they were worth preserving. Still others saw it as a duty to "correct" what they regarded as crudities and uncouth vulgarities. Since the rate at which the acculturation of the music proceeded is unknown, it is impossible to evaluate the degree of alteration in transcriptions filtered through the musical consciousness of the various transcribers. It seems safe to regard all nineteenth-century transcriptions as mere approximations of the music as it was performed, based on a single hearing or at most a few repetitions. One need only compare the versions in Harold Courlander's *Negro Folk Music, U.S.A.* with the earlier publications to see the advances made possible by the introduction of recording techniques and the theoretical and practical guidance provided by the discipline of ethnomusicology.

The nineteenth-century transcriptions are not worthless, however, for they are as close as we are likely to come to performances from an era that cannot be restored. Their deficiencies make analysis of these printed notes unsatisfactory, either for evaluating the music as it was performed or for identifying the components that might indicate its origin. For these reasons no such analysis has been attempted here. But these versions could provide a basis for reconstructing the music as it was performed, utilizing the techniques and knowledge of ethnomusicologists with a broad background of African and European musics and their performance practices. By correlating the notated versions with field recordings and written descriptions of stylistic traits, ethnomusicologists may be able to reconstitute provisional versions of what nineteenth-century listeners may have heard. Such studies would illuminate not only the development of the spiritual, but of jazz, blues, and other kinds of Afro-American music as well.

A strong impetus to nineteenth-century transcriptions (defective as they were) was provided by the Civil War, which shattered the closed society in which the slaves had been confined. The dislocations of war brought slaves for the first time into large-scale contact with the world outside the plantations, and with strangers from the North who found the blacks and their music enormously appealing. Newspaper dispatches and private letters describe how these people reacted to the music they were hearing for the first time. From these experiences grew a seminal work in American folk music, the first published collection of slave songs. The genesis of this book, *Slave Songs of the United States*, can now be traced from manuscript letters and diaries, most of them not previously examined for their musical content. It is now evident that the editors, despite the limitations of the period in which they worked, did an exemplary job, well deserving our admiration.

Much work, however, remains. No one person could hope to examine every potential source for the history of black folk music, and some classes of materials were necessarily set aside. Latin American sources remain to be examined, as does the voluminous Spanish, Portuguese, and Dutch literature on the New World. Of material in English, manuscripts and newspapers were barely touched. The Slave Narrative Collection gathered by the Federal Writers' Project in the 1930's should be carefully sifted for its musical content.

Within the United States many questions remain to be answered. When was public African dancing discontinued at Place Congo in New Orleans? How much clandestine or private African dancing took place there and elsewhere? What elements in camp-meeting songs and white spirituals are attributable to African influences? What was the connection between African music in New Orleans and the beginnings of jazz? These questions will not be easy to answer. But scholars should be encouraged by the fact that documentation has been found for the African roots of Afro-American music, its transplantation to the New World, its acculturation, and its emergence into broad public knowledge.

Appendix I: Musical Excerpts from the Manuscript Diaries of William Francis Allen

The Civil War diary of William Francis Allen is an important basic document in the history of black folk music in the United States, although its musical content is virtually unknown. It records the immediate reactions of a well-trained historian, philologist, and amateur musician to newly freed plantation slaves and their music. The excerpts, published here for the first time, include the significant references to music not already quoted in the body of this book and pertinent background material. Part of the William Francis Allen Papers at the State Historical Society of Wisconsin, the diaries cover three periods of wartime service:

St. Helena Island, South Carolina (November 5, 1863–July 13, 1864), a typewritten copy made by Allen's daughter, Katherine, of which the original has apparently been lost. The words and music of 21 slave songs are included, the music inexpertly copied.

Helena, Arkansas (September 15, 1864–January 19, 1865).

Charleston, South Carolina (April 14–July 10, 1865), Allen's original manuscript, with words and music of two songs, meticulously transcribed.

At the end of the excerpts is a list of the songs included, with the numbers assigned to them in *Slave Songs of the United States*.

The first pertinent comment was written soon after his arrival in South Carolina on November 5, 1863.

Coffin's Point, Nov. 10, 1863 . . . I was urged by a "Conservative" to give free scope to first impressions, as being more likely to be true than any reasoning upon them; and here they are. I find the people I meet much, very much, less degraded than I expected. That is to say, they seem *human beings*, neither more nor less. There is as great a difference in their faces as in the faces of whites. They are not handsome, but some of them, especially of the men, are very noble, fine-looking fellows—much superior to the *average* of whites. In their manners they are very respectful and often obsequious; less obsequious, Mr. P[hilbrick] says, than formerly. . . . In William's [Hall's] school the children seemed as bright as white children of the same age; but then I have never had much experience in the a b c's. It seems trite and common-place to say so, but I must say that the wickedness of slavery never seemed so clear as when I saw these people (about 240 on this plantation), so entirely human as they appear, and considered how they have been treated, and how little reason there is that they should be selected from all mankind for this awful abuse. I only write here first impressions; but I am struck with the fact that Mr. P., Charley [Ware] and the others speak of the negroes just as they would of whites. This one is stupid, this one lazy, this one tricky, this one industrious, this one honest, this one intelligent, exactly as we talk of Yankees or Irish.

Nov. 15 [first impressions of singing quoted in text]

Dec. 6 [1863] . . . Mary [Mrs. Allen] and Katy started a Sunday-school today, and after they were thro' I undertook to teach them to sing. They take to singing very readily—so readily that there is a constant tendency to make up as they go along. They are musical by nature, and a tune is soon very much transformed by them. . . . I have a peculiar feeling in communicating with them [the children in his school],—as if they were something between foreigners and dumb animals. Their vocabulary is so small and their ideas so little developed, that it is hard to find terms which they have in common with us, and I feel as if in reading, it was mere empty sounds I taught them. . . .

Friday, Dec. 11 [1863] . . . Until the benches were made, I had rather a hard time this week, for these 60 scholars had only two benches, and it was impossible with no regular seat, and half standing, to keep any sort of order. They do not understand how to study to themselves, and the buzzing is tremendous when they are all studying hard,—as they do study. If I can once teach them to study in a loud whisper, I shall think my school is a quiet one. Their attention cannot be kept long, and they are soon tired. They will study for a while very hard and noisily, and then all be restless and playful. I find that a song, when they are so, is a recreation to them, and lets off the superfluous steam. As I do not know their songs yet, I let either Flora or Ellen or Patty from Hope Place start it up, and the others join in, singing with great spirit, very loud, and in perfect tune. Everyone sings, and I do not know that I have noticed a discord. It is very odd to see them sing, swaying backward and forward in their seats to mark time, and sometimes striking one hand into the other, or the foot upon the ground. I have begun to teach them "the Poor

Wayfaring Man of Grief," playing the tune on my flute, and deaconing out the words. They were hugely pleased with the flute, and when I asked what it was, only one ventured to suggest that it was an organ. I only know the first and last verses, and wish someone would send me two or three of the others. . . .

Sunday, Dec. 13, 1863 . . . Katy and I went to the Praise Meeting at Peg's house—they have no Praise House here. First they had a sort of minor hymn of their own. Then Robin (Ishmael's father) deaconed out "There is a fountain filled with blood," which they sang to St. Martin's—just as I described Old Hundred before [cf. entry for Nov. 15 in text] Robin then made a prayer, a very simple one . . . Dick deaconed out another hymn, Toby spoke a benediction, and we went away. Such meetings no doubt do good—the social and devotional effects must be salutary; whether their lives are manifestly improved I don't know, but it is at any rate one of the social agencies working towards civilization.

Dec. 19 [*1863*] . . . I have been asking them [the evening class of young men] this week where they learned to read. Two . . . picked it up from their old master's children, who would tell them a letter at a time. Paris says he bought a book in Beaufort, and that several of the people could read hymns, which they know almost by heart. Dick says his master took two or three books away from Ann. . . .

Sunday, Dec. 24 [*1863*] . . . after the services were over the people sang some of their peculiar hymns—"The Lonesome Valley" which I used to sing from the *Continental* last summer. Jimmy (Lucy's husband) led, singing or rather talking in a hoarse voice "Say brudder Moses, you want to get religion?" and the rest joining "way down in de lonesome valley." But I was most pleased with one which Billy led—"Praise, true believer, praise God—I praise my God until I die," and the chorus "O Jordan bank was a good ole bank, dere ain't but one more ribber to cross—O Jordan fight was a good old fight etc." . . .

Dec. 25 [description of shout quoted in text]

Monday, Jan. 4 [*1864*] [After the New Year's celebration in Beaufort] . . . About one, Dick came in with a grin on his face, and gave us an account of his adventures. . . . rations were got for the people, and they slept on board the boat. . . . The boat came back the next morning, and altho' it was so cold, the sun warmed them a little, and they had a merry passage back, singing and "shouting." I should like to have been among them. . . .

Sunday, [*Jan.*] *10* . . . Thursday and Friday were dreary cold days, with rain. Very few scholars came, and they sat up round the fire. I had hardly any regular exercises, but taught them Portuguese Hymn, showed them my microscope, etc. . . .

Jan. 14, Thursday. . . . [describing children playing in the yard] In two minutes more the three children were "shouting" in a row a vociferous tune. . . . The children in the yard are constantly singing. Margaret, (Abraham's sister, about 12) comes to the well, draws her pail of water, puts it on her head and walks off, singing "shall I die—shall I die" (mi mi re; mi mi do); and then Tom and Abraham follow, galloping along on bamboo horses, and shouting "my body rock 'long feber," . . .

Sunday, Jan. 17 . . . go to church today, where it was rumored that Gen. Saxton would tell some good news . . . [After the speaking] the people sang "Jesus lib and reign foreber" to [the] tune of "John Brown"—other verses being "Mr. Linkum call for freedom" and "Gen'ral Saxby call for freedom"—I have never heard any black man except Billy and Limus . . . call him Saxton. . . . [After some questions and answers] they sang "Jehovia hallelujah, de Lord will perwide—de foxes hab holes and de birdies hab nests, but de son ob man hab nowhere to lay his weary head." . . .

Tuesday, Jan. 19 . . . I have . . . some story books . . . but they can't understand story books written for Northern children, and it is a great question with me what sort of reading they ought to have when they have any. . . .

Saturday, Feb. 13 . . . When I carried Mr. Harrison's boat back the other day, Paris Tony and Taffy went with me, and I got them to sing some of their boat-songs. It didn't amount to very much, because, as Paris said, "dem boy" couldn't row and sing too well; still they gave me two or three simple ones.—"Oh Michael row the boat ashore, Hallelujah Hallelujah." "My name, my name in de book ob life, Hallelujah, etc."; Paris sang the words and they the chorus. He said the boat-songs were sometimes the same as the shouting songs, and sometimes only used for rowing. One that they sang I recognized as having heard at the shout, with the chorus "Archangel open the door," Do do, mi, re, do, re,—do, do, do, do, si si,". I have only heard good boat-singing once,—in crossing the ferry to Beaufort. That crew sings finely. I haven't heard a single piece of music here that was not religious,—except the children singing "O come, come away" which I suppose they learned at church. Flora says they have songs that are not hymns, instancing "Grandmother in the grave-yard"—a very jolly carol I suppose. Phoebe divides all their music into "speriuals" and "running speriuals", that is, shouting tunes. . . .

Sunday [Feb. 14] . . . We had a small Sunday school to-day, and a good deal of it singing. They know now Portuguese Hymn (three verses) and one or two of Coronation, Poor Wayfaring Man, and Rest for the Weary.

Sunday, Feb. 21 . . . Katy and I were talking the other day about our change of feeling about slavery. I had never laid much stress upon its cruelty, that being a thing of which I could know nothing certainly; whereas the degradation of the system was manifest. But here I find the people so much less degraded than I expected, and the barbarities so much greater than I supposed, that I have been led to place more stress upon them than I ever did before. . . .

Wednesday, Feb. 24 . . . I have succeedee [*sic*] in having a sort of Lyceum to-night, or as I called it "map lesson." . . . The younger ones came first, and I had them sing several of their pieces, some of which are very pretty. They sang two "shouting" tunes (*running speriuals*), one of which was I think the sweetest tune I have heard—"I can't stay behind my lord, I can't stay behind. Room enough an' heaven all roun', I can't stay behind." *Stoback* means shouting backward, and probably is a corruption of stand back. This is the other one. [words and music of "I ax all de brudder roun',—brudder why can't you pray for me.]

March 14, 1864. [comments on "Under the Palmetto" quoted in text]

Wednesday, March 16 . . . The following is one of the best shout tunes—very simple, but very jolly. Pray all de Member [words and music]

Sunday, March 20, 1864. . . . we had wind and tide against us, and a heavy load, so we were not home until near seven . . . there was a full moon and the men sang most of the way as they rowed. It was curious to see how their rowing flagged—for they were quite tired—the moment the singing stopped. It wasn't a very good set of singers, still I was very glad to hear them, for I have heard very little boat music. They sang "Michael row", "Hold your Light," and several others, of which we were particularly struck by "de Grabeyard", "Ober yonder" and "I want to go home." The first of these is sung differently here. . . . "I hab a grandmother in de graveyard. (or dear sisters) Where d'you tink I fin' em?—I fin' em in de boggy mire. (When I asked Billy *what* he found he was completely posed.) . . . This evening we drove down to a shout—they have one frequently, after praise. As we were going, Bristol overtook us, and we asked him if he was going to the shout. "No ma'am, dey wouldn't let me in—I haint found dat ting yet, (meaning religion). Haint been out on my knees in de swamp." These people have the custom when they are "on the anxious bench", of going "out in de wilderness" as they call it—wandering by night thro' the woods and swamps like the ancient Bacchantes. It must be this that the song above refers to; and they use the expression "fin' dat ting" for getting religion.— They shouted to seven tunes—Heaven bell, Archangel open de door, I can't stay behin' my lord, Jesus die, Sinner Turn, My body rack wid feber, and Jordan roll. The Heaven bell is a pretty good type of these tunes. The introduction is sung, the shouters standing still or clapping their hands. Then begins the second part, the regular shout. I will try to send it some time. "Sinner turn" is very sweet—I hadn't heard it before this evening.

Mar. 23, Wednesday . . . Lizzie's letter of the 8th for me. Thank her for the hymns, which are just what I wanted, and enough. . . . In the brief time that there has been for the afternoon school . . . we have neglected singing this past month; but now the days are so long that the men don't come until 5, and I mean to resume it. . . .

Friday even, Mar. 25. [comments on bird-song quoted in text]

Tuesday, March 29 [descripton of Gibb and Abraham shouting quoted in text]

St. Helena, Apr. 7, 1864. . . . Sunday, after my Bible Class . . . I asked the men to sing, and they sang several of their best tunes. . . . There were two that were new to us—"Happy Morning" and "Gwine down Zion Hill." Then a shouting tune "Turn Sinner," very sweet and with a peculiarly dramatic effect. . . .

Margaret and Abraham bringing water from the well, in which occupation they seem to spend their lives, almost always singing a match [snatch?] from some shouting tune—"O Lord," "Shall I die," "My body rack long feber," "I can't stay behin' my Lord," . . .

St. Helena, Apr. 11, 1864. . . . Taft . . . brought in the bundle of hymn-books [just arrived in a schooner],—I think it a very good one, and I found in it almost every one that the men asked for. . . .

Thursday, Apr. 21 . . . Rinah, Dolly and Chloe, who had spent the night here and were kept from going home by the storm. Then they came into the entry, with Flora, and sang two of their songs, which were new to us—"I'm hunting for a city" and "Sister Dolly light de lamp and de lamp light de road."

Friday, Apr. 29 . . . To-day as I went to open the Cotton House, [where the school was held] I heard some loud singing, and presently the Hope girls appeared coming up the avenue in full numbers singing very sweetly and clearly—as they didn't know they had listeners they threw their whole voices into it, and it was as good singing as I have heard here. "I can't stan' de fire my lord," and "I'm hunting for a city."

Sunday, May 1. . . . The following shout-tune has very odd words, and besides brings up comical reminiscences of Laura or Margaret coming to "draw" painkiller for "pain in 'e head an' feber ma'am." [words and music of "My body 'rock long feber"]

Tuesday eve. [*May 17 or 24, 1864*] . . . This is the first hymn we heard down here—that Sunday at Coffin's Point. ["I believe not"—written in pencil] ["Happy morning"] They often sing it " 'Twas a happy etc. or "What a etc."

Saturday [*May 28, 1864*] . . . We got them [the Hope children] all with our children on the upper piazza and had them sing nearly an hour to us. They were in the best of humor, and sang very nicely. Patty and Chloe were the leaders for the most part, but part of the time Robert, and once when Patty forgot how to "turn" an odd piece (What John Norton) Ellen took it up with her sweet, timid voice, holding her head all the time behind Flora's back. There were several that were entirely new to us, and one or two that we only know imperfectly. Here is one that is very striking especially when sung in the open air by a number. [words and melody of I can't stan' de fire]

When the singing was thro', Katy presented the children all with little books and combs . . . and they went on their way rejoicing. Tonight we went down to the quarters, to take leave of the people. They were all very cordial and seemed really sorry to part with Mary and Katy. . . .

Sunday, May 29. This morning after Bible Class we had a concert—they sang us several that were certainly new to us, and very pretty. . . . Two or three women, Dido, Emma and Doll, came up while the singing was going on, and at Bristol's request Dido sang the "Lonesome Valley" (which is in the Continental) in a very rich contralto voice, the others "basing" her. There were a number of children, and I enjoyed having them join in the singing, but Billy objected, on the ground that they "strain" him.

Friday, June 3rd . . . The following song is a very sweet one, and particularly striking when taken in connection with the habit of going out in the wilderness to seek religion. ["Go in de Wilderness"]

Sunday, June 5, 1864 . . . Harriet [Ware] was having her sewing-school on the piazza . . . when it was over she had the children sing—some pieces among others which they do not know at Capt. John's. [Fripp?] One of them is to a tune almost like "And are ye sure the news is true?" "I saw de beam in my sister eye—Can't saw de beam in mine—I better let my sister be, An' keep my own eye clean.—I had a mighty battle like Jacob an' de angel, In der ole time of ole, Lord I nebber 'tend to let 'em go, Till Jesus bless my soul."

Another one is very pretty [words and melody of John, John of the holy order] Songs often differ on different plantations, or are peculiar to them, and the "Graveyard" they sang last night, I hardly recognized, it was so different from the way our people sing it.

Monday, June 6 . . . I . . . went with Harriet down to the quarters . . . to see a shout [at Coffin's Point], which I found did not differ from ours, except in the tunes they sang. . . . When it was time for the morning school I heard a sort of singing in the yard, and looking out saw Linnie, Mylie Minnie and others standing by the fence around the circle in front of the house and singing or rather chanting loud and with animation, shaking sticks and hands towards some object in the garden . . . a green lizard on a tree, puffing out the red pouch under his neck now and again. Then Linnie began to chant—"Lizard, lizard, mammy tell you *spread* blănkĕt—do, lizard, *spread* blănkĕt!"—The "Rock of Jubilee" is one they shouted to at Coffin's—the chorus has a noble effect a little way off, as I heard it last night.

Sunday, June 19, Coffin's Point. . . . When I first came down, I wrote in my journal my first crude impressions, and now having been here nearly eight months, I will record my final impressions, by way of comparison. My means of observation have been very limited—only a few plantations.—but so far as they go, they have been satisfactory. In the first place, it seems evident that a slave population has been turned into a free peasantry very rapidly and completely. The community is entirely self-supporting and prosperous, and has advanced in the path of independence much more rapidly and further than is generally supposed at the North. . . . Their industry is independent, and they are wholly free, but still morally dependent and very ignorant and degraded. It will be a delicate question how fast and in what way to raise them from the condition of peasants to full citizenship ... Of the moral condition of the people, I have very little means of judging. It seems to me that the family relations are well and faithfully observed, so far as I have seen. There is very strong family feeling, altho' comparatively little neighborliness. On our place there is very little thieving, but on some places a great deal. Lying is quite prevalent, but I think that the children are tolerably free from both these vices. ... As far as I have carried my scholars, I do not think that there is any inferiority to white children. ... considering the amount of schooling, I think they have all made as good progress as whites. One thing has been constantly deepening in my thoughts—the horrible crime it would be to reduce these people back to slavery, and the awful wickedness and unnaturalness of slavery itself. This one thing is worth coming down here for, if nothing else; to be able to tell the defenders of slavery that their argument of the inability of the blacks to take care of themselves is all a lie. For these people are the very lowest of the blacks, and if they succeed with free labor the question is settled. This is an *experimentum crucis*. ... My intercourse with the people has been wholly agreeable ... and I shall leave them with a great deal of regret.

Tuesday [*June 21, 1864*] ... This is one of the best shouting and rowing tunes, "I know member, know Lord" [words and music] First the introduction is sung and the shouting begins with the regular tune. The words have no regular order, and are sung first to the tune on the first staff, and then the other.

St. Helena, Sunday, June 26, 1864. ... This afternoon there was a funeral ... and ... I went to the burying-ground where the grave is. ... They didn't sing any of their own songs—all church hymns, prayers and exhortations.

St. Helena, Sunday, July 3, 1864 ... The other night I was waked up about midnight by singing, and going to the window found that it proceeded from Dick's house—very sweet and pleasant, tunes that were entirely new to me. It seems that after Praise, Dick had invited the people to come up and have a supper. Waverly, his brother-in-law, being here that night. So after supper they had singing. ... Robert has been teaching me a number of songs; *weary* is the common word for *tired*. "Me no weary yet ... tell my Jesus huddy O" [words and music] "Huddy" is "how-do," the common word for greeting.

As I sit here writing ... we can hear the very dull and distant sound of guns. ...

July 5, Tuesday. Yesterday set in with intense fierceness of heat—it was 98° at 10 ... We didn't feel much like going out, but thought we wouldn't miss the celebration at the church ... the processions ... had banners and flags, and came up singing the John Brown song. The exercises were interspersed with singing—Mr. Wells has been drilling them for two or three weeks. ... Mr. French has really a rare faculty of speaking to the people. ... He closed by reading Whittier's boatmen's song. I should have doubted their appreciating it, but he read it so well that it took right hold of them. They laughed and nodded approval with a thorough look of appreciation and enjoyment. . . . The second verse told best, particularly the lines "We sell de cow, we sell de pig, but nebber chile be sold." . . . the people sang some of their own songs. "Roll, Jordan," "One more riber to cross," "Tallest tree", "Wrestle Jacob," "Travel on, O weary soul," "Lonesome valley," "I can't stay behind my Lord," which last rolled up splendidly from that great multitude,—they sang it with more zest than any, I think. It is a favorite shouting tune, and their heads and arms at once began to move in time with the music; we were much entertained with seeing one old woman, nicely dressed, with a yellow scarf round her neck, and a white spotted turban, leaning on another woman's shoulder and wagging her head and swaying her body to the music, while she sang, and her thoughts no doubt carried her back to the days when she was a young "member" and used to shout with the best of them. . . .

Cairo [Ill.] Sept. 22, Thursday [1864] [description of sounds heard aboard steamboat quoted in text]

Memphis, Soldiers' Home, Sept. 26, 1864. . . . Yesterday morning, finding that there would be no boat until tonight, I thought I would visit the Contraband Camp on Presidents' Island . . . I . . . went to the "Praise House" (I don't know whether they use that expression), & heard an exhortation. The man talked very fast, & in a sort of chanting tone, hardly ever varying from the harmonic tones, while the audience, by way of approval, hummed & murmured in harmony. I heard the same at Holly Springs, which shows that this was not peculiar to this speaker. I heard them sing twice—a regular hymn (Balenna) [?] precisely as they sang Shirland & Ostorville at Port Royal, & one of their own hymns. I listened to this very attentively, & thought I had caught it, but have forgotten nearly all. Some of the words I remember—"Brudder, guide me
sol sol do do
home & I am glad, Bright angels biddy me to come." "What a happy
 mi sol fa fa mi   do do do do
time, chil'n." "Let's go to God, chil'n."
 ti do do

[first letter from Helena, Ark. Sept. 27, 1864]

Sunday, Oct. 2. . . . It is funny that the children here sing precisely the same hymns as at Port Royal—I don't mean their own music, but the tunes taught them at school. They sang today "In the Light" & "Glory Be to God on High"—their two favorites on St. Helena.

Sunday, Nov. 13. . . . another man came in & said that Caleb Jackson was going to preach at the Baptist church. . . . So, understanding that Jackson was a noted preacher, we went up to hear him. . . . He very rarely passed out of the chanting tone—however fast he spoke, he still modulated his voice to the musical scale, & the women sitting around him, rocking & swaying & throwing up their arms, accompanied him with a murmuring harmonic croon, which swelled like an Eolian [*sic*] harp whenever he became excited, & was sometimes very sweet indeed.

MUSIC INCLUDED IN ALLEN'S DIARY

St. Helena Island portion

Page	*Title*	*No. in* Slave Songs
70	O Jericho do worry me (1 line & base)	47
76	Praise, true belieber, praise God	5
112	Jehovia, hallelujah, de Lord is perwide	2
127	Travel on, O weary soul	3
128	A baby born in Bethlehem	3?
	Michael row the boat ashore	31
138	I ax all de brudder roun'	44
148	Hold your light	12
149	Wrestle Jacob	6
151	Pray all de member	47
154	Graveyard	21
164	De talles' tree in Paradise	4
166	Turn, sinner, turn	48
185	I'm hunting for a city	24
187	Way my brudder, better true belieb	45
195	Happy morning	13
199	I can't stan' de fire	55
206	Go in de wilderness	19
207	John, John of the holy order	22
208	De Rock o' Jubilee	33
217	I know member	46
224	Tell my Jesus huddy O	20

Helena, Ark., portion

II, 126	Little children, O won't you be glad	108

Charleston portion, beginning Apr. 14, 1865

32	Nobody knows the trouble I see	74

Appendix II: Table of Sources for the Banjo, Chronologically Arranged

Date	Term	Place	Source
1621	unnamed	Gambia	Jobson, *Golden Trade*, pp. 105–8.
1678	banza	Martinique	Dessalles, *Histoire Générale des Antilles*, III, 297.
1689	strum-strum	Jamaica	Sloane, *Voyage*, I, xlix and plate III.
1698	"espece de guitarre"	Antilles	Labat, *Nouveau Voyage*, IV, 159.
1708	bangil	Barbados	Oldmixon, *British Empire in America*, I, 123.
1739	bangil	Jamaica	Charles Leslie, *A New and Exact Account of Jamaica* (Edinburgh: Fleming, 1739), p. 326, cited in Cassidy and Le Page, *Dictionary of Jamaican English*, p. 26.
1740	bangil	Jamaica	[Leslie,] *New History*, p. 310.

Date	Term	Place	Source
1740	strum-strum	Jamaica	*Importance of Jamaica*, p. 19.
1754	banjer	Maryland	Advertisement in the *Maryland Gazette*, July 25, 1754, cited in "Eighteenth Century Slaves," p. 210.
pre-1757	bangelo	Sierra Leone	Owen, *Journal*, p. 52.
1758	"espece de guitare"	Amérique	*Encyclopédie*, II, 474, "Calinda."
1760	"kind of guitar"	French Dominions	Jefferys, *French Dominions*, II, 192.
1763	banshaw	St. Kitts	Grainger, *The Sugar-Cane; A Poem*, in Alexander Chalmers, *Works of the English Poets*, XIV, 12.
1765	banza	Amérique	*Encyclopédie*, XV, 874, "Tamboula."
1768	banza	Amérique	Ibid., 2nd ed., XI, 66, "Negres."
1774	merry-wang	Jamaica	[Edward Long,] *History of Jamaica*, II, 42.
1774	banjo	Maryland	Creswell, *Journal*, p. 19.
1774	banjo	Virginia	Fithian, *Journal & Letters*, p. 62.
pre-1775	bandore, banjer	Maryland or Virginia	Boucher, *Glossary*, p. xlix, BAN.
pre-1775	banger	Virginia	Davis, *Travels*, pp. 380–81.
pre-1775	banjor	Virginia	Smyth, *Tour*, I, 46.
1777	bonjour	Jamaica	Beckford, *Descriptive Account*, II, 387.
1780	banza	Amérique	Laborde, *Essai sur la Musique*, I, 291.
1781	banjar	Virginia	Jefferson, *Notes on the State of Virginia*, p. 257.
1784	banjah	shipboard	Schoepf, *Travels*, II, 261–62.

Date	Term	Place	Source
1785	"violon des Negres"	Guinea, Amérique	Isert, *Voyages*, pp. 207–8.
1787	banjo	Tarborough, N.C.	Attmore, *Journal*, p. 43.
1788	banjar	Antigua	Luffman, *Brief Account of Antigua*, p. 135.
1789	banjay	Barbados	Dickson, *Letters on Slavery*, p. 74.
1790	banjaw	West Indies	*Short Journey in the West Indies*, I, 90.
1791	"resembles a guitar"	Africa	Equiano, *Life*, I, 8.
1793	banja or merrywang	West Indies	Edwards, *History*, II, 84.
pre-1796	"banja or merrywang"	Sierra Leone	Winterbottom, *Native Africans*, I, 113, quoting Edwards's *History*.
1796	banjar	Barbados	Pinckard, *Notes*, I, 127.
1797	banza	St. Domingue	Moreau de Saint-Méry, *Déscription*, I, 44.
1799	bangoe	Richmond, Va.	Fairfax, *Journey*, p. 2.
1800	bangah	Guadeloupe	Macpherson, *Memoirs*, p. 186.
1804	bonjoe	Jamaica	Nugent, *Journal*, p. 219.
1806	bangie	Wheeling, [W.]Va.	Ashe, *Travels*, I, 233.
1807	banja or merrywang	Jamaica	Renny, *History of Jamaica*, p. 168.
1810	banza	Antilles	[Tussac,] *Cri des Colons*, p. 292.
1816	banjee	Jamaica	Lewis, *Journal*, p. 51.
1817	banjo	Richmond, Va.	[Paulding,] *Letters*, I, 97.
1819	unnamed	New Orleans	Latrobe, *Impressions*, pp. 50–51, with sketch.
1822	bonjaw	Jamaica	Cynric R. Williams, *Tour*, p. 21.
	bonja	Jamaica	Ibid., p. 101 and preceding plate.

Date	Term	Place	Source
1823	banja	Jamaica	*Koromantyn Slaves; or West Indian Sketches* (London: Hatchard and Son, 1823), p. 85, cited in Cassidy and Le Page, *Dictionary of Jamaican English*, p. 26.
1825	banjo	New Orleans	Marie B. Williams, "Night with Voudous," p. 404.
1826	bonja	Leeward Islands	Bayley, *Four Years' Residence*, p. 437.
1832	banjoe	Virginia	Kennedy, *Swallow Barn*, I, 110.
1833	bandjo	Virginia	John Finch, *Travels*, p. 238.
1833	banja	Louisiane	Pavie, *Souvenirs Atlantiques*, II, 320.
1835	bongau	Jamaica	Madden, *Twelvemonths' Residence* I, 184, cited in Cassidy and Le Page, *Dictionary of Jamaican English*, p. 26.
	bonjaw	Jamaica	Madden, *Twelvemonths' Residence*, II, 7.
	bonjoo	Jamaica	Ibid., II, 153.
1835	banjo	New Orleans	[Ingraham,] *South-West*, I, 162.
1838	banjo	St. Croix	Hovey, *Letters*, p. 36.
1838–39	banjo	St. Simons, Ga.	Kemble, *Journal*, p. 97.
1843	banja	Jamaica	Phillippo, *Jamaica*, p. 243.
1844	bangoe	Antigua	*Antigua and the Antiguans*, II, 107.
1846	banjo	U.S.	Mackay, *Western World*, II, 133.
1849	banjo	Trinidad	Day, *Five Years' Residence*, II, 120.
1851	banza	Louisiana	Mercier, *L'Habitation*, p. 51.

Appendix III: Earliest Published Versions of "Go Down, Moses"

Version 1. Text supplied to the New York *Tribune* by Harwood Vernon:

LET MY PEOPLE GO.

A SONG OF THE "CONTRABANDS."

When Israel was in Egypt's land,
  O let my people go!
Oppressed so hard they could not stand,
  O let my people go!

CHORUS—O go down, Moses
    Away down to Egypt's land,
    And tell King Pharaoh
    To let my people go!

Thus saith the Lord bold Moses said,
  O let my people go!
If not, I'll smite your first born dead,
  O let my people go!

No more shall they in bondage toil,
  O let my people go!
Let them come out with Egypt's spoil,
  O let my people go!

Then Israel out of Egypt came,
  O let my people go!
And left the proud oppressive land,
  O let my people go!

O 'twas a dark and dismal night,
  O let my people go!
When Moses led the Israelites,
  O let my people go!

'Twas good old Moses, and Aaron, too,
  O let my people go!
'Twas they that led the armies through,
  O let my people go!

The Lord told Moses what to do,
  O let my people go!
To lead the children of Israel through,
  O let my people go!

O come along Moses, you'll not get lost,
  O let my people go!
Stretch out your rod and come across,
  O let my people go!

As Israel stood by the water side,
  O let my people go!
At the command of God it did divide,
  O let my people go!

When they had reached the other shore,
  O let my people go!
They sang a song of triumph o'er,
  O let my people go!

Pharaoh said he would go across,
  O let my people go!
But Pharaoh and his host were lost,
  O let my people go!

O Moses, the cloud shall cleave the way,
  O let my people go!
A fire by night, a shade by day,
  O let my people go!

You'll not get lost in the wilderness,
  O let my people go!
With a lighted candle in your breast,
  O let my people go!

Jordan shall stand up like a wall,
  O let my people go!
And the walls of Jericho shall fall,
  O let my people go!

Your foe shall not before you stand,
  O let my people go!
And you'll possess fair Canaan's land,
  O let my people go!

'Twas just about in harvest time,
  O let my people go!
When Joshua led his host Divine,
  O let my people go!

O let us all from bondage flee,
  O let my people go!
And let us all in Christ be free,
  O let my people go!

We need not always weep and mourn,
  O let my people go!
And wear these Slavery chains forlorn,
  O let my people go!

This world's a wilderness of woe,
  O let my people go!
O let us on to Canaan go,
  O let my people go!

What a beautiful morning that will be!
  O let my people go!
When time breaks up in eternity,
  O let my people go!

National Anti-Slavery Standard 22 (Dec. 21, 1861) p. [4], col. 5.

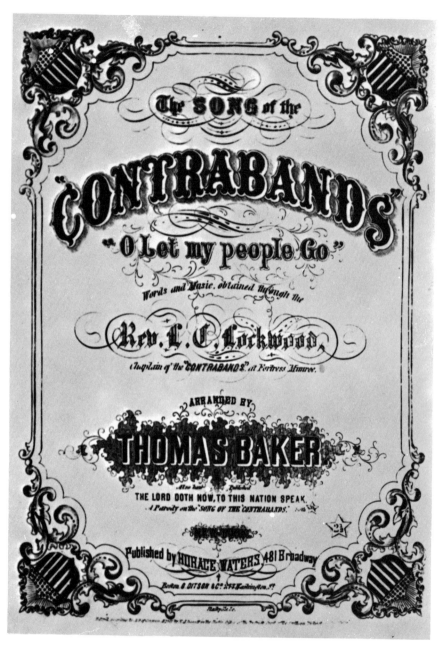

"Song of the Contrabands." In possession of the author.

THE SONG OF THE "CONTRABANDS."

"O! LET MY PEOPLE GO"

This Song, originated among the "Contrabands," and was first heard sung by them on their arrival at Fortress Monroe; and was introduced here by their Chaplain: Rev. L. C. Lockwood.

Arranged by THOMAS BAKER.

ANDANTE.

mf *ff*

1. The Lord by Mo - ses to Pha - raoh said: "O

p

let my peo - ple go!............ If not, I'll smite your

first - born dead, Then let my peo - ple go!"

O! go down, Mo - ses, A - way down to E - gypt's land, And

tell king Pha - raoh, To let my peo - ple go!

4

CHORUS.

O! go down, Moses, A - way down to E - gypt's land, And

O! go down, Moses, A - way down to E - gypt's land, And

tell King Pha - raoh,............ To let my peo - ple go!............

tell King Pha - raoh,............ To let my peo - ple go!............

2.

No more shall they in bondage toil,
  O let my people go!
Let them come out with Egypt's spoil.
  O let my people go!
    O go down, (&c.)

3.

Haste, Moses, 'till the sea you've crossed,
  O let my people go!
Pharaoh shall in the deep be lost,
  O let my people go!
    O go down, (&c.)

4.

The sea before you shall divide,
  O let my people go!
You'll cross dry-shod to the other side,
  O let my people go!
    O go down, (&c.)

5.

Fear not King Pharaoh or his host,
  O let my people go!
They all shall in the sea be lost,
  O let my people go!
    O go down, (&c.)

6.

They'll sink like lead to rise no more,
  O let my people go!
And you'll hear a shout on the other shore,
  O let my people go!
    O go down, (&c.)

7.

The firey cloud shall lead the way,
  O let my people go!
A light by night, a shade by day,
  O let my people go!
    O go down, (&c.)

8.

Jordan shall stand up like a wall,
  O let my people go!
And the walls of Jericho shall fall,
  O let my people go!
    O go down, (&c.)

9.

Your foes shall not before you stand,
  O let my people go!
And you'll possess fair Canaan's land,
  O let my people go!
    O go down, (&c.)

10.

O let us all from bondage flee,
  O let my people go!
And let us all in Christ be free,
  O let my people go!
    O go down, (&c.)

11.

This world's a wilderness of woe,
  O let my people go!
O let us all to glory go,
  O let my people go!
    O go down, (&c.)

N.B. This Song has been sung for about nine years by the slaves of Virginia. .... L. C. L.

6

THE LORD DOTH NOW TO THIS NATION SPEAK.

PARODY ON
"THE SONG OF THE CONTRABANDS."

Words by Moses.   Music Arr'd by T. Baker.

Ent'd according to Act of Congress, AD. 1861 by E. A. Daggett. in the Clerk's Office of Dist Court of New York.

Go down, Moses.

1. When Is-rael was in E-gypt's land: Let my peo-ple go,

Op-pressed so hard they could not stand, Let my peo-ple go.

Go down, Mo - ses, way down in E - gypt land,

Tell ole Pha - roh, Let my peo - ple go.

2 Thus saith the Lord, bold Moses said,
    Let my people go ;
If not I'll smite your first-born dead,
    Let my people go.
    Go down, Moses, etc.

3 No more shall they in bondage toil,
    Let my people go ;
Let them come out with Egypt's spoil,
    Let my people go.
    Go down, Moses, etc.

4 When Israel out of Egypt came,
    Let my people go ;
And left the proud oppressive land,
    Let my people go.
    Go down, Moses, etc.

"Go Down, Moses." Source: [Seward, Theodore F., comp.,] *Jubilee Songs: As Sung by the Jubilee Singers, of Fisk University, Nashville, Tenn., under the Auspices of the American Missionary Association.* New York: Biglow and Main, c 1872, pp. 22–23. Courtesy of the Joseph Regenstein Library, University of Chicago.

5.
O, 'twas a dark and dismal night,
Let my people go;
When Moses led the Israelites,
Let my people go.

6.
'Twas good old Moses and Aaron, too,
Let my people go;
'Twas they that led the armies through,
Let my people go.

7.
The Lord told Moses what to do,
Let my people go;
To lead the children of Israel through,
Let my people go.

8.
O come along Moses, you'll not get lost,
Let my people go;
Stretch out your rod and come across,
Let my people go.

9.
As Israel stood by the water side,
Let my people go;
At the command of God it did divide,
Let my people go.

10.
When they had reached the other shore,
Let my people go;
They sang a song of triumph o'er,
Let my people go.

11.
Pharaoh said he would go across,
Let my people go;
But Pharaoh and his host were lost,
Let my people go.

12.
O Moses the cloud shall cleave the way,
Let my people go;
A fire by night, a shade by day,
Let my people go.

13.
You'll not get lost in the wilderness,
Let my people go;
With a lighted candle in your breast,
Let my people go.

14.
Jordan shall stand up like a wall,
Let my people go;
And the walls of Jericho shall fall
Let my people go.

15.
Your foes shall not before you stand,
Let my people go;
And you'll possess fair Canaan's land,
Let my people go.

16.
'Twas just about in harvest time,
Let my people go;
When Joshua led his host divine,
Let my people go.

17.
O let us all from bondage flee,
Let my people go;
And let us all in Christ be free,
Let my people go

18.
We need not always weep and moan,
Let my people go;
And wear these slavery chains forlorn,
Let my people go.

19.
This world's a wilderness of woe,
Let my people go ;
O, let us on to Canaan go,
Let my people go.

20.
What a beautiful morning that will be,
Let my people go ;
When time breaks up in eternity,
Let my people go.

21.
The Devil he thought he had me fast,
Let my people go;
But I thought I'd break his chains at
Let my people go.   [last,

22.
O take yer shoes from off yer feet,
Let my people go;
And walk into the golden street,
Let my people go.

23.
I'll tell you what I likes de best,
Let my people go ;
It is the shouting Methodist,
Let my people go.

24.
I do believe without a doubt,
Let my people go;
That a Christian has the right to shout,
Let my people go.

....

Bibliography

To assist readers whose interests are more musical than historical, some suggestions for background reading may be helpful. Good general histories of the blacks in the United States are John Hope Franklin, *From Slavery to Freedom* (4th ed.; New York: Knopf, 1974), and Lerone Bennett, Jr., *Before the Mayflower: A History of the Negro in America, 1619–1964* (Rev. ed.; Baltimore: Penguin Books, 1966). Living conditions under slavery are discussed in John W. Blassingame's *The Slave Community: Plantation Life in the Antebellum South* (New York: Oxford University Press, 1972).

Two good collections of contemporary articles on black music are Bruce Jackson's *The Negro and His Folklore in Nineteenth-Century Periodicals* (Austin: Published for the American Folklore Society by the University of Texas Press, 1967) and Bernard Katz's *The Social Implications of Early Negro Music in the United States* (New York: Arno Press, 1969). The best survey of black music currently available is Eileen Southern's textbook, *The Music of Black Americans* (New York: W. W. Norton, 1971). John Lovell's *Black Song: The Forge and the Flame* (New York: Macmillan, 1972) is a comprehensive but somewhat uncritical survey of the literature on the spiritual.

To help in understanding the genesis of the first published collection, *Slave Songs of the United States*, the best discussions of the

Port Royal experiment are Willie Lee Rose's *Rehearsal for Recon-struction: The Port Royal Experiment* (Indianapolis: Bobbs-Mer-rill, 1964) and Elizabeth Ware Pearson's *Letters from Port Royal Written at the Time of the Civil War* (Boston: W. B. Clarke, 1906).

The bibliography includes listings of those works that were gen-erally most useful or were directly cited in the footnotes. A listing of the hundreds of titles that were examined for this study seemed impractical; omitted were those titles that yielded no information or that duplicated the information found in other works that were cited. The annotations emphasize the most useful information in each item, not necessarily every mention of pertinent subjects.

MANUSCRIPTS CONSULTED

Allen, Margaret Loring Andrews (Mrs. Wm. F. Allen). "The University of Wisconsin in the Days Soon After the Civil War," typescript. State Historical Society of Wisconsin.

Allen, William Francis. *Diary, 1863-1866.* State Historical Society of Wisconsin. I, typescript; II, MS.

Brinckerhoff, Isaac W. "The Port Royal Gazette." MS newspaper, Mar. 7, 1862–Feb. 6, 1863. Rutgers University Library.

Garrison Family Papers, including letters by and to Lucy McKim Garrison, Ellen Wright Garrison, their friends and relations. Sophia Smith Collection, Smith College Library.

Garrison Family Papers: letters by and to Wendell Phillips Garrison, William Lloyd Garrison II, and their relations. Houghton Library, Harvard University.

Higginson, Thomas Wentworth. *Diary,* 1862 vol. Houghton Library, Harvard Uni-versity.

———. Papers, MS. fMS 1162.7: song texts in Charles P. Ware's handwriting. Houghton Library, Harvard University.

McKim, James Miller. Papers. Maloney Collection, Manuscripts and Archives Di-vision, New York Public Library, Astor, Lenox, and Tilden Foundations.

———. Cornell University Library.

McKim, John. Letter to James Miller McKim, Aug. 4, 1860, made available by the late Mrs. Hendon Chubb, West Orange, N.J.

Manning, John Laurence. Letter dated "Clarendon, 17th Nov 1856." Caroliniana Library, University of South Carolina.

Pierpont, John. *Journal,* 1805. Pierpont Morgan Library, New York.

Group of 14 letters bound in *Slave Songs of the United States* from contributors and editors, Cornell University Library.

Tomlinson, Reuben. Letter to James Miller McKim, Oct. 5, 1862. McKim Papers, Cornell University Library.

Ware, Charles Pickard. Papers, made available by Caroline Farrar Ware.

Whitney, Henry, 2nd Lieut., 45th U.S. Colored Troops. *Diary* entry, May 22, 1864. Rutgers University Library.

Wilson, James Harrison, Maj.-Gen. Letter to Wendell Phillips Garrison, Davenport, Iowa, June 11, 1867. Field-Garrison Autograph Collection, Manuscript Division, Library of Congress.

SERIALS SCANNED

The American Missionary, 1861–65. Organ of the American Missionary Association.

American Missionary Association, *Annual Report,* 1861–67.

The Freedmen's Record, I–III, 1865–68.
  Organ of the New England Freedmen's Aid Society.
The Nation, I–VI, 1865–68.
National Anti-Slavery Standard, 1861–67.
New England Freedmen's Aid Society [earlier known as Educational Commission for Freedmen]. *First- [Second] Annual Report*, 1863–64.
———. *Extracts from Letters of Teachers and Superintendents*, I–V, 1862–64.
Pennsylvania Freedman's Bulletin, 1865–68.
Virginia Gazette. [Scattered items located through the index.]

BOOKS, PAMPHLETS, AND ARTICLES

Aaron, a Slave. *The Light a Truth of Slavery. Aaron's History*. Worcester, Mass.: Printed for Aaron, 1827.
  Worksongs: pp. 17–18.
Abrahams, Roger D. *Deep the Water, Shallow the Shore; Three Essays on Shantying in the West Indies*. Austin: Published for the American Folklore Society by the University of Texas Press, c 1974.
———. "The Shaping of Folklore Traditions in the British West Indies." *Journal of Inter-American Studies* 9 (July, 1967): 456–80.
  John Canoe: pp. 461–62.
An Abridgement of the Laws in Force and Use in Her Majesty's Plantations (Viz) of Virginia, Jamaica, Barbados, Maryland, New-England, New-York, Carolina, &c. Digested under Proper Heads in the Method of Mr. Wingate, and Mr. Washington's Abridgements. London: J. Nicholson, 1704.
  Prohibition of beating drums, blowing horns: p. 239.
An Abstract of the Evidence Delivered before a Select Committee of the House of Commons, in the Years 1790 and 1791; on the Part of the Petitioners for the Abolition of the Slave Trade. 2nd ed. Bury: Printed by R. Haworth, [n.d.].
  Dancing and singing the slaves on board slave ships: pp. 44–46.
Adanson, Michel. "A Voyage to Senegal, the Isle of Goree, and the River Gambia" [performed during 1749–53]. In Pinkerton, John, *A General Collection of the Best and Most Interesting Voyages and Travels in All Parts of the World. . . .* London: Printed for Longman, Hurst, Rees, Orme, and Brown, 1814. XVI, [598]–674.
  "Guiriots": p. 612.
"The African Slave Trade." [Review of *Captain Canot, or Twenty Years of an African Slaver*, by Brantz Mayer.] *De Bow's Review* 18 (Jan., 1855): 16–20.
  Recollection of African dancing in Congo Square, New Orleans: p. 20.
"The Africans of the Slave Bark, 'Wildfire.' " *Harper's Weekly* 4 (June 2, 1860): 344.
  Singing by newly arrived Africans.
Afro-Americana, 1553–1906; Author Catalog of the Library Company of Philadelphia and the Historical Society of Pennsylvania. Boston: G. K. Hall. 1973.
Agricola [pseud.]. "Management of Negroes." *De Bow's Review* 19 (Sept., 1855): 361.
  Lively worksongs encouraged.
Albert, Octavia V. Rogers. *The House of Bondage; or Charlotte Brooks and Other Slaves. Original and Life-like as They Appeared in Their Plantation and City Slave Life; Together with Pen-pictures of the Peculiar Institution, with Sights and Insights into Their New Relations as Freedmen, Freemen, and Citizens*. New York: Hunt & Eaton, 1890.
  Spirituals sung in Virginia and Louisiana, with texts: pp. 2–6, 9–12, 26–33.
Alexander, Sir James Edward. *Transatlantic Sketches, Comprising Visits to the Most Interesting Scenes in North and South America, and the West Indies. With Notes on Negro Slavery and Canadian Emigration*. Philadelphia: Key and Biddle, 1833.
  African drumming and instruments: p. 112; African and Creole instruments and dances: pp. 60–61.

[Allain, Hélène d'Aquin.] *Souvenirs d'Amérique et de France, Par une Créole.* Paris: Perisse Frères, [1883?]
   Place Congo in New Orleans: pp. 171–73.
Allen, William Francis. *Essays and Monographs. Memorial Volume.* Boston: G. H. Ellis, 1890.
   Biographical information: pp. 3–9.
[Allen, William Francis; Ware, Charles Pickard; and Garrison, Lucy McKim, comps.] *Slave Songs of the United States.* New York: A. Simpson, 1867.
Alston, Jacob Motte. *Rice Planter and Sportsman: The Recollections of J. Motte Alston, 1821–1909.* Ed. Arney R. Childs. Columbia, S.C.: University of South Carolina Press, 1953.
   African singing after emancipation: p. 48.
American Art Journal 39 (May 19, 1883): 80.
   Black bandsmen.
American Freedmen's Inquiry Commission. *Preliminary Report Touching the Condition and Management of Emancipated Refugees; Made to the Secretary of War ... June 30, 1863.* New York: J. F. Trow, 1863.
   "Negro songs": p. 10.
American Missionary Association. *History of the American Missionary Association: Its Churches and Educational Institutions among the Freedmen, Indians and Chinese. With Illustrative Facts and Anecdotes.* New York: S. W. Green, 1874.
   Beginnings of mission at Fortress Monroe: pp. 11–12.
"The American Missionary Association among the Freedmen. Beginnings." American Missionary Association, *22nd Annual Report.* ... New York, 1868. P. 18.
Amistad Research Center. *Author and Added Entry Catalog of the American Missionary Archives.* Westport, Conn.: Greenwood, [1970?].
Anderson, Robert. *From Slavery to Affluence; Memoirs of Robert Anderson, Exslave,* by Daisy Anderson Leonard. 1927; reprinted, Steamboat Springs, Colo.: Printed by the Steamboat Pilot, 1967.
   Slave dance: pp. 32–33; style of singing: pp. 24–25.
Andrews, Eliza Frances. *The War-Time Journal of a Georgia Girl, 1864–1865.* New York: D. Appleton, 1908.
   Style of singing: pp. 89–90.
Andrews, Ethan Allen. *Slavery and the Domestic Slave-trade in the United States.* Boston: Light & Stearns, 1836.
   Black congregation, Baltimore, 1835: pp. 89–93.
Antigua and the Antiguans: A Full Account of the Colony and Its Inhabitants from the Time of the Caribs to the Present Day. ... London: Saunders and Otley, 1844.
   "Bangoe": II, 107.
Anti-slavery Songs. A Selection from the Best Anti-slavery Authors. ... Salem, Ohio: P. Trescott, 1849.
   "Song of the Coffle Gang": p. 37.
Armstrong, Mrs. Mary Frances, and Ludlow, Helen W. *Hampton and Its Students. By Two of Its Teachers.* ... *With Fifty Cabin and Plantation Songs,* arr. by Thomas P. Fenner. ... New York: G. P. Putnam's Sons, 1874.
   Boat songs: p. 11; corn songs: p. 113; problems in notating the songs: p. [172].
Armstrong, Orland Kay. *Old Massa's People; the Old Slaves Tell Their Stories.* Indianapolis: Bobbs-Merrill, 1931.
   Reminiscence of singing aboard a slave ship: p. 52.
Asbury, Francis. *The Journal of the Reverend Francis Asbury, Bishop of the Methodist Episcopal Church* [Aug. 7, 1781–Dec. 31, 1800]. New York: Eaton & Mains, [n.d.].
   Religious conditions, 1801: III, 11.
_____. *The Journals and Letters of Francis Asbury.* Elmer T. Clarke, editor-in-chief. London: Epworth Press, [1958].
   Negroes in Methodist meetings: I, 9–10, 56–57, 222, 403, 747.

Ashe, Thomas. *Travels in America Performed in 1806 for the Purpose of Exploring the Rivers Alleghany, Monongahela, Ohio and Mississippi, and Ascertaining the Produce and Condition of Their Banks and Vicinity.* New York, 1811.
  "Bangies" played by blacks: p. 100.
Association for the Religious Instruction of the Negroes in Liberty County, Georgia. *Ninth Annual Report of the Association . . . Together with the Address . . . by the President, the Rev. Robert Quarterman.* Savannah: Printed by T. Purse, 1844.
  Protracted meeting for slaves: pp. 12–13.
————. *13th Annual Report.* Savannah: E. J. Purse, 1848.
  Disapproval of dancing: p. 22.
Atkins, John. *A Voyage to Guinea, Brasil, and the West-Indies, in His Majesty's Ships, the Swallow and Weymouth. . . .* London: Printed for C. Ward and R. Chandler, 1735.
  Description of African music and dancing: p. 53.
Attmore, William. *Journal of a Tour to North Carolina, 1787.* Ed. Lida Tunstall Rodman. Chapel Hill: University of North Carolina Press, 1922.
  Banjo in Tarborough, N.C.: p. 43.
Avirett, James Battle. *The Old Plantation: How We Lived in Great House and Cabin Before the War.* New York: F. T. Neely, c 1901.
  Black band playing for whites: p. 99; corn songs: pp. 144–45.
Bailey, Rufus William. *The Issue, Presented in a Series of Letters on Slavery.* New York: J. S. Taylor, 1837.
  Sunday dances: p. 13.
Baily, Francis. *Journal of a Tour in Unsettled Parts of North America in 1796 and 1797.* London: Baily Brothers, 1856.
  Sunday dances of slaves: p. 314.
Baird, Robert. *Religion in the United States of America. Or an Account of the Evangelical Churches in the United States.* Glasgow: Blackie and Son, 1844.
  Preference of blacks for all-black churches: p. 77.
Baldwin, Ebenezer. *Observations on the Physical, Intellectual and Moral Qualities of Our Colored Population: With Remarks on the Subject of Emancipation and Colonization.* New Haven: L. H. Young, 1834.
  Instruments played by blacks: p. 19.
Ball, Charles. *Slavery in the United States: A Narrative of the Life and Adventures of Charles Ball, a Black Man, Who Lived Forty Years in Maryland, South Carolina and Georgia, as a Slave. . . .* New York: J. S. Taylor, 1837.
  Religious conditions ca. 1800: pp. 164–65, 201–3.
Bancroft, Frederic. *Slave Trading in the Old South.* Baltimore: J. H. Furst, 1931.
  Advertisement for slave fiddler: p. 155.
Barclay, Alexander. *A Practical View of the Present State of Slavery in the West Indies; or, An Examination of Mr. Stephen's "Slavery of the British West India Colonies:" Containing More Particularly an Account of the Actual Condition of the Negroes in Jamaica. . . .* 3rd ed., with additions. London: Smith, Elder, 1828.
  African and Creole instruments: pp. 10–11.
Barrow, David C. "A Georgia Corn-Shucking." *Century Magazine* 24, n.s. 2 (Oct., 1882): [873]–78.
  Corn songs, including five texts and music of two.
Barry, William. *A History of Framingham, Massachusetts . . .* Boston: J. Munroe, 1847.
  "Nero Benson, slave," trumpeter, 1725: p. 63n.
Bascom, William R., and Herskovitz, Melville J., eds. *Continuity and Change in African Cultures.* Chicago: University of Chicago Press, 1968.
  Satire in African music: pp. 51, 55.
Bassett, John Spencer. *Slavery in the State of North Carolina.* Baltimore: Johns Hopkins Press, 1899.
  African singing: pp. 92–93; free Negro fiddlers: p. 359.

Bastide, Roger. *African Civilizations in the New World*. Trans. Peter Green. New York: Harper, c 1971.
African drum in Virginia: pp. 11–12.
———. *Les Amériques Noires. Les Civilizations Africaines dans le Nouveau Monde*. Paris: Payot, 1967.
African drum in Virginia: p. 18.
Bayley, Frederic William Naylor. *Four Years' Residence in the West Indies, during the Years 1826, 7, 8, and 9*. London: W. Kidd, 1832.
African music and dancing: p. 437.
Bear, James A., Jr., ed. *Jefferson at Monticello*. Charlottesville: University Press of Virginia, c 1967.
Interracial fife and drum team: pp. 7, 10.
Beckford, William. *A Descriptive Account of the Island of Jamaica*. . . . London: Printed for T. & J. Egerton, 1790.
African instruments in Jamaica: I, 216–20; II, 387; worksongs: II, 120–21.
———. *Remarks Upon the Situation of Negroes in Jamaica, Impartially Made from a Local Experience of Nearly Thirteen Years in That Island*. . . . London: Egerton, 1788.
Slave funerals: p. 82; singing and dancing by newly arrived slaves: p. 10.
Beckwith, Martha Warren. *Black Roadways: A Study of Jamaican Folk Life*. Chapel Hill: University of North Carolina Press, 1929.
"The Burial of the Dead": pp. [70]–87.
Bellinger, Lucius. *Stray-Leaves from the Port-folio of a Local Preacher*. Macon, Ga.: Printed for the Author by J. W. Burke, 1870.
Methodist meeting, S.C., ca. 1830: p. 17.
Benners, Alfred H. *Slavery and Its Results*. Macon, Ga.: J. W. Burke, 1923.
Black fiddler, instrumental group: pp. 22, 25–26.
Berjot, Eugène. *Un Voyage à la Nouvelle-Orléans*. [N.p., 184–?]
"La place Congo": p. 16.
Bernard, John. *Retrospections of America, 1797–1811*. Edited from the manuscript of Mrs. Bayle Bernard. New York: Harper & Brothers, 1887.
Negro dancing, ca. 1800: pp. 207, 214.
Bernhard Karl, Duke of Saxe-Weimar-Eisenach. *Travels Through North America, During the Years 1825 and 1826*. Philadelphia: Carey, Lea & Carey, 1828.
Tambourine & violins playing for a dance: I, 212.
[Berquin-Duvallon.] *Travels in Louisiana and the Floridas, in the Year 1802, Giving a Correct Picture of Those Countries*. Translated from the French, with notes, &c., by John Davis. New York: I. Riley, 1806.
Negro fiddlers: p. 27.
Berquin-Duvallon. *Vue de la Colonie Espagnole du Mississippi; ou, Des Provinces de Louisiane et Floride Occidentale en l'Année 1802, par un Observateur Résident sur les Lieux*. . . . B——- Duvallon, éditeur. Paris: A l'Imprimerie Expéditive, 1803.
Worksongs in Louisiana and Saint-Domingue: p. 274; Negro fiddlers: p. 32.
Bibb, Henry. *The Narrative of the Life and Adventures of Henry Bibb, an American Slave, Written by Himself*. With an introduction by Lucius Matlock. New York: Pub. by the Author, 1849.
Patting "juber" and banjo playing: p. 23.
Billington, Ray Allen. *Frederick Jackson Turner: Historian, Scholar, Teacher*. New York: Oxford University Press, 1973.
Turner's opinion of Allen as historian: pp. 26, 31.
Blake, James P. Letter to "Miss Stevenson." *The Freedmen's Record* 1 (Feb., 1865): 28.
Boat songs.
Blome, Richard. *The Present State of His Majesties Isles and Territories in America, Vis. Jamaica, Barbados, S. Christophers, Mevis [sic], Antego, S. Vincent, Dominica, New-Jersey, Pensilvania [sic], Monserat, Anguilla, Bermudas, Caro-*

lina, Virginia, New-England, Tobago, New-Found-Land, Mary-Land, New-York.
... London: Printed by H. Clark, for D. Newman, 1687.
African dancing in Barbados: pp. 39–40.

Board of Music Trade of the United States of America. *Complete Catalogue of Sheet Music and Musical Works, 1870.* Reprinted, New York: Da Capo Press, 1973.
Editions of "Song of the Negro Boatmen": p. 121.

Bodichon, Barbara Leigh Smith. *An American Diary, 1857-8.* Edited from the manuscript by Joseph W. Reed, Jr. London: Routledge & Kegan Paul, 1972.
Nurse distracting a child by singing while dressing it: pp. 120–21.

Botume, Elizabeth Hyde. *First Days amongst the Contrabands.* Boston: Lee and Shepard, 1893.
Singing while grinding hominy: pp. 135–36; sitting with the dead and black funeral: pp. 222–23.

Boucher, Jonathan. *Boucher's Glossary of Archaic and Provincial Words. A Supplement to the Dictionaries of the English Language, Particularly Those of Dr. Johnson and Dr. Webster.* ... London: Printed for Black, Young and Young, 1832.
Bandore: p. xlix, BAN.

Brackett, Jeffrey R. *The Negro in Maryland; a Study of the Institution of Slavery.* Baltimore: N. Murray, 1889.
Prohibition of Sunday gatherings of slaves: p. 100.

Bradford, Sarah (Hopkins). *Harriet, the Moses of her People.* New York: J. J. Little, 1901.
Songs as signals on the Underground Railroad: pp. 27–28, 51–52, passim.

Braunholtz, Hermann Justus. *Sir Hans Sloane and Ethnography.* London: Trustees of the British Museum, 1970.
African drum from Virginia: p. 35, plate 17.

Bremer, Fredrika. *America of the Fifties: Letters of Fredrika Bremer,* selected and edited by Adolph B. Benson. New York: American-Scandinavian Foundation, 1924.
Boat songs: p. 150; attribution of minstrel songs to slaves: pp. 141–42.

————. *The Homes of the New World; Impressions of America.* Trans. Mary Howitt. New York: Harper & Brothers, 1853.
African dancing in Cuba: II, 325–28, 379–83, 410–11; comparison of Cuba and U.S.: II, 442–44, 450; singing of tobacco workers: II, 509–10; singing of firemen aboard a Mississippi steamboat: II, 174; camp meeting, 1850: I, 306–17; black evening worship, Columbia, S.C., 1850: I, 393–94; disapproval of dancing: I, 285, 289–90; black churches in Cincinnati: II, 157–60.

Brewer, James Howard. "Legislation Designed to Control Slavery in Wilmington and Fayetteville." *North Carolina Historical Review* 30 (Apr., 1953): 155–66.
Prohibition of slave dancing: p. 160.

Bridenbaugh, Carl and Roberta. *No Peace Beyond the Line; the English in the Caribbean, 1624-1690.* New York: Oxford University Press, 1972.
Balafo in Barbados: p. 235.

[Brown, David.] *The Planter; or, Thirteen Years in the South.* Philadelphia: H. Hooker, 1853.
Boat songs: pp. 85–87.

Brown, Henry Box. *Narrative of the Life of Henry Box Brown, Written by Himself.* 2nd English ed. Bilston: Printed by S. Webb, 1852.
Tobacco workers in Richmond singing hymns: pp. 17–21.

Brown, William J. *The Life of William J. Brown of Providence, R.I.* ... Providence: Angell, 1883.
Black bands: pp. 54–81.

Brown, William Wells, comp. *The Anti-Slavery Harp: A Collection of Songs for Anti-Slavery Meetings.* 2nd ed. Boston: B. Marsh, 1849.
"Song of the Coffle Gang": p. 29.

_____. *My Southern Home: Or, The South and Its People.* Boston: A. G. Brown, 1880.
Marching song with text: p. 96; street cries: pp. 209–11; corn songs: pp. 91–95.
Bruce, Philip Alexander. *Social Life of Virginia in the Seventeenth Century.* 1907; reprinted, New York: F. Ungar, 1964.
Slave fiddler in 1690's: pp. 181–84.
Bruner, Peter. *A Slave's Adventures toward Freedom: The True Story of a Struggle.* Oxford, Ohio, [n.d.].
Slave coffle singing on river boat: p. [11].
Bryant, William Cullen. *Letters of a Traveller; or, Notes of Things Seen in Europe and America.* New York: G. P. Putnam, 1850.
"Making time with sticks": pp. 86–87; corn songs: pp. 84–87.
_____. "A Tour in the Old South," in *Travels, Addresses, and Comments,* v. II of his *Prose Writings.* Ed. Parke Godwin. New York: D. Appleton, 1889.
Singing of tobacco workers: II, 25–26.
Bryce, C. A., M.D. "Dusky 'Fiddlers' of Olden Days Tenderly Recalled. . . ." *Richmond Times-Dispatch,* May 22, 1921, p. 5. Clipping in files of Valentine Museum, Richmond, Va.
[Buechler, Johann Ulrich.] *Land- und Seereisen eines St. Gallischen Kantonsbürgers nach Nordamerika and Westindien . . . Naschet, Battonrouge und Neu-Orleans am Mississippi . . . in den Jahren 1816, 1817 und 1818 . . .* St. Gallen: Huber, 1820.
Slave dancing in New Orleans: pp. 129–30, 160–61.
[Burwell, Letitia M.] *Plantation Reminiscences,* by Page Thacker [pseud.]. [N.p., n.d.]
African death customs in Virginia: p. 57.
Busch, Moritz. *Travels Between the Hudson & the Mississippi, 1851–1852.* Trans. and ed. Norman H. Binger. Lexington: University Press of Kentucky, 1971.
This English translation omits Busch's chapter on Negro songs.
_____. *Wanderungen zwischen Hudson und Mississippi, 1851 und 1852.* Stuttgart: J. G. Cotta, 1854.
Discussion and German translation of "Negro songs," largely minstrel songs: I, [250]–80.
Bushnell, David I. "The Sloane Collection in the British Museum." *American Anthropologist,* n.s. 8 (1906): 671–85.
African drum from Virginia: pp. 676–77.
Butt, Martha Haines. *Antifanaticism: A Tale of the South.* Philadelphia: Lippincott, Grambo, 1853.
Reply to *Uncle Tom's Cabin* with much synthetic dancing and singing.
Cade, John B. "Out of the Mouths of Ex-Slaves." *Journal of Negro History* 20 (July, 1935): 294–337.
Slave instrumentalists: pp. 333–34; restrictions on singing: p. 327.
Caines, Clement. *The History of the General Council and General Assembly of the Leeward Islands, which Were Convened for the Purpose of Investigating and Ameliorating the Condition of the Slaves Throughout those Settlements and of Effecting a Gradual Abolition of the Slave Trade.* Basseterre, St. Christopher: Printed by R. Cable, 1804.
Worksongs: pp. 110–11.
Candler, Allen D., comp. *The Colonial Records of the State of Georgia. . . .* Atlanta: C. P. Byrd, 1913.
Drumming in the Stono insurrection: XXII, pt. 2, pp. 231–34.
Canot, Theodore. *Captain Canot; or, Twenty Years of an African Slaver. . . .* Written out and ed. from the Captain's Journals, Memoranda, and Conversations by Brantz Mayer. New York: D. Appleton, 1854. Reprinted, 1968.
Slave dancing aboard ship: pp. 99–104.

Cappon, Lester J., and Duff, Stella F. *Virginia Gazette Index, 1736–1780*. Williamsburg, Va.: Institute of Early American History and Culture, 1950.
Numerous references to slaves as musicians.

Carmichael, Mrs. A. C. *Domestic Manners and Social Conditions of the White, Coloured and Negro Population of the West Indies.* . . . London: Whittaker, Treacher, 1833.
African and Creole dances: I, 292.

Carpenter, Russell Lant. *Observations on American Slavery After a Year's Tour in the United States*. London: E. T. Whitfield, 1852.
Evening religious meeting of blacks, Charleston, 1851: pp. 33–37.

Carse, Adam. *The Life of Jullien.* . . . Cambridge, England: W. Heffer & Sons, 1951.
Thomas Baker: pp. 76–78.

Cassidy, Frederic Gomes, and Le Page, Robert B. *Dictionary of Jamaican English.* Cambridge: University Press, 1967.
Balafo: p. 21.

_____. " 'Hipsaw' and 'John Canoe.' " *American Speech* 41 (Feb., 1966): 45–51.

Castelnau, Francis de. "Comte de Castelnau in Middle Florida 1837–1838: Notes Concerning Two Itineraries from Charleston to Tallahassee" and "Essay on Middle Florida, 1837–1838." Trans. Arthur R. Seymour, *Florida Historical Quarterly* 26 (Jan., 1948): 199–255; (Apr., 1948): 300–324.
African-like instruments: p. 243.

Cate, Margaret Davis. *Early Days of Coastal Georgia*. [3rd ed.] St. Simons Island, Ga.: Fort Frederica Association, 1962.
Rice flailing song: p. 117.

_____. *Our Todays and Yesterdays: A Story of Brunswick and the Coastal Islands.* Rev. ed. Brunswick, Ga.: Glover Bros., 1930.
Boat songs: pp. 157–58.

Catterall, Helen Tunnicliff, ed. *Judicial Cases Concerning American Slavery and the Negro*. Washington: Carnegie Institution, 1926–37.
Slave professional musicians: I, 365–68; slave dancing: II, 139–41.

Caulkins, Frances Mainwaring. *History of Norwich, Connecticut: From the Possession by the Indians, to the Year 1866.* [Hartford:] Published by the Author, 1866.
Pinkster: p. 330.

Chambers, Ephraim. *Cyclopaedia; or, An Universal Dictionary of Arts and Sciences.* . . . London: Printed for J. and J. Knapton [et al.], 1728.
Slaves dancing aboard ship: II, 623.

[Champigny, Jean Bochart, Chevalier de.] *The Present State of the Country and Inhabitants, European and Indians, of Louisiana.* . . . London: Printed for J. Millan, 1744.
Bare mention of blacks: p. 26.

Chanvalon, Jean Baptiste Thibaut de. *Voyage à la Martinique, Contenant Diverses Observations sur la Physique, l'Histoire Naturelle, l'Agriculture, les Moeurs et les Usages de Cette Isle, Faites en 1751 et dans les Années Suivantes*. Paris: J. B. Bauche, 1763.
Worksongs: p. 67.

Charleston. Citizens. *Proceedings of the Meeting in Charleston, S.C., May 13–15, 1845, on the Religious Instruction of the Negroes, Together with the Report of the Committee and the Address to the Public*. Charleston, S.C.: Printed by B. Jenkins, 1845.
Black religious meetings: pp. 34–35, 51–55.

Chesnut, Mary Boykin. *A Diary from Dixie*. Ed. Ben Ames Williams. Boston: Houghton Mifflin, c 1949.
Black religious meeting: pp. 148–49.

Child, Lydia Maria. *An Appeal in Favor of that Class of Americans Called Africans.* New York: J. S. Taylor, 1836.

Slave coffle, marching to two violins: p. 33.

————. "Charity Bowery." In *The Liberty Bell. By Friends of Freedom.* Ed. Maria W. Chapman. Boston: American Anti-Slavery Society, 1839, pp. 26–43.

Suppression of black singing after Nat Turner insurrection: pp. 42–43.

Clark, George W. *The Liberty Minstrel.* 5th ed. New York: Published by the Author, 1846.

"Song of the Coffle Gang": pp. 22–23.

Clarke, Samuel. *A True and Faithful Account of the Four Chiefest Plantations of the English in America. To Wit, of Virginia, New-England, Bermudus, Barbados. . . .* London: Printed for R. Clavel [et al.], 1670.

African music and dancing: p. 69.

[Clarkson, Thomas.] *An Essay on the Slavery and Commerce of the Human Species, Particularly the African, Translated from a Latin Dissertation, which was Honoured with the First Prize in the University of Cambridge, for the Year 1785, with Additions.* London: Printed by J. Phillips, 1786.

African music: p. 170.

————. *The Substance of the Evidence of Sundry Persons on Slave-Trade. Collected in the Course of a Tour Made in the Autumn of the Year 1788.* London: J. Phillips, 1789.

Singing and dancing the slaves: pp. 14, 18, 20, 32, 35–36, 44–45, 53, 65, 76, 134–35.

Clay, Thomas Savage. *Detail of a Plan for the Moral Improvement of Negroes on Plantations.* Read before the Georgia Presbytery. [N.p.:]Printed by the Presbytery [of Bryan County, Ga.], 1833.

"Lining-out": p. 4.

Clinkscales, John George. *On the Old Plantation: Reminiscences of His Childhood.* Spartanburg, S.C.: Band & White, 1916.

Conversion of a Negro fiddler: pp. 8–12.

Coffin, Charles Carleton. *Four Years of Fighting: A Volume of Personal Observation with the Army and Navy, from the First Battle of Bull Run to the Fall of Richmond.* Boston: Ticknor and Fields, 1866.

Black church service and praise meeting: pp. 224–31.

Coffin, Levi. *Reminiscences of Levi Coffin, the Reputed President of the Underground Railroad, Being a Brief History of the Labors of a Lifetime in Behalf of the Slave.* Cincinnati: Western Tract Society, c 1876.

"Plantation songs, or hymns," 1821: pp. 69–71.

Cohen, Hennig. "A Negro 'Folk Game' in Colonial South Carolina." *Southern Folklore Quarterly* 16 (Sept., 1952): 183–84.

Derisive singing and dancing at a clandestine gathering.

————. *The South-Carolina Gazette: 1732–1775.* Columbia: University of South Carolina Press, 1953.

Coke, E. T. *A Subaltern's Furlough; Descriptive of Scenes in Various Parts of the United States, Upper and Lower Canada, New-Brunswick, and Nova Scotia, during the Summer and Autumn of 1832. . . .* New York: J. & J. Harper, 1833.

Black musicians, Lebanon Springs, 1832: I, 204.

Coker, Daniel. *A Dialogue between a Virginian and an African Minister, Written by the Rev. Daniel Coker, a Descendant of Africa, Minister of the African Methodist Episcopal Church in Baltimore. Humbly Dedicated to the People of Colour in the United States of America.* Baltimore: Printed by Benjamin Edes for Joseph James, 1810.

Religious conditions ca. 1810: pp. 33–34.

Coleman, J. Winston. *Slavery Times in Kentucky.* Chapel Hill: University of North Carolina Press, 1940.

Corn songs: pp. 70–77.

A Concise Historical Account of All the British Colonies in North-America. . . . Dublin: Printed for C. Jenkin, 1776.

Whites dancing Negro jigs: p. 213.

"Congregational Singing in Richmond, Va." *Dwight's Journal of Music* 18 (Jan. 12, 1861): 333.

Conrad, Georgia Bryan. "Reminiscences of a Southern Woman." *The Southern Workman* 30 (Feb., 1901): [77]–80; (Mar.): [167]–71; (May): 252–57; (June): 357–59; (July): [407]–11.

African songs: 30 (Mar., 1901): 168.

Conway, Moncure Daniel. *Testimonies Concerning Slavery.* By M. D. Conway, a Native of Virginia. London: Chapman and Hall, 1864.

Decline of Negro dances: pp. 3–4.

Cooke, George Willis. *John Sullivan Dwight.* Boston: Small, Maynard, 1898.

Henry Ware's editing *Dwight's Journal of Music*: p. [168].

Cooper, James Fenimore. *Satanstoe; or, The Littlepage Manuscripts. A Tale of the Colony.* (Mohawk ed.) New York: G. P. Putnam's Sons, [n.d.].

Pinkster: pp. 66–67.

Cooper, Thomas. *Facts Illustrative of the Condition of the Negro Slaves in Jamaica: With Notes and an Appendix....* London: J. Hatchard and Son, 1824.

African singing: p. 18n.

Courlander, Harold. *Negro Folk Music, U.S.A.* New York: Columbia University Press, 1963.

Coxe, Elizabeth Allen. *Memories of a South Carolina Plantation during the War ...* [N.p.:] Privately printed, 1912.

Negro church services during Civil War: pp. 54–55; dancing during Civil War: p. 89.

Craigie, Sir William A., and Hulbert, James R., eds. *A Dictionary of American English on Historical Principles.* Chicago: University of Chicago Press, 1942.

Pinkster: III, 1747; corn song: II, 630.

Creecy, James R. *Scenes in the South, and Other Miscellaneous Pieces.* Philadelphia: J. B. Lippincott, 1860.

Congo Square in New Orleans: pp. 19–23.

Creswell, Nicholas. *Journal of Nicholas Cresswell, 1774–1777.* New York: L. Mac-Veagh, Dial Press, 1924.

banjo: p. 19; "everlasting jigs": p. 53; slave funerals in Barbados: p. 40; barbecue with black musicians: p. 30.

Cripe, Helen. *Thomas Jefferson and Music.* Charlottesville: University Press of Virginia, c 1974.

Servants playing for dances: p. 7; Jefferson's lack of interest in music of blacks: p. 92.

[Crouch, Nathaniel.] *The English Empire in America....* 2nd ed. London: Printed for N. Crouch, 1692.

African dancing in Barbados: pp. 176–77.

Criswell, Robert. *Uncle Tom's Cabin Contrasted with Buckingham Hall, the Planter's Home.* New York: D. Fanshaw, 1852.

Synthetic corn songs, with texts: pp. 65–67.

Cuming, Fortescue. *Sketches of a Tour to the Western Country, through the States of Ohio and Kentucky; a Voyage down the Ohio and Mississippi Rivers, and a Trip through the Mississippi Territory, and Part of West Florida. Commenced at Philadelphia in the Winter of 1807, and Concluded in 1809.* Pittsburgh: Cramer, Spear & Eichbaum, 1810.

Drumming and dancing in New Orleans: pp. 333, 336.

Cumming, William P. *British Maps of Colonial America.* Chicago: University of Chicago Press, 1974.

Identity of Thomas Jefferys: p. 45.

Currier, Thomas Franklin. *A Bibliography of John Greenleaf Whittier.* Cambridge, Mass.: Harvard University Press, 1937.

Musical settings of "Song of the Negro Boatman": pp. 582–83.

Curtin, Philip D. *The Atlantic Slave Trade; a Census.* Madison: University of Wisconsin Press, 1969.
Slave statistics: p. 75.
Dalby, David. "The African Element in American English." In Kochman, Thomas, ed., *Rappin' and Stylin' Out; Communication in Urban Black America.* Urbana: University of Illinois Press, 1972.
Derivation of banjo: p. 177.
Darling, James S., arr. *A Little Keyboard Book; Eight Tunes of Colonial Virginia, Set for Piano or Harpsichord.* Williamsburg, Va.: Colonial Williamsburg Foundation, c 1972.
"Congo—A Jig": p. 11.
Davies, Samuel. *Letters from the Rev. Samuel Davies, and Others, Shewing the State of Religion in Virginia, South Carolina, &c. Particularly Among the Negroes.* London: J. and W. Oliver, 1759.
Delight of Negroes in psalmody: pp. 14, 15, 17, 29; lack of religious instruction: p. 9.
———. *The State of Religion Among the Protestant Dissenters in Virginia; in a Letter to the Rev. Mr. Joseph Bellamy, of Bethlem, in New-England.* Boston: Printed by S. Kneeland, 1751.
Conversion of Africans: p. 23.
Davis, John. *Travels of Four Years and a Half in the United States of America; during 1798, 1799, 1800, 1801 and 1802. . . .* London: 1803.
"Banger": pp. 378–79.
———. *Walter Kennedy, an American Tale. . . .* London: Printed for Longman, Hurst, Rees and Orme, 1805.
"Quashee's Seditious Ode": pp. 20–21.
Day, Charles William. *Five Years' Residence in the West Indies.* London: Colburn, 1852.
African drumming and instruments: I, 47.
De Beer, Sir Gavin Rylands. *Jean-Jacques Rousseau and His World.* New York: G. P. Putnam's Sons, 1972.
Creole song in Rousseau's notation: p. 22.
De la Beche, H. T. *Notes on the Present Condition of the Negroes in Jamaica.* London: Printed for T. Cadell, 1825.
African and Creole dances: pp. 40–42.
Dessalles, Adrien. *Histoire Générale des Antilles.* Paris, 1847–48.
African dancing: III, 296–97.
Dickson, William. *Letters on Slavery. . . .* London: Printed by J. Phillips, 1789.
"Banjay": p. 74.
Dillon, Merton Lynn. *The Abolitionists; the Growth of a Dissenting Minority.* De Kalb: Northern Illinois University Press, c 1974.
Abolitionists' lack of interest in black culture: p. 73.
Dixon, James, D. D. *Personal Narrative of a Tour through a Part of the United States and Canada: With Notices of the History and Institutions of Methodism in America.* New York: Lane & Scott, 1849.
Black church services, Pittsburgh, 1848: p. 94.
Dobie, James Frank, ed. *Follow de Drinkin' Gou'd.* Austin: Texas Folklore Society, 1928. Publications no. 7.
"Follow the Drinking Gourd," by H. B. Parks: pp. [81]–84.
"Documents Concerning the Rev. Samuel Thomas, 1702-1707." *South Carolina Historical and Genealogical Magazine* 5 (Jan., 1904): 39–47.
Early conversions in South Carolina.
Donnan, Elizabeth, ed. *Documents Illustrative of the History of the Slave Trade to America.* Washington, D.C.: Carnegie Institution of Washington, 1930–35.
Dorson, Richard M. *American Folklore.* Chicago: University of Chicago Press, 1959.
Evaluation of *Slave Songs of the United States*: pp. 173–74.

Douglass, Frederick. *Life and Times of Frederick Douglass, Written by Himself.* New York: Pathway Press, c 1941. First published in 1893.
Worksongs: pp. 62–63.
———. *My Bondage and My Freedom....* New York: Miller, Orton & Mulligan, 1855.
Worksongs: p. 97.
———. *Narrative of the Life of Frederick Douglass, an American Slave, Written by Himself.* Ed. Benjamin Quarles. Cambridge, Mass.: The Belknap Press of Harvard University Press, 1960. Reprint of the 1845 edition.
Worksongs: pp. 36–38.
Drake, Daniel. *Letters on Slavery to Dr. John C. Warren, of Boston.* Reprinted from the *National Intelligencer,* Washington, Apr. 3, 5, and 7, 1851. New York: Schuman's, 1940.
Slave dance in Kentucky, 1850: pp. 16–17.
Drake, Richard Bryant. "The American Missionary Association and the Southern Negro, 1861–1888...." Ph.D. dissertation, Emory University, 1957.
Beginnings of activity: p. 9.
Dresser, Amos. *The Narrative of Amos Dresser....* New-York: The American Anti-Slavery Society, 1836.
Slave coffle marching to two violins: pp. 6–7.
Duganne, A. J. H. *Camps and Prisons: Two Months in the Department of the Gulf.* New York, 1865.
Black church service, Tigerville, La., 1863: pp. 80, 82.
Dunn, Richard S. *Sugar and Slaves; the Rise of the Planter Class in the English West Indies, 1624–1713.* Chapel Hill: Published for the Institute of Early American History and Culture by University of North Carolina Press, 1972.
African culture: pp. 250ff.
Du Tertre, Jean Baptiste. *Histoire Générale des Antilles Habitées par les François.* ... Paris: T. Iolly, 1667.
First Frenchman to describe the French West Indies, 1658.
African music and dancing in the Antilles: II, 526–27.
Duties of Masters to Servants: Three Premium Essays. I. By the Rev. H. N. McTyeire. II. By the Rev. C. F. Sturgis. III. By the Rev. A. T. Holmes. Charleston, S.C.: Southern Baptist Publication Society, 1851.
Black religious singing: p. 100.
Easterby, James H., ed. "South Carolina Through New England Eyes: Almira Coffin's Visit to the Low Country in 1851." *South Carolina Historical and Genealogical Magazine* 45 (July, 1944): 127–36.
"Lining out": p. 131.
Eaton, Clement. *Freedom of Thought in the Old South.* Durham, N.C.: Duke University Press, 1940.
———. *The Waning of the Old South Civilization, 1860–1880's.* Athens: University of Georgia Press, c 1968.
Biographical information about Daniel Robinson Hundley: p. 4.
Educational Commission for Freedmen. *See* New England Freedmen's Aid Society.
Edwards, Bryan. *The History, Civil and Commercial, of the British Colonies in the West Indies....* London: Printed for J. Stockdale, 1793–1801.
African instruments used aboard slave ships: II, 116; funerals: II, 85; African instruments: II, 84.
"Eighteenth Century Slaves as Advertised by Their Masters." *Journal of Negro History* 1 (Apr., 1916): 163–216.
Runaway slave identified by "banjer": p. 210; fiddles: pp. 176, 181, 206; flute: p. 206.
Emery, Lynne Fauley. *Black Dance in the United States from 1619 to 1970.* Palo Alto, Calif.: National Press Books, 1972.
Emmer, Pieter C. "The History of the Dutch Slave Trade, A Bibliographical Survey." *Journal of Economic History* 32 (Sept., 1972): 728–47.
Slave dancing aboard Dutch ships: pp. 742–43.

Encyclopédie, ou Dictionnaire Raisonné des Sciences, des Arts et des Métiers. Paris: Briasson, 1751–65.
"Calinda": II, 474; "Tamboula": XV, 874; "Balafo": Supplement a l'Encyclopédie.
. . . Amsterdam: M. M. Rey, 1776, I, 759; "Negres": XI, 80.
_____. *Encyclopedia Selections: Diderot, D'Alembert and a Society of Men of Letters.* Trans. Nelly S. Hoyt [and] Thomas Cassirer. Indianapolis: Bobbs-Merrill, c 1965.
Le Romain, author of article on "Tamboula," identified: p. 396.
"An Englishman in South Carolina, December 1860 and July 1862. II." *Continental Monthly* 3 (Jan., 1863): 110–17.
Shout: p. 114.
Epstein, Dena J. "African Music in British and French America." *Musical Quarterly* 59 (Jan., 1973): 61–91.
_____. "The Folk Banjo: A Documentary History." *Ethnomusicology* 19 (Sept., 1975): 347–71.
_____. "Lucy McKim Garrison, American Musician." New York Public Library *Bulletin* 67 (Oct., 1963): 529–46.
_____. "Slave Music in the United States Before 1860: A Survey of Sources, pts. I–II." Music Library Association *Notes* 20 (Spring, 1963): 195–212; (Summer, 1963): 377–90.
Equiano, Olaudah. *The Interesting Narrative of the Life of Olaudah Equiano, or Gustavus Vassa, the African, Written by Himself.* New York: Printed by W. Durrell, 1791.
African music: I, 8.
Evans, Estwick. *A Pedestrian Tour of 4000 Miles in Western and Southwestern States and Territories.* . . . Concord, N.H.: J. C. Spear, 1819. (In Thwaites, Reuben Gold. *Early Western Travels, 1748–1846* . . . Cleveland: A. H. Clark, 1904. Vol. VIII.)
Slave dancing on Sunday in New Orleans: p. 336.
"Every-Day Commerce, Nos. IV and V. Steamboats and Steamboating in the Southwest." *Dollar Magazine* 8 (Oct., 1851): 148–51. Reprinted in Schwaab, Eugene L., ed. *Travels in the Old South, Selected from Periodicals of the Times.* Lexington: University Press of Kentucky, 1973.
"Fire Down Below": II, p. 398.
Ewen, David. *George Gershwin, His Journey to Greatness.* Englewood Cliffs, N.J.: Prentice-Hall, 1970.
Shout: p. 224.
"Extracts from a Letter Written by a Private in Co. F, of the 44th Massachusetts Regiment . . . Newbern, N.C., Nov. 15th, 1862." *The Liberator* 32 (Dec. 12, 1862): 199, col. 3.
Patting juba.
"Extracts from Letters of Teachers and Superintendents, 2d series." Educational Commission for Freedmen, *1st Annual Report.* Boston: D. Clapp, 1863.
Worksongs: p. 31.
Fairfax, Thomas, 9th Baron Fairfax. *Journey from Virginia to Salem, Massachusetts (1799).* London: Printed for Private Circulation, 1936.
Banjo: p. 2.
Falconbridge, Alexander. *An Account of the Slave Trade on the Coast of Africa.* London: Printed by J. Phillips, 1788.
Slave dancing aboard ship: p. 23.
Falconbridge, Anna Maria. *Narrative of Two Voyages to the River Sierra Leone, during the Years 1791-2-3.* 2nd ed. London: Printed for L. I. Higham, 1802. Reprinted [London]: F. Cass, 1967.
Mention of "bangeon": p. 80.
Fancher, Betsy. *The Lost Legacy of Georgia's Golden Isles.* Garden City, N.Y.: Doubleday, 1971.
Black bagpipe player, 1827: pp. 152–53.

Farmer, H. H. *Virginia, Before and During the War.* Henderson, Ky.: Author, 1892.
Christmas dance, Danville, Va., 1855: pp. 17, 29.

Faux, William. *Memorable Days in America.* . . . London: Printed for W. Simpkin and R. Marshall, 1823.
Boat songs in Charleston, 1819: pp. 77–78; black church services: pp. 109, 420.

Fawcett, Benjamin. *A Compassionate Address to the Christian Negroes in Virginia, and Other British Colonies in North America. With an Appendix Containing Some Account of the Rise and Progress of Christianity Among that Poor People.* 2nd ed. [London:] Salop, 1755.
Delight of Negroes in psalmody: p. 37.

Fearon, Henry Bradshaw. *Sketches of America: A Narrative of a Journey of Five Thousand Miles through the Eastern and Western States of America.* London: Longman, Hurst, Rees, Orme and Brown, 1819.
New Orleans ordinances regulating slave dancing and singing, 1817: pp. 276–78.

Featherstonhaugh, George William. *Excursion Through the Slave States from Washington on the Potomac to the Frontier of Mexico, 1834–1835.* London: J. Murray, 1844.
Slave coffle marching to slave fiddling: I, 46.

Federal Writers' Project. *Slave Narratives.* Vol. XVI: Texas, pt. 4 [microfiche of MSS].
African instruments in Louisiana: Wash Wilson narrative.

———. IV: Georgia.
Slave instruments: pt. 4, p. 194; home-made fiddle: p. 200.

———. *See also* Writers' Program.

Fedric, Francis. *Slave Life in Virginia and Kentucky; or, Fifty Years of Slavery in the Southern States of America. By Francis Fedric, An Escaped Slave.* London: Wertheim, Macintosh and Hunt, 1863.
Corn songs: pp. 47–51.

Field, Christopher D. S. "Musical Observations from Barbados, 1647–50." [Ligon's *True & Exact History*] *Musical Times* 115 (July, 1974): 565.

Finch, John. *Travels in the United States of America and Canada.* . . . London: Longman, Rees, Orme, Brown, Green, and Longman, 1833.
Black instrumentalists: pp. 237–38.

Finch, Marianne. *An Englishwoman's Experience in America.* London: R. Bentley, 1853.
Service at African Baptist Church, Richmond: pp. 297–99.

Fishburne, Anne Sinkler. *Belvidere: A Plantation Memory.* Columbia, S.C.: University of South Carolina Press, 1949.
"Native African songs": p. 25.

Fithian, Philip Vickers. *Journal & Letters of Philip Vickers Fithian, 1773–1774; A Plantation Tutor of the Old Dominion.* Edited, with an introduction by Hunter Dickinson Farish. . . . Williamsburg, Va.: Colonial Williamsburg, 1957.
Negro dancing: pp. 61–62; Sunday observance: p. 137.

Flint, Timothy. *Recollections of the Last Ten Years, Passed in Occasional Residences and Journeyings in the Valley of the Mississippi, from Pittsburg and the Missouri to the Gulf of Mexico, and from Florida to the Spanish Frontier.* . . . Boston: Cummings, Hilliard, 1826.
Congo dance in New Orleans: p. 140.

[Flügel, J. G.] "Pages from a Journal of a Voyage down the Mississippi to New Orleans in 1817." Ed. Felix Flugel. *Louisiana Historical Quarterly* 7 (July, 1924): 414–40.
Slave dancing: pp. 427, 432.

Foner, Laura, and Genovese, Eugene D., eds. *Slavery in the New World: A Reader in Comparative History.* Englewood Cliffs, N.J.: Prentice-Hall, c 1969.

Foote, William Henry. *Sketches of North Carolina, Historical and Biographical.* . . . New York: R. Carter, 1846.

Camp meetings, 1802: pp. 391–92, 402–4.

Forten, Charlotte L. *The Journal of Charlotte L. Forten.* Ed. Ray Allen Billington. New York: Dryden Press, c 1953.

Boat songs: pp. 126–28, 157, 161, 169, 170, 173; teaching new songs: pp. 132–33.

———. "Letters from St. Helena's Island, Beaufort, S.C." *Liberator* 32 (Dec. 12, 1862): 199.

Boat songs.

———. "Life on the Sea Islands." *Atlantic Monthly* 13 (May, 1864): 587–96; (June, 1864): 666–76.

Description of a shout: p. 593.

Fortier, Alcée. "Customs and Superstitions in Louisiana." *Journal of American Folklore* 1 (July, 1888): 136–40.

African instruments in Louisiana: pp. 136–137.

———. *Louisiana Studies. Literature, Customs and Dialects, History and Education.* New Orleans: F. F. Hansell & Bro., c 1894.

African instruments in Louisiana: pp. 126–27.

Fossier, Albert A. *New Orleans, The Glamour Period, 1800–1840.* . . . New Orleans: Pelican Publishing Company, c 1957.

Drums and quills in 1811: pp. 368–69.

Francklyn, Gilbert. *An Answer to the Rev. Mr. Clarkson's Essay on the Slavery and Commerce of the Human Species, Particularly the African; in a Series of Letters.* . . . London: Printed at the Logographic Press, 1789.

Negro dancing: pp. 205–6.

Franklin, James. *The Philosophical and Political History of the Thirteen United States of America . . . Also a General Survey of the . . . British American and West Indian Islands.* . . . London: Printed for J. Hinton and W. Adams, 1784.

Whites dancing Negro jigs: p. 91.

Frossard, Benjamin Sigismond. *La Cause des Ésclaves Nègres et des Habitants de la Guinée.* . . . Lyon: A. de la Roche, 1789.

Slave dancing aboard ship: I, 264, 275–76.

Fuller, Richard Frederick. *Chaplain Fuller [Arthur Buckminster Fuller]: Being a Life Sketch of a New England Clergyman and Army Chaplain.* Boston: Walker, Wise, 1864.

Negro sacred songs: pp. 199–200.

G., C. [Caroline Howard Gilman?] "A Ballad. Part First. The Plantation." *The Rose Bud, or Youth's Gazette* 1 (May 18, 1833): [149]–51.

Boat songs.

Garrettson, Freeborn. *The Experience and Travels of Mr. Freeborn Garrettson, Minister of the Methodist-Episcopal Church in North America.* Philadelphia: Printed by P. Hall, 1791.

Negroes in Methodist meetings: p. 76.

[Garrison,] Lucy McKim. "Songs of the Port Royal 'Contrabands.' " *Dwight's Journal of Music* 21 (Nov. 8, 1862): 254–55.

Worksong variety: p. 255.

Garrison, Wendell Phillips. *William Lloyd Garrison, 1805–1879; the Story of His Life Told by His Children.* New York: Century, 1885–89.

Garrison, William Lloyd. *The Letters of William Lloyd Garrison.* Ed. Walter M. Merrill. Cambridge: Belknap Press of Harvard University Press, 1973.

Georgia. Laws, Statutes, etc. *A Codification of the Statute Law of Georgia, Including the English Statutes of Force.* . . . Compiled, digested and arranged, by William A. Hotchkiss, by Authority of the Legislature. Savannah: J. M. Cooper, 1845.

Prohibition of drums and horns: p. 813; ban on black preachers: pp. 814, 840.

Gilman, Arthur. *The Gilman Family Traced in the Line of Hon. John Gilman, of Exeter, N. H.* Albany, N.Y.: J. Munsell, 1869.

Marriage date of Annie Margaret Gilman: p. 114.

Gilman, Caroline Howard. "The Country Visit, Chapter X. Singing Hymns." *The Southern Rose Bud* 2 (Aug. 9, 1834): 199.
Slave children singing hymns.

──────. *Recollections of a Southern Matron.* New York: Harper & Brothers, 1838.
Plantation fiddling: pp. 76–77; black instrumental combination: p. 76; boat songs: pp. 69–70, 106–7.

Gipson, Lawrence Henry. *The British Isles and the American Colonies: The Southern Plantations, 1748–1754.* New York: Knopf, 1960.
Prohibition of beating drums and blowing horns: p. 199.

[Girod-Chantrans, Justin.] *Voyage d'un Suisse dans différentes colonies . . .* Neufchâtel: La Société Typographique, 1785.
African singing in Saint-Domingue: pp. 192–93.

Glassie, Henry. *Pattern in the Material Folk Culture of the Eastern United States.* Philadelphia: University of Pennsylvania Press, 1968.
Fretless banjos: p. 24.

Godkin, Edwin Lawrence. *Life and Letters of Edwin Lawrence Godkin.* Ed. Rollo Ogden. New York: Macmillan, 1907.
Founding of *The Nation*: II, 51–52.

Godwyn, Morgan. *The Negro's & Indians Advocate, Suing for Their Admission into the Church: or, A Persuasive to the Instructing and Baptizing of the Negro's [sic] and Indians in Our Plantations. . . .* London: Printed by F. D., 1680.
Negro dances: p. 33.

[Goldie, William Ferguson.] *Sunshine and Shadow of Slave Life. Reminiscences as Told by Isaac D. Williams to "Tege."* East Saginaw, Mich.: Evening News Printing and Binding House, 1885.
Method of making a banjo: p. 62.

Goslinga, Cornelis Christian. *The Dutch in the Caribbean and on the Wild Coast, 1580–1680.* Gainesville: University of Florida Press, 1971.
Slave dancing on Dutch ships: p. 38.

Gosse, Philip Henry. *Letters from Alabama (U.S.), Chiefly Relating to Natural History.* London: Morgan and Chase, 1859.
Dock workers singing, Mobile, Ala.: p. 306.

Goveia, Elsa V. *Slave Society in the British Leeward Islands at the End of the Eighteenth Century.* New Haven: Yale University Press, 1965.
Prohibition of beating drums or blowing horns: p. 156.

──────. *A Study on the Historiography of the British West Indies to the End of the Nineteenth Century.* Mexico: Instituto Panamericano de Geographia e Historia, 1956. Pub. no. 186.

──────. "The West Indian Slave Laws of the Eighteenth Century." In *Slavery in the New World; A Reader in Comparative History.* Ed. Laura Foner and Eugene D. Genovese. Englewood Cliffs, N.J.: Prentice-Hall, c 1969.
Prohibition of drumming and dancing: pp. 120–21.

Grainger, James. *The Sugar Cane. A Poem in Four Books.* In Alexander Chalmers, *The Works of the English Poets, from Chaucer to Cowper.* London, 1810.
Black dance with "banshaw": XIV, 12, lines 582–99 of book 4.

Grayson, William John. "The Autobiography of William John Grayson." Ed. Samuel Gaillard Stoney. *South Carolina Historical and Genealogical Magazine* 48 (July, 1947): 125–33, (Oct., 1947): 189–97; 49 (Jan., 1948): 23–40ff.
Boat songs: 49: 24–25.

──────. *The Hireling and the Slave, Chicora, and Other Poems.* Charleston: McCarter, 1856.
Jigs at Christmas: p. 52.

Great Britain. Parliament. House of Commons. *Minutes of the Evidence Taken Before a Committee of the House of Commons, Being a Select Committee, Appointed to Take Examination of Witnesses Respecting the African Slave Trade,*

Sessional Papers, 1731–1800.

    Slave dancing aboard ship: XXXIV [London] 1791, pp. 14, 20, 22, 34, 36, 214.

Greene, Welcome Arnold. *The Journals of Welcome Arnold Greene: Journeys in the South, 1822–1824.* Ed. Alice E. Smith. Madison: State Historical Society of Wisconsin, 1957.

    Congo dances in New Orleans: p. 123.

Hachard, Marie Madeleine, Sister St. Stanislas. *Relation du Voyage des Dames Religieuses Ursulines de Rouen, à la Nouvelle Orléans.* Paris: Maisonneuve et Cie, 1872. Originally published in 1728.

Hall, Basil. *Travels in North America, in the Years 1827 and 1828.* Philadelphia: Carey, Lea & Carey, 1829.

    Boat songs: II, 228; religious conditions, 1828: II, 216.

Handler, Jerome S., and Frisbie, Charlotte. "Aspects of Slave Life in Barbados: Music and Its Cultural Context." *Caribbean Studies* 11 (Jan., 1972): 5–46.

Hardee, Charles Seton Henry. "Reminiscences of Charles Seton Henry Hardee." *Georgia Historical Quarterly* 12 (June, 1928): [158]–76ff.

    African songs with English texts: pp. 159, 165–66.

Harden, William. *Recollections of a Long and Satisfactory Life.* Savannah: Review Printing, c 1934.

    Quills: p. 48.

Harris, Joel Chandler. "Plantation Music." *The Critic* 3 (Dec. 15, 1883): 505.

    Quills.

Harris, Marvin. "The Origin of the Descent Rule." In Foner, Laura, and Eugene D. Genovese, eds., *Slavery in the New World: A Reader in Comparative History.* Englewood Cliffs, N.J.: Prentice-Hall, c 1969.

    Population figures: pp. 51–52.

Harrison, Samuel Alexander. "The Civil War Journal of Dr. Samuel A. Harrison." Ed. Charles L. Wagandt. *Civil War History* 13 (June, 1967): 131–46.

    Corn songs: p. 136.

Harrison, William Pope, ed. *The Gospel Among the Slaves. A Short Account of Missionary Operations Among the African Slaves of the Southern States. Compiled from Original Sources.* Nashville, Tenn.: Publishing House of the M. E. Church, South, 1893.

    Beginnings of missionary activity: pp. 137, 149.

Harrower, John. *The Journal of John Harrower, An Indentured Servant in the Colony of Virginia, 1773–1776.* Edited, with an introduction by Edward Miles Riley. Williamsburg, Va.: Colonial Williamsburg, c 1963.

    Balafo: p. 89.

Hart, John Seely. *The Female Prose Writers of America* . . . Philadelphia: E. H. Butler, 1866.

    Caroline Howard Gilman "Autobiography" describing her musical interests: p. 53.

Harvard College. Class of 1861. *Fifth Report.* New York: Printed for the Use of the Class, 1892.

    Biography of Wendell P. Garrison: pp. 45–47.

Harvard Dictionary of Music. 2nd ed., rev. and enl. Cambridge: Belknap Press of Harvard University Press, 1969.

    "Jig": p. 448.

The Harvard Musical Association, 1837–1912. Boston: Press of G. H. Ellis, 1912.

    Offices held by members of the Ware family: pp. [22]–23, [50]–56, 73.

Harvard University. *Historical Register of Harvard University, 1636–1936.* Cambridge: Harvard University, 1937.

    Biography of Charles Ware: p. 447.

Hawkins, William George. *Lunsford Lane; or, Another Helper from North Carolina.* Boston: Crosby & Nichols, 1863.

    Disapproval of the blacks' "native songs": p. 294.

Hecke, J. Valentin. *Reise durch die Vereinigten Staaten von Nord-Amerika im den Jahren 1818 und 1819.* Berlin: In Commission bei H. P. Petri, 1820-21.
Slave dancing on Sunday in New Orleans: II, 155.

Helps, Sir Arthur. *The Spanish Conquest in America, and Its Relation to the History of Slavery and the Government of Colonies.* London: J. W. Parker and Son, 1855.
Description of African singing in Portugal about 1445: I, 38.

Henry, Bessie M. "A Yankee Schoolmistress [Abigail Mason] Discovers Virginia." *Essex Institute Historical Collections* 101 (Apr., 1965): 121-32.
Slave dance, Christmas, 1832: p. 129.

Henry, Howell Meadows. *The Police Control of the Slave in South Carolina.* Emory, Va., 1914.
Restrictions on slave music: p. 150; black funerals: p. 144.

Hensel, William Uhler. *The Christiana Riot and the Treason Trials of 1851; An Historical Sketch.* . . . New York: Negro Universities Press, [1911; reprinted, 1969.]
Corn songs: p. 22.

Hepworth, George H. *The Whip, Hoe and Sword; or, The Gulf Department in '63.* Boston: Walker, Wise, 1864.
Style of singing in black church service: pp. 163-65.

Herbemont, H. "On the Moral Discipline and Treatment of Slaves." *Southern Agriculturist* 9 (Feb., 1836): 70-75.
Opposition to religion, approval of secular music and dancing: pp. 71-74.

Herz, Henri. *Mes Voyages en Amérique.* Paris: A. Faure, 1866.

———. *My Travels in America.* Trans. Henry Bertram Hill. Madison: State Historical Society of Wisconsin for the Department of History, University of Wisconsin, 1963.
Banjo: p. 75.

[Hewatt, Alexander.] *An Historical Account of the Rise and Progress of the Colonies of South Carolina and Georgia.* . . . London: Printed for A. Donaldson, 1779.
African religion and dancing: II, 100, 103; exclusion of the Negroes from the Christian church: II, 98-100.

Higginson, Thomas Wentworth. *Army Life in a Black Regiment.* Boston: Fields, Osgood, 1870.
Dancing, lst S.C. Volunteers, 1862: pp. 23-24.

———. "Drummer Boys in a Black Regiment." *The Youth's Companion* 61 (Sept. 27, 1888): 465.
Singing on the march: p. 465.

———. "Leaves from an Officer's Journal." *Atlantic Monthly* 14 (Nov., 1864): [521]-29; (Dec., 1864): 740-48. Reprinted in his *Army Life in a Black Regiment.* "Shout": pp. 526-27.

———. *Letters and Journals of Thomas Wentworth Higginson, 1846-1906.* Ed. Mary Thacher Higginson. Boston: Houghton Mifflin, 1921.
Ware family: p. 110.

———. "Negro Spirituals." *Atlantic Monthly* 19 (June, 1867): 685-94.

Hildreth, Richard. *The Slave; or, Memoirs of Archy Moore.* Boston: J. H. Eastburn, 1836; reprinted, Upper Saddle River, N.J.: Gregg Press, 1968.
Antagonism between secular music and dancing and evangelical religion: pp. 135-37.

Hobson, Anne. *In Old Alabama; Being the Chronicles of Miss Mouse, the Little Black Merchant.* New York: Doubleday, Page, 1903.
Survival of African animal dances: pp. 111-12, 119, 126; secular elements in sacred songs: pp. 159-60.

[Holland, Edwin Clifford.] *A Refutation of the Calumnies Circulated Against the Southern and Western States, Respecting the Existence of Slavery among Them, to Which is Added a Minute and Particular Account of the Actual Condition of Their Negro Population, by a South Carolinian.* Charleston: A. E. Miller, 1822.

Opposition to missionary activity: pp. 11–12.

Holmes, Isaac. *An Account of the United States of America, Derived from Actual Observation during a Residence of Four Years in that Republic: Including Original Communications.* London: Printed by H. Fisher, 1823.
Congo dance on Sundays in Louisiana in 1821: p. 332.

Hoover, Dwight W., ed. *Understanding Negro History.* Chicago: Quadrangle Books, c 1968.
Horn-blowing in the aftermath of the Vesey plot: p. 80.

[Hopley, Catherine Cooper.] *Life in the South; From the Commencement of the War, by a Blockaded British Subject . . . From the Spring of 1860 to August, 1862.* London: Chapman & Hall, 1863.
Tobacco workers in Richmond singing hymns: I, 152.

Hoppe, Anna. *Negro Slavery; a Review of Conditions Preceding the Civil War.* St. Louis: R. Volkening, 1935.
Satire and improvisation in corn songs: pp. 30–32.

Horsmanden, Daniel. *The New-York Conspiracy, or a History of the Negro Plot, with a Journal of the Proceedings Against the Conspirators at New-York in the Years 1741–4. . . .* New-York: Southwick & Pelsue, 1810.
Negro dancing, fiddling and drumming: pp. 76, 86, 93, 98, 148–49, 192, 213, 238, 255.

Hovey, Sylvester. *Letters from the West Indies: Relating especially to the Danish Island St. Croix, and to the British Islands Antigua, Barbadoes and Jamaica.* New York: Gould & Newman, 1838.
Banjo in St. Croix: p. 36.

Howard, Robert Mowbray, ed. *Records and Letters of the Family of the Longs of Longville, Jamaica, and Hampton Lodge, Surrey.* London: Simpkin, Marshall, Hamilton, Kent, 1925.
Musical background of Edward Long: I, 123.

Howell, George Rogers. *Bi-centennial History of Albany. History of the County of Albany, N.Y., from 1609 to 1886. . . .* New York: W. W. Munsell, 1886.
Pinkster: p. 725.

Howison, John. *European Colonies in Various Parts of the World, Viewed in Their Social, Moral, and Physical Condition.* London: R. Bentley, 1834.
African music: I, 94.

Hubbell, Jay B. *The South in American Literature, 1607–1900.* Durham, N.C.: Duke University Press, 1954.
Corn song by Thomas Holley Chivers, before 1828: p. 555; lack of interest in slave music: pp. 686–87.

Hugill, Stan. *Shanties from the Seven Seas; Shipboard Work-Songs and Songs Used as Work-Songs from the Great Days of Sail.* London: Routledge & Kegan Paul, 1961.
Exchange of songs between blacks and whites: pp. 7–17.

Humphreys, David. *An Historical Account of the Incorporated Society for the Propagation of the Gospel in Foreign Parts . . . to the Year 1728.* London: Printed by J. Downing, 1730.
Opposition to conversion of the slaves: pp. 21–31, 90–91.

Humphreys, Mary Gay. *Catherine Schuyler.* New York: C. Scribner's Sons, 1897; reprinted, 1968.
Pinkster: p. 39.

Hundley, Daniel Robinson. *Social Relations in Our Southern States.* New York: H. B. Price, 1860.
"Wild choruses and lullaloos" from Africa: p. 348; singing by steamboat deckhands: p. 345; results of conversion: p. 349.

Hungerford, James. *The Old Plantation, and What I Gathered There in an Autumn Month.* New York: Harper & Brothers, 1859.
Juber dance: pp. 196–99; boat songs, with two songs, words and music: pp. 183–92.

Hunter, Robert. *Quebec to Carolina in 1785–1786; Being the Travel Diary and Observations of Robert Hunter, Jr.* . . . Ed. Louis B. Wright and Marion Tinling. San Marino, Calif.: Huntington Library, 1943.
Negro fiddler: pp. 179–81, 206–7.

Hurault, Jean. *Africains de Guyane; La Vie Materielle et l'Art des Noirs Refugiers de Guyane.* The Hague: Mouton, c 1970.
Drums similar to Sir Hans Sloane's African drum from Virginia: pl. 40, 42, 47; p. 219.

"The Hymnody of the Blacks." [Unsigned review, written by Lucy McKim Garrison.] *The Independent* 19 (Nov. 28, 1867): p. 2, col. 7–8.

Ibn Khaldùn. *An Introduction to History: The Muqaddimah.* Trans. from the Arabic by Franz Rosenthal; abridged and ed. N. J. Dawood. London: Routledge and Kegan Paul, 1967.
African dancing: p. 63.

The Importance of Jamaica to Great-Britain Consider'd. . . . *In a Letter to a Gentleman.* . . . London: Printed for A. Dodd, [1740?].
African and Creole instruments: p. 19.

[Ingraham, Joseph Holt.] *The South-West. By a Yankee* [pseud.]. New-York: Harper & Brothers, 1835.
Congo Square in New Orleans: I, 162; cane song: I, 241.

Ingraham, Joseph Holt. *The Sunny South; or, The Southerner at Home, Embracing Five Years' Experience of a Northern Governess in the Land of Sugar and Cotton.* Philadelphia: G. G. Evans, 1860. Originally published in a periodical called *Saturday Courier* in 1853–54.
Black instrumental group in Tennessee: p. 106.

Isert, Paul Erdman. *Voyages en Guinée et dans les Iles Caraïbes en Amérique . . . tirés de la correspondance avec ses amis.* Traduits de l'Allemand. Paris: Maradan, 1793.
"Violon des Negres": pp. 207–8.

Jackson, Bruce. *The Negro and His Folklore in Nineteenth Century Periodicals.* Austin: University of Texas Press, 1967.

Jackson, George Pullen. *Spiritual Folk Songs of Early America.* New York: Dover Publications, 1964.

[Jacobs, Mrs. Harriet (Brent).] *Incidents in the Life of a Slave Girl, Written by Herself.* . . . Ed. L. Maria Child. Boston: Published for the Author, 1861.
John Canoe dance in North Carolina: pp. 179–80.

Jamaica. Laws, Statutes, etc. *The Consolidated Slave Law. Passed the 22d December, 1826. Commencing on the lst May, 1827. With a Commentary.* . . . 2nd ed. [N.p.:] Courant Office, 1827.
Prohibition of drums and horns: pp. 19–20.

———. *The New Act of Assembly of the Island of Jamaica . . . Commonly Called the New Consolidated Acts . . . Passed . . . the 6th Day of December, 1788; Being the Present Code Noir of the Island.* Published by Stephen Fuller. London: Printed for B. White and Son, 1789.
Prohibition of drums and horns: p. 7.

James, Horace. *Annual Report of the Superintendent of Negro Affairs in North Carolina, 1864.* . . . Boston: W. F. Brown, 1865.

James, Willis Laurence. *Afro-American Music; A Demonstration Recording* [brochure notes]. Asch Album AA 702, c 1970.
Claim that Africans could not have brought instruments with them to the New World: p. 1.

Janson, Charles William. *The Stranger in America, 1793–1806.* Reprinted from the London edition of 1807; with an introduction and notes by Dr. Carl S. Driver. New York: Press of the Pioneers, 1935.
Negro singing: p. 406.

[Jarratt, Devereux.] *A Brief Narrative of the Revival of Religion in Virginia, in a Letter to a Friend.* . . . London: Printed by R. Hawes, 1778.

Negroes in Methodist meetings: pp. 30–34.

_____. *The Life of the Reverend Devereux Jarratt, Rector of Bath Parish, Dinwiddie County, Virginia, Written by Himself, in a Series of Letters Addressed to the Rev. John Coleman....* Baltimore: Printed by Warner & Hanna, 1806.

Disapproval of dancing and the violin: pp. 7–8, 42–43.

Jefferson, Thomas. *Notes on the State of Virginia, Written in the Year 1781, Somewhat Corrected and Enlarged in the Winter of 1782, for the Use of a Foreigner of Distinction, in Answer to Certain Queries Proposed by Him.* [Paris,] 1782 [1785]. Banjar: p. 257.

Jefferys, Thomas. *The Natural and Civil History of the French Dominions in North and South America....* London: Printed for T. Jefferys, 1760.

"Calendoe," African dance: II, 192.

Jernegan, Marcus W. "Slavery and Conversion in the American Colonies." *American Historical Review* 21 (Apr., 1916): 504–27.

Jobson, Richard. *The Golden Trade; or, A Discovery of the River Gambra, and the Golden Trade of the Aethiopians . . . Set Downe as They Were Collected in Travelling, Part of the Yeares, 1620 and 1621.* London: Printed by N. Okes, 1623.

Music and instruments: pp. 105–8; Balafo: pp. 106–7; hand-clapping: p. 107.

Johns, John. *A Memoir of the Life of the Right Rev. William Meade, D.D., Bishop of the Protestant Episcopal Church in the Diocese of Virginia.* Baltimore: Innes, 1867.

Disapproval of dancing: p. 85.

Johnson, Guion Griffis. *Ante-bellum North Carolina, a Social History.* Chapel Hill: University of North Carolina Press, 1937.

Slave dancing in Raleigh, N.C., 1815; p. 701.

_____. *A Social History of the Sea Islands with Special Reference to St. Helena Island, South Carolina.* Chapel Hill: University of North Carolina Press, 1930.

Johnson, Guy Benton. *Folk Culture on St. Helena Island, South Carolina.* Chapel Hill: University of North Carolina Press, 1930.

Johnston, James Hugo. *Race Relations in Virginia & Miscegenation in the South, 1776–1860.* Foreword by Winthrop Jordan. Amherst: University of Massachusetts Press, 1970.

1734 advertisement for fiddle-playing runaway: p. 276, n. 31; opposition to Negro preachers: pp. 135–36.

Johnstone, Abraham. *The Address of Abraham Johnstone, a Black Man, Who Was Hanged at Woodbury in the County of Glocester, and State of New Jersey, on Saturday the Eighth Day of July Last; to the People of Colour....* Philadelphia, 1797.

Condemnation of "frolicking": p. 28.

Jones, A. M. *Africa and Indonesia; the Evidence of the Xylophone and Other Musical and Cultural Factors.* Leiden: E. J. Brill, 1964.

Jones, Charles Colcock. *Religious Instruction of the Negroes in the United States.* Savannah: T. Purse, 1842.

Teaching hymns: pp. 265–66.

_____. *Suggestions on the Religious Instruction of the Negroes in the Southern States....* Philadelphia: Presbyterian Board of Publication, [n.d.].

Discouragement of spontaneous responses: pp. 39–40; black religious song: p. 56.

Jones, Eldred D. *The Elizabethan Image of Africa.* [Washington, D.C.:] Published for the Folger Shakespeare Library by the University Press of Virginia, 1971.

A convenient summary of English knowledge of Africa at the time of the settlement of North America.

Jones, F. O., ed. *A Handbook of American Music and Musicians....* Canaseraga, N.Y.: 1886; reprinted, New York: Da Capo Press, 1971.

Biography of Carl Wolfsohn: p. 177.

Jones, J. Ralph. "Portraits of Georgia Slaves" [a collection of interviews]. Ed. Tom

Landess. *Georgia Review* 21 (Spring, 1967): 126–32; (Summer, 1967): 268–73; (Fall, 1967): 407–11; (Winter, 1967): 521–25; 22 (Spring, 1968): 125–26; (Summer, 1968): 254–57.
Use of pot to deaden sound: 21 (Spring, 1967): 129, (Summer, 1967): 270.
Jones, Thomas H. *The Experience of Thomas H. Jones, Who Was a Slave for Forty-Three Years. Written by a Friend, as Related to Him by Brother Jones.* New Bedford: E. Anthony & Sons, 1871.
Attempt to suppress a religious meeting: pp. 26–27.
Jordan, Winthrop D. *White Over Black: American Attitudes toward the Negro, 1550-1812.* Chapel Hill: University of North Carolina Press, 1968.
Balafo: p. 303.
Joyaux, George J., ed. "Forest's Voyage aux États-Unis de l'Amérique en 1831." *Louisiana Historical Quarterly* 39 (Oct., 1956): 457–72.
Dancing in New Orleans: p. 468.
Jubilee Songs. See [Seward, Theodore Frelinghuysen, comp.]
Kalm, Peter. *Travels into North America.* Trans. John Reinhold Forster. Barre, Mass.: Imprint Society, 1972.
Rate of conversion of Africans in 1748: pp. 201–2.
Kaplan, Sidney. *The Black Presence in the Era of the American Revolution, 1770-1800.* Washington, D.C.: National Portrait Gallery, 1973.
John Marrant: pp. 95–99.
Kearney, Belle. *A Slaveholder's Daughter.* 6th ed. St. Louis: St. Louis Christian Advocate, 1900.
"Lining out": p. 57.
Kelly, James. *Jamaica in 1831: Being a Narrative of Seventeen Years' Residence in That Island....* Belfast: Printed by J. Wilson, 1838.
African and Creole dances and instruments: pp. 20–21.
Kemble, Frances Anne. *Further Records, 1848-1883; a Series of Letters Forming a Sequel to Records of a Girlhood and Records of Later Life.* New York: Holt, 1891.
James Leigh's visit to Butler's Island.
————. *Journal of a Residence on a Georgian Plantation in 1838-1839.* New York: Harper, 1863.
Prohibition of melancholy songs: p. 129; boat songs: pp. 106–7, 127–29, 159, 218–19; slave dance: pp. 96–97; slave funeral: pp. 112–13.
Kennedy, John Pendleton. *Swallow Barn; or, A Sojourn in the Old Dominion.* Philadelphia: Carey & Lea, 1832.
Banjo playing: I, 110–13.
[Kilham, Elizabeth.] "Sketches in Color." *Putnam's Magazine* 14 (Dec., 1869): 741–46; 15 (Jan., 1870): 31–38; (Feb., 1870): 205–10; (Mar., 1870): 304–11.
Black church service: pp. 304–9.
Killion, Ronald, and Waller, Charles, eds. *Slavery Time When I Was Chillun down on Marster's Plantation: Interviews with Georgia Slaves.* Savannah: Beehive Press, 1973.
Instruments, including quills: pp. 24–25.
[Kingsley, Zephaniah.] *Treatise on the Patriarchal or Co-operative System of Society as it Exists in Some Governments, and Colonies in America, and in the United States, under the Name of Slavery, with its Necessity and Advantages. By an Inhabitant of Florida.* 2nd ed. [N.p.:] 1829.
Tolerance of African customs: pp. 14–15; fear of religion: p. 13.
[Kinnard, J., Jr.] "Who Are Our National Poets?" *Knickerbocker Magazine* 26 (Oct., 1845): 331–41.
Boat songs: p. 338; improvisation: p. 336.
Kmen, Henry A. *Music in New Orleans; the Formative Years, 1791-1841.* Baton Rouge: Louisiana State University Press, 1966.
————. "The Roots of Jazz and the Dance in Place Congo: A Re-appraisal." *Yearbook for Inter-American Musical Research* 8 (1972): 5–16.
[Knight, Henry Cogswell.] *Letters from the South and West, by Arthur Singleton* [pseud.]. Boston: Richardson and Lord, 1824.

Slave funerals in Virginia: p. 75, 77; slave dancing on Sunday in New Orleans, 1819: p. 127.

Knox, William. *Three Tracts Respecting the Conversion and Instruction of the Free Indians and Negro Slaves in the Colonies. Addressed to the Venerable Society for Propagation of the Gospel in Foreign Parts.* [London, 1768.]
Opposition to converting the slaves: p. 36; teaching Negroes to sing hymns: p. 39.

Kochman, Thomas, ed. *Rappin' and Stylin' Out: Communication in Urban Black America.* Urbana: University of Illinois Press, 1972.
Africanisms in American English, including "Bamboula," "Banjo": p. 177.

Krehbiel, Henry Edward. *Afro-American Folksong: A Study in Racial and National Music.* New York: G. Schirmer, c 1914.

Labat, Jean Baptiste. *Nouveau Voyage aux Isles de l'Amerique....* The Hague, 1726.
African music and dancing: IV, 152–60.

Laborde, Jean Benjamin de. *Essai sur la Musique Ancienne et Moderne.* Paris: P. D. Pierres et E. Onfroy, 1780.
Balafo: I, 217–18; banza: I, 291.

Laborie, P. J. *The Coffee Planter of Saint Domingo; with an Appendix....* London: Printed for T. Cadell and W. Davies, 1798.
Dancing to drumming: pp. 157, 178, 181–83.

Lambert, John. *Travels through Canada and the United States, in the Years 1806, 1807 and 1808....* London: C. Cradock and W. Joy, 1814.
Boat songs, with text: II, 253–54.

Lanier, Sidney. *Florida: Its Scenery, Climate, and History.... Being a Complete Hand-book and Guide.* Philadelphia: J. B. Lippincott, 1876.
Characteristics of black music with notation of whistling: pp. 30–31.

———. *The Science of English Verse.* New York: C. Scribner's Sons, c 1880.
Rhythm of patting juba: pp. 186–89, 247.

Lanman, Charles. *Adventures in the Wilds of the United States and British American Provinces.* Philadelphia: J. W. Moore, 1856.
"Fire Down Below": II, 150.

———. *Haw-Ho-Noo; or, The Records of a Tourist.* Philadelphia: Lippincott, Grambo, 1850.
Corn songs: pp. 142–43.

Latrobe, Benjamin Henry Boneval. *Impressions Respecting New Orleans: Diary & Sketches, 1818–1820.* Edited, with an introduction and notes by Samuel Wilson, Jr. New York: Columbia University Press, 1951.
Slave dancing on Sunday: pp. 49–51.

Laussat, Pierre C. de. *Mémoire sur ma Vie Pendant les Années 1803 et Suivantes ... à la Louisianne....* Pau, France, 1831.
Bamboula and contredanse in New Orleans: p. 395.

Lehmann, Theo. *Negro Spirituals: Geschichte und Theologie.* [Berlin?:] Eckart-Verlag, 1965.

Leiding, Harriette Kershaw. *Street Cries of an Old Southern City.* Charleston: [Daggett Printing,] 1910.

Leigh, Frances Kemble (Butler). *Ten Years on a Georgia Plantation since the War.* London: R. Bentley & Son, 1883.
Comments on music: pp. 59, 228–229, 254.

Leigh, James Wentworth. *Other Days....* London: Macmillan, 1921.
Style of singing: pp. 155–57.

Le Jau, Francis. *The Carolina Chronicle of Dr. Francis LeJau, 1706–1717.* Ed. Frank J. Klingberg. Berkeley: University of California Press, 1956.
African dances: pp. 61, 77, 120–21.

Leland, John. *The Virginia Chronicle: With Judicious and Critical Remarks under XXIV Heads....* Norfolk: Printed by Prentis and Baxter, 1790.
Slave religion: p. 11.

Le Page du Pratz. *Histoire de la Louisianne.* Paris: De Bure l'ainé, 1758.
"Calinda," worksongs: I, 352.

———. *The History of Louisiana, or of the Western Parts of Virginia and Carolina*

... Trans. from the French ... A New Edition. London: Printed for T. Becket, 1774.
"Calinda": pp. 380, 384, 387; worksongs: p. 384.

[Leslie, Charles.] *A New History of Jamaica from the Earliest Accounts, to the Taking of Porto Bello by Vice-Admiral Vernon. In Thirteen Letters from a Gentleman to His Friend.* ... London: Printed for J. Hodges, 1740.
Bangil: p. 310; black funerals: pp. 307–10.

A Letter to an American Planter from His Friend in London. London: Printed by H. Reynell, 1781.
Conversion of the Negroes: pp. 5–7.

A Letter to the Right Reverend the Lord Bishop of London, from an Inhabitant of His Majesty's Leeward-Carribee-Islands. In Which is Inserted, A Short Essay Concerning the Conversion of the Negro-Slaves in Our Sugar-Colonies: Written in the Month of June, 1727, by the Same Inhabitant. London: Printed for J. Wilford, 1730.
African singing and dancing: pp. 90–94.

Levine, Lawrence. "Slave Songs and Slave Consciousness." In *American Negro Slavery.* Ed. Allen Weinstein and Frank Otto Gatell. 2nd ed. New York: Oxford University Press, 1973.

Lewis, Matthew Gregory. *Journal of a West India Proprietor, Kept during a Residence in the Island of Jamaica.* ... London: J. Murray, 1834.
African instruments in 1816: pp. 73, 81.

"Life and Travel in the Southern States." *Great Republic Monthly* 1 (1859): 80–84. Reprinted in Schwaab, Eugene L., ed. *Travels in the Old South Selected from Periodicals of the Times.* [Lexington:] University Press of Kentucky, c 1973.
Cotton pickers singing: II, 491.

Ligon, Richard. *A True & Exact History of the Island of Barbados.* London: Printed for H. Moseley, 1657.
African music and dancing: pp. 46–49, 50, 52, 107; balafo: pp. 48–49.

Little, Nina Fletcher. *The Abby Aldrich Rockefeller Folk Art Collection: A Descriptive Catalog.* Boston: Colonial Williamsburg, 1957.
"The Old Plantation": p. 132.

Lofton, John. *Insurrection in South Carolina: The Turbulent World of Denmark Vesey.* Yellow Springs, Ohio: Antioch Press, c 1964.
Victimization of a black boatman accused of blowing his horn: pp. 162–65.

[Long, Edward.] *The History of Jamaica.* ... London: Printed for T. Lowndes, 1774.
African music, instruments and dancing: II, 242–43; style of singing: II, 423; John Canoe: II, 424.

Long, John Dixon. *Pictures of Slavery in Church and State.* 3rd ed. Philadelphia: Author, 1857.
Patting juba: p. 18; worksongs with texts: pp. 197–98; religious songs by blacks: p. 383; camp meeting: pp. 159–60.

Lovell, Caroline Couper. *The Golden Isles of Georgia.* Boston: Little, Brown, 1932.
Boat songs: p. 230.

Lovell, John. *Black Song: The Forge and the Flame; The Story of How the Afro-American Spiritual Was Hammered Out.* New York: Macmillan, c 1972.

Luffman, John. *A Brief Account of the Island of Antigua ... In Letters to a Friend. Written in the Years 1786, 1787, 1788.* London: Printed for T. Cadell, 1789.
African instruments: pp. 135–36.

Lyell, Sir Charles. *A Second Visit to the United States of North America.* New York: Harper & Brothers, 1849.
Boat songs: I, 244–45; disapproval of secular music by missionaries: I, 269–70.

McConnell, Roland C. *Negro Troops of Antebellum Louisiana; A History of the Battalion of Free Men of Color.* Baton Rouge: Louisiana State University Press, c 1968.
Slaves singing Jacobin songs: pp. 26–27.

McCormack, Helen G. "A Provisional Guide to Manuscripts in the South Carolina

Historical Society." *South Carolina Historical and Genealogical Magazine* 47 (Jan., 1946): 53–57.
  MSS contributed by Charles P. Ware: p. 54, Accession No. 452.
McCrady, Edward. *History of South Carolina under the Proprietary Government.* New York: Macmillan, 1901.
  Boat songs: p. 516.
[McDougall, Frances Harriet (Whipple) Greene.] *Shahmah in Pursuit of Freedom; or, The Branded Hand. Translated from the Original Showiah, and Edited by an American Citizen.* New York: Thatcher & Hutchinson, 1858. Reprinted, Freeport, N.Y.: Books for Libraries Press, 1971.
  Patting juba: pp. 276–77.
McDowell, Tremaine. "The Negro in the Southern Novel Prior to 1850." *Journal of English and Germanic Philology* 25 (1926): 455–73.
  Caroline Howard Gilman's writings about Negroes: pp. 463–64.
Mackay, Alexander. *The Western World; or, Travels in the United States in 1846–1847. . . .* 3rd ed. London: R. Bentley, 1850.
  Banjo: II, 133.
McKim, James Miller. *The Freedmen of South Carolina. An Address Delivered by J. Miller M'Kim, in Sansom Hall, July 9th, 1862.* Philadelphia: P. Hazard, 1862.
  Organization of the Port Royal Relief Committee: p. 4.
[McKim, James Miller.] "Negro Songs." *Dwight's Journal of Music* 21 (Aug. 9, 1862): 148–49.
  Reprint of pp. 11–13 of his *Freedmen of South Carolina.*
McKim, Lucy. *See* [Garrison,] Lucy McKim.
McNeilly, James Hugh. *Religion and Slavery; A Vindication of the Southern Churches.* Nashville: Publishing House of the M. E. Church, South, c 1911.
  Black singing at camp meetings: pp. 83–84.
Macpherson, Charles. *Memoirs of the Life and Travels of the Late Charles Macpherson, Esq., in Asia, Africa and America. . . .* Edinburgh: Printed for A. Constable, 1800.
  "Bangah": p. 186.
Madden, Richard Robert. *A Twelvemonth's Residence in the West Indies, During the Transition from Slavery to Apprenticeship. . . .* Philadelphia: Carey, Lea and Blanchard, 1835.
  Black funerals: I, 371 [i.e., 137].
Malet, William Wyndham. *An Errand to the South in the Summer of 1862.* London: R. Bentley, 1863.
  Slave fiddler: p. 49.
Mallard, Robert Q. *Plantation Life before Emancipation.* Richmond, Va.: Whittet & Shepperson, 1892.
  Decline of dancing: pp. 162–63.
"Manner of Living of the Different Ranks of Inhabitants of Virginia. Hardships of the Negro Slaves. Traits of Their Character. Their Passion for Music and Dancing." *American Museum* 1 (Mar., 1787): 245–48.
  "Banjor and quaqua": p. 247.
Marcuse, Sibyl. *Musical Instruments, a Comprehensive Dictionary.* Garden City, N.Y.: Doubleday, 1964.
  Balafo: p. 32; banza: p. 36.
Marly; or, A Planter's Life in Jamaica. Glasgow: R. Griffin, 1828.
  African instruments: pp. 46, 293; John Canoe: pp. 293–94.
Marrant, John. *A Narrative of the Lord's Wonderful Dealings with John Marrant, a Black, (Now Going to Preach the Gospel in Nova Scotia) Born in New York, in North America.* Taken down from His Own Relation, Arranged, Corrected, and Published by the Rev. Mr. Aldridge. London: Printed and sold by Gilbert and Plummer, 1785.

His training as a musician: pp. [7]–11.

[Marsden, Peter.] *An Account of the Island of Jamaica; with Reflections on the Treatment, Occupation, and Provisions of the Slaves . . . By a Gentleman Lately Resident on a Plantation.* Newcastle: Printed for the Author by S. Hodgson, 1788.
Worksongs: p. 36; African dancing: p. 34; acculturated dancing: pp. 33–34.

Martin, François-Xavier. *The History of Louisiana, from the Earliest Period. . . .* New-Orleans: Printed by Lyman and Beardslee, 1827.
Slave amusements restricted to Sunday: II, 112.

Mason, Edward G. "A Visit to South Carolina in 1860." *Atlantic Monthly* 53 (Feb., 1884): 241–50.
Prohibition of drumming at night: p. 244.

Mathews, Mitford McLeod. *A Dictionary of Americanisms on Historical Principles.* Chicago: University of Chicago Press, 1951.
Pinkster: II, 1249.

Meacham, James. "A Journal and Travels of James Meacham. Part I, May 19 to Aug. 31, 1789." Trinity College. *Historical Papers*, ser. 9 (1912): [66]–95.
Slave evangelism: pp. 79, 88, 90, 94.

————. "A Journal and Travels of James Meacham. Part II, 1789–1797." Trinity College. *Historical Papers*, ser. 10 (1914): [87]–102.

Mead, Whitman. *Travels in North America. . . .* New York: Printed by C. S. Van Winkle, 1820.
North Carolina scamper dances, 1817: p. 67; black fiddler: p. 29; stevedores singing, Savannah, 1817: pp. 13–14.

Meade, William. *Sermons Addressed to Masters and Servants, and Published in the Year 1743, by the Rev. Thomas Bacon, Minister of the Protestant Episcopal Church in Maryland. Now Republished with Other Tracts and Dialogues on the Same Subject, and Recommended to All Masters and Mistresses to Be Used in Their Families.* By the Rev. William Meade. Winchester, Va.: J. Heiskell, Printer, [1813?].
Slave dancing aboard ship: "The Sorrows of Yamba," p. 184; opposition to dancing: pp. 197–206.

Memorial, R[obert] G[ould] S[haw]. Cambridge, [Mass.:] University Press, 1864.
Charlotte Forten's efforts to "copy" slave songs: p. 145.

Menard, Russell R. "The Maryland Slave Population, 1658 to 1730: A Demographic Profile of Blacks in Four Counties." *William and Mary Quarterly*, 3rd ser., 32 (Jan., 1975): [29]–54.
Negro drums: p. 37.

Mercier, Alfred. *L'Habitation Saint-Ybars; ou Maîtres et Éscalves en Louisiane, Récit Social.* New Orleans: Imprimerie Franco-Américaine, 1881.
Method for making a "banza": p. 52.

Merolla da Sorrento, Jerom. *A Voyage to Congo . . . by Father Jerom Merolla da Sorrento, a Capuchin and Apostolic Missioner in the Year 1682.* In Pinkerton, John, ed., *A General Collection of the Best and Most Interesting Voyages and Travels in All Parts of the World*, XVI, 195–316. London: Printed for Longman, Hurst, Rees, Orme, and Brown, 1816.
Balafo: p. 245.

Michaux, Richard Rudolph. *Sketches of Life in North Carolina. . . .* Cutler, N.C.: W. C. Phillips, 1894.
Black religion: pp. 23–24.

Middleton, Arthur Pierce. "The Colonial Virginia Parson." *William and Mary Quarterly*, 3rd ser., 26 (July, 1969): [425]–40.
Disapproval of dancing: [425].

"A Mississippi Planter." "Management of Negroes upon Southern Estates." *De Bow's Review* 10 (June, 1851): 621–27.
Patting juba: p. 625; fiddler supplied by planter: *ibid.*

Montule, Edouard de. *A Voyage to North America, and the West Indies, in 1817.*
London: Printed for Sir R. Phillips, 1821.
Worksongs in Santo Domingo: p. 25.
Moody, Vernie Alton. *Slavery on Louisiana Sugar Plantations.* "Reprinted from the
Louisiana Historical Quarterly, April, 1924."
Prohibition of slave drumming or dancing: p. 89.
Moore, Charles. *The Life and Times of Charles Follen McKim.* Boston: Houghton
Mifflin, 1929.
Marriage of Lucy McKim Garrison: p. 15, Appendix I. Chronology: entries for
1865–66.
Moore, J. Roderick. "Folk Crafts." *Arts in Virginia* 12 (Fall, 1971): 22–29.
Fretless banjos in the present day.
Moore, Lillian. "Moreau de Saint-Mery and Danse." *Dance Index* 5 (Oct., 1946):
231–59.
Mordecai, Samuel. *Richmond in By-gone Days; Being Reminiscences of an Old
Citizen.* Richmond: G. M. West, 1856.
Sy Gilliat, black fiddler: p. 251–52, 352–54.
Mordell, Albert. *Quaker Militant: John Greenleaf Whittier.* c 1933; reprinted, Port
Washington, N.Y.: Kennikat Press, 1949.
Evaluation of "At Port Royal": p. 212.
Moreau de Saint-Méry, Médéric Louis Élie. *Déscription Topographique, Physique,
Civile, Politique et Historique de la Partie Française de l'Isle Saint-Domingue....*
Philadelphia: Chez l'Auteur, 1797.
African instruments: I, p. 44; training of Negro fiddlers: I, 51.
————, ed. *Loix et Constitutions des Colonies Françoises de l'Amérique Sous le Vent.*
Paris: l'Auteur, 1784–90.
Laws forbidding African dances: I, 417; IV, 234; V, 384.
Moreton, J. B. *Manners and Customs in the West India Islands....* London: Printed
for W. Richardson, 1790.
Negro dancing and singing: pp. 155–56; worksongs: p. 152.
Morgan, Julia. *How It Was; Four Years Among the Rebels. . . .* Nashville, Tenn.:
Publishing House Methodist Episcopal Church, South, 1892.
Slave jigging, Augusta, Ga., during the war: p. 120.
Mott, A[bigail]. *Biographical Sketches and Interesting Anecdotes of Persons of
Color....* New York: M. Day, Printer, [1839].
Clarinda, black woman fiddler: pp. 74–81.
Mott, Frank Luther. *A History of American Magazines. . . .* Cambridge: Belknap
Press of Harvard University Press, 1938–59.
Founding of *The Nation*: III, 333.
Mousnier, Jehan. *Journal de la Traité des Noirs, Dam Joulin, Charles le Breton la
Vallée, Garneray-Mérimée.* Présente et Commenté par Jehan Mousnier. Paris:
Éditions de Paris, c 1957.
Dancing aboard slave ships: pp. 202–3.
Mullin, Gerald W. *Flight and Rebellion: Slave Resistance in Eighteenth-Century
Virginia.* New York: Oxford University Press, 1972.
————. "Rethinking American Negro Slavery from the Vantage Point of the Colo-
nial Era." *Louisiana Studies* 12 (Summer, 1973): [398]–422.
The Musical Gazette (Boston) 1 (July 6, 1846): 91.
Earliest notice of black religious songs in a musical periodical. Untitled paragraph.
Myers, Robert Manson, ed. *The Children of Pride; A True Story of Georgia and the
Civil War.* New Haven: Yale University Press, 1972.
Black revival meeting, Chattanooga, 1859: pp. 482–83.
Nathan, Hans. *Dan Emmett and the Rise of Early Negro Minstrelsy.* Norman:
University of Oklahoma Press, c 1962.
"Let Us Pity the Poor White Man": pp. 6–7.

The Nation 1 (Aug. 10, 1865): 162;(Oct. 19, 1865): 508.
Notices of Blind Tom.

"Negro Melodies." *De Bow's Review* 18 (Mar., 1855): 335–36.

"Negro Superstition Concerning the Violin." *Journal of American Folk-Lore* 5 (Oct., 1892): 329–30.

Neilson, Peter. *Recollections of a Six Years' Residence in the United States*. . . . Glasgow: D. Robertson, 1830.
Black religious songs with texts: pp. 258–59.

Nettel, Reginald. "Historical Introduction to 'La Calinda.'" *Music & Letters* 27 (Jan., 1946): 59–62.

Nettl, Bruno. *Folk and Traditional Music of the Western Continents*. Englewood Cliffs, N.J.: Prentice-Hall, c 1965.
Quills in Africa: p. 140; "African Music South of the Sahara": pp. 118–46.

New England Freedmen's Aid Society. *Extracts from Letters of Teachers and Superintendents of the New England Educational Commission for Freedmen*, 4th ser., Jan., 1864. Boston: D. Clapp, Printer, 1864.
Children singing "native" and new songs in school: p. 11.

New Orleans. Ordinances, etc. *Police Code, or Collection of the Ordinances of Police Made by the City Council of New-Orleans*. . . . New-Orleans: Printed by J. Renard, 1808.
Slave funerals, dancing and singing: pp. 48–50, 254.

[Nisbet, Richard.] *Slavery Not Forbidden by Scripture. Or, A Defence of the West-India Planters, from the Aspersions Thrown out against Them, by the Author of a Pamphlet, Entitled, "An Address to the Inhabitants of the British Settlements in America, upon Slave-keeping." By a West-Indian*. . . . Philadelphia, 1773.

Nissen, Johan Peter. *Reminiscences of a 46 Years' Residence in the Island of St. Thomas, in the West Indies*. Nazareth, Pa.: Senseman, 1838.
African music and dancing: p. 165.

Nordhoff, Charles. *The Freedmen of South Carolina: Some Account of Their Appearance, Character, Condition and Peculiar Customs*. New York: C. T. Evans, 1863.
Appreciation of the blacks' "native songs": pp. 9–10.

Norman, Benjamin Moore. *Norman's New Orleans and Environs, Containing a Brief Historical Sketch of Louisiana, and the City of New Orleans*. New Orleans: B. M. Norman, 1845.
"Circus Place . . . once known as Congo Park": p. 182.

Northup, Solomon. *Twelve Years a Slave: The Narrative of Solomon Northup, a Citizen of New-York, Kidnapped in Washington City in 1841 and Rescued in 1853, from a Cotton Plantation near the Red River in Louisiana*. Auburn, N.Y.: Derby and Miller, 1853.
Patting juba: p. 219; life of a slave fiddler: pp. 216–17.

Nugent, Lady Maria (Skinner). *Lady Nugent's Journal of Her Residence in Jamaica from 1801 to 1805*. A new and revised edition by Philip Wright. Kingston: Institute of Jamaica, 1966.
African instruments, including a nose flute: pp. 75, 219.

"OP Publishing: The New Look in Reprints." *Saturday Review* 48 (June 12, 1965): 37.
Slave Songs reprinted.

"The Old Plantation: A Poem." *The Countryman* 3 (Nov. 24, 1862): [65].
Corn song.

Oldmixon, John. *The British Empire in America, Containing the History of the Discovery, Settlement, Progress and Present State of All the British Colonies on the Continent and Islands of America*. London: J. Brotherton, 1708.
African religion, instruments and music in Barbados: I, 113, 118, 122–24.

Oliphant, Laurence. *Patriots and Filibusters; or, Incidents of Political & Exploratory Travel.* Edinburgh: W. Blackwood and Sons, 1860.
Negro spirituals: pp. 140–43.
Oliver, Paul. *Savannah Syncopators: African Retentions in the Blues.* New York: Stein and Day, 1970.
Includes a fascinating discussion of the professional musicians of twentieth-century Senegal, the *griots.*
Olmsted, Frederick Law. *The Cotton Kingdom.* Edited, with an introduction, by Arthur M. Schlesinger. New York: Knopf, 1953.
Singing by steamboat deckhands: pp. 270–71.
————. *A Journey in the Seaboard Slave States in the Years 1853–1854, with Remarks on Their Economy.* . . . New York: G. P. Putnam's Sons, 1904. Originally published in 1856.
Field holler: II, 19–20; black funeral: I, 26–29.
Olson, Edwin. "Social Aspects of the Slave in New York." *Journal of Negro History* 26 (Jan., 1941): 66–77.
Pinkster: pp. 71–72.
O'Neall, John Belton. *The Negro Law of South Carolina.* Columbia: Printed by J. G. Bowman, 1848.
Black religious meetings: p. 24.
Owen, Nicholas. *Journal of a Slave-Dealer.* "A View of Some Remarkable Axcedents in the Life of Nics. Owen on the Coast of Africa and America from the Year 1746 to the Year 1757." Edited, with an introduction, by Eveline Martin. Boston: Houghton Mifflin, 1930.
Mention of "bangelo" and drums: p. 52.
Padgett, James A. "A Yankee School Teacher in Louisiana, 1835–1837: The Diary of Caroline B. Poole." *Louisiana Historical Quarterly* 20 (July, 1937): [651]–79.
Blacks mourning for the dead: p. 677.
Page, John W. *Uncle Robin in His Cabin in Virginia, and Tom Without One in Boston.* Richmond: J. W. Randolph, 1853.
Disapproval of dancing: pp. 155, 159ff.
Paine, Lewis W. *Six Years in a Georgia Prison. Narrative of Lewis W. Paine, Who Suffered Imprisonment Six Years in Georgia, for the Crime of Aiding the Escape of a Fellowman from that State, after He had Fled from Slavery. Written by Himself.* New York: Printed for the Author, 1851.
"Patting juber": pp. 179–80.
Parrish, Mrs. Lydia (Austin). *Slave Songs of the Georgia Sea Islands.* Music transcribed by Creighton Churchill and Robert MacGimsey. New York: Creative Age Press, 1942.
Ring shout: pp. 54–[92].
Parsons, Charles Grandison. *Inside View of Slavery; or A Tour among the Planters.* Boston: J. P. Jewett, 1855.
Blacks singing religious songs in a circle: p. 276.
Patten, J. Alexander. "Scenes in the Old Dominion. Number Two—A Tobacco Market." *New York Mercury* 21 (Nov. 5, 1859): 8. Reprinted in Schwaab, Eugene, ed., *Travels in the Old South, Selected from Periodicals of the Times.* [Lexington:] University Press of Kentucky, 1973.
Negro whistling: II, 541.
[Paulding, James Kirke.] *Letters from the South. By a Northern Man.* New York: Harper & Brothers, 1835.
Banjo: I, 97.
Pavie, Théodore M. *Souvenirs Atlantiques. Voyage aux États-Unis et au Canada.* Paris: Roret, 1833.
African dancing and instruments: II, 319–20.

Pearse, James. *A Narrative of the Life of James Pearse.* . . . Rutland, [Vt.:] Printed by W. Fay for the Author, 1825.
"Lining-out": p. 10.

Pearson, Elizabeth Ware, ed. *Letters from Port Royal, Written at the Time of the Civil War.* Boston: W. B. Clarke, 1906.
Boat songs: pp. 134, passim.

Peck, John Mason. *Forty Years of Pioneer Life. Memoir.* . . . Edited from His Journals and Correspondence by Rufus Babcock. Philadelphia: American Baptist Publication Society, c 1864.
Slave dancing on Sunday in St. Louis, 1818: p. 90.

Pennington, James W. C. *The Fugitive Blacksmith; or, Events in the History of James W. C. Pennington, Pastor of a Presbyterian Church, New York, Formerly a Slave in the State of Maryland, United States.* London: C. Gilpin, 1849.
Religious conditions before 1827: pp. 66–68.

Perry, William Stevens, ed. *Historical Collections Relating to the American Colonial Church. V. 1: Virginia.* [N.p.,] 1870.
Reports of the colonial clergy on the infidels in their parishes: pp. 265, 267, 278, 283.

Peytraud, Lucien. *L'Esclavage aux Antilles avant 1789, d'après des documents inédits des Archives Coloniales.* Paris: Hachette, 1897.
"Calinda": pp. 232–35.

Phillippo, James Mursell. *Jamaica: Its Past and Present State.* With a new introduction by Philip Wright. 1843; reprinted, London: Dawsons, 1969.
African music and dancing: pp. 241–43.

Phillips, Thomas. "A Journal of a Voyage Made in the Hannibal of London, Ann. 1693–1694, from England to Cape Monseradoe, in Africa; and Thence along the Coast of Guiney to Whidaw, the Island of St. Thomas, and so forward to Barbadoes." Reprinted in *Documents Illustrative of the History of the Slave Trade to America.* Ed. Elizabeth Donnan. Washington, D.C.: Carnegie Institution of Washington, 1930–35.
Slaves dancing aboard ship: I, 392.

Phillips, Ulrich Bonnell. *American Negro Slavery; a Survey of the Supply, Employment and Control of Negro Labor as Determined by the Plantation Regime.* c 1918; reprinted, Baton Rouge: Louisiana State University Press, 1969.
Approval of dancing: p. 315.

[Pierce, Edward Lillie.] "The Contrabands at Fortress Monroe." *Atlantic Monthly* 8 (Nov., 1861): 626–40.
————. *Major John Lillie, 1755–1801. The Lillie Family of Boston, 1663–1896.* Revised ed. Cambridge: J. Wilson and Son, 1896.
Identification of Eliza Dodge and Annie Bowen: p. 114.

Pilcher, George William. *Samuel Davies, Apostle of Dissent in Colonial Virginia.* Knoxville: University of Tennessee Press, 1971.
Delight of Negroes in psalmody: p. 112.

Pinckard, George. *Notes on the West Indies.* 2nd ed. London: Baldwin, Cradock and Joy, 1816.
Slave dancing aboard ship: I, 97–103.

The Planter; or, Thirteen Years in the South. See [Brown, David.]

"The Planter's Son." *The Rose Bud, or Youth's Gazette* [ed. Caroline Howard Gilman] 1 (Sept. 29, 1832): 18.
Child singing while braiding a straw basket.

Playfair, Robert. *Recollections of a Visit to the United States and British Provinces of North America in the Years 1847, 1848 and 1849.* Edinburgh: T. Constable, 1856.
Banjo applied to an instrumental ensemble: p. 174.

Poe, Edgar Allan. *The Complete Works of Edgar Allan Poe.* Ed. James A. Harrison. New York: G. D. Sproul, 1902.
Rhythm of patting juba: XVII, 22.

Pollard, Edward Alfred. *Black Diamonds Gathered in the Darkey Homes of the South.* New York: Pudney & Russell, 1859.

Black religious songs, with text: pp. 28, 35–36.

Pollard, John Albert. *John Greenleaf Whittier, Friend of Man.* Boston: Houghton Mifflin, 1949.
Lydia Maria Child's judgment of "At Port Royal": p. 236.

Pomfret, John E., and Shumway, Floyd M. *Founding the American Colonies, 1583–1660.* New York: Harper & Row, c 1970.

Porter, Dorothy, ed. *Early Negro Writing, 1760–1837.* Boston: Beacon Press, c 1971.
John Marrant: p. 402; disapproval of dancing: p. 132.

Porteus, Beilby. "An Essay towards a Plan for the More Effectual Civilization and Conversion of the Negroe Slaves, on the Trust Estate in Barbadoes, belonging to the Society for the Propagation of the Gospel in Foreign Parts. First Written in the Year 1784 and Addressed to the Society; and Now Considerably Altered, Corrected and Abridged," pp. 167–217. In his *Tracts on Various Subjects. . . .* London: Printed by L. Hansard & Sons, 1807. 2nd ed., London: T. Cadell and W. Davies, 1807.

Practical Considerations Founded on the Scriptures, Relative to the Slave Population of South-Carolina . . . By a South-Carolinian. Charleston: Printed by A.E. Miller, 1823. (Attributed to Frederick Dalcho.)
Black preachers blamed for Vesey conspiracy: pp. 33–36.

Prescott, Harriet E. "Down the River." *Atlantic Monthly* 16 (Oct., 1865): 468–90.
Opposition to secular music and dancing: p. 469.

Pringle, Elizabeth Waties (Allston). *Chronicles of Chicora Wood.* New York: C. Scribner's Sons, 1922.
Dancing and singing by "turbulent" freedmen after emancipation: pp. 269–73.

Pryor, Sara Agnes Rice (Mrs. Roger A.). *My Day; Reminiscences of a Long Life.* New York: Macmillan, 1909.
Disapproval of dancing: pp. 54–57; slave funeral: pp. 146, 157–58.

[Pyle, Curtis B.?] "Letters from the South. By Our Corresponding Editor." *Masonic Mirror and American Keystone* 2 (April 6–May 25, 1853): 125–26. Reprinted in Schwaab, Eugene, ed., *Travels in the Old South, Selected from Periodicals of the Times.* [Lexington:] University Press of Kentucky, c 1973, II, 527–35.
Negro whistling: II, 528.

Quarles, Benjamin. *The Negro in the American Revolution.* Chapel Hill: Published for the Institute of Early American History and Culture at Williamsburg, Virginia, by the University of North Carolina Press, c 1961.
Negro drummers: p. 58, 77.

Ramsay, David. *The History of South-Carolina, from Its First Settlement in 1670, to the Year 1808.* Charleston: Published by D. Longworth, for the Author, 1809.
Boat songs: II, 545; conditions on Edisto Island, ca. 1769: pp. [539], 543–45.

Randolph, Peter. *Sketches of Slave Life: or, Illustrations of the 'Peculiar Institution.' By Peter Randolph, an Emancipated Slave.* 2nd ed., enl. Boston: Published for the Author, 1855.
Sitting with the dead: p. 49.

Rankin, John. *Letters on American Slavery, Addressed to Mr. Thomas Rankin, Merchant at Middlebrook, Augusta County, Va.* Boston: Garrison & Knapp, 1833.
Slave convoy, marching to two violins: p. 46.

Ravenel, Henry William. "Recollections of Southern Plantation Life." *Yale Review* 25 (June, 1936): [748]–77.
African jig: pp. 768–69; African culture and dances: pp. 750, 774–75.

Ravitz, Abe C. "John Pierpont and the Slave's Christmas." *Phylon* 21 (Winter, 1960): 383–86.

Read, William A. *Louisiana-French.* Rev. ed. Baton Rouge: Louisiana State University Press, 1963.
African words: pp. 118, 120.

"Records of the Superior Council of Louisiana, July–November, 1741." *Louisiana Historical Quarterly* 12 (Jan., 1929): [119]–52.
"Service in African style and language": p. 145.

Reed, Andrew, and Matheson, James. *A Narrative of the Visit to the American Churches by the Deputation from the Congregational Union of England and Wales*. London: Jackson and Walford, 1835.
Black church service, Lexington, Va.: I, 217–22.
Reid, Ira De A. "The John Canoe Festival." *Phylon* 3 (4th quarter, 1942): 349–77.
Reid, Whitelaw. *After the War: A Southern Tour, May 1, 1865 to May 1, 1866*. Cincinnati: Moore, Wilstach & Baldwin, 1866.
Style of singing in black churches: pp. 103–5.
Renny, Robert. *An History of Jamaica. With Observations on the . . . Negroes. . . .* London: Printed for J. Cawthorn, 1807.
"Banja or merrywang": p. 168.
"Report of the [Presbyterian] Synod of South Carolina [and Georgia] in Regard to the Religious Instruction of the Colored Population." [By Charles Colcock Jones?] *The African Repository* [Publication of the American Colonization Society] 10 (Aug., 1834): 174–75.
Religious conditions, 1834.
"Review of Current Literature. Miscellaneous." [Review of *Slave Songs of the United States*, by H. G. S., i.e., Henry George Spaulding?] *Christian Examiner* 84, n.s. 5 (Jan., 1868): 121–22.
Riland, John. *Memoirs of a West-India Planter*. London: Hamilton, Adams, 1828.
Slave dancing aboard ship: pp. 46–60.
Riley, Edward. *Riley's Flute Melodies. . . .* New York, [1814].
"Negro Dance": I, 31.
Robin, Claude C. *Voyages dans l'Interieur de la Louisiane, de la Floride Occidentale, et dans les Isles de la Martinique et de Saint-Domingue, Pendant les Années 1801–1803, 1804, 1805 et 1806*. Paris: F. Buisson, 1807.
Dancing aboard slave ships: III, 167–70.
[Robinson, Solon.] "Negro Slavery at the South." *De Bow's Review* 7 (Sept., 1849): 206–25; (Nov., 1849): [379]–89.
Slave dance near Natchez, 1849: p. 382.
[Rochefort, Charles de.] *The History of the Caribby-Islands, viz. Barbados, St. Christophers, St. Vincents, Martinico, Dominico, Barbouthos, Monserrat, Mevis* [sic], *Antego, &c. in all XXVIII . . . Rendred into English by John Davis. . . .* London: Printed by J. M., 1666.
Prohibition of African dances: p. 202.
Rogers, Seth. "Letters of Dr. Seth Rogers [to his Daughter] 1862–1863." Massachusetts Historical Society, *Proceedings* 43 (Feb., 1910): 337–98.
Boat songs: pp. 341–42.
Rolph, Thomas. *A Brief Account, Together with Observations, Made during a Visit to the West Indies, and a Tour through the United States of America, in Parts of the Years 1832–3. . . .* Dundas, Upper Canada: G. Heyworth Hackstaff, 1836.
African drumming and instruments: p. 21.
Root, George Frederick. "Congregational Singing among Negroes." *New-York Musical Review and Choral Advocate* 6 (Mar. 29, 1855): 107.
Rose, Willie Lee. *Rehearsal for Reconstruction: The Port Royal Experiment*. Indianapolis: Bobbs-Merrill, c 1964.
Rothschild, Salomon de, Baron. *A Casual View of America: The Home Letters of Salomon de Rothschild, 1859–1861*. Trans. and ed. Sigmund Diamond. London: Cresset Press, 1962.
Negro dancing on Sunday in Louisiana: p. 112.
Rush, Benjamin. "An Account of the Diseases Peculiar to the Negroes in the West-Indies, and Which Are Produced by Their Slavery." *American Museum* 4 (1788): 81–82.
Negro singing: p. 82.
[Rush, Benjamin.] *A Vindication of the Address, To the Inhabitants of the British Settlements, on the Slavery of the Negroes in America, in Answer to a Pamphlet,*

Entitled, *"Slavery Not Forbidden by Scripture; or a Defence of the West-Indian Planters from the Aspersions Thrown out against Them by the Author of the Address." By a Pennsylvanian.* Philadelphia: Printed by J. Dunlap, 1773.

Negro songs: p. 30.

Russell, William Howard. *Pictures of Southern Life, Social, Political and Military. Written for the London Times.* New York: J. G. Gregory, 1861.

Slave dancing on Sunday in Natchez, Miss.: pp. 93–96.

[Ryland, Robert.] "Reminiscences of the First African Baptist Church, Richmond, Va. By the Pastor." *American Baptist Memorial* 14 (Sept., 1855): 262–65; (Oct., 1855): [289]–92; (Nov., 1855): [321]–27; (Dec., 1855): [353]–56.

Black choir: [289]–92.

S., M. R. "A Visitor's Account of Our Sea Island Schools." *Pennsylvania Freedman's Bulletin* (Oct., 1866): 5–7.

Sack, Albert, Baron von. *A Narrative of a Voyage to Surinam; of a Residence There during 1805, 1806, and 1807; and of the Author's Return to Europe by the Way of North America.* London: Printed for G. and W. Nicol by W. Bulmer, 1810.

African dancing: p. 62; balafo: pp. 82–83.

Saint-Amand, Mary Scott. *A Balcony in Charleston*; with a foreword by Archibald Rutledge. Richmond, Va.: Garrett and Massie, c 1941.

African instruments and dancing: p. 57.

"Sassafras and Swinglingtow: or, Pinkster Was a Holiday." *American Notes & Queries* 6 (June, 1946): 35–40.

Satineau, Maurice. *Histoire de la Guadeloupe sous l'Ancien Régime, 1635–1789.* Paris: Payot, 1918.

African and Creole dances: pp. 275–76.

Scarborough, Dorothy. *On the Trail of Negro Folk Songs.* Cambridge: Harvard University Press, 1925.

Use of pot to deaden sound: p. 25.

[Schaw, Janet.] *Journal of a Lady of Quality; Being the Narrative of a Journey from Scotland to the West Indies, North Carolina, and Portugal, in the Years 1774 to 1776.* Ed. Evangeline Walker Andrews, in collaboration with Charles McLean Andrews. New Haven: Yale University Press, 1921.

Slave behavior at funerals in North Carolina: p. 171.

Schoelcher, Victor. *Des Colonies Françaises. Abolition Immédiate de l'Esclavage.* Paris: Pagnerre, 1842.

Worksongs: p. 23.

Schoepf, Johann David. *Travels in the Confederation, 1783–1784. . . .* Trans. and ed. Alfred J. Morrison. Philadelphia: W. J. Campbell, 1911.

Singing and dancing aboard ship: II, 260–62; Sunday observance in Charleston, 1784: II, 222.

Schoolcraft, Mrs. Mary. *The Black Gauntlet; a Tale of Plantation Life in South Carolina.* Philadelphia: J. B. Lippincott, 1860.

Quoted description of Congo Square in New Orleans: pp. 31–33.

[Schoolcraft, Mrs. Mary.] *Letters on the Condition of the African Race in the United States. By a Southern Lady* [pseud.]. Philadelphia: T. K. and P. G. Collins, 1852.

Boat songs: p. 13.

Schouler, James. *Historical Briefs. With a Biography.* New York: Dodd, Mead, 1896.

Schouler's musical activities: pp. 170, 202–308.

Schultz, Christian, Jun. *Travels on an Inland Voyage through the States of New-York, Pennsylvania, Virginia, Ohio, Kentucky and Tennessee, and through the Territories of Indiana, Louisiana, Mississippi and New-Orleans; Performed in the Years 1807 and 1808; Including a Tour of Nearly Six Thousand Miles.* With maps and plates. New-York: Printed by Isaac Riley, 1810.

African dancing to drums in New Orleans: p. 197.

Schwaab, Eugene L., ed. *Travels in the Old South, Selected from Periodicals of the*

Times. Ed. Eugene L. Schwaab with the collaboration of Jacqueline Bull. [Lexington:] University Press of Kentucky, c 1973.

[Scott, Michael.] *Tom Cringle's Log.* New ed. Edinburgh: W. Blackwood and Sons, [1881, originally 1833].
African funeral: pp. 131, 145–47.

A Selection of Scotch, English, Irish and Foreign Airs, Adapted for the Fife, Violin or German Flute.... Glasgow: J. Aird, 1782.
"Pompey Ran Away. Negroe Jig": I, 57.

Sellers, James Benson. *Slavery in Alabama.* University: University of Alabama Press, 1950.
Negro band in Montgomery, Ala.: p. 121; original Negro hymns: p. 300.

Serment, Jacques Henri. *La Question des Nègres et la Reconstruction du Sud aux États-Unis. Meeting du 29 Mars 1866 et Rapport du Comité Genevois en Faveur des Esclaves Affranchis.* Genève: J. G. Fick, 1866.
French translation of "Go Down, Moses": pp. 44–45.

[Seward, Theodore Frelinghuysen, comp.] *Jubilee Songs: As Sung by the Jubilee Singers, of Fisk University, Nashville, Tenn., under the Auspices of the American Missionary Association.* New York: Biglow & Main, c 1872.

Sharpe, John. "Proposals for Erecting a School, Library and Chapel at New York." MS 841, Lambeth Palace Library. Dated New York, March 11th, 1712/13. New-York Historical Society, *Collections* (1880): [341]–63.
African funeral ceremony: p. 355.

Shillitoe, Thomas. "Journal of the Life, Labours and Travels of Thomas Shillitoe, in the Service of the Gospel of Jesus Christ." *Friends' Library* 3 (1839): [74]–486.
Slave coffle singing: p. 461.

A Short Journey in the West Indies.... London: Printed for the Author, 1790.
"Banjaw": I, 90.

Simpson, John Hawkins. *Horrors of the Virginia Slave Trade and of Slave Rearing Plantations. True Story of Dinah, an Escaped Virginian Slave, Now in London.* London: W. Bennett, 1863.
Black religious service: pp. 28–29.

Sims, Alexander Dromgoole. *A View of Slavery, Moral and Political.* Charleston: A. E. Miller, 1834.
"Native harmony": pp. 25–26.

Singleton, John. *A General Description of the West-Indian Islands, as far as Relates to the British, Dutch, and Danish Governments, from Barbados to Saint Croix. Attempted in Blank Verse.* Barbados: Printed by G. Esmand and W. Walker, 1767.
Negro funeral: pp. 115–18.

Slaughter, Linda Warfel. *The Freedmen of the South....* Cincinnati: Elm Street Printing, 1869.
Teaching new songs: p. 134.

"Slave Songs of the United States." [Unsigned review.] *Lippincott's Magazine* 1 (Mar., 1868): 341–43.

"Slave-Songs of the United States." [Unsigned review.] New York *Citizen* (Nov. 23, 1867): p. 3, col. 3–4.

"Slave Songs of the United States." [Unsigned review, probably by Charlotte L. Forten.] *Freedmen's Record* (Dec., 1867): 185–86.

"Slave Songs of the United States." [Unsigned review written by Lucy and Wendell Garrison.] *The Nation* 5 (Nov. 21, 1867): 411.

Sloane, Sir Hans. *A Voyage to the Islands of Madera, Barbados, Nieves, S. Christopher and Jamaica, with the Natural History of the . . . Last of These Islands....* London: Printed by B. M. for the Author, 1707.
African dancing and instruments: I, xlviii–xlix, lii.

"A Small Farmer." "Art. III.–Management of Negroes." *De Bow's Review* 11 (Oct., 1851): 371–72.

Fiddler supplied by planter.

Smith, Charlotte Turner. *Letters of a Solitary Wanderer; Containing Narratives of Various Descriptions.* London: S. Low, 1800–1801.

African drums and shells played by Maroons: II, 93–94, 101, 139.

Smith, James L. *Autobiography . . . including, also, Reminiscences of Slave Life, Recollections of the War, Education of Freedmen, Causes of the Exodus, etc.* Norwich: Press of the Bulletin, 1881.

Black religious meetings, ca. 1836: pp. [162]–65.

Smith, William. *A New Voyage to Guinea. . . .* London: J. Nourse, 1744.

Balafo: p. 21 and frontispiece.

Smith, William. *A Natural History of Nevis, and the Rest of the English Leeward Charibee Islands in America . . . in Eleven Letters from the Revd. Mr. Smith, Sometime Rector of St. John's at Nevis. . . .* Cambridge: Printed by J. Bentham, 1745.

Worksongs: pp. 230–31.

Smith, William B. "The Persimmon Tree and the Beer Dance." *Farmer's Register* 6 (Apr. 1, 1838): 58–61.

Clapping juba to a banjo: pp. 59–60; persimmon beer dance.

Smyth, John Ferdinand Dalziel. *A Tour in the United States of America. . . .* London: Printed for G. Robinson, 1784.

"Banjor & quaqua": I, 46.

Snowden, Frank M., Jr. *Blacks in Antiquity; Ethiopians in the Greco-Roman Experience.* Cambridge: Belknap Press of Harvard University Press, 1970.

African dancers and musicians: pp. 106, 165, 190–91.

Society for the Preservation of Spirituals. *The Carolina Low-Country.* New York: Macmillan, 1931.

African singing: p. 94; shouts: pp. 199–201.

Society for the Propagation of the Gospel in Foreign Parts. *Classified Digest of the Records of the Society . . . 1701–1892.* 5th ed. London, 1895.

Eagerness of the slaves for instruction: p. 16.

A Soldier's Journal, Containing a Particular Description of the Several Descents on the Coast of France Last War; with an Entertaining Account of the Islands of Guadeloupe, Dominique, &c. . . . London: Printed for E. and C. Dilly, 1770.

African and Creole music and dancing: pp. 106–9.

South Carolina. Laws, Statutes, etc. *The Statutes at Large of South Carolina.* Ed. Thomas Cooper and David J. McCord. Columbia: Printed by A. S. Johnston, 1836–41.

Prohibition of gatherings of slaves: VII(1840): 354; ban on drums, horns or other loud instruments: VII(1840): 410.

Southall, Geneva. "Blind Tom: A Misrepresented and Neglected Composer-Pianist." *Black Perspective in Music* 3 (May, 1975): [141]–59.

Southern, Eileen. *The Music of Black Americans: A History.* New York: W. W. Norton, 1971.

_____, ed. *Readings in Black American Music.* New York: W. W. Norton, c 1971.

Souvenirs d'Amérique et de France, par une Créole. See [Allain, Hélène d'Aquin.]

Spaulding, Henry George. *Times Hab Badly Change' Old Massa Now; Song of the Freedmen.* Boston: O. Ditson, 1866.

[Spaulding, Henry George.] "Under the Palmetto." *Continental Monthly* 4 (Aug., 1863): 188–203.

"Negro 'Shouts' and Shout Songs": pp. 196–200.

Starobin, Robert S. *Industrial Slavery in the Old South.* New York: Oxford University Press, 1970.

Singing while spinning hemp: p. 18.

Stearns, Marshall and Jean. *Jazz Dance; The Story of American Vernacular Dance.* New York: Macmillan, c 1968.

Stevenson, Robert. "The Afro-American Musical Legacy to 1800." *Musical Quarterly* 54 (Oct., 1968): 475–502.

Largely devoted to Spanish colonies.

[Stewart, John.] *An Account of Jamaica, and Its Inhabitants. By a Gentleman, Long Resident in the West Indies.* 2nd ed. Kingston, Jamaica, 1809.

African and European music: p. 178; slave funerals: p. 179.

———. *A View of the Past and Present State of the Island of Jamaica; with Remarks on the Moral and Physical Condition of the Slaves, and on the Abolition of Slavery in the Colonies.* Edinburgh: Oliver & Boyd, 1823.

African and Creole music and dancing: p. 272.

Stoddard, Amos. *Sketches, Historical and Descriptive, of Louisiana.* Philadelphia: M. Carey, 1812.

Slave amusements restricted to Sunday: p. 335.

Stoutamire, Albert. *Music of the Old South: Colony to Confederacy.* Rutherford, [N.J.:] Fairleigh Dickinson University Press, c 1972.

Slaves singing hymns, 1782: p. 44; runaways identified by ability to play the fiddle: pp. 27, 32.

Stowe, Harriet Beecher. "Sojourner Truth, the Libyan Sibyl." *Atlantic Monthly* 11 (Apr., 1863): 473–81.

Style of singing: pp. 476–77.

Stroyer, Jacob. *My Life in the South.* New and enl. ed. Salem, Mass.: Observer Book and Job Print., 1891.

African songs: p. 47.

Stuckey, Sterling. "Through the Prism of Folklore: The Black Ethos in Slavery." In *Blacks in White America Before 1865.* Ed. Robert V. Haynes. New York: D. McKay, 1972.

The Suppressed Tract! and the Rejected Tract! . . . submitted to the Publishing Committee of the Am. Tract Society. . . . New York: J. A. Gray, 1858.

Identification of James W. Alexander: pp. 71–72.

Svin'in, Pavel Petrovich. *Picturesque United States of America, 1811, 1812, 1813, Being a Memoir on Paul Svinin, Russian Diplomatic Officer, Artist and Author, Containing Copious Excerpts from His Account of His Travels in America* . . . by Avraham Yarmolinsky. New York: W. E. Rudge, 1930.

Singing style in a black Methodist church: p. 20.

Sweet, William Warren. *Religion on the American Frontier. The Baptists, 1783–1830; a Collection of Source Material.* New York: Holt, c 1931.

Cane Ridge camp meeting: pp. 610–11.

Swint, Henry L., ed. *Dear Ones at Home; Letters from Contraband Camps.* Selected and ed. Henry L. Swint. Nashville: Vanderbilt University Press, 1966.

Patting juba, Craney Island, Va., Sept., 1863: pp. 89–90; disapproval of dancing: pp. 246–47; dancing and style of singing: pp. 88, 90; church service: pp. 117, 124.

Taylor, Joe Gray. *Negro Slavery in Louisiana.* [Baton Rouge:] Louisiana Historical Association, c 1963.

Special regulation to permit evening practice of the Shreveport Ethiopian Band: pp. 228–29.

Teas, Thomas S. "A Trading Trip to Natchez and New Orleans, 1822: Diary of Thomas S. Teas" [Philadelphia Quaker, 1794–1850]. Contributed by Edward Teas, ed. Julia Ideson and Sanford W. Higginbotham. *Journal of Southern History* 7 (Aug., 1941): [378]–99.

Slave dancing in Red Church, La., 1822: p. 391.

Thomas, Henry Goddard. "The Colored Troops at Petersburg." *Century Magazine* 34, n.s. 12 (Sept., 1887): [777]–78.

Improvising a new song: pp. 777–78.

Thomas, Samuel. "Letters of Rev. Samuel Thomas, 1702–1710." *South Carolina Historical and Genealogical Magazine* 4 (July, 1903): [221]–30; (Oct., 1903): [278]–85; 5 (Jan., 1904): [21]–55.

Early conversions in South Carolina: 4 (July, 1903): 225, (Oct., 1903): 280.
Thomas Jefferson and His Unknown Brother Randolph; Twenty-Eight Letters. . . . Introduction by Bernard Mayo. Charlottesville: Tracy W. McGregor Library, University of Virginia, 1942.
Black people dancing and fiddling: p. 22.
Thompson, Robert Farris. *African Art in Motion, Icon and Act.* Los Angeles: University of California Press, c 1974.
Contemporary descriptions of African music and dancing: pp. 30–41.
Thornton, Thomas C. *An Inquiry into the History of Slavery. . . .* Washington, D.C.: W. M. Morrison, 1841.
Corn songs: pp. 120–22.
Tinker, Edward Larocque. "Gombo Comes to Philadelphia." American Antiquarian Society, *Proceedings* 67 (1957): [49]–76.
Creole songs: pp. 51–53, 71.
Toll, Robert C. *Blacking Up; The Minstrel Show in Nineteenth-Century America.* New York: Oxford University Press, 1974.
Banjo: p. 44.
Torian, Sarah Hodgson, ed. "Ante-Bellum and War Memories of Mrs. Telfair Hodgson." *Georgia Historical Quarterly* 27 (Dec., 1943): [350]–56.
Boat songs: p. 351.
Towe, Joseph. "Old Time Music of the Negroes." New York *Times*, June 15, 1875. Reprinted in Booker T. Washington, *The Booker T. Washington Papers, vol. 2: 1869–89.* Ed. Louis R. Harlan. Urbana: University of Illinois Press, 1972.
African origins of spiritual melodies: II, 58, 60.
Towne, Laura Matilda. *Letters and Diary of Laura M. Towne, Written from the Sea Islands of South Carolina, 1862–1884.* Ed. Rupert Sargent Holland. Cambridge: Riverside Press, 1912.
[Tryon, Thomas.] "A Discourse in Way of Dialogue, between an Ethiopian or Negro-Slave and a Christian that Was His Master in America." In *Friendly Advice to the Gentlemen Planters of the East and West Indies . . . by Philotheos Physiologus* [pseud.]. London: Printed by A. Sowle, 1684.
Slave dancing: pp. 146–48.
[Tucker, George.] *Letters from Virginia, Translated from the French.* Baltimore: F. Lucas, 1816.
Slave coffle singing: pp. 29–34.
_____. *The Valley of Shenandoah; or, Memoirs of the Graysons.* New York: C. Wiley, 1824.
Black instrumentalists: II, 121; corn songs: II, 116–18.
[Turnbull, Gordon.] *An Apology for Negro Slavery: or, The West-India Planters Vindicated from the Charge of Inhumanity. By the Author of Letters to a Young Planter. . . .* London: Printed by Stuart and Stevenson, 1786.
Singing and dancing by newly arrived slaves: pp. 21–25.
Turnbull, Jane M. and Marion. *American Photographs.* London: T. C. Newby, 1859.
Negro dance, Montgomery, Ala., 1853: II, [60]–72; tobacco workers in Richmond singing hymns: II, 214–17.
Turner, James K. "Slavery in Edgecombe County [N.C.]." Trinity College *Historical Papers*, ser. 12 (1916): [5]–36.
Use of pot to deaden sound: p. 27.
[Tussac, Fr. Richard de.] *Cri des Colons contre un Ouvrage de M. l'Evèque et Senateur Grégoire, Ayant pour Titre, De La Littérature des Nègres. . . .* Paris: Les Marchands de Nouveautés, 1810.
Banza: p. 292.
Tyson, Bryan. *The Institution of Slavery in the Southern States, Religiously and Morally Considered in Connection with Our Sectional Troubles.* Washington, D.C.: H. Polkinhorn, 1863.
Slave dancing, Chatham Co., N.C., 1862: pp. 12–13.

Underwood, Francis Henry. *John Greenleaf Whittier, A Biography.* Boston: Houghton, Mifflin, 1892.
Whittier's wish for a "song worthy of the [black] people": p. 235.

Vaissière, Pierre de. *Saint-Domingue, 1629–1789. La Société et la Vie Créole sous l'Ancien Régime.* Paris: Perrin, 1909.
Slave dancing aboard ship: p. 161.

Venable, W. H. "Down South before the War; Record of a Ramble to New Orleans in 1858." Ohio Archaelogical and Historical Society, *Publications* 2 (Mar., 1889): 488–513.
Musical bow: p. 498; patting juba: p. 497; iron workers' songs with texts: p. 490.

Victor, Mrs. Metta V. *Maum Guinea, and Her Plantation "Children"; or, Holiday Week on a Louisiana Estate. A Slave Romance.* New York: Beadle, c 1861.
Black instrumental group: p. 37; song texts of unknown authenticity: pp. 76–77, 108–9, passim.

Villard, Henry. *Memoirs of Henry Villard, Journalist and Financier: 1835–1900.* Boston: Houghton, Mifflin, 1904.
"Original songs" of the blacks: II, 24.

Virginia (Colony). Laws, Statutes, etc. *An Exact Abridgment of All the Public Acts of Assembly of Virginia, in Force and Use.... By John Mercer.* Williamsburg: Printed by W. Parks, 1737.
Enlistment of Negro drummers or trumpeters in the militia: p. 189.

Wade, Richard C. *Slavery in the Cities: The South, 1820–1860.* New York: Oxford University Press, 1964.
Slave dance in Mobile, 1851: pp. 90, 104; arrest of blacks in New Orleans for attending black religious meetings: pp. 83–84.

Walker, Susan. "Journal, March 3d to June 6th, 1862." Ed. Henry Noble Sherwood. Historical and Philosophical Society of Ohio, *Quarterly Publication* 7 (Jan., 1912): 3–48.
Boat songs: p. 19.

Walvin, James. *Black and White; The Negro and English Society, 1555–1945.* [London:] A. Lane, Penguin Press, 1973.
African musicians in England: pp. 70–71.

Ware, Emma Forbes. *Ware Genealogy; Robert Ware, of Dedham, Massachusetts, 1642–1699, and His Lineal Descendants.* Boston: C. H. Pope, 1901.
Relations of the Ware and Allen families: p. 158.

Ware, John. *Memoir of the Life of Henry Ware, Jr., by His Brother.* Boston: J. Munroe and Company, 1846.

Warner, Charles Dudley. *Studies in the South and West, with Comments on Canada.* Hartford, Conn.: American Publishing Company, 1904.
Voodoo ceremony in New Orleans in 1885: pp. [75]–82.

Washington, Booker T. "Christmas Days in Old Virginia." *Suburban Life* 5 (Dec., 1907): 336–37. Reprinted in *The Booker T. Washington Papers.* Ed. Louis R. Harlan. Urbana: University of Illinois Press, 1972. I, 395.
Sacred songs at corn-shucking.

Waterbury, Maria. *Seven Years among the Freedmen.* 2nd ed., rev. and enl. Chicago: T. B. Arnold, 1891.
"The Heavenly Dance": pp. 195–96.

Waters, Horace. *Harp of Freedom (Part I), a New and Superior Collection of Anti-Slavery, Patriotic and "Contraband" Songs, Solos, Duets and Choruses....* New York: H. Waters, [1862].
"The song of the 'Contrabands.' 'O! Let My People Go.' & parody": pp. 2–3.

Watson, Elkanah. *Men and Times of the Revolution; or, Memoirs of Elkanah Watson, Including His Journals of Travels in Europe and America, from the Year 1777 to 1842.... Ed. His Son, Winslow C. Watson.* 2nd ed. New York: Dana, 1856.

Boat songs: p. 52.

Watson, John Fanning. *Annals of Philadelphia and Pennsylvania in the Olden Time.* . . . Philadelphia: Published for the Author, 1850.

Pinkster: II, 265.

[Watson, John Fanning.] *Methodist Error; or, Friendly Christian Advice, to Those Methodists, Who Indulge in Extravagant Religious Emotions and Bodily Exercises. By a Wesleyan Methodist.* Trenton, N.J.: D. & E. Fenton; Cincinnati: Republished by Phillips & Speer, 1819.

Black music at camp meetings: pp. 15–16.

————. "Notitia of Incidents at New Orleans in 1804 and 1805." *American Pioneer* (Cincinnati) 2 (Mar., 1843): 227–37.

Slave dances on Sunday: p. 232.

Watson, Richard. *A Defence of the Wesleyan Methodist Missions in the West Indies; Including a Refutation of the Charges in Mr. Marryat's Thoughts on the Abolition of the Slave Trade etc. and in Other Publications; with Facts and Anecdotes Illustrative of the Moral State of the Slaves and of the Missions.* London, 1817.

"Dance to a tom-tom": p. 60.

Wax, Darold D. "A Philadelphia Surgeon [William Chancellor] on a Slaving Voyage to Africa, 1749–1751." *Pennsylvania Magazine of History and Biography* 92 (Oct., 1968): 465–93.

Boat songs in Africa: p. 478.

Weise, Arthur James. *History of the City of Troy.* . . . Troy, N.Y.: W. H. Young, 1876.

Pinkster: pp. 63–64.

[Weld, Theodore Dwight.] *American Slavery as It Is: Testimony of a Thousand Witnesses.* New York: American Anti-Slavery Society, 1839.

Slave singing with text: Hurra, for good ole Massa: p. 13.

Western Freedmen's Aid Commission. *Second Annual Report.* Cincinnati: Printed at the Methodist Book Concern, 1865.

"Hymns of their own": p. 33.

Whipple, Henry Benjamin. *Bishop Whipple's Southern Diary, 1843–1844.* Ed. Lester B. Shippee. Minneapolis: University of Minnesota Press, c 1937.

Black band, St. Mary's, Ga., 1843: pp. 50–51.

White, Newman Ivey. *American Negro Folk-Songs.* Cambridge: Harvard University Press, 1928.

Worksongs: p. 148; oral transmission of minstrel songs: passim.

Whitefield, George. *Journals.* A New Edition, Containing Fuller Material Than Any Hitherto Published. [London?]: Banner of Truth Trust, 1960.

Disapproval of dancing: pp. 378–82.

————. *Three Letters from the Reverend Mr. G. Whitefield.* . . . Philadelphia: Printed by B. Franklin, 1740.

African dancing and piping: p. 14.

Whitten, Norman E., Jr., and Szwed, John F., eds. *Afro-American Anthropology: Contemporary Perspectives.* Foreword by Sidney W. Mintz. New York: Free Press, c 1970.

Evaluation of *Slave Songs of the United States*: p. 31.

Whittier, John Greenleaf. "At Port Royal. 1861." *Atlantic Monthly* 9 (Feb., 1862): 244–45.

Wilgus, D. K. *Anglo-American Folksong Scholarship since 1898.* New Brunswick, N.J.: Rutgers University Press, 1959.

Afro-American worksongs: p. 320; "Appendix One: The Negro-White Spiritual": pp. 345–64.

Wilkes, Laura Eliza. *Missing Pages in American History Revealing the Services of Negroes in the Early Wars in the United States of America, 1641–1815.* [Washington, D.C., n.d.] Reprinted in *The Negro Soldier; A Select Compilation.* New York:

Negro Universities Press, c 1970.
Negro musicians in French and Indian War and the American Revolution: pp. 27, 31, 47.

Williams, Cynric R. *A Tour through the Island of Jamaica, from the Western to the Eastern End, in the Year 1823*. London: Printed for Hunt and Clarke, 1826.
African and Creole music and dancing: pp. 23–29.

Williams, Eric. *From Columbus to Castro: The History of the Caribbean, 1492–1969*. New York: Harper & Row, c 1970.
Ratios of black to white population: pp. 104–7.

Williams, Marie B. "A Night with the Voudous." *Appleton's Journal* 13 (Mar. 27, 1875): 403–4.
Ceremony with African instruments, 1825: p. 404.

Williamson, Joel. *After Slavery; the Negro in South Carolina during Reconstruction, 1861–1877*. Chapel Hill: University of North Carolina Press, c 1965.
Characterization of Reuben Tomlinson: p. 361.

Willis, Nathaniel Parker. *A Health Trip to the Tropics*. London: S. Low, Son and Co., 1854.
African drumming and instruments: p. 410.

Winchester, Elhanan. *The Reigning Abominations, Especially the Slave Trade … Delivered in Fairfax County, Virginia, December 30, 1774. …* London: Printed by H. Trapp, 1788.
Lack of interest in converting the Negroes: p. 25.

Winterbottom, Thomas Masterman. *An Account of the Native Africans in the Neighborhood of Sierra Leone*. 2nd ed. London: Printed by C. Whittingham, 1803. Reprinted, [London:] F. Cass, 1969.
Description of African music: I, 111–14; satire and improvisation: I, 108.

Wise, Jennings C. *Ye Kingdome of Accomacke; or, The Eastern Shore of Virginia in the Seventeenth Century*. Richmond: Bell Book, 1911.
Slave fiddler in the 1690's: pp. 322–24.

Wood, Peter Hutchins. *Black Majority; Negroes in Colonial South Carolina from 1670 through the Stono Rebellion*. New York: Knopf, 1974.
Boat songs in Africa and South Carolina: pp. 124, 202; rice cultivation to work-songs: pp. 61–62; slave drummer: p. 104.

Woodberry, George E., ed. "The Poe-Chivers Papers." *Century Magazine* 65 (Jan., 1903): 435–47; (Feb., 1903): 545–58.
Rhythm of patting juba: p. 555.

Woodward, Arthur. "Joel Sweeney and the First Banjo." Los Angeles County Museum *Quarterly*, 7 (Spring, 1949): [7]–[11].

Wright, Constance. *Fanny Kemble and the Lovely Land*. New York: Dodd, Mead, c 1972.
James Leigh's visits to Butler Island: pp. 190–97.

Writers' Program. *See also* Federal Writers' Project.

———. Georgia. *Drums and Shadows; Survival Studies among the Georgia Coastal Negroes*. Savannah Unit, Georgia Writers' Project, Work Projects Administration. Athens: University of Georgia Press, 1940.
Drums: pp. 62, 101, passim; funeral ceremonies: pp. 62, 67, 71, 106–7, 125, 130, 140–41, 143, 155, 180, 184.

Wyeth, John Allan. *With Sabre and Scalpel; the Autobiography of a Soldier and Surgeon*. New York: Harper & Brothers, 1914.
Method of making a banjo: pp. 61–62; corn songs: p. 58.

Yates, John Ashton. *Colonial Slavery. Letters to the Right Hon. William Huskisson, President of the Board of Trade, &c. &c. on the Present Condition of the Slaves, and the Means Best Adapted to Promote the Mitigation and Final Extinction of Slavery in the British Colonies*. Liverpool: Printed by Harris & Co., 1824.
New Orleans ordinances regulating slave dancing and singing, 1817: pp. 16–17.

Yetman, Norman R. *Life under the "Peculiar Institution"; Selections from the Slave Narrative Collection.* New York: Holt, Rinehart and Winston, [c 1970].
Quills: p. 170; slave fiddler: p. 282; same fiddler played for slaves and whites: p. 190; worksongs; pp. 221–22: spinning and weaving songs: p. 163; corn songs: pp. 124–25, 259, 267; conversion of a fiddler: pp. 330–33; restrictions on singing: pp. 11–13, 55–56, 261–62.
Young, Sir William. "A Tour through the Several Islands of Barbadoes, St. Vincent, Antigua, Tobago, and Grenada, in the Years 1791 & 1792." In Edwards, Bryan. *The History, Civil and Commercial, of the British West Indies.* London: Printed for J. Stockdale, 1793–1801. III, 261–301.
Slave dancing aboard ship: p. 268; balafo: p. 276; African and acculturated dancing: p. 276.
Zilversmit, Arthur. *The First Emancipation: The Abolition of Slavery in the North.* Chicago: University of Chicago Press, c 1967.
Slave contract mentioning fiddling: p. 31.
Zurara, Gomes Eannes de. *The Chronicle of the Discovery and Conquest of Guinea.* Trans. C. R. Beazley and E. Prestage. London: Hakluyt Society, 1896–97.
Description of African singing in Portugal about 1445: I, 81.

Index